Management science
Decision making through systems thinking

WITHDRAWN

JAN 5 2018

UOIT & Durham College
LIBRARY

0 1341 07812759

Management science
Decision making through systems thinking

Hans G. Daellenbach
Donald C. McNickle

University of Canterbury, Christchurch, New Zealand

First published 2005 by
PALGRAVE MACMILLAN
Houndmills, Basingstoke, Hampshire RG21 6XS and
175 Fifth Avenue, New York, N. Y. 10010
Companies and representatives throughout the world

PALGRAVE MACMILLAN is the global academic imprint of the Palgrave Macmillan division of St. Martin's Press LLC and of Palgrave Macmillan Ltd. Macmillan® is a registered trademark in the United States, United Kingdom and other countries. Palgrave is a registered trademark in the European Union and other countries.

ISBN 1–4039–4174–2

This book is printed on paper suitable for recycling and made from fully managed and sustained forest sources.

A catalogue record for this book is available from the British Library.

A catalog record for this book is available from the Library of Congress.

10   9   8   7   6   5   4   3   2   1
14   13 12 11 10 09 08 07 06 05

Printed and bound in China

*"If we investigate our ideas, we have
to be willing to give them up."*

Gordon Hewitt, PhD
Wellington

Contents

Part 2   Management science methodologies: Introduction

Part 4   Hard MS/OR methods

Preface

This text is a substantive revision of *Systems and Decision Making*, published by John Wiley & Sons Ltd, Chichester, UK (1994). As the subtitle indicates, its aim is to explore Management Science/Operations Research (MS/OR) firmly within a broad systems thinking framework. It is this aspect that sets it apart from most other introductory texts in MS/OR, whose emphasis is mainly on mathematical techniques of what has become known as hard operations research.

The aim of MS/OR projects is to provide insights for informed decision making. The vast majority of that decision making occurs within organizations or, in other words, within systems. Therefore MS/OR can be viewed as a way of thinking with a systems focus, i.e. a form of systems thinking. This necessitates a fair general understanding of systems, systems concepts, and systems control. What is included in the system defined to analyse a particular problem and what is left out—the system boundary choices—may have important consequences for the people actively involved, as well as those passively affected.

Rather than assume that the usual starting point for an MS/OR project is a relatively well-structured problem, with clearly defined objectives and alternative courses of action, the text steps back to the inception phase for most projects, namely the presentation of a problematic situation, where the issues are still vague, fuzzy, and not yet seen in their proper systemic context. It demonstrates several aids to capturing the problem situation in its full context. This will facilitate gaining a more comprehensive understanding of the various issues involved, which in turn increases the likelihood that the problem formulation addresses the 'right' issue at an appropriate level of detail to provide insights into the problem and answers relevant for decision making.

These are the topics of Part 1, together with graphical aids for depicting systems or views of important aspects of a particular system. Their aim is to make systems modelling more accessible to the beginner.

Part 2 gives an overview of the two major strands of Management Science, i.e. hard OR approaches and soft OR approaches, and their overall methodologies, and contrasts them. While most analysts who use hard OR agree on the general form of the hard OR methodology, soft OR covers such a wide range of approaches that no single methodological framework can capture them all. Not only do they differ in terms of their specific aims—problem structuring, learning, conflict resolution, and contingency planning, as well as problem solving—but also in terms of their suitability for specific problem situations. By necessity, the chapter devoted to it can only scratch the surface of this vast area. It restricts itself to an introductory survey, contrasting three of the most used approaches with the same case.

Part 3 looks at two topics that any successful modeller needs to be familiar with. First, most projects involve costs and benefits. These may be of a monetary or intangible nature. Which costs and benefits are relevant for a particular problem? Second, much decision making involves the timing of various events or their temporal incidence, as well as the sequencing of decisions as an integral aspect of the problem. How does this affect the decision process and how can it be captured by the models?

Part 4 is largely devoted to hard OR. A number of MS/OR techniques borrow a leaf or two from managerial economics, in particular the principle of marginal analysis. This leads us to study the nature of cost and benefit functions and their marginal behaviour.

A variety of restrictions may be imposed on the decision process, relating to limited resources or properties that the solution has to satisfy. What effects does this have on the solution and the process of obtaining it? What kind of insights can we derive from analysing these effects? The concept of shadow prices is introduced here in general terms and in the context of linear programming.

Most decisions are made under various degrees of uncertainty about the outcomes. What is uncertainty? How do we react when faced with uncertainty? How can we model uncertainty? We make an excursion into waiting lines, simulation, and decision and risk analysis.

We return to the topic of decision making over time by exploring, albeit all too briefly, how to capture the dynamics of system behaviour.

Finally, there is a brief discussion on how the decision process needs to be adapted if we explicitly acknowledge the fact that the decision maker may be faced with conflicting goals.

Part 4 thus gives an introduction to several of the well-known OR techniques. However, the emphasis is not on the tools themselves, but on how these tools are used within a systems thinking framework, and what insights we can get from their use in terms of the decision process. The text is not an elementary introduction to MS/OR techniques. At an introductory level, although interesting and fun, these techniques are often reduced to the triviality of cranking a computational handle for a drastically simplified toy problem, devoid of most practical relevance.

Rather than discuss concepts in the abstract, they are demonstrated using practical case studies that we have been involved in or that have been reported in the literature. By necessity, some of them have had to be trimmed to reduce their complexity and render them amenable for inclusion in the limited space of a textbook, but most of them have retained the essentials of their original flavour.

In Parts 3 and 4, whenever possible the quantitative analysis is demonstrated using the power and flexibility of PC spreadsheets. The text uses Microsoft Excel©, but this choice is more one of convenience rather than preference. Any other spreadsheet software with optimizer or solver capability and the facility for generating random variates will do. When we use this text in a first-year undergraduate course or at the MBA level, we supplement it by giving the students an introduction to spreadsheets.

The use of spreadsheets implies that the level of mathematics involved remains at a fairly elementary level and does not go beyond high school mathematics and statistics. In Parts 3 and 4, the emphasis is not on the mathematics, but on the concepts and the process of quantitative decision making. The book lives on the principle of 'never let the mathematics get in the way of common sense!'

By the time the reader has studied this text and digested its wealth of learning opportunities offered, he or she will approach all types of problem solving — not just that suitable for quantitative modelling — from a more comprehensive, enlightened and insightful perspective. Hopefully, the reader will also have been encouraged to reflect on and become more critical of her or his own way of looking at the world.

The text has a new feature: an extensive glossary of most technical terms and concepts used, complementing the detailed index. References to the bibliography at the end of the text are indicated by author and/or year, shown in square brackets.

The main audience of the text is at an introductory undergraduate or MBA level for a 50 to 80 hour course on quantitative decision making, where the emphasis is on methodology and concepts, rather than mathematical techniques. This is the use we have put it to at the University of Canterbury. It is sufficiently challenging for the MBA level, where the focus is in any case on insight, rather than techniques. The real-life case studies used in many chapters make the text particularly relevant and attractive to mature MBA students. However, it is also suitable for self-study and as recommended background reading to set the stage for an introductory course in MS/OR, systems thinking, and computer science. It puts the techniques into their proper perspective in the decision-making process. They are then seen for what they are, namely powerful aids used for what usually does not make more than a small portion of the effort that goes into any project, rather than the most important core of the project. It is not the tools that 'solve a problem', but the process in which they are used.

Thanks go to several people who have contributed in various ways to this text: Ross James, Shane Dye, and Nicola Petty who have used the precursors to this text and made numerous valuable suggestions for improvements. Nicola Petty is also the artist who rendered many of the more complex diagrams into an attractive form. And then there are the thousands of students who read the text and whose questions and queries for explanations have led to saying some things more simply and clearly.

The scholar and teacher who has undoubtedly shaped the whole approach to systems thinking and MS/OR more than anybody else is C West Churchman. This text is dedicated to him.

The accompanying website to this text can be accessed at http://www. palgrave.com/business/daellenbach. Students can download Excel files of all the spreadsheets used within the text, and may edit them for their own use. Lecturers who adopt this text for class use may access worked solutions of all the exercises set within the text (including any Excel spreadsheets used to compute the solutions). Please contact your local Palgrave Macmillan sales representative for further information.

1
Introduction

This chapter aims to whet your appetite to learn more about the complexity and challenge of effective problem solving. We will briefly describe five real-life situations that each involved making recommendations as to the best course of action to take. Three look at commercial situations, while the other two deal with issues of public decision making and policy. They are intended to give you a feel for the great variety of decision-making problems in terms of area of application, types of organizations involved, the degree of complexity, and the types of costs and benefits, as well as their importance. In each instance a systems approach, based on systems thinking, will lead to more insightful decision making.

1.1 Motivation

Emergency services call centre

In recent years, most countries have centralized their telephone call centres for emergency services, such as the fire service, ambulance service, or civil emergencies — the 111 or 911 service — from a regional basis to a single, national centre. The telephones at such centres have to be staffed by real people on a 24-hour basis. The processing of each incoming call consists of recording the name, the address and telephone number, the type of emergency, its urgency, etc. Some of this information must be evaluated for its accuracy and whether the call is genuine. Each incoming call may take as little as one minute or may sometimes exceed five minutes to process and then liaise with the appropriate service.

The aim of the service is to trigger an appropriate response as quickly as possible. The faster the response, the greater the likelihood of preventing loss of life or reducing serious injury and loss of property. The response rate can be kept to a minimum by scheduling a very large number of operators on duty at all times, such that the chance of having to wait for an operator for more than ten seconds is almost nil. As a result, many operators would be idle most of the time. Not only would this be very boring for the operators, but it would also be very costly in terms of both salaries and equipment. Government funds are limited and have to be allocated to a large number of competing uses. The emergency services call centre is only one of these uses, albeit a very important one, but so are health services, policing, education, welfare, etc.

Determining the staffing levels of an emergency call centre boils down to balancing the centre's operating costs and its callers' waiting times (measured for instance by the average and the 99th percentile). In a well-managed system it is not possible to reduce both. If one is decreased, the other will inevitably increase.

The problem is made more difficult by the fact that some aspects, such as salaries and equipment, can be expressed in monetary terms, while others largely defy any attempt to express them in this way. How do you evaluate a 10 per cent increase in the waiting time which may result in a 40 per cent increase in the likelihood of loss of lives or of serious injury?

This is a type of problem faced by many organizations, private or public, called a **waiting line** problem. Here are other examples:

- the number of tellers that a bank, insurance office, or post office should open during various times of the business day; the number of automatic bank teller or cash dispensing machines to install for 24-hour access.

- the number of crews needed by a repair or service outfit, such as an appliance service firm or a photocopying machine service firm.

- the number of nurses and/or doctors on duty at an emergency clinic during various hours of the week.

- the degree of redundancy built into equipment to prevent failure breakdown.

Vehicle scheduling

Pick-up and delivery firms, like courier services, pick up and drop off goods at a number of places. The locations of these pick-ups and drop-offs may differ daily or even hourly, with new locations added to the list of locations to visit. Certain of the customers may specify a given time period or 'time window' during which the visit must occur. The vehicle used may have a limited carrying capacity. The length of time drivers can be on the road in one shift may be subject to legal restrictions. Add to this the problem of traffic density on various city arterial roads and the consequent change in travel times between locations during the day. It is also clear that even for a small problem, the number of possible distinct sequences for visiting all locations is very large. For example, for 10 locations, there are $10! = 3,628,800$ different itineraries, while for 20 this number grows to about 2,432,902,000,000,000,000. Although a majority can easily be ruled out as bad, it is still a non-trivial task to select the best combination or sequence of pick-ups and deliveries from those that remain, such that all complicating factors are taken into account. It may even be difficult to decide which criterion should be chosen for 'best'. Is it minimum distance, or minimum time, or minimum total cost, or a compromise between these considerations?

Similar types of combinatorial sequencing problems are faced by airlines for the scheduling of aircraft and air crews, public bus or railroad companies for the scheduling of buses or engines and drivers, or the city rubbish collectors for determining their collection rounds.

A mission statement for an organization

It seems that in today's world no organization is viewed as responsible, forward-looking, and success-oriented without having a formal 'mission statement'. Gone are the days when it was good enough to have a group of like-minded people, under the leadership of an energetic person with good interpersonal skills, who all shared a vision, albeit often somewhat vague. Now most organizations prominently exhibit a mission statement of what they are all about. It is proudly shown as a framed document in the CEO's office and on the organization's website. These statements are rather curious documents that literally promise the moon, but all too often hardly bring about any substantive change in how the organization goes about its business, except maybe to increase the amount of paperwork to fill the many reports that claim to measure how well the organization meets its missions.

Producing a meaningful mission statement is a rather difficult project. It has to be relevant for the purpose of the organization, set achievable goals that can be measured and, most importantly, get the active cooperation of its members. The trouble is that even in an *a priori* like-minded group of people there will be conflicts and differences in preference about the aims they would like the organization to pursue and their vision for its future, as well as how they see their own role in that scheme. Unless the CEO can simply impose her or his will in a dictatorial manner, coming to a meeting of minds that satisfies the three properties of 'relevant', 'achievable', and 'measurable', and secures the active cooperation of everybody, a mission statement has to be a compromise. It is usually obtained by a lengthy process, starting out with canvassing the views of some or all members, followed by assembling them in some organized fashion, combining similar ones, eliminating those that are subordinate to others (e.g. if A serves to achieve B, A can be dropped), restating them such that their achievement level can be measured in a meaningful way, and finally reducing the number to an essential few. This process will involve many meetings and negotiation. One of the so-called **soft operations research** approaches or **problem structuring methods**, surveyed in Chapter 7, could provide the right vehicle for this process. In most cases, to be successful it will also need a skilful facilitator to guide and control it.

Environmental and economic considerations: the Deep Cove project

The water discharged in Deep Cove from the Manapouri Power Station in Fiordland National Park at the bottom of New Zealand's South Island is so pure that it does not need any chemicals to neutralize harmful bacteria or other contaminants. Several years ago, a US firm applied for the rights to capture this water and transport it with large ocean-going tankers to the US West Coast and Middle East. It would have entailed building a floating dock close to the tail race of the power station, where up to two tankers could berth simultaneously. The project would provide employment for about 30 people in an economically depressed area of NZ, and the NZ Government would collect a water royalty. It would thus make a substantial contribution to both the local and national economies.

The firm showed considerable responsibility in planning the whole operation to keep the environmental impact in the fiord as low as economically feasible. For instance, all staff would be flown into Deep Cove daily, allowing no permanent residence. All rubbish would be removed. No permanent structures would be erected. Tanker speed in the fiords would be reduced to keep swells low. There would be extensive safety measures to avoid oil spills, etc.

Not surprisingly, environmental groups were opposed to this project. Here are some of their reasons: First, it would introduce non-tourist commercial activities in the waters of a national park, which is against the charter of national parks. They feared that the removal of up to 60% of the tail race water for extended periods would alter the balance between fresh water and salt water and affect the sound's unique flora and fauna that have evolved over millions of years. The big tankers would speed up the mixing of the fresh water layer on top of the salt water base, affecting the ecological balance even further. Due to the severe weather conditions in that part of NZ, accidents resulting in oil spills would be difficult to prevent, even with the best of intentions, with potentially disastrous consequences. It could introduce rats, endangering rare birds. It would make poaching of rare birds easier.

The NZ Government had the final say. What should it do? Given the potential environmental impact, a decision for or against it could not be made on economic grounds alone. It required a careful balancing of important economic, political, and environmental factors. There were conflicting objectives, i.e. maximizing the economic welfare of NZ versus minimizing irreversible environmental impacts to preserve a unique wilderness area for the enjoyment of future generations, as well as limiting the intrusion of commercial activities into a national park.

Problems of multiple and conflicting objectives occur frequently, particularly in the public sector. **Multicriteria decision making** approaches may help in dealing with such conflicts. Similarly, problem structuring methods can be used for clarifying different viewpoints and resolving conflicts.

Breast cancer screening policies

Breast cancer is currently the biggest single cause of mortality for women in developed countries. The incidence in NZ is particularly high. About 1 in 11 women will develop breast cancer and of these 40% will die as a result of the disease. Breast cancer incidence and aggressiveness vary with the age of the patient. The disease usually starts with a small growth or lump in the breast tissue. In its early stages such a growth is usually benign. If left untreated, it will enlarge and often become malignant, invading adjacent tissue and ultimately spreading to other parts of the body — so-called metastasis. The rate of progression varies from person to person and with age. The age-specific incidence of breast cancer rises steadily from the mid-twenties through the reproductive years. At menopause there is a temporary drop, after which the rate climbs again.

About 95% of all potentially cancerous growths discovered at a preinvasive stage can be cured. It is thus crucial that it can be detected as early as possible. In the 1970s screening trials were made in Sweden, England, and the USA in an effort to reduce breast cancer mortality. It is now generally accepted that mammography is the most effective method for detecting abnormal tissue growth. Research shows that for women of age 50 mammography can detect about 85% of all abnormal tissue growths that could develop into breast cancer within the next 12 months after screening. This is significantly higher than for other methods of screening. The percentage of potentially cancerous growths detected at an early stage drops substantially as the time interval between screenings becomes longer.

As the need for the introduction of an effective screening policy finally became recognized by both health professionals and governments, there was still some controversy as to the 'best' screening policy to use. A screening policy is defined by the age range of women to be screened and the frequency of screening, e.g. all women between the ages of 48 and 70 at yearly intervals.

In addition to the medical factors and partially avoidable loss of human life involved, there were economic aspects to be considered. In 2000, the cost of a screening was between $50 and $100, while the equipment cost was in the range of $200,000 to $300,000. Each machine can perform around 6400 screenings per year. As the age range and frequency of screening is increased, the number of machines and trained personnel needed also increases. Acquiring these machines and training the personnel required thus involved an enormous capital outlay and could not be done 'overnight'. So, the problem faced by health providers in many countries was (and still is) what policy offered the best compromise between economic considerations and human suffering, and how the policy finally chosen should be implemented. Similar, to the Deep Cove project, such decisions made by publicly funded health providers are not devoid of political considerations.

1.2 Systems thinking

What have all these problem situations in common? A number of things! First, there is somebody who is dissatisfied with the current situation or mode of operation and sees scope for doing something better or more effectively, or sees new opportunities or new options. In other words, this somebody would like to achieve one or several goals, or maintain currently threatened levels of achievement.

Second, the answer to the problem, or the solution, is not obvious. The problem situation is complex. The interested party may not have enough information about the situation to know or discover all the consequences of decision choices, or to be able to evaluate the performance of these options in terms of their goals. Elements of this are present in the Deep Cove and breast cancer problems.

Third, the interactions between various elements or aspects have a degree of complexity that the limited computational capacity of the human mind cannot evaluate in the detail necessary to make an informed decision. All of the problems discussed above are of this nature.

Finally, the settings within which these problems exist are systems. What is a system? Chapters 2 and 3 explore various system concepts in detail. So for now, we define a system as a collection of things, entities, or people that relate to each other in specific ways, i.e. that are organized and follow specific rules of interaction. Collectively, they have a given purpose, i.e. they aim to achieve or produce outcomes that none of its parts can do by themselves. However, let me also quickly add that in the real world systems do not exist or create themselves spontaneously, ready made for us to discover. No! Systems are human inventions. We conceive or view something as a system for our own purposes. This is an important insight, and we will come back to it again.

If we are to deal effectively with the complexity of systems and decision making within systems, we need a new way of thinking. This new way of thinking has evolved since about 1940 and could be labelled 'systems thinking'. **Operations research (OR), systems engineering** or **systems analysis** are strands of this mode of thinking that are particularly suitable if most of the interactions between the various parts of a system can be expressed in quantitative terms, such as mathematical expressions. Since the early 1970s, these so-called **hard OR/hard systems approaches** have been complemented by a number of non-quantitative approaches that go under the label of **soft OR/soft systems approaches**. Some are based on formal systems ideas, whereas others use *ad hoc* processes that have proved successful for certain types or structures or problems, while still being rooted in systems thinking. All are decision processes which help decision makers to explore problems in much of their complexity, to find a good or best compromise solution, and frequently to give answers to important 'what if' questions, such as "How is the best solution affected by significant changes in various cost factors?" or "What is the effect of uncertainty in a critical aspect?" Thus, they provide the decision maker(s) with useful information and insights on which to base an informed decision, rather than be mainly influenced by intuitive, emotional, or political considerations alone. Although political considerations may be unavoidable and may in the end sway the decision one way or another, the use of such decision processes increases the degree of rationality in decision making, be it in the private or public sector. Note, however, that they are not intended to replace the decision maker. The final say still rests with her or him.

1.3 Overview of what follows

As we have seen, most decision making in today's world deals with complex problem situations. They are often ill-defined, subject to conflicting forces and goals. One of the major reasons for this complexity is that these problem situations occur within a systems context. Most systems are created and controlled by humans. The human element can therefore not be excluded from the decision process.

Although we, as humans, are endowed with amazing faculties of reasoning and insight, most of us are unable to cope with more than very few factors at the same time. Without computers, our computational abilities are slow and limited. We have difficulties processing and digesting large quantities of information and tracing complex interrelationships and interactions between various elements or factors. Borrowing a notion from Professor Herbert Simon, the 1978 Nobel Prize Laureate in Economics, we assume that human decision making is limited by **bounded rationality**. It is therefore all the more important that decision making is guided by a systematic and comprehensive methodology that helps us make effective use of our extensive but still limited powers of reasoning.

This text is an introduction to a group of methodologies that go under the general label of **Management Science (MS).** They are not a panacea, capable of handling all problematic situations. They have proved successful for problem situations that involve management problems which lend themselves to rational analysis. Usually they deal with questions of the effectiveness and/or efficiency of various activities or operations. The discussion looks at how systems thinking forms the basis for MS approaches and what is good and bad practice. The methodologies are not intended to deal with dilemmas of a psychological or ethical nature.

Part 1 covers systems thinking and system models, regardless of what specific problem-solving approach is applied. This implies an understanding of essential system concepts. Problems do not occur in a vacuum, but are embedded in **problem situations** — their context. In order to identify the right problem, we need to understand this context in much of its richness and complexity.

Part 2 gives a somewhat succinct overview of the two prominent strands of MS approaches: hard OR, where problems lend themselves to quantification, and soft OR, where the problem situation has high human complexity with conflicting values and perceptions of the stakeholders involved.

Much decision making involves costs and benefits. Which costs and benefits are relevant for a particular decision? Some costs and benefits occur over time. How should their timing be correctly dealt with? And many decision problems involve not simply a single decision point, but a sequence of decisions over time, where later decisions depend on earlier ones. These aspects are the topic of Part 3.

Finally, Part 4 explores how constraints on the decision choices affect decision making, how to deal with uncertainty and incorporate it into the decision process, and how to balance conflicting multiple objectives. Several of the best known hard OR techniques — marginal analysis, linear programming, queueing, simulation and system dynamics, decision and risk analysis, and multicriteria decision making methods — are used for demonstrating these aspects, where the emphasis is not primarily on the intricacies of the mathematical models and their solution methods, but on conceptual aspects of the approach to gain greater insight for informed, rational decision making.

PART 1
Systems and systems thinking: Introduction

Except for the most trivial daily actions, most decision making happens within the context of systems — all sorts of organizations, from family units to major corporations, from local government to international institutions, and all sorts of activities and operations. You may wonder: "Since science has been one of the major driving forces of modern civilization, why don't we simply use the scientific method for decision making? Hasn't it proved itself highly successfully in the biological and physical sciences and, by extension, in all branches of engineering?" There are a number of reasons! First, experts in science and the philosophy of science do not agree on what the scientific method really is. There are also serious claims and much anecdotal evidence that what sets scientists and researchers on the path of successful breakthroughs are often ingenious hunches and that the scientific method is only used after the fact to confirm the results. But even disregarding these controversies, most real-life decision making does not neatly fall into a pattern of observation, followed by generating hypotheses, which are then confirmed or refuted through experimentation.

Most importantly though, while scientific research attempts to understand the various aspects of the world we live in, decision making attempts to change aspects of this world. Furthermore, decision making does not occur under idealized conditions in a laboratory, but out in the real and often messy and turbulent world. So the methodology has to be able to cope with the complexity of the real world, and must be comprehensive and flexible while still delivering the results in the often short time frame within which most decision making has to occur. Nor is it so important that the methodology used satisfies strict scientific principles of inquiry. It is more important that it leads to good decision making.

Part 1 sets the platform of concepts and ideas needed for applying one of these MS methodologies. Chapter 2 gives a few examples of the complexity in today's decision making, discusses effectiveness and efficiency — concepts often misunderstood — and shows that systems may exhibit unexpected counterintuitive behaviours.

It then contrasts the traditional reductionist and cause-and-effect thinking that underlies the scientific method with systems thinking.

Chapter 3 studies basic systems concepts and types of system in detail and highlights them with examples. Since viewing something as a system is a human conceptualization, it is by definition subjective. We explore the meaning of this. The behaviour of systems is the prime concern of systems thinking, and we study various modes of controlling system behaviour.

In order to identify the right problem, we need to understand the context or problem situation in which it occurs and its stakeholders — the roles that various people play. This and how to describe and summarize the problem situation are the topics of Chapter 4. We will study mind maps, rich pictures, and cognitive maps. Chapter 5 studies system models, effective approaches to the process of modelling, and good properties of models. It explores how to capture aspects of special interest in the form of diagrams.

2
Systems thinking

Why is there a need for systems thinking in dealing with many of today's decision situations? Why are the traditional analytic methods used by engineers, economists, and accountants for the last 100 years no longer adequate to come up with the 'right' solutions? After reading this chapter you will be able to give a tentative answer to these two questions.

2.1 Increased complexity of today's decision making

What is 'complexity'? W.R. Ashby, one of the fathers of modern systems thinking, defined complexity as the quantity of information required to describe something ['Some peculiarities of complex systems', *Cybernetic Medicine*, 1973, v9 no2, 1–6]. This includes the number of parts and their interrelations that make up that something, that 'whole'. Complexity is thus in the eye of the beholder. For example, the neurosurgeon views the brain as a highly complex system, while for the butcher the brain of a calf is only one of some 30 different cuts of meat. It seems that the more we know about something, the more complex we see it. The same is true for decision making.

The 20th century, and particularly its second half, was marked by the unprecedented realization of the complexity of even everyday decision making, let alone decision making in government and business. Where before we saw few and only limited interdependencies, technological progress has raised the awareness of many complex interactions. Untold innovations in agriculture, industrial and chemical processes, engineering, and air travel have encroached on our natural environment on a huge scale, a scale so large and unforeseen that we are only now beginning to realize its potential impact on the future of humankind. Similarly, the communication/information explosion since the introduction of television, computer information processing technology, satellite communications, and virtually instant electronic communication via the Internet has revolutionized private and commercial activities and the world of entertainment. Its cultural impact on both developed and developing countries may well turn out to be the greatest leveller the human race has ever experienced and have profound effects on the values and mores of humanity — maybe equalled only by the advent of the world religions like Christianity or Islam.

Hand-in-hand with the accelerating rate of innovation in technology and communications has been the ever increasing complexity of various large infrastructures that regulate our daily lives and supply services that we take for granted, such as water, sewage, power, gas, transport, health, police, fire fighting, emergency and civil defence, education, a multitude of government regulations and laws, and so on. Few of them stand alone. They are heavily interdependent. A planned change, or a hiccup or breakdown in one, may have serious consequences for another.

The lowering of trade barriers and the easing up of the flow of investment funds over the last three decades has given untold power to a few huge multi-national corporations — the names of the industrial and commercial giants like Shell, General Motors, Du Pont, Mitsubishi, Nestlé, Microsoft, or world bankers like Chase Manhattan, Citigroup, Mitsubishi Bank, Sekura Bank spring to mind — with financial and human resources and technical know-how which give them means to influence world events that far exceed the power and control of all but a few national governments. Nor do we fully know the sinister penetration of crime syndicates, like the Mafia, triads, Japanese yakuzas, and more recently Russian crime bosses, into legitimate business ventures and the effects of this.

Along with these developments also came the widening gap between the rich developed countries, with their ever-increasing demand for energy and raw materials, their consumption and waste mentality, and the poor underdeveloped and developing countries, where traditional subsistence farming has been replaced by large-scale planting of cash crops subject to widely fluctuating world prices, leading to unsustainable indebtedness towards the developed countries and hopeless impoverishment of their rural population.

Add to this the problems of overpopulation, the collapse of the communist power bloc, the resurgence of ethnic-based nationalism and religious fundamentalism, both erupting in bloody conflicts and insurgencies, the legitimate call for women's equality in this male-dominated world, the 1998 economic crises that started with the collapse of the banking systems in several of the Asian 'economic miracle' countries and soon threatened the world economy, the uncertainties and unanswered questions of genetic engineering in both agriculture and medicine, and the looming environmental threats (deforestation, ozone depletion, greenhouse gases) of a planet that continues to be exploited and abused for the sake of profit and greed, economic growth, and political and economic power. Today's world has thus increased in complexity and interdependence to a point where the traditional methods of problem solving based on the cause-and-effect model cannot cope any longer. Let us study briefly some examples.

Construction of the Aswan High Dam in Egypt

Many of the 'great' technical achievements have not just brought the increased well-being used to justifying them, but have also had unexpected undesirable consequences, some of which may far outweigh the benefits claimed. The construction of the Aswan High Dam in Egypt is cited as an example. Heralded as the key to Egypt's entry into the world of plenty, it initially increased agricultural production in the Nile Delta. However, it also caused an unprecedented increase in schistosomiasis — a highly debilitating disease spread by water snails that thrive in the irrigation canals. In the 1970s it was claimed that 60% of Egypt's fellahin (farm workers) were affected. Fertile silt, which prior to the building of the dam annually renewed the fertility of the land it inundated, is now trapped behind the dam. In its place a massive increase in the use of fertilizers is needed to maintain output. That, together with poor drainage, causes salinization, annually rendering large tracts of land unsuitable for agriculture. The loss of the silt previously carried past the Delta into the Mediterranean has caused the sea to encroach onto the land, leading to further loss of land. The loss of the nutrients previously fed into the Mediterranean destroyed the sardine fisheries which provided an essential part of the population's diet. Finally, uncontrollable growth of water hyacinth in Lake Nasser causes excessive loss of water through evaporation. So the erection of the Aswan High Dam had a number of unexpected consequences, some of them disastrous. Few were predicted and taken into account when the decision to build the dam was made. That decision, in fact, was largely a political power play between the USA and the old USSR, both hoping to incorporate Egypt within their sphere of influence.

Deterioration of urban transport

A second example is the increasing deterioration of urban public transport. In response to the suburban population drift and increased car ownership after the Second World War, it looked like a very responsible public policy of city planners to improve the road network and city centre parking facilities. It unfortunately also led to reduced patronage of public transport facilities. That in turn resulted in fare hikes and a curtailment of service frequency and coverage, which accelerated the shift from public to private transport, and the story continues. The end result was the virtual demise of public transport in many cities and ever more serious traffic congestion on the access roads used by commuters. Again we see that seemingly good responsible decision making resulted in unexpected outcomes which only temporarily improved access to the city centres. It is interesting to speculate what would have happened if city mayors had opted to upgrade public transport to bring the people from the suburbs into the city, rather than upgrading the road network.

Assessment of unit production costs

Many firms compute the unit production cost at each machine centre by adding up all the material, energy, and labour costs incurred at that machine centre and then dividing the total by the number of parts produced. The efficiency of a machine centre is assessed on the level of its unit production costs: the lower the unit production costs at a machine centre, the higher its efficiency. This rule works fine for simple one-stage production processes, where the firm works at full capacity and has no difficulties in selling all its output.

However, the above rule runs into serious trouble when we are faced with complex multi-product production processes. Usually, each machine centre produces many different parts — often in small lots — which are used as input into later stages of the production process. If the centre supervisor is judged on the basis of unit production costs, then he or she will have a strong incentive to have all machines and operators producing parts all the time. If subsequent machine centres do not require the parts immediately, they will temporarily be stored in a warehouse or on the production floor. The costs of keeping these stocks are normally not attributed to the machine centre that produced them. So the machine centre's efficiency looks good, but the firm ends up with excessive intermediate parts stocks that are costly to finance and maintain and furthermore run the risk of becoming obsolete before they are required.

Activity: For each of the above three examples list three aspects that contribute to the complexity of the situation.

2.2 Efficiency and effectiveness

Efficiency

The last example demonstrates how the concern with efficiency for a particular operation or division of a firm may lead to an overall deterioration of the performance, in this case profit generation, of the firm as a whole. The firm may be very efficient in the use of its resources, but this efficiency is not put to effective use in terms of the firm's overall objectives or goals.

So what is efficiency and what is effectiveness? Everyday language often confuses these concepts. Efficiency looks at how well resources are used in a given activity. The higher the level of output achieved for a given set of inputs or resources or, alternatively, the lower the inputs or resources needed for producing a given level of output, the higher the **technical efficiency** of the activity. For example, driving a car so as to maximizes the ratio of distance travelled to fuel consumption is technically efficient. This may mean that you travel at between 60 and 80 km per hour, always accelerate very gradually, and plan your speed so as to avoid any unnecessary use of the brakes. However, if the vehicle is used for commercial purposes, e.g. a bus service, such a mode of driving may be economically inefficient, since it ignores wage costs for the driver as well as the potential earning power of the vehicle. For **economic efficiency**, in terms of maximizing the difference between revenues and total costs, the vehicle may often have to be driven in a technically inefficient way. The gain in added revenue may well outweigh the increased costs of a technically inefficient operation.

Effectiveness

Effectiveness, on the other hand, looks at how well the goals or objectives of the entity or activity are achieved. For example, the bus service may be part of a city's public transport system. Its objectives may be to provide convenient but cost-effective commuter transport, where 'convenient' may be defined as 'no residents having to walk more than five minutes from their home or workplace to catch public transport'. Economically efficient operation of each vehicle is now only one aspect of the system operation. The choice of bus routes, the frequency of service at various times of the day, and the type of vehicles used and how they are maintained, as well as the fare structure, all enter into determining the effectiveness of the transport system in terms of its objectives and the resource constraints imposed on it. Trade-offs between these variables will affect overall effectiveness of the system.

Efficiency versus effectiveness

Operating various parts of a system in their most efficient manner does not necessarily mean the system as a whole is effective in terms of achieving its ob-jectives. Consider the operation of a hospital. The fact that its testing laboratory, its physiotherapy service, its blood bank service, etc., are all operated efficiently in a technical and economic sense is not sufficient for the hospital as a whole to operate effectively. For instance, the tests ordered from the laboratory may be the wrong type or may be redundant in the sense of not adding any additional information for correct diagnoses. The fact that they are executed efficiently does not imply that their use was effective. Effectiveness implies that these services are used and coordinated properly to achieve the objectives of the system as a whole.

Why do managers of all sorts of organizations, profit-making as well as non-profit-making, private and public, seem to be so much concerned with efficiency? When working with a fixed budget — a limited amount of funds to spend over a given period of time — any pound spent on a given activity means a pound less for another activity. Hence the overriding concern to make every pound go as far as possible. Now, most firms or organizations operate with some waste or not fully utilized resources. Most managers' natural reaction is to eliminate such waste or underutilised resources. As we have seen above, the consequences for the firm as a whole may, however, not turn out to be as beneficial as expected.

Here is another example. Walk through any factory and you will see machine spare parts accumulating dust. They tie up the funds spent to purchase them. These funds are seemingly 'idle'. Hence, it looks like a good idea to reduce the stock of spare parts, freeing the funds for productive use elsewhere in the firm. But wait a minute! The reason why the spare parts were purchased was to keep any down-time resulting from a machine part breaking down as short as possible. If the parts are in stock, no time is lost waiting to get them. If the supplier is overseas, procuring them could easily imply a few weeks' delay, or expensive air freighting. So lack of adequate stocks of spare parts may result in prolonged down-time during which the machine is 'idle'. The loss of profit from the loss of output may far outweigh the cost of funding adequate stocks of spares. Therefore, elimination of such seemingly 'idle' spares may not be cost-effective. The real problem is not one of being efficient in the sense of eliminating idle resources, but rather one of being effective in terms of the operation of the firm as a whole. In this example, this translates itself into finding the proper balance between the cost of the investment in stocks of spares and the cost of machine down-time incurred if the firm is short of spares.

This same theme occurs with respect to productive capacity of all sorts — machine capacities, runway capacity at airports, or employee levels in service industries, to name just a few. The difficult question to answer is: at what point is there real excess capacity in terms of the overall costs for the organization as a whole, rather than in terms of seeming 'idleness' over long periods of time?

Complementarity of efficiency and effectiveness

This discussion may have given the impression that efficiency is the enemy of effectiveness. Far from it! It is only the narrow concern with efficiency at the exclusion of the overall goals of the organization which is detrimental. True efficiency looks at the overall goals. Hence the effectiveness of decisions and policies taken by the decision makers is enhanced. The goals of the organization will be achieved at lower costs, with fewer resources, or with increased benefits — in other words, more efficiently. The two are thus complementary. Effectiveness deals with 'doing the right thing', efficiency with 'doing things right'.

Activity:
- What actions on your part would make studying this text more efficient? (Example: agree with your flatmate(s) not to be disturbed.)
- How would you judge that your studying of the text was effective?

2.3 Unplanned and counterintuitive outcomes

In all these cases we see a common theme: seemingly rational decisions are made on the basis that 'Action A will cause the desired outcome B to be realized.' But in addition to B the decision also causes C, D, and E. Some of these outcomes are unintended and unpredicted, and may partially or wholly negate the sought-for economic or social benefits of the intended outcome B.

Responsible decision making clearly must consider the undesirable and/or additional beneficial effects of unplanned outcomes on the system as a whole. Consideration of such outcomes may well sway the decision. A comprehensive systems analysis is more likely to uncover most of the unplanned outcomes than a narrow cause-and-effect analysis (see Section 2.4 for cause-and-effect thinking).

Some of the outcomes actually realized, both planned and unplanned, may be 'counterintuitive' — what happens appears at first glance to contradict what common sense and intuition tell us should occur. Here are two examples.

A production example

It is a generally accepted business principle that a firm should push those products which offer the highest profit margin. Consider the following simple example: A firm produces two products on the same assembly line as shown in Figure 2-1. Both cost the same to produce, i.e. £90/unit, but product A has a profit margin of 50%, while B only achieves 40%. (The profit margin is [profit/selling price] × 100%.)

Figure 2-1   A production situation.

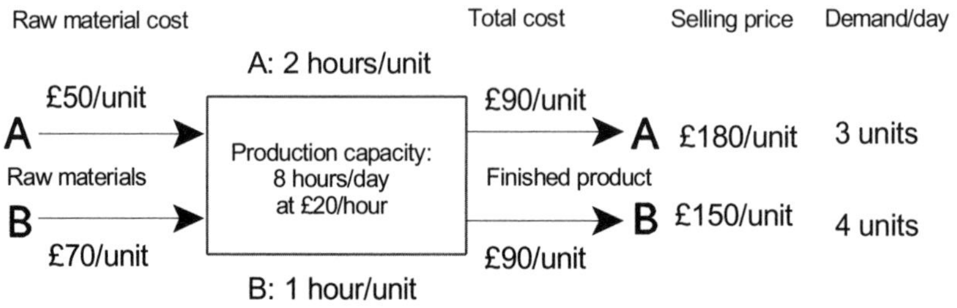

Given the limited demand for each product, it seems intuitively appealing that the firm should produce as many of A as it can sell, i.e. four, and then use up the remaining production capacity of 2 hours to produce two units of B. The daily profit is then 3 × £90 + 2 × £60 = £390.

Interestingly, in this example a reversal of the above business principle produces a better result. Namely, the firm should produce as many as possible of the product with the lower profit margin and only then use the remaining production capacity to produce the one with the higher profit margin. The resulting output of four units of B plus 2 units of A has a total profit of £420 — higher by £30.

This is a counterintuitive result. Why does it happen? The answer is simple. The business principle ignores vital system interactions: in this case, the different profit contribution per unit production capacity used of each product. Every hour of capacity used by product B produces a profit of £60, while an hour of work on product A only achieves £45.

The Hawthorne experiments

A famous example is given by experiments conducted around 1930 among workers of the Hawthorne Works factory of the Western Electric Company in Illinois. A group of workers were subjected to a number of successive changes in their work environment to determine the effects on their performance or work output. One of these experiments involved changing the light luminosity in their work space. As expected by the researchers, improved work space lighting increased the productivity of those workers affected, but contrary to expectations the control group who had not benefited of any change also showed improved productivity. When the lighting was restored to its original level as part of further experiments, rather than causing a decrease in productivity it resulted in a further increase. Both results were completely counterintuitive. How could this be explained?

The explanation was found in the discovery by the researcher of what became known as the 'Hawthorne effect' — an increase in worker productivity, produced by the psychological stimulus of being singled out and made to feel important. Somebody seemed to care about their lot, looking for how their work environment could be improved — factors initially overlooked. This was perceived not only by the group subjected to the changes, but also by the control group.

In conclusion, outcomes that at first seem counterintuitive are usually not mysterious happenings. Most often, they can be explained by taking a sufficiently comprehensive systems view.

> Activity: For each of the three examples in Section 2.1 list:
> - the planned desirable and undesirable outcomes (Example answer for the 'emergency services call centre' in Section 1.1: low waiting time is a planned desirable outcome, while idle staff is an planned undesirable outcome.)
> - the unplanned desirable and undesirable outcomes (Example continued: low waiting times will lead to a low rate of complaints against the service, which is desirable and usually not planned and vice versa for high waiting times.)
> - Can you identify any counterintuitive outcomes? (Example continued: long waiting times or slow response rate may lead to an increase in the number of calls received. Explanation: Some calls, such as fires or accidents, may trigger several repeated calls if the waiting time increases.)

2.4 Reductionist and cause-and-effect thinking

How is it that, all too frequently, our decision-making process seems to be so singularly linear? There is the desired outcome Y — here is action X which will cause Y to happen! Russell L. Ackoff — a philosopher, operations researcher, and systems thinker — gives us an answer in his paper 'Science in the Systems Age' [*Operations Research*, May-June 1973]. He says that the intellectual foundations of the traditional scientific model of thought are based on two major ideas. The first is reductionism: the belief that everything in the world and every experience of it can be reduced, decomposed, or disassembled into ultimately simple indivisible parts. Explaining the behaviour of these parts and then aggregating these partial explanations is assumed to be sufficient to allow us to understand and explain the behaviour of the system as a whole.

Applied to problem solving, this translates into breaking a problem into a set of simpler subproblems, solving each individually and then assembling their solutions into an overall solution for the whole problem. 'Division of labour' and 'organizational structure along functional lines', such as finance, personnel, purchasing, manufacture, marketing, and R&D are clear manifestations of this. However, we know that even if each is operated with the highest economic efficiency, the sum of the individual solutions does not necessarily produce an overall solution that is best for the system as a whole. The hospital example in Section 2.2 is an instance of this.

The second basic idea is that all phenomena are explainable by using cause-and-effect relationships. A thing X is taken to be the cause of Y if X is both necessary and sufficient for Y to happen. Hence, 'cause X' is all that is needed to explain 'effect Y'.

If we view the world in this way, everything can be explained by decomposing it into parts and looking for cause-and-effect relationships between the parts. But we have seen in the examples above that it may be inadequate to examine the causal relationships one by one. New relationships or properties may emerge through the interaction between the various parts or aspects of a situation — so-called **emergent properties** or relationships. Some of these are usually planned, while others may be unexpected and counterintuitive. Furthermore, causal relationships may not be simply one-way. There could be **mutual causality** or **feedback** between two things, i.e. X affects Y, but is in turn affected by Y. The two are interdependent. Dealing with one alone, while ignoring the other, may not achieve the desired results. For example, poverty may result in poor health, which may in turn lead to further poverty. Dealing with both simultaneously, rather than just with each individually, is likely to be much more effective in improving both. Chapter 3 will pick up mutual causality and feedback in more detail.

2.5 Systems thinking

From about 1940 on, a number of researchers from various scientific disciplines — biology, mathematics, communication theory, and philosophy — started to recognize that all things and events, and the experience of them, are parts of larger wholes. This does not deny the importance of the individual elementary parts or events. But the focus shifts from the parts to the wholes, namely to the **systems** to which the parts belong. This gave rise to a new way of thinking — **systems thinking**. Something to be explained is viewed as part of a larger whole, a system, and is explained in terms of its role in that system.

This new mode of thought has immediate consequences for decision making within a systems context, namely that for effective action in terms of the system as a whole it may not be sufficient to use reductionist and cause-and-effect thinking by studying the individual parts or aspects in isolation. In order to get a true picture, it is essential to study their **systemic** role in the system.

However, this does not imply that we should discard reductionist and cause-and-effect thinking in favour of systems thinking. Both approaches are in fact complementary. We cannot conceive of parts if there is no system to which they belong, nor can we talk of a whole unless there are constitutive elements that make up the whole. Reductionism gives attention to the details of each component, systems thinking to their systemic role in the system. Each may ignore or miss crucial aspects. More often than not, both modes of thinking are needed to gain a fuller understanding of a system. When we emphasis one, the other is implied. They are like the object and its shadow.

The next chapter defines systems and studies various aspects and properties of systems. Chapter 5 explores how to define a system and capture certain systems aspects using diagrammatic methods.

> Activity: Remember how you learned to drive a car. Analyse the learning process you went through and list three tasks you mastered using:
> • reductionist thinking (e.g. starting the motor),
> • cause-and-effect thinking (e.g. pressing the brake pedal to slow down).
> Give two examples of why mastering each task of driving a car separately is insufficient for learning to drive safely.

2.6 Chapter highlights

- Today's world in a modern society is becoming increasingly complex.
- Traditional rational thinking is still largely based on reductionist and cause-and-effect modes. These may not be able to cope with complexity, leading to narrowly focused, piece-meal decision making which may result in unplanned outcomes and which from an overall point of view may be ineffective.
- Systems thinking takes a more comprehensive view, focussing on the whole and trying to explain the role or behaviour of the parts in terms of the whole, rather than the other way round.
- Systems thinking strives for effectiveness in terms of the system as a whole, rather than narrow efficiency of its parts.
- Systems exhibit not only the planned and desired outputs, but also unplanned and often undesirable outputs. Some outputs may seem counterintuitive.

Exercises

1. The University Energy Committee held a meeting discussing ways to save power. The following argument between two committee members was overheard:

   A: 'Clearly, every light turned off means some power saved. Hence, one of the major tasks of this committee is to educate all members of the university, and in particular all staff, to turn off lights whenever they are the last to leave a room, a lecture hall, or a corridor.'

   B: 'Admittedly, a policy of turning off lights may generate some immediate power savings. But the greater frequency of turning lights on and off will burn out lights more quickly and result in higher light bulb replacement costs. Furthermore, dark corridors and lecture halls may also increase the incidence of accidents and the potential for crime, possibly imposing higher costs on the university community as a whole.'

A: 'The brief of this committee is to save power. The things you mention are not our concern!'

What are the desired planned outcomes and what could be the undesired, unplanned and unexpected outcomes of the action proposed by A? Discuss the arguments put forth by A and B in terms of efficiency and effectiveness.

2. Consider the Deep Cove Water Export Project briefly described in Section 1.1.
   (a) Contrast the different views, in terms of efficiency and effectiveness, taken by the firm, the Government, and environmental protection groups.
   (b) List the planned outcomes and the unplanned outcomes of the proposal.

3. Consider the Breast Cancer Screening Policy Project described in Section 1.1.
   (a) Contrast the different views, in terms of efficiency versus effectiveness taken, by the Government, health professionals, and the female population in the 50–70 age range.
   (b) List the planned outcomes and the unplanned outcomes of the example policy stated.

4. For each of the following examples discuss the relevance of efficiency versus effectiveness:
   (a) The Aswan High Dam Project in Egypt (Section 2.1)
   (b) The deterioration of urban transport (Section 2.1)
   (c) The emergency services call centre (Section 1.1)

5. For each of the following examples list one or more counterintuitive outcomes:
   (a) The Aswan High Dam Project in Egypt (Section 2.1).
   (b) The deterioration of urban transport (Section 2.1).
   (c) The assessment of unit production costs (Section 2.1).

6. Some systems experts stress the importance of the three Es, i.e. efficiency, effectiveness, and efficacy. Compare the brief definitions given in the glossary, and show their relationship and differences. What does 'efficacy' add that is not contained in efficiency and effectiveness?

7. In your own words, discuss the difference between efficiency and effectiveness. Give two real-life practical examples for each. Give an example where a narrow view of efficiency interferes with effectiveness and one where efficiency enhances effectiveness.

8. In the spare part example in Section 2.2, the assumption was that any delay in output of the machine causes a loss of sales of finished products. Assume now that there is no loss of sales for a (reasonably small) delay in output. How does this change the argument about stocking or not stocking spare parts? Answer the same question if there are other machines available with sufficient capacity that can produce the same output, possibly at a somewhat higher cost?

9. Briefly discuss an example of mutual causality present for the following:
   (a) The Aswan High Dam Project in Egypt (Section 2.1).
   (b) The deterioration of urban transport (Section 2.1).
   (c) Poverty and educational achievement.
   (d) The inflationary spiral (relating prices to wage levels).

3
System concepts

In Chapter 2 you saw why it is useful to know about systems. This chapter discusses in more detail the most important system concepts. Sections 3.2–3.7 explore how to define systems, what is so special about them, and what differentiates them from a mere collection of parts. Section 3.8 studies system behaviour and the importance of emergent properties of systems — the main reason for viewing something as a system. We then briefly look at various classifications of systems in Section 3.9. Our main interest is the control of systems — control aimed at achieving certain desired goals. This is the topic of the last section.

3.1 Pervasiveness of systems

In the 1950s, with the exception of a few pioneering scientists, the term **system** was hardly used except in words like **systematic**. This is rather surprising, since we are constantly surrounded by things we view as systems or that belong to systems. Similarly, new systems are conceptualized or invented by the thousands every day.

Planet Earth is viewed as a part of the **solar system**. Our whole life is spent in, and shaped and controlled by **social systems**, like the family, the neighbourhood, the school, our workplace, and various interest groups we join, participate in, and drop out of. Some of us exploit **political systems** or are frustrated by them. Life without a **telephone system** would be difficult to imagine. The Internet system has become our favourite **communication system**. In high school or university we learn about **number systems**. Modern management practices would collapse without **information systems**. We expect our rights to be protected by the **legal system**. When our **digestive system** strikes, we suffer. Indeed, the most important part of us, which differentiates us from other animals, is our brain, part of our **central nervous system**.

At first sight, these things seem to have little in common. So, why are they all referred to as systems? They are all assemblies of things or entities that we view as interconnected or standing in clearly defined relationships with each other. They may have evolved to these relationships through natural physical processes, like the solar system or a biological system. These are **natural systems**. Or they have been created by humans, such as **human activity systems**, like most social systems, business and industrial entities or parts of them, or **abstract systems**, like number systems or information systems. In this text, we will be mainly interested in human activity systems, how to describe them, how to control them, and what aspects and considerations lead to effective decision making.

Figure 3-1 is an excerpt from *Webster's 9th New Collegiate Dictionary*. It lists more than a dozen different meanings for the word 'system', including the everyday language use as a procedure or scheme, or as a derogatory term for 'the ruling social order' or 'the establishment'. Have you recently 'beaten the system', implying you got around some rule you did not like?

Figure 3-1   Excerpt from *Webster's 9th New Collegiate Dictionary*.

sys-tem n [**LL** systemat-, systema. fr Gk systemat-, systema. fr. synistanai to combine, fr. syn- + histanai to cause to stand – more at STAND] (1619) **1 :** a regularly interacting or interdependent group of items forming a unified whole {a number ~}: as **a** (1) : a group of interacting bodies under the influence of related forces {a gravitational ~} (2) : an assemblage of substances that is in or tends to equilibrium {a thermodynamic ~} **b** (1) : a group of body organs that together perform one or more vital functions {the digestive ~} (2) : the body considered as a functional unit **c** : a group of related natural objects or forces {a river ~} **d** : a group of devices or artificial objects or an organization forming a network esp. for distributing something or serving a common purpose {a telephone ~} {a heating ~} {a highway ~} {a data processing ~} **e** : a major division of rocks usu. larger than a series and including all formed during a period or era **f** : a form of social, economic, or political organization or practice {the capitalist ~} **2 :** an organized set of doctrines, ideas, or principles usu. intended to explain the arrangement or working of a systematic whole {the Newtonian ~ of mechanics} **3 a** : an organized or established procedure {the touch ~ of typing} **b** : a manner of classifying, symbolizing, or schematizing {a taxonomic ~} {the decimal ~} **4** : harmonious arrangement or pattern : ORDER {bring ~ out of confusion – Ellen Glasgow} **5** : an organized society or social situation regarded as stultifying: ESTABLISHMENT 2 – usu. used with the syn see METHOD – sys-tem-less.

Our view of a 'system' will be much more restrictive. The key terms are 'interacting', 'interdependent', and 'forming a unified whole'. Furthermore, it is not the notion of 'systematic', in the sense of carefully using a rational method or following a well laid-out plan or procedure, that primarily concerns us here, although we will go about any applications of system concepts in a systematic way. The key emphasis is on **systemic**, i.e. 'pertaining to systems', using systems ideas, or viewing things in terms of their role in a system. The term 'organized' captures much of the system idea.

3.2   Out-there and inside-us view of systems

One of the prime sources of confusion when calling an organized assembly of things a system is what could be termed the **out-there** view of systems in contrast to the

inside-us view of systems. When we talk about our solar system we have in mind the Sun and its nine planets, of which Earth is one, and how the planets are linked to the Sun and each other by gravitational forces. Similarly, an electric power system is viewed as the collection of power stations and their equipment, the power transmission grid, the local distribution network, with its transformers and power lines, and the various control stations that regulate the flow of power, as well as what the power system does, i.e. generate electric power and distribute it to its users where it is 'consumed'. A computer information system consists of the pieces of data collected, the rules used for collecting the data and their transformation into pieces of information, the storage of this information in computer files, the programs for processing, storing, cross-referencing, manipulating, retrieving, and presenting this information on screens or in printed form, the computer equipment needed to perform all these activities, and finally the users.

In each of these examples, the system **is seen** as the physical and abstract things that make up the whole assembly, their relationships, and what the system does. This is the out-there view of systems. It is seen as absolute; it exists or will exist sometimes out there; it is viewed as independent of the observer.

While most informed people today would agree on the same definition of the solar system, no such agreement can be expected for what things make up a particular electric power system or a computer information system. The hydro reservoirs, the water catchment areas that feed them, and the annual water inflow patterns as part of the system were not listed. This is a seemingly arbitrary choice of what is viewed as belonging to that system. Another observer might have included these aspects as integral parts. One of our colleagues, who is an expert in the efficient operation of such systems, would have included the pricing structure for electricity as part of the system, something partially controllable by the power company. So we see that different people may define the same 'system' in different ways, deliberately choosing what to include and what to exclude.

The choice of what to include or exclude will largely depend on what the person viewing something as a system intends to do with this definition, i.e. the purpose of defining something as a system. The system is no longer seen as existing independently of the observer; it is not out there; it has become a mental construct, personal to the observer! This is the inside-us view of systems.

The confusing thing is that in everyday language the word is usually used in an out-there meaning. This even happens if the assembly of components is a human construct or view, such as an industrial or business operation. It is described as if it existed independently of the observer. Unfortunately, even systems experts sometimes fall into this trap. So, when we say 'something is a system', what we really mean is that we '**view something as a system**' for a given purpose. Most often it is simply a convenient means to express and organize our thoughts.

Systems as a human conceptualization

In this text, it is the inside-us view of systems that is important. Systems are seen as human conceptualizations. Although they may exist out there, it is only the human observer that views something as a system. For instance, the grandfather taking his grandchild for a walk along an estuary may see the estuary as a beautiful place to share the wonders of nature with his grandchild, while the jogger, crossing their path, may be hardly aware of anything more than a few feet away from the path. The biology student studying the estuary will see it as an ecological system, where plants, insects, and all sorts of aquatic life forms interact with each other and are affected by the tides. The engineer working for the local catchment authority will also see it as a system, in fact, a subsystem of a larger water drainage system under her management. The grandfather or the jogger will hardly view the estuary as a system, while the biology student and the engineer each see different systems. But when the engineer takes her wind surfer onto the estuary, she too will not see it as a system, but simply as an enjoyable playground.

The point that systems are human conceptualizations is clearly driven home by the fact that the majority of systems we conceive in our role as analysts are not our personal view of some existing real assembly of things out there in the real world. They are visions (i.e. mental conceptualizations) of things that may not exist yet, things we plan to realize, such as a major planned change to an existing operation, still to be implemented. Sometimes these visions are idealizations of what we would like to see, idealizations that we know will never come fully true, but which we strive to realize at least partially.

3.3 Subjectivity of system description

The way something is viewed as a system depends on the personal interest of the observer. The purpose of studying an organized assembly of things as a system will determine the type of system seen. However, any two people viewing the same situation with the same purpose in mind may well form surprisingly different conceptualizations of that organized assembly of things. The reason for this is that the way an individual views a situation is affected by factors highly personal to that individual — aspects that the person may not even be fully aware of.

The world view of the observer

These personal factors are such things as the upbringing, cultural and social background, education, practical experience, and values or beliefs of the individual. For example, the three co-owners of a firm may each view their firm as a different system: the first (the materialist) views it as a system to increase his wealth, the second (the idealistic artist) as a system to exercise her creative drive, and the third (the humanitarian) as a system to provide employment for the people in the town he lives in. So one of the skills that all budding management scientists have to learn is to see a situation through other people's eyes. Hopefully, this will also make them more aware of their own way of looking at the world.

These personal factors are all captured in the concept of the ***Weltanschauung*** of the individual. This German word loosely translates as **world view**. It operates like coloured spectacles that taint things: distorting a few, emphasizing some, and obscuring others. It works as a filter that channels a person's view in a given personal direction and allows her or him to attribute meaning to what he or she observes that is congruent with his or her *Weltanschauung* or world view.

Effect of previous knowledge

Reality is even more diverse and confusing. Partial knowledge, or an *a priori* obvious interpretation, or what we are told about something may affect what we observe or end up seeing. Consider the three shapes in Figure 3-2. We immediately recognize them as an isosceles triangle, a circle with a point at its centre, and a sector of a circle.

Figure 3-2   Geometrical shapes.

In fact, each of these shapes is a different view of the same object, seen from a different angle. Can you guess what that object is? To verify your guess, look at Figure 3-3 over the page.

The triangle is the silhouette of the cone seen level with its base. The circle is the view from above, while the sector is its silhouette as seen from a hill in front.

System definitions are subjective

For all these reasons, the way you view something as a system is to a large extent subjective. It is important for you to recognize that other people, viewing the same system, may not share your definition. Not only may they attribute a different purpose to the system, they may also include and exclude different aspects. But, and this is an important 'but', one definition cannot be labelled 'right' or 'valid' and another one 'wrong' or 'invalid'. As long as each is logically consistent, each one is valid for its owner. The only judgement that may be made is that one may be more effective, insightful, useful, or defensible in terms of the aim or purpose for building it. This is an important aspect of systems thinking that may be difficult for a novice to accept. It is simpler, more comforting, and less threatening to think in terms of a single unique answer or solution — the right answer. However, systems thinking is not a matter of black-and-white, but of shades of grey.

Figure 3-3 A cone.

Naturally, this discussion deals with the age-old controversy of **objective** versus **subjective**. Is there objectivity? From what you have read so far, you must conclude that we are firm believers that objectivity, at least in its traditional meaning of 'the expression or interpretation of facts or conditions as perceived without distortion by personal feelings, prejudices — in other words, independent of the observer's mind' — is an illusion. It is not an operational concept. What is out there in the real world can never be fully known. All we have are perceptions of an unknown reality, constructed and reconstructed as we learn more and gain more insights. Our mind can only capture our personal perceptions coherent with our world view. The only operational meaning that objectivity may have is what the systems thinker R.L. Ackoff [1974] calls 'the social product of the open interaction of a wide variety of individual subjectivities' — a sort of **consensual subjectivity**. So, a wide consensus of interpretations on many things is not excluded. Modern scientific knowledge is based on such a consensus. But, as the two examples below show, this is all that it is: a consensus. Or to quote Albert Einstein: 'The only justification for our concepts is that they serve to represent the complex of our experiences; beyond this, they have no legitimacy.'

Consider the interpretation of 'what is insanity?' We look at past views of 'possessed by the devil' either with abhorrence or a benign smile. Future generations may think of the current view of 'deep-seated emotional disturbances due to maladjustment to the social environment, particularly in childhood' as rather naive.

Probably the most famous example comes from physics. Newton's laws of dynamics have been and still are some of the most successful scientific theories of profound theoretical and practical importance ever put forward. Not only were these laws corroborated by countless experiments and observations, but they also fully proved their practical value in mechanics — the building and working of all machinery on which modern life is based. Yet, at the beginning of the 20th century, Einstein showed that, when considering motions with velocities comparable to that of light, or when attempting to analyse the mechanics of atoms and subatomic elements, Newton's laws, seen as inviolate for over two centuries, break down and must be replaced by postulates of relativity and quantum theory. Nevertheless, this in no way diminishes the continued importance of Newton's laws for operations with bodies of ordinary size, as dealt with in industry and much of space science.

So if you hear somebody state with emphasis 'The facts prove it!' or 'Looking at it objectively, ...' be suspicious. The person is either a fool, possibly a naive one, or he or she is trying to make you uncertain and cow you into submission.

3.4 Formal definition of the concept 'system'

We choose to define a system as follows:

1. A system is an organized assembly of components. 'Organized' means that there exist special relationships between the components.

2. The system does something, i.e. it exhibits behaviours that are unique to the system.

3. Each component contributes towards the behaviour of the system and its own behaviour is affected by being in the system. No component has an independent effect on the system. (A part that has an independent effect and is not affected by the system is an input. See (5) below.) The behaviour of the system is changed if any component is removed or leaves.

4. Groups of components within the system may by themselves have properties (1), (2), and (3), i.e. they may form **subsystems**.

5. The system has an outside — an environment — which provides inputs into the system and receives outputs from the system.

6. The system has been identified by someone to be of special interest for a given purpose.

The relationships between components may be uni-directional and/or causal, i.e. part A affects part B, but is not in turn affected by B. They may be mutual, i.e. A and B both affect each other. Mutual influences or causality increase the complexity of system behaviour.

The crucial ingredients of a system are therefore its **components**, the **relationships** between the components, the **behaviour** or the **activities** of the system, its **relevant environment**, the **inputs** from the environment, the **outputs** to the environment, and the **special interest of the observer**. This is depicted in Figure 3-4, which shows two overlapping systems.

A system is not a mere collection of parts that do not interact with each other, i.e. it is not a **chaotic aggregate**, such as a pile of rocks. Adding a few parts to a chaotic aggregate or removing some does not change its nature. Doing so in a system will affect its behaviour. Similarly, a chaotic aggregate does not do anything, while a system does or at least is capable of doing things under specific conditions.

Figure 3-4   Environment, systems, subsystems, and components.

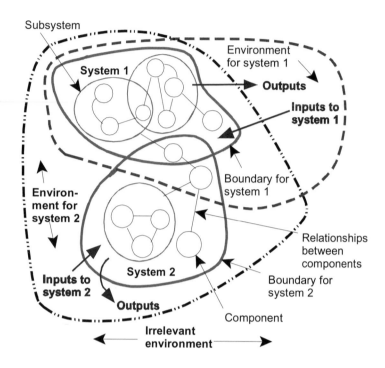

System components do not have to be physical things. They can be abstract things, such as information, numerical variables that measure things, like cumulative costs or levels of achievement, and relationships between physical or abstract things. In fact, most systems of interest in decision making may often consist of abstract things and their relationships alone.

An example of two overlapping systems is the operation of a fire service and an ambulance service, sharing the same facility and communication subsystem.

What a system does — its activity — is of prime interest to the observer, a decision maker or an analyst. The system behaviour consists of a **transformation process**, i.e. **inputs from the environment are transformed into outputs**. Examples of such transformation processes are living plants, which when exposed to light transform water and carbon dioxide (inputs) into carbohydrates and oxygen (outputs), or a manufacturing firm, which transforms raw materials (inputs) into finished products for sale to customers (outputs), or resources, such as funds, labour and expertise of people (inputs), into profit (outputs).

The relevant environment of a system consists of all those aspects that affect system behaviour in any form, and those aspects that are affected by it but do not in turn affect it. (If they did they should be included as part of the system.) They are viewed as being outside the system. They provide inputs to the system or receive outputs from the system. Inputs are things the system needs to function but does not produce for itself, or if so only in insufficient quantities, such as resources or information. Inputs may also be in the form of constraints on the behaviour of the system, e.g. by setting quality standards or equipment capacities.

Many of the inputs are **uncontrollable** or assumed to be so. They are given and cannot be affected by the decision maker. However, aspects over which the decision maker has control are **controllable inputs**. The control may be in the form of being able to select the value of a decision variable, choosing one of a range of actions to take, a decision about the amount of certain resources, such as funds, to be made available to the system, or a set of decision rules to follow whenever the behaviour of the system exhibits certain conditions or a specified event occurs.

Outputs are things the system 'releases' or gives to the environment, such as goods and services, information, funds, and waste products. They also include **measures of performance** or other indicators of system behaviour. The purpose for studying a system determines which ones an observer may want to measure.

The relevant environment is in turn embedded in an even larger environment — 'the universe' — which is assumed not to affect the system; nor is it affected by the system, i.e. it is irrelevant and can be ignored.

Finally, the person studying a system has a purpose for doing so. This could be to gain a better understanding of system behaviour, e.g. for a natural system. For human activity systems the 'observer' is usually the decision maker, interested in how to control system behaviour, e.g. how to achieve maximum output.

3.5 System boundary and relevant environment

The separation between the system and its environment means that there is a **boundary**. In fact, **boundary selection is the most critical aspect of systems thinking**. Boundary choice determines not only the nature of the system transformation process and the form of the outputs, but also who will benefit from the desirable outputs and who will suffer undesirable consequences. For example, the productivity of a system operation may be enhanced to the detriment of another operation viewed as outside the system. Is this good and intended, or on the contrary bad and unintended, and why? Hence, we must question, in a critical sense, our **boundary judgements**, i.e. justify the boundary choices made in terms of their consequences and reassess them as we learn more about the system.

Similarly, what is considered the relevant environment and what is ignored as irrelevant gives also rise to critical boundary judgements, i.e. the choice of boundary for the relevant environment. For example, at what point can an aspect in the environment be viewed as insignificant and hence be ignored, i.e. judged as irrelevant? Or which undesirable consequences of system outputs can be ignored as insignificant or irrelevant to the study, such as effects of pollutants discharged into waterways, etc., or the social consequences resulting from closing a factory, or splitting a community in two by siting a four-lane divided highway through its middle. Each of these choices involves value judgements that the analyst needs to evaluate carefully.

For each boundary choice, the analyst must be on the lookout for implicit assumptions or boundary judgements. For example, a system for the future operation of an entity or parts of an entity, such as a firm or government department, that uses past data to estimate inputs contains several implicit assumptions: future behaviour of the environment will be similar to past behaviour (e.g. the demand for an entity's products or services will remain stationary, i.e. be the same or the current trend will continue); changes in the system outputs will have no effect on relevant inputs into the system (e.g. it will not stimulate or curtail demand for the entity's products or services); and the system has no control over these aspects, when in fact such control is possible (e.g. demand for the entity's products or services can be affected through promotion).

3.6   Some examples of system descriptions

Let's look at some examples to clarify and elaborate on these concepts. For the sake of brevity, the examples used are somewhat coarse. Chapters 4 and 6 study real-life situations with much of their intricacies.

A traffic system

A network of roads and their connections, i.e. road intersections, road forks, and highway interchanges, and their physical characteristics and traffic controls which affect their carrying capacity, as well as the vehicles using the roads at any given point in time, can be viewed as a traffic system. The relationships between the components consist of their geographic location relative to each other and how they are linked together.

Does a traffic system do anything? The road network connects places with each other and thus allows vehicle movement from each point in the road network to all other points. It transforms vehicles at given source locations (inputs) into vehicles at given destination locations (outputs). If a road segment (such as a critical bridge over a river) or a road connection is removed, some locations may become isolated from the rest of the system or more difficult to access. So the traffic behaviour changes. In a traffic system, the interrelationships between many components, such as the traffic flow on various streets, affect each other mutually.

The traffic system of, say, a country, may contain subsystems, such as city road networks, which also have these properties.

What constitutes the environment of a traffic system? To answer this question we need to look at the inputs and outputs of the system. The major input consists of the people who want to go from one place to another and the type of vehicles they intend to use. These inputs enter the system, become components of the system, and then leave the system at their destinations. Abstract inputs may consist of the operational settings for various traffic controls at traffic intersections, or green waves, etc. Note that if the physical inputs (vehicles entering the network) are removed, the road network ceases to be a traffic system, since it lacks one of its major components, namely its users. There is no transformation process present.

The person viewing the assembly of components as a system could be a traffic engineer. His aim may be to observe some system performance measures, such as the rate of traffic flow along crucial road segments and the degree to which the road segments' capacities are used during periods of peak traffic and how they are affected by various traffic control inputs. These are some of the abstract outputs of the system. The driver of a vehicle or the scheduler of a fleet of pick-up and delivery vehicles may be another person interested in the road network as a traffic system. The driver's aim is finding the fastest or shortest path from point A to point B. The scheduler's aim is determining the sequence of pick-ups and deliveries for a given vehicle that has the shortest distance or takes the shortage time.

A motor vehicle

A car is often cited as a typical example of a system. It is a complex assembly of thousand of individual parts. Its major components — the engine, its steering mechanism, its suspension, the electric parts — are complex subsystems by themselves. Their relationships consist of how they are fitted together and how they interact. It is an easy trap to view an assembled car as a system — indeed in its out-there meaning, existing independently of the observer. But a car by itself, say parked on the road, in a garage, or exhibited in a car museum, is not a system in a useful sense. It does not and cannot do anything on its own. More is needed for a system. To be a means for transporting people and goods, it also needs a driver with some goal about where to go, plus fuel, plus a road network for a road vehicle. The road network and all its properties form the environment of the car–driver system. Without all the components and the environment needed to fulfil its intended activity, a mere assembly of car parts is not a system for a means of transport.

Cars could, however, form parts of different systems. For example, for a car collector cars become a hobby — part of a personal enjoyment system. For the car salesperson, the cars in the sales yard are part of a profit-making system.

Note that most cars have many components — trim, interior comforts, a stereo, a central locking subsystem — that do not contribute to their intended role as a means of transport. It is still part of a transport system without these. (Naturally, if the primary purpose is as a means of self-expression for the owner, these extras may be more important than its ability to carry passengers, as is demonstrated by competitions for who has the loudest car stereo subsystem.) However, remove the wheels, and the car ceases to be a system for a means of transport. If it has an external power pickup link, like some cross-country vehicles or tractors, it may be used as a system to provide motive power for the operation of machinery, such as an electric power generator. Its purpose changes.

A sawmill

A sawmill cuts up logs into a variety of products — planks, beams, framing materials, posts, and trim. An industrial engineer may see a sawmill as a system for converting raw materials in the form of various types of logs into a wide range of different finished products, including by-products, such as off-cuts and sawdust. The aim is to determine a facility and equipment layout and processing rules that provide an efficient and safe operating environment. The owners of the sawmill may see it as a system for producing a financial return on their investment. A management scientist may see parts of it as a system for cutting logs into end products intended to satisfy a given composition of customer demands at the lowest possible cost. Table 3-1 lists the components, activities, relationships, inputs and outputs, and the transformation process for each of these three views.

The industrial engineer takes a highly detailed view of the physical characteristics of each piece of equipment, such as its dimensions, its maintenance and safety requirements, its potential location, its processing rates, and the various ways in which different pieces of equipment may interact with each other. The inputs and outputs of the system are both physical (logs, products) and abstract (operating rules, operating statistics, such as output capacities, bottleneck locations, etc.).

In contrast, the owners have little interest in the details of the physical side of the operation. Seeing the firm as a profit-generating system, they take a much more aggregate view. For them the firm consists of several interdependent subsystems, each with its own mission. The outputs of one become the inputs into others. Their prime concern is the effective coordination of subsystems' interactions and the financial consequences in terms of profit and cash flows for the firm as a whole. These are the firm's major outputs and performance measures, not the products it produces. Inputs are mainly financial (funds) and abstract (policies on pricing, etc.). Its outputs are also abstract (projections of profits and cash flows).

An MS study has some aspects of both the preceding systems. It keeps much of the details on the physical product flow as in the engineering system, but possibly at a lower level of resolution. In fact, best operating rules and processing capacities derived in the engineering study become abstract inputs into its system definition. But it also retains the financial implications for all activities which are associated with the multi-stage process of converting logs into finished products, as in the profit generating system. Again, it is not the physical product that is the output of the system, but the overall cost implications of the operations.

Level of resolution in system description

As these three views of a sawmill demonstrate, the purpose of studying the operations as a system strongly influences the level of detail or the degree of **resolution** used for representing the various components and the system inputs and outputs. The industrial engineer's system adopts a very high level of resolution, showing minute details of equipment operations. On the other hand, the owners' system has a much

Table 3-1   Three different systems views for a sawmill

Systems view	Industrial engineer	Owners	MS analyst
Purpose of viewing entity as a system	study physical lay-out of equipment, product handling, & diff. operating rules	assess financial return on investment	study effect on costs of different cutting patterns to meet given demand
System components	• buildings, yards, equipment, vehicles • operators • logs in yards • intermediate products	• subsystems, such as procurement of logs, production, warehousing, mar-keting, finance • funds invested	• processing subsystems • intermediate product stocks
Activities of system	• cutting operations • moving of cuts • drying of cuts • planing of cuts • storage	• purchasing of logs • conversion of logs • storage of logs • sales of logs • control of funds	• subsystem product conversions • storage of interme-diate products
Relationships between components	• sequencing of tasks • location of fixed equipment • feasible combina-tions of cutting patterns	• subsystem outputs become inputs to other subsystems • communications between subsystems • financial aspects	• subsystem outputs become inputs to other subsystems • feasible cutting combinations • financial aspects
Inputs from environment	• types of logs • supplies (oil, fuel) • processing rates & capacities • operating rules	• funds • personnel • product demands • commercial laws • pricing policy	• log availabilities • cost data • processing rates & capacities • operating rules • product demands
Outputs to environment	• finished products • by-products (saw-dust, off-cuts) • processing capacity • bottlenecks • equipment cap. use	projections for • net profit • cash flows • return on investment • market share	projections for total operating costs to meet customer demands
Transformation process of system	logs into finished products and opera-ting statistics	wealth and production capacity at time t into wealth and production capacity at time $t+1$	production capacity, logs available, and customer demands into total operating cost

lower level of resolution, where complex details of, say, the production subsystem are aggregated into a few relationships that use capacity to convert logs into products and the associated financial implications of that operation. The MS analyst may go for an intermediate degree of resolution. Its exact level will depend on the purpose of the study — a low level of resolution for aggregate monthly planning, a high level of resolution if the study is to come up with a detailed daily operating schedule.

Arbitrariness of system description

This discussion drives home the point that there is considerable arbitrariness in how a system is defined, where its boundary is placed, and its level of detail or resolution. As a rule, the choice should be the smallest system needed for achieving the purpose for which the system is defined. Furthermore, the analyst may make simplifications and approximations to reduce the system complexity to a level that he or she can handle with the resources available. Both are a matter of judgement.

Activity: The principal views her high school as a human activity system.
- List its major components, inputs, and outputs, and its environment. (Examples: teachers, government minimum contact hours, number of students suspended, location of school, respectively.)
- Do you see your description as an 'out-there' or 'inside-us' view?
- What is the underlying world view of the school principal? (Example: maintaining discipline is essential.)
- What is the system transformation process? (Hint: Which major input is transformed into the major output?)
- List three performance measures. (Example: number of students suspended.)
- List three (possibly arbitrary) choices you made as to where to draw the system boundary. (Example: Computing facilities assumed unchangeable.)
- Redefine the boundary by including one of these aspects as an integral part of the system. How might this affect the major transformation process? (Example: Changes in computing facilities open up new ways of teaching.)

3.7 Systems as 'black boxes'

The complexity of real life may be such that we have no or only incomplete knowledge of the inner workings of a system, even if we are able to identify the physical components. Often the major reason for this lack of knowledge is that the system behaviour is affected by random aspects. In other cases, the relationships between components are only partially understood. This is the case for human brain functions. So, there is no full understanding of how humans learn. Similarly, in spite of the enormous progress made in meteorology, weather systems are only partially understood. As a result, weather predictions are unreliable. Computers or other machinery fail for a myriad of reasons. It may be impractical to keep track of individual causes which often exhibit mutual causality. So only aggregate records are compiled.

In each of these examples, the inside of the corresponding system is left largely empty. All we know are the inputs to and outputs from the system. For the lay observer it looks like one of those black control boxes, with lots of wires into and out of the box, but no way of knowing what is under the cover. If our aim is to predict the output of such a system in response to various inputs, we may indeed not have to know the details of its inner workings, even if this were possible. In such instances, all we need to discover is the form of the functional relationship between inputs and outputs, i.e. the mathematical form of the transformation process. Various statistical tools may help in this task. After proper testing, these relationships can then be used for predicting the corresponding phenomena, such as the most likely weather pattern resulting from certain meteorological (input) conditions, or the long-run daily breakdown patterns for, say, 24 looms in operation at a carpet or cloth factory — information needed for planning a repair service.

In other situations the transformation process is known exactly. However, rather than represent it in full detail, it may be adequate to view the inner working as a black box and simply express the various activities of the transformation process by a single functional relationship. Examples of this are intricate multi-stage chemical processes, like in an oil refinery, where a yield table is used for transforming, say, crude oil into a range of refined products. This approach is frequently used as a substitute for the transformation process of a subsystem which receives inputs from and provides outputs to other components of the system. For example, the subsystem for the conversion of logs into finished products in the sawmill profit-maximizing system is most likely to be included in the form of a black box.

3.8 Hierarchy of systems

The purpose of viewing something as a system affects what aspects should be included as part of the system and what aspects are more appropriately placed into the relevant environment; in other words, where to place the **boundary of the system**. The two systems for the sawmill — a profit-making system and the cost minimization system — clearly demonstrate this. The latter assumes a given input of logs available for conversion into finished products to meet a known customer demand. For a profit-maximizing system, the value of the logs purchased and the value of the stocks maintained are system components. They are affected by the decision rules imposed by management on the purchasing function.

The sawmill shows a further important point. The cost minimization system is completely contained in the profit-making system. It is unimportant that the degree of detail shown for the two systems is different. Those aspects of the profit-making system not included in the cost minimization system, such as the procurement of logs, are part of the environment of the latter. So we have a system within a system.

In fact, these are only two of a whole sequence of nested systems related to the sawmill. The firm itself is embedded in a system of regional sawmills, all sharing the same forest resources. The system of regional sawmills is embedded in the system covering the national wood processing industry. The latter in turn is included in the system for the whole national economy. This nesting of systems within systems within systems is referred to as a **hierarchy of systems**. It is depicted in Figure 3-5. The containing system becomes the environment.

Figure 3-5   Hierarchy of systems.

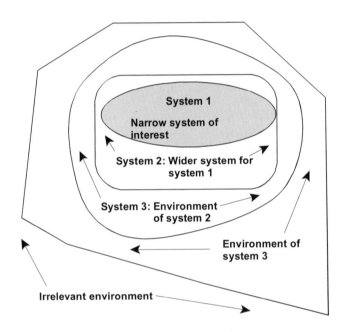

In many instances, the containing system exercises some control over the contained system. The controlling system may set the objectives of the contained system, monitor how well it achieves these objectives, and have control over crucial resources needed by the contained system. The controlling system is then referred to as the **wider system of interest**, while the contained system becomes the **narrow system of interest**. The wider system (including its own relevant environment) thus becomes the relevant environment of the narrow system. For example, if the sawmill cost-minimizing system is the narrow system of interest, then the sawmill profit-maximizing system and its environment are its wider system of interest.

The advantage of viewing two systems in a hierarchy of a narrow and a wider system is that their relationships are shown in their correct context. It may show that improvements in the performance of the narrow system requires action to be taken in the wider system. Similarly, the relationships between various inputs into the narrow system are clarified. For example, two inputs first seen as independent of one another may turn out to be highly affected by the same factors when seen in their proper relationship within the wider system. This could be the case for the cost of labour in the sawmill cost minimization system for the various subsystem operations. All labour costs may depend on the same union contract.

Activity continued (high school as a system):
- Describe two subsystems and their major components.
- Describe briefly the wider system of interest.
- Define a hierarchy of three systems, with high school as the smallest one.

3.9 System behaviour

System state

As pointed out earlier, the behaviour of the system is of prime interest to the person studying it. How do we describe the behaviour of a system? We show how various characteristics, properties, or attributes of each component change. Consider the road network as a traffic system. The behaviour of this system over a short interval of time is known if we note down exactly for both the beginning and the end of the time interval which road segments and road connections are open for travel and where each vehicle is located and what direction and speed it is travelling. The attribute of interest for each road segment and road connection is thus whether it is open or closed. The attributes of a car consist of its location, its direction of travel, and its speed of travel. We usually refer to these attributes as **state variables**. At any point in time each state variable has a given numerical value (e.g. "speed" and "geo-graphical coordinates" for each car) or categorical value ("open" or "closed" for the road segment). The set of values assumed by all state variables at a given point in time is referred to as the **state of the system** at that time. The behaviour of a system is therefore completely known if we know how the state of the system changes over time.

When we start observing a system the initial values of these state variables are inputs (either observed ones or arbitrarily assigned ones). Their values change in either of two ways:

1. The change in a state variable is the result of an input provided by the person who has a means of affecting the behaviour of the system. For instance, the traffic engineer specifies that at 9 a.m. the four-lane road segment between X and Y is to be reduced to two lanes for 4 hours in order to undertake road work. In many instances, the control may be in the form of an automatic decision rule, such as the green phase at a traffic light being triggered by an approaching vehicle between the hours of 8 p.m. and 6 a.m.

2. The change in a state variable of a component is a consequence of the activity of the component itself or of the relationship with other components. For example,

as a vehicle travels in the network it constantly changes the value of some of its state variables, in particular the ones recording its location and speed. Similarly, the speed at which a vehicle can travel is affected by the traffic intensity along that stretch of road or by a bottleneck emerging ahead of it. Both of these aspects will slow down the vehicle's progress.

Variety of system behaviour

System behaviour can be almost infinitely varied, even for very simple systems. To demonstrate this we borrow the fascinating example in the (British) Open University text (J. Beishon, see references). Consider one of those old-fashioned newscaster strips, where advertising and news headlines march across, each letter being spelled by a specific pattern of on and off light bulbs. In their modern version the bulbs become pixels on a video screen. Assume that the display panel is 7 light bulbs high and 100 light bulbs long, allowing for only 20 letters to be shown at one time. The behaviour of this system is given by the changing patterns of light bulbs on and off. Each possible pattern is one state of this system. How many different states does this system have?

Since each light bulb can either be on or off, the state variable for each light bulb has two values. If there are only two light bulbs, then for each of the two states of the first bulb there are two states for the second bulb, i.e. there are 2 times 2 or 2^2 possible states. For three light bulbs it is 2 times 2 times 2, or 2^3. You now see the pattern. For 700 light bulbs it is 2^{700} different states. This is slightly larger than 10^{210}, i.e. a number consisting of a 1 followed by another 210 zeros. Most of us have great difficulties in grasping how big this number really is. To put it into perspective, consider the number of atomic particles contained in the entire universe. This has been estimated as being of the order of 10^{73}, an infinitesimally small number compared to the number of states for the 700 light bulb newscaster, which is a rather small one compared to the one that existed in the 1960s and 1970s on London's Leicester Square, which had 30,000 bulbs! And this is dwarfed by the capacity of a high-resolution computer monitor that can display up to 1024×768 or almost 800,000 individual dots or pixels. we will not even try to express the number of possible states.

In real-life systems studies we are rarely interested in the minute details of the system behaviour. This would quickly outstrip our cognitive capabilities. Our concern is rather with the aggregate or average system behaviour. For example, in the road network the traffic engineer is hardly interested in the movement of every vehicle, but rather with 15-minute or half-hour averages of the capacity use or the traffic flows along certain road segments and road intersections over the course of a given day, such as a 'typical' Saturday. This will indicate which road segments and intersections are prone to become traffic bottlenecks. Or the traffic engineer may want to collect information on the number of trips made from a given suburb of the city to various other parts of the city for planning future road needs. This means that only a few crucial systems variables are kept track of in any detail, and they are usually in the form of summary measures for all state variables of a given class or subgroup of components, like the number of vehicles travelling past a given location in the road network over a certain interval of time. The performance of the system as a whole or of various subsystems is evaluated on the basis of these aggregate or summary state variables.

The huge variety of system behaviour is another dimension that adds complexity to decision making.

Emergent properties

The behaviour of the road network as a traffic system highlights another important aspect. A traffic bottleneck at a given intersection as a result of high traffic flow cannot be associated with an individual vehicle travelling through that intersection. Similarly, the traffic density at a given point in the network is a product of many components acting together. So **the system exhibits behaviours or properties that none of its components individually may exhibit**. Such behaviours or properties are new or different from the behaviours or properties of the individual components. It makes no sense to associate a traffic density with a single car. Such properties only emerge from the joint interaction or behaviour of the components that form the system, hence their label '**emergent properties**'. This phenomenon is often summarized by 'the whole is greater than the sum of its parts'.

Human activity systems are usually created or formed in order to produce desired emergent properties. Consider again the car/driver as a system of components (engine, wheels, etc., plus driver, plus road network). This system is more than simply a complementary collection of components arranged in a given pattern; it was created specifically as a mode of transport. None of its parts or a subset of parts has this property by itself.

Similarly, the various subsystems that make up a sawmill, each one viewed by itself, are not capable of producing a profit. Only if their individual activities are properly coordinated does the potential for producing a profit emerge. Again this is a planned emergent property.

Unfortunately, all too often some emergent properties are not desirable or even planned. The examples in Chapter 2, such as the side effects of building the Aswan High Dam, the deterioration of urban transport, or the effects of the traditional method of assessing machine efficiencies, clearly highlight this. One of the compelling reasons for using a systems approach to problem solving is exactly to predict planned desirable emergent properties and unplanned undesirable emergent properties resulting from a given decision better. It is then possible to take suitable countermeasures or alter the original design to alleviate or avoid undesirable emergent properties at the planning stage, before they occur.

Activity continued (high school as a system):
- List three state variables and their attributes. (Example: state variable — contact hours for a given student; attribute — number of hours.)
- List two desirable planned and two undesirable unplanned emergent properties of the high school system? (Example: socialization of students — planned, desirable; vandalism — unplanned, undesirable.)

3.10   Different kinds of system

As in all scientific disciplines, systems are classified along various distinguishing properties. Being aware of them helps you to understand system behaviour.

Discrete systems

In the newscaster light bulb display the state of the system is any one of a huge number of individual states, each characterized by a pattern of on-and-off bulbs. The pattern changes so fast that our eyes are deceived into seeing a continuously moving string of letters. However, that apparent movement consists of a sequence of displays of individual patterns, each one held for a fraction of a second. The patterns do not fade from one display into another. So the state of the system jumps through a sequence of discrete states. Such systems are called **discrete systems**. A discrete system changes its state at discrete points in time. Between these times, the state of the system remains unchanged.

Here are a few other examples of discrete systems: (1) In the emergency services call centre discussed in Chapter 1, the number of telephone lines or the number of operators busy are two of the important state variables. Each can only be an integer. (2) In a predator/prey system, the state is described by the number of predators and number of prey alive at any point in time. Both are discrete variables. (3) In the loom repair system, two state variables of prime interest are the number of machines operating and the number of machines broken down at any given point in time — again discrete variables.

Continuous systems

In contrast, some state variables of the road network system (such as the location and speed of each vehicle, or the density of traffic flow over a given road segment) change continuously over time as vehicles move along the road segments or through intersections. Hence the state of the system also changes continuously. Since the state variables are continuous variables, the number of possible states is infinitely large, even if each variable may be restricted to a small range of values. This is an example of a **continuous system**. Many industrial processes, particularly in chemical and petrochemical plants, should be viewed as continuous systems. Similarly, the process used by warm-blooded animals to maintain the body temperature within a narrow range is also a continuous system.

Some state variables that may assume any real value may nevertheless change their values only at discrete points in time. For example, the cargo load of a ship, measured in tons, is a continuous variable, but only changes when the cargo is loaded or unloaded (or some containers are lost overboard).

Although a continuous system may change continuously, in practice its state is usually also observed and recorded only at regular discrete points in time, say, every 10 minutes. The closer consecutive recordings are in time, the more accurately the system actual behaviour is approximated.

Many systems have both discrete and continuous state variables that may change their value continuously or only at discrete points in time. Furthermore, the 'observer' of the system may for reasons of simplicity approximate a continuous state variable as discrete or a discrete variable as continuous.

Deterministic and stochastic systems

If the behaviour of a system is predictable in every detail the system is **deterministic**. For example, for most studies the solar system is viewed as a deterministic system. The trajectory of every planet can be predicted almost exactly. Animated neon advertising signs that go through a regular pattern can be viewed as deterministic systems. A sequence of traffic lights along a one-way street is set at a fixed pattern during certain hours of the day so as to produce a green wave. When operating in this mode, it is a deterministic system. Given the same starting conditions, a deterministic system will always exhibit exactly the same behaviour, i.e. go through the same sequence of system state changes.

However, few phenomena in real life, particularly those involving people, behave in deterministic ways. They are generally not completely predictable. Some behaviour may be affected by **random** or **stochastic** inputs. Such systems are called **stochastic systems**. ('Stochastic' derives from the Greek *stochos*, meaning 'guess'.)

If the variations in behaviour are minor, we may still approximate it by a deterministic system. For example, the Swiss railroads, known for their almost pedantic punctuality, can for most purposes be adequately approximated as a deterministic system. On the other hand, trains in India rarely keep to the published timetable. So they form a stochastic system, but then by nature (or necessity) Indians show more patience than the Swiss.

Closed and open systems

The father of General Systems Theory, Ludwig von Bertalanffy, introduced the concepts of **closed and open systems**. A closed system has no interactions with any environment. No inputs, no output. In fact, it has no environment. In contrast, open systems interact with the environment, by receiving inputs from it and providing outputs to it.

In real life there exist no truly closed systems. Any real-life system has an environment with which it interacts, even if only in a small way. So, the concept of a closed system is a theoretical concept. With no interactions with an environment, its behaviour is regulated entirely by the interactions among the components of the system and its initial or starting conditions. These determine to the last detail how the system behaves. Hence, it must be deterministic.

Scientists, particularly in the biological or physical sciences, may try to create artificially closed systems that are as far as physically possible insulated from their environment. Their only inputs are initial starting conditions. (Since these are control inputs, these systems are not truly closed.) By providing different initial states the analyst can observe how the system behaviour responds to different initial inputs. Unfortunately, some social scientists give 'closed system' a different meaning — a rather unhelpful misuse of the term, leading to confusion.

Systems defined for decision-making purposes are always open systems, since by definition the decisions or the decision making rules are inputs into the system. Stochastic systems are also open systems, since the factors that introduce the randomness in the behaviour are the result of forces or events not included inside the system, usually because their causes of randomness are not fully understood.

The steady state of a probabilistic system

A stochastic system may exhibit some remarkable and surprising characteristics in its behaviour. It may become trapped in the same final state, if one exists, even if it starts out from different initial conditions or initial states of the system. However, more commonly, stochastic systems in the long run tend to approach a **state of equilibrium**, also called a **'steady state'**. This state of equilibrium is independent of the state the system starts out from.

The term 'steady state' is an unfortunate misnomer. It is not a particular state that once reached is maintained in perpetuity. Rather, it refers to the system's **long-run behaviour**. The state of equilibrium is characterized by the values which certain state variables that measure long-run averages tend to approach if the system 'functions' or operates for a sufficient length of time. In an emergency services call centre, they are the long-run average number of operators busy and the long-run average length of time that callers have to wait prior to receiving service. In a predator–prey system, they are the long-run average size of each population.

Few stochastic systems ever reach their state of equilibrium. Small or large random disturbances, e.g. a sudden random surge of emergency calls, or a severe storm in an ecological system, may disrupt system behaviour and push it away from these long-run averages. But in each case, the system will gradually approach the same or a new state of equilibrium again.

> Activity: For each type of system (discrete, continuous, deterministic, stochastic), give two examples and show why they are that type of system.

3.11 Feedback loops

As mentioned in Section 2.4, the behaviour of system components may exhibit mutual causality, i.e. component A affects component B, which in turn affects component A. This is known as a feedback loop. Such feedback may be indirect via other components, e.g. A affects B, which affects C, which in turn affects A. This is depicted in the top loop of Figure 3-6. The arrow inside the loop shows the direction of the influence relationships. Note that it is usually the state of a component that affects the state of another component, and so on.

Feedback is a common feature of most systems, both human activity systems and natural systems. They often are the main cause of complexity. The filling mechanism of a toilet cistern is based on feedback. Figure 3-6 captures this.

Figure 3-6   Feedback loops.

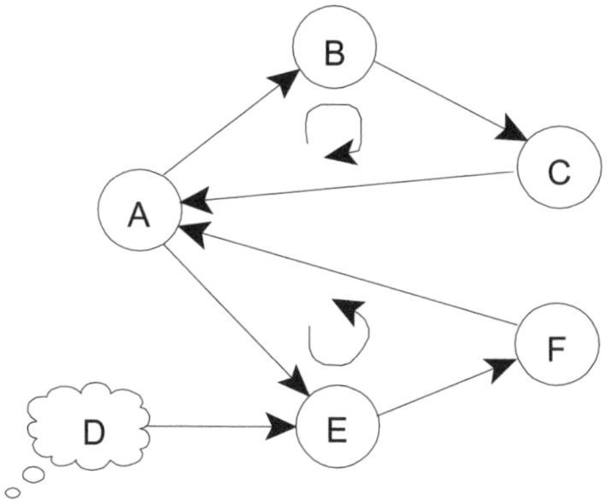

Water flows into the cistern via an inflow valve B and out via outlet E. The water level is the state of the cistern A. It affects the opening of the inflow valve B which controls the inflow C. If the cistern A is full, its level is at its maximum, B is closed and C is zero. If the flushing lever D (an external disturbance of the system) is activated, E opens, causing the outflow F to be positive. This in turn lowers the level of cistern A, which opens B, causing C to become positive (usually C is at a much lower maximum rate than F). Once the cistern A has emptied out, i.e. its level is at its minimum, outlet E becomes blocked, reducing F to zero. This now allows the level of cistern A to rise. When full, B is closed, cutting C to zero.

Negative and positive feedback loops

Feedback can act positively or negatively. Positive feedback increases the discrepancy between the future state of the system and some reference state, such as an equilibrium state or a desired target state. In other words, the system state tends to deviate more and more from its reference state. In contrast, negative feedback decreases the discrepancy between the future state and the reference state. (Note that 'positive' and 'negative' are not used in their colloquial meaning of 'good' and 'bad'.)

In the cistern example, a full cistern A, i.e. its level at its maximum, is the desired target state. If a disturbance occurs (lever D is activated), the level of A is displaced from its target, but is brought back to it by the two feedback loops A–B–C–A and A–E–F–A. Both loops act negatively, restoring the level of A back to its target.

Positive feedback tends to lead to instability. The system either explodes, for example, by having some of its state variables take on larger and larger values, or it kills itself. The meltdown of a nuclear reactor, without the presence of a counter-mechanism, is an example of positive feedback.

Although a number of theoretical examples, particularly from mathematics and economics, exhibit positive feedback, most natural and human activity systems rely on negative feedback. They either try to reach a goal or strive to maintain or preserve existing relationships, properties, or equilibria. In all cases, the system has built-in mechanisms that steer the system back towards the goal or the desired relationship or equilibrium if it is displaced from it through some external event.

Section 5.5 of Chapter 5 shows how diagrams help identify feedback loops and whether they are positive or negative.

Feedback loops play a central role in the control of most systems.

Activity: Describe the feedback loop for
* a thermostatically controlled heating system;
* the market system assumed to balance supply and demand for a product.

3.12   Control of systems

Our main reason for viewing something as a human activity system is to exercise effective control over its behaviour. Control is achieved by imposing something on the system in the form of inputs — a set of decisions, or decision rules, or simply an initial state for the system — that will affect some activities in the system and therefore the behaviour of the system in desired ways. We shall refer to them as **control inputs**. Note that if we impose decision rules on the system it may seem, at least superficially, as if the system exercises control by itself. The fact that its behaviour will change if the system is made to obey a different set of rules clearly shows that this apparent self-control is imposed from outside.

Three conditions are needed to exercise control over system behaviour:

1. A target, objective, or goal for the system to reach. For a deterministic system this may be a particular state of the system. For stochastic systems it may be a desirable steady state.

2. A system capable of reaching the target or goal. This is rather obvious! The difficulty is that for stochastic systems there may be no way of guaranteeing that this goal is ever reached.

3. Some means of influencing system behaviour. These are the control inputs (decisions, decision rules, or initial states). How these control inputs affect system behaviour is an important aspect of studying systems.

Systems theory distinguishes between three types of control: **open loop controls**, **closed loop** or **feedback controls**, and **feed-forward controls**.

Open loop controls

Open loop controls are inputs imposed on the system based only on the prediction of how the system behaviour responds to them. No account is taken of how the system actually responds to the control inputs. Open loop controls are often in the form of a recipe or a set of rules to follow. For example, in the sawmill cost-minimizing system the control inputs will be in the form of a schedule of very detailed cutting patterns to apply for each log to be processed.

We will find that for many MS projects the recommendations derived for controlling the system are in the form of open loop controls. However, for many situations open loop controls are not adequate or effective. Assume you use the following four steps for starting the engine of your vintage British sports car:

1. Insert ignition key into ignition lock.

2. Depress clutch pedal and use gear lever to shift into neutral (assume you always leave the car in gear when the engine is off).

3. Pull choke button half way out. ('What is a choke?' may ask. That is why it is a vintage car!)

4. Turn ignition key clockwise to red mark (this engages the starter motor), hold for two seconds, and then return key to black mark.

It is clear that this does not guarantee that you can start the car's engine successfully. For example, the person who used the car before you may have left it in neutral. Touching the gear lever will immediately indicate this, so you will skip step 2. The engine may still be hot from a previous run, hence no choke is needed; or it may be very cold, and the choke has to be pulled out completely. The engine may start after only one second, so you return the key to the black mark without waiting two seconds. The engine may not start within the two second interval, in which case you may continue holding the key to the red mark for much longer. In fact, what you are doing is adjusting the controls used for starting the engine to how the car responds to the controls. The behaviour of the system becomes a source of feedback to adjust your controls.

Closed loop or feedback controls

Under this type of control, information about the system behaviour, possibly in response to previous control inputs, is fed back to the controller for evaluation. This may lead the controller to adjust the control signals. The classic example of this is how most people control the temperature of a shower. Standing safely outside the shower, we turn the shower control valve to a setting somewhere midway between 'cold' and 'hot'. After a few seconds we tentatively put in a hand to test the temperature of the water flowing from the shower rose. This information is interpreted by our brain. We turn the control valve either clockwise to increase the flow of hot water relative to the flow of cold water if the temperature feels too cold or counterclockwise if it is too hot. We then wait again a second or two to check the result. This process continues until the water temperature feels right. The final temperature chosen may not necessarily always be the same. It will be affected by the air temperature and by our internal metabolism.

In systems terms, the controller supplies some initial control inputs to a **feedback control mechanism.** The latter is a component of the system, while the controller itself is outside. The initial control inputs are usually in the form of decision rules or a decision strategy (… if such and such is true, do this and that …). These decision rules are used by the control mechanism to issue **control signals** that steer the system in a desired direction. Information about the resulting system behaviour or outputs is then fed back to the control mechanism for evaluation. The latter adjusts the control signals in accordance with the decision rules. So the loop from the control mechanism to other parts of the system is closed by a feedback loop from these parts back to the control mechanism. For this reason, such types of control are referred to as **closed-loop controls** or **feedback controls**. The top part of Figure 3-7 shows this.

Figure 3-7   Feedback control and self-regulation.

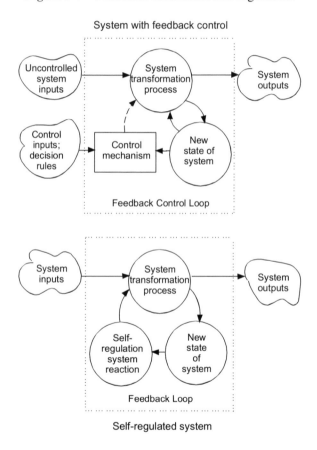

Self-regulation

Feedback loops also occur in many natural systems, particularly biological and ecological systems, where they help regulate the behaviour of these systems. For example, for a given form of tidal action and fresh water inflows, an estuary has a natural state of equilibrium, where the various ecological symbiotic relationships and interdependencies, like predator–prey subsystems, are in balance. If this balance is disturbed it will redress itself slowly over time to its previous equilibrium, provided no new disturbance occurs or no permanent change has occurred. In fact, self-regulation in biological and ecological systems is as a rule based on negative feedback. This returns such systems to their natural state of equilibrium.

Assume, for instance, that a large proportion of the predator population has been wiped out through a storm. This will lead to an explosion of the prey population. The predator population thus finds very favourable conditions for multiplying beyond its original level. This added pressure will reduce the prey population, with excess predators now also dying off due to lack of food, and so on. Through a series of oscillations of ever-decreasing magnitude the previous natural balance will re-establish itself after a while.

This feedback has nothing to do with control. There are no human inputs that influence the behaviour of the system. What is happening is a natural self-regulation, which is different from control. Self-regulation returns such a system to its natural equilibrium. Human control of natural systems usually has different goals, such as the eradication of some aspect of nature considered a pest or a health menace. Unfortunately, many attempts at human control of natural systems have had disastrous results.

The classical example is the use of DDT for combatting mosquitos and agricultural insect pests between 1950 and 1980. Although DDT admirably accomplished this desirable goal, it also had unplanned consequences, such as weakening the egg shells of a number of predatory birds. As a consequence, these bird populations crashed almost to the point of extinction. Only belated banning of DDT use and other rescue measures saved a number of species, like the American eagle, the condor, and the pelican, from being wiped out.

There is obviously a lesson to be learned from such events: namely that a systems approach might have prevented such near-disasters. In fact, state agencies dealing with environmental issues are now very cautious in giving permission for the introduction of new biological controls without having seen sufficient evidence that these controls will not develop into problems themselves.

The present controversy over genetic engineering of animal populations or genetically modified foods is another case in point. Should we believe the claims of private industry and some scientists that the use of GM technologies is safe and will greatly benefit society in the long run or should we be more cautious and demand much more extensive and long-term testing, done by agencies and scientists without any vested interest, thereby seriously delaying the vaunted benefits? Just keep in mind that it took over 20 years before the full effects of DDT use became apparent, and it took half a century before we discovered that chlorofluorocarbons or CFCs, hailed as harmless gases, safe for all sorts of uses, are the prime cause of the ozone depletion that occurs each year over the Antarctic and to a lesser extent in the upper northern hemisphere. Not to mention the billions of dollars of profit at stake for some of the giant and powerful multinationals at the forefront of GM seed production. The tobacco industry has taught us that we must be cautious when evaluating claims from powerful vested interests as to the safety of their products.

Feedback control and self-regulation

The lower portion of Figure 3-7 shows that feedback control and self-regulation differ in important ways. Feedback control receives an extra input of decision rules supplied by a human controller. The rules governing self-regulation are internal to the system. They are usually the result of natural evolution, such as a predator–prey system, or the process to maintain the body temperature of all warm-blooded animals.

Feed-forward control

A feedback control mechanism **reacts** to changes in some critical state variables or outputs. Rather than react to events after they have happened, a feed-forward control mechanism **predicts** how changes in inputs (uncontrollable or controllable) are likely to affect system behaviour and then sends control signals that will maintain system behaviour as closely as possible on the desired course, thereby counteracting the effects of input disturbances. This is the type of control used by an experienced driver of a car. It is also commonly used for the control of chemical processes. Similarly, most successful firms attempt to forecast future economic and demand trends and technological change in order to take advantage of growth opportunities or avoid potential disasters due to an economic downturn or a change in technology. Again, these are applications of feed-forward control.

Naturally, feed-forward and feedback controls are often combined into a single control strategy.

Response lags in systems

Let us briefly return to the temperature control of the shower water. You will have observed that an adjustment of the shower valve does not result in an instantaneous change in the water temperature. In fact, the response is delayed for a short time and then occurs gradually, either increasing or decreasing to a new level. The time delay between the moment when the control signals are applied and their effects have been fully realized is called a **lag**.

For example, if the water flow into a canal bringing water to a hydro power station is increased, it may take a few minutes or even hours before the increased water flow reaches the pressure pipes leading to the turbines, allowing additional turbines to be operated. Such a lag is a **transport lag** (also referred to as a pipeline lag in analogy to a pipeline operation). Such lags are quite common in industry and commerce. An increase in the production level may take considerable time before it results in increased deliveries from the factory, and even longer until it finally leads to an increase in sales from the retail outlets. Most feedback loops are also subject to a transport lag. By the time the information on the state of the system has been processed by the control mechanism that information may already be out-of-date; hence the need for feed-forward controls.

A second kind of lag of great importance is the **exponential lag**. Here, the control signal has an immediate effect, but it is gradual in terms of its size. An example of this type of lag is the temperature change in a gas oven. Although the temperature starts rising immediately if the temperature controls are raised, say from 175 °C to 250 °C, the oven will take several minutes to reach that new temperature. Since an increase in the supply of gas has an instant effect in terms of increased heat output, the initial temperature response will be fairly fast as the air in the oven is heated. Some of that heat is lost to heat the oven walls, so the rate of increase in temperature gain will slow down as the temperature approaches its new target level.

Stochastic systems tend to approach their steady state asymptotically. This is an example of an exponential lag response.

The response of a system to control signals may exhibit both a transport lag and an exponential lag. Furthermore, response lags also occur as a consequence of non-controllable inputs, such as the traffic flow response lags as the input of vehicles into the network increases or decreases during certain times of the day. Natural systems also exhibit response lags to changes in inputs.

> Activity continued (high school as a system):
> *   Who provides control inputs to the system? Give at least two 'controllers'.
> *   What type of control inputs are they? Open loop, feedback, feed-forward? Are any feedback controls positive or negative? (Do not confound 'positive' and 'negative' with the type of criticism offered by teachers.)
> *   Are there any response lags and of what type?

3.13 Chapter highlights

*   This text, in common with most social and natural sciences, thinks of systems as human conceptualizations — the inside-us view. System descriptions are therefore subjective to the person viewing something as a system. They are affected by the world view assumed by the person(s) defining the system. Different people (or different world views) may define different systems for the same entity or phenomenon studied, and each one may be an effective or good view for the intended purpose. The definition will also be dependent on the resources (time, funds, training, tools and equipment for analysis) available to the analyst.
*   The choice of system boundaries is a critical aspect of a system definition. It assigns each aspect or thing to be a component of the system or to be part of its environment. The central concept of a system is that it transforms inputs from the environment into outputs to the environment.
*   Two or more levels of nested system form a hierarchy. The containing system is the wider system of interest to the contained or narrow system.

- Systems have emergent properties that none of its part or subsets of parts have by themselves.
- Finding good ways of controlling a system to enhance desirable emergent properties or reduce the effects of undesirable emergent properties is often the reason for 'building' systems. These controls can take the form of open loop, closed loop (or feedback), and feed-forward controls.

Exercises

1. Consider a university as a system. Identify a possible relevant world view of the observer, the transformation process of the system, the mission or objective of the system and what system aspects are used for measuring the system performance, the inputs into the system, including control inputs, and the outputs from the system, and the major system components, including possible subsystems, from the following viewpoints:
   (a) A student attending the university to acquire theoretical and practical training for a professional career.
   (b) An academic staff member who sees the university as a system for pleasant gainful employment.
   (c) The chief executive officer of the university who sees the university's major role as one of advancing knowledge.

2. Consider the operation of a small urban fire department as a system. It is funded and operated by local government on behalf of its tax-paying residents. Identify a possible relevant world view of the observer, the system transformation process, its mission or objectives, its measures of performance, its inputs, including control inputs, its outputs, and its major components, and the explicit and implicit boundary judgements made, from the point of view of
   (a) the local tax payers.
   (b) the chief of the fire department.

3. A local hospital blood bank collects blood from volunteer donors. The donors do not get any compensation for donating blood. Each donor donates one pint of blood one to three times per year. Attrition of blood donors, due to age, illness, or moving away, causes the pool of blood donors to decrease over time. To restore the pool of donors the blood bank periodically organizes a drive to recruit new donors. The amount collected obviously depends on the number of active donors and on the frequency with which they are called up for donations. For various reasons, the amount collected also fluctuates on a daily basis. All blood collected is tested for various diseases. If it is disease free, it is added to the blood bank's stock of blood, available for transfusions to patients. The demand for fresh blood originates either in the hospital's accident and emergency unit or from surgeons' requests for scheduled surgery. Hence the requirements for blood also fluctuate on a daily basis. Fresh blood has a shelf life of 35 days. Thus any blood not used within 35 days of collection is outdated, i.e. removed from stock and destroyed. Some fresh blood is put aside for the production of by-products, such as platelets and plasma, immediately after collection and testing. It is by such withdrawals of fresh blood that the director of the blood bank controls the daily stock of fresh blood. Her objectives are (i) to avoid, as far as possible and reasonable, having to notify surgeons that their requests for blood cannot be met due to stock shortages, and (ii) to avoid having too much blood outdated.

(a) Define a relevant system, including its boundary, its environment, and the world view implied.

(b) The director of the blood bank uses the following rules to control the stock of blood for each blood type. At the end of each day she determines the amount of fresh blood that is 32 days old. If that amount is larger than some critical number, she withdraws an amount of blood equal to the excess above the critical number, using the most recently collected blood. What type of control is she using? Why do you reach that conclusion?

(c) List some of the state variables used for specifying the state of the system.

(d) Discuss the boundary judgements made by the system you defined.

4. Give an example of a hierarchy of systems:
   (a) in a governmental setting.
   (b) in an educational setting.
   (c) in a sports setting.
   (d) in a law enforcement setting.

5. List some of the state variables used for defining the state of the system for
   (a) the university as a professional training system (refer to Question 1(a)).
   (b) the fire department (refer to Question 2(a)).

6. In 100 words or fewer, state what the main reasons are for using a systems approach for problem solving.

7. Give examples of emergent properties for the following types of system:
   (a) A river system receiving untreated chemical or sewage discharges.
   (b) A computer information system.
   (c) An intersection traffic control system.
   (d) A firm.
   (e) The police department.

8. Give two examples (different from any listed in the text) for
   (a) discrete systems.
   (b) continuous systems.
   (c) deterministic systems.
   (d) closed systems (as an approximation).
   (e) open systems.
   (f) probabilistic systems.

9. For the following situation/systems, identify the type of control/regulation mechanism present:
   (a) Assembly instructions for a kitset.
   (b) Filling air into a car tire at a service station air pump.
   (c) The driver/car system on a motorway or freeway, where constant speed can be maintained.
   (d) The driver/car system on a curvy, hilly two-lane road with traffic in both directions.
   (e) An automatic wage payment system, where wages are directly credited to the recipients' accounts.
   (f) A firm has the following system to replenish its raw material stocks: whenever the stock level falls below a critical level, called the reorder point, a quantity of X tonnes is ordered.
   (g) The fermentation process for converting the sugar in the grapes into alcohol works as

follows: After the yeast starter has been mixed with the grapes, the yeast cells multiply many-fold and convert the sugar in the grapes into alcohol. As sugar is depleted or the concentration of alcohol builds up, the growth in the number of yeast cells is inhibited until it stops, and most yeast cells die. At that point, fermentation stops.

(h) A stockbroker constantly watches the price changes in various company shares and tries to predict future price movements. This information is then used for making buying or selling decisions on various shares.

(i) The system used for controlling filling of the toilet water tank.

10. Identify the types of lags found in the following systems: (Note: there may be several types of lags present.)

(a) The system for replenishing products from a supplier who will deliver the goods 10 days after receipt of the order.

(b) The cheque clearing system used by banks, where all cheques presented before 4 p.m. on each day are processed overnight for credit or debit to the corresponding accounts.

(c) A system of reservoirs used for hydro-electric power generation.

(d) The temperature of an unheated swimming pool.

4
The problem situation

Before we can apply the concepts studied in Chapters 2 and 3 to describe a relevant system for an issue of concern or problem we want to study, we need to come to grips with the context within which the issue or problem occurs, i.e. the problem situation. Seeing the problem in its proper full context will facilitate identifying its stakeholders — the people involved — and come up with a definition of the problem and its elements. This is the subject of Sections 4.1 and 4.2. Next we explore three effective ways to capture the problem situation. These are mind maps and rich pictures (Sections 4.3–4.6), and cognitive maps (Sections 4.7 and 4.8).

A full grasp of the problem situation and its stakeholders is also a prerequisite in our critical search for setting appropriate boundaries to both the narrow system of interest and its relevant environment or the wider system of interest. Section 4.9 broaches that topic. All this provides the basis for defining a relevant system, in terms of both its focus and its detail. Chapter 5 studies several diagrammatic aids or approaches to capturing or representing core aspects or relationships of systems.

4.1   The problem situation and what is a 'problem'?

The **problem situation** is the context within which the problem occurs. It is the sum or aggregate of all aspects that can or may affect or shape the problem or issue of concern. Figure 4-1 attempts to capture this.

It is the complex of relationships and conflicts, stemming from the people involved, their world views, and their goals and aims, the physical relationships and constraints impacting on the situation, the structures and processes used or potentially available that govern the behaviour, the control and actions made possible by the resources, the uncertainties associated with any of them, and last, but not least the consequences stemming from their interactions for all those involved, or directly and indirectly affected, where the latter may include not only people, but also other species and the environment.

Figure 4-1   Issue context — the problem situation.

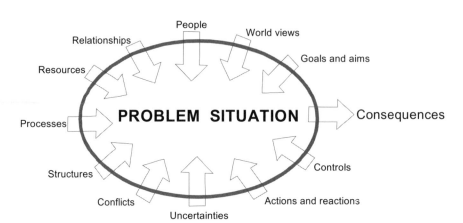

But first, what is a 'problem'? How do problems manifest themselves? For a problem to exist there must be an individual (or a group of individuals), referred to as the **problem owner** — usually its decision maker — who:

- is dissatisfied with the current state of affairs within a real-life context — does not like what is happening, or has some unsatisfied present or future needs, i.e. has some goals or objectives to be achieved or targets to be met;

- is capable of judging when these goals, objectives, or targets have been met to a satisfactory degree; and

- has control over some aspects of the problem situation that affect the extent to which goals, objectives, or targets can be achieved.

The six elements of a problem are (1) the **decision maker**, (2) the decision maker's **objectives** and (3) the associated **decision criterion**, (4) the **performance measure**, (5) the **control inputs** or **alternative courses of action**, and (6) the **context** in which the problem occurs.

To clarify these concepts somewhat, consider again the sawmill example in Section 3.6. The owner may have become concerned about the firm's decrease in profitability over recent times. The decision maker is the sawmill owner–manager. His objective is to achieve a satisfactory return on his investment in the firm. One possible decision criterion used for judging whether or not the decision maker's objective has been achieved is 'the rate of return on the owner's investment reaches at least 18% before taxes', a rate considered satisfactory by the owner. Its associated measure of performance is the ratio of net profit over the owner's investment. Any alternative course of action, such as any combination of the type and quantities of logs to purchase, the type and quantities of products to produce, and the best rules for processing logs into finished products, and so on, that reaches or exceeds 18% satisfies the criterion and is a solution.

An alternative decision criterion could be to 'maximize annual profit', with the annual level of profit being the measure of performance. Once we find a course of action where no other action exists that has a higher profit, the criterion is satisfied.

The context of the problem is all aspects that directly or indirectly affect the measure of performance and over which the decision maker has no immediate control or which are taken as 'givens', such as the current location of the firm, its potential sources of raw materials, and the demand for its products.

Distinction between objective and decision criterion

Unfortunately, these two terms are often confused in the MS literature. *Webster's Collegiate Dictionary* defines *objective* as 'the end towards which effort is directed, an aim, goal or end of action'. Examples are: achieving the highest profit, gaining a 40% share of the market, finding the shortest distance between two locations in a road network, a water purity that safeguards the survival of flora and fauna in a river or estuary, equity between various interest groups, and so on.

Criterion, however, is defined as 'the principle or standard on which a judgment or decision is based.' Both 'principle' and 'standard' imply a rule. So a criterion is the rule used for judging whether or how well the objective has been achieved.

Another example may help. An ambulance service wants to find the 'best' location in a small city, where 'best' is interpreted as 'reaching any emergency as quickly as possible'. This is the objective. We need a criterion for judging whether or how well a location achieves this objective. One criterion could be to minimize "the sum of all times to reach every road location in town". The words in double quotes define the relevant measure of performance associated with this criterion. This would locate the ambulance service at the centre of gravity of the city with the largest part of locations reachable in a relatively short time, but some only after extremely long times. A second criterion is to minimize "the sum of the squared times". This would penalize long times more than short times, thus favouring a solution to keep the long times shorter. A third is to minimize "the maximum time between the ambulance service and any locations in the city". This would tend to reduce the longest time. With each criterion we associate a different performance measure and each will yield a different 'best' location.

In many situations, there may only be one relevant criterion to evaluate how well an objective has been achieved, such as 'maximize profits' for the objective of 'achieving highest profits'. Criterion and objective then coincide.

Complexities of problem definition

In real life, determining the six problem elements may not simply be a question of asking the decision maker. The dissatisfaction felt may just be a vague feeling that things could be better. The analyst's job is then to explore and clarify the problem situation in order to shed more light on the real issue(s) of concern. A decision maker may also be vague or fuzzy about objectives and, consequently, about performance standards and decision criteria. The analyst will then have to help the decision maker to externalize objectives and preferences. Setting of realistic performance standards may have to wait until the analysis is well advanced, because only then will it become possible to explore the range of available solutions. If it turns out to be easy to improve performance, the decision maker may aspire to a higher level of achievement, and vice versa if it is difficult. Furthermore, the decision maker may not be aware of the full range of alternative courses of action open. Discovery of new decision choices is one of the exciting and rewarding aspects of MS work.

Further complexities arise if there are multiple decision makers who may have different world views and who may see the problem situation differently, and hence may have potentially conflicting objectives. Such conflicts can usually only be resolved by a compromise. One of the **problem structuring methods,** discussed in J. Rosenhead and J. Mingers [2000], may help to bring about at least a partial consensual understanding about the problem situation that will allow agreement on a choice of action, even if no consensus can be reached on objectives. (Our Chapter 7 gives a succinct survey and demonstrates some applications.)

Many projects are also initiated by interested parties other than the decision maker(s) and who have no direct control over the problem situation, the possible courses of action, and the resources needed. For example, some of the first studies dealing with breast cancer screening were initiated by consumer groups and medical organizations, rather than by a Government agency responsible for funding it. Often such projects are undertaken with the aim of convincing the 'real' decision maker(s) to take action, if the results of the analysis show that this is in the interest of the wider community. While the project is undertaken, the real decision maker may not be involved. The objectives assumed are likely to be the ones of the interest group and may not necessarily coincide with those of the final decision maker(s).

In most real-life applications, problem definition will not be achieved in a single pass. The initial definition usually goes through a series of progressively more detailed reformulations and refinements, as deeper insight into the problem is gained. In fact, to some extent problem formulation continues until the project ends. It is, however, in these early stages where the ultimate success or failure of a project most often has its roots!

Activity: Referring to Section 1.1, define the six problem elements for:
• the emergency call centre project.
• the Deep Cove project.

4.2   Stakeholders or roles of people in systems

As we have seen in the previous section, any human activity, particularly problem solving within a systems context, involves people. We mentioned the problem owner, the decision maker, other parties affected but without any control over the situation, and the analyst. They all assume various roles. We refer to these roles as **stakeholders**. Let us now formalize this. They are:

- The **problem owners**, who are the persons exercising control over certain aspects of the problem situation, in particular over the choice of action to be taken. Most often, they are also the decision makers. There may be several levels of problem owners: those who have the ultimate power over all controllable aspects in the wider system of interest, and in particular the level of controllable resources made available, but may have delegated part of that power to others, and those who have been given limited powers to make decisions and initiate change within the narrow system of interest or some subsystem.

- The **problem users**, who use the solution and/or execute the decisions approved by the problem owners or decision makers. They have no authority to change the decision or initiate new action. Any apparent decision making is simply an application of prescribed rules. If any discretionary powers are given, they are very limited in scope and again within specified rules.

- The **problem customers**, who are the beneficiaries or victims of the consequences of using the solution. In many instances, they may be given no voice or have no means to affect the analysis or its outcomes. They may also include future generations or even other species. Which ones should be included in the analysis gives rise to critical boundary judgements (see Section 3.5 and 4.9).

- The **problem analysts or solvers**, who analyse the problem and develop a solution for approval by the problem owners.

All roles are always defined with respect to the narrow system. Definite identification of who the various stakeholders of a problem situation are becomes fully clear only once the relevant system has been defined, although the analyst may have a fair idea about who most of them are very early in the analysis.

Some examples will clarify these roles. Recall the emergency call centre at the beginning of Chapter 1. The call centre manager is the problem owner. He or she has the final say over any decision made and hence assumes the role of decision maker. The manager may have delegated the implementation and continued day-to-day management of that aspect of the business to the technical supervisor, who then assumes the role of problem user, with a limited amount of discretionary power, such as setting the best staffing levels at various times of the day. The customers are the people placing calls and the emergency services responding to these calls. They are the beneficiaries or victims of the service quality and access offered. They may have no direct voice in the process, but only through the use of a complaints process. Finally, the decision maker hired a specialist in waiting line problems — a university lecturer — to study the problem and make recommendations. That person assumes the role of problem analyst.

In this case, each role was assumed by a different person. For many situations, the same individual may act in different roles. Assume that you are considering the replacement of your current car. You have limited finance and borrowing capacity, a wish list of desirable and absolutely essential features that your new car should meet, and a wide choice of options: a range of new cars, as well as suitable pre-owned cars. In this case, you are the problem owner, the problem user, and the problem customer, as well as the problem analyst — all roles coincide.

Note again that the terms *problem owner*, *user*, *customer*, and *analyst* refer to the roles that people assume and not to the people themselves. As we have seen, one person may assume more than one role simultaneously or consecutively.

Importance of clear role definition

Why are we concerned about role definition? Firstly, any one of these roles can in fact be the initiator of an MS project. The role of the sponsor will colour the nature of the project, i.e. stamp it with a corresponding focus and world view. If initiated by the decision maker, the project will usually be of a substantive nature, leading to real change, with a relevant system for the project clearly defined within the span of control of the decision maker. The relevant world view is the one held by the decision maker. If it is initiated by any of the other roles, its nature is usually descriptive. Its initiator will tend to use it as a means for educating or persuading other actors of the problem situation. It will only become substantive if its findings are adopted and acted upon by the real problem owner. The appropriate choice of the relevant system for such projects and an appropriate world view may be more problematic and possibly controversial.

Unless the problem analyst is fairly clear about the roles of the various participants in the problem situation to be studied, the project may head off in the wrong direction from the very start. It goes without saying that the analyst must attempt to see the problem situation through the relevant world view of the project sponsor, and not her or his own, while remaining aware of her or his own!

Consider the breast cancer study of Chapter 1. If the study is initiated by the Director of Public Health, the highest level of decision maker for health issues in the governmental administrative structure, the prevailing world view is likely to be 'the effective allocation of public funds'. This would ultimately lead to evaluating trade-offs between allocating funds to breast cancer screening and other uses within the health system. The entire health system becomes the wider system of interest. The output of the study would be a recommended screening policy and a schedule for its implementation, and a total cost. If that total cost exceeds the budget allocation, this may lead to cuts somewhere else or to a revisiting of the breast cancer screening project to bring its cost in line with initial expectations. In contrast, if initiated by a group of medical practitioners — a problem users' group, or by the 'Women for Health' — a problem customer group, the relevant world view would be achieving the greatest reduction in breast cancer mortality, with the relevant system limited to the relationship between screening policies and breast cancer mortality. Wider issues of allocation of public funds may not be considered. The study would be used as evidence to persuade the Health Department to divert funds for a national screening policy.

Similarly, identification of the problem users is essential for effective implementation of any recommendations. The recommendations should be appropriate to the training and educational level of the users. Furthermore, unless the users perceive implementation as being in their personal interest, they may easily be tempted to sabotage the project or the implementation of the recommendations, regardless of how successful the technical aspects of the project turn out to be — a case of 'the operation was successful, but the patient died!'

Furthermore, if the results of the study affect future generations or non-human species, e.g. by destroying a wilderness area through open-cast mining or wildlife habitat in a tropical forests through clearfelling, it is essential that somebody takes up the defence of their interests — gives them a voice.

One of the difficulties sometimes encountered at this stage is that the existing assignment of 'stakeholder roles' is inappropriate. For example, the person having the control over the decision process may not have access to the information needed for effective decision making, while the person with the information may have no decision-making authority. For effective decision making it may first be necessary to change the organization's structure and to reassign decision-making roles. Only then will the climate of the organization be conducive to embarking on an MS study proper. One of the problem-structuring methods may be useful for bringing about the appropriate change in the organizational structure.

Activity: Who are the stakeholders for the Deep Cove project of Section 1.1?

4.3 Problem situation summary — mind maps

Acquiring a sufficiently complete and detailed understanding of the problem situation is a necessary condition for a successful system intervention. The analyst must get a thorough 'feel' for anything that may impact on the outcome. Figure 4-1 gives a list of things to look out for. **Mind maps**, **rich picture diagrams** and **cognitive maps** are highly effective diagrammatic aids to capture these aspects.

What is a mind map? When you think about something — a phenomenon, an issue, or a problem — a host of thoughts are evoked in your mind: things, aspects, and concepts, including fears and aims, data and facts, and the possible actions and reactions by yourself or other people or entities involved and their consequences, both planned and unplanned, desirable and undesirable, that result from such actions, and the wider context or environment of it all. A mind map is all this (or a judiciously chosen subset) put down on paper in headings, slogans, or sentences.

The things are arranged in a meaningful way by showing aspects closely related in groups, by lines that connect things which are related, and by arrows that indicate causal relationships between items. No formal conventions are used. You may introduce your own, such as using solid lines for strong relationships, broken lines for weak ones, or enclosing items that form a subgroup inside a circle or 'cloud'.

Figure 4-2 is a mind map of what gets evoked in the mind of one of the authors when he ponders the mode of transport for going to work on some mornings.

Figure 4-2   Mind map of dilemma for going to work by bicycle.

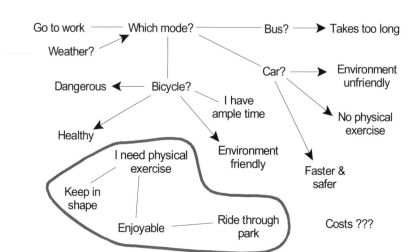

Mind maps can easily be used for capturing and consolidating the thoughts and ideas of several people, borrowing rules of brainstorming. An effective way to go about it is to write down each item on a sticky note as it is evoked. These are initially stuck on a whiteboard or big flipchart. As more and more concepts and relationships are elicited from the participants, the sticky notes are rearranged and appropriately connected by lines or arrows. This is an effective way to help bring about a consensus among the participants on the problem situation. Differences of view or disagreements can also easily be depicted by showing alternative configurations side-by-side. Once complete, the final version can be digitally photographed or copied on paper.

In contrast to a formal written description, which by necessity has to be sequential, a mind map shows the situation in much of its complexity at a glance, so to speak. It can be 'read' in any direction, with all aspects remaining 'present' for instant reference. The information contained in it can be processed in parallel, while a verbal description can only be processed serially. It is thus a much more effective and potent vehicle to present a situation or to use it as a basis for communication than a formal write-up. The same is true for rich pictures, introduced next.

Activity: Draw up a mind map for the Deep Cove Project in Section 1.1.

4.4 Rich picture diagrams

Rather than show the various aspects in words or short sentences, P. Checkland [1993/99] suggests drawing a cartoon-like pictorial summary of everything (or almost everything!) the observer knows about the situation studied.

Note that term 'rich picture' does not, in the first place, mean a drawing. It is simply a more colourful term for a situation summary. Its cartoon-like representation is called a rich picture diagram. However, this is rather clumsy and long. So if it is clear from the context, we will refer to the diagram simply as a rich picture.

'But I'm no good at drawing!' you object. Neither are we. The representations used are very simple: stick-like figures, clouds, blobs and boxes, some slogan-type writing, and arrows depicting connections or time sequences. Figure 4-3 is a rich picture for the dilemma of whether or not to go to work by bicycle.

Figure 4-3   Rich picture of dilemma for going to work by bicycle.

Figure 4-4 shows some types of items and symbols commonly used. You will quickly discover that the talent needed is not the ability to draw well, but simply a bit of imagination. In fact, drawing rich pictures is fun. Note that the temptation to use computer clipart is great. Don't! The result is usually stilted and contrived.

Although your prime concern may only be with a particular aspect of the situation, for both mind maps and rich pictures, it pays to assemble as wide a picture as is reasonably possible. Only then will you have some assurance of not missing inter-actions and relationships that could turn out to be essential for the particular issue that you wish to analyse in detail. Hence it is advisable to depict all facets you are aware of from your familiarization of the situation and not only those that

Figure 4-4   Sample symbols for rich pictures.

seem directly related to the original issue that triggered the study. Even so, you will
have to use your judgement as to what details to include and what to leave out, or as
to the appropriate level of resolution. You will have to strike a sensible balance
between the desires for completeness and parsimony. For instance, you may draw a
book entitled 'rules' as a reminder in place of the rules. Slogans, coming out of some
person's head, are often highly effective summaries of details.

As you have discussions with other people involved, you may discover new
aspects or other angles of the situation. So you add new items and reorganize or discard old material. In some sense, a rich picture is never finished. It is often redrawn.
It will remain a central point of reference during the entire project and a useful
reminder for all involved, even after moving on to other things.

Naturally, you can only give your perception of the situation. So, be aware that it will be affected by your world view. Therefore, you will need to remind yourself as you proceed to keep an open mind, avoid introducing preconceived ideas, refrain from imposing an assumed structure on the situation or viewing it as 'the problem of ...'. The latter is particularly important, since other people may see different aspects of the situation as 'the real problem'. At this point, you do not want to commit the analysis unwittingly to a given direction before you have gained a full understanding of its complexity and crucial interrelationships.

All of this is easily said, but more difficult to stick to. We all have a natural tendency to classify problem situations and give them a name. It gives the illusion 'of having the situation under control'. For example, consider truancy at primary school or at high school. 'Oh this is simply a lack of discipline in the home!' The 'problem' has been labelled and hence 'solved' — end of discussion. Taking such a view will narrow our focus of attention. It may lead us to overlook the social complexity of truancy and effective means to limit its adverse effects on the truant, the family, and society.

Most importantly, as is the case for a mind map, a rich picture — the diagram or the concept — is not a system description. The term *system* implies that any inter-connectedness is organized and not coincidental. By assuming such organized interconnections you may impose a structure on the situation which may not be present or, if present, focuses your attention in a given direction, rather than encouraging you to keep a completely open mind. Only once you have identified the aspect of the situation of particular interest to you, or the issue to be analysed, will you be ready to define a system relevant for that aspect or issue.

Expressing a problem situation in the form of a rich picture diagram is obviously only one mode of making a situation summary. In some instances, it may be instructive to capture certain aspects with other diagrams, such as a flow chart of either material, documents, or information. For example, a manufacturing operation may best be captured by a flow diagram depicting how material moves from workstation to workstation, the tasks performed at each station, the quality inspection points, the locations where data are collected about the processes, etc. It is important though to include pointers for alternative ways to accomplish the same thing. It may be supplemented by notes about difficulties encountered at each workstation and various options suggested for alleviating them. (More on such diagrams in Sections 5.5 and 5.7.)

4.5 Guidelines for mind maps and rich pictures

Three major components are represented in mind maps and rich pictures:

1. **Elements of structure:** All aspects or components of the situation that are relatively stable or change only very slowly in the time frame implied in the situation. This would include all physical aspects, like physical structures, buildings and equipment, and products involved, but also logical, functional, or intellectual structural aspects and their properties, possible alternatives, advant-

ages and disadvantages, departmental divisions, information and data, rules of how things are and could be done, or services rendered.

2. **Elements of process:** All dynamic aspects that undergo change or are in a state of flux, like activities that go on within the structure, flow and processing of material or information, and any decision making that goes on.

3. **Relationship between structure and process and between processes:** How does the structure affect or condition processes? How does one process affect or condition other processes? What things or aspects are direct or indirect results of such relationships? For example, if all information on aircraft flight schedules and reservations is stored in each airline's own individual computer data bank (a structure), then booking a flight (a process) necessitates that the customer deals through a travel agent who has access to all these data banks and not just some, or else the flight choice may be drastically reduced.

For human activity systems, a mind map or rich picture should include not only **'hard' facts**, but also **'soft' facts**. Hard facts are the physical structure and processes, data records and their statistical interpretation, information links, and anything on which there is widespread agreement, or what might be labelled 'objective'. Soft facts include opinions, gossip, hunches, interpersonal relationships (friendships, hostilities, power, egos) coming to the surface, perceived agendas and sacred cows, synergies, and symbiotic relationships — or what could broadly be called 'the climate' of the situation. This climate is often an important determinant of the various world views held by the people involved in the situation. Unless the climate is sufficiently well understood, essential aspects of these world views may escape the analyst.

All known areas of concern and actual or potential issues or problems should also be shown. In rich pictures this can be done in a number of ways. One is to use the focus symbol of Figure 4-4 pointing at the area of concern. Another is to show a balloon, coming out from an area of concern or a person, containing a question or a short slogan with a question mark or an exclamation mark. If opposing values, or benefits versus costs, have to be weighed, this can be depicted by scales with the baskets containing appropriate words, possibly with a question mark at the top of the scales. Opposing or conflicting views by various people involved can easily be shown by two crossed swords.

The rich picture should also be annotated to define symbols that are not self-explanatory or provide brief footnotes on why certain aspects are excluded or represented in only a cursory way, etc. It may also be interesting and revealing to indicate where you enter into the picture: your interests or roles.

Novices may believe that each item shown needs to be connected to one or more other items. They end up with a map or picture where every item is connected directly or indirectly to every other item. Some connectors and arrows between some items may be crucial and useful to indicate relationships, such as cause-and-effect, symbioses, precedence, or processes. However, excessive use of connections may inadvertently impose a system structure. Remember again: a mind map or a rich picture is not a system description.

If your map or picture looks like a flow chart, depicting the flow of documents, information, or material, or a precedence diagram of how activities have to be executed or like a flow chart of the decision process, as you will encounter in Chapter 5, you may again have imposed a system structure on it. There could well be some aspects of the problem situation which call for a flow chart of some sort. For example, the sequence of cartoons and arrows in the rich picture in Figure 6-2 on page 127, starting at the Sandpoint Refinery and ending at the Warehouse, depicts the flow of material from the refinery, through the mixing and filling plants, to the warehouse, and finally on to the customer. However, this flow is mainly included to pinpoint other aspects that are of managerial concern, provide other important information about the situation, or sketch statistical data.

Beginners often fail to include focus pointers to highlight potential issues.

4.6 Uses and strengths of rich pictures and mind maps

The main use of rich pictures and mind maps is for communicating with other people about complex and problematic situations. They are rarely included in a formal report, since they need to be talked about rather than just shown. The reaction of many analysts to rich pictures, in contrast to mind maps, is one of scepticism. 'Cartoons have no place in serious analysis!' Give the rich picture a chance! You will discover that precisely because they are unconventional, unexpected, and a fun tool, they are more likely to catch and retain your listeners' attention and interest — in fact, have them become active participants.

Interconnections, relationships, and direct and indirect consequences become more clearly visible; understanding is considerably enhanced. Since the whole map or picture is constantly present, references to aspects previously discussed do not have to rely on the listener's memory, but can be directly pointed out or referred back to. Queries can also refer to the map or picture and hence will be more focussed and more precise. Misunderstandings are reduced. Missing aspects become more obvious.

It allows identification of the people who own the problematic situation, the people in positions of power, such as the decision makers, the people who will execute any decisions taken, and the people who will enjoy the benefits or suffer the consequences of the results. It pinpoints the sources and types of data. But most importantly, it will help identify existing or potential issues, conflicts, and problems. It may point out that the particular issue is embedded in other areas of concern that may have to be resolved before the original issue can be tackled. Sometimes, particularly in a learning context, a mind map or rich picture is drawn simply to gain a better understanding of a complex situation as a whole. However, more often, the map or picture constitutes the first step towards analysing a particular issue. It will firm up the choice of the problem to be studied. It will show that problem within its complete context. This will help in selecting appropriate boundaries for the system and the scope of the analysis.

Activity: Draw a rich picture for what aspects and considerations have relevance for deciding whether or not to study at a tertiary educational institution or to complete your degree. Clearly show your world view.

4.7 Cognitive mapping

Cognitive mapping is a tool that C.L. Eden [1983] adapted from G.A. Kelly's (1955) personal construct theory. In contrast to mind maps and rich pictures, which are suitable to represent an individual's personal as well as a group's aggregate perception of the problem situation, a **cognitive map** only captures the subjective, personal perception of an individual. It takes the form of a network of statements, expressing concepts — ideas, goals, concerns, preferences, actions — and their contrasts or opposites. The concepts are linked together by arrows, which indicate the direction of connections, i.e. which concept leads logically to which other concept(s). Figure 4-5 gives a simple example. Cognitive maps have some similarity to mind maps that capture means–end or cause-and-effect relationships. (They are also related to **causal loop diagrams**, taken up in detail in Section 5.5.)

Figure 4-5   Constructs and links.

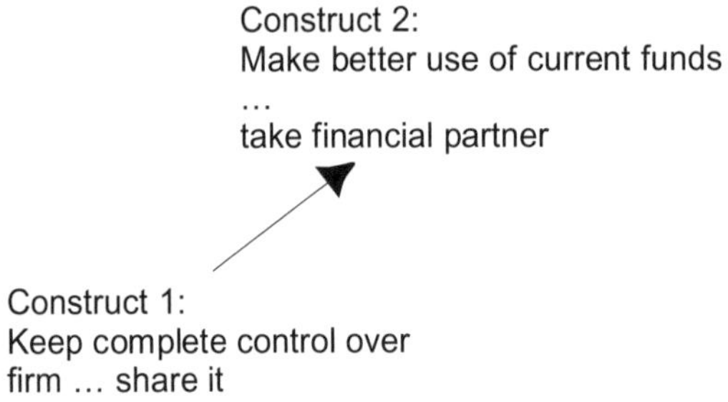

Construct 2:
Make better use of current funds
...
take financial partner

Construct 1:
Keep complete control over
firm ... share it

As we have seen in Chapter 3, we can never describe reality in an interpretation-free or objective way. All we can do is to express our subjective perceptions. (If enough people substantively agree, then we achieve a degree of 'consensual inter-subjective objectivity'.) Personal construct theory is a model that explains how individuals make sense of their world — attribute meaning to events and experiences, and develop and understand connections between experiences, via linked concepts, called **constructs**. Unless we act or react instinctively, we are guided by this framework of constructs to anticipate the consequences of any action potentially available to us. What may appear as irrational behaviour may be understood as rational in terms of this subjective framework. Furthermore, the framework is not context-independent. Experiences in different situations may produce and elicit a different set of constructs, and new experiences may change them in the same way as they may change a person's world view.

Constructs are usually composed of two **poles**. The first or preferred pole expresses a given desirable concept (idea, meaning, goal, or action) and the second or undesirable pole denotes a contrast or opposite. The opposites are not necessarily logical opposites, but perceived subjective contrasts. For example, the first pole of Construct 1 in Figure 4-5 states: 'keep complete control over firm', contrasted by 'share it' (with another person) as the second pole. Other opposites are plausible contrasts, such as a rather vague 'give up total control', 'sell firm and be an employee', or 'take a silent financial partner with no operational involvement'. In the diagram the two poles are separated by an ellipsis (…) which is read as "*rather than*". So the construct becomes: 'keep complete control over firm *rather than* share it.' If the logical opposite can be inferred as the contrast of the first pole, it is not shown explicitly after the ellipsis. A final goal, a constraint, or information may have no relevant opposite, and hence only one pole is stated.

Both poles should be expressed in the individual's own words, since the way in which something is said may have associated connotations that go beyond the words themselves, such as the strength of a preference, ambiguities, conflicts, or even contradictions that may need clarification when the map is analysed. If possible, the wording should be action-oriented — a verb or noun implying an action.

In Figure 4-5, the first pole of Construct 1 leads to the first pole of Construct 2. If this is not the case, i.e. the first pole of a construct leads to the second pole of another construct, then a negative sign (–) is attached to the head of the arrow. Similarly, a negative sign on the tail of an arrow implies the second pole leads to a new construct. It is not implied that the second pole of a construct logically always leads to the second pole of the next construct (as is true in Figure 4-5).

4.8 Cognitive map for NuWave Shoes

Let us now develop a cognitive map for a personal problem of Elly Schuhmacher, the owner–manager of NuWave Shoes. We will first give a short verbal description of the 'difficulties' she faces and then show how her perceptions can be mapped out. (Ignore the numbers in square brackets on your first reading.)

Elly Schuhmacher's nightmare

A little more than a year ago Elly jumped at the opportunity to go into business on her own, taking over a failing niche-market, high-fashion shoe factory from an old family friend and converting it into one offering funky shoes to the yuppy generation. With a €90,000 overdraft from a sympathetic bank and her own savings of a little more than €40,000, plus a loan from her parents, her funky shoes were an instant success rather than a flop [1], as some sceptics predicted, with sales only restricted by limited production capacity rather than demand [2]. However, her cash position was tight and not as good as expected [3], due mainly to two reasons: a three-fold rise in raw material stocks [4], locking up cash [5], and the slow rate of collections from the retailers, the latter taking an average of 50 days to pay, rather than the 30 days net asked for by NuWave [6].

Elly knows that she can easily double sales with little additional effort [7] if she gets new machinery more suitable for her style of goods [8]. How to raise the €140,000 needed for that is her immediate dilemma [9]. The bank turned down her loan application unless she injects more equity capital [10]. She has no other funds, and neither can she raise more from her parents [11]. *A priori*, her only option seems to be to take a financial partner [12]. But NuWave is her baby, and she wants to keep complete control rather than share it [14]. Last night she had a nightmare that somebody else was sitting at her desk and giving her orders. She looks again over her options:

1. Do nothing, i.e. continue with the current mode of operation [7]. Another few years of deprivation on a measly €400 a week for slaving 60 to 70 hours a week? It would take her three to four years to build up enough retained earnings to up-grade the machinery [8]. Can she wait that long? Competition may grab the opportunity and step in to fill her potential market [15].

2. Get a business partner to inject €70,000 [12]. Together with an equal-size bank loan this would cover the new equipment cost and provide the additional working capital needed, but would reduce her equity share to 50% — her nightmare come true [13]!

Could she perhaps make better use of her current funds [16]? For instance, offer a discount for prompt payment [17] to speed up collections from retailers. It will reduce her margin and hence profit [18], but if it frees half of the current €150,000 tied up in accounts receivable [19], she is already halfway home.

She again studies the latest balance sheet. Her gaze is caught by the investment in raw materials (RM). 'Do we really need over €90,000 dollars of RM stocks? Could we not operate efficiently with less?' she asks herself [20]. The current stocks are 4 to 5 months' worth of usage! Admittedly, when they started out with only €30,000, a few deliveries had to be delayed [21]. In the long run that will give NuWave a reputation of unreliability — something she wants to avoid [22] since it will ultimately have a negative impact on sales and hence profits [23].

A cognitive map for Elly's dilemma

Rather than read this narrative several times, highlighting pertinent aspects, you will get a more truthful picture of how Elly perceives her problem by developing the map sentence by sentence. We take the sequence of statements as a reflection of her thought processes, and that in itself may reveal crucial aspects, such as contrasts and juxtapositions in their immediate context, rather than deliberately separated from it, and the strengths of preferences and dislikes. So, reread the first paragraph of the narrative again. Ignoring the historical reference, the first statement leading to other constructs is 'her funky shoe sales were an instant success, rather than a flop, as some sceptics predicted' (labelled [1]). This becomes our first construct, stated as '[1]

Funky shoes instant success … a flop', which mirrors the essential meaning of the words used. (Recall that the ellipsis reads as 'rather than'.) We enter this about 2/3 down a blank page (at least A4 format, but A3 is even better), or on a sticky note that we stick on a big whiteboard. This will hopefully leave enough space to add other constructs below as well as above. (In our case, no other constructs lead to it. Hence it shows up at the bottom of Figure 4-6.) The second part of that sentence gives the next construct '[2] Sales restricted by production capacity … demand'. Construct [2] is a natural successor or follow-on thought of construct [1], as indicated by the arrow from one to the other. The next two sentences contain four related constructs ([3] to [6]) which have no direct relationship with constructs [1] and [2], so we place them a bit to the side.

The first sentence of the second paragraph provides the next two constructs. Construct [7] is a successor to construct [2], while [8] follows [7]. The sentence following refers to her dilemma of how to raise the €140,000 (construct [9]) needed to finance the new equipment. Some thought indicates that raising these funds sounds like a goal that she wants achieve. This is why the opposite pole is often dropped. Furthermore, it is a mapping convention to show goals or final outcomes at the very top of the map, with actions that lead to the goals below. Rather than show it directly above construct [8], we insert it close to the top of the sheet. (At this point we do not know if there are even higher order goals, so we leave some free space above.)

Continuing in this fashion we develop Figure 4-6. We hasten to say that this is a sanitized version, carefully reworked and reorganized to avoid most intersections of arrows and to have the constructs spread out evenly on the sheet. Most first drafts will look cluttered, with new constructs squeezed in between other constructs, some constructs or arrows crossed out, and many arrows intersecting.

A problem owner can develop such a map on his or her own, expressing the personal train of thought. In practice, cognitive maps are usually drawn by an analyst trained in the method, either while interviewing the problem owner or on the basis of a taped interview. It goes without saying that a map drawn during an interview will need considerable tidying up. The analyst will invariably have to go back to the problem owner for clarification on exact wording of poles, particularly second poles, or eliciting missing second poles, and verifying correct direction of arrows. This may result in substantive changes in wording, as well as the addition of new constructs and links. In fact, critical analysis and discussion of the map will shed considerable further insight into the problem situation and result in a better understanding for both the problem owner and the analyst.

Note that for many real-life problem situations the number of constructs in a map may go into the hundreds. Hence, it may be a good idea to break the map into several submaps, with labelled links between the submaps.

C. L. Eden (the inventor of the problem structuring method SODA) and his associates at the University of Strathclyde have developed 'Decision Explorer', a PC software package, as an aid in drawing and analysing cognitive maps interactively. Although hardly appropriate for use during an interview, it is of great help for producing the final draft of the map.

Figure 4-6   Cognitive map for NuWave's owner–manager.

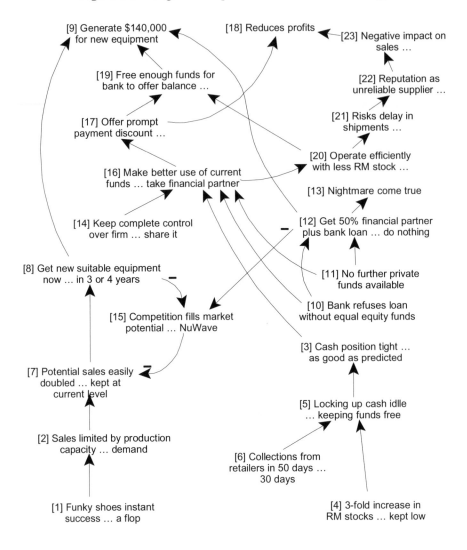

Analysing the map

Once the problem owner is satisfied that the map is a sufficiently true representation of her or his thought processes and vision of the problem situation, the map should be analysed along a number of lines. We start out by working through the map in detail. The aim is to make sure that the various paths from information, via actions, to goals are correct and complete. This is done either from top to bottom, or from bottom to top. In both approaches, it is important to question whether there are other, yet uncharted, possible actions that may also achieve the desired goals (top-down approach) or whether a given action opens up the possibility for other, yet uncharted, actions (bottom-up approach). This may lead to the discovery of new options and possible courses of action.

In Elly's map, a bottom-up analysis reveals that construct [20] ('Run operations efficiently with less RM stock ...) should lead to more positive actions, rather than mainly undesirable consequences. How could operations be run efficiently with less RM stock? One obvious action is to predict RM usage carefully in the light of planned production on a daily basis [24] and arrange express supplies to avoid shortages [25], even if this increases costs [26]. Maybe even more crucial is to find out why RM stocks have increased so dramatically. It turns out that this is the result of the production supervisor's policy of ordering all RMs only once at the beginning of each shoe season — summer or winter — and also keeping high safety stock in case a second run for a given shoe model is made. Neither of these policies makes sense to Elly. Why not schedule supplies in the exact quantities needed for a given shoe model to arrive shortly before production is about to begin — a just-in-time policy — and not weeks or months before [27]? It might be a bit more costly. Furthermore, since production capacity is so tight, and is likely to remain that way even with the new equipment, it makes little sense to keep safety stocks just in case. Simply plan for only one production run for each shoe model [28]. 'And is it not more important right now to get the new equipment and capture the market than trying to reduce costs [29]?' she argues. 'Keeping costs low can always come later.' That still leaves current excess supplies from previous seasons' models. 'I could design shoe models that use up these stocks [30].'

Figure 4-7 shows the revised map which incorporates these ideas, changing construct [20] to a different wording in the process. It now offers considerably more options for effective decision making than the original map.

Another line of analysis checks for **feedback loops** and, in particular, for destabilizing (positive) feedback loops (see Section 3.11). Elly's revised map contains a loop from construct [8] back to construct [7] via construct [15]. Given that two arrows have a negative sign attached (the one from [8] to [15] signifying that the second pole of [8] leads to [15]), it is a positive feedback loop and its effect is reinforcing, i.e. waiting 3 to 4 years and risking competition to fill the gap makes it even more likely that sales may never go beyond the current level and by inference may even decrease.

The third type of analysis looks for so-called **core constructs** and **emerging themes**. A core construct is one that has relatively many arrows issuing from it and/or leading to it, in comparison to other constructs in the map. In Figure 4-7, construct [16] sticks out with eight links — four arrows in and four out. Except for goal construct [9] and constructs [12], [20], and [27], with four links each, all the remaining ones have fewer than four links. Construct [16] is therefore a pivotal construct. Any attempt to find a solution or answer to Elly's dilemma is likely to revolve around it, i.e. involving paths that lead through it to the final goal.

Figure 4-7 Amended cognitive map for NuWave.

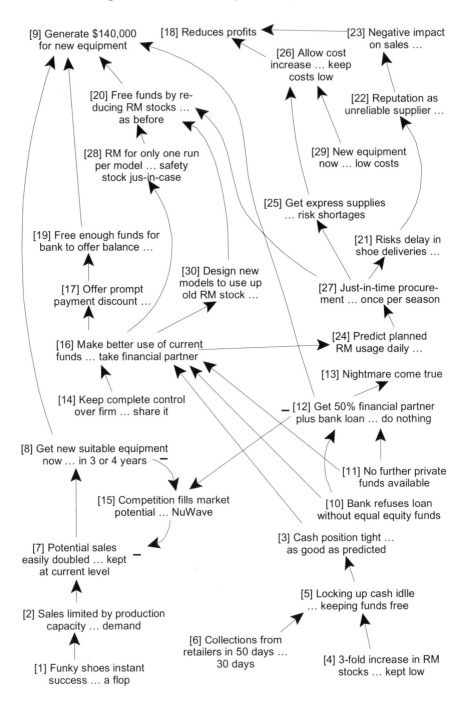

Emerging themes are highly interlinked groups of constructs with few links to the rest of the map. Emerging themes may again be singled out for detailed attention, either giving rise to an issue that will become a focus for further analysis or holding the key to finding a solution to the problem in question. If a large map is broken into smaller submaps, they are likely to be along clusters of constructs.

Some sobering comments on cognitive mapping

Although deceptively simple-looking, the method requires considerable skill and experience to produce a map that captures the problem owner's view of the problem situation with sufficient accuracy and reliability. In a mind map and a rich picture links do not necessarily have a cause-and-effect connotation, but simply mean that there is some loose connection or relationship between the items shown. In contrast, the links between constructs in a cognitive map imply a definite logical predecessor–successor relationship. However, faced with real-life situations, we have often found that the direction of the relationship may be far from clear and could go either way. For example, construct [14] ('Keep complete control over firm ... share it') could legitimately be viewed as a goal, rather than a motive for action resulting from it, in which case the direction of the arrow between construct [16] and [14] would be reversed.

Furthermore, analysts must be constantly on guard not to distort the problem owner's account with their own perceptions. As with all such aids, there could always be a certain inadvertent or intended contamination coming from the analyst.

If the aim is mainly to get a good grip on a problem situation which will help to select the right issue, identify the stakeholders, and justify boundary choices, we find mind maps and rich pictures easier to use. The strength of cognitive maps is that they are more than simply a summary of the problem situation, but, as we have seen when analysing and enhancing Elly's map, they are the first phase for practical problem solving via SODA (more on this in Chapter 7).

4.9 Problem definition and boundary selection

Recall that the purpose of getting a sufficient understanding of a problem situation is to delineate the problem to be analysed. This does not simply mean identifying the correct issue of concern, but also its scope, form, and level of detail or depth. These should all be appropriate to generate useful insights and answers for decision making or problem solving. Part of this involves a critical evaluation of which aspects of the problem situation should be included in the analysis and which aspects can be ignored. Those included either become part of the narrow system of interest or its environment. In other words, we have to select the boundaries for both the narrow system of interest and its relevant environment. As pointed out in Section 3.5, boundary selection is the most critical facet of systems thinking. **Critical systems heuristics**, developed by W. Ulrich in 1983 [Ulrich, 1996], is currently the most comprehensive and systematic framework for subjecting boundary selection to thorough scrutiny. Several problem-structuring methods [Rosenberg and Mingers, 2000] devote considerable effort to assessing which aspects should be considered and which ones can be ignored during a particular phase in the analysis. We will limit our comments to some general points.

Boundary selection will largely fix the scope, direction, and focus of all subsequent analysis. It not only determines which inputs are considered controllable, but also whose benefits and costs are included in the performance measure, and in particular which potential stakeholders are reduced to problem customers, possibly mere victims without any say or recourse. Inappropriate boundary selection often means that the benefits or advantages derived for the narrow system of interest are partially or completely negated by losses or disadvantages in the wider system.

It may also be highly instructive to contrast different world views and analyse their effect on the appropriate boundary choices. The added insights invariably gained will contribute towards a more comprehensive understanding of the problem situation and a revised definition of the problem.

Selecting the wrong boundaries may result in solving the wrong problem. It may make it difficult or even impossible to implement the solution or may reduce the potential benefits that could have been derived.

Let us now use the summary portrayed in Figure 4-7 to define Elly's problem. Her initial concern was how to raise the €140,000 needed to finance the new equipment. Her statements indicate that she does not want to consider taking a financial partner — it's her nightmare! That either leaves doing nothing, which is potentially crippling, or finding most of the funds internally, as shown by constructs [16] and [20]. With this focus, the critical problem elements become:

- Decision maker: Elly Schuhmacher.

- Objective: Generate enough funds to purchase the new equipment.

- Decision criterion: Funds generated are at least equal to €140,000.

- Performance measure: Amount of funds freed.

- Alternative courses of action: The combination of: size of discount offered to customers; form of just-in-time procurement policy; imaginative model designs to absorb excess RM stock from previous seasons; express in-freighting to avoid shortages; no safety stocks for just-in-case second production runs.

- Boundaries for narrow system of interest (as indicated by major system inputs): Old and new production output capacity and cost structure; potential demand and shoe wholesale prices.

- Boundaries for wider system of interest: no countermove by competition within the near future; bank amenable to making up shortfall (e.g. in the form of a mortgage on equipment) if sufficiently small.

Of the stakeholders affected by, but not involved in, the decision-making process, the retail stores are not adversely affected, being offered a new option of taking advantage of the discount or paying within the net period. Only NuWave's competitors could be adversely affected by Elly's preemptive move to expand production capacity, but then that is in the nature of competition.

(As an aside, the set of constructs from [16] to [9] via [17], [30], [24], and [28] strongly suggests that one of the first things Elly needs to do is to carefully analyse the effects of these actions on her cash flow, i.e. come up with month-by-month cash flow projections over the coming year or two. This will tell her how close she might get to goal [9] of generating €140,000 from internal sources before approaching the bank for a second time. If shown favourable figures, the bank may be more amenable than if asked for a commitment without such information.)

4.10   Some conclusions

As we have seen, how problem owners and/or analysts perceive the problem situation involves a fair degree of arbitrariness. It is strongly affected by the purpose of the analysis, the world views of the analysts and/or problem owners, and the resources (time, funds, people) available for the job. You should therefore not be surprised if different people see the problem situation differently and may disagree on which issues need to be studied first. Such a disparity of views is to be expected. No view can be ruled out as invalid, unless it lacks internal logic or is incompatible with the person's own world view. However, this does not imply that all problem situation summaries are equally useful, particularly if they are incomplete or their focus is biased. Furthermore, a problem situation summary should not be in the form of a systems description, since this may impose a given structure that may again bias the analysis. At this stage, it is crucial to keep an open mind. Nevertheless, a sufficient degree of shared appreciation of the various views is needed to reach a partial consensus on the problem situation. Only then is it likely that an agreement will emerge as to which issue is to be studied and how.

4.11   Chapter highlights

- The problem situation is the context in which a problem is embedded. Most problem situations involve a collection of interconnected issues, each of which could become the focus for analysis. Seeing a problem within its full context is essential for correctly defining the problem.
- Identifying a problem means defining the decision maker, her or his objective(s), the criterion for judging when the objective has been achieved, the performance measure for assessing the level of achievement towards the objective, the alternative courses of action, and the relevant context or environment in which the problem is embedded.
- The stakeholders are the various roles that the people or entities assume when they are in one way or another connected to the problem, either as the person(s) owning or having the problem and controlling crucial aspects of the problem, the person(s) who will use the results of the analysis, the person(s) who will analyse the problem, or those that are affected by the results and may or may not have any

direct or indirect influence over the actions taken. Since stakeholders are roles, a person may assume more than one role at the same time.

• Mind maps, rich pictures, and cognitive maps are useful vehicles for representing the problem situation summary. They serve as a basis for discussion with other people who have a stake in the problem. They show the problem in its full context and help identify and define the issue or problem to be analysed, the stakeholders, and facilitate selecting appropriate boundaries of the analysis.

Exercises

1. Draw a mind map for the emergency service call centre in Section 1.1 of Chapter 1.

2. Draw a mind map for the Deep Cove project situation in Section 1.1 of Chapter 1.

3. (a) Draw a mind map for the balance of your tertiary education in view of the kind of job career you envisage for yourself and the possible obstacles to it.
   (b) Identify the various stakeholders of the problem.
   (c) List the six problem elements.

4. (a) Draw a mind map for the breast cancer screening situation described in Section 1.1 of Chapter 1.
   (b) Identify the various stakeholders.
   (c) List the six problem elements.

5. Draw a rich picture diagram, showing the issues and the world view of the project owner, for the following situation. E. Lim E. Nate, or Lim for short, recently joined Steel Fabricators (SF) as their new production manager. Two years ago, after successfully completing an MBA, Lim had taken up a position as production planner for a sizable steel mill. He had liked that job since it allowed him to practice some of the theory he had encountered during his studies. After a year, the planner's job lost its challenge. It became largely a repetitive routine. Although SF is a much smaller outfit, he felt ready for a change, particularly since it seemed to be a step up in responsibility.

SF produces a variety of steel products, mostly to special customer specifications. It has acquired a reputation for its high-quality work and its ability to meet promised delivery dates. So, in spite of the general economic downturn facing the steel processing industry, SF has been able to attract enough new work to operate close to full capacity. In particular, its machine tool shop No. 3 has maintained a four-week order book up to now, while still keeping its high profit contribution, in contrast to most other machine centres. However, it is only a question of time before the considerably lower prices offered by the competition will force SF to lower its prices also in the No. 3 shop. Furthermore, some competitors are offering delivery lead times of three weeks or less compared to SF's 6 to 8 weeks. There is therefore considerable pressure on Lim to remain competitive in terms of both price and delivery lead times. Lim's concerns are being heightened when he reviews the latest report on the rate of defectives produced by the various machine centres. The No. 3 shop sticks out like a sore thumb, with an average rate of over 8%. This is way beyond what could be expected from the type and age of machines operated there. He figures that if the rate of defectives could be reduced to a reasonable 2%, SF could afford to lower prices by 5% without affecting profits, and also trim a few days from its delivery lead times. He therefore decides to have a closer look at the No. 3 shop operation and pick the brains of the shop foreman and some of the operators for possible ideas on how to reduce the rate of defectives.

An extended visit to the No. 3 shop turns up some interesting facts. Most of the defectives seem to come from two particular machines. In fact, their rates regularly reach 1/3 of the machines' total output, while the remaining machines are not out of line with the rest of the plant, with rates of around 1.5 to 2%. Although the foreman is well aware of the problem, he assures Lim that the operators are following the guidelines for maintenance and machine adjustments issued by the machine's manufacturer to the last detail. He says that he regularly checks that this is so. Indeed, some months ago when he had been promoted to foreman at the No. 3 shop and had discovered that the rate of defectives of these two machines was around 25% he had called up the technical service of the machine's manufacturer for advice. For the particular job the machines were doing then, they tended to get out of adjustment with time, with a resulting increase in the rate of defectives. Readjusting the machine at regular intervals should therefore keep the rate of defectives at a reasonable level, still considerably higher than for other machines and other work. At that time, the machine operators adjusted the machines whenever they thought that the rate of defectives was getting too large, somewhere between every 40 and 50 minutes. The manufacturer's guidelines call for an adjustment every 60 minutes. Lim also finds out that each adjustment takes on average 6 minutes to perform — the time needed to produce three parts. Since the product mix has remained essentially the same, this is the rule that is still followed, but without any success in lowering the rate of defectives. In fact, it has since increased to an average of over 30%. The foreman thinks that machine age can be the only logical explanation. He recommends that the machines be replaced.

Lim also finds out that about half of the defective parts can be reworked on another machine. So the loss of output from defectives is not 30% or more, but only about 15 to 16%. If this could be lowered substantially, delivery lead times from this machine could be reduced by at least a week.

Back in his office, Lim checks the files for the date of purchase of these machines. They are currently five years old. He also finds in the same folder the latest update on the range of machines offered by this manufacturer. To his consternation he discovers that no changes have been made to the specifications for this particular type of machine and the manufacturer indicates that its average productive life is still around 12 years. This essentially rules out advanced age as a serious reason for the problem. A call to the cost accounting office shows that the cost of the raw materials used is £16 per part, the cost of reworking defective parts amounts to £4 per part, and the parts sell for a net price of £21. The labour cost for the machine, including all fringe benefits, is £18.00 per hour. One operator is needed for each machine.

Taking stock of his finding, he notes down the following major points: The high rate of defectives of the No. 3 shop is exclusively due to two identical machines, with rates of over 30% defectives, half of which could be reworked at a cost. The manufacturer's guidelines on maintenance and hourly adjustment for these machines are followed strictly. The manufacturer has no other advice to offer. Solving the No. 3 shop's defectives problem could only justify price decreases and shorter delivery lead times for the parts produced on these two machines, but not for the remainder of the machines. The output of these two machines amounts to just over 20% of the No. 3 shop's total output. Pressure for increasing shop efficiencies for other products still remains. He is rather frustrated. This morning he was all fired up to tackle the defectives problem of the No. 3 shop. And now the situation looks rather hopeless, particularly since the manufacturer seems to be of no help!

Clearly show all possible issues.

6. Consider Exercise 5 above.
   (a) Identify the stakeholders for the issue of finding a suitable interval for adjusting the two machines of the No. 3 shop.
   (b) List the six problem elements.

7. Consider the situation summary for the blood bank operation in Exercise 3 of Chapter 3. Draw a rich picture diagram for it.

8. Consider the following interview between a young graduate (Y) from the University of Mexico and the priest (P) his mother called in to settle the dispute with his father about what he should do over the next year or two.
   P: Son, tell me about how you see your future.
   Y: I am torn between wanting to take a year off rather that go for a job now, you know, travelling around Europe, not stay home, spend some time in St Tropez, you know, and enjoy the girls …
   P: St Tropez, where they bathe topless? Mm … Go on.
   Y: … yes, rather than settle down, you know, no more playing around. That would please dad.
   P: And marry Iñez now?
   Y: I guess, rather than wait a year or two. But it may already be a bit late this year to find a good job. I mean, the really good jobs always go first. Maybe one of father's friends might help.
   P: You know what kind of job you would like?
   Y: Yeah, a job with one of those big international consulting firms. Many of their projects involve travel all over the world. That would be awesome! No dull factory job for me.
   P: Travelling seems really important to you. Why?
   Y: I want to see the world, meet people, have excitement.

9. In late 200X, Bill Dodge, the supervisor or Customs at the Christchurch International Airport (or CIA), became increasingly concerned about a number of aspects of the customs operation under his management. He received approval to call in an MS/OR consultant to study the operations. The interview reproduced below took place between Bill Dodge (B), the supervisor of Customs and the consultant (C). Draw a cognitive map for (B) from this.
   C: So that I can put things into context, what is Customs' primary role at CIA?
   B: Clearly, it must be border protection, i.e. prevention of importation of illegal goods (drugs, pornographic material, etc.), prevention of entry into NZ of prohibited aliens, and full assessment of import duties.
   C: And I guess that you are not achieving these goals to your satisfaction, right?
   B: Yes, for a number of reasons. Most critically, there is insufficient staff capacity to deal properly with all the tasks loaded onto us. It is obvious to me that our current staff ceiling is too low, although HQ considers it about right. We have been given processing standards that require us to process all passengers of an incoming flight within a set maximum of 30 minutes — rather than taking as much time as needed to perform our duties properly. Secondly, our present shift schedule was OK 8 years ago, when most of our flights arrived during the day time, but it does not fit the current flight pattern any longer. Our flight arrivals and departures are spread over almost 24 hours each day. And so far, the Customs Officer Union has insisted on continuing the present schedule, rather than allowing us to adapt it to the current needs.
   C: Why is that?

B: The present shift schedule results in large amounts of overtime and numerous special call-outs. As a consequence, officers have their wages topped up by very high overtime pay, rather than just getting their normal salary. This is in fact one of their major reasons for choosing to work at CIA rather than at other Customs jobs, such as sea freight import processing or investigations. It's ironic, but my reading of the situation tells me that, although most officers are keen on the extra pay for the first one or two years, they begin to resent it in the long run. They dislike the disruption of their family or social life. The extra money does not compensate enough for it. They particularly dislike the special call-outs.

C: What are special call-outs?

B: Calling in off-duty officers for a duration of 2 to 4 hours to process an incoming flight, either because no shift is on duty or the shift on duty is short-staffed and unable to handle the traffic.

C: Would it be possible to eliminate most overtime and call-outs by changing the shift schedule?

B: Not so much for overtime, since late arrivals of incoming flights might still require the staff to finish processing beyond their scheduled quitting time, but it would reduce the number of special call-outs needed to process scheduled flights outside the current shift schedule. There still would be special call-outs to meet non-scheduled flights and the highly irregular Deep Freeze traffic from and to Antarctica, which seem to fall mainly into the hours between 02.00 and 06.00 hours. I think if we could come up with a shift schedule that still offers a reasonable amount of overtime, say maybe about 50% of the current level, and eliminate all special call-outs for scheduled flights, leaving only the occasional unscheduled flight, the majority of officers would vote for it. So, one of the aims of this exercise is to demonstrate to the staff that it is possible to leave sufficient overtime opportunities for those who want it, rather than forcing it on everyone. With a hefty reduction in overtime pay we could live within our current budget allocation, rather than having to apply for special funding every six months to cover the cost overrun. I hate getting the heat from HQ over that twice each year. It does not look good on my annual job evaluation. In fact, I think that if I can show a permanent and guaranteed reduction in overtime costs they might even be willing to give favourable consideration to increasing my staff ceiling. That would allow larger shift crews and hence enable us to meet the processing standard more regularly, rather than the 70% or less as at the present. Meeting these processing standards is a real problem. How can we meet them 100% all the time? It would require excessively high staff levels with a large portion of the staff being idle much of the time.

C: I am afraid that is correct. What is the current shift schedule?

B: We run two shifts each day: 06.30 to 15.30, and 15.00 to 23.00, with a 30-minute lunch break somewhere around the middle of the shift. The overlap is needed for a proper hand-over of work in progress, such as processing a flight. With the second shift ending at 23.00 we have to schedule overtime or special call-outs every day to process several incoming flights between 22.00 and 01.00 Same, there are five days a week when we have departing and incoming flights between 05.00 and 06.00, i.e. before the first shift is fully operational, since they have 15 minutes to change into uniforms and we need at least 15 minutes to brief the team.

C: However, I presume that other work can be postponed and executed later when there are no flights.

B: Yes, administration and answering correspondence can wait for up to a week, rather than having to be done right away. Some other jobs can be postponed for a day or two.

But two people are needed to staff the customs office for airport freight every weekday from 9.00 to 16.00.

C: I see, but it seems that two shifts would not cover the current flight schedule.

B: No. We would still need some overtime or special call-outs, but not every day. Also, on mornings where there are early departing flights, but no incoming flights, only two officers are needed. Maybe we should look into the possibility of having shifts of various sizes, rather than each shift with a full complement of 15 officers. It would also help if the union agreed to flexible shift start times, as long as they only differ by up to four hours, rather than insisting that a given shift has the same start time every day. Flexible shift times would allow us to have officers on duty when they are needed, rather than having a mismatch between staff needs and availability.

C: To come back to the union: is their position on shift schedules very entrenched or a bargaining strategy?

B: A bit of both, I guess. The current schedule gives high pay, and as a former union member I can understand that the union delegates wish to protect that and not be seen as being soft on anything that threatens current conditions. Also the union contract will be up for negotiation later this year, and they want to start from a strong position, rather than compromise before then. Mind you, they are reasonable chaps, not bloody minded, and if we can come up with an acceptable compromise that shows them as having firmly protected their members' interests, I am fairly confident that they will be willing to put it up for a vote. The important aspect is that it must satisfy both those officers who want to top up their salary though overtime and those who would rather not have these disruptions to their daily lives.

C: Are there any other aspects about the union contract that I should know about?

B: Let me see. Yes. All staff get four weeks vacation plus seven days statutory holiday. Each officer also has the right to attend up to two weeks of training courses each year, and they also have sick leave provisions. All in all, these entitlements add up to about 18% of their regular working hours. We call this the X-factor.

5

Systems models and diagrams

We are now ready to define a relevant narrow system of interest for the issue identified as the problem. This is often referred to as **systems modelling**. Section 5.1 discusses various types of system model, while Section 5.2 describes two common approaches to systems modelling. The next two sections give some pointers on good modelling.

Diagrams are an attractive and effective approach to highlight certain aspects of systems, such as their structure, internal system interactions between components, cause-and-effect and precedence relationships, inputs from and output to the environment, material and information flows inside the system, and the logic of decision rules. These topics are taken up in Sections 5.5–5.7.

5.1 System models

The word 'model' has many meanings. The one of interest to us is defined in *Webster's Collegiate Dictionary* as 'a description or analogy used for helping to visualize something (as an atom) that cannot be directly observed,' although in some cases we may be able to observe certain aspects of it. This seems to be exactly what we do when we define a system. Therefore **a system model is a representation of all essential parts of a system**. As a system is an abstract mental construct — a personal conceptualization and hence not independent of that person (recall the concept of 'consensual subjectivity', Section 3.3, pp. 24–27) — so a model is another abstraction at a different level. It is not the real thing.

A model may be **iconic**, **analogous**, or **symbolic**. Iconic models are reproductions of physical objects, usually to a different scale and with less detail. A car model, the small-scale aircraft tested in a wind tunnel for the aerodynamics of the real thing, or an architectural mock-up of a building are all iconic models.

Analog models are representations which substitute the properties or features of what is modelled by alternative means such that the model is able to mimic whatever aspect of the real thing is of interest to the modeller. For instance, the constantly updated picture that an air traffic controller observes on a radar monitor is an analog of the air traffic in a given sector of the air space. Similarly, the three-dimensional vision produced by computer software on the screen, allowing the observer to see an object from any desired direction or angle, or enabling the observer to walk through a building, is an analog model.

Symbolic models

Symbolic models are representations of the relationships between various entities or concepts by means of symbols. By the time you reached tertiary education, you had encountered and been bombarded with thousands of all sorts of symbolic models. Every newspaper, technical magazine, or school book contains graphs, depicting how a given variable varies as a function of another variable, such as the stock exchange index over time, or statistical charts, e.g. pie charts of how funds are allocated or bar charts comparing the values of various variables of interest. Geographic maps, hierarchical charts of the command structure in an organization showing who reports to whom, flow diagrams depicting how material and information flow through an organization, or diagrams depicting the sequence of decisions that need to be made are all examples of symbolic models. Such models are extensively used for communicating all sorts of data and information. In Sections 5.5–5.7 we will study several graphical and diagrammatic models.

However, the most common symbolic models are the mental pictures we form in our minds or the word descriptions that we make verbally or in writing about something: an object, an entity, an operation, a process, or an interconnected set of abstract concepts, such as a logical argumentation or a theory. Our daily life is literally a never ending journey from model to model, although most of the time it remains outside our formal awareness. What we call 'experience' is a huge memory bank of mental models to which we add new ones daily. This is what allows us to recognize a car when we see one, and not mistake it for a rubbish container, although closer inspection of what people keep in cars makes us wonder whether many cars are in fact used as rubbish containers. But, as Nicola Petty pointed out while proofreading this chapter, this is preferable to dumping it out of the window.

Mathematical models

Another type of symbolic model extensively used in hard OR is the mathematical models. The relationships between entities are represented in the form of mathematical expressions, like functions, equations, and inequalities. You may have come across the mathematical expression for the distance s that a free-falling object travels in t seconds: $s = 0.5gt^2$, where g is the constant of gravity. This is a mathematical model, although your high school teachers may not have called it that. The methodology of hard OR is taken up in Chapter 6.

This book focuses on symbolic models — mental, diagrammatic, and mathematical — although even the last two invariably start with a verbal model.

Models as approximations

As Webster's definition states, a model is only a partial representation of what it is supposed to capture. It will contain various approximations and simplifying assumptions, some of little importance, but others of great consequence. However, it is essential that the analyst carefully records the form of the approximations and assumptions made. There are three major reasons for this: (1) to ensure that all stakeholders of the model are aware of the model's limitations; (2) to highlight the need to study changes in system behaviour by modifying these approximations and assumptions if this is possible; and (3) to ensure that, if the model is revisited at some time in the future with a view to making modifications, the analyst is fully aware of any approximations and assumptions incorporated in it.

The type of approximation and assumptions made will reflect the training, experience, and personality of the analyst and the resources, particularly in terms of time and funds, available, as well as the purpose of the study. There is always a degree of arbitrariness present. Hence there may be several good models for the same system. However, for any model that claims to be a valid representation of the systemic content of a problem it must be clear what its transformation process, system boundary, inputs (including which ones are control inputs), and outputs (in particular the system performance measure(s)) are.

Unfortunately, analysts may introduce assumptions into a model without being fully aware of doing so. For example, data used in the model, such as demand for a product or service, are often based on past experience. They may even have been collected while a different mode of operation was in use. If the model is used for predicting or controlling future behaviour of the system, the implicit strong assumption is that the nature, form, and pattern of past data are valid predictors for the future after the new system has been implemented, which may or may not be the case. Furthermore, what may be obvious to you may not be obvious to somebody else. So it pays to record all assumptions carefully.

> Activity: For each of the following, indicate the type of model and explain why it is of that type: (a) the wiring diagram of a TV set; (b) a thermometer; (c) a weather chart; (d) a PlayStation game; (e) a porcelain statue; (f) the normal distribution.

5.2 Approaches for describing a relevant system

A system description or model consists of specifying:

(a) the **transformation process(es)** or activities of the system;

(b) the **boundary** of the system, i.e. what is inside the system — the narrow system of interest — and what makes up its environment or the wider system of interest;

(c) the **components** and **subsystems** of the narrow system involved in the transformation process, and the **dynamic relationships**, and **stable relationships** or the **structure**;

(d) the **uncontrollable inputs** into the system from the environment, the **control inputs** or **decision and decision rules;** and

(e) the **outputs** of the system, desired and undesired, planned and unplanned, and which ones serve as the **performance measures** for the system.

How should we go about this task? There are two main approaches: (a) identifying and fitting a known basic structure, and (b) analysing the processes and defining a suitable structure from first principles.

A structural approach

The issue chosen for detailed study may strongly suggest a typical structure usually found for situations of that sort. For instance, the issue may be the excessive length of time that the customers of a given bank may have to wait for service. This immediately suggests a 'waiting line' structure, as depicted in Figure 5-1, with customers arriving randomly at a service facility, joining the queue in front of the servers, and advancing in the queue by one position each time a customer ahead of them has been served, until it is their turn to be served by the next server who becomes free. The system transforms customers in need of service into customers served.

Figure 5-1   Waiting line structure.

| Customer Population | Arrival Process Population | Queue | Service Facilities |

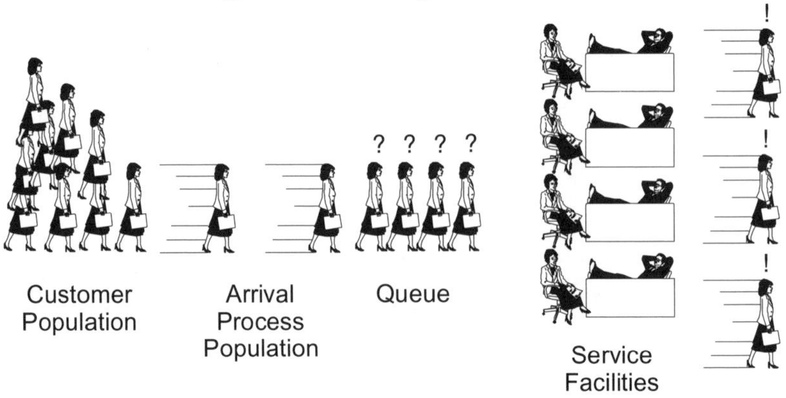

In a waiting line structure, the components of the system are customers, one or several queues, and the server(s). The stable structure of the system is given by how customers pass through the system. After arriving, they wait in the queue in front of the service facility, are served by the server(s) in a specified sequence or priority, e.g. first-come first-served, and then depart from the system. The dynamic aspects or processes are given by the random arrivals of customers from a given 'population' in the environment to join a queue of the system, the ordered advancement of these customers to the front of a queue, and the service activity where both a customer and a server are engaged jointly — a transient relationship.

Customer arrival times and service times constitute the uncontrollable inputs into the system. The control inputs are the number of servers on duty and the service priority rules imposed. The arrivals obey a given (assumed) known arrival pattern, such as each arrival being independent of all other arrivals and completely random. Once 'arrived', each customer becomes a temporary component of the system. The novice will take customer departures as the output of the system. This, though, is of little use. Typically, the analyst is interested in several performance measures, such as the average waiting time of customers in the queue, the average total time that a customer spends in the system, and the average time the servers are idle. Customer departures are only of interest in that they help determine how long each customer spent in the system.

Using a known basic structure allows fast progress towards a complete system description. Once the basic structure has been identified, the analyst will immediately know which aspects of the situation form the narrow system of interest and which ones are part of the environment, the type of components to look for, the usual relationships between them, the underlying processes, the usual inputs and outputs of the system, the type of input data needed, and suitable system performance evaluators. The analyst will also have a fair idea which quantitative tools, if any, are most appropriate for analysing the situation. He or she may in fact have access to commercial computer software specifically developed for such problems.

A structural approach is clearly the preferred way to go if the situation is well understood and the world view implied by the system performance evaluators of the structure chosen closely fits the one identified in the problem situation. However, for situations with some degree of ambiguity there is a serious risk that the issue is 'forced' into an inappropriate structure.

This approach also presupposes that the analyst is familiar with the most common system structures, not simply on a theoretical level, but also through practical experience. The theoretical knowledge, particularly for quantitative or diagrammatic models, can be acquired through university MS/OR courses.

The experienced analyst, on the other hand, will very quickly recognize which known structure, if any, is an appropriate system description for a given problem. If none can be identified, he or she will have to fall back on a process approach. Note though that stories abound of experienced analysts who have their one favourite structure and by hook or crook will force any problem into it or give up.

A process approach

Here, no assumptions about the possible system structure are made. Rather, the observed processes and relationships of interest between the various components of the system are used for discovering a good structure. The world view dictates which system performance evaluators are to be observed. Often several different possible structures may be suitable. This approach is more challenging, but also more difficult. Chapter 6 demonstrates its use for a real-life case.

What is the best way to go about it? A good starting point is to determine from whose standpoint to view the system and then define the prime transformation process. This delineates the system boundary and points to what inputs the system uses, what outputs it provides, and what system components participate in the transformation process. The following four rules help in identifying the components, the inputs (both uncontrollable and controllable), and the outputs of the system:

1. Any aspect, controllable or uncontrollable, that affects the system, but in turn is not affected by it, is a system input.

2. Any aspect that is directly or indirectly affected by the transformation process, but in turn does not affect any other aspect of the system, is a system output.

3. Any aspect that is part of the system's structure or is affected by an input (uncontrollable or controllable) or by other aspects of the system and in turn affects other aspects of the system, including outputs, is a component or a relationship.

4. Any aspect that does not affect the system, or is not affected by it, or is not part of its structure is irrelevant and can be ignored.

Table 5-1 neatly summarizes these rules. By rules 1 and 2 there should be no feedback loops between the system and its environment. All aspects in such a feedback loop, except external control and data inputs, should be contained within the system. Any transactions across the system boundary are therefore either inputs or outputs. In fact, it is probably advisable to start out by identifying the desired outputs and known control inputs, followed by data inputs, and only then look into the inside of the system.

Table 5-1   Systems identification rules.

Question	Is aspect affected by system variables or inputs?		
	Answer	YES	NO
Does aspect affect system?	YES	component or relationship	input
	NO	output	irrelevant

Naturally, in the real world things may not be as clear-cut as assumed by these four rules. A given aspect may affect the system only marginally. The recurrent question is therefore: 'At what point does such an influence become a significant factor that should be taken into account?' If time and funds allow it, a prudent analyst will include rather more than less. If it turns out that the relationship is negligible, it can always be discarded later on.

A simple, effective way of finding out whether an aspect is irrelevant or only marginally relevant is to look at the opposite or absence of that aspect. If it does not change the relevant system definition or its relevant inputs, then that aspect can be ignored.

Novices get confused by the fact that a control input may only exercise partial control, since random aspects may also be at work and affect how the system responds. This is best represented by separating it into a known control input, following immediately by an uncontrollable input — the stochastic disturbance, such as a probability distribution. The system component is then correctly seen to be affected by two inputs.

Activity:
* View a tertiary institution as a system for educating people. Look at it from the point of view of its chief executive (president or vice-chancellor). It transforms students who satisfy the entrance requirements into graduates (or dropouts) in a given field of study. The underlying world view is that this is a worthwhile thing. Define the control inputs, uncontrollable inputs, outputs (including at least one performance measure), and the components of this system.
* Do the same, but now from the point of view of a student who sees education as a means to a rewarding career.

5.3 Essential properties of good models

Since models are not primarily for the analyst but for the problem owner or decision maker, they should satisfy some essential properties. In his article 'Models and Managers: Concepts of Decision Calculus' [*Management Science*, April 1970], J.D.C. Little gives some useful hints for mathematical models. However, his comments apply to any symbolic model. Models should be:

1. **Simple**. Simple models are more easily understood. A decision maker will more easily follow the logic of a spreadsheet than of a complicated mathematical expression, which may do little more than the computations performed in a spreadsheet — admittedly more elegantly. To get simple models, the analyst may have to make suitable approximations and simplifications to the real situation. For example, although a given phenomenon (such as the demand for a product) is subject to small and possibly random fluctuations over time, it is approximated as occurring at a constant rate per period.

    To get a model that is transparent, i.e. where interactions and relationships are easily tractable, aspects of minor significance may even be deleted. For example, minor exceptions to the general rule are left out.

    However, sometimes an analyst may have no choice but to build a complicated mathematical model. In such cases, the decision maker will gain confidence in the model if he or she has the opportunity to experiment with it, e.g. by exploring whether changes in the input parameters produce intuitively reasonable changes in the best solution and, if not, whether counterintuitive results can be explained convincingly.

2. **Complete**. A model should include all significant aspects of a problem situation that affect the measure of performance. The problem here is to know, before the model is built, whether an aspect is likely to affect the 'best' solution in a significant way. Experience will obviously help. It may be necessary to build two models, one with these aspects present, the other without them, compare their answers, and only then judge the significance of a particular aspect.

3. **Easy to manipulate and communicate with**. It should be easy for the analyst and/or the user to prepare, update, and change the inputs and get answers quickly and with a reasonable amount of effort and resources. In today's world of interactive user-friendly computer software, this property has become one of the standard selling points. (I am reminded here of the situation faced by meteorological services in the 1970s, where they could produce accurate 7-day weather forecasts only by having very fast mainframe computers churn away for 5 days, ending up with an out-of-date 2-day forecast! Clearly, the computation time needed then was excessive, robbing the answers of much of their value.)

4. **Adaptive**. Usually, reasonable changes in uncontrollable inputs and the structure of the problem situation should not completely invalidate the model. If they do, it should be possible to adapt it to the new situation with only relatively minor modifications. This is more likely if the model consists of a sequence of small modules that each perform a separable task or operation. Any structural changes in the problem situation may then require only modifications to one or a few modules.

An adaptive model is often referred to as a **robust** model.

Note that some of these properties put conflicting demands on the modelling process. A simple model may not capture all significant aspects of the problem situation. A robust model may not be simple. A model that includes all significant aspects may not be easy to manipulate. Model builders have to balance these conflicting demands and come up with a suitable compromise. This compromise will by necessity reflect not only the training of the analyst, but also the amount of resources in terms of time and funds available for the analysis. It should also reflect the likely benefits that can be achieved. It may be economically more advantageous to use simple quick-and-dirty rules that only capture 50% of the potential benefits, rather than develop a sophisticated and expensive mathematical model that may capture 90%. The costs of developing a mathematical model, collecting the required input data, computing the best solution, implementing the model, and finally operating and maintaining it all increase much more than proportionately as the sophistication of the model increases, while the additional benefits go up less than proportionately (the economic principle of decreasing marginal return and increasing marginal cost).

However, satisfying these properties to a high degree may not be enough to convince a problem owner and/or user to implement the answers of the model. That depends to a large extent on the **confidence** the latter has in the model's ability to produce useful information or, loosely speaking, in the model's **credibility**. This will in the end determine the model's fate. This adds a new dimension to the notion of desirable properties of models. In fact, it may be more useful to talk about **desirable properties of the modelling process**, since user credibility and confidence are more related to that process and the interactions between user and modeller than to the model itself.

5. **A model must be appropriate for the situation studied.** By this is meant that the model produces the relevant outputs **at the lowest possible cost** and **in the time frame required for effective decision making**. For example, for the NuWave case of Chapter 4 a simple spreadsheet for a month-by-month cash flow projection may well be an appropriate choice of model if the objective is to provide a quick estimate of the firm's cash flow and its profits, whereas a simulation study which models the progress of every single shoe along the production line will not, unless it also produces suitable financial measures. Even then, its level of detail may be excessive and therefore inappropriate for the situation studied. On the other hand, if our objective is to estimate the maximum possible rate of production, or the size of buffer space needed between operations or machines, a detailed simulation model will be appropriate, whereas a financial spreadsheet will not. There are two conclusions from this: (a) A 'good' model may not necessarily show details of or resemble the physical system we are trying to study and/or improve, and (b) the model must enable the analyst to measure how well the objectives of the decision maker have been achieved.

6. **A model has to produce information that is relevant and appropriate for decision making.** This means that the output of a model has to have direct bearing on the decision process, has to be useful for decision making, and has to be in a form that can be used directly as an input for decision making, without the need for further extensive translation or manipulation. This does not imply that the decision maker may not have to use judgement in interpreting the information produced, but the information should lead to insights that the decision maker could not easily obtain by other means.

If a model satisfies the last two properties this will enhance the decision maker's confidence in the model and her or his willingness to use its answers. Confidence in and credibility of the model are not necessarily the result of a logical analysis of the model or even of an understanding of how the model works. It may be largely intuitive, based on a demonstration that the model gives usable, sensible, expected, and explainable answers in a timely fashion and with a reasonable effort and expense. It will also be strongly influenced by the working relationship between modeller and problem owner/user and their involvement in the modelling process.

5.4   The art of modelling

One of the aims of this text is to render modelling more of a scientific process. However, there still remain aspects which are more akin to art than science. This means that some people will discover that they possess a natural talent for modelling, while others find it hard going. So how should one go about modelling?

Here are a few useful guidelines — some little more than common sense when approaching any new task, but, surprisingly, often ignored by the inexperienced.

Ockham's razor

William of Ockham, a 14th century English philosopher stated a useful heuristic rule: 'Things should not be multiplied without good reason.' (Since Ockham was reputed to have a sharp and cutting wit, this heuristic has become known as Ockham's razor!) In terms of modelling it means that the modeller has to be highly selective about which aspects to include in a model. All aspects that are not absolutely essential or that contribute little to its 'accuracy' or 'predictive power' should be excluded. A good model is as parsimonious as possible in terms of the variables or aspects included. In other words, it should be simple.

An experienced modeller is often capable to slice through a messy situation and quickly select all aspects essential for a good model and only those. But how should a novice go about applying Ockham's razor?

An iterative process of enrichment and reformulation

Successful analysts confirm that building a model is a process of successive rounds of **enrichment** and **reformulation**. We begin with a simple model — possibly quite removed from reality — and move in an evolutionary fashion towards a more elaborate model that more closely reflects the complexity of the perceived problem situation.

This advice seems harmless enough, yet it does require a certain amount of 'guts' to back off from the real problem situation in its full complexity, and knowingly commit the sins of omitting or distorting certain aspects. The aim is to discover how much of reality can be captured by a simple model. For example, our first model may ignore most aspects of uncertainty.

On the second round, we enrich the model without changing its basic form and structure by trying to incorporate additional aspects that may be important. In other words, we add bells and whistles and see how far we get. For example, we may allow some aspects to exhibit random behaviour and then trace the consequences of this for the rest of the system. This may indicate the need to introduce slack in the form of excess capacity or buffers to provide a reasonable level of protection against a sustained run of adverse effects.

If seemingly important aspects still remain excluded, we may need to abandon the original model and reformulate the problem. This may imply changing the structure and form, or even the nature of the model. For example, rather than using a normal feedback control (i.e. steering the system in reaction to system outputs and events actually observed), we may use feed-forward control (i.e. predicting system outputs and future events to steer the system). Sometimes it may be advisable or necessary to switch to a different modelling or problem-solving methodology, such as switching from a quantitative approach, which by necessity largely ignores the human element, to a qualitative approach that is capable of catering for interpersonal conflicts.

The new model may itself undergo another round of enrichment. Sooner or later we will reach a point where including further aspects adds little to the accuracy or predictive power of the model, or where the additional complexity may jeopardize its successful implementation.

Use an incremental approach

Often the system for the problem of interest consists of a number of interacting subsystems with strong connections within each subsystem, but only one or a few relationships with other subsystems. Rather than modelling the system as a whole, it may pay to gain experience by initially concentrating only on one of the subsystems. Once mastered, a second subsystem is modelled, taking care to include the interactions between the two. This may require some changes to the first subsystem. Proceeding in this incremental fashion, gaining experience at each step, the analysis is extended to cover the entire system. In many instances, it may even be possible to implement the intermediate results of the subsystems analysis at each step.

Working out a numerical example

For problems with strong quantitative content, a piece of advice which we often apply ourselves is to construct an example with representative numbers and play around with them. We carefully observe how variables of interest behave. Any recurrent regular patterns found may suggest a suitable mathematical structure. We may also find analogies with other problems that we analysed at another time. These may suggest reasonable approximations or assumptions which make it easier to translate the relationships or the average behaviour over time into mathematics. But even if we do not discover anything earth-shattering, working through a numeric example often provides valuable insights into the behaviour of the system.

Diagrams and graphs

If you are a visual person, like many of us, you will find it helpful to see things in the form of graphs or other drawings that express relationships or patterns. Typical patterns, such as nonlinear trends, regular fluctuations, or outliers in data plots, are more readily visible from a graph than from sequences of numbers.

The shape or pattern in the graph may suggest analogies with possible completely unrelated problem situations that you have encountered in other problems. The same approach as used there may turn out to be suitable or can be adapted suitably. Often breakthroughs in finding a suitable model are made from such analogies.

Sections 5.5–5.7 introduce a number of diagrammatic systems models and/or essential aspects of system behaviour.

Revisiting the rich picture, mind map, or cognitive map

System modelling invariably leads to the discovery of aspects, both soft and hard, that may be missing or different from the depiction in the rich picture, mind map or cognitive map that describes the original problem situation. It is good practice for the analyst to revisit the map and fill in additional details, i.e. alter, add, enrich, or blow up relevant parts. Critical scrutiny of the changes within the full problem situation also adds an element of reality check — are they consistent with all other aspects present or do the changes raise further questions? It may show the need to go back to various stakeholders and revisit the facilities and/or data sources for clarifications and more detailed analysis and data collection.

5.5   Causal loop diagrams

As a rich picture or mind map is able to convey the complexities of an unstructured situation more effectively than prose, so can various diagrammatic representations help in clarifying both structure and process for many systems. We will find **causal loop** and **influence diagrams** particularly insightful for bringing out the transformation process of the system in terms of the structural and causal relationships between system components. It is often the first step for the process approach to modelling. Both are based on the idea of cause and effect or the producer–product idea, i.e. A may affect or influence B, or A causes or produces B. Causal loop diagrams, developed in the early 1960s, are formally used in **system dynamics** to map out diagrammatically the dynamic behaviour of complex systems that may contain lagged feedback loops (see Sections 17.6–17.8).

Causal loop diagrams and feedback loops

Causal loop diagrams depict **cause-and-effect** relationships between various aspects, entities, or variables. If item A affects item B, this causes one or more attributes of item B to change, such as its numeric value or its status. This is shown by connecting the two with a directed arrow. A change in B may in turn become the cause of a change in C, and so on, resulting in a chain of cause and effects.

A positive sign (or the letter 's' for 'same direction') attached to the arrow head means that an increase in the value of item A causes an increase in the value of item B, while a negative sign (or the letter 'o' for 'opposite') indicates that the increase in A results in a decrease in B. An arrow from an item farther down in the cause-and-effect chain to an earlier item is a feedback loop, as discussed in Section 3.11 of Chapter 3. If the number of negative signs attached to the arrows on the entire loop is odd, the loop is negative, dampening the cumulative effect of the causes, while an even number of negative signs indicates positive feedback or a destabilizing cumulative effect.

Figure 5-2 is a causal loop diagram depicting a production/inventory system. 'Orders received' from customers are added to the 'order book' (the backlog of orders not yet shipped). 'Orders received' affects the 'order pattern observed', which in turn influences the 'sales forecast'. Increases in the 'order book' or the 'sales forecast' both cause an increase in 'production'. However, the response in 'production' will be delayed by the time it takes to initiate an increase and by the time to produce the finished goods, labelled 'production lead time'. A rise in 'finished goods stocks' has a dampening effect on 'production'. Obviously, 'production' increases 'finished goods stocks'. Figure out the remaining relationships.

Figure 5-2   Causal loop diagram for production/inventory system.

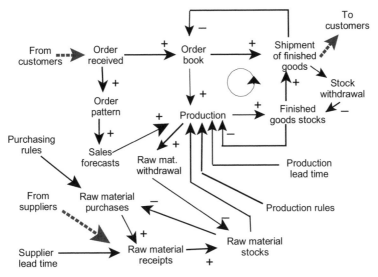

Some arrows have no signs attached. They are either constant inputs, such as the current production lead time, or they constrain an item or variable. For example, 'production' can only happen if 'raw material stocks' are sufficient. Can you explain the relationship between 'finished goods stocks' and 'shipment of finished goods'?

The diagram contains two simple feedback loops and one complex one (the latter shown by the circle arrow), all of them negative, as desired. Find the other two.

Figure 5-3 reproduces an amended version of a causal loop diagram for the New Zealand Wine Industry (for details see R.Y. Cavana *et al.*, "A policy making framework for the NZ wine industry, *System Dynamics,* IX(1) 1997, 1–19). The model makes the strong simplification that the wine industry is homogeneous, i.e. that all grapes and wines follow the same behavioural patterns. The NZ wine industry grew from a few hundred hectares in the early 1970s to over 10,000 ha by the year 2000. The diagram explains what factors affect wine production and the planting of new vineyards.

Figure 5-3   New Zealand Wine Industry planning model.

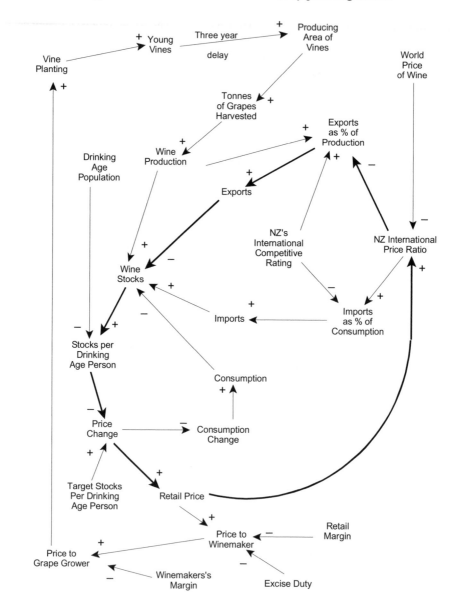

One feedback loop is highlighted by the arrows with thick lines. There are four more, one of them positive. Try to identify them and find which one is the positive one. Fortunately, its destabilizing effect is counteracted by another loop with which it shares most of the causal links.

Since all aspects shown can be expressed quantitatively, the relationships can be captured in mathematical form. Using system dynamics software, such as Stella or *ithink*, it is possible to trace out numerically the effect of various policies of grower support, of the Government excise duty, or of the world price of wines.

5.6 Influence diagrams

Influence diagrams are more formal versions of causal loop diagrams. They are particularly useful when using a process approach. They depict diagrammatically the system transformation process. Figure 5-4 shows the diagrammatic conventions used.

Figure 5-4   Diagrammatic conventions for influence diagrams.

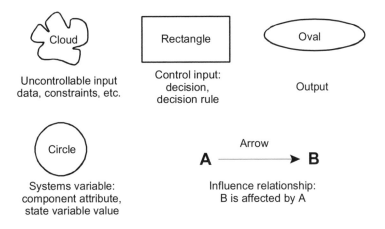

The notation clearly identifies the nature of the various elements included: control inputs, uncontrollable inputs, outputs, and system components. The system components are represented by their attributes, since it is the latter that are affected or changed by the influence relationships. Each attribute is shown separately. We shall refer to them as **system variables**.

For attributes that can be measured numerically, a system variable is the value of the corresponding state variable. For instance, in the production/inventory system, 'raw material withdrawal' becomes a system variable and the quantity or the rate of raw materials withdrawn is its value. It reduces the value of 'raw material stocks', another system variable, by the same amount.

However, influence diagrams are equally effective for depicting non-quantitative relationships, such as the presence of virgin forests increasing the enjoyment experienced by tourists visiting an area, or the severity of pain suffered by a patient affecting the timing of the relieving surgery required. The system variable indicates the presence or absence of some (critical) aspect or quality, or an arbitrarily defined gradation of something, such as a five-point word scale: 'very strong', 'strong', 'average', 'weak', 'absent'.

Figure 5-5 shows the influence diagram for an investment decision in company shares. Assume the investor considers putting £10,000 into company shares for one year. Being a prudent person, she only considers shares from highly reputable companies, so-called blue-chip stocks. The shares differ in terms of their dividend payout over the one-year period, as well as in their final value at the end of the period. Obviously, the investor would like to determine a portfolio of shares (i.e. a combination from various firms) that yields the highest return on the £10,000 available. However, the influence diagram does not show that maximization process, but only what happens if the investor chooses a given portfolio of shares.

Figure 5-5   Influence diagram of investment system.

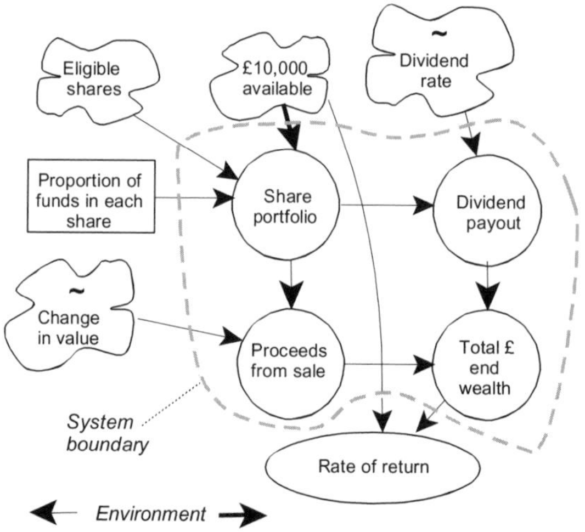

What is the transformation process of this system? It transforms the input of £10,000 at the beginning of the period into an amount of X pounds at the end of the period. This determines the output of interest, i.e. the 'rate of return' achieved on the initial investment of £10,000. The control input (or decision) is the 'proportion of funds invested in each share'. Other inputs are the 'eligible shares', the likely 'dividend payout rates' during the period, and the 'change in value' (capital gain or capital loss) of each eligible share by the end of the period. The last two are not known with certainty, i.e. they are random. This is denoted by a tilde (~) over their name. The system variables are the 'share portfolio', the total 'dividend payout' over all shares, the total 'proceeds from sale' of the shares at the end of the period, and the 'total end wealth', all in monetary units. The last three of these are also uncertain or random, given that some of the inputs are random. The boundary of the system is delineated by the half-tone broken line which encloses the four system variables (done here only for demonstration).

Note that this diagram does not show a physical flow of money or funds over the year. Recall that the arrows simply indicate an influence of one aspect or item on another aspect or item, but not necessarily a physical flow of anything. For instance, the 'share portfolio' is a list of amounts invested in each 'eligible share', each amount being a fraction of '£10,000' corresponding to the control input. Even the two arrows into 'total £ end wealth' do not represent an actual flow of funds. They simply indicate that the 'total £ end wealth' is a function of the other two system variables (in fact, the sum of 'proceeds from sale' and 'dividend payout'). Although in this example all system variables are in the same unit, i.e. pounds, there is no requirement that this be so.

The arrows only give the direction of the influence relationship, but no indication as to its strength or form. Sometimes the form of the relationship is obvious, as we have just seen for the 'total £ end wealth'. However, in general such information has to come from other sources. It usually requires further research, data gathering and analysis, or developing the information from first principles. Without it, the influence diagram only allows qualitative inferences.

Figure 5-6 shows the influence diagram that corresponds to the causal loop diagram of the production/inventory system in Figure 5-2 on page 93. Note their similarity, including the feedback loops. However, the influence diagram clearly shows the nature of the various items. Unfortunately, neither can explicitly show the passage of time implied in the process. For instance, 'finished goods stocks' are affected by the 'production rate', by 'stock withdrawals', both occurring over time, and by the 'finished goods stocks' carried forward from before. This explains the arrows leading back from 'finished goods stocks' to itself.

Although on first glance it may seem that several of the arrows show a flow of material, this is not so. For instance, the arrow from 'raw material stocks' to 'production rate' relates information as to the availability of raw materials. Obviously, the rate of production is restricted by the amount of raw materials on hand. It does not signify a flow of raw material to the production process. Similarly, the arrows from 'production rate' back to 'raw material stocks' convey information as to the amount of raw material used in production.

Here are a few ground rules to remember: By the very definition of an input, arrows can only leave a cloud (an input) or a rectangle (a control input), but must never enter either of them. Again by the definition of an output, arrows can only end at an oval (an output), never leave one. Circles (system variables) must have at least one arrow entering that originates either at a cloud, rectangle, or another circle, and at least one arrow leaving to another circle or an oval. They cannot be the head or the end of a chain of influences.

Figure 5-6   Influence diagram of the production/inventory system.

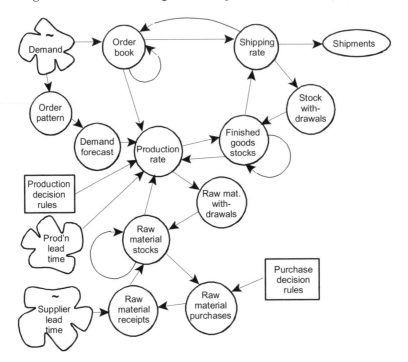

Influence diagrams and causal loop diagrams help in exploring the complexity in a system. As mentioned earlier, an influence diagram is often a very effective means to define a relevant system for the issue studied. In such instances, it can thus be used as a substitute for a more formal system definition based on the four-rule scheme summarized in Table 5-1 on page 86. Like rich pictures, both facilitate and clarify the communication process between analysts, and between analysts and clients. However, there are situations where an influence diagram may not be a suitable vehicle to bring out the structure of a decision problem unambiguously and clearly. One or the other of the diagrammatic aids in the next section may be able to shed more light on the problem and its structure.

Activity:
- Develop a causal loop diagram of all the aspects that may influence you (or should have influenced you) on whether or not to pursue graduate studies after completion of an undergraduate degree. Does it have any feedback loops?
- Develop an influence diagram for the emergency call centre described in Section 1.1. The diagram should show the two output measures: the total cost of the operation and the frequency distribution for the length of time callers have to wait until their call is answered. Both depend on the number of operators on duty.

5.7 Other system diagrams

Flow charts are another type of diagram that depict specific aspects of a system, in particular the logical or temporal sequence of some process, operation, or activity. The process could be the temporal flow of material through a system, how information is processes and used, the temporal sequence in which a set of tasks has to be performed to complete a project, or the logical sequence of steps and checks in a complex decision process.

Material (or information) flow charts

Figure 5-7 shows the water flow through a large hydroelectric power system. Water from large catchment areas flows into natural or artificial storage reservoirs along the river system. Most of the water is then channelled through canals to power stations which generate electricity, and back into storage reservoirs farther downstream. This sequence repeats itself six times. Some water is released into the original river beds to allow recreation and to maintain fisheries.

Figure 5-7   Flow chart of the Waitaki power system on NZ's South Island.

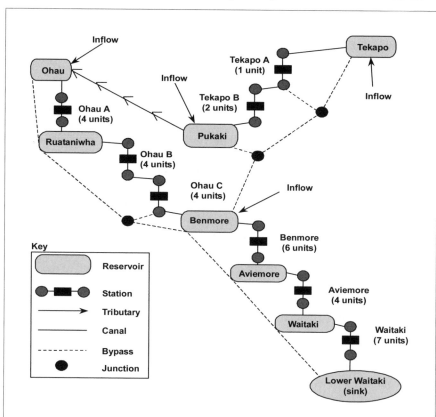

It is obvious that such a diagram allows you to visualize the system quickly and without much explanation, except for a table of keys to the symbols used. It is much more effective than verbal descriptions that would be tedious and difficult to follow.

Most manufacturing firms use material flow charts to introduce new employees or visitors to their operations. The flow chart shows how raw material is processed into intermediate products through various operations and equipment, how these become the raw materials for subsequent operations, until finally a range of finished products is either shipped to customers or stored in warehouses, ready to be sold.

Precedence charts

Many projects consist of a large number of individual tasks that have to be performed in a specific sequence. While some may be done simultaneously, others can only be started after one or several other tasks have been completed. The tasks may also have to share scarce resources, such as equipment or specific job skills. Construction jobs, overhauls and maintenance of large installations, research and development projects, a major move into new facilities, even the production of a film, all require a coordinated plan for the execution of the various tasks that make up the project. Figure 5-8 shows the task precedence relationships for building a house.

'Prepare detailed plans' takes two weeks, as indicated by the number on the left of the box. 'Obtain building permit' and 'Arrange finance' can only be started once 'Prepare building plans' is finished, i.e. two weeks after the start of the project. 'Obtain building permit' is completed four weeks later, i.e. by the end of week 6 (2 + 4), as shown by the bold number to the right of the box. The three tasks including 'Build floor' take another three weeks and are completed at the earliest by week 9. The subsequence 'Arrange finance' through 'Prebuild wall framing' can be done in parallel with the other sequence. It takes five weeks and can be finished at the earliest by week 7. Since 'Erect wall framing' has to wait for both these subsequences to be completed, it can be started at the earliest at the beginning of week 10, i.e. after 'Build floor' has been completed. Note that the second subsequence could be delayed by up to two weeks without delaying the start of 'Erect wall framing'. But a delay in the first subsequence will delay completion of the project. Using the same logic, verify that the earliest the house can be accepted is 23 weeks after its start.

There is at least one path of consecutive tasks from the start to the end where any delay will cause the project as a whole to be delayed. These are called **critical tasks**. Which are critical in Figure 5-8? One of the reasons for drawing up precedence charts is to determine which sequence of tasks is critical. These are the ones that need to be tightly controlled so as to avoid any delays. **Critical path analysis** (or CPA) and PERT are tools to analyse scheduling problems of this sort. They are extensively used for initial planning and later day-to-day control of all sorts of project work.

Figure 5-8   Precedence chart for building a house.

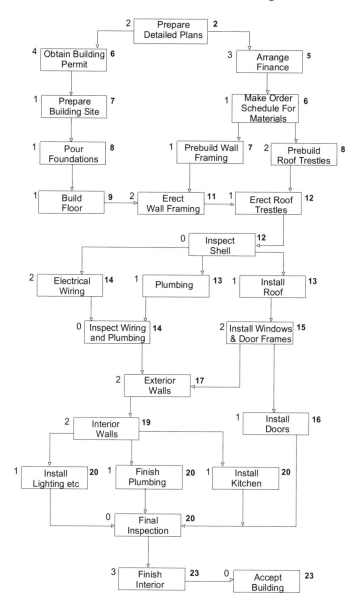

Spray diagrams and fault trees

Both are a special version of cause-and-effect diagrams. The complexity of today's life means that a given outcome is usually not the result of one or two causes, but of a myriad causes. Some may trigger the outcomes by themselves, while others only affect the outcome when combined with other events or causes. Often a given cause may in turn be the effect of its own cause-and-effect subchain.

Figure 5-9 shows a **spray or fish-bone diagram** for what factors may lead to customer dissatisfaction with the products of a firm. There are three main causes: product unsuitable, product quality, and service. Each of these may be the result of other causes, as explained in the circled portion of the diagram.

Figure 5-9   Spray diagram exploring the causes of customer dissatisfaction.

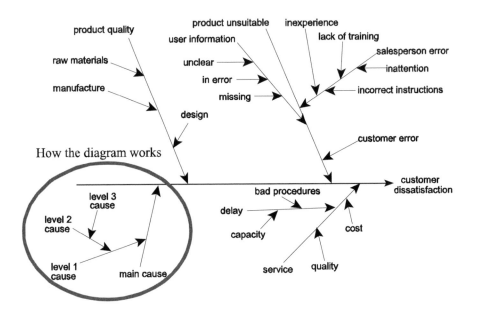

Figure 5-10 is a **fault tree** that explains which combination of causes needs to happen simultaneously to produce an accident at a controlled railway crossing. A collision between a car and a train only results from the joint occurrence of event 'train about to enter crossing' and either of 'vehicle attempts crossing' or 'vehicle stuck on crossing'. They are useful for the investigation of accidents or disasters and for developing plans and countermeasures for their prevention. For example, if the investigation of a fatal accident points to 'track visibility obstructed' by a high hedge, steps may be taken to lower or remove the hedge.

In Figure 5-9, it is assumed that each cause may trigger the final outcome independently of all other causes. In contrast, in Figure 5-10 some effects can only be produced by the joint occurrence of a combination of causes. We indicate this by connecting these causes to a small circle from which issues the arrow that leads to the effect (resulting from the joint occurrence of these causes). Occurrence of one of these causes alone is not sufficient. The presence of all of them is a necessary condition, and together they form the sufficient condition for the effect.

Figure 5-10   Fault tree for an accident at a controlled railway crossing.

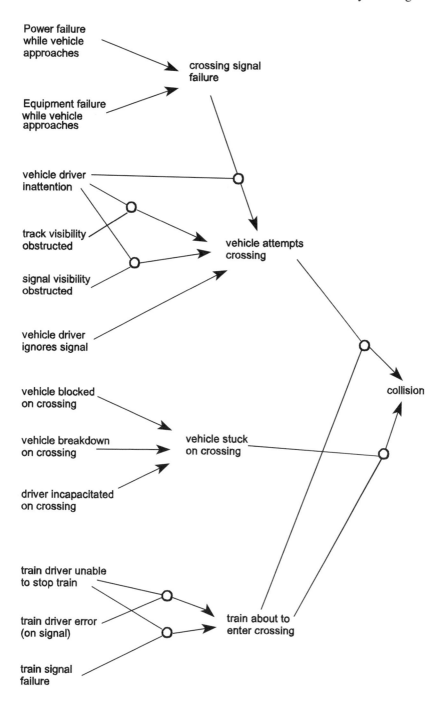

Decision flow charts

A decision flow chart shows the logical sequence of tests performed, actions taken for each test result, decision choices available, and so on, for each possible path that leads to a final outcome. You may have been introduced to decision trees in an introductory course in statistics. They are a type of decision flow chart.

We will use the Lubrication Oil Division problem analysed in Chapter 6. The firm produces various types and grades of oil. Customer orders for these products vary in size quite considerably: small orders from local service stations; large orders from wholesalers and big national department store chains. A customer order received for a given product can be executed in two different ways. The first is to make a special production run for the exact amount ordered and directly ship it to the customer. The second is to withdraw the product requested from inventory and ship it. Since small production runs are uneconomic, small orders are usually met from inventory. Special production runs are only made for large orders. The customer order processing clerk uses the following criterion to decide whether a customer order is small or large: If the order is equal to a cutoff point L or larger, the order is considered "large", if smaller than L, it is "small".

Meeting small orders from inventory gradually reduces the stock level. Sooner or later there is not enough left in stock to meet the last small order received. At this point, a new production run of size Q is scheduled to replenish the inventory. Once the product has been added to stock, the small customer order that triggered the replenishment is shipped.

Congratulations if you understood this fully at the first reading. Now study the corresponding decision flow chart of Figure 5-11 below. Most people will find the diagram much easier to follow.

Figure 5-11   Decision flow chart for a production/stock control problem.

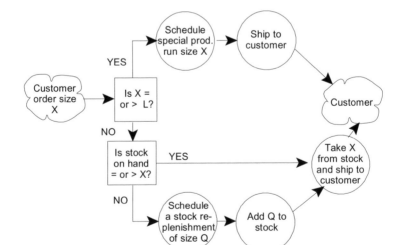

Activity:
- Draw a material flow chart for the following situation. A blood bank collects blood from donors. The blood is first tested for various pathogens (hepatitis, HIV, etc.). Contaminated blood is discarded. The good blood is stored in refrigerator A. Whenever surgery is scheduled (both elective or emergency), the surgeon requests that a certain amount of the right blood type is set aside. That blood is removed and stored in a separate refrigerator B. If not used within 24 hours it is returned to A. Every day, all blood stored in A is checked for its age. Any blood that is older than 49 days is removed and discarded.
- Construct a precedence chart for a market survey (the letters in brackets list the predecessor tasks; the number is the length of the task in days):
  A: design preliminary questionnaire [2]
  B: determine sampling design [3]
  C: test preliminary questionnaire [A; 4]
  D: prepare final version of questionnaire [C; 1]
  E: prepare list of people to be surveyed [B; 2]
  F: print required number of questionnaires [D, B; 5]
  G: recruit interviewers [B; 4]
  H: train interviewers [G, D; 2]
  I: conduct interviews [E, F, H; 10]
  J: process questionnaires [I; 3]
  K: analyse results [J; 5]
  L: write survey report for sponsor [K; 2]
  Can you determine the number of days required to complete the survey? Which tasks are critical?
- You are inviting a group of friends to a formal dinner party. Draw a decision flow chart for the various decisions you need to make. Include such aspects as, cleaning, who to invite, whether you do the cooking yourself or cater out for parts of it, etc.
- Draw up a spray diagram for the possible causes that may make you fail a given course at university.

5.8 Chapter highlights

1. The system definition is a symbolic model. This model should clearly indicate the system boundary, the controllable and the uncontrollable inputs into the system, the transformation process, and the outputs of the system.
2. A structural approach makes use of typical known structures or configurations, while a process approach defines the system from first principles.
3. Good models are simple, complete, easy to manipulate and communicate with, adaptive to changes in the problem situation, appropriate and relevant for decision making for the problem studied. Some of these properties are in conflict.
4. Modelling is an iterative process of enrichment and reformulation. Few models are 'final' after a single pass.
5. Causal loop diagrams and influence diagrams show the influence relationships between system components, controllable and uncontrollable inputs, and system outputs, thereby delineating the system boundaries.

6. Other diagrammatic models highlight the sequence of processes, the flow of material, precedence relationships between different activities, or the logic of the decision process.

Exercises

1. Use a process approach to define a suitable system for exploring how many telephone operators the emergency services call centre should hire, so as to explore the trade-off between waiting time and centre operating costs (see the situation summary in Section 1.1).

2. Use a process approach to define a suitable system for exploring the consequences of different breast cancer screening policy choices on the various conflicting goals (see the situation summary in Section 1.1). Use a governmental point of view.

3. Develop a causal loop diagram for the blood bank operation described in exercise 3 of Chapter 3.

4. Draw a causal loop diagram for the breast cancer screening problem described in Section 1.1.

5. Develop a causal loop diagram for the NuWave Shoes problem in the first part of Section 4.8. How does it differ from the Elly's cognitive map?

6. Consider the relationships between unemployment, poverty, public health expenditures, family breakdown, and crime. Draw a causal loop diagram.

7. Draw an influence diagram for Lim's problem discussed in Exercise 5 of Chapter 4. What boundary judgements are implied by the system defined in the diagram?

8. Draw an influence diagram for exploring the outcome of a given breast cancer screening policy for the situation summary in Section 1.1 of Chapter 1. What boundary judgements are implied by the system defined in the diagram?

9. Draw an influence diagram for the blood bank operation described in exercise 3 of Chapter 3. It should clearly show the direct or indirect effects of the controllable actions and decisions on the two performance measures of shortages and outdating. Note that the aspect of optimization is not shown, only the results of decision choices, etc. What boundary judgements are implied in the system defined by the diagram?

10. The production process for an electric toothbrush consists of the following operations: PVC compounds are procured from a local supplier. PVC is used for moulding the toothbrush (motor case and battery) case, the housing of the recharging unit and the holder of the brushes (which slots into the recharging unit). Rechargeable batteries are purchased and built into the toothbrush case. The firm produces its own electric motors from parts purchased from suppliers. It also makes its own brushes, using purchased bristle material that is moulded into PVC. Once assembled, all parts plus one spare brush and an instruction booklet are packaged into a cardboard box. Draw a material flow chart for this process.

11. Draw a material flow chart for the bread-making operation in a commercial bakery.

12. The tasks for making kite kits are as follows: [predecessors; time in minutes]
    A: cut cloth to shape of kite [2]
    B: sew seams and sleeves on cloth, attach dowel slots [A; 8]
    C: cut plastic dowels [3]
    D: attach metal end pieces to dowels [C: 2]
    E: measure and cut string, spool on roll [4]
    F: preassemble parts of the frame [B, D; 1]
    G: role up kite around remaining dowels [F; 1]
    H: package rolled up kite, string, and assembly and flying instructions [E, G.; 2]
    If one person does all the tasks, how long does it take for one kite? Which tasks are critical?

    If two persons can work at the same time, side by side, each doing different sets of tasks simultaneously, how does that change things?

13. Assume that you have at most £10,000 available to buy a 'pre-loved' car. Draw a decision flow chart for this purchase decision. You may not want to spend all the money. You may buy from a dealer or privately. You may want to have the car professionally inspected.

14. Draw a spray diagram or a fault tree, whichever is more suitable, for what may lead to a drowning fatality when using a small pleasure boat.

PART 2
Management science methodologies: Introduction

Part 2 gives a brief survey of how systems thinking is applied in the two major strands of management science, i.e. the hard OR/hard systems approaches and the soft OR/soft systems approaches. In order to gain a better understanding of the paradigms underlying each strand and the general nature of their processes and practice, it is helpful to consider first their scope and areas of application.

M.C. Jackson and P. Keys [1984] classify problem situations along two dimensions: **complexity** and **divergence of values and interests**. As we have seen in Chapters 2 and 3, complexity can be understood as the number of elements, aspects or factors and their interactions in a problem situation. Few elements and well-defined, linear, stationary interactions imply low complexity, while many elements, many interrelationships, dynamic and poorly understood relationships in a turbulent environment imply high complexity.

These authors divide divergence of views into **unitary**, **pluralistic**, and **conflicting/coercive**. 'Unitary' implies agreement of views and values of the stakeholders involved, i.e. genuinely shared common world views. 'Pluralist' implies multiple views and values within a shared common core, i.e. compatible world views that differ in emphasis and degree of preference, but allow trade-offs and hence form the basis for mutually acceptable compromises. In their classification, 'conflicting/coercive' implies irreconcilable, usually competitive values and views, i.e. radically different world views that render voluntary compromise difficult if not impossible, and where differences in the power relationships (economic and/or authoritarian) between stakeholders usually imply that one party is coerced into accepting a 'solution' imposed by another party. This constitutes an extreme. In practice, the differences in power may range from the subtle effect of claims to expertise, seniority, or status to the dependent employee/employer relationship and ultimately to the coercive force of the absolute dictator or law enforcer. It also covers attempts at deception by one party. A term such as 'asymmetry or distortion in communications' would be a more accurate description than 'coercive', nor are any real-life situations ever entirely free of such distortions [Ulrich, 2003]. The unitary, pluralistic, and conflicting/coercive classification are abstractions. Most practical situations involve aspects of all three.

For our purposes, it is useful to differentiate between two types of complexity: **technical complexity,** associated with the physical and logical relationships and/or the mathematical and computational nature of the problem and its context, and the **degree of uncertainty** present in the situation — the higher the degree of uncertainty, the higher the level of complexity. Consider for example the problem of which of m factories should supply known quantities q_n to n distributors so as to minimize total transportation costs. This exhibits low technical complexity in terms of both its logical structure (a simple transportation network consisting only of sources and destinations) and computational effort, and there is no uncertainty. In contrast, scheduling minimum cost itineraries for m vans for pickups from and deliveries to a multitude of customers, subject to vehicle capacities, fixed driver shifts, and possibly time windows specified by customers, has high technical complexity, in terms of both its logical structure and its computational difficulties, but with no uncertainty if all pickup and delivery requests are known. Since both involve cost minimization as the objective, they fall into the 'unitary' sphere. If the quantities q_n in the transportation network are random variables or customer requests in the van scheduling problem are generated dynamically over time and only become known when a request is received, these uncertainties raise that level of complexity while not necessarily affecting the degree of technical complexity.

The breast cancer situation, discussed in Chapter 1, can be viewed as falling into the pluralist sphere (multiple stakeholders with partially conflicting but reconcilable values and interests), with relatively low technical complexity (the physical structure is well known), and with moderate uncertainty (extensive data on statistical incidences and treatment outcomes available). On the other hand, the 'greenhouse gas' problem is at the other extreme: highly conflicting world views and extreme differences in economic power between various stakeholders (i.e. multinationals and various countries with radically different vested interests, e.g. USA versus Pacific island states), high technical complexity (incomplete understanding of the physical processes), and high degree of uncertainty as to future technological and economic developments.

These three dimensions classify the three main streams of management science approaches, as depicted in Figure 1 over the page. (The boundaries of the three areas are fuzzy. The areas overlap considerably. The volume of each area is not intended to reflect the number of problem situations contained.)

Functionalist systems approaches assume that systems catch or represent aspects of existing or future reality, largely independent of the observer. Different observers would basically agree on the same system and share the same goals or objectives — sometimes referred to as 'objective' (i.e. a consensual subjectivity). Note that this does not imply that different observers and modellers may not draw their system boundaries differently, or put the main emphasis on different systems aspects, or select a different degree of resolution to model the system. Their main concern is mainly with "How to do it" questions,

Figure 1   Problem situation classification and systems approaches.
(adapted from Jackson [2000])

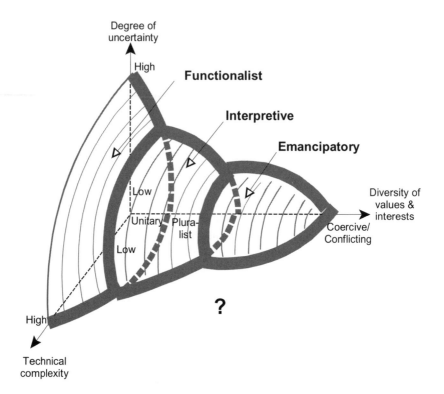

assuming that the "What to do" questions are resolved. Hard OR, systems engineering, systems analysis, and cybernetics are prime examples of functionalist approaches. Over the last 50 years, they have seen numerous successful applications in problem situations that may have considerable technical complexity and uncertainty which can be expressed in the form of probability distributions, but in general they can only cope with low human complexity and a low to medium divergence of interests (such as multiple objectives rather than differences in values).

Few activities or operations in today's world are not fully or partially affected by the results of a hard OR analysis, from private business and industry to public and environmental issues, and from Government policies to personal leisure activities. When you flip your light switch, you have just become a customer of a hard OR project, i.e. controlling power generation and/or pricing. When you use your cell phone, you have become the customer of half a dozen different hard OR analyses. Even sporting activities, such as cricket, baseball, and yachting have been successfully subjected to hard OR. In most cases, you had no involvement in it whatsoever — you were simply a voiceless 'customer'.

Interpretive systems approaches adopt a 'subjectivist' approach to systems thinking. The system defined for a given problem situation reflects the observer's world view and perceptions. It is not assumed to exist in more or less this form in reality, but is seen as a personal conceptualization of what the observer views as a useful and convenient representation of interrelationships between the various aspects and stakeholders. Although interpretive approaches allow a certain divergence of interests and views, they assume there is a sufficient sharing of interests that the various stakeholders consider it in their interest to cooperate. They focus mainly on "What?" issues, rather than on "How?" issues. The main aim of interpretative approaches is to learn more about the behaviour of the system in view of bringing about, if not a shared set of values, at least a shared commitment to action. They can cope with a fair degree of diversity of interests and values, but have greater difficulty in dealing with technical complexity and uncertainty, responding to the latter mainly on an intuitive level. These approaches are increasingly being applied for practical problem solving in both the private and public sectors.

Emancipatory systems approaches also take a 'subjectivist' view of systems. However, the various stakeholders may have partially or even radically different, conflicting or opposing world views that may be irreconcilable. They may disagree on which 'facts' are relevant and on their interpretation, see essentially different relevant systems and, in particular, choose substantively different boundaries for both the narrow and the wider system of interest, while strongly contesting the boundary judgements made by other stakeholders. They may be in a conflicting or confrontational relationship with each other and possibly unequal in terms of their power over the situation, with some being potentially in a victim role. The main focus is again on "What?" issues. For extreme cases of 'coercion', strikes, direct political action or civil disobedience may be the only options open to the 'coerced'. Less extreme approaches, such as negotiation, mediation, law suits, and political campaigns have difficulties coping with high technical complexity and high uncertainty. 'Resolutions' of such problem situations may involve reforms and changes in the current social and political order. So far, MS/OR has offered little in this respect; some *ad hoc* Community OR interventions and Critical Systems Heuristics (see Section 7.8) are the exception.

The label 'emancipatory' is somewhat ambitious. True emancipation of all stakeholders can only occur if all parties are willing to acknowledge and appreciate all other parties' views and interests, fully share all relevant information, and set aside economic and political power differences to seek a resolution of problems as equal partners, rather than imposing their will from a position of power — a utopian view of human nature.

Interpretive and emancipatory systems approaches may resort to a functionalist methodology to deal with those "How?" aspects that lend themselves to quantification.

Chapter 6 describes our version of the hard OR methodology and demonstrates parts of it with a real-life case. As you will discover, the hard OR methodology cycles through a well-defined set of steps, from exploring the problem within its context — the problem situation — to implementation of the solution. By necessity, the discussion is succinct. Its aim is to give you an informed appreciation of the methodology, without going into all its details. A more comprehensive and detailed treatment, complemented with aspects of practical experience, is given in Daellenbach [2001], covering 120 pages.

Loosely speaking, the label 'soft OR' covers a subset of the interpretive systems approaches, whereas 'soft systems approaches' is a catch-all term that includes both interpretive and emancipatory systems approaches, some of which have their origin in critical philosophy, sociology, psychology, and organization theory. Chapter 7 briefly elaborates on some of the common aspects found in many soft OR/soft systems approaches and gives a brief survey of several. Three are studied in somewhat more detail. However, the treatment never goes beyond an appreciation level. Unfortunately, competent use of these methods requires considerable experience and exposure. Most cannot be mastered by reading a textbook, even one devoted exclusively to a given method, but are learned by hands-on practice under the guidance of an experienced facilitator or by participating in specialized workshops.

Finally, Chapter 8 covers the process of implementing the results and recommendations of an MS/OR analysis and the difficulties associated with it, and also briefly comments on professional and personal ethics of the analyst.

6
Overview of hard OR methodology

Operations researchers broadly agree on the basic steps of what is a good hard OR methodology, although they may packet some activities slightly differently or place their emphasis on different parts. This chapter gives our preferred version of the hard OR methodology — together with points of practical experience.

The first six sections cover a general overview of the hard OR methodology, while the remainder of the chapter demonstrate the various steps with a real-life practical application.

6.1 Hard OR paradigm and diagrammatic overview

Hard OR approaches assume that

1. the problem has been clearly defined, implying that
   - the objectives of the decision maker are known and there exist criteria to ascertain when they have been achieved,
   - if there are conflicting objectives, trade-offs can be defined,
   - the alternative courses of action are known, either as a list of options or a set of decision variables,
   - the constraints on the decision choices are known, and
   - the input data needed are available;

2. the problem is relatively well structured, meaning that
   - the relationships between the variables are tractable,
   - system behaviour can be captured in mathematical models, and
   - the computational effort for determining solutions is economically feasible;

3. the problem can be sufficiently well insulated from its wider system.

4. optimization of the objectives, whenever possible, is the ideal.

5. the problem is of a technical nature, devoid of politics; people are mainly seen as passive objects.

6. if there are multiple stakeholders, a consensus can be reached about all aspects that affect how well the objectives can be achieved.

7. the decision maker has the power and authority to implement the 'solution' or enforce implementation through the hierarchical chain of command.

(In Chapter 7 we shall contrast these assumptions with those for soft OR.)

Although in practice not all of these properties may be satisfied for a particular problem, a hard OR approach may still provide valuable insights to the decision maker(s), provided the nature of the approximations and assumptions made and their implications are clearly spelled out and understood, and extensive "What-if" analysis is performed.

The particular hard OR version presented in this chapter relaxes some of these assumptions. In particular, it does not assume that the problem is presented in a fully defined form, ready for building a mathematical model, but must first be extracted and identified from the problem situation. Similarly, a high degree of implementation can only be achieved if human factors are not ignored.

With this proviso in view, any OR project with a happy ending goes through three major phases: (1) problem formulation or problem scoping, (2) problem modelling, and (3) implementation of recommendations. Each phase consists of several steps. This is depicted in Figure 6-1. As shown, it is not a linear process, starting with 'summarizing [the] problem situation' and ending in 'following up solution use'. In practice, it is an iterative process where we may have to go back to earlier phases or steps to overcome unexpected difficulties, fill in omissions uncovered at a later stage, and alleviate or eliminate undesirable consequences. There are also forward linkages. At each step, we keep future steps in mind and are on the lookout for difficulties we may encounter. It may lead us to alter our initial approach and look for countermeasures, whenever possible.

The process starts out in the real world — a concrete world. For the modelling phase, we move into the world of systems — an abstract world. As we proceed to implementation, we return to the real world. On the other hand, the nature of the analysis goes from the qualitative and possibly ill-structured world in the early stages of the problem formulation to the quantitative and more structured world in the modelling phase, and then back to the qualitative world for implementation.

6.2 Problem formulation or problem scoping

The first phase aims to identify the issue to be analysed and define a relevant system for it. The level of depth, the detail, and the level of resolution of this definition depend on a number of factors — prior knowledge about the problem, its complexity, and the relationship between problem owner and problem analyst.

If the potential benefits are certain and justify the cost of the analysis, the first phase takes the form of a complete **problem formulation**, culminating in a detailed definition of the relevant system. On the other hand, if not enough is known about the potential benefits and costs of a project, or the project is big and highly complex,

Figure 6-1 Hard OR methodology.

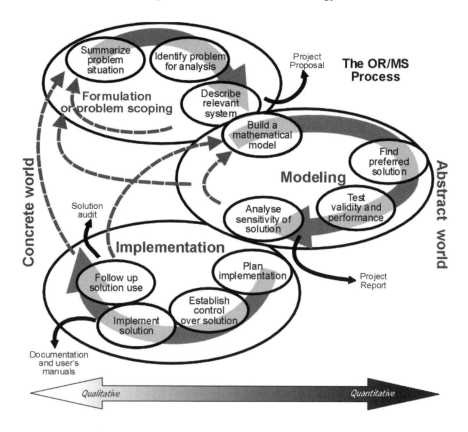

it may be advisable to **scope the problem** first. Scoping means identifying the nature of the problem and assessing what an in-depth analysis could produce and whether its likely costs justify its likely benefits. The relevant system is only defined in broad terms by identifying the major subsystems and delineating its boundaries. A complete system definition will wait to see whether the project proceeds to the problem modelling phase. This is the reason why in Figure 6-1 'Describe relevant system' is shown straddling the first two phases.

If the problem owner and analyst are one and the same, a scoping exercise may gradually turn into a full problem formulation, as the analyst/problem owner learns more about it. If the two are different people, then problem scoping usually leads to a formal **project proposal**, submitted to the problem owner for evaluation and approval.

Problem formulation and problem scoping follow the same steps. They only differ in the depth of the analysis. We will study both at the same time, although problem scoping will receive more emphasis. Any differences will be flagged.

You are already familiar with what is involved in the three steps of problem formulation or scoping from our discussion in Chapters 4 and 5. The first step — summarizing the problem situation — is preferably done by means of a rich picture or a mind map. It helps us to focus on the problem or issue to be analysed within its full context and helps us in step 2 to identify the right problem. We suggest that at this point you briefly remind yourself again of the material in Sections 4.1 and 4.2 (pages 53–59) on the six elements that define a problem, the complexity of problem definition, and the stakeholder roles.

For the third step — defining a relevant system, we usually have recourse to dia-grammatic aids. In particular, influence diagrams are often ideal for bringing out which aspects are inputs and outputs, and which systems variables form the trans-formation process of the narrow system of interest.

However, for problem scoping we will not necessarily define the system in all its intricacies. We are mainly interested in where to draw the boundaries of the narrow system and wider system of interest. At this point, we do not need a highly detailed understanding of all the interrelationships and interactions between the various system components. We only need to understand enough to make a competent project proposal. There is little justification to invest large efforts in analysis when we do not even know if the project will go ahead. So how far we proceed in defining a relevant system depends on many factors. For problems that fit into a well-known structure for which commercial software is available, definition may limit itself to assessing the suitability of that structure and identifying the boundaries of the system. All details will be fleshed out at the beginning of the modelling phase. For simple situations that do not fit a known structure, the phase may end with a detailed influence diagram that provides a complete definition of the relevant system. For highly complex situations system definition may remain somewhat coarse and tentative and at a low level of resolution. Rather than draw a detailed influence diagram, we make do with a sim-plified causal loop diagram or other diagrammatic representation.

In fact, sometimes not enough may yet be known about the problem situation and the nature of the problem to be in a position to make a definite proposal for a full-scale study. In such instances, the more prudent approach is to suggest a preliminary study with the aim of assessing whether a full-scale study is justified.

6.3 The project proposal or go-ahead decision

Once the analyst has obtained a sufficient understanding of the problem and has drawn the boundaries of the relevant system, he or she has to make a judgement about whether hard OR can be successfully applied to find a 'solution' to the problem. The analyst must weigh the following questions:

(a) Can the problem be expressed in quantitative terms?

(b) Are the required data available or can they be generated at a reasonable cost?

(c) Does the cost of the analysis justify the likely benefits to be derived from the implementation of the results? To what extent can the project sponsor's expectations be met?

To answer some of these questions, the analyst must give cursory consideration to the modelling and implementation phases. We see the forward linkages in action almost from the start. Obviously, previous OR experience will be of great help here — though this is of little comfort to the novice management scientist. If the analyst is reasonably satisfied that the answer to all these questions is affirmative, the scoping phase may conclude with a recommendation to go ahead with the project, i.e. writing a formal project proposal to the problem owner. The latter will base the decision on whether or not to give the go-ahead for a full study largely on this document.

Even if the project skips the project scoping phase, it will still be useful to answer carefully these three questions. The insights gained so far may well change the assessment of the project's benefit and/or costs and lead to a change of direction or its abandonment before large efforts are wasted.

The formal project proposal is no doubt a most critical piece of work in any study. The quality of its presentation and soundness of the reasoning used often make the difference between its acceptance or rejection. In some sense, it is the analyst's sales pitch. However, in contrast to most sales transactions, where the relationship between seller and buyer is often terminated with the goods passing hands, the acceptance of a project proposal by the problem owner signals the beginning of an even closer relationship. It is therefore important that the analyst gains the confidence of the problem owner by being scrupulously honest as to likely benefits and costs.

The analyst should not promise more than he or she knows can be delivered with the resources likely to be available. It would be unethical to do otherwise. If he or she is an external consultant, the client may have the legal powers to insist on promises to be kept without covering the cost of the additional work needed.

Major potential difficulties that could derail or delay the project should be brought into the open and discussed, and responsibilities for action clearly assigned. Since OR modelling claims to have much in common with scientific investigations, it should also be guided by the ethics of scientific research.

Estimation of project cost and likely benefits

The likelihood that a project is undertaken will largely depend on whether its predicted benefits will justify its costs and whether the problem owner's expectations can be reasonably met. If both benefits and costs can be expressed in monetary terms, a project is beneficial if the total **present value** of the difference between all benefits and its total cost over the useful life of the project is positive.

For projects dealing with environmental, health, or social issues, many of the benefits cannot be adequately captured in currency. Take the preservation of nature or scenic beauty, or the prevention of fatal accidents. How much is it worth to prevent the destruction of some ecologically important estuary or a wildlife habitat? Similarly, the monetary evaluation of the benefits of noise abatement or pollution control or the social benefits of pre-school education can hardly be measured in dollars, pounds, or euros. A comparison of benefits and costs may therefore be far from simple.

But even if we look only at monetary benefits, providing a reliable answer for what the likely benefits are going to be may not be straightforward. At this point in the life of a project, the analyst may have only scant information about the potential size of the benefits. As pointed out earlier, the analyst may then find it advisable to propose a preliminary study for assessing the economic feasibility of the project. Such projects are similar in nature to research and development ventures. These have to be funded based on vague potential, rather than hard facts. Some will succeed and reap great benefits; others will fail. The expectation in undertaking such projects is that on balance long-term benefits will outweigh long-term costs.

However, the analyst should make a serious and honest attempt at predicting the likely benefits beyond mere guesses. It may require developing a simplified model of the proposed operation or system. This can then be used for computing approximate lower bounds to estimates of benefits. It will also give a better picture of the likely costs for undertaking the project, although these are usually easier to estimate.

Frequently, the sponsor of the project may have certain expectations about what the project should achieve and the time frame within which it should be completed. Even if the project is beneficial from a cost–benefit point of view, it may not meet these expectations. The sponsor should be made aware of this. It could well be that the expectations or the time frame offered are unreasonable. The analyst may then try to alter these expectations through reasoned arguments, based on a preliminary study or experience from similar projects. Analysts must also keep in mind that they may inadvertently encourage the formation of unreasonable expectations. Proper and diplomatic management of the sponsor's expectations is an important aspect of any project. Inappropriate expectations may easily result in implementation failure.

Format of project proposal

A project proposal should be relatively short — three to six pages — and presented to a professional standard, with correct spelling, grammar and syntax, and consistent formatting. Its visual effect is also important.

Your language should be concise, clear, and simple. Be weary of pompousness, fad words, or 'business speak'. Do not use OR jargon, unless you know for certain that the readers are fully conversant with it. Reasoning should be logically developed and complete, with one point leading to the next. This sounds obvious, but it is often violated!

Writing a competent, well-presented report is an integral part of the professional image you wish to convey to the problem owner. One of the most common causes for complaint that we hear from employers of novice OR analysts is the often abysmal writing skills of many fresh graduates. It is difficult to come across as credible and professionally competent if your boss has to rewrite your reports before they can be presented to the sponsor of a project. In fact, it is the quickest way to lose your job.

The report should briefly summarize the problem situation, motivate the proposed approach in non-technical terms, list the steps of the analysis, the data and the resource needed (time, funds, computational capabilities), indicate the nature and approximate size of the benefits (if this is possible at that stage, or justify why this may not be possible), show a list of costs and a detailed time-table for completing the project, and give a recommendation on whether the project should proceed. If relevant, it is also advisable to indicate briefly why other potential approaches were discarded. External consultants must provide supporting evidence of competence and address questions of confidentiality (e.g. how to deal with confidential data). The proposal should start out with an executive summary.

We recommend that the analyst offers an oral presentation to the problem owner and the problem users. Do not hesitate to use the rich picture. It may be a catalyst for an animated discussion. Questions, doubts, and anxieties — which invariably crop up — can be dealt with, clarified, and alleviated on the spot.

Such an oral presentation again must be professional, i.e. clear, to the point, and logically developed, and should not go much beyond half-an-hour. It also needs careful preparation of good overheads, flip charts, or a software-based show. Most important though, rehearse your entire talk and time yourself carefully. In fact, one rehearsal may not be enough!

If the problem owner or decision maker finds that the likely results justify the cost of the analysis, including cost of eventual implementation, and has confidence in the analyst's competence to bring the project to a successful completion, he or she will normally give the go-ahead to proceed with the project.

6.4 The problem modelling phase

It is this phase that distinguishes the hard OR methodology from soft OR. Often hard OR is viewed as synonymous with a collection of powerful mathematical tools and techniques, such as linear programming, computer simulation, and statistical methods. We shall see that this is a rather limited view which we find unhelpful (even detrimental) in achieving the full potential of hard OR modelling.

The problem formulation or scoping phase may not have come up with a detailed definition of the relevant system. Therefore, step 4, building a mathematical model, may start out by finalizing the definition of the relevant system in the detail and resolution needed for translating it into quantitative terms. If the analysis done for step 3 showed that the problem fits a well-known structure, this simply means fleshing out the details. However, for a complex problem that does not fit a known structure, step 3 may only have delineated the boundary of the system. Hence considerable further work needs to go into defining a relevant system, usually using a process approach. This may be in the form of a detailed influence diagram. Sometimes it may be useful to have two or more levels of diagrams: a high-level system structure diagram, showing categories of inputs, the interactions between subsystems, and the major outputs, supplemented by a detailed influence diagram for each subsystem.

However, even if step 3 ended in a complete definition of the relevant system, it is advisable to revisit it carefully. The passage of time may have changed your perception of the problem.

Once satisfied with the system definition, we build a mathematical model. Sometimes a spreadsheet is all that is needed to capture the quantitative relationships between the inputs, the system variables, and the outputs. If the problem fits a well-known structure, such as a linear program or a network, readily available commercial software can be used for formulating a mathematical model and finding a solution. However in many instances, we may have no choice but to build a special-purpose model that expresses the relationships between control inputs, system variables, and outputs. Such models may consist of numerous equations and inequalities. Notice that at this point we are well into the abstract world. The model is not the real thing.

As discussed in Section 5.4, building a mathematical model is in part an art. The final version of the model may be the result of a process of enrichment and re-formulation.

In step 5 — finding the preferred solution — we manipulate this model in order to explore the response of the system performance to changes in controllable and uncontrollable inputs, i.e. we explore set of feasible solutions or the **solution space**. The aim is to find the preferred solution in terms of the problem owner's objective(s). If the problem owner is interested in one major objective, this means finding the optimal solution. For example, if profits are the performance measure, the optimal solution is the one that maximizes profits.

Testing and validation of model and solution

Step 6 — testing and validation — establishes the model's credibility. Validation has two facets:

1. **Internal validity or verification**: Checking that the model is logically and mathematically correct and that the data used is correct. It means carefully verifying that all mathematical expressions correctly represent the assumed relationships and that they have been correctly implemented in the computer program, achieved by printing out detailed intermediate results step-by-step. If computationally feasible, these should be verified by checking the results numerically with a hand calculator for a sufficiently wide range of inputs. This also involves verifying that each expression is dimensionally consistent. For example, if the right-hand side of an equation is in terms of kilograms per hour, so must be the left-hand side. The correctness of all numerical constants should be verified. In spreadsheets this is simplified if all such constants are provided as input into unique data cells, referenced by all formulas that use them, rather than being inserted as numbers separately into each formula. This ensures that any changes will automatically be carried forward to all formulas where that constant

is used.

The prudent analyst does much of the checking for internal validity while developing the model. Establishing internal validity can thus not be divorced from the actual model building—a clear example of how various steps overlap or happen concurrently, at least in part.

Complex models consisting of many separate but interrelated mathematical expressions also have to be checked for logical consistency. Have the parts been fitted together correctly?

2. **External validity** (also simply referred to as **validation**): Is the model a sufficient representation of reality? Does it provide insight and answers useful and in the appropriate form for decision making? This is far more difficult to establish than internal validity. 'What is or is not a close enough approximation?' is largely a question of judgment. The answer should depend on the purpose for building the model and the intended use of its solution. A rough approximation may well be good enough for an exploratory planning model, while a model intended for detailed operational decisions may need to be a fairly accurate representation of reality. So again we see that validation overlaps with both the definition of the relevant system (step 3 of the MS/OR methodology) and the model building (step 4) (see M. Landry *et al.* [1983]).

All stakeholders should be recognize that it is not possible to prove that a model is externally valid. It is only possible to show that it is wrong. Hence external validation is a question of establishing the **credibility** of the model. The importance of a model's credibility and appropriateness have already been stressed in Section 5.3, dealing with the essential properties of good models. If the model is credible, the user will have confidence in it.

External validity can often be assumed if the model mimics reality accurately. Hence, the analyst needs to ascertain the responses of the model to changes in inputs — are they as expected and if not, why are they different? Complex systems often exhibit counterintuitive behaviour. A model's validity is put into question unless such behaviour can be convincingly explained.

Testing looks at how the model and its solution perform. What improvement in benefits or cost does it offer over the current mode of operations? If the project deals with a proposed future system, what is the range of the potential benefits that can be expected? The answers to these questions will determine whether the project is abandoned, reoriented, or allowed to continue on its current course.

What-if or sensitivity analysis

Finally, in step 7— sensitivity analysis — we ask 'what if' questions. How is the preferred or optimal solution affected by individual or simultaneous changes of uncontrollable inputs into the system? How costly are errors in inputs in terms of reduced benefits achieved if a solution based on incorrect inputs is implemented? Both are referred to as **sensitivity analysis**.

Sensitivity analysis is without doubt the most important step of hard OR. It must become second nature for any operations researcher. The insights gained from it may be more valuable than finding a good or even the optimal solution.

Extensive sensitivity and error analysis are also an integral part of checking external validity — another instance of the linkage between various steps.

Project report

For projects that need the owner's approval for implementation, the modelling phase ends with a detailed project report on the analysis done, its findings, and the analyst's recommendations about implementation. Further action will largely depend on this document. Its format is a more detailed and extended version of the project proposal, again preceded by an executive summary of the findings and recommendations. By this point, the analyst is ready to give firm estimates of the potential benefits and costs of implementation. The appendices should give details on technical aspects of the quantitative model(s) used, justify of the assumptions and simplifications made in the analysis and their likely effects on the findings, list the input data used, and report on important findings of the sensitivity analysis performed. The project report must be complete and stand on its own. To be credible, it must be to a high professional standard in terms of content and presentation.

Both the strengths and weaknesses of the analysis and the conclusions reached should be spelled out. This is also for the analyst's own protection. He or she can then not be accused of negligence, or of having misled the problem owner by hiding important aspects. It forms part of the analyst's professional ethics!

Should the project be abandoned?

As the analysis progresses, the analyst must periodically assess whether the project should continue or be abandoned. The viability of a project is put in question when the likely benefits that can be derived from implementing its results do not justify the additional cost to be incurred for completing it. If this seems to be the case, professional ethics require that the analyst report this fact to the problem owner(s) or sponsor(s). The points raised on estimation of project costs and benefits are all relevant here.

Note that this assessment does not take into account the costs already spent up to this point, but only the additional costs for completing the project. Why do we ignore the costs already spent? The reason is that nothing can be done about them any more; they are a so-called sunk cost (see the detailed discussion on this in Chapter 9). However, if any further costs are justified by the likely benefits, it is still worthwhile to proceed.

We cannot undo costs already spent. It is therefore important that we discover as early as possible that further costs may not be recovered by the project's benefits. This will allow a project to be culled before large amounts of resources are wasted; hence the need to regularly assess a project's continued viability.

6.5 The implementation phase

If the problem owner agrees that the performance standards are likely to be met, the project enters its last phase: solution implementation. Step 8 — planning implementation — prepares a detailed plan of all implementation tasks, their assignment to individuals, and a schedule for their coordination.

Step 9 establishes procedures for maintaining and establishing controls over the solution. It specifies for what range of values for crucial uncontrollable inputs the current solution remains valid and the exact procedure for updating the solution when inputs stray outside these ranges, including who is responsible for it.

Step 10 — actual implementation of the solution — executes the changes required to switch from the current to the proposed mode of operation. Preparation of complete documentation of the model, any software developed for its use, and self-contained user manuals form an integral part of the implementation process.

Although implementing the solution comes almost at the end of a project, planning for implementation starts at the very outset of any project, when the first contacts are established with the problem owners and users, and continues through all other steps. It implies establishing good lines of communications, exploring and managing prior expectations, particularly unrealistic ones, and keeping the problem owners and users informed about the progress of the project and consulting with them. Experience shows that the more the problem owners and users are actively involved in the project, the more they own the results, and the keener they are to implement the results and make them work.

Finally, after the new solution has been in use for some period, the analyst returns and performs an audit of the solution (step 11). This consists of establishing the extent to which the solution fulfils its promises in terms of the benefits achieved and the costs incurred, as well as checking for continued proper use of the solution and recommending possible changes in the light of the practical experience gained. This may give rise to a final project audit report.

Chapter 8 discusses the implementation process and obstacles to implementation, and how to overcome them, in more detail.

6.6 The nature of the hard OR process

Forward and backward linkages

The various steps are usually initiated in the sequence shown, but each step may overlap with both the preceding as well as the subsequent steps. For example, when we start identifying the problem to be analysed, we may need to gather more specific and more detailed information about the problem situation, which is then added to the rich picture, i.e. we return from step 2 to step 1. By the time we get to the project proposal (end of step 3), we may already have explored, at least tentatively, a general form of the mathematical model (step 4). Not only may this allow us to determine rough estimates of the potential benefits, but it may also affect the boundary choices and the level of resolution for the relevant system.

The choice of the most suitable mathematical model should be influenced by how costly both its detailed development and ultimate implementation are expected to be. For example, if its use presupposes a level of training and skills which goes far beyond the norm for the type of employee in that position, we may opt for a simpler model or for rules that only approximate the optimal solution. This is likely to capture less of the potential savings or benefits, but will have a better chance of successful implementation. The experienced analyst will constantly be on the look-out for such forward and backward linkages between phases, as well as between steps within a phase.

Iterative process

The methodology is iterative. This means that the analyst may go back to previous steps and redo or modify part of the analysis already done. For example, attempting to define a relevant system may point to contradictions or missing aspects in the problem situation. Before proceeding, this should be resolved. It may in turn lead to changes in the relevant system. During the solution step, the analyst may discover that the software and computing facilities needed to find the optimal solution are very costly, negating most or all of the expected financial benefits. Implementation of the model might therefore not be justified. The analyst may have to iterate back to the model-building step and formulate a computationally less demanding model. Unfortunately, it may even happen that during implementation, crippling oversights in the problem formulation are discovered which render part or most of the model irrelevant or even change the nature of the issue. If the problem owner agrees, the analyst may have to start almost from scratch with a new problem formulation.

Few projects sail through all the various steps without iterating back to earlier steps in the analysis. You should therefore clearly keep in mind that even if we discuss the steps separately in their natural sequence, they overlap.

Data collection

Many OR texts show a separate 'data collection' step. Figure 6-1 shows none. This is not an oversight! The reason is simple. Data collection does not occur at a given point in the analysis as a separate step. We start collecting and assessing data and identifying data sources when we meet the problem situation for the first time. As we proceed, we continue collecting more data for describing the relevant system. For some projects, the major part of data has to be available when building a mathematical model. The specific form of the quantitative relationships may only be discovered if we know the major characteristics of the data (such as 'Are the relationships linear?', 'Is the probability distribution approximately normal?'). In other cases, the data have to be directly incorporated into the mathematical relationships. In other instances, the bulk of data collection can wait until the model is ready for implementation in step 10. Collecting and evaluating data occurs in parallel with any of the 11 steps, even the audit at step 11.

In many instances, the data may not be in the form required or may not even exist. It is important that the analyst ascertains before step 3 whether the required data sources exist and in what form. If the data are missing or not available in a useful form, action has to be initiated to start the collection of the data in the form required. Furthermore, an assurance by various stakeholders that all the data are available and easily accessible should be treated with a healthy degree of scepticism. It pays to show a lively interest for inspecting the data sources and their format. Lack of sufficient data may seriously delay completion of the project.

One further important word about data. Most data available reflect the current or past mode of operation. If the proposed project substantially changes that mode, such data may not be relevant any longer. What we really want are data as they will be once the proposed system has been implemented. However, such data are not yet available, so we have to make do with what we have, but it may need adjustment to become relevant for the proposed system. For instance, if demand for products shows a trend, up or down, that trend needs to be extrapolated. If equipment is replaced, the labour cost for the new equipment has to be ascertained. The blind use of past data implies hidden, unintended system boundary judgements.

6.7 The Lubricating Oil Division — a situation summary

We now demonstrate these eleven steps of the methodology with a case in which one of the authors was the principal analyst.

How is the project initiated?

The project deals with the operations of the Lubricating Oil Division (LOD) of a major US oil company. The LOD produces and stores about 400 types of automotive and industrial lubricating oils and greases, for ultimate sale to over 1000 customers. The impetus for the project is a report by the firm's internal auditors to the Vice-President of Finance that in their judgement the current average stock turnover achieved by the LOD of 12 times per year is well below the company target of 24. (Stock turnover measures how many times per year the entire stock is renewed.) As a result, the funds tied up in inventories are seen as excessive. This concern is passed on to the Vice-President of Manufacture who, in turn, informs the manager of the LOD with a request to report to him in due course. In response, the manager of the LOD approaches the OR group in the company headquarters for help. That is where the analyst comes in.

The initial request is somewhat vague — the manager wants advice. Therefore the first phase of the project is clearly in the nature of problem scoping. There is no guarantee that the project may ever get approval.

Learning the stakeholders' technical jargon

The analyst's first action is to arrange a guided tour of the offices and facilities of the LOD. Remembering people's names is one of his weaknesses. So, whenever he meets new people, he immediately notes down their name and function on a notepad. He makes a conscientious effort to understand, learn, and use the largely unfamiliar technical terminology which he encounters. If he does not understand something, he is not ashamed to ask — even at the risk of looking a bit dumb. It is important not to assume that somebody else's technical meaning of a term is the same as yours. So he checks it out to avoid any confusion and misunderstanding.

Details of the operations

If he had been familiar with rich pictures at that time, he would have drawn up something like Figure 6-2 shown opposite. Starting in the top left-hand corner, it shows what triggers the study and the implied world view, namely a concern for the economic efficiency of investments. The core of the picture describes the various operations of the LOD and its relationships with other parts of the refinery operation and its customers. Here are some additional comments.

Production of lube oils and greases is done in batches in size from 400 litres to 100,000 litres. Many products are sold in several container sizes — from large drums to small cans. The LOD carries 804 different product–container size combinations. As shown in the rich picture, some customers place such large orders for a single product that they are met by special production runs and directly shipped to them. Only orders from small customers are met from warehouse stocks. As these stocks are sold off, they are replenished by an appropriately sized production run. The LOD follows a policy of shipping any goods to the customer within two days after receipt of the order, i.e. the delivery lead time is two days.

Various base oils and additives are mixed to specified recipes in mixing vats. The vat size chosen depends on the size of the mixing batch. The base oils are drawn from storage tanks, fed from the refinery. After mixing, the finished product is tested to ensure that it meets the desired specifications. Once a batch has passed the tests, the finished lube oil is filled into containers, usually within 4–6 hours. The pattern for grease production is similar.

The LOD's existing mixing and filling capacities are sufficiently large that with few exceptions all production runs are completed in 24 hours. The production lead time is therefore one day. It is this aspect which makes it possible to schedule special production runs for large customers after receipt of their orders and still ship the products within the planned two-day delivery cycle. The same aspect also means that a stock replenishment has to be scheduled only once sales have depleted stocks to a level too small for meeting the last small customer order received. As a result, all customer orders are always met within the planned delivery lead time. No shortages or unmet customer demands can occur.

Packaged goods are moved by forklifts. Goods supplied from stock are moved twice, once from production to the stock location in the warehouse and a second time from there to the shipping docks. Goods for big customer orders, in contrast, are only moved once, i.e. from production to the shipping docks. Hence the total workload for forklift operators and the corresponding wage bill can be reduced by having more goods bypass the inventory stage. The larger the fraction of customers classified as big, the lower the wage bill for forklift operators.

Figure 6-2   A rich picture for the LOD.

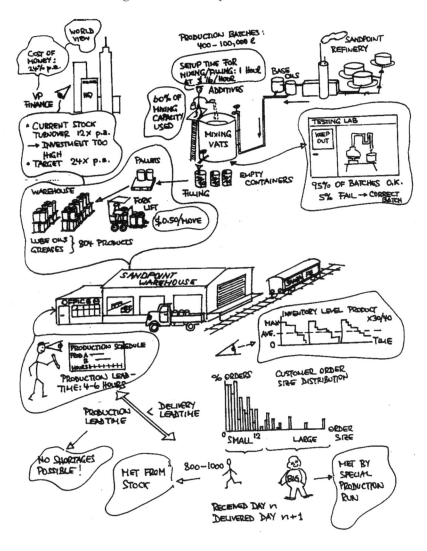

Assessing document flows and data sources

The analyst follows up the guided tour of the facilities by an extended visit to the offices of the LOD. He draws detailed diagrams of the document and information flow for processing customer orders, from receipt to shipment, and for initiating and processing of stock replenishment, and verifies them on the spot with the people doing each task.

Naturally, the analyst's intense curiosity in seeing all data files is interpreted as enthusiasm for the project. He asks for photocopies of all documents used and checks how far back data files are kept and whether during that period changes in operations and in processing information or in data file formats have occurred, so as to make sure that the right data in the right form is available when needed.

Once back in the office, he immediately organizes all information gathered in a systematic form, filling in any gaps from memory, and highlights aspects that need further clarification or verification on subsequent visits.

6.8   Identifying the problem to be analysed

Identifying the issue to be analysed

The rich picture indicates a number of possible issues, such as the process of scheduling production runs to achieve tight coordination of the mixing and filling operations and reduce the cost of changing over from one product to another, particularly on the filling machines; or the decision of which customer orders are classified as big and which ones as small (the decision flow chart in Figure 5-11 on page 104 depicts this process); or whether it is advantageous to allow a lengthening of the production lead time from the current 1-day period. The latter would allow for better smoothing and coordination of the mixing and filling workload and may possibly reduce the number of operators needed to perform the same tasks. The constraint on maintaining the current level of customer service clearly seems to preclude the latter course of action.

The stimulus for the project in the first place is the concern voiced by the Vice-President of Finance. Her statement about the inadequate average turnover of stocks in the LOD carries the implication that she considers that too much money is tied up in stocks. The average stock turnover for the LOD as a whole is a weighted average over all products. As shown in the rich picture, the normal inventory behaviour over time for each product has a typical saw-tooth pattern. Each tooth corresponds to one stock replenishment and represents one complete stock turnover for that product. The fewer stock turnovers per year, the larger must be the stock replenishment. For example, if the demand for a given product is 120,000 litres per year and the size of each stock replenishment is 5,000 litres, the stock turnover is 24 times per year. If the stock turnover is reduced to 12 times per year, then each stock replenishment must be equal to 10,000 litres. So we see that the stock turnover for each product is directly linked to the size of the corresponding stock replenishment, which is controllable by the LOD. This issue is taken as the focus of the project.

Discussions with the LOD manager indicate that he shares the world view revealed by the Vice-President of Finance, namely to assure the most efficient use of the LOD's resources. The latter sees funds tied up in stocks as lying idle, whereas a high stock turnover is interpreted as a sign of efficiency. From this narrow perspective, reducing the size of stock replenishment will increase the stock turnover. This would allow meeting the Vice-President's goal or prior expectation of a stock turnover of

24 times per year, thereby reducing the total investment in stocks. However, from the rich picture we see that every mixing and filling run also involves a setup — the time operators spend to prepare a mixing and filling run — and the lab technician needs to test the products. Increasing the turnover rate for a given product means more stock replenishment and hence more production setups. As a consequence, the time spent by operators on setups will also increase. At $16 per hour, this can well mean that any savings made by reducing investments in stock may be lost by higher annual labour costs.

The size of the stocks needed also depends on how small orders are defined. Lowering of the cutoff point reduces the demand met from stock. Consequently, smaller stocks are needed, which in turn translates into a reduction in stock investment. But lowering the cutoff point means that more customer orders are met by special production runs, causing an increase in the annual production setup costs.

Each of these possible actions causes some costs to decrease and others to increase. A narrow efficiency approach focussed only on investments may thus not be in the best interest of the firm (unless for other reasons the firm wishes to reduce its investments regardless of its effect on operating costs). We need to consider all costs that are affected by a change in policy. In other words, we are looking for the most effective production/inventory control policy — a policy that keeps the total cost of the operations as low as possible, while at the same time maintaining or even improving the current level of customer service. Even if the relevant system is confined to the production/inventory control operations, the perspective taken should be one that looks at the effects on the firm as a whole, rather than simply the narrow (sub)system involved. (Recall the discussion on efficiency and on boundary judgements in Sections 2.2 and 3.5.) If this also meets the Vice-President's target stock turnover, all the better, but her expectation should not be the driving force. The problem owner — the LOD manager — should, however, fully understand the reasons for this and agree with them. Hence some management of prior expectation may be required right at the start of the project.

The hierarchy of systems involved

The problem is embedded in a hierarchy of systems. The widest system of concern is the company as a whole, with the refinery as one of its subsystems. The LOD in turn is a subsystem of the refinery system. Within the LOD system, production/inventory control operations form one of its major subsystems. It is the latter which is the narrow system of interest here. Since the LOD operation as a whole has control over the resources needed by the narrow system, as well as having the final say in terms of the project, it becomes the wider system of interest.

Stakeholders

With the narrow system of interest tentatively chosen, the analyst knows enough about the situation to identify the various stakeholders. These are defined with respect to this narrow system of interest. Here, the role of analyst is assumed by a consultant internal to the company.

There seem to be several levels of problem owners or decision makers. This is typical of problem situations with a hierarchy of systems, as is the case here. At the top is the Vice-President of Finance, who coordinates the use of funds within the firm. She states the criteria by which investments of funds are to be evaluated. The Vice-President of Manufacture (refinery system) operates within these criteria. He has delegated the authority for making day-to-day operational decisions on production and stock control for packaged products to the manager of the LOD (LOD system). For projects that do not involve any major investments, the latter is the immediate decision maker of the situation. However, he will have to refer the decision on large investments to the Vice-President of Manufacture.

A priori, the only new use of funds is the cost of the project itself. Once the project has been completed, the analyst may recommend a change in the level of investment in inventories. Any such recommendations will then be evaluated in terms of the investment criteria specified by the Vice-President of Finance. At this point in the analysis, the project cost is the only use of funds which has to be evaluated. As it turns out, even that exceeds the manager's authority and hence has to be referred higher up. But once approved, any changes to the day-to-day operation of the LOD are under his control. It is his world view that the problem solver must use as a basis for determining the goal or aim of the project.

It is important to confirm that the world views of all levels of problem owners are compatible. If not, the stakeholders at the various levels should be made aware of the conflicts and the need to have them resolved prior to proceeding further. Resolution of such conflicts in world views is usually beyond the scope of a hard OR project, since it deals with basic organizational issues and requires a soft systems approach. Persistence of conflicting world views between various levels of decision makers is likely to result in serious suboptimization, i.e. the benefits gained may be wholly or partially negated by additional costs inflicted elsewhere in the organization, e.g. in another subsystem at the same or at a different level. For the LOD, the analyst has already ascertained that there is basic agreement between the world views of the Vice-President of Finance and the LOD manager in terms of profit maximization. However, one source of conflict can arise if the optimal solution does not meet the stock turnover target set by the Vice-President of Finance. This aspect needs to be addressed in the project proposal.

To determine the problem users, we need to identify who is in charge of initiating production runs for stock replenishment or large customer orders. These 'decisions', within the policy defined by the problem owner — the LOD manager — are made by the stock officer. Any changes to the rules of the inventory/production control policy will have to be such that she is capable of applying them without a need for extensive further training.

The customers for the LOD's products are the problem customers. One of the first points raised by the LOD manager is that any new policy will have to maintain or improve the current level of service offered to all customers, in particular with respect to the two-day delivery lead time.

In addition to this requirement, there are other constraints that any proposed production/inventory control policy has to meet. The warehouse space and production capacity requirements of any new policy have to remain, at least in the short to medium term, within the current capacities available.

Problem elements

In summary, the six elements of the problem are:

- Immediate decision maker: the LOD manager.
- Objective: achieving low operating cost for the LOD's operation, subject to maintaining the same level of customer service.
- Performance measure: the total operating costs of the LOD.
- Decision criterion: minimizing total costs.
- Alternative courses of action: the size of stock replenishment batches and the cutoff point for classifying customer orders as big or small.
- Wider system of interest: the LOD operation and the refinery.

6.9 Relevant system for stock replenishment problem

Having settled on the problem to be analysed, we can now proceed to define a relevant system. A cursory inspection shows the presence of all the usual inventory/production control aspects. An experienced analyst may be tempted to use a structural approach, selecting one of the standard production/inventory control models. This, together with an identification of the products to be controlled, will delineate the system boundary. But a more careful analysis reveals that there are aspects not normally found in a typical production/inventory structure; in particular, different rules apply to meet big and small customer orders. Hence a process approach, starting from first principles, is more appropriate.

What is a suitable level of resolution for the system definition? At this point, little is known about the potential savings the project may produce. So opting for problem scoping, rather than a full problem formulation, is more appropriate. Hence only a high-level system structure diagram is needed, such as in Figure 6-3, which connects the various subsystems and indicates the system boundaries.

The uncontrollable inputs that the LOD wants to manage effectively are incoming customer orders and the existing operation facilities. Orders are grouped into 'large' and 'small'. The processing of each is a separate subsystem, i.e. a subsystem that meets large orders by scheduling a special production run, and another that meets small orders from stock and replenishes stocks periodically. Existing production facilities and capacities, including the forklift operation to move stock, are taken as given (uncontrollable inputs). They are shared by both subsystems. Similarly, existing warehousing capacity is given and used by the 'small order subsystem'. Specifying the inputs, both controllable and uncontrollable, delineates the boundaries of the narrow system of interest in sufficient detail for problem scoping.

Figure 6-3   High-level system structure diagram for LOD.

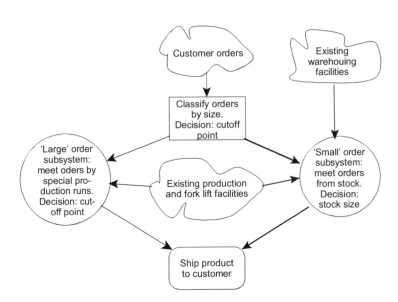

It is also important to notice that the two input controls, i.e. the **cutoff point** clas-sifying a customer order as large, and the **stock replenishment size**, must be specified individually for each of the 804 products. What may be a good pair for one product may be bad for another. The products are independent of each other. In some sense, there is not one big problem, but 804 small problems, one for each product. Their only interdependence is that they share the same production and warehousing faci-lities. Their combined usage of these facilities cannot exceed the existing capacities.

There is one more consequence of this. The measure of performance of the narrow system, i.e. the total operating cost of the LOD for meeting customer demands, is the sum of the 804 costs for the individual products.

Boundary judgements, explicit and implicit

Figure 6-3 shows customer orders and existing warehouse, production and forklift facilities as inputs. Strictly speaking, this means that the LOD takes all these as givens or aspects outside its control. The assumption is in fact even stronger. They are outside the wider (controlling) system's control, i.e. the firm as a whole. This is hardly true for the operating facilities. What is assumed here is that the firm deliberately chooses not to use that control and leaves them unchanged in terms of types and capacities. However, how they are used is assumed controllable and is bound to change as a result of the study.

The demand for the firm's products can also be affected by promotion and other actions. Since a large part of the 'customers' are company-owned wholesale distributors, even the pattern of demand can be controlled. For example, the firm could give each of these 'customers' a schedule of when they have to place orders. That schedule would be coordinated between these outfits to achieve certain desirable patterns, such as an even flow of orders or synchronizing ordering for certain products to allow them to be combined into a special joint production run. Again, the LOD deliberately decided that such controls are not part of this study.

There are also assumptions made about cost factors, various operating capacities of facilities, and the availability of the base oils and additives used for the blending of oils, such as that additives are always available when needed.

Activity:
- Before you proceed to the next section, reread the three questions at the beginning of Section 6.3 on page 116. Try to answer each from the information and discussion in Sections 6.8 and 6.9. If you cannot, indicate why or what additional information you would need to do so.
- List the additional boundary judgements made in the LOD case for costs, base oil availabilities, and operating capacities, and discuss their implications.

6.10 Project proposal for LOD

At this point, we can answer the first two of the questions listed in Section 6.3, i.e. the problem can easily be expressed quantitatively and the required data seems to be available or can be determined at a reasonable cost. The LOD has a complete computer database on all customer orders processed for at least the last two years, from which customer order patterns can be determined. Cost data on products and the production and warehousing operations can be obtained either directly from cost accounting data or computed without major expenses by observing operators' time and materials required for various tasks.

The third question about potential benefits and costs of the analysis is somewhat more difficult to answer without actually solving the problem, which begs the question. We have not yet formulated a mathematical model, nor has detailed product input data been collected. All we have are rough ranges for the product cost factors and a general idea of the form of the measure of performance.

The way to deal with this is to make simplifications. With the help of the stock officer, half a dozen representative products are identified, covering the range from small to large volumes. She also has access to approximate product values and information about the mixing and filling operations from which a rough guess as to the setup cost can be derived. A call to the Finance Section of the firm confirms that investments are supposed to achieve a return of at least 18% per year. This is the opportunity cost for the use of funds. At this stage, it seems appropriate to have recourse to one of the most basic inventory control models that are part of the hard OR tool box. This model determines the best stock replenishment size under the assumption that all orders are met from stock. The model we shall develop is much more sophisticated and therefore likely to produce larger savings. Consequently, the cost estimates produced by the simple model are a very conservative lower bound. This cost is then compared with the annual the cost of the current practice and the resulting cost savings are extrapolated for all 804 products.

In the actual case, the cost savings for the six products used as a sample ranged from $32 to $253 per year, with an average of about $114 and a standard deviation of 30. Using standard statistical estimation principles, a 95% interval estimate for the predicted savings over all 804 products is $90,000 to $94,000.

A rough estimate as to the total time input by analysts, cost accounting and data processing, as well as LOD staff, was about 120 days. At an internal charge-out rate of $400 per day, the cost of the analysis would be recovered within about half a year from implementation of the results — lower than the acceptance criterion of one year used by the company for 'research' projects of this type.

However, a more prudent approach is first to do a preliminary study to get a more reliable savings estimate, based on a version of the proposed model, and using a stratified random sample of around 5% of all products. If the results confirm the above guesstimates, then a recommendation for a full-scale study can easily be supported. On the other hand, if a more detailed preliminary study shows that the potential savings are much smaller than initially estimated, then this fact is discovered before a costly full-scale commitment has been made — a more sensible approach here. Such a study can be completed in about 16 workdays.

In this project much of the ground work done in a preliminary study can also be carried forward to a full-scale study. As a consequence, the total expense of a preliminary study followed by an extension to all products will not be appreciably higher than undertaking a full-scale study from the start. This is due to the fact that a substantially larger portion of the total cost of a full-scale study is incurred for data collection and computation of the optimal policies (and their implementation), while the cost of the modelling phase is relatively small.

A further reason for opting for a preliminary study is that we are dealing with a fairly large number of products. For only a few dozen products, much of the justification for a preliminary study would disappear. The cost of a full-scale study would then be only be minimally larger.

An important factor for whether to go for a preliminary or a full-scale study hinges on which phase of the OR methodology incurs the most substantial portion of the cost of the analysis. If it is the modelling phase, the tendency would be to opt directly for a full-scale study. If it is the implementation phase, as in the LOD case, a preliminary study is less risky.

Appendix 1 to this chapter contains a project proposal for a preliminary study. If it were written by external consultants, a short description of the mathematical model would be included as an appendix. Study it now before continuing!

6.11 A complete definition of the relevant LOD system

For the LOD problem the project proposal, reinforced by an oral presentation,

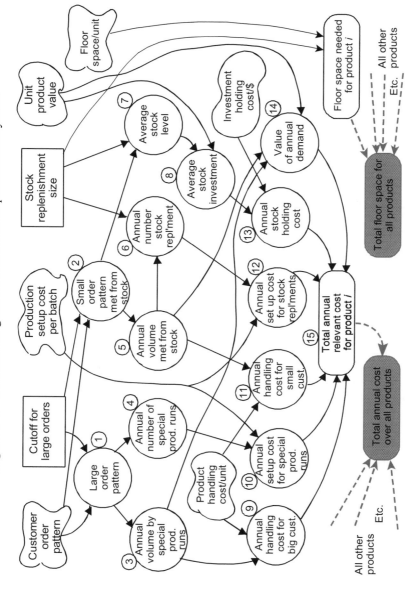

Figure 6-4 Influence diagram for LOD stock replenishment system.

completes Phase 1 of the OR process. A detailed definition of the relevant system will only be needed if the project is approved, which was the case here. Our discussions will be based on the influence diagram in Figure 6-4.

An influence diagram shows the transformation process of control inputs and uncontrollable inputs via system variables into outputs. It does not show the optimization aspect. That is another system. We have already identified the control inputs for each finished product, namely the size of stock replenishments and the cutoff point for classifying customer orders as big or small. The system performance measure and main output of interest is the sum of operating costs over all products of the LOD. The total warehouse floor space needed is another output of interest.

'Total operating cost' is rather vague. Costs are incurred over time. But we are not really interested in the total cost for a particular year, say the most recent 12-month period. Instead, the aim is to devise decision rules for the future. Since that future is unknown we assume it will remain similar to the past — a fair assumption for a stable system like the LOD. So we take the total long-run average cost over a given time interval, such as one year, as the measure of performance. This choice is arbitrary. An interval of one month would work equally well.

The total operating cost is made up of those costs that change as we change the control inputs and those costs that are not affected by it. There is little point in including the latter at this time. They can always be added in at the end, if need be. So the term 'total operating cost' only relates to those costs that, for the firm as a whole, change if we change the control inputs. They are the **relevant costs**.

Furthermore, as we have already seen, the total cost is the sum of the individual costs incurred for each of 804 products. The cost structure for each product is in principle identical; only the data inputs vary from product to product. So all we need is an influence diagram covering one generic product. Once translated into a mathematical model, it can be applied to each product individually.

Figure 6-4 is our version of an influence diagram. It shows full details for one product, i. The same pattern is repeated for all other 803 products. The overall performance measure (shown in grey at the bottom) is the sum of the individual 'total annual relevant costs'. Similarly, the total warehouse space required (also shown in grey) is the sum over all 804 products.

We find that the easiest approach is first to insert the rectangle(s) for the control input(s) — in our case 'cutoff for large orders' and 'stock replenishment size' — at the top of the diagram and the oval(s) for the output(s) at the bottom. Next we map out the transformation process in a logical top-down sequence. The 'cutoff for large orders' splits the 'customer order pattern' — a data input — into two groups: large orders met by special production runs and small orders met from stock. Therefore two sets of arrows issue from 'cutoff for large orders' and 'customer order pattern' to the two system variables 'Large order pattern' (circle 1) and to 'Small order pattern met from stock' (circle 2). The system variable 'Large order pattern' determines the 'Annual volume [met] by special production runs' (3) and the 'annual number of special production runs' (4). Recall that products shipped directly from production are handled only once. So if we know the 'annual volume by special production runs' and the input data 'product handling cost/unit) we can determine the 'annual handling cost for large customers' (9). Similarly, each special production run incurs a setup cost. The 'annual number of special production runs' and the data input 'production setup cost per batch' determine the 'annual setup cost for special production runs' (10). The system variables 9 and 10 are contributors to the output 'total annual relevant cost' (oval 15). As an exercise, explain all the other relationships yourself.

The influence diagram allows us to trace the effect of any choice of decisions on the two output measures. The choices over all 804 products only yield a feasible solution if the total floor space required is no more than the space available. If this constraint is violated, we either have to reduce all stock replenishment sizes so that they fit into the warehouse or get approval to build more warehouse space. If we propose to add more warehouse space, we are dealing with a new project — an investment evaluation (covered in Chapter 10). The difference in total costs between the restricted solution (that fits into the current warehouse) and the cost of the unrestricted optimal solutions is the saving resulting from building a new warehouse of an appropriate size. If these savings, discounted over the life of the warehouse, exceed the discounted sum of construction, maintenance, and operating costs, building a new warehouse is financially attractive.

6.12 Mathematical models

A mathematical model expresses, in quantitative terms, the relationships between the various components, as they were defined in the relevant system developed in the formulation phase. Sometimes, it may be possible to represent these relationships in a relatively simple table using a spreadsheet. Often it may be more convenient or necessary to formulate the relationships by a mathematical expression or a whole system of mathematical expressions, such as equations (e.g. $Q=ax+by$), inequalities (e.g. $ax+by \leq c$), or functions (e.g. $f(x) = ax+[b/x]$).

Before proceeding, it will be useful to define some terminology. The controllable aspects of a problem are referred to as the **decision variables** or the **alternative courses of action**, the latter term being mainly used if the choices available are discrete and usually few in number. For example, when you consider replacing your car with another one, the alternatives may be: do nothing (i.e. keep the current car), or replace it with a car of type A, B, C, ..., or K. A decision variable, on the other hand, can be any integer or any real-valued variable in a given range. In the LOD problem, the 804 pairs of 'size of a replenishment' and 'cutoff level for classifying customer orders as big or small', one set for each product, are the decision variables. Both may assume any non-negative integer value (number of containers, e.g. drums, or cases of containers, e.g. cartons of litre cans).

Those aspects that measure how well the objectives of the decision maker are achieved are called the **performance measure** or **measure of effectiveness**. If it can be expressed as a function of the decision variables, then we usually call it the **objective function**. For the LOD problem, the relevant performance measure is the sum of total annual costs over all 804 products carried.

Our aim may be to find values for the decision variables that maximize or minimize the objective function, whichever is relevant. In the LOD case, we want to minimize the total annual cost. This is the optimizing criterion used.

The uncontrollable inputs are often referred to as **parameters, coefficients**, or **constants**. For example, the initial purchase price and the fuel consumption are input parameters into the car replacement decision, while the value of a product or the production setup cost are input parameters in the LOD problem. They are uncontrollable inputs from the wider system or the environment.

Mathematical expressions that limit the range of values that a decision variable can assume are called **constraints**. For instance, you may impose conditions on the minimum size of the engine or on the maximum rate of fuel consumption that a car must satisfy to be a possible candidate. Similarly, the total amount of warehouse floor space available to store all products in the LOD problem may be limited to 2000 square metres. Any solution, i.e. combination of decision variables, that requires more than that is not viable, i.e. is **infeasible.**

Since the early 1950s researchers into hard OR have developed many **general-purpose models**, such as linear programming and its numerous extensions, network models, such as critical path scheduling, and waiting line models and so on. They have a clearly defined mathematical structure and an associated solution method, usually in the form of an algorithm (Section 6.19 has a brief discussion of solution methods). They are commonly referred to as OR techniques and form the core of most OR teaching and textbooks.

For problems which do not fit a particular OR technique, the analyst uses a process approach to build a **special-purpose model** with a structure tailored to the problem. It may also imply devising a suitable solution technique. Such problems are often more difficult to formulate and to solve, but also offer more challenge.

If all inputs and all relationships are known with certainty, the model is **deterministic**. If certain inputs are uncertain or random, then the outputs of the model are also uncertain or random. If probability distributions can be specified for the random inputs, the resulting model is **probabilistic** or **stochastic**.

Why build mathematical models?

A pharmaceutical company which does research to develop a medical treatment will test a large number of compounds or a combination of compounds on laboratory animals, and then the one or two that have shown exceptional promise also on humans. In contrast, when a management scientist wants to determine the best mode of operation for an existing process, there are no convenient guinea pigs available, nor is experimentation on the existing facilities a viable option. It would be far too disruptive, too risky, and usually too expensive. Frequently, the problem deals with potential projects that are still on the drawing board. Hence real-life tests are not even possible. But even if real tests could be done, the time delay caused by testing one configuration, let alone several dozen different ones, means that real-life testing is out of question. In most cases such tests may take several months or years to become conclusive. The final answer may only be available when the problem has long become irrelevant! Mathematical models are therefore the only practical way to obtain answers to such problems quickly and reasonably inexpensively.

With today's interactive mathematical modelling packages, such models can be developed fairly easily — often within a few hours or days of analysis. The exception may be models that attempt to represent the entire operation of a firm, such as an entire oil company, consisting of the extraction of crude oil, the transportation to the refineries, the detailed operation at each refinery, and finally the distribution of the refined products. Such a project may take several person-years to complete. The major costs are the salaries of the analysts.

Mathematical models are usually easy to manipulate. This allows for quick exploration of the effects of changes in the inputs on the objective function, particularly with the help of computers. In contrast to real-life experiments, a new or updated answer can often be found within a few seconds of computer time, although there are some notable exceptions. It is these attributes which make mathematical models the workhorse of hard OR.

Important considerations when building mathematical models

When building a mathematical model, analysts must keep the **essential properties of good models**, discussed in Section 5.3, firmly in their mind. In particular, the model should be as simple as possible, while still capturing all essential aspects. It should be robust and, above all, appropriate for the situation and provide the output relevant in a useful form for decision making.

As we have seen in Section 3.5, any system definition implies **boundary judgements**. Analysts make some deliberately to keep the problem within manageable bounds or by necessity because some aspects may be beyond their control. Good practice requires that these be critically justified and recorded. Similarly, when capturing the system's structural relationships analysts may introduce further assumptions or boundary judgements. Some may be implied by the form of model used. Again, it is essential that these are critically evaluated. Are they appropriate or a sufficiently good approximation to reality? How may they affect the outputs from the model or even possibly invalidate some?

Two types of boundary judgement may be made without deliberate consideration. The first, the validity of using past data to predict the future, has already been covered. The commonly implied second boundary judgement is more pernicious and difficult to deal with. As the discussions on efficiency in Section 2.2 and the hierarchy of systems in Section 3.8 show, most systems are in reality only subsystems of some bigger entity; they share resources with other subsystems and receive inputs from and give outputs to other subsystems. The implicit assumption we make when 'optimizing' a particular subsystem is that all other subsystems are already operating at their optimum and that any changes made will not affect that — a rather big ask! There may be little analysts can do about how the operations of other subsystems affect the their subsystem, except making those in control aware of it. However, it is crucial that they check out how changes in their subsystem may affect the operation of other subsystems. Little is gained if their own improvements cause a deterioration in other subsystems.

> Activity: For each of the following descriptions, indicate whether it involves the use of a mathematical model. If yes, identify its components, i.e. decision variables, uncontrollable inputs, performance outputs (incl. objective function), constraints, etc., and discuss the boundary judgements made.
> - The height of males of age 20 in a given city tends to follow a normal distribution with an average of 178 cm and a standard deviation of 4 cm. Current policy states that all recruits to the police force must be at least 174 cm tall. Hence a certain proportion of persons interested in police work are excluded by this criterion.
> - The distance that you can throw a rock depends on the weight of the rock, the angle of your throw, and the initial velocity once the rock leaves your hand.
> - The amount that an addicted gambler is willing to bet in a casino.

6.13 Mathematical model for LOD: first approximation

The next two sections will demonstrate the modelling process of enrichment and reformulation, discussed in Section 5.4.

We have already discovered that the only connection between products is given by the constraints on total warehouse space available (and also the mixing and filling capacities). A first obvious simplification is to ignore these constraints. If the best unconstrained solutions for all products satisfy the constraints, then these are not restricting and ignoring them was a good guess. If any one of the constraints is violated, e.g. more space than available is needed, we try to enrich the model by appropriately amending the unconstrained solutions or by embarking on a new round of building a more comprehensive model.

We identified two decision variables: the cutoff point for what customer order size is classified as big and the stock replenishment size. As a first simplification, we would rather deal with only one decision variable per product. Note that the original issue raised by the manager of the LOD deals with the size of the investment in stocks. So our first simple model deals only with that. Checking back with the influence diagram, we now consider only the consequences that follow from system variable (2). This is the stock replenishment subsystem in Figure 6-3. However, rather than simply ignoring the decision variable for the cutoff point, we fix it at an arbitrary value, say $L = 12$. In other words, we do not use it as a decision variable, but treat it as another fixed input. Together with the overall customer order pattern it determines the order pattern for demand met from stock, as shown in the influence diagram (Figure 6-4). Furthermore, the subsystem for dealing with large orders (circles 1, 3, 4, 9, and 10 in Fig. 6-4) is not affected by the stock replenishment policy and can be ignored at this point.

We are now ready to build the first approximation of a mathematical model for the LOD. From the influence diagram, each system variable or outcome is expressed as a function of all inputs and/or other system variables which have arrows terminating at that variable or outcome. Proceeding stepwise down, we can assemble an expression for the 'Total annual relevant cost for product *i*' (oval 15).

We start arbitrarily with circle 6. The incoming arrows indicate that the 'Annual number of stock replenishments' is a function of the annual volume of demand met from stock, denoted by D_1 (originally the system variable of circle 5, but now an input), and the stock replenishment size, Q (the single decision variable). The larger the value of Q, the fewer replenishments are needed to fill that demand. A little bit of thought (or trial and error) shows that

$$\text{Annual number of stock replenishments} = D_1/Q.$$

The annual setup cost for stock replenishments (circle 12) is a function of the annual number of stock replenishments (circle 6) and the production setup cost per batch, s. In fact, it is the product of the two:

$$\text{Annual setup cost for stock replenishments} = [D_1/Q]s.$$

The rich picture (Figure 6-2 on page 127) shows that the inventory for each product follows a saw-tooth pattern over time — each time stocks are filled by a replenishment (the decision variable), they are gradually reduced by withdrawals to meet the pattern of small customer orders (circle 2). Approximating these stock withdrawals as a constant rate, it follows that each tooth is a right-angled triangle and hence the average stock level is half its height, or

$$\text{Average stock level} = 0.5Q.$$

If each unit in stock has a value of v, the

$$\text{Average stock investment} = 0.5Qv.$$

Each dollar invested per year incurs a penalty of r, so

$$\text{Average stock holding cost} = 0.5Qvr.$$

A bit of thought shows that circle 14 is a product of two inputs (recall that 'Annual volume met from stock' is an input in the first approximation):

$$\text{Value of annual demand} = vD_1$$

Circle 11 is also the product of two inputs:

$$\text{Annual handling cost for small customers} = h_1 D_1.$$

Summing up these intermediate results gives the total annual relevant cost for the first approximation, denoted by $T(Q)$:

$$T(Q) = 0.5Qvr + (sD_1/Q) + h_1D_1 + vD_1 \qquad (6\text{-}1)$$

$T(Q)$ is a function of one decision variable, Q. Naturally, it is also a function of other inputs in the form of cost and demand parameters. It is customary not to show these explicitly as arguments in $T(Q)$. However, it would be useful to indicate that $T(Q)$ is in fact expressed for a given fixed cutoff point L.

Our decision criterion is to find a value for Q that minimizes expression (6-1). Note that for any given cutoff point L, the last two parts of (6-1) are constants that do not depend on the decision variable Q. Hence the value of Q that minimizes (6-1) is the same that minimizes

$$T(Q) = 0.5Qvr + (sD_1/Q) \qquad (6\text{-}1\text{A})$$

By differential calculus it can be shown that the optimal value of Q which minimizes (6-1A) is given by

$$Q^* = \sqrt{\frac{2sD_1}{vr}} \qquad (6\text{-}2)$$

Expression (6-2) is known as the **Economic Order Quantity Formula (EOQ)**. It is the simplest OR inventory control model, but also the most widely used one. In fact, it is the model incorporated in most inventory management software packages commercially available.

Consider the following example: a given product Y has a total demand in drums of $D = 7132$. For a cutoff point of $L = 12$, only $D_1 = 4140$ are met from stock, the rest is met by special production runs. The product value is $v = \$320/\text{drum}$, the production setup cost $s = \$18$, and the holding cost penalty $r = \$0.18/\$$ invested/year. By Expression (6-2), the optimal EOQ is

$$EOQ = \sqrt{2(4140)(18)/(320)(0.18)} = 50.87.$$

Since Q is an integer, we round to 51. By (6-1A) the relevant annual cost is

$$T(EOQ) = 0.5(51)320(0.18) + 18(4140/51) = \$2,930.$$

Activity: For the following input data: $D_1 = 3600$, $s = \$20$, $v = \$15$, $r = 20\%$, $h_1 = \$0.50$, determine
- the annual relevant total cost $T(Q)$ for $Q = 300$.
- the optimal $Q^* = EOQ$ and its associated annual relevant total cost $T(Q^*)$.

6.14   Second approximation for LOD model

For the first approximation, we fixed the cutoff point for classifying customer orders arbitrarily at $L = 12$. This allowed us to discover that the EOQ formula could be used for finding the optimal stock replenishment size Q. The annual volume of demand met from stock, D_1, is one of the input parameters of the EOQ formula. That formula is still applicable even if D_1 changes, for instance, as a result of a change in the cutoff point L. Is it then not possible to find the best joint values of Q and L by a simple process of enumeration? Right! For all possible values that L can assume we determine the optimal value of Q and also compute the total cost associated with the corresponding combination of L and Q. The lowest of these total costs will allow us to identify the jointly optimal values of L and Q.

An interesting feature emerges. The first simple model developed for finding the optimal stock replenishment size becomes a submodel of the new model. Such **nesting** of one model inside another model occurs reasonably often.

The total cost now also has to include those costs associated with special production runs. Since it is a function of two decision variables, L and Q, we will denote it as $T(L,Q)$. The influence diagram in Figure 6-4 shows that there are two additional costs associated with L, the annual setup cost for special production runs (circle 10) and the annual handling cost for big customer orders (circle 9). Here are the corresponding expressions:

$$\text{Annual handling cost for big customers} = h_2 D_2,$$

where D_2 is the annual demand from large customers, i.e. the sum of orders equal to or larger than L, and h_2 is the corresponding unit handling cost, and

$$\text{Annual setup cost for special production runs} = sN,$$

where N denotes the annual number of special production runs for big customer orders. It is given by the number of customer orders equal to or larger than L. For any given L, both D_2 and N can easily be determined.

The total relevant cost for $T(L,Q)$ is therefore as follows:

$$T(L,Q) = [sN] + [h_2 D_2] + [0.5Qvr + sD_1/Q] + [h_1 D_1] \tag{6-3}$$

The annual handling cost for small customers increases or decreases as the cutoff point L is increased or decreased. In contrast to the simple EOQ model, where this cost remained constant and could be ignored, it is now affected by one of the decision variables and becomes part of the total relevant cost.

6.15 Exploring the solution space for $T(L,Q)$

Figure 6-5 shows the output from a spreadsheet for product Y. It calculates, for a range of values of L, the associated optimal value of Q (using the EOQ formula), and the various cost components, as well as the total relevant cost.

The annual product value still remains constant for all combinations of L and

CHAPTER 6 — Overview of hard OR methodology

Figure 6-5
Spreadsheet
computations for
$T(L,Q)$ of the
LOD two decision
variable model.

The spreadsheet (Microsoft Excel - FIG6-5) contains:

SECOND MODEL FOR LOD STOCK CONTROL

Decision variables:

Stock replenishment size Q	
Special production run cutoff level L	

INPUT DATA

Total Demand	7132	drums/year
Product value	$320.00	/drum
Production setup cost	$18.00	/production run
Product handling cost	$1.10	/drum via storage
	$0.45	/drum by special production runs
Investment holding cost	$0.18	/dollar invested per year

COMPUTATION OF T(L,Q) (base period: one year)

cutoff point	Demand from stock	Demand met by special prod runs	Number of special prod runs	Setup cost special prod runs	Total handling cost	Corresp. EOQ	Corresp. relevant EOQ cost	Total relevant cost
1	0	7132	1266	$22,788	$3,209	0.0	$0	$25,997
2	134	6998	1132	$20,376	$3,297	9.2	$527	$24,200
3	846	6286	776	$13,968	$3,759	23.0	$1,324	$19,052
4	1131	6001	681	$12,258	$3,945	26.6	$1,531	$17,734
5	1875	5257	495	$8,910	$4,428	34.2	$1,972	$15,310
6	2045	5087	461	$8,298	$4,539	35.8	$2,059	$14,896
7	2717	4415	349	$6,282	$4,975	41.2	$2,374	$13,631
8	3445	3687	258	$4,644	$5,449	46.4	$2,673	$12,765
9	3580	3552	243	$4,374	$5,536	47.3	$2,725	$12,635
10	4140	2992	187	$3,366	$5,900	50.9	$2,930	$12,196
12	5160	1972	102	$1,836	$6,563	56.8	$3,271	$11,670
15	5340	1792	90	$1,620	$6,680	57.8	$3,328	$11,628
16	6108	1024	42	$756	$7,180	61.8	$3,559	$11,494
20	6568	564	19	$342	$7,479	64.1	$3,690	$11,511
24	6856	276	7	$126	$7,666	65.5	$3,770	$11,562
36	7036	96	2	$36	$7,783	66.3	$3,820	$11,638
48	7132	0	0	$0	$7,845	66.8	$3,846	$11,691

DEMAND INPUT DATA

Cust. order size	Number	Cumula-tive number
0	0	0
1	134	134
2	356	490
3	95	585
4	186	771
5	34	805
6	112	917
8	91	1008
9	15	1023
10	56	1079
12	85	1164
15	12	1176
16	48	1224
20	23	1247
24	12	1259
36	5	1264
48	2	1266

Q. Therefore, this is not a relevant cost even for this more complete model and is not shown explicitly in the spreadsheet. The lowest cost of $11,494 is obtained for the combination of $L = 20$ and $Q = 61.8$. However, both L and Q have to be integers. So Q is rounded to the nearest integer 62. Therefore the optimal policy is to meet all customer orders of size $L = 20$ and larger by scheduling a special production run, supply customer orders of less than 20 from stock, and replenish inventory by $Q = 62$ whenever it does not cover the last small customer order received. This occurs about every third day. The volume of demand met from stock is 6108 drums. The balance of 1024 is supplied by special production runs.

It turns out that goods are stored on pallets of four drums each. Management may therefore prefer to use a Q that is a multiple of 4. The actual policy recommended is most likely to be the pair $(L = 20, Q = 60)$. Verify that the corresponding total annual relevant cost is

$$T(L = 20, Q = 60) = \$756 + \$7,280 + \$3,560 = \$11,495,$$

or about one dollar larger than the minimum cost.

Figure 6-6 shows the total relevant cost as a function of L. Note that it is fairly flat. Hence small adjustments to the optimal values of L and Q, so as to have more 'appealing' numbers, will cause only negligible cost increases above the minimum total relevant cost.

How does the second model compare cost-wise to the policy of $L = 12$ and $Q = 80$ currently used by the LOD? By expression (6-3), the total annual relevant cost of the current policy is equal to

Figure 6-6   Total relevant cost $T(L,Q)$ for product Y.

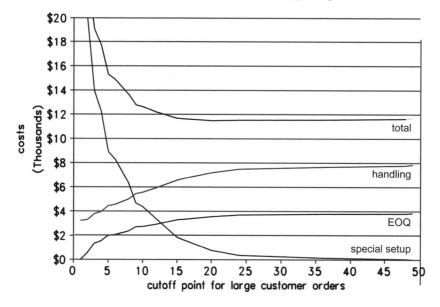

$$T(L=12,\ Q=80) = (18)187 + (0.45)2992 + [0.5(80)320(0.18)$$
$$+ (18)4140/80] + (1.10)4140 = \$12{,}502$$

or about $1007 higher than the recommended policy for the second model — a rather substantial saving. Furthermore, the average investment in stock is reduced by $3,200, a reduction of 25%. (Verify these numbers, using expression (6-3).)

Are there any aspects that the second model has not captured? Since it deals with each product separately, it still ignores the constraints on the productive capacity and the warehouse space. But as we have already outlined, those will only be considered once the optimal policy has been found for all products. At that point the overall effect on capacities can then be assessed. Otherwise, the model seems to be a good representation of the real situation.

There are still some possibilities to streamline the model. Some of you may have wondered whether the LOD would make more than one special production run if several customer orders of size L or larger are received for the same product on the given day. Why not combine them into one larger run and split them only at the time of shipping, thereby saving on production setup cost?

Combining orders leads to a new idea. If one or more small customer orders are also received on the same day as large customer orders, they could all be combined into a single large special production run. Hence even some small orders will in such cases be met without the goods going through the inventory stage. The effect of this is that a slightly larger fraction of the total demand is supplied by special production runs, leading to a further small decrease in stock investments.

The logical extension to this idea becomes quite obvious. Rather than look at single customer orders to decide whether or not to schedule a special production run, all customer orders for a given day are totalled up, regardless of size. If this total is equal to or larger than the cutoff point, all orders received on that day are supplied by a special production run. If the total is less than the cutoff point, they are supplied from stock. (Note that the optimal cutoff for this modified policy may not be equal to the cutoff point found best for the original model.) So we see an opportunity for another round of enrichment.

This is an example of generating a new form of policy — always an exciting aspect of OR modelling. This extension was in fact adopted. The fortunate aspect is that the same model can handle this extension. The only difference is that the demand data now has to be compiled in the form of a daily demand frequency distribution, rather than an order size distribution. So as not to further complicate the issue, we shall, however, ignore this extension here and base all further discussions on the original $T(L,Q)$-model developed earlier.

Another possibility would be to take advantage of special production runs to also replenish stocks for that product. This would further reduce production setup costs and at the same time also lower the size of stock replenishments. This third model was explored and abandoned, because the computational effort required to find the optimal solution became prohibitive.

Activity: Using expression 6-3 in Section 6-14, verify the results in Figure 6-5 for a cutoff point of 8.

6.16   Testing the LOD model

The LOD model is based, at least in part, on well-tested production/inventory control theory. Hence there is little doubt about its external validity. Internal validity is tested by verifying the spreadsheet calculations by hand for a typical product.

Testing of the solution of the second LOD model for its performance pretty much follows the steps outlined in the project proposal (Appendix 1). The 804 products are grouped into four classes: three classes for lubrication oils and one for all greases. The classification of oils is based on the distribution by annual sales-value volume — the method commonly used for grouping products for production/inventory control purposes. The high-volume A Class products comprise the group of biggest selling products that make up about 50% of the total annual sales value, the low-volume C Class products comprise the slowest selling products that make up about 10% of the total sales value. All other products fall into the medium-volume B class. Usually, the breakdown in terms of number of products in each class is roughly 10% for A, 40% for B, and 50% for C.

A stratified random sample of about 5% of all products is considered to be appropriate. Fixing the size of each subsample proportional to the annual sales-value volume recognizes the fact that the larger the sales volume of a given product the larger the potential savings are likely to be. The results are shown in Appendix 2 to this chapter. They show that the annual expected savings in costs amount to over $90,000.

Since testing is done product by product, other aspects of importance, such as the variations in the daily workload for mixing and filling and warehouse space usage, cannot be observed. However, rough extrapolations of capacity usage on an annual basis indicate a workload similar to the current one. This is due to two opposing changes in the pattern of operations that cancel each other closely. The proposed policies in general have higher cutoff points and hence less capacity usage for special production runs, but they have smaller stock replenishments and hence have higher capacity usage for that part of the operations.

6.17   Sensitivity and error analysis of the LOD solution

Once the optimal solution has been found, two further issues need addressing:

1. How does the optimal solution respond to changes in the input parameters?
2. What is the error, in terms of loss of benefits or savings, incurred for using the model based on wrong values for input parameters?

Although both may be called **sensitivity analysis**, we reserve this term for the first, while the second is more appropriately referred to as **error analysis**.

Sensitivity analyses

Sensitivity analysis explores how the optimal solution responds to changes in a given input parameter, keeping all other inputs unchanged. We will demonstrate this using the total cost expression (6-1A). If expression (6-2) is inserted in (6-1A) and simplified and rearranged, we get

$$T(EOQ) = \sqrt{2Dsvr} \tag{6-4}$$

(Expression (6-4) is only valid for the optimal EOQ, not for other values of Q!)

How do expressions (6-2) and (6-4) respond to changes in the input parameters D, s, v, and r? Assume that one of them changes by a factor k, i.e. [new value] = [original value] $\times k$. Then $T(Q)$ changes by a factor of $\sqrt{k}$, while the EOQ changes by a factor of $\sqrt{k}$ for D and s, but a factor $1/\sqrt{k}$. for v and r. So, a 50% (k=1.5) increase in the demand or the setup cost increases both the EOQ and its total cost by a factor of $\sqrt{1.5} = 1.225$, or by about 22.5%. But a 50% increase in the product value reduces the EOQ by a factor of $1/\sqrt{1.5} = 0.8165$ or 18.35% (100% − 81.65%), while $T(Q)$ still increases by 22.5%. For a more modest and more likely short-term increase in demand of, say, 5%, the increase in the EOQ and its cost is only about 2.5%.

Sensitivity analysis has three main purposes:

1. If the optimal solution is relatively insensitive to reasonably large changes in input parameters, the solution and the model are said to be robust. It increases the credibility of the model. The decision maker and user can place more confidence in the validity and usefulness of the model. It is true for the EOQ model.

2. For scarce resources, sensitivity analysis finds information about the value of additional amounts of each resource. (This is a concept of high importance to both economics and OR and is taken up in more detail in Chapter 13.) So, if warehouse space turns out to be limiting, then sensitivity analysis with respect to warehouse space will tell us by how much total costs will change.

3. There may be considerable uncertainty about the value of some input data. Sensitivity analysis is used for exploring how the optimal solution changes as a function of such data. If the best solution remains unchanged or is only slightly affected for reasonably large departures of these data from their most likely range, then the decision maker can put much confidence into the solution. On the other hand, high sensitivity of the best solution to minor changes in these data would be a signal for caution. Either greater effort must be expended to obtain highly accurate estimates for the data or a play-safe policy is implemented instead.

Activity: Current values are: $D = 4140$, $s = \$18$, $v = \$320$, $r = 0.18$. Find the percentage change in the optimal EOQ and the associated minimum cost $T(EOQ)$ for:
- an annual change in demand D from 4140 to 2070.
- a decrease in the annual cost per dollar invested r from $\$0.18$ to $\$0.09$.

Can you explain why the change in $T(EOQ)$ is the same in both cases, while the changes in the EOQ are in opposite directions?

Error analysis

Many of the input parameters are estimated on past data. They are then used for optimizing the operation in the future. There is no guarantee that the future will be similar to the past. For instance, demand for a product may increase or decrease appreciably. The holding cost may increase due to a world-wide rise in interest rates, etc. So incorrectly estimated input parameters may have been used in the model. The 'optimal' solution derived on that basis is only optimal on paper, but not in reality. How much does the use of incorrect input data cost in terms of the loss in potential benefits or potential savings? Error analysis explores this aspect.

Say the (incorrect) value p actually used is equal to k times the correct value P, or $p = kP$. $k < 1$ means it is smaller, and $k > 1$ means it is larger than the correct value. The percentage increase of the true cost over the minimum cost is given by

$$\{[(k+1)/2\sqrt{k}] - 1\} \times 100\%$$

A rather surprising fact emerges. This percentage error is only a function of k and not the actual values of the parameters. The table below lists some examples:

value of k	0.2	0.5	0.8	1.2	1.5	2	4
implied % error in parameter used from correct value	−80%	−50%	−20%	+20%	+50%	+100%	+300%
cost increase over minimum	34%	6.1%	0.6%	0.4%	2.1%	6.1%	25%

For example, overestimating any of D, s, v, or r by 100% results in an increase of actual costs incurred over the minimum possible cost of only 6.1%. These numbers show that EOQ model is very insensitive to fairly large errors in the input parameters, confirming again its robustness. There is little need for highly sophisticated and hence very accurate demand forecasts when using the EOQ model, nor is there a need to estimate the various cost parameters to a high degree of accuracy.

Error analysis is done for two main reasons:

1. To determine the accuracy needed for estimating input data; the more sensitive the solution is to input errors, the more accurate the input parameters need to be.

2. To establish control ranges for changes in all input parameters over which the current optimal policy remains near-optimal; as long as the input parameters stay within these limits, there is no need to recompute the optimal policy. The gain in benefits or savings is too small to warrant the cost of updating. This is an im-

portant input for step 9 of the hard OR methodology, namely, control and maintenance of the solution.

Activity: Using the data in the activity for sensitivity analysis, determine the percentage error in true costs incurred for incorrect setup costs used of $14.40 and $25.90, and incorrect holding cost penalties used of 0.144 and 0.259.

6.18 Project report and implementation

We are now ready to prepare a project report. Given the favourable net savings projected, the report recommends extending the preliminary study to all products. Study now our version of the project report in Appendix 2. Note again its format.

The project report also touches on implementation, in particular the fact that the effects of the new policy will occur gradually, as more and more of the product stocks fall within the new range of the Qs recommended by the policy.

Human factors become important considerations that need to enter the planning for implementation and the transition itself. Chapter 8 discusses these aspects in more detail.

6.19 Deriving a solution to the model

The optimal solution for the EOQ model was derived by calculus, but we could have used trial and error. For many mathematical models more powerful approaches are needed. We briefly review the common approaches used in MS/OR.

Enumeration

If the number of alternative courses of action is relatively small, say in the tens rather than the thousands, and the computational effort to evaluate each alternative is relatively minor, like in the LOD case, then finding the optimal solution by simply evaluating the performance measure for each alternative course of action or each discrete value of the decision variable may be simple and fast. The best solution is the one which achieves the best value of the performance measure — a minimum or a maximum value, whichever corresponds to the objective.

Enumeration is commonly used if the problem deals with a one-off situation. Rather than spending considerable resources in time and funds to develop a more elegant and efficient solution approach, enumeration may be the cheapest way to find the best alternative.

Search methods

If the performance measure to be optimized is in the form of an objective function in one or several decision variables, various search methods may reduce the computational effort to find the optimal solution. Several successful search methods are based on the idea of eliminating successively more and more of the solution space which has been identified as not containing the optimal solution until an arbitrarily small interval remains which will contain the optimal solution. For this reason they are called interval elimination methods. Some of the more famous interval elimination methods developed by mathematicians have been given colourful names, like 'golden section search'. Interval elimination methods, however, only work if the objective function is well behaved. If the objective function contains only one decision variable, this implies that the function is either U-shaped or unimodal, i.e. has only one single maximum (for a maximization problem) or one single minimum (for a minimization problem), as depicted in Figure 6-8 further on in this section.

Algorithmic solution methods

The most powerful solution methods are based on an **algorithm**. This is a set of logical and mathematical operations performed repeatedly in a specific sequence. Each repetition of the rules is called an **iteration**. To start off the algorithm, an initial solution has to be supplied. At the first iteration, the incoming solution is improved upon, using the rules of the algorithm. The new solution so generated becomes the incoming solution for the next iteration. This process is repeated until certain conditions — referred to as **stopping rules** — are satisfied. These stopping rules either indicate that the optimal solution has been found, or that no feasible solution can be identified (if the initial solution supplied was also not feasible), or that a certain maximum number of iterations has been reached or a maximum amount of computer time has been exceeded. Most search methods are based on some algorithm. Figure 6-7 summarizes this approach as a flow diagram.

To be a practical solution method, an algorithm has to meet four properties:

1. Each successive solution has to be an improvement over the preceding one.
2. Successive solutions have to converge, i.e. get closer and closer to the optimal solution.
3. Convergence arbitrarily close to the optimal solution should occur in a reasonable number of iterations.
4. The computation effort at each iteration has to be sufficiently small to remain economically acceptable.

For practically all real-life problems, the computations invariably have to be performed by computer. Many of the general-purpose MS/OR techniques, such as linear programming (discussed in Chapter 14), use algorithms for finding the optimal solution. Becoming thoroughly familiar with these algorithms is usually the major part of most MS/OR university curricula.

Classical methods of calculus

In some instances, classical methods of mathematics, in particular differential

Figure 6-7   General flow diagram for an algorithm.

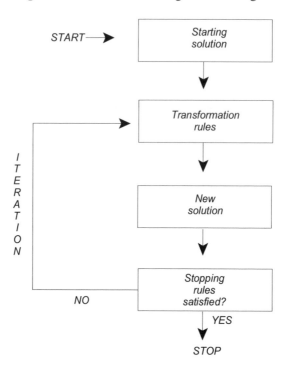

calculus, can be used for finding the optimal solution. This is the case for problems involving an objective function with one or two decision variables that can assume any real-valued number, as is the case for the EOQ. The basic idea can easily be grasped graphically. Consider the U-shaped function $f(x)$ in the variable x of Figure 6-8. It first decreases as x increases from a to b and then increases as x increases further. Additional insight is gained by studying how the slope of the function changes as x increases. The slope of the function at any point $x = p$ is simply given by the tangent to the function at the point p. Observe that to the left of b, the tangent is downward sloping, i.e. its slope is negative, while to the right b it is upward sloping, i.e. its slope is positive. As x increases from a, the slope becomes less and less negative, at b itself it is horizontal or 0, and as x moves away from b it becomes more and more positive. The minimum of $f(x)$ is assumed at b, where the slope is 0. (Note, however, that there may be other points where the slope of the function is zero and where no minimum or maximum occurs!)

The **derivative** of $f(x)$ measures the slope. It is denoted by $df(x)/dx$ or simply by $f'(x)$. To determine the minimum, we find the derivative $f'(x)$ and determine the value of x_0 for which $f'(x) = 0$. (We also check that $f(x_0)$ is a minimum by verifying that for a value of x just less than x_0 the derivative is negative, while for a value of x just larger than x_0 it is positive.)

Figure 6-8 A function and its derivative.

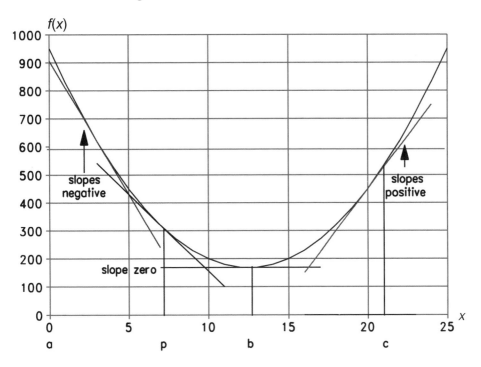

The analogous reasoning can be used for finding the maximum of a function that has the shape of an upside down U. We leave it up to you to work out the details.

Heuristic solution methods

Some models are of such a degree of complexity, or computationally so intractable, that it is impossible to find the optimal solution with the computational means currently available. There are also instances where it is possible to find the optimal solution, but the potential benefits do not justify the computational effort needed. Heuristic solution methods may then be the only practical alternative.

Heuristic methods use the human mind's ingenuity, creativity, intuition, and experience to find good solutions or to improve on an existing solution. It is a process of learning how the objective function responds to various solution strategies and then of using the insight gained to devise or discover better solution rules. Sometimes it may be possible to find explanations of why the rules are successful for finding a good or even the best solution. At other times, they may be adopted simply because trials show that they work.

We all use heuristic problem solving in our daily lives. For example, assume you want to travel from point A to point B. You know that in general the shortest way to reach your destination is travelling on a route that is as close to a straight line as possible. However, experience also tell you that travel through the centre of town is slow. Making a detour around it, maybe using the one-way system, is faster, although the distance is longer. You may also discover side streets with little traffic which allow you to travel at the speed limit, rather than be slowed down.

When packing boxes of various sizes into a container you will discover after some trials that unless you put the biggest boxes into the container first you may not be able to fit them in later on. So the insight gained is that it is best to put the biggest boxes into the containers first, and then fill the space with smaller ones.

Although it may be possible sometimes to prove that a given heuristic solution method finds the optimal solution, this cannot be guaranteed. The analyst may have to be satisfied with finding a good, rather than optimal, solution. The famous American Nobel Laureate for Economics, Herbert Simon, coined the word '**satisficing**' for this. So, heuristic solution methods are usually associated with satisficing, rather than optimizing.

Simulation

As we have seen in Chapter 3, the behaviour of a system can be accurately described by how the state of the system changes over time. Keeping a detailed record of these state changes and extracting statistics about the average value of critical variables can give useful information about the performance of the system in response to different operating policies. Collecting such data from the observation of the 'real' system may not be possible for a number of reasons — it may be too costly or too time-consuming, or the system may not exist yet, etc. So we imitate, step by step, how the system would behave over time. This can be done with paper and pencil, but is usually more efficient by computer. Such an imitation is called **simulation**. For complex dynamic systems, particularly if they also involve random aspects, simulation may be the only way to collect information about how the system performs under various policies. Again, as for heuristic problem solving, all the analyst can expect is to be able to identify good policies, rather than the optimal one.

Simulation is one of the more important tools for the MS/OR analyst. It is not only used for identifying good, if not optimal solutions, but it is the ideal vehicle for verifying how well the solution derived by other methods is likely to perform in the real world, as well as demonstrating the solution to the problem owners and problem users.

Simulation is discussed in detail in Chapters 17 and Sections 18.6 and 18.7.

6.20 Reflections on the hard OR methodology

We have seen that Phase 1 of the hard OR methodology ends with a definition of a relevant system for the problem of interest. Phase 2 takes that system and translates it into a mathematical model. It then applies mathematical methods to find a 'solution', usually one that optimizes some measure of performance. Some of the methods used are traditional, such as calculus, while others have been specifically developed for this purpose, such as linear programming, dynamic programming, various search techniques, simulation, and so on. Often the solution is found by trial and error with the help of a spreadsheet.

It is revealing to view this process as a linked sequence of systems, where the output of one becomes the input into the next. This is depicted in Figure 6-9.

Figure 6-9 Structure diagram for hard OR.

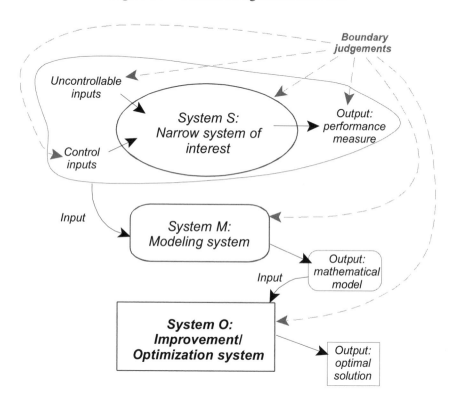

Phase 1 develops the narrow system of interest, S. The process of building a mathematical model can itself be viewed as a system — a **modelling system**, M. It uses as input system S, and then translates the transformation in S into mathematical expressions — a model. This is its output. That model in turn becomes the input into an **improvement/optimizing system**, O. System O manipulates the mathematical model by exploring the model's solution space, often in view of finding improvements in the performance outputs of system S. This manipulation could involve the use of sophisticated techniques, particularly if the aim is to find the best or optimal control inputs to system S that optimize its performance level. Note how boundary judgements affect all aspects.

6.21 Chapter highlights

- The hard OR methodology is an iterative process that covers three well-defined phases: problem formulation, mathematical modelling, and solution implementation, each consisting of several steps, with forward and backward linkages.
- Phase 1 takes the form of either a complete problem formulation or a problem scoping study.
- Problem scoping usually leads to a project proposal that makes a recommendation as to whether, and if so, how to proceed.
- Phase 1 may produce a complete definition of the relevant system, e.g. in the form of an influence diagram, the identification of a typical known system structure to be fleshed out in the problem modelling phase, or only a low-resolution description, delineating the boundaries of the relevant system, e.g. in the form of a high-level structure diagram. Boundary choices must be critically evaluated for their implications.
- A mathematical model expresses the system relationships in quantitative form. By manipulating the inputs (both controllable and uncontrollable) it is possible to explore the solution space of the system and often find the solution that achieves the best value of the performance measure.
- By necessity, mathematical models are always approximations to the 'real thing', not the 'real thing' itself. They may imply further boundary judgements.
- Its final version is usually not derived in a single pass, but is the result of an iterative process of reformulation and enrichment. This process terminates when the analyst is satisfied that the model approximates and captures most significant relationships of the real situation and that it will produce answers that are insightful, relevant, and appropriate for decision making. The analyst must find a suitable compromise between simplicity and completeness.
- For problems that involve finding an optimal solution, a number of often powerful techniques, methods, and approaches have been developed. Familiarity with them forms a core aspect of training in hard OR.
- Sensitivity analysis explores how the optimal value of the performance measure responds to changes in uncontrollable inputs, while error analysis establishes the loss in true benefits incurred if a solution based on erroneous uncontrollable inputs is used (instead of the truly optimal solution). It helps establish how robust the model and its solution are.
- Verification of the model and its input data and validation of both the model and the modelling approach are important features for establishing the credibility of a model and the sponsor's and user's confidence in its results.
- The project report is the document that allows the problem owner to decide if the findings should be implemented. It should disclose both the strengths and the weaknesses of the model and its solution.
- Concern for implementation is an ongoing process from the start of a project.
- The hard OR methodology can be viewed as a sequence of linked systems: a formulation system, a modelling system, and an improvement system.

Exercises

1. Read the Champignons Galore Situation Summary in the Appendix to Chapter 9, pages 245–250. That case is used there as an exercise in identifying various types of costs. Here we want to use it for the purpose of identifying a suitable system, etc.
   (a) Draw a high-level system structure diagram, similar to Figure 6-3, delineating the boundaries of the relevant system.
   (b) Discuss the boundary judgements implied by your boundary choices.
   (c) List stakeholders and the six problem elements.
   (d) Draw an influence diagram for computing the annual cost as a function of the number of flushes per growing/harvesting cycle.
   (e) Assume that you have been asked to do a scoping study and prepare a project proposal for finding the optimal policy for the number of flushes. The problem can be solved without any special MS/OR techniques. Assume that at the time you write the project proposal no cost data, nor yield and picking rate data, have been collected yet. Such collection is therefore part of undertaking the project. Also, based on the situation summary no estimates of potential savings can be derived.

2. Consider the 'Sawmill as a profit-maximizing system' in Section 3.6 of Chapter 3.
   (a) Identify the stakeholders of the problem.
   (b) List the six problem elements.
   (c) Draw a high-level diagram, similar to Figure 6-3, showing the boundary of the relevant system and its major subsystems.
   (d) Discuss the boundary judgements implied by your boundary choices.

3. Consider the machine adjustment problem described in exercise 5 of Chapter 4. The objective is to find the time between adjustments or the number of adjustments per hour so as to maximize the hourly net profit contribution.
   (a) Use the influence diagram developed in exercise 7 of Chapter 5 to formulate a mathematical model. Build it up step by step by finding the expression corresponding to each state variable and output variable in the influence diagram. Once completed, combine them into a single expression which shows the hourly net profit contribution as a function of the decision variable. You will need the following additional information to find the relationship between defectives produced and machine running time. Lim makes 5 test runs of one hour each, recording the cumulative number of defectives produced at regular intervals. Prior to each run the machine was properly adjusted. The number of defectives were:

	Test run	1	2	3	4	5
Machine	6 minutes	0	0	1	0	0
run	12 minutes	1	1	2	0	0
time	24 minutes	2	3	3	1	1
	36 minutes	5	5	5	4	2
	48 minutes	8	7	9	7	4
	60 minutes	11	11	13	12	8

   (b) Develop a spreadsheet with a row for each system and output variable and columns for machine adjustments after every 12, 18, 24, 36, 48, and 60 minutes (which includes the adjustment time). Plot the net profit as a function of the time between adjustments. Indicate the range where the optimal solution seems to lie.
   (c) By trial and error or systematic search, find the time between adjustments that maximizes the net profit contribution per hour. In the spreadsheet simply use one of

the columns for these trials, such as, the 60-minute column. Determine this time accurate to one decimal place. Determine the loss in net profit for rounding the optimal time to a convenient number, such as a multiple of 5 minutes.

(d) List all major approximations made for the model in (c). How reasonable are they?

4. ELMO, a manufacturer of electric motors, has just purchased a machine tool for winding coils of electric motors. Initial trials with the machine indicate that the number of rejects produced varies with the running speed of the machine. The results of the six trials for various speed settings are as follows:

machine speed	30	40	50	60	70	80	90 coils/hr
trial 1	1	2	3	5	6	8	11 rejects
2	0	1	4	6	7	9	10 rejects
3	1	3	4	4	5	7	9 rejects
4	2	3	2	4	5	7	11 rejects
5	2	1	2	4	7	10	10 rejects
6	1	2	3	5	6	7	10 rejects

Rejects have to be scrapped. The material cost of each coil is €2.60. The machine operator is paid at a rate of €22/hour. It costs €6 to operate the machine for one hour. 10,000 good coils have to be produced for a given type of motor. The total cost of producing this batch is used as the performance measure for setting the machine speed. Note that to end up with 10,000 good coils more than 10,000 coils will have to be wound. The size of the batch that needs to be scheduled is equal to $10,000/(1 - \text{fraction of rejects})$. The fraction of rejects is a function of the machine speed.

(a) Develop an influence diagram showing the relationship between the running speed of the machine and the total cost of producing the batch of 10,000 coils.

(b) What boundary judgement are implied by the system defined in (a)?

(c) Use that influence diagram to derive mathematical expressions for each system variable and the performance measure of total costs. Combine these expressions into a single expression for total costs as a function of the machine speed setting. Does that model make additional boundary judgements? If so, what are they? (Note such further assumptions may be in the form of simplifications.)

(d) Develop a table or a spreadsheet containing one row for each variable and one for the total cost and columns for the running speeds listed above. Graph the results and identify the range in which the lowest cost is likely to lie. Use the table to determine the best speed setting.

5. (a) Develop a spreadsheet to compute the total annual cost corresponding to expression (6-1) in the text for values of $Q = 24, 32, 40, 48, 56, 64, 72$, using the data listed on page 142. Find the optimal solution to the nearest integer value by trial and error.

(b) Develop a spreadsheet to reproduce the content of Figure 6-5, using the same data.

6. One of the products in the LOD is only sold in multiples of 4 drums. A total of 120 orders were received last year as follows:

Order size	4	8	12	16	20
Number of orders	70	32	11	5	2

They were evenly spread over the entire year, with very few days having more than one order. The sales pattern for the coming year is expected to be fairly similar. The combined mixing and filling setup cost is $15. The product handling cost is $1/drum for orders supplied from stock, and $0.40/drum for orders met by a special production run. Each drum has a value of $400. The stock holding cost is $0.18/$1/year. (It is suggested that you develop a spreadsheet similar to Figure 6-5.)

(a) Assume that all orders of more than 8 drums are met by a special production run. What is the optimal inventory replenishment size, its total annual cost, and the overall total annual cost for meeting the entire demand?

(b) Find the combined optimal policy for meeting customer demand, i.e. an optimal cutoff point for special production runs and an optimal stock replenishment policy. What is the minimum cost associated with the optimal policy?

7. Consider the following data for another LOD product: product value $180/ drum, production setup cost $12/setup, product handling cost $1.50/drum via storage, $0.30/drum via special production run, investment holding cost 25% on the value invested per year; and the demand distribution as follows over a period of one year covering 250 working days:

demand	0	2	4	6	8	12	16	20	24	32
days	82	65	32	23	17	10	8	5	4	4

(a) Using the EOQ model, to find the optimal stock replenishment size if the cutoff point for direct replenishments is set at 12 drums. Note that the demand is not given as a frequency distribution by customer order size, but by total demand for each day. The implication is that special production runs are made to cover all customer orders for a given day, rather than individual customer orders. (This is the extension briefly mentioned in Section 6.8.)

(b) Develop a spreadsheet similar to Figure 6-5 for finding the joint optimal values for the stock replenishment size and the special production run cutoff point.

8. A liquid is mixed in a mixing vessel and then packed into one-litre cans on an automatic filling machine. It takes the mixing technician 2 hours to mix the liquid, regardless of the amount to be mixed. The cost of the ingredients used is £1.60/litre. Two machine operators take 30 minutes to prepare the machine for a filling run. Cans are filled at a rate of 60/minute. Both machine operators have to be present while the machine is filling cans. The cost of a can, including its label, is £0.15. The labour cost for the technician and the machine operators, including the cost of fringe benefits earned, amounts to £18 per hour worked. The firm aims for a rate of return on its investments of 24% per year.

(a) Determine the cost of preparing a batch of 3600 cans for the product in question.

(b) The annual demand for that particular product is 180,000 cans. Use the EOQ formulas to find the optimal batch size and its relevant total annual cost.

(c) The cans are packed into cartons of 48 cans each. Cartons are stored on pallets. Each pallet holds 24 cartons. The practice is to always produce a batch which results in a multiple of full pallets, i.e. a multiple of 24 times 48 cans. If this practice is to be continued, what batch size would you recommend as best in terms of total costs?

9. Last year, Q-Imports sold 750 sets of stainless steel cutlery, imported from Germany at a cost of £60 per set, including airfreight. The firm sells the sets to retailers at £96. Sales occur at a fairly steady even rate throughout the year. The sets were imported in two shipments, the first of 250, the second of 500. For each shipment, the firm incurs clericalcosts, bank charges, and custom agent clearing charges, totalling £200. Q-imports usually finances most of its purchases by bank overdrafts. The current overdraft rate is 18% per year. There are also insurance costs for storing goods in inventory amounting to 2% of the value of the goods. The manager of Q-Imports expects that sales this coming year will be about 1/3 higher than last year's. He therefore plans to place two orders of 500 sets each.

(a) What would be the total annual cost of the proposed ordering policy?

(b) Could he do better? Why and how?

10. A-Electronics sells about 2000 of its new sim chips per month at a price of $35/chip. The production cost are $25/chip. The current policy is to replace any chips that fail within the first six months of installation. The dealer doing the replacement also gets $10 to cover the labour cost for the replacement. The competition has recently increased its guarantee period from 6 to 9 months. A-Electronics is now under pressure to follow suit or even go to a 12-months guarantee period. The engineering department has collected extensive data on replacements of chips, both under guarantee and after the guarantee period. They show the following picture, where time refers to the number of months after the initial installation of the chip:

Time	3	4	5	6	7	8	9	10	11
Replacements	0	1	2	2	5	5	6	6	9

Time	12	13	14	15	16	17	18	
Replacements	9	13	14	18	22	23	27	per 1000 chips

(a) Management would like to know the increase in annual costs of extending the guarantee period from six months to 9, 12, 15, or 18 months. You need to find a functional relationship between the time and the number of replacements. What approximations, assumptions or boundary judgements do you make?

(b) By how much would monthly sales have to increase to recover the increase in guarantee costs?

Answer both questions by building an appropriate spreadsheet.

11. A manufacturer assembles pumps from parts purchased from subcontractors. For a particular type of pump, it takes a technician 8 hours to set up the assembly line. His pay, including all fringe benefits, is £24/hour. Other production setup costs, such as picking up the required number of parts from subcontractors, amount to £80. Once the technician has set up the assembly line, four people perform the actual assembly of the pumps. They can assemble 24 pumps per day. The value of the assembled pump, including all parts and labour costs, is £216. The firm estimates that its stock holding cost is 25% per year on the average stock investment. The annual demand for that pump is about 1250. The replenishment policy used is to start a new assembly run of Q pumps whenever the stock for that pump has been depleted. Hence the technician will prepare a new assembly run one or two days prior to the time the inventory for that pump has been sold. Once assembly has been started, each day's production of 24 pumps is added to the inventory of that pump. These pumps are then available for sale. In other words, during production, some of the pumps are sold. As a result, once a batch of size Q has been completed, fewer than Q pumps still remain in stock. (Note that this situation is slightly different from the EOQ model developed in this chapter, where the entire batch Q is added to stock as a single lot.)

(a) Adapt the influence diagram of Figure 6-4 for this situation. Note that there is no special production run option, so that whole section is not relevant. On the other hand, the section dealing with the average inventory investment is now more complex and needs more detail.

(b) Using this influence diagram, develop a set of expressions that will ultimately culminate in a total relevant annual replenishment and inventory cost.

(c) List the approximations that you made to develop the total cost expression.

(d) Using enumeration by spreadsheet, find the optimal replenishment size and its relevant annual cost.

The following computational exercises on sensitivity and error analysis are most conveniently done using the spreadsheets developed for the original exercises above.

12. For the example used in Figure 6-5, explore the effect on the optimal *EOQ* and its cost for the following changes in input parameters:
   (a) Changes in the replenishment setup cost from $18 to $12, 24, and 36.
   (b) Changes in the investment holding cost from 18% to 12%, 24%, and 30%.

13. For the optimal solution to the machine adjustment problem derived in exercise 3 above perform the following sensitivity analysis:
   (a) Changes in the net selling price of –10%, –20%, and +25%.
   (b) Changes in the fraction of reworkable defectives from 0.5 to 0.4, 0.6, and 0.75.
   (c) Changes in the slope of the defectives function from the 10 to 8, 6, and 12/hour.

14. For the optimal solution to the ELMO coil production problem in exercise 4 above do the following sensitivity analysis:
   (a) Changes in the size of the order from 10,000 to 5,000, 20,000, and 40,000.
   (b) Changes in the rate of defectives per hour, which currently runs at $0.0125 \times$ (running speed of the machine)^2, to 0.0015, and $0.001 \times$ (running speed)^2.

15. For the example in Figure 6-5, perform error analysis for the following cases:
   (a) A true replenishment setup cost of $12 and $24, rather than the $18 used.
   (b) A true investment-holding cost of 12% and 24%, rather than the 18% used.
   (c) The table of errors for the EOQ in Section 6.17 is not only valid for errors in the annual demand, but for errors in the replenishment setup costs or the ratio of replenishment setup costs and investment holding cost. Hence estimate the approximate effect of the following errors:
   – an error of –80%, –20%, +50%, and +100% in the setup cost;
   – true setup costs and investment holding cost penalties of [$12 and 12%], [$15 and 25%], and [$24 and 15%].

16. For the machine adjustment problem of exercise 3 above, perform the following type of error analysis (note that the results of exercise 2 above will be useful):
   (a) An error in the net selling price of –20%.
   (b) An error in the rate of defectives that can be reworked of +25%, –33.33%.
   (c) An error in the slope of the function for the rate of defectives of +25%, –16.67%.

17. For the ELMO coil production problem of exercise 4 above, perform the following type of error analysis (note that the results of exercise 4 above will be useful):
   (a) A true size of the order of 20,000 rather than 10,000.
   (b) A true coefficient for the rate of defectives of 0.001 rather than 0.00125.

18. Discuss the following apparent contradiction: If at the start of an MS/OR project all costs and potential benefits were known accurately, the project would not get off the ground. However, if the total costs and potential benefits can only be ascertained with some confidence after the model has been tested for performance, but prior to its implementation, the correct decision may be to proceed with implementation. What implications does this have for evaluating costs and benefits of MS/OR projects?

19. Based on your analysis of the ELMO case in exercise 4 and 17 above, as well as additional analysis as to the potential savings of the best solution over the current policy, write a short project report, following the format in Appendix 2.

20. What information/insights is the (a) manager or decision maker, and (b) the problem analyst looking for in sensitivity and error analysis? Say it in your own words.

21. Why is establishing internal and external validity important for (a) the decision maker/user of the solution, and (b) the analyst of the problem.

Appendix 1

PROJECT PROPOSAL
PRODUCTION/INVENTORY CONTROL STUDY
LUBRICATION OIL DIVISION, SANDPOINT REFINERY

Table of Contents

1. INTRODUCTORY STATEMENT

In the middle of March, Mr Black, Manager of the LOD, approached the Management Science Group at the Company's Headquarters with a request to study the LOD production/inventory operations of packaged goods and make recommendations concerning appropriate stock levels. It is my understanding that this request is a follow-up on remarks in the Company's internal auditors' report about the current level of investments in stocks at the LOD. In particular, the auditors pointed out that the LOD's stock turnover of packaged goods was well below the Company's target of 24 times per year, resulting in a level of funds tied up in packaged goods judged as excessive.

I arranged for a visit to the LOD's production and warehousing facilities at Sandpoint on March 27 and 28, during which I had extensive discussions with Mr Black, Mary Clarke, the stock control clerk, Bill Quick, the data processing supervisor, and all four operations supervisors. I also consulted with the Cost Control Department at Headquarters. The following report outlines my recommendations for a preliminary study, briefly motivates and describes the proposed analysis, and lists the resources required and a time-table for undertaking the study.

2. EXECUTIVE SUMMARY OF RECOMMENDATIONS

It is recommended that the Company's Management Science Group undertakes a preliminary study of the production/inventory operations. The study would develop a model for finding optimal stock replenishment sizes as well as the minimum size when it becomes more economical to meet individual customer orders by a separate mixing and filling run. Based on this model, reliable estimates of the potential savings in operating costs can be computed with the aim of establishing whether a full-scale investigation can be justified. The results of the study would be available within 4 weeks and the internal charge to the LOD would amount to $6,400.

3. STATEMENT OF THE PROBLEM SITUATION

The auditors' report states that the LOD's stock turnover rate over the last two years averaged 12 times per year and hence is well below the company's target rate of 24. As a result, they conclude that the amount of funds tied up in stocks is about twice as high as it should be.

What are the cost implications of a given stock turnover rate? For the current customer delivery policy and production lead time, the average amount of funds tied up in

page 2

stocks and hence the cost of carrying this investment for any given product, is proportional to the size of its stock replenishment batches. On the other hand, the annual production setup cost is inversely proportional to the size of replenishment batches. Any reduction in average stock levels and the annual cost of carrying the corresponding investment can therefore only be achieved by increasing the annual production setup cost. It can easily be shown that there is a best size for each replenishment batch for which the sum of these two costs is at its lowest possible level. This also implies a best turnover rate for each product, which is likely to be different from product to product. Only by coincidence will the average turnover rate over all products be equal to the target rate of 24. A target turnover rate of 24 may thus not achieve the lowest total cost for the LOD operations.

If the objective is to reduce the total investment in inventories, it is preferable to set an upper limit of the total amount, rather than a target turnover rate. The models can then be used for finding the least expensive policy to stay within this limit. This recognizes the fact that the best turnover rate is different from product to product.

The current customer delivery policy offers the possibility of scheduling special production runs for direct delivery to customers, with the goods by-passing the inventory stage. They will then only be handled once, rather than twice. This is currently done for those products where large customer orders occur frequently. A decrease in the cutoff point for which customer orders are met by special production runs reduces the fraction of the total demand satisfied from inventories. This in turn will reduce the best replenishment size and hence the average investment in stocks, and decrease product handling costs, but increase the annual number of setups incurred for special production runs and hence the annual setup cost. It will also affect the best stock turnover ratio for the portion of the total demand met from stock.

The best policy is the one which sets a cutoff point for special production runs and a stock replenishment batch size that minimizes the sum of all relevant costs.

Approximate calculations indicate that the annual reduction in operating costs varies from $32 to over $250, depending on the product. This extrapolates to at least $90,000 per year over all products. The cost of a full-scale study would amount to about $48,000, based on about 120 person days at the internal charge-out rate of $400/day.

However, rather than embark on a full-scale study right away, it is advisable to undertake first a preliminary analysis. Its aim is to establish beyond doubt if the potential savings of a full-scale study are justified by the cost of such a study. The reasons for such a recommendation are that (1) at this stage it is difficult to give any reliable estimates of the potential savings that could be achieved without substantial additional effort and collection of data, and (2) the cost of extending the analysis to all products is roughly proportional to the number of products. Therefore, most of the work undertaken for the preliminary study can be carried forward to the full-scale study.

If the findings confirm that all further costs for a full-scale study can be recovered within the first year of changing over to the new policy, i.e. within the payback period required for such projects by the Company, a recommendation and timetable for such a study will be submitted for approval.

4. BRIEF DESCRIPTION OF PROPOSED ANALYSIS

The preliminary analysis will be done for a random sample of products. Its results will be extrapolated to all products carried by the LOD. The following major steps are involved:

page 3

(a) **Development of model:** After further on-site study, a model for the total annual relevant cost, suitable for use on all products carried by the LOD, will be developed. It will be used for determining the best combination of stock replenishments and cutoff point for special production runs for each product. The objective is to minimize the total annual operating costs. The model will be in the form of a computer spreadsheet.

(b) **Sample selection and data collection**: With a view to increasing the accuracy of potential savings estimates for the new policy, products will be grouped according to annual sales and a representative sample selected from each, making up about 5% of all products. Demand and cost data will be estimated for all products in the sample using readily available data from the LOD data base of customer orders and costing data from the Cost Control Department.

(c) **Estimation of total saving:** The total annual operating cost for the best policy will be determined individually for each product in the sample. These costs will be extrapolated for each product group and finally to the entire product line. This extrapolation is an estimate of the total annual cost of using the best policy for all products. This estimate will be compared with the annual costs incurred for the current policy. The difference represents the potential annual savings. No change in the expected office costs of running the new policy is expected.

(d) **Estimation of further expenses for a full-scale study**: The expense in terms of internal employee charge-out rates, materials, and computer running costs for undertaking a full-scale study will be estimated.

(e) **Forming of recommendations and preparation of project report**: The recommendation will state whether a full-scale study should be undertaken, based on the normal company criterion that all expenses for such a study must be recovered by the savings generated within one year of implementation of the recommendations. If appropriate, the project report will also present a detailed budget of resources needed and a timetable for undertaking the full-scale study.

5. RESOURCES REQUIRED AND TIMETABLE

Task	Analyst time	Other staff time	Elapse time
Model development	2 days	1 day (LOD staff)	2 days
Sampling design	1 days	2 days (LOD staff)	4 days
Data collection	4 days	3 days (cost control) 3 days (LOD staff)	8 days
Savings estimates	2 days	1 day (cost control) 2 days (LOD staff)	4 days
Writing recommendations	3 days		4 days
Totals	12 days	4 days (cost control) 8 days (LOD staff)	22 days

Chargeable costs: 12 days at $400/day   **$4,800**

Date: April 11, 200X   Project analyst: H. G. Daellenbach
Management Science Group

Appendix 2

PROJECT REPORT

PRODUCTION/INVENTORY CONTROL FOR PACKAGED GOODS AT THE LUBRICATION OIL DIVISION, SANDPOINT REFINERY

Table of Contents

1. INTRODUCTORY STATEMENT

This report contains the findings of a preliminary study covering the production/inventory control operations for packaged goods in the LOD warehouse at Sandpoint Refinery. Mr Black, Manager of the LOD, approved this study on April 18, on the basis of the project proposal submitted to him by the Management Science Group on April 11. We undertook the preliminary study during the period from May 27 to July 5.

The aim of the study was (1) to develop a mathematical model for finding the best production and stock replenishment policy which minimizes the sum of all costs affected by the choice of policy, and (2) to estimate the potential savings in operating costs that can be achieved by using such a policy for all products.

2. EXECUTIVE SUMMARY OF FINDINGS AND RECOMMENDATIONS

The following major findings were made:

(a) Implementation of the policy proposed in this report for the entire product line of the LOD is estimated to result in annual savings of operating and investment costs of over $90,000. It will increase the average stock turnover to about 32 times per year.

(b) The additional cost for developing the necessary computer software for implementing the policy and assuring its continued updating, and for the actual implementation of the policy, amounts to about $32,000 at internal charging rates.

(c) The new policy could be fully implemented within 14 weeks.

In view of this highly favourable ratio of savings to costs, it is recommended that the LOD immediately proceeds with implementing the proposed model.

3. STATEMENT OF THE PROBLEM

The current production and stock replenishment policy for packaged goods followed by the LOD distinguishes between two groups of products: group 1 includes only high-volume products with frequent large customer orders, and group 2 includes all other products. Group 1 currently covers 78 products (all packaged in drums of 200 litres),

page 2

while group 2 covers the remaining 726 products. Each group accounts for about 50% of the total dollar throughput of packaged goods. The production and stock replenishment policy is characterized as follows:

1. Group 1: any customer order equal to or larger than a given cutoff point is supplied by scheduling a special production run, while any customer orders below the cutoff point are met from stock. Stock is replenished periodically. Currently, the cutoff point for all products is 12 drums, while the stock replenishment size varies from product to product and covers between 2 to 6 weeks of customer orders supplied from stock.

2. Group 2: all customers orders are supplied from stock. Stock replenishments vary in size with the sales volume and cover 3 and 12 weeks of sales.

Our analysis indicates that, in principle, the policy followed for group 1 products can be applied to all products: drums as well as products packaged in other containers. Furthermore, the choice of the best cutoff point depends not only on the customer order pattern, but also on the various production and warehousing costs.

Rather than classifying products arbitrarily into these two groups, we decided, after discussions with Mr Black and other LOD staff, to build a model that allows all products to follow the group 1 policy, but with individually determined cutoff points and stock replenishment sizes. If the cutoff point for a product is set at a level larger than the largest customer order likely to be received, the policy for that product corresponds to the entire demand being supplied from stock.

Although some products exhibit a mild seasonal pattern, the model is based on the premise that the average demand remains constant over the year. The effect of this simplification is negligible. To adjust for trend, the optimal policy should be updated annually.

As a result of opting for a uniform policy for all products, the problem becomes one of developing a model which finds for each product a cutoff point and stock replenishment size so as to minimize the sum of all operating costs affected by these two variables. The relevant costs are (a) the product raw material and production costs, (b) the mixing and filling operation setup costs, (c) the product handling costs, and (d) the cost of holding products in stock, which consists mainly of the cost of funds invested in stocks.

The second aim of the study, namely the estimation of the potential savings that would accrue if the model is applied to all packaged goods, was to be done by extrapolating the results obtained from a sample to all products.

4. MAJOR STEPS OF ANALYSIS

These followed the steps outlined in the project proposal.

(a) **Developing a suitable model:** My initial visits to the LOD on March 27 were followed up by further visits on May 26 and 27. After extensive discussions with Mr Black and his staff we concluded that a model based on the group 1 policy should be used, in principle, for all products. A computer spreadsheet program was developed for finding the best policy. The details of the model and a sample output from the spreadsheet are shown in the Appendices to this report.

(b) **Data collection for the sample of products to be analysed:** In view of the large number of products, the model was applied to a sample of 5%, with the results to be extrapolated to all products. In order to achieve higher accuracy of the estimate, the products were grouped into relatively homogeneous classes. The usual distribution by annual dollar sales volume was applied, with three classes: high, medium, and

page 3

low dollar volume. Since the production setup costs of greases are considerably higher than for oils, a fourth class for all greases was created. The composition of the classes and the subsample sizes is summarized in the top portion of Table 1 below. Products to be analysed were selected by random sampling methods. The customer order pattern for each sample product was extracted from the 200X customer order file, the most recent complete year of customer data available. Figures for all relevant cost factors were supplied by the Cost Control Department or were computed based on rough time trials.

(c) Estimation of total savings: For each product in the sample, the best policy, consisting of the cutoff point for large customer orders and the stock replenishment size, was computed using the spreadsheet developed.

A simple simulation program was written to simulate the performance of the proposed and of the current policy for a given product. This program was used for estimating the total cost difference between the two policies for each product in the sample. This in turn provided all the input required for extrapolating the results obtained to the entirety of all products. The findings are summarized in Table 1.

Table 1   Estimation of potential annual savings.

Class	High volume oils	Medium volume oils	Low volume oils	Greases
Overall:				
Percent of total volume	45%	35%	12%	8%
Number of products	64	205	411	124
Subsample size	20	15	5	4
Ratio (class #/subsample)	3.2	13.67	82.5	31
Per product:				
Average cost difference	$431	$147	$74	$39
Standard deviation	$125	$26	$21	$19
Extrapolation to class:				
Cost difference	$27,584	$30,135	$30,414	$4,836
Standard error	$1,000	$372	$425	$212
Estimate of total cost difference:		$92,969		
Standard error (of total estimate):		$1,168		

5. MAJOR FINDINGS

Table 1 summarizes the results of extrapolating the savings to the entire packaged goods product line carried by the LOD. It shows that implementation of the best policy for each product would generate savings over the current operating costs of over $90,000 per year.

A detailed comparison of the current and proposed best policy indicates the following:

(a) As expected, the best cutoff point differs from product to product. As a rule, it tends to be between 3200 and 4400 litres per order—somewhat higher than the current 2400 (which is equivalent to 12 drums). Hence, a larger proportion of all sales are supplied from stock than is currently the case.

page 4

(b) For most products, the best stock replenishment size is also smaller than the current policy, this in spite of the higher cutoff point.

(c) A consequence of (b) is a substantial reduction in total investments, as well as warehouse space needed. This could well ease the current shortage of easily accessible warehouse space suffered by the LOD.

(d) The average stock turnover associated with the best policy seems to be substantially higher than the company target of 24 times/year. A rough estimate is around 32 times/year.

(e) The proposed best policy is relatively insensitive to reasonable shifts in the total annual demand and in most cost factors, i.e. changes in any of these of up to 25% that occur after implementation of the best policy for a given product will only result in a small reduction in the potential savings. As a consequence, it will in most instances be adequate to update the best policy once each year, unless a given product is subject to major changes.

6. RECOMMENDATIONS FOR IMPLEMENTATION

Implementation of the model for all products will require computationally efficient programs to be developed for finding the best joint values of the cutoff point and stock replenishment. Furthermore, the format currently used for recording customer order data requires substantial data manipulation. Hence considerable time savings can be gained in the future when the control variables are updated if some small additions are made to the existing programs for recording customer orders and storing them in an annual database. Implementation involves therefore mainly staff time, with all other costs being negligible. Table 2 shows the staff time for the various tasks. According to this schedule, the new policies could be in use by the end of October.

Table 2   Staff resources required for full implementation.

Task	(time in days) Analyst	Other staff	Completion
(a) Programs for use of model	12	1 (LOD)	week 4
(b) Alterations to data files	3	30 (EDP)	week 9
(c) Data collection	5	20 (LOD)	week 8
		10 (cost control)	
(d) Computation of policies	5		week 12
(e) Preparation of implementation plan	2	2 (LOD)	week 12
(f) Instruction of users	3	5 (LOD)	week 13
(g) Change-over to new policy	2	2 (LOD)	week 14
(h) Follow-up monitoring	8		week 26
Totals	40	30 (LOD)	
		40 (other)	
Chargeable cost:	80 days at $400/day	$32,000.	

page 5

The estimate of potential annual savings indicates that the cost of full implementation would be recovered by the new policies within less than four months. However, it should be noted that the savings will only rise to their full potential level after a transition period. During this period excess stock levels of those products with lower recommended replenishment sizes will be gradually reduced to their new lower levels, while products with higher recommended replenishment sizes will reach their new levels very quickly. Therefore the savings in investment costs will only become fully realized once the new average levels have been achieved for all products. This may take up to 6 months.

Based on this analysis, I recommend that the model developed is implemented.

Date: July 10, 200X

Project analyst: H.G. Daellenbach, Management Science Group

APPENDIX: SPREADSHEET COMPUTATIONS FOR FINDING OPTIMAL POLICY FOR PRODUCT Y

(Figure 6-5 reproduced here)

APPENDIX ON COMPUTATIONS PERFORMED

(Not shown here in detail.) This appendix gives for each product full details on input parameters used for finding optimal policies and the resulting solution in a table form. It also shows the results of the simulation runs and the cost incurred for the current policy. These form the basis for estimating the potential savings in Table 1. Details on sensitivity analysis performed are also included.

APPENDIX: DETAILED DESCRIPTION OF MODEL

(Not shown here in detail.) This appendix shows an annotated formulation of the total cost function for the $T(Q,L)$-model. It also lists all important assumptions, in particular that there are no warehouse or production facility capacity restrictions. If such a constraint turns out to be binding, once the optimal policies for all products have been computed, suitable adjustments would need to be made. It also refers to the possibility to generate additional savings if the stock level is reviewed whenever a special production run is scheduled for a given product, and topped up at the same time. This would have increased the complexity of the model substantially at only modest further saving. However, no tests were made to confirm this conclusion.

7
Soft Systems Thinking

Coverage follows the material in Jackson [2000], Rosenhead and Mingers [2000] and Ulrich [1996].

In 1960, C.W. Churchman, a pioneer of OR, voiced his serious misgivings about the ever-increasing mathematical bias and narrow focus on optimization of MS/OR. Rather than dealing with important executive-type decision problems, these trends condemned MS/OR to become tools for low-level operational problems. He challenged our MBA class at the University of California to step beyond the shackles of mathematics and address our efforts to the really important problems humanity was facing. His call for a change of heart remained a lonely voice for almost another decade. Stafford Beer, the originator of the **viable systems model**, was the only exception — in fact a precursor. In the 1970s, other voices took up the call: Russel L. Ackoff (University of Pennsylvania), Peter Checkland (University of Lancaster), and Colin Eden (University of Bath) being some of the most prominent ones.

Rather than accept the narrow rationality of economic thought, they recognized that human decision making is far more complex and varied and that it is also governed by other than economic values. Imposing a 'solution' that ignores this simply shifts the problem to a new dimension. They discovered that the process of decision making greatly affects whether or not a 'solution' is accepted. They expanded the narrow quantitative optimization focus to include ideas from other disciplines, primarily critical philosophy, sociology, and organizational behaviour, in order to tackle those important executive-type decision problems. This blurring of boundaries between disciplines can be seen as part of the growing awareness that problems do not respect discipline boundaries, that a narrow economic focus alone is insufficient, and that human striving for quality of life, happiness, aesthetics, equality, and justice is equally valid and legitimate.

This chapter introduces the philosophy and processes of these alternative approaches to decision making. The basic properties and working modes of soft OR are presented first. The next five sections demonstrate three prominent and radically different problem structuring approaches: Checkland's soft system methodology, Eden's strategic option development and analysis (SODA), and Friend and Hickling's strategic choice approach. The final two sections give a brief summary of philosophical and methodological issues in systems thinking.

7.1 Soft system paradigm and working modes

The proponents of soft OR/soft systems approaches correctly point out that the majority of real-life problem situations in business, industry, and government violate many, if not most of the assumptions underlying hard OR approaches. Furthermore, the human aspects inherent in the problem situation and the intervention process used should not be treated as separate unrelated issues. We will now contrast the hard OR properties, listed in Section 6.1, with those of soft systems approaches. (Please review the beginning of Section 6.1 to refresh your memory.)

Properties of PSMs and soft systems approaches

Soft systems approaches were designed to deal with complex problem situations, which are messy, ill-structured, ill-defined, and not independent of people; in other words, where different stakeholders with different world views have different, possibly conflicting perceptions about the problem situation and the major issues, and where there may be no agreement about the appropriate objectives. These methodologies are characterized by:

1. Structuring the issues in a problem situation, rather than narrowly focussed problem solving.

2. Facilitating dialogue between the various stakeholders with the aim of achieving a greater degree of shared perceptions of the problem situation, rather than providing a decision aid to decision makers.

3. Addressing "What" questions first and only then "How" questions, i.e.
   - What is the nature of the issue?
   - What are appropriate objectives, given the various world views of the stakeholders?
   - What is the appropriate definition of the system for the issue considered?
   - Which changes are **systemically desirable** and **culturally feasible**?
   - How are these changes best brought about?

4. Eliciting the resolution of the problem from the stakeholders themselves, rather than from the analyst.

5. Changing the role of the problem solver to one of becoming a facilitator and resource person who relies on the technical subject expertise of the stakeholders.

Note that 'how' questions, i.e. which means are the best for achieving the desired objectives, must ultimately also be addressed by soft systems approaches. But they are often an anti-climax, almost obvious, rather than being centre-stage as in most hard OR projects.

Chronological list of PSMs and soft systems approaches

Here is a list of PSMs and soft systems approaches. Some are full-fledged methodologies, others have more the flavour of techniques, while still others provide a philosophical basis for sound professional practice (developers in parentheses).

1950s	**Gaming** (The Rand Corporation)
1960s	**Metagame analysis** (US Arms Control and Disarmament Agency)
1969	**Strategic choice approach** (J. Friend, A. Hickling)
1969/81	**Strategic assumption surfacing and testing** (R.O. Mason, I.I. Mitroff)
1971	**Social systems design** (C.W. Churchman)
1974	**Social systems sciences**, also as **Interactive Planning** (R.L.Ackoff)
1975	**Soft systems methodology** (P. Checkland)
1979	**Strategic option development and analysis** (C. Eden)
1980	**Hypergame analysis** (P.G. Bennett)
1980	**Robustness analysis** (J. Rosenhead)
1980s/90s	**Theory of constraints** (E. Goldratt)
1983	**Critical systems heuristics** (W. Ulrich)
1990/3	**Drama theory** (P.G. Bennett, M. Bradley, J. Bryant, N. Howard)
1991	**Total systems intervention** (R.L. Flood, M.C. Jackson)
1995	**Multimethodology** (J. Brocklesby, J. Mingers)

Essential characteristics

In contrast to hard OR, it is difficult (possibly even questionable) to capture the characteristics and working mode of all PSMs and soft systems approaches by a single diagram as in Figure 6-1 on page 115. The reason for this is that the majority use quite different, often *ad hoc*, processes that have evolved through practical use and have proven themselves successful for specific types of problem situations.

Several approaches were developed through **action research**, often within a practical consulting context. Some, such as Checkland's soft systems methodology, Churchman's social system design, and Ulrich's critical systems heuristics, are firmly based on philosophical foundations and systems theory. Gaming, metagame and hypergame analysis, and drama theory originate in the ideas of **game theory**, but abandon its rigorous axiomatic foundations and only retain its outer form, i.e. two or more players with opposing views. Other approaches, such as aspects of strategic option and development analysis and drama theory have psychological roots. Total systems intervention and multimethodology are meta-methodologies that help analysts determine which paradigm and method or combination of methods is most suitable for a given problem situation.

They all have one thing in common. While hard OR deals mainly with the 'content' of the problem, giving only limited concern to 'process', soft approaches put equal emphasis on both content and process. At the very start of an intervention, process is used for extracting content and the underlying value systems. The methods seek to attain a reasonably comprehensive view of the issues within their wider context, although they recognize that true comprehensiveness is impossible, nor may it be needed to get to a workable solution or resolution of the problem. The main aim at that stage is to gain a shared understanding and mutual appreciations about values, interests, objectives, choices for action, and the environment, and identify clusters of highly connected aspects. System and environment boundary choices are subjected to critical assessment and evaluation. They also recognize that a resolution of a problem does not necessarily require a full convergence of views, and that a mutual appreciation of views may be sufficient to bring about an acceptable compromise and a commitment for action.

Iteration through or flexible switching between various modes of working are a prime feature. Several methods use software to aid in the structuring process and the exploration of choices. Most require a facilitator with thorough training and experience in the method and, most importantly, good interpersonal and negotiation skills.

Figure 7-1 is a compromise to capture general aspects of the working mode of the majority of methods. In parallel with hard OR, there are three major phases: Formulation of the problem, system and action modelling, and implementation.

Figure 7-1   General working mode of PSMs.

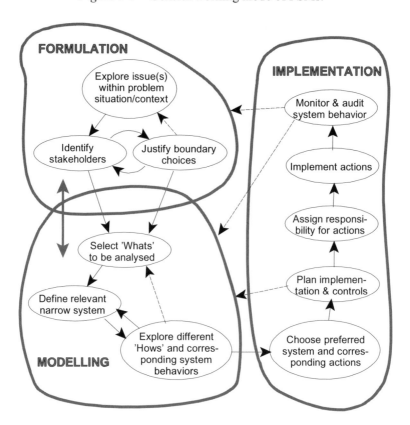

As mentioned above, most approaches are iterative, both between different steps within a phase and between phases, with forward and backward linkages. Different steps may be dealt with at the same time. For several methods, the first two phases have considerable overlap and the working mode may switch from one to the other several times (as indicated by the solid grey double arrow), since different "Whats" may involve different sets of stakeholders and imply different boundary judgements.

Activity: From your reading in Chapters 2–4 and 6, discuss why concern with process is essential when dealing with problem solving in human activity systems.

7.2 Checkland's soft systems methodology

Peter Checkland's soft systems methodology or SSM is without doubt one of the most researched and rigorously based in terms of its theoretical systems premises and underlying philosophical reasoning. Although difficult to judge, it also seems to be the most widely applied, with numerous known applications, many of them documented in the literature. Its track record seems reasonably good. Based on a program of action research at the University of Lancaster started in the late 1960s, the methodology slowly evolved, using itself as a learning system. Although in their 1990 book, Checkland and Scholes profess a more flexible use, its best known version, and the one most easily understood by a novice, is the one presented in Checkland's *Systems Thinking, Systems Practice* [1983/1999]. Any serious student of management science should carefully study this text.

The methodology is a seven-stage process, as shown in Figure 7-2. The brief review below does not intend to give you a full understanding of the methodology, but only a flavour of its process and some of the underlying ideas.

Figure 7-2 A flow diagram of Checkland's SSM.
(Adapted from P. Checkland [1983])

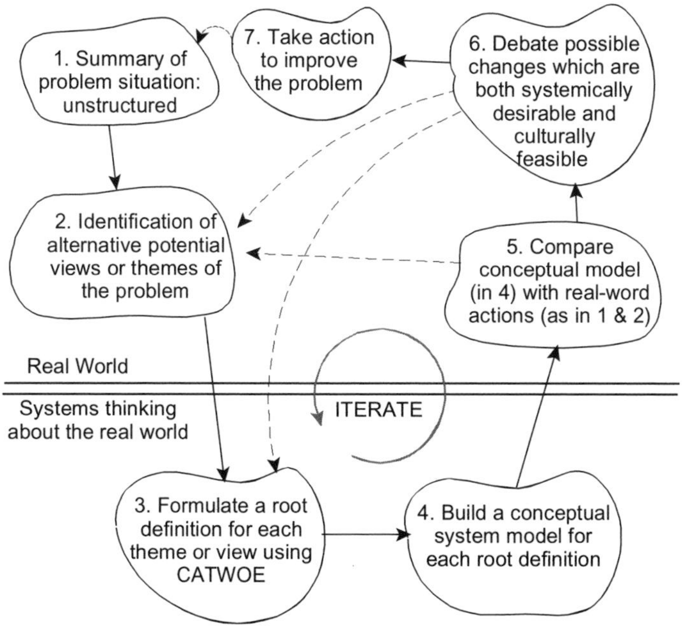

Checkland sees problem solving within a management or social science context as a never-ending learning process. It starts out with one or more people viewing a situation as problematical, with its own history and various stakeholders, all having possibly different perceptions of the situation and different world views. The first two stages —'finding out'— assemble a **situation summary** or a **rich picture** (see Figure 6-2 on page 127 for an example) which should contain elements of structure and process, as well as the 'climate' of the problem situation. This should throw up a variety of alternative and contrasting visions or themes of the problem, each possibly reflecting a different world view or seen from a different angle. The aim is to a gain deeper, broader and more varied understanding of the problem.

The methodology now leaves the real world and enters the abstract world of systems thinking. At stage 3, each vision or theme is expressed as a so-called **root definition** — a succinct unambiguous statement, specifying the owners of the problem (O), the prime system transformation (T) to be achieved by one or more users/actors (A), the owners' world views (W) that makes that transformation a meaningful activity, the customers (C), i.e. the victims and beneficiaries of the system, and the environmental constraints (E) on the system transformation, implying the boundary choices made. (The three sets of stakeholders, O, A, and C, correspond to the definitions given at the beginning of Section 4.2 on page 57.) In the guise of a memory aid, Checkland captures these six elements by the mnemonic letter sequence CATWOE.

Root definitions can either be **issue-based**, placing emphasis on the prime issue(s) the system is supposed to deal with, such as 'resolve conflicts in resource allocations to different uses', or **primary-task** based, specifying the primary tasks that need to be executed, such as 'allocate and efficiently use resources for different uses', or a mixture.

Broadly speaking, the first three stages correspond to the formulation phase of Figure 7-1.

Stage 4 builds so-called **conceptual models** of the **human activity systems** corresponding to each of these alternative root definition. Each conceptual model is expressed in six to twelve activities — usually verbs. Arrows show the logical influence relationships and the precedence sequence between these activities. It is important to keep in mind that Checkland sees human activity systems as intellectual constructs. There is no implication that the various components and relationships necessarily exist, or should exist, in the real world. The models are idealizations of the minimum number of activities needed for the system transformation defined in the root definition to happen. They should only be developed from the corresponding root definition and nothing else. However, Checkland recommends that they are also checked against the principles of formal systems models. In particular, in addition to the 'operating system' that does the system transformation, there may be the need to have a subsystem for monitoring and controlling the performance of the system and another for updating the performance criteria and assessing and evaluating critical inputs, particularly those of a dynamic nature.

Some activities may refer to subsystems which in turn could be decomposed further into submodel of activities at a higher level of resolution.

Stage 5 returns to the real world. It compares the conceptual models with the rich picture, i.e. with what is perceived to exist in the real world. The aim is to develop an **agenda of discussion topics** with the stakeholders for stage 6. So we look for similarities and differences between conceptual models and the real world. The emphasis should be on "Whats", e.g. "What activities are missing or problematic?" rather than in terms of "Hows", such as "How is this activity done in the real world?". There may be several "Hows" to achieve a given "What".

The **debate** at stage 6 should, whenever possible, involve all types of stakeholders. The purpose of this debate is to subject the implications of possibly conflicting world views to the collective judgement of the group in an open and non-defensive manner. The aim is to develop new ideas for change in the real world that are **systemically desirable and culturally feasible**.

As stated above, each root definition is processed through stages 4 to 6 (some in full detail, others in only a cursory manner), depending in whether or not a particular vision promises new insights and new learning. The broken arrows from stages 5 and 6 indicate that the process may, in fact, iterate right back to stage 2 at that point. This iterative process corresponds to the modelling phase in Figure 7-1.

Regardless of whether any changes are implemented or not, each completed cycle of this process will transform the original problem situation into a new one. The new situation should find the stakeholders with a shift in perception and at a higher level of understanding. That new situation may then become the starting point for another learning cycle, i.e. the methodology returns to step 1.

By involving all stakeholders in the process, it is hoped that change or **implementation** (stage 7) is facilitated.

Note that nowhere in this short description of the process was the analyst mentioned. In fact, ideally, there is not one analyst, but the various stakeholders or a subgroup of them do the analysis themselves. If there is an analyst, her or his role is largely one of facilitation and advice about important dos and don'ts at various stages. As the stakeholders become more confident with the SSM process, the facilitating analyst becomes superfluous.

Activity: SSM explores changes which are 'systemically desirable and culturally feasible'. How does that differ from hard OR approaches?

7.3 SSM applied to the NuWave Shoe problem

(Before continuing your reading, we suggest you quickly refresh your memory about Elly Schuhmacher's dilemma in Section 4.8 on pages 67–68.) Rather than developing a rich picture (stage 1), we shall take the cognitive map in Figure 4-6 (page 70) as sufficient to capture the essential aspects of the problem situation and bring forth alternative visions or themes. It also allows us to identify corresponding CATWOE candidates for each vision, as needed for formulating alternative root definitions at stage 3.

Potential stakeholders include: Elly as the problem owner; Elly, the production supervisor, and possibly even the bank loan manager as possible users/actors; and the bank, the retailers, and the production workers as potential customers. Aspects of Elly's world view include: 'reaping the benefits of capturing a major share of potential market is desirable', 'keeping control over firm is desirable', 'operating efficiently in the long-term is desirable', and 'getting enjoyment from the challenge of making NuWave Shoes a success'. The potential market for funky shoes, the retailers' response to prompt payment discounts and a tighter credit policy, the current production technology and its cost structure, the raw material procurement process, including lead times, and the loan conditions by the bank are potential constraints that shape the environment, depending on the boundary choices made.

This map allows us to infer a number of interrelated issues (stage 2), such as 'capture the potential market', 'keep financial control over firm', 'expand the production capacity', 'run an efficient operation', 'enjoy running the firm', and last but not least 'convince bank to advance additional funds'. These also happen to be the major "What?" questions. Tasks include: 'purchase new production equipment' and 'free up currently invested funds for other uses', which in turn can be subdivided into a number of detailed tasks.

A mainly task-based root definition could read (CATWOE in parentheses):

Root definition 1: "A system controlled by Elly (O + A) for increasing production capacity (W), achieved through the purchase of new equipment (T), financed via freeing up funds by tight credit control and offering prompt payment incentives (T) to retailers (C), and by reducing current raw material stock levels, the latter by having the production supervisor (A) institute new purchasing policies (T) from suppliers (C).

A mainly issue-based root definition, addressing the immediate task of getting a bank loan, could read:

Root definition 2: "A system which allows Elly to convince the bank to advance sufficient additional funds for the purchase of new production equipment needed to capture the potential market for funky shoes, while keeping financial control over the firm.'

While the root definition 1 gives details of necessary activities for operating the system with the higher production capacity, root definition 2 shifts the focus to a new crucial element, namely that Elly's immediate need is to convince the bank to change its initial refusal and come to the party.

Neither of these root definitions spells out all six CATWOE elements in detail. Unless it gives rise to ambiguity, those that can be inferred implicitly, such as the customers/beneficiaries/victims, a full list of all actors, additional aspects of the world view, or parts of the environment may not be listed explicitly. If all elements are explicitly included in full detail, the root definitions tend to become rather long-winded and clumsy statements.

Activity:
* Identify the CATWOE elements in root definition 2. Which are missing?
* Try to define another issue-based root definition dealing with Elly's aversion to have a financial partner in her business.

Figure 7-3 shows a possible conceptual model for the first root definition. In addition to the operating subsystem that deals with increasing the productive capacity and its efficient use, there is a monitoring and controlling subsystem for evaluating the effects on sales, raw material stocks, and the cash flow of the new policies, and a so-called 'awareness subsystem' which determines and adjusts the criteria for the new policies based on the inputs from the monitoring subsystem.

Figure 7-3   Conceptual model for root definition 1.

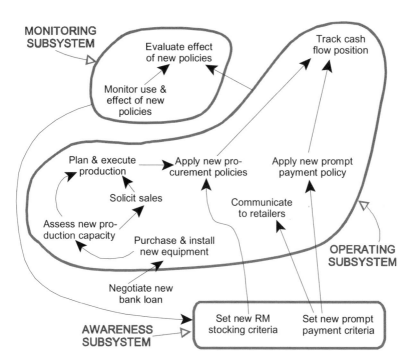

Figure 7-4 shows the conceptual model for the second root definition. Since its theme is to produce convincing arguments for the bank to come to the party with additional funds, its whole focus is on the prediction of cash flow over time in response to various possible policies for raw material stocking and prompt payment incentives. The aim is to bring about a match between the perceived bank lending rules and the need for additional loan funds, if this is possible.

Figure 7-4   Conceptual model for root definition 2.

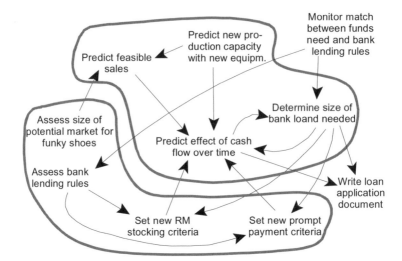

Activity: In Figure 7-4, identify which activities form the operating subsystem, the awareness subsystem, and the monitoring subsystem.

The stage 5 comparison between what is present is the real world and each conceptual model highlights the following points:

- Existing raw material stocking policies claim to be based on cost minimization and ignore cash flow effects, while both conceptual models focus mainly on the latter. Which is more relevant at this point? The debate should also attempt to assess the cost effect of abandoning cost minimization.

- The conceptual model for root definition 1 focuses on buying new equipment and on operational changes, monitoring and control needed for its effective use, while the one for root definition 2 focuses on what information is needed to convince the bank to grant the additional loan, culminating in a loan application. Which focus is the appropriate one? Are both relevant, but for different purposes?

- Neither conceptual model directly addresses the important issue of financial control of the firm. In fact, both make a boundary judgement that sharing such control is not on the cards. Hence, only ways to capture the potential market with Elly remaining in full control are considered 'technically feasible and culturally acceptable'. Is this an immutable constraint? Maybe further insights could be gained by relaxing it. At this point it might be desirable to iterate back to stage 3 and explore a suitable root definition along that line, such as

Root definition 3: 'A system that allows Elly to increase production capacity to capture the potential market for funky shoes by taking a financial partner, while keeping sole operational control over the firm.'

Since our aim is to give the reader some appreciation of the methodology only, we will not pursue this avenue.

The 'debate' at stage 6 will be one of self-searching for Elly. However, it would be advisable to include the production supervisor and possibly even the previous owner/friend of the firm. Such an outsider might contribute a more 'unbiased' view to the exploration for coming up with a recommendation on how to proceed.

If such a debate confirms Elly's absolute horror of sharing financial control of the firm, then root definition 2 shows another way to proceed, i.e. map out the effects on the cash flow over time of (1) different raw material procurement policies that reduce and keep stocks to an absolute minimum and (2) different levels of incentives to retailers for prompt payment, always under the assumption of having the increased production capacity of the new equipment. This will show how much additional loan funds are needed and for what period. If the gross profit margin is healthy, that period could possibly be shorter than Elly's original estimate. Obviously, there is no guarantee that the amount of loan funds required can be kept within a level acceptable to the bank. If it is not, then Elly may have to look seriously at root definition 3 and reconsider her position on taking a financial partner.

Concluding remarks on SSM

The version of SSM presented above follows a well-defined seven-stage iterative process. It tackles both the intellectual problems of interpretation, analysis, and synthesis involved in conceiving ideas for change, and the practical problems of facilitating the change process itself. With a bit of experience, it can be used by a group of people facing a dilemma or decision problem without the need for a facilitator. Probably the most difficult aspect is the formulation of effective alternative root definitions that introduce sufficiently varied and contrasting viewpoints and themes and thereby offer new insights into the problem. Although the methodology calls for a debate between different stakeholders, it offers little help and no guidelines on how to deal with disagreements and conflict in views and values between stakeholders beyond stating that the debate at stage 6 should be open and non-defensive, where all stakeholders should feel safe to state their case. If there are fundamental conflicts between world views and they are firmly entrenched and refuse to shift, no meeting of minds may be possible. If power differences tend to dictate the outcome, free and open debate is highly unlikely. SSM therefore lends itself best to situations in which the stakeholders share similar interests, and views differ mainly in emphasis and detail, rather than substance. This will allow accommodation between stakeholders without the need to accept or impose compromises that satisfy no one.

In principle, nothing prevents a single decision maker from using the seven-stage process without explicitly involving other stakeholders. All that is needed is the ability to place oneself into the different stakeholder roles with an open mind — in Churchman's terminology, being able to play the devil's advocate to one's own ideas and views — and debate with oneself.

However, SSM is more than a problem-structuring method: it is a mode of thinking that can be internalized and become second nature, the same as the process of the hard OR methodology. It will then be applied on a more informal, heuristic basis, or only in parts, the debate remaining largely internal to the person doing it.

Activity: Assume you are enrolled in a university course that involves regular lectures, additional tutorials, considerable reading, and the completion of one assignment and a final examination for getting credit for the course. Formulate two alternative root definitions and identify the CATWOE elements explicitly included. Root definition 1 assumes that you enrolled in the course as a requirement towards completing a degree. Root definition 2 assumes that the course material is of high interest to you (but obtaining credit for it is not important). Construct a conceptual model for root definition 1.

7.4 Strategic option development and analysis

Strategic option development and analysis (SODA) [Eden, 1983] is a method used by an analyst/consultant to facilitate group decision making in complex problem situations that involve several **stakeholders**. These may have different perceptions of the problem, different values and goals, and possibly different vested interests.

SODA is based on four interacting perspectives:

- **Personal construct theory:** Cognitive psychology is the theoretical basis of the method. Individuals use language to express concepts and ideas. These are subjective and the language used is rich in meaning. An individual's perceptions of a problem situation can be captured by a **cognitive map** (see Section 4.7).

- **Nature of the organization:** Organizational decision making involves politics, forming of coalitions, and negotiation between stakeholders. Change in organizations often occurs through management of conflict.

- **Nature of consulting practice:** The role of the consultant is to help problem solving and securing commitment to action through facilitation and negotiation.

- **Technology and technique:** Cognitive mapping, quantitative analysis, dedicated computer software (Decision Explorer, previously known as COPE), and SODA workshops, all designed to explore and manage complexity.

SODA is run by a consultant, skilled in the method, with a group of two to ten people, who are all actively and substantively involved in the problem situation. The method is based on the premise that a sufficient degree of appreciation of the different views and interests among the stakeholders will allow the group to commit itself to an agreed set of actions. It consists of four main steps:

Step 1:   The consultant constructs a cognitive map for each stakeholder involved, based on one or two extended individual interviews with each.

Step 2:   The consultant discusses each map with its owner, clarifies ambiguities and contradictions and works with them through the map, checking for consistency and completeness. They explore it for possible uncharted actions and goals. Through this process, each member should gain a good understanding of his or her own views and perception of the situation.

You are already familiar with these two steps from Section 4.7, where the principles of cognitive maps are discussed in some detail, and Section 4.8, which demonstrates the process for NuWave Shoes.

Step 3: The consultant merges the maps into a **strategic map** by combining identical or similar constructs, retaining the richer construct wording. Substantive conflicts between maps may be highlighted by alternative paths. The aim of the strategic map is to develop **emerging themes** and **core constructs**. Emerging themes are in the form of clusters of constructs with many links between them and fewer links with clusters outside the group. Core constructs are those that either have many arrows leading into it or many leading away. 'Decision Explorer' is interactive software for merging of maps and identifying and analysing clusters.

Step 4: All participants are now brought together in a so-called **SODA workshop** with the consultant as an active facilitator for the process. The strategic map becomes the vehicle for discussion and negotiation. The consultant starts out by taking the group through the merged map, its emerging themes and core concepts, and any still unresolved conflicts. The idea is to enable all group members to recognize their views as part of the greater picture. Then one or more related clusters are chosen for deeper analysis with the aim of getting a shared view, if not on goals then at least on actions. The consultant will attempt to bridge major differences in views and goals between stakeholders through negotiation. The workshop ends in success if the consultant can get the stakeholders to commit themselves to a set of clearly defined and spelled-out actions.

The perspective of 'personal construct theory' underpins steps 1 and 2. Principles of organizational behaviour are recognized in step 4. Technology, in particular the Decision Explorer software, is used in steps 1 and 3, while consulting practice guides the process through all four steps. Unlike SSM, where conflict resolution hinges on open and free debate, SODA provides specific mechanisms. Merging the individual maps into a strategic map depersonalizes the issues and places its ownership with the group as a whole, while at the same time allowing each member to see her or his own map reflected in it. It allows conflict to be managed, first by exposing it in the strategic map and then through negotiation in the SODA workshop.

In terms of Figure 7-1, problem formulation and modelling occur hand-in-hand in the first three steps, with the emphasis shifting more and more to modelling as the process moves towards and into step 4. There is no proper implementation phase, unless the commitment for action includes the planning for its execution and the assignment of responsibility for who does what.

In contrast to SSM, SODA heavily relies on the competence of the outside consultant. Not only does this person need to have excellent interpersonal and facilitation skills, but he or she must also be a skilful interviewer (for developing the strategic map) and a skilful and experienced negotiator. Given the critical role of the consultant throughout the entire process — interpreting each stakeholder's views through individual cognitive maps and working on each map with its owner, the consultant's choices and interpretations made while merging the maps, and finally the process of facilitation and negotiations in the SODA workshop — it is also clear that the consultant does not remain an 'objective' or neutral outsider, but becomes an active participant and thereby an interested stakeholder in the process and by extension in the problem situation, shouldering a heavy responsibility.

NuWave Shoes continued

You may wonder how the process we started in Section 4.8 with the creation and analysis of Elly's cognitive map (pages 70 and 72) would proceed further with the SODA method. So far, we only have Elly's contribution. Who could be other stake-holders? The production supervisor, in charge of raw material procurement, comes to mind immediately. His perspective on the efficient running of procurement and shoe production, in terms of costs and maintaining the current reputation of reliability in meeting promised delivery dates, is in partial conflict with Elly's view that in the current crisis cost efficiency can be sacrificed and reliability may not be seriously compromised if a few deliveries are delayed by a few days. Another, possibly more interesting, stakeholder is the bank's loan manager. A satisfactory solution to Elly's problem requires that the bank comes to the party. Including the loan manager in the process directly, rather than simply as a customer whose views Elly can only second-guess, could well enhance the chances of a successful conclusion. (If the bank is more than simply a conditional provider of funds, but takes a more intimate interest in the venture, such an inclusion could be on the cards.)

If, in Section 4.8, Elly developed and analysed her own cognitive map, we now need a consultant who does this for the other two stakeholders and then merges the three maps into a strategic map. The most likely emerging theme would remain concept 16 ('Make better use of current funds …'). If a bit of quantitative analysis in the form of cash flow projections over the next two years confirms that the bank loan can be repaid fully within that period, the bank may well commit itself to a further loan. A SODA (mini-)workshop would be mainly concerned with the terms of such a loan: security offered, its size, its duration, and the monitoring conditions the bank may want to impose, i.e. a close watch on how raw material stocks and balances owed by retail stores behave over time and the steps to be taken if they go against the expected pattern.

7.5   Strategic choice approach

In the words of one of its developers, John Friend, the origins of the strategic choice approach (SCA) [Rosenhead and Mingers, 2000] "are to be found in the experience of two pioneering research projects, in which operational researchers and social scientists worked together in observing strategic decision makers in action. ... The insights obtained ... were to provide the foundations for the development of a set of relatively open, participative methods for representing the structure of interrelated decision problems and the various sources of uncertainty — technical, political, structural — which made them difficult to resolve." During the 1970s, the approach was further developed and refined in a program of action research in the Tavistock Institute of Human Relations. SCA attempts to formalize the way a group of people learn to cope with complexity and uncertainty in decision making. It has proved to be particularly appropriate and useful for contingency planning, where the group participants represent the stakeholder interests of several possibly only loosely connected organizations, such as local or national governmental agencies, educational institutions, or departments within a private organization, and where there is strong pressure for early decisions and early commitment to action.

In contrast to SSM and SODA, SCA has no formal theoretical foundation, but instead consists of a set of four *ad hoc* complementary modes of working flexibly with a group of six to eight interested participants in intensive workshop sessions that are managed closely by a skilled consultant/facilitator.

Fundamental to SCA are the stakeholders' perceptions of the importance of three types of uncertainty (lack of knowledge, lack of externalization, ambiguities, and fuzziness are other intended meanings):

- **UE: Uncertainties about the working environment**, mainly of a technical nature: These can usually be overcome fully or partially by forecasting, surveys, in-depth technical or costing studies of insufficiently known aspects, using statistical and other quantitative and qualitative techniques.

- **UV: Uncertainties about values, objectives, priorities, and vested interests:** These are the most difficult to come to grips with since they touch the world views of the stakeholders or how they are perceived by their representatives. It may call for policy guidance from higher authority, ways to externalize values and preferences, and open disclosure of vested interests, all leading to a high level of shared understanding and appreciation of each other's positions.

- **UR: Uncertainties about the relationships/interconnectednees/interactions between decision areas or issues:** How do decision choices for a given issue affect decision choices in other issues? What aspects are unknown, unclear, or fuzzy, or open to different interpretations?

Answers to these uncertainties often involve boundary judgements for both the narrow and the wider system of interest. In some sense, SCA can be viewed as a learning approach to manage these three types of uncertainty when faced with complex problem situations. The process of SCA consists of working in four modes, as shown in Figure 7-5. They are:

Shaping involves identifying issues or so-called **decision areas** and deciding which ones to include or exclude. It is in the form of a decision graph — a network that shows which decision areas are linked with each other, the strength of the connections, and the importance, urgency, or priority of the decision areas. The

Figure 7-5   Four working modes of SCA.
(Adapted from J. Friend and A. Hickling, *Planning under Pressure*, Pergamon, 1987)

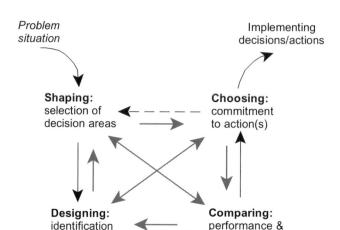

output of this mode is an agreement on which subset of highly interconnected decision areas should be the (first tentative) **problem focus** for further study. This basically comes down to making boundary choices and boundary judgements about the narrow and wider system of interest.

Designing (analysis of interconnected decision areas or AIDA) consists of defining mutually exclusive **action options** or alternative decision choices for each decision area in the problem focus. For situations that involve decision making over time, action options will include a timing element, such as 'now' or '12 months from now'. Action options in different decision areas are superimposed on each other and tentative answers are given on whether action options in different decision areas are compatible, incompatible, or whether compatibility is uncertain/questionable/unknown. Each set of compatible (or feasible) action combinations is referred to as a feasible **decision scheme**.

Comparing consists of defining a set of quantitative or qualitative objectives or performance measures and associated decision criteria (see Section 4.1, page 55, for a discussion of the difference between objectives and criteria) for evaluating or assessing the strength and desirability of the various decision schemes. This comparison is done for each pair of decision schemes, resulting in a balance sheet or **comparative advantage graph** that may involve objective numerical outcomes or qualitative (arbitrary) point scales.

Choosing is a two-stage process, i.e. (1) evaluating decision schemes in terms of how they are affected by uncertainties and what remedial actions or **exploratory**

options will help reduce critical uncertainties or clarify ambiguities, and (2) developing a final **action scheme** or commitment package, detailing the chosen action options and exploratory option and their timing, as well as what contingencies to keep in reserve for managing future uncertainties.

Although these four modes of working may be initiated in the order shown, the effectiveness of the method is considerably enhanced if the facilitator allows flexible switching between modes in any direction, backwards, forward, or across, as depicted in Figure 7-5, whenever working in a given mode tends to become bogged down or insights gained from working in a given mode lead naturally to reconsideration of a previous mode, such as a redefinition of the problem focus, changes in the action options, or the reassessment of action compatibilities and of uncertainties. In particular, areas of uncertainty and ambiguity should be noted down as they are discovered during all stages of the process, rather than just at the choosing stage.

In terms of Figure 7-1, shaping and the identification of the action options of designing are the formulation phase, while the rest of designing, comparing, and the first step of choosing form the modelling phase. Only the second step of choosing can be viewed as implementation planning.

Activity: For the Deep Cove project described in Section 1.1, determine aspects of uncertainty/ambiguity/fuzziness and identify and justify their nature.

7.6 SCA applied to NuWave Shoes

The developers of the method provide the STRAD (for 'strategic adviser') interactive software to streamline the process. STRAD has proved helpful for small informal groups to make quick progress while working interactively around a desktop computer. However, we will now demonstrate some aspects of SCA using only the low-tech diagrammatic aids and tables suggested by Friend and Hickling [1987].

The NuWave Shoes problem has only one major involved stakeholder, Elly. In this problem, the group interactions which form a vital part of SCA are missing. The treatment is, therefore, rather one-sided and demonstrates mainly the technical aids used, lacking the human interaction flavour — an aspect difficult to put into print. However, it shows that the basic process of working in the four modes nevertheless provides valuable insights as a mode of systems thinking.

Shaping

Figure 7-6 lists seven major potential decision areas and arranges them as a network. Note how different representations are used for indicating the 'importance', 'urgency', and 'strength' of the links between decision areas.

The three decision areas inside the gray bordered shape are the subset for the initial problem focus. They include the two urgent decision areas, as well as the promising area of freeing up internal funds to reduce the need for external funding.

Figure 7-6   Decision (areas) graph.

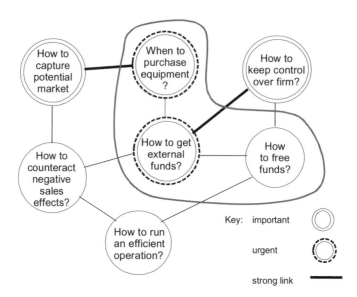

Designing

The set of mutually exclusive action options — deliberately kept small — is:

• When to purchase equipment:	– now
	– later
• Freeing up of internal funds:	– offer cash discounts to retailers
	– tighter credit for slow payers
	– reduce raw material stocks
	– all three
• Procuring external funds:	– get additional bank loan
	– take a financial partner
	– both

These options are now checked against each other for compatibility and all combinations arranged in a logical option tree that allows identification of feasible decision schemes, as shown in Figure 7-7. Usually, the decision areas are arranged in their order of urgency — purchase equipment, external funding, freeing internal funds in our case — their chronological order — all three to occur more or less at the same time — and logical sequence. The sequence in Figure 7-7 reflects the fact that the need and size of external funding depends on freeing up internal funds.

Elly also arbitrarily decides that she will not consider decision schemes for a later equipment purchase that rely on partial financing by taking on a financial partner. Furthermore, all four action options for 'freeing internal funds' result in the same pattern for 'getting external funds', so they are shown combined.

Figure 7-7   Option tree showing feasible decision schemes.

Purchase equipment	Freeing internal funds	Getting external funds	Feasible decision schemes
Now	Cash discounts	Bank loan X	
		Financial partner X	
		Both ?	A?
	Tighter credit	Bank loan X	
		Financial partner	B
		Both	C
	Low RM stocks	Bank loan X	
		Financial partner	D
		Both	E
	Cash discounts & low RM stocks	Bank loan ?	F?
		Financial partner ?	G?
		Both	H
Later	Cash discounts	Bank loan ?	I?
	Tighter credit	Financial partner X	
	Low RM stocks	Both X	
	Discounts & low RM		

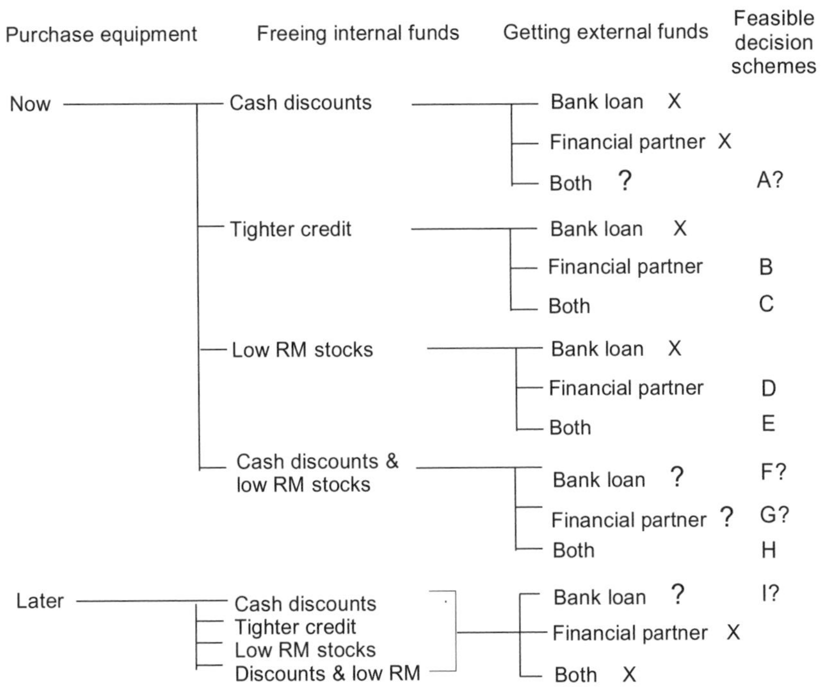

Infeasible action option combinations are marked by an x and doubtful ones by a question mark (?). The feasible (and questionable) decision schemes are labelled {A} to {I}.

Comparing

A subset of feasible decision schemes is chosen for further evaluation in terms of their performance. Elly considers the following objectives or performance measures:

- Her degree of control of firm
- The firm's share of potential market
- Her share of profits
- Low need for external funding

Each scheme is ranked, either on an arbitrary point scale or by an objective measure. Some assessments may give rise to the use of hard OR techniques, such as linear programming or multi-criteria approaches, particularly if the action options consist of a loosely defined set of decision variables, such as 'high output' which may need to be allocated optimally to a number of activities.

Armed with such assessments, the decision schemes are compared pairwise with each other. Figure 7-8 depicts one way of displaying such comparisons.

Figure 7-8   Comparative advantage analysis between schemes {C} & { F?}.

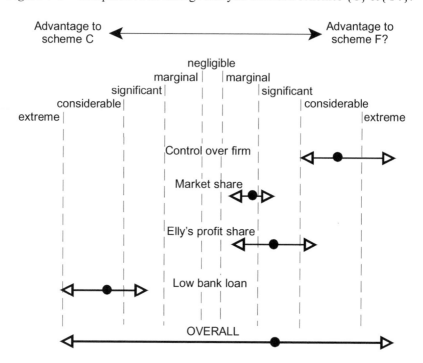

Uncertainties, particularly of the UE type, are now also taken into account. This is displayed by showing the perceived range of advantage — the double-pointed arrows — rather than simply the most likely value or the mode — the dot on the arrow lines. The overall score reflects the entire possible range. The mode of the overall score is not simply an average of the modes, but takes into account that the various objectives may differ in terms of importance. Clearly, in Elly's case, control over the firm and market share are considerably more important than her profit share and the size of the bank loan needed.

Such pairwise comparisons are made for all combinations. This shows whether some schemes clearly dominate other schemes. The dominated schemes can then be eliminated. In this manner the schemes are whittled down to a few preferred ones which become the input into the choosing mode.

Choosing

As pointed out at the end of the previous section, as the analysis progresses, areas of uncertainty and ambiguity will be discovered and recorded. It is not uncommon, for aspects that have been chosen as decision areas or objectives also to turn out to be areas of uncertainty. They now have to be classified as to type (UE, UV, UR). Some may straddle more than one type. For NuWave Shoes the list shows:

Area of uncertainty	Uncertainty type
• Share of the market that can be captured	UE + UR
• Potential response of retailers to discounts and tighter credit	UE
• Credit limit of the bank	UR
• Effects of actions on Elly's profit share	UR
• Effect of loss of control over firm due to an external partner	UV

Recall that UR means that the uncertainty is caused by the interaction between decision areas. So, the share of the market is affected by whether or not tight credit controls are instituted. (This is why scheme {C}, with tight control, is disadvantaged against scheme {F?} which does not, as shown in Figure 7-8.) The effect of how loss of control affects Elly is largely an issue of values, hence it is a UV type.

Next, the areas of uncertainty are assessed as to their relative importance or **salience**. This may lead to proposing possible remedial steps or exploratory options that could reduce highly salient uncertainties. Such steps may render action schemes affected by these uncertainties more attractive. This is particularly crucial for action schemes which have been labelled questionable or doubtful, such as scheme {F?}. For example, Elly might want to sound out the bank as to their assessment of a loan for various amounts of internal funds freed (with the balance of funds needed to be covered by the bank). Similarly, if it is perceived that scheme {C} has a fair degree of uncertainty in term of how retailers will respond to tighter credit controls, this may lead Elly to undertake a survey of retailers.

She might also do some soul searching about why she feels that she wants to retain absolute control over the firm (recognizing that the simple act of getting a loan from the bank already means a certain loss of control). It may affect the importance she assigned to this area of uncertainty/ambiguity. In turn, this may lead to changes in the comparative advantage of various pairs of schemes, causing the process to recycle back to the comparing mode.

The outcome of this process is a commitment package or action scheme, such as the one listed in Figure 7-9. The timing of actions and options becomes important, hence the action scheme may differ from the preferred decision scheme in detail and composition. Before Elly can commit herself to the purchase of the equipment, she needs to explore how the cash flow over time is affected by offering discounts to retailers for prompt payment and by reducing investments in RM stocks.

This presupposes that she makes firm forecasts for her planned production schedule and traces the schedule's effects on the time pattern of RM usage, shoe deliveries to retailers, and the resulting collection pattern from retailers. Armed with these cash flow projections, she can enter into negotiations with the bank that will hopefully permit placing her equipment order. The major contingency provision in case the bank declines the loan is to reconsider finding a 'silent' financial partner — silent in the sense that he or she takes only a financial, not an operational, interest.

In the usual multi-stakeholder case, each step involves extensive discussions, the interchange of ideas, and negotiations between the workshop participants, carefully facilitated by the consultant, who would manage the process by judicious switching of working modes to encourage progress towards reaching a commitment package.

Figure 7-9   Commitment package for Elly in NuWave Shoes project.

Decisions now		Future decisions	
Explorations	Actions	Deferred actions	Contingency plans
Purchase equipment: Make cash flow forecast based on exploratory option below	Place equipment order if bank offers loan		
Freeing internal funds: Find best discount level	Offer discounts	Explore feasibility of tighter credit controls	
Develop tighter RM usage forecasts and Just-in-time scheduling	Reduce RM stock levels	Find ways to use RM remainders from previous seasons	
External funding: Prepare funding case	Negotiate with bank		Find silent financial partner if bank declines loan

7.7 Survey of other problem structuring approaches

Strategic assumption surfacing and testing (SAST)

SAST evolved in the 1970s [Mason and Mitroff, 1981] and owes much to C. West Churchman's dialectic approach of playing devil's advocate, i.e. the deliberate contrasting of opposing perspectives. Its main area of use is for strategic planning and controversial policy decisions in complex situations involving several interconnected issues, where the situation challenges the status quo and there is polarization between groups of entrenched protagonists. The core aspect of SAST is the adversarial testing and questioning of assumptions, beliefs, values and world views that underlie strategies and, by extension, the strategies themselves.

The method consists of four stages:

Group formation: The participants, often the stakeholders or their representatives, are grouped into two or more small homogeneous teams, such that the members within each team share similar views and values and may have similar vested interests, while the views and values between groups are highly diverse. Consider a proposal to create a marine reserve along an ecologically vulnerable stretch of coast. One team may be made up of recreational anglers for whom this area is a favourite fishing spot and who put a high value on their right to enjoy this leisure activity. A second is a team of ecologically minded individuals and government representatives from the Department of Conservation who wish to protect a unique ecological asset, and a third is a team of commercial fishing firms whose livelihood may be threatened by the proposal.

Assumption surfacing: Each team is asked to identify the stakeholders, both those involved and those affected by their preferred strategy, and the assumptions and value judgements they have made about them. These often boil down to making boundary choices and judgements, which may or may not be seen as valid by other teams. Each team then positions their assumptions on an **assumption rating chart**, as shown in the Figure 7-10. The horizontal axis measures how important an assumption is and the vertical axis how certain or confident the team is that the assumption is correct.

Figure 7-10   Assumption rating chart.

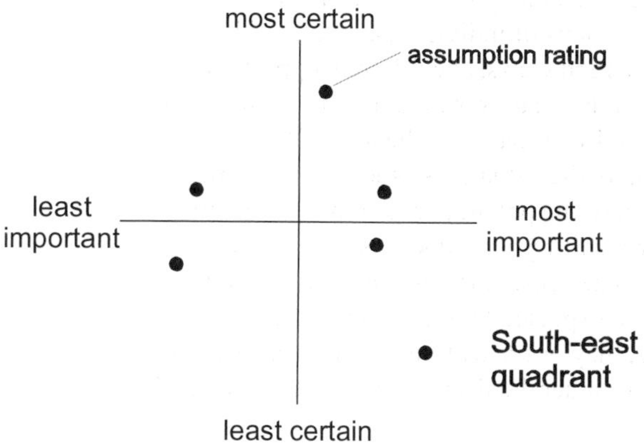

The assumptions in the south-east quadrant (important but uncertain) represent a weakness that other teams will certainly challenge. They are candidates for further research in an attempt to increase their degree of certainty.

Dialectic debate: An external consultant facilitates an adversarial debate between the pairs of opposing teams where each team critically evaluates the assumption-rating chart of the other. The aim is to identify weaknesses in the other team's assumptions, thus causing them to rethink their approach. Prime candidates for being challenged are: (a) questionable boundary judgements, such as the omission of potential stakeholder groups, including future generations or flora and fauna, (b) a failure to recognize assumptions made about them, and (c) logical flaws in assumptions.

Synthesis: Each team revisits their preferred strategy in the light of the learning gained during the dialectic debate. They meet again with the other team with the aim of forging a new approach to which both sides can commit themselves.

The consultant becomes an active participant in the process, both to manage the dialectic debate and to help in the strategy synthesis. SAST seems to be most suitable for issues that involve groups of professionals of equal rank and status.

Activity: For the NuWave Shoes case, give and justify your perception of the degree of importance and uncertainty for the following aspects:
- the share of the market that may be captured;
- the potential response of retailers to discounts; for tighter credit policy;
- the bank's credit limit;
- the potential loss of control due to taking an external financial partner.

Problem structuring methods based on a game metaphor

Operational gaming, **hypergame analysis**, **metagame analysis**, and **drama theory** all borrow concepts from game theory, but abandon its rigorous axiomatic foundations. They only retaining its outer form, i.e. two or more players, opponents, competitors, or groups of individuals, with conflicting perceptions, different vested interests, motives and views, and different opportunities and decision choices, facing a complex decision situation where the final outcome depends on the joint effect of the actions taken by all parties. The aim of the methods is to help decision makers gain insights into the situations, such as their own and other players' potential decision dilemmas, the potential reactions of other players to decisions or strategies chosen, and the resulting consequences or outcomes, *before* the situation is played out in real life. In some sense, they are simulations in preparation for the real events or conflict situation expected to arise. They differ from the type of simulations done in hard OR in that they occur with real individuals who interact or role-play with each other in real time under the firm control of a consultant. The latter plays an active and central role.

Operational gaming grew out of war games developed by the Rand Corporation in the 1950s. It has found uses in education (e.g. business games), job training, disaster planning, marketing, and so on. It follows a strict format with rules clearly spelled out to the participants. The game controller prepares a detailed game plan and sets the game rules and the starting conditions. The participants then play the game, usually through several rounds, where at each round they have to make certain decisions or take actions. The game controller determines the outcomes for each party and feeds that information back to them. At the end, the game play is analysed through all its moves and conclusions are drawn about the effectiveness of the strategies used. If used for learning or as a training device, this is done jointly with the participants.

Metagame and hypergame analysis are both 'played out' under the control of a consultant. Usually only one side or party involved in the conflict situation is physically present. It 'simulates' their own and their opponents' possible play. Metagame analysis explores in detail possible scenarios that could eventuate under the assumptions that all parties can predict each others' choices and their reactions to such knowledge, including their emotional responses to threats and promises and their credibility. As a result of the insights gained, the party will be much better prepared to behave rationally in the real situation. Metagame analysis has been used for exploring international conflict situations and policy and management conflicts in business organizations.

In hypergame analysis each player is assumed to construe the game in possibly quite different terms. This is captured by the client defining for each player a perceptual game — her or his own strategies and the perceptions of the possible strategies and preferences for each of the other players, including emotional aspects, such as their willingness to honour an agreement, their sincerity, and their fears. Again, all feasible combinations of strategies by all players are explored. This reveals the strengths and weaknesses of the client's strategies, promoting better insight and hence better decision making.

In the late 1990s, the learning from these two methods led to the development of drama theory (also known as confrontation analysis), where the conflict situation is actually played out, so-to-speak, on the stage as dramatic episodes, with all their existing emotions and irrationality. The method assumes that strong emotions, expressed in the confrontation, are often a precursor to changes in preferences. This in turn may bring about a redefinition of the game for which a common position can be achieved that the players all trust will be implemented.

Robustness analysis

One of the serious problems in strategic planning is how to cope with high degrees of uncertainties about the future, and in particular how to develop strategies that do not foreclose potential future options, but leave the door open to cope with a large number of likely scenarios about what the future may look like. Conventional strategic planning approaches try to reduce or tame future uncertainties and identify the most likely future. In contrast, robustness analysis is a low-tech planning approach to cope with such uncertainties, mainly of the UE and UR type (in SCA's terminology). It is often true that several future strategies all imply the same initial action or commitment. Each set of strategies that shares the same initial commitment is tested for success or acceptability over a reasonably wide range of possible future scenarios. The larger the fraction of all future scenarios for which a given initial commitment is acceptable, the higher the robustness of this commitment. Robust commitments offer flexibility and are desirable candidates to be implemented.

Unlike most other PSMs, robustness analysis, developed in 1980 by Rosenhead [2000] needs no facilitator. It can also be used informally as a mode of thinking. In fact, it is good MS/OR practice to look for strategies that keep future options open.

There are other methods or approaches that can be viewed as PSMs, such as **decision conferencing** (a type of brainstorming and systems designing, using interactive computer software that allows a group of people to network and interact with each other from different locations), **scenario analysis** (developing of representative futures or scenarios for a given problem situation, usually as inputs into further analysis), **stakeholder analysis** (a systematic procedure to identify all stakeholders of a project, their 'stakes' or interests and values, etc., and then analyse the relationships between them), and the **theory of constraints** (a mode of thinking about technical and/or organizational change and how to deal with all sort of constraints, physical, intellectual, and relational, often in the form of bottlenecks).

7.8 Critical systems heuristics, critical systems thinking, meta-methodologies

This last section looks at more recent developments in systems thinking and briefly considers some of their philosophical motivation.

Critical systems heuristics (CSH)

One of the recurrent themes in this text is the vital importance of choosing appropriate boundaries for the system of interest and its relevant environment. The effectiveness and legitimacy of any system intervention depends on this. So far we have been somewhat vague about how to select appropriate boundaries. W. Ulrich's **critical systems heuristics** (CSH) [1983/94] is the first and still only systematic procedure for critically examining boundary choices and their underlying boundary judgements. It is derived from rigorous theoretical and philosophical reasoning.

Space does not allow us to develop the philosophical origins of CSH. We limit ourselves to a motivational overview, as we understand Ulrich's extensive writings. As seen in Chapter 3, we, as humans, interpret the 'real world' through our perceptions. These are affected by our interests, values, and world view. Which 'facts' we view as relevant for a given purpose and our interpretation of them depend on our interests, values, and world view. Hence, **facts and values are not separable**. This is well captured by the simple folk wisdom of "we only see what we want to see." Similarly, human activity systems are conceptualizations for a given purpose, usually to improve the effectiveness of an existing or planned entity, operation, activity, or organization. Different people may define the corresponding relevant system and its environment differently. In other words, the associated boundary choices involve a fair degree of subjectivity. But boundary choices determine which 'facts' and values are considered relevant and which ones are ignored. Values and world views, in turn, may shift as a result of a systems analysis. Ulrich refers to these relationships as the 'eternal triangle of reference system, facts, and values'.

Boundary choices also limit the nature of improvements derived from the implementation of the system and how these improvements are distributed among the potential stakeholders. As the discussion on efficiency and effectiveness in Chapter 2 shows, improvements in the narrow system of interest may be at the cost of a worse performance in the wider system. Both aspects raise serious ethical questions.

Churchman, the first systems thinker to raise these questions in the 1960s, argued that ideally the answer lies in considering the totality of all relevant aspects, i.e. effectively pushing the boundaries for both the system of interest and its relevant environment out farther and farther. Only then can we judge whether an improvement is real and not to the detriment of somebody or something else. Leaving aside the difficulty of judging what is 'relevant', such a quest is both impossible and impractical in the light of uncertainties about effects, conflicts of interest, cognitive difficulties, the often limited time frames within which decisions have to be made, and the power differences between stakeholders.

We cannot avoid making (possibly arbitrary) boundary choices. In Ulrich's words "The implication of the systems idea is not that we must include as much as possible in the system of interest, nor that we must understand all systemic relationships and their effects on all stakeholders, but rather that **we need to deal critically with the fact that we never will.**" ('Critically' in the sense of exercising careful judgements without bias and guarding oneself against error; making transparent the value judgements underlying them.) CSH is Ulrich's approach to doing this.

Its core consists of critically assessing for each of four types of stakeholder involved in or affected by the system a set of three boundary question about "who and what is" and contrast the answers with "who and what ought to be". Ulrich does not claim that answering these questions will produce the 'correct' boundaries. In fact, he stresses that there does not usually exist a single right answer, but that this process will lead to reflection, appreciation, and debate about legitimate alternative views and values. This in turn will hopefully result in more informed and appropriate boundary choices. The twelve questions are (note carefully that his classification of stakeholders differs from the one listed in Section 4.2, page 57):

- About the **client** (i.e. those for whom the system is designed):
  1. Who is (ought to be) the client of the system?
  2. What is (ought to be) the objective, goal, or improvement of the system?
  3. How is (ought to be) the improvement in the system measured?

- About the **decision maker** (i.e. those who yield control over the system):
  4. Who is (ought to be) the decision maker?
  5. What aspects are (ought to be) controlled by the decision maker, such as resources (in a broad sense)?
  6. What aspects are not (ought not to be) controlled by the decision maker, i.e. the system environment?

- About the **planner** (i.e. the professionals or analysts who develop the system):
  7. Who is (ought to be) involved in planning the system?
  8. What is (ought to be) the knowledge and expertise of the planner?
  9. Who guarantees (ought to guarantee) that the system developed achieves its planned purpose effectively?

- About those **affected by the system, but not involved in it** (i.e. the voiceless victims or beneficiaries, including flora and fauna, who have no say in the control or development of the system, but may be affected negatively, as well as positively, by its consequences):
  10. Who of those involved in the system represent/argue (ought to represent/argue) the interests of those affected but not involved?
  11. What opportunities are (ought to be) offered the voiceless affected to represent themselves?
  12. Whose world views of those involved and of those affected are (ought to be) underlying the system design?

As a rule, the 'ought' mode implies shifts in boundaries to cover concerns, usually of the voiceless group of stakeholders, that are ignored or violated by the original boundary choices.

In Ulrich's words [Daellenbach and Flood, 2002, pp. 72–3] the checklist points "can be used, first, to identify boundary judgements systematically; second, to analyse alternative reference systems for defining a problem or assessing a solution proposal; and third, to challenge in a compelling way any claim to knowledge, rationality or 'improvement' that relies on hidden boundary judgements or takes them for granted." The last can be particularly helpful when confronting experts who, knowingly or un-knowingly, hide value judgements behind references to facts or claims of expertise (such as "you don't understand that because you lack subject expertise."). The interpretation of facts is not value-free, and values cannot be justified through a claim of expertise or using the 'correct' methodology.

Boundary critique along the lines of CSH **should be standard practice for any systems study**, hard or soft. Its use is essential for public policy issues and public projects. In fact, Ulrich says that CSH enables individuals to become competent citizens in public debates. However, as we shall see in the next subsection, CSH is more than a checklist for systematically uncovering boundary judgements.

Activity: Give answers to the 12 questions of CSH and justify them for
* the Deep Cove project;
* the NuWave Shoes case.

Critical systems thinking

The name 'Critical systems thinking' (CST) was coined in the late 1980s as a common label for two distinct research strands that called for a more comprehensive and critical approach to systems thinking [Ulrich, 2003]. The first of these is Ulrich's work on CSH in the late 1970s and early 1980s. His major driving force was to develop a philosophical foundation, viz. CSH, for sound professional practice, as well as proposing a practical framework for the applied disciplines and, in particular, those claiming to use systems thinking. It is based on the work and philosophical and social theories of Kant (1781), Peirce (1878), Churchman [1968, 1971], and Habermas [1971]. As we have seen above, its core concept is boundary critique.

The second is the work done at Hull University in the mid to late 1980s by M. Jackson, P. Keys, and others, aimed at developing a framework for critical profes-sional practice through critical awareness and understanding of the strengths and weaknesses of methodologies and the nature of the problem situation in question. Particular emphasis was placed on the implications of differences in power relation-ships between stakeholders. One of its criticism is that the kind of open, unfettered, and participative debate between stakeholders, presupposed by many soft OR approaches, is unattainable, and that specific mechanisms for emancipating all stake-holders have to be provided to produce results that address their aspirations in the presence of coercive power. Flood and Jackson [1991] developed a meta-methodo-logy, based on methodological pluralism, to guide professional practice in the use of management science approaches. It is briefly covered in the next subsection.

The Hull School's aim for emancipation of all stakeholders has yet to produce an effective mechanism beyond the call for direct political action. (In fact, Ulrich's polemical employment of boundary critique via CSH is so far the only approach for concerned citizen to make their voices heard, challenge the stated or implied boundary judgements made by planners, and pursue such endeavours in various forums of the public sphere. Although this is no guarantee of complete emancipative success, there are numerous instances where the concerns of citizens, repeatedly and insistently raised in the public sphere, has finally prevailed [Ulrich, 2003]).

Ironically, the Hull School's strongly proclaimed commitment to emancipation as an act of faith precludes critical questioning of one's own boundary judgements. Gordon Hewitt's short quote on page *v* ("If we investigate our ideas, we have to be willing to give them up.") is highly pertinent.

Total systems intervention (TSI)

TSI is an ambitious meta-methodology [R. Flood and M. Jackson, 1991] for critical guidance of the practice of systems intervention.

Flood and Jackson use the following metaphors or systems analogies for viewing an organization:
- **a machine** with coordinated division of labour, a clear chain of command, and fixed (open-loop control) rules or procedures for doing things, all controlled from above, such as a bureaucracy (e.g. a military unit, local government administration, or the manufacturing operation of most firms;
- **an organism**, consisting of systemically interrelated parts, with feedback loops and controls, where each part has its own needs to be met, with long-term survival of the organization as a primary goal (e.g. a firm promoting flexible responsiveness to its economic and technological environment);
- **a brain**, with high information gathering and information processing ability, which emphasizes learning, self-enquiry, creativity, dynamic goal seeking (e.g. a consulting firm, an R&D department, or a highly decentralized firm with quasi autonomous operating units);
- **a culture**, consisting of individuals with shared interests, values, and beliefs, and interacting with a cooperative community-like spirit (e.g. a sports club, a professional association, or lower, middle, and upper management levels in firms with highly shared goals and views and high loyalty);
- **a political system**, consisting of groups or coalitions of individuals with different vested interests and values and who use power to achieve their goals (e.g. parliament, a coalition government, the or upper management level of a firm made up of various factions who compete strongly for power and scarce resources);
- **a coercive system**, held together through sanctions and/or authority enforced consensus (e.g. a prison, a single-party cabinet of government ministers who must support all majority decisions, the sole, or ruthless employer in an economically depressed area).

For a given problem situation, an organization may exhibit features of several metaphors. Different analysts may therefore end up selecting different metaphors as the most appropriate one.

TSI consists of three phases:

Creativity: Use the organizational metaphors to think creatively about the problem situation faced and choose the most appropriate one for the next phase.

Choice: Select a system-based methodology or a set of complementary methodologies and techniques that is judged as most suitable and effective for both the metaphor and the problem situation. If a set of methodologies is chosen, then one is used in a dominant role and the others in supporting roles as needed and appropriate within the framework of the dominant one.

Implementation: The chosen methodology (or set of methodologies) is applied to bring about a coordinated change to the problem situation — a solution, resolution or dissolution — that enhances the organization's efficient, effective, and ethical functioning. (The term 'implementation' departs from the traditional meaning of putting the final results of the analysis to work.)

The 'creativity' and 'choice' phases correspond to the problem formulation stage in Figure 7-1, while 'implementation' covers primarily the modelling stage. Again, as for other hard and soft systems approaches, TSI is used iteratively, possibly on more than one metaphor, with continual linkages backward and forward, and possible switching of dominant and supportive methodologies as more is learned about the problem situation and the suitability of the metaphor used.

A thorough theoretical and practical knowledge of a wide range of methodologies, both hard and soft, is an essential prerequisite for the competent use of TSI. Only then will the analyst/consultant be able to identify the most fitting organizational metaphor and the most suitable methodologies. Currently few analysts/consultants, except some academics, have such a background. This is clearly one of the major weaknesses of TSI, limiting its use. Having heterogeneous teams of analysts may partially overcome this weakness, but will increase the costs of analysis. Furthermore, although not explicitly included in TSI by Flood and Jackson, both the creativity and choice phases will be remiss unless complemented by a rigorous boundary critique along the lines of Ulrich's CSH. It is also questionable whether the 'correct' choice and 'correct' use of methods provides sufficient validation for TSI's claim to bring about critical professional practice.

TSI practice is still evolving, with Flood and Jackson going in different directions.

Multimethodology

Multimethodology shares some of the same aims as TSI, i.e. plurality of methodologies and methods. Rather than using a single best hard or soft OR approach, multimethodology, put forth by J. Brocklesby and J. Mingers [Mingers and Gill, 1997], seeks to combine approaches so as to better match the richness, complexity, and peculiarities of a particular problem and its organizational context. Several methods or parts of methods may be applied to different stages of the analysis or parts of a method are combined with another one at the same stage. For example, the hard OR methodology presented in Chapter 6 recommends the use of rich pictures (stage 1 of SSM) or cognitive mapping (step 1 of SODA) as the most effective way for capturing the problem situation (step 1 of 'formulation'). To overcome difficulties of or constraints to implementation of a hard OR solution, the various stakeholders may be brought together in a workshop for a PSM exercise. While using a soft systems approach, hard OR techniques may be used for evaluating or comparing of system performance, such as for the comparing phase of SCA, steps 6 of SSM, or in preparation for step 4 of SODA. Similarly, the SAST assumption rating chart may be a useful device for assessing the relative salience of uncertainties in SCA. Multimethodology recognizes a practice that analysts have informally used almost from the inception of MS/OR.

As is true for TSI, effective practice of multimethodology requires good theoretical and practical competence in a wide variety of systems approaches.

7.9 Concluding remarks

It is fair to say that so far the major use of soft systems approaches, except for multimethodology, comes from the developers themselves, often within a consulting practice, and from a small group of acolytes, predominantly academics. Few users are sufficiently familiar with more than one approach, although this is changing with several universities, as well as some of the developers, offering courses and intensive workshops. However, such exposure alone is not sufficient for expertise. As has been pointed earlier, the consultant also needs to have good skills in interpersonal relations, in facilitation and negotiation, skills that come naturally to a few, while others struggle to acquire them through long years of working with people.

None of the soft systems approaches seem to explicitly address the various issues of implementation. It is true that the active participation of many stakeholders in the project intervention process will hopefully pave the way for the implementation of the commitment package or recommendations made, since the stakeholders are more likely to own the solution. However, owning the solution is only a beginning — it removes some of the human constraints to implementation. Planning for the actual process of change, assigning responsibilities for who does what when, and monitoring implementation and the performance of the new system are other essential aspects that need to be dealt with. The 'monitoring subsystem' of SSM provides for the latter, provided it gets translated into action.

Finally, it is interesting to view PSMs as within a systems context, similar to the structure diagram for hard OR in Figure 6-9. This is done in Figure 7-11. In contrast to hard OR, it is not a sequence of systems whose outputs become the input into the next system. System S is 'created' or defined within system M. Note again how boundary judgements affect all aspects.

Figure 7-11   Structure diagram for PSMs.

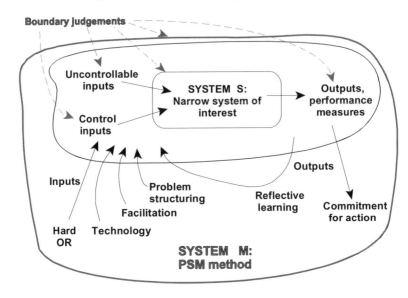

7.10   Chapter highlights

- While hard OR approaches stress mainly 'content', PSMs put equal emphasis on process. They use participative debate to enhance understanding of differences of interests and views. They address primarily "What" questions. All profess to be 'learning systems', used iteratively and flexibly.
- Most PSMs are the result of practical consultancy and/or action research and rely on a consultant/facilitator to guide the process through its phases.
- While some PSMs are firmly based on systems theory, others are also based on critical philosophy and/or borrow ideas from psychology, sociology, and organization theory.
- The version of SSM presented is a seven-step learning process that iterates through several alternative potential views or root definitions of the problem, develops a conceptual systems model for each, and compares what "is" in the real world with what "ought to be" to gain greater insights into the problem.
- SODA merges individual stakeholders' cognitive maps into a joint strategic map that helps discover emerging themes and core ideas which become the focus for a decision-analysis workshop, culminating in a commitment for action.
- SCA is a four-phase approach to explore and deal effectively with various types of uncertainties that may impede decision making. Its outcome is a commitment package for immediate and exploratory actions and future contingencies.
- CSH is a practical approach to evaluate system and environment boundary choices and reveal boundary judgements, particularly with respect to those stakeholders that are affected, but have no voice in the project. It should be the front-end of any systems analysis, hard or soft.

- CST attempts to address principles of critical professional systems practice and the difficulties any systems methodology faces in the presence of differences in economic, political, and authority-based power between the stakeholders.
- TSI views problem situations through one or more of six organizational metaphors and then matches it with an appropriate MS/OR methodology or combinations of methodologies.
- Multimethodology advocates the judicious combining of methods or parts of methods for various phases or aspects of an MS/OR intervention to enhance its effectiveness and success.

Exercises

1. Consider the staffing problem situation faced by Bill Dodge in exercise 9 of Chapter 4. Formulate two alternative root definitions, both seen from his point of view, the first task-based, reflecting his objectives for border control, the second issue-based reflecting his desire for efficient and effective staff management. Identify the CATWOE elements.

2. Consider again the Customs staffing problem situation in exercise 9 of Chapter 4. Take now the point of view of the consultant and formulate a task-based root definition for providing the client, i.e. Bill Dodge, with an effective tool for exploring his problem. Identify the stated and implied CATWOE elements.

3. Consider the situation summary for the blood bank operation in exercise 3 of Chapter 3 and the rich picture diagram for it in exercise 7 of Chapter 4. For the following issue-based root definition draw a conceptual model:

    "A system which allows the director of the blood bank to reconcile the conflict of potential blood product shortages versus outdating of fresh blood so as to derive a medically defensible policy for managing limited shelf-life blood stocks, collected from voluntary donors and needed for transfusions to patients in emergency and scheduled operations and for conversion into blood components administered to patients with blood deficiencies."

4. Exercise 1 continued: Draw a conceptual model for each root definitions formulated.

5. Consider exercise 8 in Chapter 4. Combine your map for Y with the one shown below for his father (F) into a strategic map. Identify any emerging themes and/or core concepts.

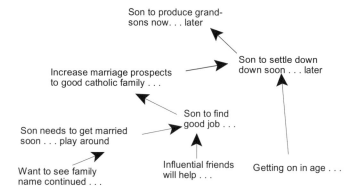

6. For the Customs staffing problem situation in exercise 9 of Chapter 4:
   (a) Identify which aspects belong to each type of uncertainty: UE, UV, and UR.
   (b) List the various decision areas.
   (c) Draw a decision (areas) diagram, similar to Figure 7-6, showing both the importance and urgency of the decisions and their links.
   (d) Select a subset that you judge is most important for Bill Dodge to investigate first. Develop an option tree, showing all feasible decision schemes, similar to Figure 7-7.

7. For the blood bank problem of exercise 3 in Chapter 3:
   (a) Identify which aspects belong to each type of uncertainty UE, UV, and UR.
   (b) List the various decision areas.
   (c) Draw a decision (areas) diagram, similar to Figure 7-6, showing both the importance and urgency of the decisions and their links.

8. From the interview answers given by Bill Dodge for the Customs staffing problem situation in exercise 9 of Chapter 4, draw an assumption rating chart, similar to Figure 7-10, for the following aspects: (A) prevention of entry into the country of prohibited aliens; (B) prevention of importation of illegal drugs; (C) meeting Government guidelines for processing commercial flight passengers; (D) processing correspondence within three days; (E) meeting custom officers union demand for no flexible shifts, no short shifts, and no part-timers; (F) eliminating (most) overtime that are extensions of regular shift hours; (G) eliminating (most) special call-outs; (H) the reliability of passenger numbers supplied by the airlines prior to arrivals of aircraft; (I) arrival times of scheduled flights.

9. Discuss the distinction between "what" and "how" questions. Referring back to Figure 1 on page 110, why do soft OR approaches tend to address the former, while hard OR approaches generally address the latter?

10. It seems obvious why a proposal for introducing a change in a system or organization must be "systemically desirable". Explore why it also needs to be "culturally feasible" to be successful and accepted by the various stakeholders, particularly the users.

8

Implementation and code of ethics

The majority of MS/OR projects are aimed at improving the operation of an existing system or finding the best mode of operations for a new proposed system. The potential benefits of such a project can, however, only be secured if the solution to the problem is implemented. Contrary to the belief of most novice MS/OR analysts, implementation is not something tacked on to the end of the modelling phase. Rather, it must be a prime concern underlying all earlier steps in the analysis. Planning for implementation starts right from the outset of any project. This is the topic of the first two sections of this chapter.

Once a solution has been implemented, procedures and rules have to be put in place for the continued control, updating, and maintenance of the solution. These are the topics of Section 18.3 and 18.4.

The chapter concludes with a discussion of aspects of personal and professional ethics for the analyst, particularly for projects that involve and affect stakeholders other than the analyst him- or herself.

8.1 Implementation and its difficulties

As shown in Figures 6-1 and 7-1, implementation of an MS/OR project is putting the results of the modelling phase to work. This means translating the mathematical solution for a hard OR analysis, or the new system and processes for a soft OR analysis, into a set of easily understood operating procedures or decision rules; preparing detailed user guides that give instructions on preparing inputs for any quantitative models used and on performing all computations, or on the correct application of new decision rules and procedures; and finally assigning responsibility to all individuals involved in using the new rules and procedures.

This is followed by training all people involved for the proper application of these rules, executing the transition from the existing to the proposed mode of operation, and preparing complete documentation for future reference. These seem like straightforward tasks that are easily handled by a systematic approach, good organization and coordination. Unfortunately, the process of implementation is fraught with difficulties that are largely of a human nature. This is particularly pronounced for projects that deal with improving an existing operation.

To get a better 'feel' for one of these human aspects, just put yourself into the position of the stock clerk in the LOD in charge of the day-to-day replenishments of stocks (case of Chapter 6), or into the position of the personnel scheduler of a 24-hour service operation in charge of rostering individual employees to tasks and shifts. You have done these tasks for a number of years and considered that you did a competent job. Along comes this MS/OR analyst, called in by your boss or even sent in by somebody higher up in the hierarchy. Few people will not see this as a sign of lack of confidence in their ability to do the job properly, and hence will perceive it as a threat. What may make it even worse is that this whiz kid is probably fairly young and university-trained, but with seemingly little practical understanding of the intricacies of your job. It would be rather surprising if you did not view any 'solution' that this analyst proposes with a fair degree of suspicion, unless you were yourself intimately involved in the analysis.

Problems of implementation can stem from three causes:

1. Those relating to the physical task of implementation, such as the complexity of the solution, the sensitivity of the benefits or costs (both tangible and intangible) to deviations from the formally prescribed rules, and the extent to which the proposed solution deviates from current practice. The greater any of these, the greater the problems which have to be overcome.

2. Those relating to the problem user and other individuals affected by the solution, such as their personalities, their motivation and pride in the job (e.g. does the proposed solution restrict their freedom of action, take away their responsibility, reduce their relative status, transform a challenging job that required years of experience into one of merely feeding data into a computer which then feeds back what action to take?), their ages (routine becomes more entrenched with age, change is more difficult to accept), their background and level of education, and the importance of the tasks associated with the proper use of the solution in relation to their other job activities (the less important they perceive these tasks to be, the less attention these tasks will receive).

3. Those relating to the environment of the project, such as the support given to the project and its solution by the problem owners (the less visible and explicit the support given to the project, the less cooperation it will receive from the problem users), the organizational implications of the solution (if a problem user department becomes more dependent on another department, or the problem users see the solution as a threat to their job security, the less support the solution will receive from them), and the incentive systems for pay and promotions used by the organization (if implementation reduces pay or threatens promotional prospects, individuals may find ways to 'show' that the new system does not work).

Generally, hard MS/OR analysts pay full attention to the first factor, which is a question of technology, largely devoid of human aspects. The tendency is to neglect or overlook the human factors of (2) and (3). They are qualitative in nature and evade the formal treatment that can be given to the technological factors, but can nevertheless act as serious constraints on implementation. It should come as no surprise that neglecting these human constraints in a system can easily lead to a 'solution' that is one on paper only and is not workable in practice. From this point of view, implementation can be viewed as a problem of relaxing the human constraints versus adjusting the technical solution.

The nature of a soft OR approach is to give more attention to the factors of (2) and (3), sometimes to the detriment of (1).

The human constraints may be relaxed in a number of ways. More involvement of problem user(s) from the outset of the project and more training may both increase the understanding of the solution. Individuals who could become obstacles to proper implementation could be transferred to other jobs of equal importance or status. The technical solution can be adjusted by simplifying the policy or solution rules, e.g. by going to quick-and-dirty rules that capture the major part of the benefits, but are much easier to use and implement.

The literature on implementation is unanimous on one point — implementation and continued use of a solution are almost guaranteed if the problem owners and problem users 'own' the results of the analysis. Again, soft OR approaches are geared to produce ownership as an integral part of the methodology, while for hard OR projects, the analyst may have to proactively develop a climate of analysis for this to happen. Users will develop a feeling of ownership if they can contribute to the project in meaningful ways with their experience and in-depth knowledge of the operations. A wise analyst will therefore keep them appropriately informed, submit all or most ideas to their scrutiny, and solicit their advice. If they feel that they have contributed in significant ways to the project and that their inputs have been valued, they will wish to see the solution put into practice and will take an active role in the implementation process.

In the LOD project, the stock clerk was the most important user stakeholder. She was pulled in as an active project team member from the outset and given the responsibility of liaising with all other potential problem users and problem customers. Similarly, the LOD manager was kept fully informed and regularly consulted during the project. Rather than have the analyst present the proposed solution to the staff of the LOD and interested refinery personnel, the LOD manager was briefed to give that presentation. The whole project conveyed a strong impression of active LOD participation and management support.

8.2 Planning for implementation

Planning for implementation starts at the outset of any project, when the first contacts are established with the sponsor(s). As the project progresses, the groundwork for implementation is laid throughout all other phases. This truth cannot be overemphasized. Except for purely technical projects, largely devoid of any human aspects, it is not sufficient to start planning for implementation once the solution to the model has been tested and the project report submitted to the sponsor. Not only could this result in serious delays in getting the solution implemented, because crucial input data may not be available, but the human aspect discussed in the previous section will most certainly have been neglected.

Planning for implementation consists of the following elements:

1. **Identifying all stakeholders** of a problem situation, in particular the problem owners and problem users: the former because they will ultimately have to give approval for implementation, and the latter because their full cooperation is needed for continued use of the solution.

2. **Establishing effective lines of communication** with the problem owners and problem users. Which channels, formal or informal, does the analyst use to communicate with various people in the sponsor organization? Who are the liaison people? To be effective, the lines of communication must be open, and there must be mutual respect and trust between the problem owners and users and the analyst.

   If the project is the first contact that the analyst has with them, trust and respect must be explicitly established and nurtured, because, as discussed above, the problem owners and problem users are likely to feel threatened by the project. Any attitude revealing condescension or superiority by the analyst will only reinforce mistrust of the problem users, in particular. The analyst has to be aware that such messages are more often than not conveyed by non-verbal body language, such as signals of impatience or 'knowing smiles'.

   As a rule, the analyst should start from the premise that the problem users have done their best, based on their training, education, and resources available. The analyst may know more about MS/OR modelling, but they know much more about the problem, not only those aspects that are easily visible, but also those that may require extensive experience and exposure. It is easy to withhold such information, which will then become an obstacle to proper implementation. So, at least initially, it is the analyst who has to rely on them and learn from them before he or she can start contributing to the problem.

3. **Exploring and managing prior expectations for the project.** As discussed in Section 6.3, a problem owner and/or problem user may have formed prior expectations about what the project will deliver in terms of benefits or in terms of the time frame for its execution. If these expectations cannot be met, these stakeholders may withdraw their support from the project, either actively or passively. This may jeopardize implementation of the results. For this reason, the prudent analyst will explore and evaluate all prior expectations. If they are unrealistic or difficult to meet within the time frame and resources available, they should be confronted in a diplomatic manner. The analyst must also be aware that he or she could unwittingly contribute to the formation of unrealistic expectations by indirectly promising more than can be delivered.

4. **Keeping the problem owners and problem users regularly informed** about the progress of the project. Get feedback and solicit new ideas from them.

5. **Checking out availability and sources of all input data needed.** Are the data available in the form, quantity and quality needed? It may take months to accumulate missing data, such as product demand. Unless such data collection is initiated

right from the start, undesirable delays in implementation of any results will be unavoidable. It is also crucial to ascertain that over the data period selected no changes in recording practices have occurred, e.g. no recording change from gross figures to net figures. What is to be done with bad or unreliable data? Should they be corrected or deleted?

6. **Ordering of special equipment and commercial computer software** may have to be done well in advance of implementation. This includes the computer hardware and networking.

7. **Developing all software** needed for implementation and continued use of the new solution. Such software has to be fully tested on real-life data. It should flag errors in data input or data that are clearly wrong, e.g. falling outside their operational range. It is not acceptable that a newly developed computer system breaks down or becomes quickly overloaded shortly after being implemented.

8. **Planning and executing the actual process of implementation.** Planning and executing the various steps of changing over from the current mode of operation to the new mode of operation requires a detailed information of the sequencing and timing of all tasks, and their assignment to the people best equipped to execute them. This includes:
   - Preparation of all databases in the exact format needed for implementation and continued use of the solution.
   - Preparation of special stationery or forms needed for using the solution, user manuals, and material for training sessions with problem users. Special care needs to be given to user manuals, particularly those involving the use of computer software. They have to be complete, covering not only the normal operations, but also how to handle exceptions and troubleshooting, as well as all procedures for updating, controlling, and maintaining the solution (see the next section). The importance of complete user manuals cannot be stressed enough. Incomplete, inaccurate and badly written user manuals are a prime cause of implementation failure or rapid deterioration in the proper use of the implemented solution.
   - Training sessions with problem users.
   - 'Physical' changeover to a new mode of operation: for large projects it may be advisable to schedule implementation in stages rather than in one go in order to avoid straining resources and facilities. For example, the solution for the LOD case provided a decrease in the stocking levels for low-volume products but an increase for high-volume products. Depletion of the stock levels for low-volume products was predicted to take up to three months. Implementation of the policy for all products simultaneously could thus have resulted in serious warehouse space shortages. Hence the policy for the low-volume products was implemented immediately, while implementation for the high-volume products only proceeded at the rate at which warehouse space was freed up by the low-volume products.

   For the NuWave Shoes case, successful implementation of prompt payment discounts to retailers was more likely if all retailers were explicitly informed about the change in policy prior to the season, rather than by a small print statement at the bottom of the invoice.

9. **Regular follow-up sessions with problem users** during the early stages of the new mode of operation to eliminate or overcome any problems that may arise and could threaten the proper use of the solution.

Planning for implementation may call for the use of an MS/OR technique called the **project evaluation and review technique** (PERT) or the **critical path method** (CPM). They are a topic in most texts on MS/OR techniques or production management (see Figure 5-8 on page 101 for an example).

In particularly complex and sensitive cases, the implementation planning and execution for the results of a hard MS/OR projects may be facilitated via recourse to a soft OR approach, such as SSM.

8.3 Controlling and maintaining the solution

The environment in which most organizations operate is constantly undergoing change. This means that inputs to the system modelled and its environment are also changing. Such change may be quantitative or structural. Any changes that only affect the magnitude of inputs into the model, such as the volume of the annual demand for the LOD or the travel time from point A to B in a delivery problem, say due to road alterations, are referred to as quantitative. In most cases, the model remains a valid representation of the system. However, the optimal solution derived from the model usually changes. If the changes in the inputs are sufficiently large, then the current solution may need to be adjusted. Sensitivity and error analysis will provide guidelines as to when such an adjustment may be desirable, hence the importance of performing systematic sensitivity and error analysis with respect to all important inputs into the model.

A change in the form or nature of an input or in the systems environment is structural if it affects the influence relationship with one or more system components or variables in the model. The original model may cease to be a valid representation of the system. Affected functional or systemic relationships in the model may have to be reformulated. For example, in the LOD problem, installation of new mixing and filling equipment may result in substantial savings in production setup costs if stock replenishments are scheduled in such a way that all container sizes of the same oil are filled from one single mixing batch, rather than having separate mixing setups for each container size. The current model deals with each oil/container size combination individually. This structural change requires a new model that finds a joint optimal policy for several related products — a much more complex problem. Similarly, for NuWave Shoes, if the major foreign supplier introduces substantial quantity discounts for large purchases, the potential cost impact of that could lead to a rethink of the just-in-time ordering policy.

Procedures have to be set up to monitor such quantitative and structural changes in the environment, so that corrective action is initiated when the changes become significant. These form an important part of the user manuals. A change is judged significant if the improvement in the benefits that can be gained by adjusting the solution exceeds the cost of making the adjustment. If the solution is regularly updated, say once every six months, the improvement in benefits only covers the period remaining until the next regular adjustment.

Establishing controls over the solution consists of:

1. Listing for each input (parameters, constraints) — for those that are explicitly included in the model as well as those that have been excluded as insignificant — the quantitative change in values for which the present solution remains optimal or near-optimal. Rather than indicating such permissible changes in absolute terms, it is more useful to give percentage changes. The latter often remain valid even after successive updates of the solution, while absolute changes could become out of date already after one or two updates. For example, for the LOD project, any change in the rate of demand for a given product in excess of 50% became a signal for an update of the control parameters, unless an annual update was less than three months away.

2. Listing of the structural form of all influence relationships between inputs and system variables, and system variables and outputs assumed by the current version of the model, again both for those explicitly included and those excluded. Any MS/OR analyst will then be able to judge whether a given subsequent structural change in relationships invalidates the current version of the model. For the LOD project, any changes in equipment and processing procedures for customer orders could imply structural changes.

3. Specifying in detail how each input should be measured to assess if a change is significant, how frequently such measurements should be made, and specific events that may call for such measurements to be taken. For the LOD project, the product demand distributions were updated monthly by computer using a forecasting method called **exponential smoothing**. Using standard statistical control charts, if an updated monthly average was signalled as out of control, this triggered a review of that product. The introduction of possible substitute products was also used as a trigger for a possible update.

4. Assigning responsibility for the control of each item and who is to be notified if significant changes have been detected. Rather than name a specific individual, such responsibilities should be part of a job description for a given position. This will ensure continuity if personnel changes occur. For the LOD project, the stock clerk was responsible for the majority of the control tasks, except those of a purely financial nature, like changes in the cost of capital or changes in labour costs. Control of these was assigned to a position in the Cost Control Department. In the NuWave Shoe case, Elly would be in charge of monitoring the payment habits of retailers, while the production supervisor would be in charge of monitoring RM levels.

5. Specifying in detail how the solution has to be adjusted in response to quantitative changes in inputs and by whom, and what action has to be initiated to deal with possible structural changes detected. For the LOD project, the stock clerk was put

in charge of updating the solution for quantitative changes in the input parameters. She was also in charge of updating all control parameters once each year. She would notify the head of the Management Science Group at headquarters if events occurred that could imply structural changes.

8.4 Following up implementation and model performance

Monitoring implementation

The job of the MS/OR analyst is not finished once the solution has been implemented. There is always the danger that, after some time, enforcement of the rules for using the solution becomes lax. Shortcuts may be taken which do not cause any immediate visible deterioration of the performance, but which will ultimately lead to problems. Certain rules or their reasons may have been misunderstood or misinterpreted. Furthermore, even with the most comprehensive planning and greatest care, events unforeseen by the analyst will occur and remedial action may be taken by individuals who do not have the right information or training to make the proper changes. For all these reasons, it is essential that the analyst keep monitoring the performance of the model for some time after implementation.

If any misapplications or misinterpretations of the solution show up, corrective action must be initiated. This may consist simply of again going over the rules for using the solution correctly with the individuals in question, or issuing corrections to the user manuals, or organizing follow-up training sessions, or even adjusting the solution rules to circumvent a recurrence of errors. It is crucial that the analyst does not underestimate the importance of such follow-ups. Neglecting this aspect could well result in the actual operation reverting to the previous mode within a few weeks or months and the new solution being 'shelved'. Resurrecting it at that time may be quite difficult, due to the negative attitude that most users will have developed towards it by then. It is quite natural that they will blame the solution or the analyst for the failure, rather than the improper use of the solution.

For example, follow-up monitoring revealed that the supervisor of the LOD grease operation continued using the old rules. He had worked in that plant for over 40 years and was not going to 'take orders from anybody who did not know the first thing about how to make greases', as he put it to the LOD manager. In the end, implementation of the solution for the grease plant could only be obtained by shifting him to another job. Sadly, he could not adjust to the new job either and was offered early retirement at full pension, which he accepted.

Performance audit

One of the final duties of the analyst is to make a performance audit on the solution. This means checking the extent to which the projected new benefit or reduced costs (both pecuniary and intangible) have been realized. The benefits actually generated by the use of the new solution are computed or estimated, based on the solution's actual performance. These are then compared with the performance of the old solution. To be valid, the comparison should be made using the same basis. For quantitative problems, this means the same input data. Any serious discrepancy between the projected and actual benefits should be fully examined and properly explained.

This audit is not only important for the sponsor of the project, but also for the analyst. **Only then does the analyst get valid quantitative and qualitative feedback on her or his own performance**.

The final audit for the LOD project was done one year after implementation. The cost savings were estimated at $72,000 for that year. Given that the new policy was implemented in stages and only became fully effective after a four-month transition, this fairly well confirmed the original savings estimates. However, the costs of implementation were slightly more than $40,000. This was largely due to significant additions to the software produced, in particular, a demand forecasting system.

Full versus partial implementation

Full implementation of all recommendations is rare. It is more useful to talk about the degree of implementation achieved. The aim of the analyst should be to achieve a sufficiently high degree of implementation to capture the major portion of the potential benefits. As for mathematical modelling, to capture the last bit of benefits may not be justified by the additional cost incurred.

8.5 Ethical considerations

Ethics is the code of moral principles and values that govern the behaviour of a person or a group of people with respect to what is judged right or wrong by the society they live in. Sounds pretty straightforward! Unfortunately, this is not the case. There are a number of difficulties and grey areas. There are genuine conflicting views among people and societies about what constitutes ethical behaviour and what does not. - Different societies and subgroups of society will tend to abide by different ethical standards. What is acceptable behaviour for one group may be very objectionable for another. Nor do such standards remain static over time. Even religious moral principles acquire new interpretations over time. Certain generally accepted industrial practices in the 19th century are now viewed as morally detestable. Many aspects of the new free market society that has sprung up in Russia with the demise of communism would be highly frowned upon even by the bastion of the free market, the USA.

Furthermore, we are also highly selective and inconsistent in choosing which ethical principles to apply or ignore in various situations. Many of us follow one code of ethics in our interactions with relatives and friend, another when interacting with people at large, and a third in our dealings with the tax authorities.

Ethics has occupied philosophers and religious leaders for as long as humanity has existed in the form of organized societal structures. The discussion that follows will therefore hardly scratch the surface of this fascinating subject.

Ethics as a basis for decision making

Ethics is relevant for decision making in at least two ways. First, it goes without saying that ethical principles should form the basis for all decision making. Without following ethical principles, decision making degenerates and becomes opportunistic, self-centred, inconsistent, and destructive to all stakeholders. What forms a minimal set of ethical norms has puzzled philosophers, from Pythagoras (6th century BC, better known for his mathematical discoveries) to Bertrand Russell (1872–1970). Its discussion goes beyond the scope of this text. However, what is relevant is that in recent years decision-making methodologies have been proposed that are largely based on ethical considerations. They consist of check lists for evaluating the decision process, the decisions, and the outcomes and their effects on all stakeholders. The process of boundary critique in CSH is an effective approach to uncover questionable ethical judgements.

Personal ethical considerations for analysts

But even within the MS/OR methodology, ethics and ethical considerations must concern analysts at a personal and professional level. Analysts must assume moral responsibility for the effects that their own involvement in a project and the recommendations derived have on the various stakeholders, in particular the problem users and problem customers, i.e. third parties that benefit from or are the victims of the results of the project, but have no direct say in it — in Ulrich's classification [1983, 1996] those affected by the system but not involved in its planning, including other species, fauna and flora. For example, the project may involve increasing the efficiency of personnel use, such as the nurses and doctors in a public hospital, which, depending on the decisions taken, could result in a considerable number of nurses losing their jobs, subjecting the others to increased work stress, while patients face potential increases in waiting lists for elective surgery, reduced quality and safety of care, and possible increased risks of medical misadventure. While the nurses and doctors may be consulted to some extent, the patients usually have no say in the matter. Or the project may deal with the siting of a nuclear power station or the extension of an airport runway, adversely affecting large numbers of people, as well as ecological systems.

How should analysts deal with such situations? If an analyst has personal, moral, or environmental objections to the possible outcomes of the project, then clearly he or she should decline participation. At the very least, the analyst should make a full disclosure of her or his moral objections and the possible outcomes, or other possible conflicts of interest (such as personal gain or loss), and leave it up the problem owner(s) to make a judgment about whether any involvement in the project should continue. If yes, then the analyst must confront the issue of how these moral objections could influence the analysis and the results, and attempt to keep the analysis as far as humanly possible free of these personal biases.

The analyst must also be aware that in public advocacy processes he or she cannot assume the role of modeller and also be an advocate of vested interest without having the role of unbiased modeller put into question. For example, as a member of the official publicly funded project team modelling an environmentally controversial project, you are supposed to take a neutral view. Both the model and your own credibility are jeopardized when you also become an advocate for some vested interest, such as an environmental lobby group or the mining company who would benefit from the project.

This does not imply that analysts should not draw the problem owners' attention to any adverse consequences of both the project process and its final recommendations. In fact, this is one of their responsibilities, regardless of their own personal views on the project for or against.

If a project involves rare undesirable or dangerous outcomes, such as contamination of an environment or the accidental exposure of people or animals to dangerous substances, care must be taken when making statements about their likelihood. Such outcomes are often the consequence of the simultaneous or conditional occurrence of a large number of separate events. Their interdependence may be difficult to assess, and the temptation to assume independence may be great. Unfortunately, true independence is rarely present, particularly if many events are subject to human failure. History is replete with such instances. One form of Murphy's law says that if one thing goes wrong, all hell breaks lose.

But even if the analyst is personally neutral or favours the outcomes, there still remains the ethical responsibility not only to point out the positive aspects of the expected outcomes, but also to fully disclose the negative consequences, including ethical ones, without belittling them. The analyst must point out the ethical dilemma involved in trading off cost savings against the potential of loss of life, permanent injuries, and irreversible detrimental environmental changes, regardless how small their probabilities. It is part of critical boundary judgements.

It is not the analyst's place to judge these consequences as to their desirability or otherwise, but to provide the decision maker with a relevant basis and complete information for making a fully informed decision.

Professional ethics of the MS/OR analyst

The analyst must make sure that the analysis performed is not flawed from a professional point of view. This implies:

- Disclosing any vested interest in the project or its outcomes.

- Approaching the problem situation from the world view of the problem owner(s) as far as this is possible and being aware of one's own biases.

- Keeping the problem owner(s) regularly informed about the project's progress and immediately reporting the discovery of new aspects or a higher severity of undesirable consequences that may call for a reassessment of the project.

- Fully documenting the model, such that any other analyst of similar training can understand and verify it. This implies recording of any assumptions, simplifications, and known omissions made, and data ignored or discarded, as well as the proper justification of these things.

- For any data used as input, recording their sources, keeping data specifically collected for that purpose in raw form, or saving operational data that in the normal course of events would be destroyed after some limited time period. Without such data it is impossible for a third person to verify the analysis.

- Verifying and validating the model; performing sensitivity analysis to evaluate the robustness of the model and its recommendation; and establishing ranges of critical input parameters for which the recommendations remain valid.

- Supplying the problem owner(s) with a report on the project, the analysis done, and its recommendations, at an appropriate level agreed upon beforehand. It should cover what was accomplished by the study, as well as (even more importantly) what was not accomplished, and any possible weaknesses and limitations of the analysis done. Projects involving quantitative analysis should give technical details, intended for persons trained in MS/OR, that describe in sufficient detail the model and solution method used.

- Scrupulously observing any ground rules about confidentiality for the disclosure of data and any reports produced, as laid out at the inception of the project. This should also cover what material may be removed from the premises of the sponsor and by whom. (That does not rule out whistle-blowing if written, well-founded, and documented reports on adverse effects are repeatedly ignored by those in charge of the project.)

These points just cover the most important ethical considerations. There are other obvious rules of moral conduct not unique the MS/OR projects, such as:

- Do not undertake a project that requires you to rubber stamp a conclusion or decision already reached, or do it only with the clear (written) understanding that you are in no way bound by such prior decisions or conclusions.

- Do not omit aspects (such as data, alternatives, sensitivity analysis, weaknesses, limitations) that you know will weaken your case. The temptation to do that may sometimes be strong. Mistakes, and their consequences for the validity of the findings, that are discovered after the report has been submitted should be disclosed immediately. Your own loss of credibility by admitting to mistakes may be of minor importance in comparison with the possible risks for other stake-holders if you fail to come clean.

- The report and its analysis should be written in such a manner that neither can be easily misrepresented or used for implying more than it should.

8.6 Chapter highlights

- The aim of most MS/OR projects (at least for those of a substantive nature) is to improve the performance of some existing or proposed entity or operation. The benefits of the project can only be achieved if the recommendations are implemented to a high degree.

- Problems of implementation relate to the physical task of change and to the human aspects involving the problem stakeholders. Neglecting the human aspects is the prime cause of implementation failure.
- Helping the problem owners and users to get a feeling of ownership over the solution is often the key to successful implementation. This is often an integral part of a soft OR approach, but has to be planned for in hard OR projects.
- Planning for implementation starts at the outset of a project.
- Only by following up on the implementation and assessing the proper use and performance of the implemented solution will the analyst discover what works well and learn from her or his own mistakes.
- Following an accepted code of personal and professional ethics is a moral obligation and enhances the credibility of the analyst.

Exercises

1. Professor Churchman, after reviewing the introductory chapter of another OR text we co-authored, casually observed: 'Don't you know that implementation is the first phase of any MS/OR project?' This remark initially startled us, particularly since Churchman's own text shows implementation as the final step of the analysis. However, as we pondered this, we came to agree. In the light of the coverage you have seen of the 11-step hard OR methodology of Chapter 5 or the 11-step soft OR working mode of Chapter 7, critically discuss Churchman's statement. It may be helpful to clearly distinguish between the physical process of implementing the results and the substantive issues involved in implementation.

2. Do you see any parallels between the major MS/OR implementation principle of 'get the problem owners and problem users to own the project' and your own personal experiences of getting family members, friends or colleagues to go along with some new activity or way of dealing with recurrent daily problems, or being at the receiving end of such pressures coming from them?

3. Assume that your project report for the ELMO case (exercise 19 of Chapter 6) convinced management to implement the solution. Prepare a detailed list of steps to implement, maintain, and audit your recommended solution. Note that the machine operators (i.e. the users) are trained mechanics, but have no higher education.

4. When we looked at desirable properties of models in Section 5.3 and validation in Section 6.4, the concept of model 'credibility' was mentioned. We also pointed out that it may be more useful to talk about 'desirable properties of the modelling process', rather than of the model itself. Integrating this with the material in this chapter, develop a list of such desirable properties that enhance the likelihood of full implementation and facilitate implementation.

PART 3
Assessing costs and benefits, and dealing with time

The focus in Parts 1 and 2 was systems thinking and systems methodologies in general, both hard and soft. The emphasis in Parts 3 and 4 now shifts more toward hard OR analysis, although even soft OR practitioners should be capable of assessing the relevance and treatment of the cost concepts and have at least a rudimentary knowledge of the most basic hard OR methods presented in Part 4.

Most MS/OR analyses involve costs and benefits, expressed in monetary terms. A good understanding of the nature of costs and benefits is therefore essential. Only then will the analyst be able to identify those costs and benefits which are relevant for a given decision problem and those which can be ignored. Briefly expressed, the relevant costs and benefits are those which, for the system as a whole, change for different decision choices. A proper understanding of how costs and benefits arise and how they vary also helps the analyst to incorporate them correctly in the analysis. Chapter 9 explores the nature and types of costs.

Often costs and benefits occur over time. How can we aggregate costs and benefits that occur at different points in time? This leads us to study discounting and to express future cash flows in terms of their present value — the topic of Chapter 10.

Time enters the analysis also in a different way. A project may involve making decisions at various points in time in an environment that does not remain stable, but also changes in predictable ways in the future. Chapter 11 studies how this affects the decision process.

9
Relevant costs and benefits

If the word 'system' is used in various different ways, the word 'cost' has even more varied uses in our language, and each may imply different value judgements. Business people speak of the cost of goods and materials purchased for production or resale, the cost of equipment, the cost of operating the equipment, and the cost of workers and employees — referring to wages and salaries paid. It is relatively easy to put an exact monetary figure to each of these. But business people also talk of the cost of delivering goods late to customers, the cost of a strike, either within their own organization or that of a supplier or a big customer, or the cost of rescheduling production to meet a rush job to a major customer. It is usually not possible to assess the exact amounts that such events 'cost' the firm.

In everyday language, the use of the word 'cost' becomes even more fuzzy: consider the social cost of unemployment in terms of despair, low self-esteem, increased suicide rate, increased crime, increased family breakups; or the environmental cost of pollution; or the hidden cost of government actions and policies; or simply the cost of a missed opportunity! The possibilities for ambiguity are compounded by the differing use and classification of costs by the major professions dealing with costs, i.e. accountants and economists.

This chapter first looks at how these two disciplines define and use various types of costs. Section 9.3 studies which costs are relevant for decision making. In MS/OR modelling, we are usually concerned with how costs and benefits change in response to a change in policy or the mode of operation. Hence, like managerial economists, management scientists are interested in incremental changes in costs and benefits.

These concepts are explored for a real-life case in Sections 9.4 to 9.8.

9.1 Explicit, implicit, and intangible costs

Some of the ambiguity when dealing with cost concepts arises from the fact that some costs involve an 'out-of-pocket' transfer of funds from one party to another, while others do not. The first are called **explicit costs**, the second **implicit costs**. The payment by a firm for goods or equipment purchased from a supplier is an explicit cost. The annual reduction in the value of a piece of equipment, called depreciation, recorded by accountants, is an example of an implicit cost. No funds change hands. It is simply a convention used by accountants to reflect the fact that through use and aging a piece of equipment has lost some of its original value. By the time the firm disposes of this equipment, its 'book value' recorded in the accounts is expected to have been reduced from the original purchase price to its current disposal value, say as scrap or second-hand machinery.

Several of the instances of costs mentioned in the introduction, like the cost of late delivery, the cost of reduced productivity and disruption caused by rescheduling production in response to some emergency, the social cost of unemployment, etc., are also examples of implicit costs.

The difference between these examples and depreciation is that it is relatively easy to put an exact figure on the amount of depreciation, while it is usually very difficult to assess the 'cost' of a late delivery. If a late delivery is a very exceptional occurrence, happening for reasons beyond the control of the firm, and the customer has been notified prior to the delivery due date, there is probably no cost. However, if late deliveries occur several times for the same customer, the firm runs a high risk of ultimately losing that customer. The 'cost' for the firm is the possible loss of profits that future sales to that customer could have generated. The potential for future profits through sales is also called **goodwill**. So the firm may suffer a loss in goodwill with its ensuing financial impact. Such costs are also referred to as **intangible costs**. Their assessment is often based on guesswork and is therefore highly subjective to the assessor.

The amount of depreciation assessed on a piece of equipment will usually have no effect on decision making, except in so far as it affects the timing of taxes paid (given that depreciation reduces the taxable income). On the other hand, intangible costs clearly should be taken into account in decision making.

Accountants have their own type of intangible costs, i.e. goodwill, and reserves for doubtful accounts receivables (credit customers who are seriously in arrears in their payments). The balance sheet item 'goodwill' usually arises from the acquisition of a going concern where the purchase price exceeds the net value of the assets acquired. This excess is seen as representing the growth in potential earnings of the firm. It is recorded as an asset. It is depreciated in the same way as most fixed assets. Similarly, the reserve for doubtful accounts receivable is recorded as a form of asset value reduction or liability in the balance sheet. Although accountants refer to these items as intangible assets or intangible costs, their use of the term 'intangible' is somewhat different from MS/OR. They refer to actual entries in the accounts of the firm. In MS/OR, we refer to potential future costs or loss of benefits that should be recognized as relevant for the correct evaluation of decision alternatives. However, no cash transaction or entry in the accounts of the firm is implied or will occur if a decision is implemented.

9.2 Accounting versus economics concepts of costs

Accountants' view

In general, accountants are historians. They record costs in terms of the amount of cash expended to acquire goods and services, like the raw materials and supplies needed for a manufacturing operation, goods for resale, employees' time, equipment and facilities, and the sources of funds. This then allows them to determine the financial position of a firm as of a given point in time, i.e. what the firm owns in the form of various assets, and what the firm owes to its creditors. The difference between these two represents the equity position of its owners. These three aspects are summarized in the **balance sheet**. Furthermore, accountants record in detail how this equity position changes over time, usually over a 12 month period. This gives rise to the **profit-and-loss statement**.

The balance sheet and the profit-and-loss statement allow current and potential investors in the firm to assess how well the current investments in the firm are doing. Producing these two documents is also a legal requirement for all firms, for assessment of taxes as well as for the protection of creditors of the firm. These are the main purposes of financial accounting.

In order to help management in pricing decisions, and the monitoring and control of costs, accountants have extended the concept of costs to the notion of **standard costs** — a measure indicating what it should cost on average to produce a given item or service under normal operating conditions. Actual historical costs vary from standard cost in the short run due to unexpected events, like price fluctuations of raw materials or varying productivity of the workforce. Significant deviations (or what cost accountants call 'variances') from standard costs are flagged and brought to the attention of management. In the absence of inflation or deflation, actual average historical cost will approximate standard costs in the long run, since the latter are in fact derived from the former.

Economists' view

In contrast, economists measure the cost of a resource in terms of the earning power or the opportunities foregone by not applying the resource in question to some other potentially available use — in fact, the best alternative use of the resource. Economists thus argue that the implicit cost of a resource is equal to what it could earn if used for its best available alternative activity now or at some future point in time. This cost is called the **opportunity cost** of the resource. Being an implicit cost, no funds change hands. For resources already owned by the firm it is not the original cost of acquiring the resource that is relevant any more, but the return on its best alternative use that counts.

Economic theory shows that applying this principle consistently will lead, in theory, to the optimal use of all resources available to a firm and hence to the maximum possible profit. If all firms behave in this manner, this should, again in theory, lead to the optimal allocation of resources for the economy as a whole. In practice, the world is not quite that simple. Individuals and firms do not pay the true cost of the use of many resources, particularly for so-called 'free goods' like the environment (air, water, land), by polluting it, and for 'public goods', like the road network (damage to road surfaces by trucks exceeding heavy vehicle road taxes), or the public health system (the health cost of alcohol or smoking far exceeding the tax revenue on such goods).

The most common application of the opportunity cost concept concerns situations in which a resource enjoys several potential uses at the same point in time. Using the resource for one purpose precludes its use for any other purpose.

Accountants' classification of costs

Accountants classify costs either by product identification or by variability. In the first classification (by product identification), costs are grouped into **prime or direct costs** and **overhead or indirect costs**. Prime costs are those directly identifiable with a specific end product or service. This includes the purchase costs of goods or materials used in the production process and the costs of all labour directly attributable to the production of that product or service. Prime costs tend to increase or decrease (often proportionately, but not necessarily so) with the volume of output. It is fairly obvious that if the level of output doubles, the amount of materials needed to produce the goods also doubles. Similarly, a doubling of the level of service offered will in most cases also double the labour input and its cost.

Overheads cover the cost of all support activities that are not directly attributable to a particular product or service or that are shared by all or a group of products or services. Examples are the salaries and fringe benefits of executives, managers, supervisors, and various support staff, like maintenance, personnel, and other administrative services, including vacation and holiday pay for these employees. The cost of borrowed funds, such as loans or mortgages, are also overheads.

Most overheads, but not all, remain fixed over a wide range of output levels. For example, the same administrative support staff may be needed even if the output of the firm decreases or increases within a fairly wide range around the current level. Only a change in output level beyond that range may result in a change in overheads, e.g. by requiring more staff or additional shared production facilities. The interest cost of loans taken up to finance the purchase of plant and equipment will have to be paid regardless of the level of output of the plant.

For product costing purposes, all overheads will ultimately be allocated on some suitable basis to the individual products or services. This allocation by necessity involves a varying degree of arbitrariness. The most commonly used basis for allocating overheads is in proportion to the amount or the cost of direct labour involved in producing each product or service.

The distinction between prime cost and overheads is often not clear-cut, particularly if the costs do not vary proportionately with output. Furthermore, some costs may be classified as overheads because the efforts or 'cost' of identifying which portion is directly attributable to each product or service may be excessive, while increasing the accuracy of their unit costs in only a minor way.

Economists' classification of costs

The main classifications used by economists are **fixed costs** and **variable costs**, on the one hand, and **short-run costs** and **long-run costs** on the other. Fixed costs are those that are not affected by changes in output level, in contrast to variable costs. There is thus some analogy between the accountants' distinction of direct costs and overheads and the economists' distinction of variable and fixed costs. However, the analogy is far from perfect. Direct costs may include charges which can be directly attributed to a given product, but are essentially fixed in character. For example, a given machine may be exclusively dedicated to the production of a single product or an office may solely be used for providing a given service. The cost of either may remain constant over a wide range of output levels. The cost associated with their use (depreciation or decrease in disposal value for the machine, actual or imputed rental of the office) may be constant per period (say a year). They are classified as direct costs by accountants, but as fixed costs by economists.

In the short run, investments in capital goods, such as equipment, buildings, and land, are taken as given. They are not easily changed without often substantial new investments of funds. They restrict the firm's output to a given range. Hence the cost of using these resources is fixed. On the other hand, other aspects of a firm's operations, such as the amount of raw materials and labour used, usually vary in proportion to the output level. Hence they are variable costs.

In the long run, however, the composition of all inputs into a firm's operation can be altered. The number and type of machines, the number and size of facilities, and so on, can be changed. Hence, in the long-run all costs become variable.

In general, economists use costs to derive normative statements about how a firm should operate under market conditions. The economists' view of costs is thus more akin to the prescriptive focus of the management scientist. Hence, we will find the economists' classification of costs more useful for decision making.

9.3 Relevant costs and benefits

Which costs and benefits should a decision maker take into account when evaluating the monetary effects of alternative decision choices? The short answer is:

> **All those that change as a consequence of any of the decision choices! Any cost or benefit now or in the future that for the system as a whole remains the same in total terms, regardless of the decision choice, is irrelevant.**

As is true for most short answers, this only tells part of the story. In many instances it may be difficult to determine which costs and benefits change until the analysis has been completed. Fortunately, any costs included in the analysis that are not affected by the decision choice will not influence which decision is best, provided such costs are included in the correct manner. It is obvious that if the same constant is added or subtracted from the monetary outcome of each decision choice, their ranking is not changed. (If you have doubts about this principle, test it with a practical example. Alternatives A and B have outcomes of 8 and 5, respectively. Outcome A is highest. Adding the number 3 to both does not affect that ranking. We already used this principle when we ignored the annual value of product costs for the LOD case of Chapter 6; see pages 141–142.) It is therefore more important to include costs in the correct manner, rather than worrying about whether a cost item should be included or not.

Having said this, we will nevertheless review which costs and benefits are relevant. This discussion will clarify grey areas and improve your understanding. For each cost and benefit we attempt to answer the following question: Does this cost item (in terms of its current or future impact for the system as a whole) increase or decrease if any of the decision choices is implemented or does it remain the same, regardless of which decision is taken? If it changes, it is a relevant cost item; if it remains the same, it can be ignored. Let us consider a few examples!

Explicit costs

It is quite obvious that explicit costs incurred by a decision choice, whether fixed capital investments or variable with the output level, are relevant costs. However, this does not tell us what the correct way of including explicit costs is, particularly if they are of a fixed nature — more about that later. Any explicit cost, incurred regardless of the decision choice, is not relevant. But what about costs incurred in the past and clearly associated with the project or activity in question?

Sunk costs

To answer this question, let us assess whether or not the results of an MS/OR project should be implemented. Consider the LOD case study in Chapter 6. The LOD manager has received the final project report. For discussion's sake, assume that this report states that the potential cost savings amount to $35,000 per year (considerably smaller than the correct figure quoted in the Appendix 2 to Chapter 6) and that a further $30,000 will have to be spent for implementation of the new policy. This is in addition to the $8000 already charged to the LOD for the preliminary study so far. Recall that the firm's criterion for accepting any investment of this nature requires that the estimated first-year benefits must exceed the cost of the project. Should the LOD manager give the go-ahead for implementation or not?

One line of reasoning is to state that the results of the project should not be implemented, since the total cost of the project (consisting of the initial $8000 for the preliminary study plus the additional $30,000 for implementation of the results) exceeds the estimated first-year savings of $35,000 by $3000. The firm would be worse off by $3000 if it proceeded.

What is wrong with this reasoning? It is true that the total cost for the project, including the additional work needed for implementation, is $3000 larger than the estimated first-year savings. On the other hand, the expenditure of a further $30,000 will provide estimated first-year savings of $35,000, a gain of $5000. Hence, within one year of implementation the firm would be better off by this amount compared to abandoning the project now. So, if the LOD manager uses 'the recovery of all further costs within one year' as the criterion for accepting new projects, then he should go ahead with implementing the recommendations.

The fallacy in the first line of reasoning is that the $8000 has already been spent. Nothing can be done about it. None of the decision choices available to the LOD manager will recover the funds already spent. They are a so-called **sunk cost**. Sunk costs are irrelevant for decision making. Had the LOD manager known prior to engaging in the preliminary study that the total cost for the project would be $38,000, while the estimated first-year's savings would only come to $35,000, the project would never have got off the ground. The $8000 cost of the preliminary study would not have been spent. However, the manager did not know this at that time. He made the best choice on the basis of the information available then. Hindsight shows that this was the wrong choice. Taking the funds already spent into account again now would only lead to making another error in choice — one that can be avoided!

Sunk costs may sometimes be hidden in cost data derived from accounting records. Depreciation charges on a machine included in the unit production costs for a given item may be a case in point. If the annual depreciation charge is only an accounting entry made to reduce the initial purchase cost to zero over the productive life of the machine (and to reduce the incidence of tax on profits), then it is not a relevant cost item. The initial purchase price of the machine is a sunk cost and hence is irrelevant. However, if it reflects the loss in value due to its use, such as wear and tear, then it is a relevant cost item. (Note that the loss in resale value of the machine due to aging may be relevant for a different decision, such as whether or not to keep the machine for a further time given its earning potential or to dispose of it right now and replace it by a more efficient machine, as we shall see in Chapter 10.)

This is not to deny that, in the long-run, the continued survival of the firm depends on whether or not it can generate enough funds to replace all existing equipment and buildings at the end of their productive life. Hence even the loss in value due to aging becomes a cost that has to be recovered from the sale of the products or services produced.

As is often the case in MS/OR, answers are not clear-cut, but depend on the circumstances and purpose of the analysis. This reminds us of that firm that advertised for a 'one-armed' operations researcher. When the chief executive was asked why the firm wanted a 'one-armed' operations researcher, he answered that he was sick and tired of being told by them that 'on the one hand, you should do this; on the other hand it may be advantageous to do that!'

Opportunity costs

Firms own or are in control of many resources, such as raw materials, machinery, buildings, and funds. These resources may have been bought or created by the firm's own operations. They may be used currently for some purpose or the firm may be considering putting them to an alternative use. In either case, how should these resources be valued? What is the 'cost' of their use? These are important questions. Their correct answer will determine whether these resources are put to their best use or not.

Consider again the LOD problem, and in particular the investment of funds in finished goods. What is the cost of these funds? You may say that this depends on the source of these funds. You could reason that if they are raised through loans from a bank, the cost of these funds is the interest charged by the bank. On the other hand, if they come from retained earnings (profits accumulated and not paid out as dividends to the shareholders), there is no cost. What is wrong with this reasoning?

It ignores the return that the firm could earn on these funds from alternative uses. Assume the firm has alternative investment opportunities, such as the acquisition of shares of another company that earn a high return or the purchase of a machine that can produce a highly marketable and profitable product, thus raising the firm's profits. Using the funds for investment in finished goods means that these same funds cannot be used for the best of these alternative investments. Therefore the firm foregoes the return on this lost opportunity. The return foregone becomes the real cost of using these funds for investment in finished goods.

Since the assessment of this cost is based on the best alternative opportunity foregone, it is called an **opportunity cost.** All resources available to the firm or, for that matter, to any organization should always be valued at their opportunity cost. This will ensure that these resources are used efficiently.

Here is another example. What is the cost of the current warehouse space available to the LOD? As was the case for the use of funds, this item is relevant for assessing the cost of holding goods in stock for future sale. The cost accountant would claim that the cost of warehouse space is equal to the total maintenance costs incurred for the warehouse, the operating costs, such as electricity, cleaning, and heating, depreciation on the warehouse, and the cost of the funds originally invested in its construction. The opportunity cost, on the other hand, depends on the return that could be earned for the best alternative use of the warehouse. This cost is not recorded in the accounting records, which only show historical costs. The latter may be larger or smaller than the opportunity cost.

Assessing opportunity costs requires that the analyst goes beyond accounting records. It may need some research into potential alternative uses. In the LOD case, some analysis may show that due to its location, there is no alternative use for the warehouse as such, only for its land. The best alternative use for this land is as parking space for refinery employees, which currently has to be rented from the city at $528 per parking space per year. This cost, expressed on an equivalent square metre basis (say 12 m^2 per parking space) would then correspond to an opportunity cost for warehouse space at the LOD of $44 per square metre per year. Alternatively, if another division of the firm currently has to rent warehouse space adjacent to the refinery at $56 per square metre per year, and the LOD warehouse would be a suitable alternative, the opportunity cost would amount to $56 per square metre.

Should maintenance and operating costs be added? The answer is yes if these costs vary as a function of the warehouse space used by the LOD and no if they are incurred regardless of the level of usage. In general, interest charges on the funds invested in the warehouse land and building are irrelevant since they do not depend on the level of usage of the warehouse. They are a consequence of a sunk cost. If no alternative use exists for the warehouse, including its possible disposal, and maintenance and operating costs do not depend on the level of usage, the opportunity cost of warehouse space could well be zero.

Replacement costs

The historical cost paid for a resource or for goods is not a relevant measure for the value of this resource or these goods. Rather, it is the replacement cost which is relevant. For example, a cable manufacturer purchased a large quantity of copper wire at £1.63 per kilogram. A few weeks later, the price of copper wire increased to £1.84. It would then be incorrect to value the copper wire still in inventory at its original purchase price of £1.63. Any copper wire used up would have to be replaced right now at the higher value of £1.84. Furthermore, copper being a world commodity, any stock on hand presumably could be sold also at the new higher price of £1.84/kg. Replacement costs are thus a type of opportunity cost.

Future costs and benefits

Opportunity costs could well be in the form of the value of the resource for use at some future point in time. Future costs may, however, often happen in the form of explicit costs. For example, at the end of the productive life of a piece of equipment, a plot of land used for mining, or a facility built on some rented land, a substantial removal, disposal, or restoration cost may have to be incurred. This cost is a direct consequence of the decision choice and hence is a relevant cost. The huge decommissioning costs of nuclear power stations are a case in point.

The converse could also be true, i.e. the resource has some residual value at the end of the planning horizon for the project in question. This is particularly true for land and buildings, but also for equipment, if it has a positive disposal or **salvage value.**

Intangible costs

As pointed out earlier, the intangible costs may significantly reduce the worth or effectiveness of a decision alternative. For example, in terms of explicit costs (wages, etc.) alone, it is clearly much cheaper for a store to have few cashiers to serve customers. But excessive waiting times for customers may ultimately cause some customers to switch to another store. This potential loss of future business may be far more costly in the long run than the cost of additional cashiers. A decision on the best number of cashiers to have on duty should take into account the possible incidence of intangible costs.

Given the difficulty and ambiguity in assessing intangible costs, the analyst may be tempted to ignore them. This is not advisable. Every effort should be made to determine a valid monetary equivalent for these costs. **If this is not possible, the analyst should perform extensive sensitivity analysis to ascertain how the best decision changes as the (assumed) value of intangible costs varies.** If intangible costs have been ignored, this fact should be clearly stated in any report on the project. This will forewarn the decision maker that her or his final conclusion should take the possible presence of intangible factors into account in qualitative ways. Armed with extensive sensitivity analysis, the decision maker will find that this task is greatly facilitated.

Activity: Find an example of each type of cost discussed in this section for
* owning and operating a car.
* your cost of living.

9.4   Champignons Galore — problem formulation

We now look at an account of an MS/OR project, where the major effort of the analysis was the correct assessment and use of various costs, and their presentation in a convincing form. You should now carefully study the situation summary in the Appendix to this chapter. It is crucial that you get a clear understanding of the Champignons Galore (CG) problem situation before you continue with this section. You may have to read it more than once. If you have not done so yet as part of exercise 5 in Chapter 5, it will even be helpful to represent the situation as a rich picture diagram and to identify the various issues to be analysed.

Problem definition

The discussion is confined to only one of the options considered by Gérard Mousse, namely the reduction of the number of flushes in each production cycle from the current five to either 4, 3, 2, or 1. The aim is to learn if this will increase the annual output of mushrooms and its associated effect on the firm's profits. In accordance with this option, Gérard Mousse would like to know the best number of flushes to use. We shall assume that he interprets 'best' as that policy which maximizes the annual profit for the current production facilities available.

The annual profit is the difference between the annual revenue and the total annual costs. While annual revenue is simply the product of the total annual output of mushrooms and other products and their net unit selling price, determining total annual costs is more involved. We need to study in detail the nature of the various costs. This allows us to identify which ones are affected by changing the operating policy — therefore relevant — and to determine the form of the relationships between the number of flushes per production cycle and annual revenue and costs. Influence diagrams are the ideal tool for establishing these relationships. So we will now formally define the problem, summarize the relevant system, and then construct the associated influence diagram.

Referring to Section 5.2, the essence of the problem is defined by identifying the decision maker, her or his objectives, the performance measure(s), the decision criterion, and the alternative courses of action. The decision maker is Gérard Mousse. His objective is to achieve a high annual profit. The performance measure is the annual profit and the decision criterion is maximizing this measure. Finally, the alternative courses of action are the number of flushes in each cycle. To keep things simple, we will assume that none of the potential constraints, such as the size of the market and the availability of raw materials, particularly straw, will become effective.

System definition

The firm's annual profit is mainly affected by how the various costs of inputs into the process (raw materials, labour, etc.) and revenues from the outputs produced change as a function of the number of flushes. The system description thus only needs to focus on these relationships. Little additional insight will be gained by expanding the system definition to also include the biological details of mushroom growing. We will simply treat those aspects as black boxes. As a consequence, the system can easily be divided into a number of subsystems, each concerned with a given task or operation and its associated costs and revenues. Our choice is:

1. Subsystem 1: the operations of phase 1 (composting and tray preparation). Its major external inputs are raw materials and supplies for compost making, power, and labour, and the unit costs of all external inputs. The empty trays, after they have been removed from the sheds and cleaned (an output of subsystem 2), are also an input. Its outputs are trays ready for the growing phase and tray preparation costs. Peak heating is included as part of that subsystem. Trays are the major systems component relevant to this subsystem.

2. Subsystem 2: the operations associated with loading and emptying sheds. Its major inputs are the trays prepared by subsystem 1 (output of subsystem 1), sheds having completed the harvesting phase (output of subsystem 3), supplies, compost packing material, labour, and the unit costs of all external inputs. Its outputs are sheds ready for the harvesting phase, empty trays, and spent compost, ready for sale, the costs of its operations, and the sales revenue of spent compost. The systems components of prime concern to us are trays and sheds.

3. Subsystem 3: the harvesting operation. Its major inputs are sheds ready for harvesting (output of subsystem 2), labour picking rates for each successive flush, and labour pay rates. Its outputs are mushrooms (measured in kilograms), ready for sorting, the cost of picking mushrooms, and sheds having completed a full cycle. Sheds and kilograms of mushrooms are its major systems components of interest.

4. Subsystem 4: the sorting and packing operations. Its inputs are mushrooms (output of subsystem 3), packing material and supplies, and labour, and the unit cost of all external inputs. Its outputs are mushrooms delivered to customers and the canning factory, the cost of its operations, and the revenue of mushrooms sold. Its major systems components are mushrooms.

5. Subsystem 5: the biological and climate control subsystem. Its inputs are some supplies and power, and labour. Its outputs are sheds climatically controlled for best growth and harvesting, and the cost of this control. The latter is the only part of interest to us. Sheds are its major systems components.

Each subsystem receives external inputs and provides some outputs, some of which become inputs to other subsystems. These form the links between the subsystems. They are also linked together by the decision variable, namely the number of flushes in each harvesting cycle, which affects the system as a whole. Furthermore, various subsystems are subject to biological factors, such as the length of time needed to produce compost, the duration of the growing phase, and the duration of each flush.

A suitable influence diagram

You need to keep clearly in mind that the influence diagram shows the significant influence relationships between inputs, systems variables, and outputs. So it is a limited view of the system. For the systems definition above we listed aspects and relationships which reflect the tasks that a given subsystem performs, while for the influence diagram our concern is only with those aspects that directly or indirectly affect the measure of performance defined for the system. The annual profit is the measure of performance for the CG problem — the output of prime interest. All other aspects of the system are left out. Remember also that the influence diagram only shows the transformation of inputs into outputs, not the decision criterion, i.e. the optimization process.

Before you study our version of a suitable influence diagram for the CG problem, we strongly recommend that you draw up your own. Not only will this be a valuable exercise in becoming more proficient in this useful tool, but it will also force you to think thoroughly through the problem. Only then should you compare your diagram with the one in Figure 9-1.

We chose to show each of the first four subsystems as a separate sequence of relationships, each receiving external and internal inputs and having costs and/or revenues as the output to the system as a whole. While the cost relationships of each subsystem are fairly straightforward, the relationship between the decision variable, i.e. the number of flushes in each cycle, and other systems variables, such as the length of each cycle, the number of cycles per year, and the output per cycle, may need some explanation.

Recall that the duration of the growing phase is 28 days, while each flush takes on average 7 days. Together these two determine the length of a complete cycle (circle 1). The shorter each cycle, the more cycles can be scheduled per year for

Figure 9-1 Influence diagram for the CG problem.

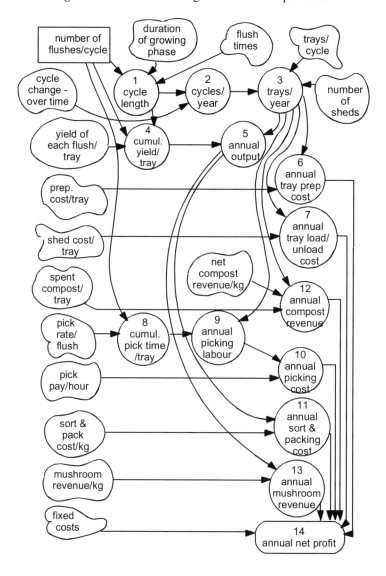

each shed. With each of the 65 sheds constantly in use carrying 400 trays per cycle, the number of cycles per year (circle 2) determines the annual number of trays needed per year (circle 3). The latter is one of the internal inputs into subsystems 1 and 2. Similarly, the length of each cycle (circle 1), together with the yield of mushrooms of each successive cycle determines the cumulative yield per cycle per tray (circle 4). This in turn, with the annual number of trays (circle 3), fixes the annual output of mushrooms (circle 5), the output of subsystem 3.

Explain the relationship between the system variables for the length of the cycle, the picking efficiency, and the amount of picking time required per tray.

The next task is to examine all cost and revenue items listed in the Appendix and associate them with the inputs to the subsystems in the influence diagram.

9.5 Champignons Galore — analysis of costs

To determine which cost factors are relevant, we answer for each the question: Does the annual cost for the firm as a whole change if the decision changes from its current value of 5 flushes per cycle? If the answer is 'yes', that particular cost factor is relevant; if 'no', it can be ignored. Note that we may still wish to add it in as a cost that remains constant for all decision choices. We then get a complete picture of the net profit. However, including or excluding such fixed costs in the measure of performance will not affect which decision choice is optimal.

As is clear from the influence diagram, the effect of the number of flushes on the total annual cost may not be direct, but indirect via other system variables.

Table 9-1 states the relevance of each cost factor listed in the Appendix to this chapter, its nature, and the corresponding input parameter that captures its effect.

There is little question that some costs, such as raw materials and wages, are proportional to either the number of trays prepared per year or the mushroom output in kg per year. Fringe benefits, like vacation and sick pay, pension fund, and other employer contributions on wages vary in proportion with the wage payment. As the wage bill changes, so will such items. Hence they are a variable cost. Note that accountants may include some of these costs for reasons of convenience and tradition, particularly fringe benefits, as part of various overheads. (The prudent analyst will analyse the composition of overheads for such items and, if necessary, reallocate them appropriately.)

Table 9-1 Analysis of CG cost factors.

Section	Relevance	Nature of effect	Input parameter	
Compost/tray preparation:				
raw materials	yes	prop./tray	prep. cost/tray	(1)
electricity	yes	variable/tray	prep. cost/tray	(2)
diesel fuel	yes	prop./tray	prep. cost/tray	(3)
maintenance on vehicles	yes	variable/tray	prep. cost/tray	(4)
vehicle depreciation	no	constant	fixed cost	
yard/build. maintenance	no	constant	fixed cost	
yard workers wages	yes	prop./tray	prep. cost/tray	(5)
salary J.Brownsey	no	constant	fixed cost	
Shed loading and maintenance:				
supplies & diesel fuel	yes	prop./tray	shed cost/tray	
compost pack material	yes	prop./tray	shed cost/tray	

tray repair & maint'nce	yes	prop./tray	shed cost/tray
vehicle maintenance	yes	variable/tray	shed cost/tray
vehicle depreciation	no	constant	fixed cost
shed workers' wages	yes	prop./tray	shed cost/tray
salary of M. McTrae	no	constant	fixed cost
Climate control:			
electricity	no	approx. constant	fixed cost
materials	no	approx. constant	fixed cost
lab. maintenance	no	constant	fixed cost
equipment depreciation	no	constant	fixed cost
new equipment	no	sunk cost	excluded
Picking, sorting, packaging:			
packing materials	yes	prop./kg	sort/pack. cost/kg
supplies & electricity	yes	variable/kg	sort/pack. cost/kg
new equipment	no	sunk cost	excluded
maintenance equip.	yes	variable/kg	sort/pack. cost/kg
equip. depreciation	no	constant	fixed cost
diesel fuel trucks	yes	prop./kg	sort/pack. cost/kg
maintenance trucks	yes	variable/kg	sort/pack. cost/kg
depreciation trucks	no	constant	fixed cost
wages sort/pack	yes	prop./kg	sort/pack. cost/kg
wages for drivers	yes	variable/kg	sort/pack. cost/kg
salary J. Fleurette	no	constant	fixed cost
wages picking	yes	variable/hour	pick pay/hr
vacation/sick pay	yes	variable/hour	pick pay/hr
Local marketing:			
salary J. Marchand	no	constant	fixed cost
travel J. Marchand	no	approx. constant	fixed cost
Other costs:			
office supplies	no	approx. constant	fixed cost
new equipment	no	sunk cost	excluded
company cars running cost	no	approx. constant	fixed cost
depreciation company cars	no	constant	fixed cost
office salaries	no	approx. constant	fixed cost
gardener	no	constant	fixed cost
maintenance office	no	constant	fixed cost
depreciation office bldg	no	constant	fixed cost
insurance, mortgage interest	no	constant	fixed cost
salaried employees accident insurance, pension fund	no	constant	fixed cost
worker accident insurance & pension fund	yes	prop./€ paid	prep. cost/tray & shed cost/tray & sort/pack. cost/kg & pick cost/hour
salary C. Mousse	no	constant	fixed cost
travel C. Mousse	no	approx. constant	fixed cost

Other costs, such as the purchase of equipment, are clearly irrelevant and must be excluded from consideration. Salaries, including the associated fringe benefits, in general are constant, at least over the variation in the output level considered. Hence they are fixed costs. Depreciation, insurance, and mortgage interests on buildings, etc., are not affected by the level of activity. Hence, they are fixed costs. Depreciation on equipment and vehicles depends on whether it is mainly affected by usage or by age. In the first case, it is a variable cost, while in the second it is fixed. Given the relatively small amounts involved, we shall arbitrarily assume for simplicity that such depreciation is a fixed cost.

Most supplies and electricity usage are affected by the level of activity, but not necessarily proportionately. Again, to keep things simple, we assume that these costs are approximately proportional to the level of activity, i.e. either the number of sheds prepared or the output of mushrooms. The exception is the section dealing with climate control. The sheds are in constant use for either the growing or harvesting phases, except for the two days of changeover from one cycle to the next. But even during those two days, the cooling of the sheds continues; hence the annual power cost is constant. Similarly, since the firm cultivates its own mycelium, the annual cost of supplies, etc., is not affected by fairly large variations in the output level. All costs of the climate control section can thus be treated as constant.

Maintenance of yard equipment and vehicles, and of the sorting and packing equipment is likely to be affected by the level of activity. Hence it is viewed as a variable cost, for simplicity approximated as proportional to the output level.

The travel costs of both the marketing manager and Gérard Mousse are partially affected by the mushroom output. The more mushrooms available, the larger must be the selling effort, which requires more travel. However, it would be difficult to determine a suitable mathematical relationship between output and travel cost. Given the small amounts of funds involved, we simply take them as fixed.

The tray maintenance, repair, and replacement costs are proportional to the level of activity. Most damage to the trays occurs during handling. The more handling, the higher this damage, so it is assumed to be proportional to the number of trays prepared.

The mushroom picking costs are clearly affected by the output level of mushrooms. But the relationship is somewhat complex, since the picking rate decreases with each additional flush. We shall analyse this aspect in more detail when we look at the mathematical model of total costs.

The two revenue sources are sales of mushrooms and sale of spent compost, both proportional to the volume of output of each.

Activity: Consider the costs listed in Table 9-1.
• Under what conditions is it correct to treat yard and building costs as fixed?
• The picking, sorting, and packaging section currently employs two drivers. Jennifer Fleurette guesses that a third driver is only required if the mushroom output goes up by more than 20% (resulting though in considerable idle time), while an

increase in output of more than 8% but less than 20% can be handled by overtime in the short run. Does this change the nature and relevance of that cost? Why or why not? (Note that such cost behaviour is quite common when 'work' capacity increases in discrete steps. Explain why an assumption of proportionality is a reasonable approximation once the number of 'work' units gets large or workers can be used for other tasks.)

- Some costs, such as electricity or maintenance have the following form: cost = [fixed portion] + [variable portion], where the latter is a function of output. How would you deal with that?
- The section supervisors receive an annual bonus, based on productivity increases in their section. How would you treat this?

9.6 Mathematical model for annual profit

We now list the mathematical form of the relationships represented in the influence diagram of Figure 9-1. Rather than using mathematical notation, we explain the relationships in plain English. Most of the expressions are simple enough to be self-explanatory. If you have doubts about any of them, we suggest that you check them out by working out a few examples using assumed numbers. That usually helps.

All expressions are defined for a decision choice of n consecutive flushes in each cycle, where n can be 5, 4, 3, 2, or 1. The expressions are labelled by the numbers shown in each circle or output.

1. Length of each cycle:

   [cycle length] = [growing phase duration]+[average flush length] $\times n = 28 + 7n$

2. Number of cycles per year:

   [cycles/year] = [days in year]/([cycle length] + [cycle change-over time])
   $$= 365/([\text{cycle length}] + 2)$$

3. Number of trays prepared per year:

   [trays/year] = [number of sheds] $\times$ [trays/shed] $\times$ [cycles/year]
   $$= 65 \times 400 \times [\text{cycles/year}]$$

4. Mushroom output per cycle per tray: The data collected by Jennifer Fleurette for sheds 5 and 6 allow us to compute the average yield for each consecutive flush. In practice, it would be advisable to collect data on about a dozen cycles, rather than just two. Verify from the data listed that a new flush seems to start at regular intervals of about 7 days. (A graph highlights this pattern clearly.) So we add up the amount picked for each consecutive 7-day interval for both sheds and divide this sum by two. This gives the average yield for each flush per shed. Dividing these numbers by 400 gives the following average yields and cumulative average yields per tray for each consecutive flush:

flush $n =$	1	2	3	4	5
average yield kg/shed	9189	6432	2841	1711	1044
or kg/tray	22.97	16.08	7.10	4.28	2.61
cumulative yield kg/tray	22.97	39.05	46.15	50.43	53.04

5. Annual output of mushrooms:

    [annual output] = [trays/year] × [cumulative yield/tray for n flushes]

6. Annual tray preparation cost:

    [annual tray preparation cost] = [preparation cost/tray] × [trays/year]

7. Annual shed loading and unloading cost:

    [annual shed cost] = [shed cost/tray] × [trays/year]

8. Mushroom picking time per tray: The picking time per kg increases with each consecutive flush. As for the yield, Jennifer's figures allow us to compute an average picking rate for each consecutive flush. To test your understanding, compare the answers you compute with the ones shown below:

flush	1	2	3	4	5
kg picked/hour	10.804	9.629	6.938	5.085	4.176
hours per tray	2.126	1.670	1.024	0.841	0.625
cumulative hours/tray	2.126	3.796	4.820	5.661	6.286

9. Annual number of hours required for picking mushroom output:

    [annual picking labour] = [trays/year] × [cumulative hours/tray]

10. Annual cost of picking labour:

    [annual picking cost] = [annual picking labour] × [picking pay/hour]

11. Annual sorting and packing cost:

    [annual sorting & packing cost] = [annual output] × [sort. & pack. cost/kg]

12. Annual compost revenue:

    [annual compost revenue] = [spent compost/tray] × [trays/year]
    × [net compost selling price/kg]

13. Annual mushroom revenue:

    [annual mushroom revenue] = [annual output] × [mushroom revenue/kg]

14. Annual net profit: total revenue less total costs

    [annual net profit] = [annual mushroom revenue]
    + [annual compost revenue]
    − [annual tray preparation cost]
    − [annual shed cost]
    − [annual picking cost]
    − [annual sorting & packing cost]
    − [annual fixed cost]

To apply this model, we now have to compute the various cost factors used in expressions 6, 7, 10, and 11.

9.7 Computation of cost factors for each subsystem

We will demonstrate how some of the cost coefficients are computed for use in the mathematical model. It is important to remember that all costs compiled by the accountant and reported in the Appendix refer to the preceding financial year. During that year, the policy used was to let each harvesting cycle go through five flushes, i.e. $n = 5$. We shall also assume that there is no inflation. This implies that the cost factors derived will remain valid for the future.

Preparation costs per tray

This covers all costs of the compost making and phase 1 tray preparation that vary proportionately with the number of trays prepared per year. They are thus best expressed in the form of an average preparation cost per tray.

For $n=5$ flushes per harvesting cycle, the cycle length is $28 + 7(5) = 63$ days. The number of cycles per year is then $365/(63 + 2) = 5.6154$ cycles on average. With 65 sheds in constant use and each shed carrying 400 trays, the annual number of trays required is $65(400)(5.6154) = 146,000$ trays.

Applying the classification of Table 9-1 to the data for tray preparation in the Appendix, the costs that vary proportionally to the number of trays prepared amount to €6,243,310 (items numbered 1 to 5 in table), including €428,211 for wages. The total cost of waged labour also has to include the cost of any fringe benefits and other wage-related contributions paid by the employer. We can assume that the figure on the total wage payments compiled by the accountant includes vacation and sick pay. So no adjustment for this is needed. However, the accountant also lists under other costs accident insurance and pension fund contributions, totalling €784,906. These contributions are incurred on the totality of all wages paid. The percentage contribution rates for each are 2.5% for accident insurance and 4% for employer's pension fund contributions, or a total of 6.5%. This amounts to €27,834 on the €428,211 wages paid for this section. The total variable cost for this section is thus

Materials, power, fuel, etc.	€5,815,099
Waged labour	€428,211
Fringe benefits 6.5%	€27,834
Total waged labour cost	€456,045
Total variable cost for 146,000 trays	€6,271,144

This gives an average tray preparation cost of €42.96.

Shed cost per tray

Using the classification of costs in Table 9-1 for this section, verify that the analogous reasoning as for the tray preparation leads to a shed cost per tray of €5.40.

Mushroom pickers gross pay per hour

The accountant lists the hourly pay rate for mushroom pickers at €9.20. This is exclusive of all fringe benefits supported by the employer. The accountant also quotes that the vacation and sickness pay is limited to the equivalent of 8% of the total annual pay of a picker. Adding to this the accident insurance and pension fund contribution, total fringe benefits of 6.5% + 8% = 14.5% have to be added to the hourly pay rate. The hourly cost to the firm is thus €10.53.

Sorting and packing costs per kilogram of mushrooms produced

The total variable cost for materials, etc., and labour, including the 6.5% cost of fringe benefits, amounts to €6,353,911. The annual output is equal to the cumulative yield per tray multiplied by the number of trays per year, i.e. 53.043(146000) or 7,744,205 kg. This gives a sorting and packing cost of €0.8205 per kilogram of mushrooms produced. (It is here important to show sufficient decimal places, since it will be multiplied by millions. Any small rounding error will be magnified.)

9.8 Analysis of Champignons Galore by spreadsheet

The input data for the mathematical model shown in Section 9.6 is reproduced in Figure 9-2, while Figure 9-3 is a reproduction of the spreadsheet computations. It first computes the various intermediate variables as a function of the number of flushes per cycle. These are then used in the cost and revenue computations. The last line shows the difference in annual profits in comparison with the current policy of five flushes per harvesting cycle.

The annual profit is higher for 2, 3, and 4 flushes than for the current policy. The highest profit increase is obtained for 3 flushes (shown shaded) per harvesting cycle. The increase is almost 1 million euros per year. It also results in an increase in mush-room output of 844,245 kg or slightly more than 10%. It is a highly interesting aspect of the policy of 3 flushes per cycle that it also achieves another of Gérard Mousse's objectives. Based on this analysis, he would be advised to reduce the number of flushes from 5 to 3 per harvesting cycle. This would achieve his objectives of both increasing output and profits at the same time. The increase in output is the equivalent of 7 additional sheds if the current policy of 5 flushes were maintained. Any decision as to adding more sheds can thus be postponed by another few years.

9.9 Chapter highlights

- Traditional accounting practices record the historical financial performance of an organization. Accounting cost control focuses on allocating all costs, variable and fixed, to individual products or services in view of determining average costs or

Figure 9-2   Spreadsheet evaluation for CG problem.

CHAMPIGNONS GALORE LTD.					
INPUT DATA:					
Picking cost:					
Labour/hour		9.20			
Fringe benefit 14.5%		1.33	(incl. 8% vacation pay, 2.5%		
Total/hour		10.53	accident ins., 4% pension		
Tray preparation:					
Materials		5815099			
Labour	428211				
Fringe benefit 6.5%	27834	456045	(incl. 2.5% accident ins.,		
Total for 146,000 trays		6271144	4% pension fund)		
per tray		42.9560			
Shed cost:					
Materials, etc.		588343			
Labour	188231				
Fringe benefit 6.5%	12235	200466	(as above)		
Total for 146,000 trays		788809			
per tray		5.4032			
Processing cost:					
Materials, etc.		4121198			
Labour	2096444				
Fringe benefit 6.5%	136269	2232713	(as above)		
Total for 7,744,205 kg		6353911			
per kg		0,8205			
SUMMARY OF INPUT DATA:					
Number of trays/shed	400		Flush	Yield (kg)	Picking hrs
Number of sheds	65		1	9189	850.5
Revenue/kg	€3.60		2	6432	668.0
Sort & Pack cost/kg	0.82047		3	2841	409.5
Picking cost/kg	€10.53		4	1711	336.5
Preparation cost/tray	€42.96		5	1044	250.0
Shed cost/tray	€5.40				
Fixed cost/year	€2914294				
Compost revenue/tray	€8.40				

so-called standard costs. These may be used for pricing decisions and to assess current performance under the assumption of no change in the level of activity or operation.

Figure 9-3   Cost and Revenue Computations for Champignons Galore.

EVALUATION					
Flushes per cycle	1	2	3	4	5
Tray and volume computations					
Cycle length in days	37	44	51	58	65
Number of cycles/year	9.865	8.295	7.157	6.293	5.615
Yield/tray in kg	22.973	16.080	7.103	4.278	2.610
Cumul. yield/tray in kg	22.973	39.053	46.155	50.433	53.043
Picking hours/tray	2.126	1.670	1.024	0.841	0.625
Cumul. picking hr/tray	2.126	3.796	4.820	5.661	6.286
Number of trays/year	256,486	215,682	186,078	163,621	146,000
Total output/year in kg	5,892,136	8,422,914	8,588,450	8,251,800	7,744,205
Revenue and cost computations					
Mushroom revenue	21,211,689	30,322,491	30,918,420	29,706,482	27,879,138
Compost revenue	2,154,486	1,811,727	1,563,059	1,374,414	1,226,400
Tray preparation cost	11,017,629	9,264,824	7,993,182	7,028,487	6,271,573
Shed cost	1,385,840	1,165,366	1,005,414	884,071	788,863
Picking cost	5,744,763	8,625,051	9,447,924	9,757,619	9,668,026
Sorting & packing cost	4,834,338	6,910,773	7,046,591	6,770,379	6,353,911
Fixed cost	2,914,294	2,914,294	2,914,294	2,914,294	2,914,294
Net profit	(2,530,689)	3,253,910	4,074,075	3,726,045	3,108,871
Difference	(5,639,560)	145,040	965,204	617,174	0

Postscript: When this solution was submitted to the management for consideration, the chief executive's response was disbelief. His answer was the one attributed in the case write-up in the Appendix to the father of Gérard Mousse. However, three years later, the firm nevertheless went ahead and reduced the flushes per harvesting cycle, a delay that could have cost them up to three million euros!

• In MS/OR projects, we are only interested in those costs and benefits that change, for the organization as a whole, if the mode of operation or the level of activities change. Often fixed costs remain unaffected and are not relevant. If they change they need to be taken into account as totals rather than in the form averages per unit output, usually as part of a financial project evaluation (as discussed in detail in Chapter 10).

• Accounting data of standard costs may thus not be inappropriate. Furthermore, accounting records do not show opportunity costs, but include sunk costs which are irrelevant for decision making.

Exercises

1. Compare opportunity costs and intangible costs and discuss their differences and similarities, if any.

2. Discuss why opportunity costs are a form of implicit costs.

3. Why are opportunity costs relevant for decision making?

4. Give an example of explicit costs, implicit costs, fixed costs, variable costs, opportunity costs, sunk costs, and intangible costs for each of the following types of entities:
   (a) An industrial firm, such as a manufacturer of household appliances.
   (b) A merchandising firm, such as a department store.
   (c) A service industry firm, such as a restaurant.
   (d) A public service organization, such as a hospital.
   (e) A local government agency, such as the water supply authority.

5. The following questions all refer to Table 9-1 of the Champignons Galore case:
   (a) The depreciation for yard vehicles is currently classified as a fixed cost. Assume now that CG adopts the optimal cycle length of three flushes. The number of trays to be prepared increases from 146,000 to 186,078, a 27% increase. When Charles Brun hears this, he casually mentions to Roger Munny that this implies that the yard vehicles may have to be replaced earlier than under the previous scheme. What implications, if any, has this on the relevance of depreciation?
   (b) Charles Brun also points out that, while the compost stacking machine can easily cope with the increased workload, this is not the case for the current assortment of forklift tractors. In fact, he reckons that at least one additional forklift tractor will have to be purchased. Its operating and maintenance costs, as well as its depreciation, would be identical to the ones for the current tractors. What is the effect of purchasing another tractor on the annual costs under the new system?
   (c) The amount of work for climate control is considerably more intensive during the 26–28 day growing phase than during the harvesting phases. Under the new system, the number of cycles per year also increases by 27%. Karl Scharf worries that he and Tina Paille will not be able to handle the increased workload without getting a part-time assistant. How does this affect the relevance of costs for climate control?
   (d) The increase in the level of operations due to the higher volume of mushrooms requires additional working capital (funds invested in inventories of all sorts, an increase in the level of outstanding customer bills, increased bank account balances required for daily operations, etc.). Gérard Mousse proposes raising the additional funds by getting a bank loan of €300,000 at an interest rate of 15%. The loan will be paid off through retained earning. How does this affect the imputation of costs?

6. A firm produces various types of adhesive tape, like flesh-coloured vinyl for bandages, electrical insulating tape, etc. Depending on the type of tape, it is either produced on the older and more expensive Classic line or the newer and more efficient Modern line. Both lines are currently used for about 1.5 shifts per day. In an effort to reduce production costs, the production engineer experiments with various different setups and comes up with a proposal, which he claims will reduce production costs substantially. The proposal implies that the equivalent of about ½ shift of work is moved from the Classic line to the Modern line. This would increase the workload of the Modern line by about ¼ shift. He presents the following summary of savings for switching bandage vinyl from the Classic to the Modern line:

	Classic line	Modern line	Savings
Speed of production (m² /hr)	600	1200	
Adhesive applied (kg/m²)	0.275	0.25	
Adhesive cost/year at €15/kg for 140,000 m²	€577,500	€525,000	€52,500
Machine hours for production	233.33	116.67	
Size of batches in m²	5000	10000	
Annual setup time in hours	28	14	
Total machine hours required (hrs)	261.33	130.67	
Labour cost €20/hr + 25% fringe ben.	€6533	€3267	€ 3,266
Overhead* allocation/machine hour	€102	€78	
Total overhead allocation	€26,656	€10,660	€15,996
Total net savings			€71,762

* Overhead also includes recovery of the initial cost of the machine, i.e. machine depreciation.

Upon seeing this statement, the accountant reports that switching production from the Classic line to the Modern line would result in the overhead allocation rate changing. Reducing the work load on the Classic line by ½ shift would increase its overhead rate to around €123. Given the greater efficiency of the Modern line, its overhead rate would decrease by about 14% only. As a result, all the remaining products produced on the Classic line would increase substantially in cost, either reducing the profitability of these products or forcing corresponding price increases, with a potential drop-off in sales. The firm might even have to stop production of some of the previously profitable products due to decreased sales. The increased profitability of products produced on the Modern line would probably not justify any price reductions in these products, or if prices were reduced marginally this was unlikely to increase sales noticeably. He therefore recommended against this move. When asked if the overhead allocation rate on the Classic line could not simply be left at its present level, he was quite adamant that this would violate company policy that each machine had to recover all its costs, including its proper overhead allocation. If this were done in this instance, then pressure would build to use this kind of ploy in other instances also. This would invalidate all attempts to properly cost products.

Analyse these costs and discuss their relevance for the decision to switch production lines. Discuss the accountant's arguments.

Are there any relevant costs that the engineer missed?

7. A firm sells a range of chemical products in a variety of containers: 0.3 and 1 litre plastic bottles, 1 and 5 litre cans, etc.. Each product goes through the following production process. The first stage is to mix the basic ingredients. This is done in vats of 100, 500, 1000, 4000, and 10000 litres. An operator measures out the ingredients and adds them to the vat chosen for mixing in a prescribed sequence, with the mixing blades activated at various times. The ingredients are stored in the nearby chemicals warehouse. For safety, each ingredient has to be handled individually, i.e. removing the desired quantity from the stock of ingredients if it comes in containers of the correct size, or else bringing a drum or bag from the storage area to the scales and measuring out the required amount, and then returning the balance in the warehouse. Most products use between 5 and 20 ingredients, but some are made up of up to 50. Once mixed, some of the products have to go through a homogenization process, i.e. the mixing vat is covered and the mixing blades rotated at very high speed. The entire mixing operation can take anywhere from 1 to 6 hours.

When mixing is completed, a 0.5 litre sample undergoes a series of tests in the lab. About 5% of all batches mixed fail one or several of these tests. If this happens, the lab technician returns an upgrading report to the mixing operator. That report spells out what additional quantities of ingredients have to be added to bring the batch up to specifications. The time taken for this is on average about 60% of the original mixing setup time. It occasionally means also that the size of the batch becomes larger than originally ordered. Naturally the upgraded batch has to be retested. Over the last 5-year period no batch has failed a test twice. Test results are usually available within 30 minutes.

Once a batch has been cleared, it is filled into containers. Plastic or rubber lines are hooked up to connect mixers to filling machines: one for each size container. To eliminate any contamination which could potentially be hazardous to the operators and the users of the products, these lines have to be thoroughly cleaned after each use. Furthermore, the lines deteriorate with use and have to be discarded after 80 uses. A new line has a cost of €60.

Prior to filling a new batch, the containers have to be made ready, the labels inserted into the machine, the filling machine adjusted for the viscosity of the product filled (this controls the quantity filled), and the lines from the mixer hooked up to the filling machine. Two operators are engaged in these preparations for a total of 15 minutes each. A trial batch of 12 containers is then filled and inspected. The last three containers are tested for weight. One of the containers is also returned to the testing lab for confirmation of its content. This container is then labelled by the batch number and date, and kept for at least 8 months. The time taken for these final tests is 15 minutes, during which time the filling machine is stopped. Although the two machine operators keep busy, such as making final readjustments to the machine, the production engineer views this time as essentially unproductive. Once the sample can has been cleared by the lab, filling takes place at full machine speed. The containers are packed into cardboard boxes by hand by up to four labourers. The boxes are sealed and labelled and then placed on pallets, which are stored in the finished goods warehouse. During the machine setup and testing, these labourers are kept busy by other productive work. Their wages during setup are therefore not chargeable to the product being filled. Filling time depends on the batch size. The 1 litre machines can fill up to 300 cans or 180 bottles per minute.

Consider product X. Its ingredients cost €5.50 per litre of finished product. Preparation for mixing takes 2 hours. This includes the cleaning of the vat. The actual mixing operation is proportional to the size of the batch and takes 20 minutes for every 1000 litres of mix. The two laboratory technicians test 20 to 40 products each day. They also spend some 2 hours per day testing raw materials shipped by suppliers. Hooking up the mixers to the filling machine takes 5 minutes. This is done by the mixing operator. The actual filling occurs at a rate of 200 cans per minute. Four packers are needed for packing the cans into boxes, etc. Cleaning the filling machine and the hookup lines after a run takes another 10 minutes for two people. Cleaning is done using cleaning solvents and neutralizers. For this particular product it takes 12 litres of fresh cleaning solvents to clean the vat, filling machine, and hookup lines at a cost of €1.50 per litre. Furthermore, the first two cans filled cannot be used, since even after thorough cleaning, there may still be some small amounts of residue left in the filling mechanism, which is washed out by the flow of chemicals to fill the first two cans. Consumption of power during all these operations is about €0.16 per 1000 litres of product. Can labels cost 2 cents/can, while a carton for 24 cans has a cost of 60 cents, including the label.

The wage rate for the mixing operator and the two filling machine operators is €16 per hour, while the packing labourers at the filling machine are paid €12 per hour. The weekly salary of lab technicians is €800 for a 40-hour week. Any increase in the lab workload of more than 10% requires overtime or the addition of a part- or full-time technician.

Other costs involved in inventory control include clerical costs at the accounting department. Currently about 3 persons are fully occupied in maintaining computerized inventory records, including the processing of customer orders, preparation of customer delivery documents, preparation and processing of stock replenishments. It is estimated that each stock replenishment takes about 20 minutes of clerical time for all processing involved. Only about 20% of their time is taken up by processing stock replenishments. Clerks are on monthly salaries of €2,000 and work a 40-hour week.

There are two types of overhead. Plant overhead is charged at 50% of direct labour cost. General overhead is assessed at a rate of 64% on direct labour cost. General overhead also includes fringe benefits of 30%, such as vacation pay, pension fund contributions, health and accident insurance, cafeteria subsidies, etc. The company wishes to earn a return on its investment of 15% after taxes. The current marginal tax rate is 33%.

The company rents its premises. The cost accountant has figured out that each square metre of floor space has an annual cost of €40. One pallet stored in the warehouse requires 1.44 square metres of floor space. Pallets are stored three high. For each pallet area, 0.56 square metres of floor space is needed for access aisles. The filling machine requires a floor space of 10×15 metres, while a vat needs about 9 square metres of floor space. The premises consist of a separate building. It is not subdividable and has to be rented as a whole unit. Currently, there is ample floor space available for expansion. Maintenance of the plant area has an annual cost of €12 per square metre.

The current inventory replenishment policy used by the firm is based on the economic order quantity model. Identify all costs relevant for determining the EOQ for the product in question. Develop a table similar to Table 9-1 for classifying all costs mentioned. You may wish to review some of the material in Chapter 6 dealing with the EOQ model. Recall that there are two types of relevant costs for the EOQ model: those that are fixed for each replenishment, regardless of its size, and those that are associated with the cost of holding goods in stock, usually assessed on the average inventory level.

8. For the cost factors developed in exercise 7, find the optimal replenishment size and its annual cost, using the EOQ model of Chapter 6, for an annual demand of 160,000 litres.

Appendix: Champignons Galore — situation summary

Champignons Galore (CG) is a French commercial grower of mushrooms. Cultivated mushrooms grow under carefully controlled climatic and hygienic conditions, usually in complete darkness in caves, cellars, or specially constructed sheds. CG uses sheds.

The production process

Mushrooms are grown on a base of specially prepared compost. CG makes its own compost. It buys straw from the surrounding farms and wheat growers. In fact, CG buys well over 50% of all straw locally available. This straw is mixed with animal manure and other organic materials. The mixture is stacked into long snakes or rows of about 2×2 metres dimension. This operation is done by a special-purpose stacking machine. Once stacked, the mixture naturally undergoes a fermentation from inside out which transforms it slowly into compost. This creates a substantial amount of heat which further contributes to the process. Outside temperatures and the amount of natural rain can affect the speed of fermentation. Sprinkler systems are used for controlling the humidity level of the mixture. After 1 to 2 weeks, when the insides of the stacks have become compost, the stacking machine turns the stacks inside out. This speeds up complete fermentation of all material. The whole process takes anywhere from 2 to 4 weeks, depending on the time of the year and the outside temperature. New stacks of compost are started at regular intervals to guarantee a constant supply of fresh compost for the production process.

The mushroom production itself consists of three phases. In phase 1 the compost is put into 30-centimetre deep wooden trays. These are topped with peat. The trays and their contents are then sterilized to kill any diseases or unwanted seeds, etc. Once sterilized, the trays are injected with laboratory-grown mycelium (mushroom spawn), covered with casing soil, and treated in a process called 'peak heating'. Phase 2 is the mycelium growing stage. The trays are stored on shelves in growing sheds. The inside of the sheds is almost completely dark and kept within carefully controlled temperature and humidity ranges. The growing phase lasts about 26 to 28 days. During this time the mycelium invests the entire bed in each tray. The third phase is the cropping stage. The mushrooms which are the fruiting bodies of the plant appear in a sequence of 'flushes' at intervals of 6 to 8 days. Within 1 to 2 days of breaking through the casing soil, the mushrooms are harvested. The yield of the first two flushes is substantially higher than for the subsequent flushes. Also, the size of the mushrooms becomes smaller for the later flushes. As a result, the amount of labour needed to pick the mushrooms appearing in the later flushes increases markedly over the first two flushes. The reason for both these phenomena is that each flush reduces the nutrient content of the compost until, after about 5 to 6 flushes, it has been almost exhausted. At that point, the trays are removed from the sheds, the 'spent' compost packed into bags for resale as mulch to home gardeners or commercial vegetable growers, and the trays cleaned and returned to the compost filling station, ready for use in a new production cycle. Emptying a shed, preparing it for the next cycle, and loading it with a fresh batch of trays takes about 2 days.

Like composting, phase 1 of the production process is done on a continuous basis, with new trays prepared daily for phase 2. With the number of sheds currently in operation, a new shed starts on phase 2 practically every day. As a consequence the sheds are on a continuous rotation, with each shed at a different stage in the process. This provides a fairly constant output level for the operation as a whole.

Picking of mushrooms is done by hand. For this reason, the width of the trays and their spacing on the shelves in the sheds is such that a picker can easily reach to the middle of each tray, working either from the floor for the lowest shelf or from a ladder that rolls along the shelves for the upper two shelf levels. In order to maintain strict hygiene, any person entering a growing shed has to pass through a lock where shoes and clothing are automatically sterilized. The freshly picked mushrooms are sorted by size and quality. The very small ones are used by a canning factory, operated by CG at a different site. Most of the high-quality product is exported to England and Scandinavia, while the second grade mushrooms are sold on the local French market or used in the canning operation.

The firm currently operates 66 sheds, each capable of storing 400 trays. 65 sheds are continuously in use for the growing and harvesting phases, except for the 2 days needed to clean a shed and prepare it for the next cycle. At all times, one shed is not in use on a rotational basis and undergoes major maintenance/repair work, which takes 5 to 6 days. Trays also need regular repairs and replacement. On average a tray last four years.

The people

Gérard Mousse is the principal owner of the firm, having taken over from his father as managing director two years ago. Before that he was the firm's marketing manager. He has six people in supervisory positions reporting to him. Roger Munny is the chief accountant and also serves as office manager. The compost and tray preparation sections are managed by Charles Brun. It is said of him that with his super-sensitive nose, which is a most striking feature of his face, and by sticking his right index finger into the fermenting stacks he is able to judge the correct temperature and humidity level of the stacks as well and with less effort than the scientific tests Gérard Mousse tried to convince him to use. His portion of the operation is highly mechanized, using the rather expensive compost stacking machine, forklift tractors, the automatic sprinkler system, the tray filling machine, and the sterilization and peak heating ovens. Michel Boîte is in charge of the gangs filling and emptying the sheds, shed maintenance and cleaning, and repair and maintenance of trays, as well as disposing of the spent compost. Karl Scharf and his laboratory assistant, Tina Paille, are responsible for the climatic control of the sheds. They are by far the most scientifically trained employees of the firm. Picking and sorting of the mushrooms and their dispatch to customers, all highly labour-intensive operations, are managed by Jennifer

Fleurette. Jean Marchand has recently been hired as the marketing manager in charge of domestic sales as the sole member of that department. Gérard Mousse retained control over international marketing contracts and promotion.

The problem

When Gérard Mousse took over control of the firm after his father's retirement, his initial efforts went mainly into developing the export markets in England and Scandinavia. This led to increasing requirements for top-quality product. To meet the additional demand, ten new sheds were added to the original 56 in operation at the time Gérard assumed the top position. Otherwise, Gérard did not make any major changes to the operation or its management. The exception was hiring the German scientist Karl to improve quality control. It may also be worth mentioning that, as one of his first actions after taking over the management of the firm, he upgraded the staff cafeteria and the staff changing facilities — a deed that earned him the respect and loyalty of his waged and salaried staff and strongly contributed to staff morale and productivity.

Given the potential for increased export sales, Gérard now sees upgrading the production capacity for top-grade product as one of his priorities. The firm's current facilities do not really allow the construction of more sheds, unless the firm adopts the rather expensive two-level sheds. A plot of land, two kilometres to the south of the existing plant and suitable for a maximum of 32 sheds, had recently been offered for sale. This opens up the option of going to a two-site growing operation, with the composting and phase 1 done on the current premises for both sites. Gérard doubts that the firm will need more than about 10 to 16 additional sheds within the next five years. Hence, only a small portion of the site would be used productively. However, this option would provide the firm with sufficient breathing space for further expansion for a long time. The increase in transportation cost for trays and mushrooms is an added disadvantage of the two-site option.

Gérard wonders whether it would be possible to increase the output of top-grade mushrooms at the current site without the need to construct new sheds. He has always wondered about the reasons why his father had used a 5-flush harvesting cycle, although he was aware that practically all commercial mushroom growers, using the same system as CG, seem to follow this policy. In fact, he recently discussed this issue with his father when he visited him with his young family at a weekend. His father was very sceptical that any gains could be made by adopting a policy with a smaller number of cycles. His main argument was that if this were advantageous, the mushroom industry would have adopted it long ago. Gérard was not convinced by this argument, since the mushroom industry was hardly known for its initiative in researching anything else but how to grow the perfect mushroom.

Being a cautious businessman, he decides to cost out the three options. He remembers bumping into his old university buddy, John Smart, at a recent function in London, where he discovered with some envy that John Smart had continued his university study, getting a PhD in MS/OR at a British university. He recently accepted a teaching position at his old *alma mater*. He mentioned that he was looking for potential student projects. Would this problem not be an ideal project? He contacts John who asks him to gather some data on various aspects of the operation, like costs of various tasks and the yield for each consecutive flush.

Data collected

Gérard asks Roger Munny to compile a preliminary list of various cost items incurred in the production of mushrooms. Jennifer willingly agrees to keep an exact tally of the quantity of mushrooms harvested each day over the entire harvesting cycle for sheds 5 and 6 which where just coming on-stream for producing mushrooms. It turns out that Jennifer goes a step further by also recording for each day the number of hours worked by the pickers harvesting mushrooms in these two sheds.

Here is a list of the various items of data compiled or collected.

Cost data compiled by Roger Munny, based on the preceding financial year:

1. **C. Brun's section** (composting and tray preparation):
    - €5,493,557 for raw materials (straw, manure, peat, casing sand, sterilization agents, etc.). Most raw materials were purchased regularly, some like straw almost daily, with raw material stocks being small and remaining fairly constant over the entire year.
    - €267,844 for electricity for peak heating, operation of tray filling equipment, etc.
    - €27,911 diesel fuel for yard vehicles.
    - €25,787 maintenance and repair costs on yard vehicles.
    - €123,000 depreciation on yard vehicles and equipment.
    - €86,520 yard ground and building maintenance and repair costs.
    - €428,211 for yard workers' wages, including vacation pay.
    - €36,400 salary of C. Brun.

2. **Michel Boîte's section** (shed loading and unloading):
    - €51,333 for supplies (sterilization and cleaning chemicals for sheds).
    - €219,102 packing material for spent compost.
    - €24,451 for diesel fuel.
    - €12,211 for vehicle maintenance and repairs; €35,600 depreciation on vehicles.
    - €44,898 repairs and maintenance of sheds.
    - €281,346 for replacement, repairs, and maintenance of trays.
    - €188,231 wages, including vacation pay.
    - €31,200 salary of M. Boîte.

3. **Karl Scharf's section** (climate control):
    - €37,866 electricity for climate control.
    - €34,613 for materials (mycelium, laboratory supplies, etc.).
    - €12,452 laboratory maintenance, cleaning, etc.
    - €33,200 depreciation on climate control and lab equipment.
    - €55,800 new climate control and lab equipment.
    - €68,400 salary of K. Scharf and Tina Paille.

4. **Jennifer Fleurette's section** (picking, sorting, and packaging):
    - €4,071,758 for packing materials.
    - €14,881 for supplies; €6,554 for electricity.
    - €24,600 for new sorting machine.
    - €4,212 for sorting and packing equipment maintenance.

- €14,600 depreciation on sorting and packing equipment.
- €5,602 maintenance and repair of sorting and packing shed.
- €18,006 for diesel fuel for trucks.
- €5,787 for truck maintenance and repairs; €37,800 depreciation on trucks.
- €2,044,324 wages for sorting and packing staff only, including vacation pay.
- €52,120 wages for drivers.
- €36,000 salary of J. Fleurette.
- Pickers hourly wage: €9.20; vacation and sick pay allowance: 8% on wages.

5. Local marketing:
- €34,800 salary of J. Marchand.
- €26,922 travel and daily allowances.

6. Other costs:
- €48,766 for office supplies.
- €32,688 for new office equipment and computers.
- €3,435 for office building electricity.
- €12,111 fuel and maintenance costs for two company cars.
- €6,600 depreciation on company cars.
- €288,420 salaries of office staff; €22,600 gardener.
- €8,688 office building maintenance.
- €190,000 depreciation on all buildings and sheds.
- €1,360,000 mortgage interest; €124,005 fire and property insurance.
- €301,887 accident insurance on waged workers (2.5%).
- €8,517 accident insurance on salaried employees (1.5%).
- €483,019 pension fund contribution on waged workers (4%).
- €34,069 pension fund contribution on salaried employees (6%).
- €72,000 salary of G. Mousse.
- €35,210 travel cost for G. Mousse

Current revenue, net of sales commissions:

Mushrooms	€3.60/kg
Spent compost	€8.40/tray

Yield and picking data collected by Jennifer Fleurette:

Day		Kilograms picked in		Hours pickers spent in	
		shed 5	shed 6	shed 5	shed 6
February	2	452	576	45	66
	3	912	797	78	83
	4	1463	1620	124	140
	5	2043	1304	191	119
	6	2495	2710	220	241
	7	1302	2003	129	176
	8	496	205	55	34
	9	0	298	0	48
	10	983	1160	94	103
	11	1224	1567	131	172
	12	1498	1364	161	129
	13	1373	1112	141	120
	14	1057	761	118	71
	15	467	0	48	0
	16	0	421	0	65
	17	232	365	36	64
	18	786	613	109	81
	19	848	907	123	112
	20	595	426	81	61
	21	264	225	46	41
	22	0	0	0	0
	23	0	289	0	43
	24	323	180	69	35
	25	368	423	71	81
	26	404	407	80	82
	27	301	198	61	42
	28	115	172	25	34
March	1	242	0	50	0
	2	0	0	0	0
	3	175	204	39	44
	4	238	153	49	36
	5	98	311	24	54
	6	307	144	56	34
	7	118	121	26	27
	8	94	87	23	21
	9	56	69	15	17

10
Discounted cash flows

Many MS/OR projects involve costs and benefits, occurring not at a single point in time, but spread over several periods. For example, a project may involve big initial investments in plant and equipment, followed one or two years later by a stream of cash inflows over many years, as that plant and equipment produces goods or services to meet customer demands. Should this project be undertaken?

You have already come across a similar example. The project report in Appendix 2 of Chapter 6 recommended a full-scale study to find the optimal replenishment policies for all finished products carried by the Lubricating Oil Division. That recommendation entailed spending some $32,000 now, with the promise of generating annual total savings in costs of about $93,000 for several years. The decision for going ahead with this study hinged on whether the flow of promised savings over several years justified spending the additional development costs. The criterion used was whether these costs would be recovered in less than a year by the promised savings. For the majority of OR/MS projects, this type of analysis will have to be done as part of the recommendations for implementation.

To determine the net monetary outcome of projects with costs and benefits spread over several years, we have to aggregate the costs and benefits into a summary measure. Is the net monetary outcome of a project simply equal to the difference of total benefits and total costs, regardless of what points in time the individual items occur? The answer to this question depends on whether a pound received, say, one year from now is worth exactly the same as a pound received now. If this is so, then the answer is yes; otherwise, adding costs or benefits occurring at different points in time would be like adding apples and oranges.

This chapter studies how costs and benefits, that are spread over several time periods, can be aggregated into a single meaningful measure which allows valid comparisons between different streams of cash flows. In Section 10.1 we will first study the time value of money. This will lead us in Section 10.2 to the concept of discounting future costs and benefits. Section 10.3 shows how any uneven cash flow can be expressed as an equivalent sequence of equal cash flows. We will find this concept useful when we need to compare projects with different productive lives in

Section 10.7. Section 10.4 discusses criteria for accepting or rejecting a project from a purely financial point of view, while Section 10.5 looks at the implications of the choice of a suitable discount rate. The last section applies these concepts to finding the best replacement age for piece of equipment.

All numerical computations — laborious by hand — will be demonstrated in spreadsheets. In fact, nowadays no financial calculations are ever done by hand any more. However, in order to fully understand the principles involved, we cannot avoid delving into some aspects of 'financial mathematics'.

10.1   The time value of money

Compounding

Under normal economic conditions, money in a savings account will earn interest. Say the current interest rate is $r = 8\%$ per year. Then putting £100 into a savings account and leaving it there for one full year will earn 8% of £100 interest. So after one year the balance of the account will be £108. If we leave this amount in the account for a second year, it will earn interest of another 8% of £108, or £8.64. By the end of the second year, the original £100 will have grown to £116.64.

It is useful to look at this process in a mathematical way. Let r be expressed as a decimal fraction — in our case $r = 0.08$. Then at the end of year 1, the investment has grown to £100(1 + 0.08) = £108. By the end of year 2, this in turn has grown to £108(1 + 0.08) = £116.64. Substituting £100(1.08) for £108, the result at the end of the second year becomes [£100(1.08)](1.08) = £100(1.08²).

This growth process of the original investment, as interest gets added to it, is called **compounding**. The original investment of C_0 at time 0, compounded at a rate r per period, will grow by the end of n periods to a future value F_n of

$$F_n = C_0(1 + r)^n \qquad (10\text{-}1)$$

This is depicted graphically in Figure 10-1. (Recall that any number to the power 0 is simply equal to 1. So $1.08^0 = 1$.)

A period can be of any length — a year, 6 months, 1 month, or even 1 day. The compounding rate r is simply adjusted accordingly. For example, if the annual rate is equal to $i = 0.08$, then rate r is reduced to $i/2$ or 0.04 for a half-year period and to $i/12$ or 0.00667 for a one-month period.

Figure 10-1   Compounding at a rate r.

time	0	1	2	3
	$C_0(1 + r)^0$	$F_1 = C_0(1+r)^1$	$F_2 = C_0(1+r)^2$	$F_3 = C_0(1+r)^3$
example for $r = 0.08$	100(1.08⁰)	100(1.08¹)	100(1.08²)	100(1.08³)
	100(1)	100(1.08)	100(1.1664)	100(1.259712)
or	100	108	116.64	125.97

(Note that these rates are approximations only, but for most purposes they are good enough. The approximation gets worse the shorter the compounding period. For instance, £100 compounded half-yearly at the rate $r = 0.04$ grows to £108.16, i.e. £0.16 more than annual compounding at $r = 0.08$. For monthly compounding the difference is £0.30.)

Discounting

Assume that you have won a cash prize of £108. The snag is that you will receive it only one year from now. But you need the money now. You also know that a friend of yours has some spare cash that she would like to invest for at least one year at the going annual rate of 8%. So you ask her for a swap, namely that she gives you cash in exchange for your prize worth £108 one year from now. How much should she be willing to pay you? We just saw that £100 invested at an interest rate of 8% will grow to £108 by the end of one year. So we can infer from this that £108 received in one year is worth right now £100, namely £108/1.08. Similarly, £116.64 to be received two years from now has a value right now of £116.64/$(1.08)^2$ or also £100.

The process of converting a future value into its worth right now — its **present value** — is called **discounting**. It is the reverse of compounding. The rate at which the future value diminishes is the **discount rate**. In our example the annual discount rate is $r = 0.08$ or 8%. In general, the present value, PV, of a payment, C_n, received at the end of n periods, discounted at a rate r per period, is given by

$$PV = C_n / (1 + r)^n \qquad (10\text{-}2)$$

While the factor $(1 + r)^n$ multiplies C_n in expression (10-1), it divides expression (10-2). The latter is therefore the inverse of the former.

As for compounding, the discount rate r can refer to a period of any length, not exclusively to annual periods. Its size is simply adjusted proportionately. However, if not specifically specified, it is assumed to be an annual discounting rate.

Note that (10-2) can be expressed as $PV = C_n[1/(1 + r)^n]$. The ratio $1/(1 + r)$ is referred to as the **discount factor**, often denoted by the Greek letter α. α^n represents the present value of one pound received at the end of n periods. So $PV = \alpha^n C_n$. We will use this short-hand notation most of the time. The following table demonstrates these concepts and then shows the results of discounting a sum of £100 received at the end of n years:

end of year n	1	2	3	...	8
discount factor	$1/(1+r)^1$	$1/(1+r)^2$	$1/(1+r)^3$	...	$1/(1+r)^8$
or for $\alpha=1/(1+r)$	α^1	α^2	α^3	...	α^8
example for $r = 0.08$					
$\alpha = (1/1.08)$	0.925926	0.925926^2	0.925926^3	...	0.925926^8
equals	0.925926	0.857339	0.793832	...	0.540269
PV of £100	£92.59	£85.73	£79.38	...	£54.03

There exist extensive tables for discount rates. Their importance and usefulness have diminished dramatically since the widespread availability of pocket calculators. And now the availability of electronic spreadsheets for personal computers has made these tables largely superfluous, at least for commercial use.

Opportunity cost concept of discount rate

From the above discussion it is clear that the discount rate is an opportunity cost concept. By receiving funds only n periods from now, the recipient foregoes the return that could be earned if the funds were available right now. Hence, these funds are worth less now. Similarly, in order to make a payment n periods from now, a lesser amount needs to be invested now. The amount less is equal to the compound interest that can be earned during these n periods.

The size of the discount rate depends on the alternative uses available for any funds between now and some future point in time. The higher the earnings potential for funds, the higher is the discount rate. It is also affected by the degree of risk inherent in the 'promise' of the future payment. The riskier the promise, i.e. the higher the chance that the promise will not be kept, the higher is the discount rate. This explains why a second mortgage carries a higher interest rate than the first mortgage or why loan sharks charge a higher interest rate.

Activity: To test your understanding, answer the following:
- If £1000 grows to £1125 in one year what is the rate of compounding?
- If £500 received one year from now is worth £400 now, what is the discount rate?
- Give reasons why a higher risk justifies a higher discount rate.

10.2   The present value of a series of cash flows

We will now apply these concepts to determine whether a given investment proposal is an attractive proposition from a purely financial point of view. Note that even if this is so, the proposal may still be rejected for other reasons. For instance, it may be riskier than the investor is willing to accept or it may result in a highly uneven and hence undesirable cash flow pattern. The financial analysis developed below only considers the net monetary worth of the proposed investment.

Recall the Champignons Galore case in Chapter 9. We explored whether CG should reduce the number of flushes per growing cycle from the current five to less than five. We discovered that by going to three flushes per cycle, the annual profit would increase by about €965,000. Some additional analysis indicates that at least initially, the increased output could only be disposed of by decreasing the selling price, while at the same time increasing sales promotion. This would reduce the annual net savings as follows:

Year	1	2	3	4	5
Profit increase	€320,000	€360,000	€450,000	€600,000	€800,000

Furthermore, the increased output would require the acquisition of additional yard equipment and trays at a total cost of €1,200,000. This additional equipment and the trays would have a productive life of 5 years. In other words, at the end of 5 years, continued increased output would require its replacement. This would give rise to a new evaluation and investment decision at that time.

After consultation with the accountant, the owner of CG, Gérard Mousse, concluded that any new investments in the firm would have to earn an annual return of at least 18%, otherwise the investment was not attractive financially.

What is the meaning of a required annual return of 18%? It means that if Gérard Mousse lends somebody €1,200,000 for N years, he would expect, in return, to get annually a payment of 18% of €1,200,000 or €216,000 for the use of the funds, as well as receiving back his initial capital advanced at the end of the N years. This situation is depicted in Figure 10-2 for $N = 5$ years.

Figure 10-2   Cash flow pattern earning 18%.

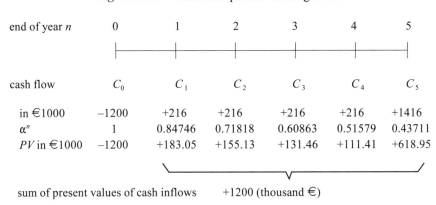

end of year n	0	1	2	3	4	5
cash flow	C_0	C_1	C_2	C_3	C_4	C_5
in €1000	−1200	+216	+216	+216	+216	+1416
α^n		1	0.84746	0.71818	0.60863	0.51579	0.43711
PV in €1000	−1200	+183.05	+155.13	+131.46	+111.41	+618.95

sum of present values of cash inflows   +1200 (thousand €)

The initial loan of €1,200,000 is shown as a cash outflow (negative number) at the beginning of year 1 (= time 0). It is followed by four payments of €216,000 and a final payment of €216,000 plus the initial capital of €1,200,000 also returned at that time. The row underneath lists the discount factors for converting each payment to its present value. The row labelled *PV* shows the product of the cash flow and the corresponding discount factors. Each payment is thus expressed in terms of its worth as of the same point in time, namely the beginning of a 5-year period. As required, the sum of the present values for the cash inflows from year 1 to year 5 add up to the initial cash outflow of €1,200,000. At a discount rate of 18%, the initial cash outflow is thus exactly recovered by the present values of the cash inflows.

The sum of the present values of all cash flows — cash outflows and cash inflows — is called the **net present value** or **NPV** of the project. Since in our example the cash flows were fixed such that they exactly meet the required 18% return per year, the *NPV* = 0. From this we can conclude that if the *NPV* is positive at a rate of discount of 18%, the project has a higher return than 18%. If its *NPV* is negative, then the project returns less than 18%. Therefore, we now have a criterion for deciding whether the proposed expansion of CG returns more or less than 18% per year, and by extension whether Gérard Mouse will find the project financially attractive or not.

Evaluation of the CG expansion project

Figure 10-3 shows the computations for finding the *NPV* for the cash flow associated with the CG expansion project, executed in a spreadsheet using the financial functions available in a spreadsheet package, like Lotus 1-2-3®, Corel Quattro Pro®, or Microsoft Excel®.

The first four columns reproduce the computations for a discount rate of 18%. The *NPV* for the project is given by the sum of the entries in column 4. It comes to €262,777, i.e. the sum of the present values of the inflows exceeds the initial investment of €1,200,000 by €262,777. This signals that the project has a better return than 18%. It is thus an attractive project.

Columns 5–7 repeat the calculations for discount rates of 12, 24, and 30%, respectively. For 12%, the *NPV* is substantially larger than for 18%, while for 24% it is substantially smaller. As the discount rate increases, the *NPV* decreases. For 30% it has become negative. This relationship is depicted in Figure 10-4 (an Excel graph produced with additional entries for the discount rate).

Figure 10-3   Net present value calculations for CG expansion.

Champignons Galore Expansion Project: Detailed NPV Computation						
Year	Cash flow	Discount factor for 18%	Present value for 18%	Present value for 12%	Present value for 24%	Present value for 30%
0	−1,200,000	1.000000	−1,200,000	−1,200,000	−1,200,000	−1,200,000
1	320,000	0.847458	271,186	285,714	258,065	246,154
2	360,000	0.718184	258,546	286,990	234,131	213,018
3	450,000	0.608631	273,884	320,301	236,019	204,825
4	600,000	0.515789	309,473	381,311	253,784	210,077
5	800,000	0.437109	349,687	453,941	272,886	215,463
Net present value			262,777	528,258	54,885	-110,464

The internal rate of return

In Figure 10-4 we see that there is a discount rate for which the *NPV* is exactly equal to zero. Verify that this occurs for a discount rate of 25.84755%, shown as 25.85 in the graph. The discount rate for which the *NPV* is equal to zero is called **the internal rate of return** (IRR) or **the marginal efficiency of capital**.

Figure 10-4   Relationship between discount rate and *NPV*.

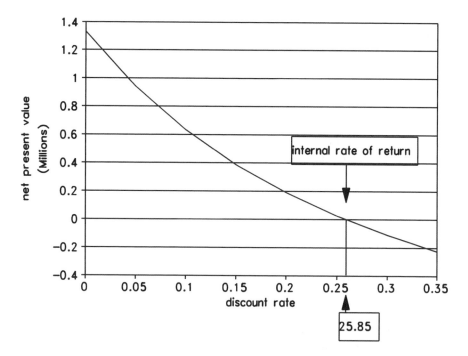

10.3   Annuities and perpetuities

The computations of the *NPV* are somewhat simpler if the cash flow is the same in each period of the project's productive life. An equal cash receipt or payment at annual intervals is called an **annuity**. By extension, any equal cash flow at regular intervals of any length is also referred to as an annuity. If it occurs at the beginning of each year, it is a **prepaid annuity**, if at the end a **post-paid annuity**. For example, assume that at the end of each of the coming five years, you receive a payment of €84,030.40, i.e. a post-paid annuity for five years. What is the present value of this annuity at a discount rate of 18%? Figure 10-5 shows the computations. Since the amount is the same in each period, the *NPV* is simply equal to the product of this constant amount and the sum of the discount factors.

Figure 10-5   NPV of an annuity

period	1	2	3	4	5
amount	84,030.40	84,030.40	84,030.40	84,030. 40	84,030.40
α^n	0.847458	0.718184	0.608631	0.515789	0.437109

Sum of discount factors   3.127171
NPV   (84,030.40) 3.127171 = 262,777

If the constant cash flow occurs for ever — a so-called **perpetuity** — then the *NPV* (for the post-paid case) is given by this simple formula:

$$NPV_r = C/r$$

C is the amount of the perpetuity occurring at the end of each period. For example, the *NPV* of a perpetuity of €47,299.90 at a discount rate of $r = 18\%$ is equal to €47,299.90/0.18 = €262,777.

Equivalent annuity

These two examples demonstrate an interesting concept. The original cash flow for the CG project has a *NPV* of €262,777. The annuity of €84,030.40 received at the end of each of five consecutive years also has a *NPV* of €262,777. Two different cash flows over 5 years have the same *NPV*. They are equivalent to each other in terms of their *NPV*. This property allows us to express any sequence of unequal cash flows as a sequence of equal cash payments or receipts, or as a so-called **equivalent annuity**, covering the same number of periods. The annuity of €84,030.40 for five years is thus the equivalent (post-paid) annuity for the original stream of cash flows of the CG project. This is an important concept.

Similarly, to generate an annual cash payment of €47,299.90 over all future periods, i.e. a perpetuity, all that is needed is an investment of €262,777, earning interest at 18% per year. So this perpetuity is also an equivalent stream of cash flows to the original CG project (although for a different number of periods).

Expressing uneven cash flows in terms of equivalent annuities turns out to be very useful when comparing of projects that have different productive lives.

10.4   Accept/reject criteria for financial projects

The previous discussion provides us with two alternative criteria for deciding whether to accept or reject a project from a purely financial point of view, as shown in the box on page 259. The two criteria give the same answer if the project's cash flow consists of an initial cash outflow, followed by a string of cash inflows. The CG project has this pattern. So, if the target rate of return is $r^* = 18\%$, then the project is accepted under both criteria, since $NPV = €262,777 \geq 0$ and $IRR = 25.84755\% \geq 18\%$.

> **Given a target rate of return of r^*,**
>
> **if $NPV_r^* \geq 0$ (Net Present Value Criterion)**
> **or if $IRR \geq r^*$ (Internal Rate of Return Criterion)**
> **accept the project,**
> **otherwise reject the project.**

Unfortunately, if the cash flow is not so well behaved, e.g. has more than one reversal of cash flow from negative to positive and vice versa, there may be two or more distinct *IRR* values for which the $NPV = 0$. For example, the cash flow pattern of –£720, £1700, –£1000, has two *IRR* values of 11.11% and 25%. If the target rate of return is 20%, the $NPV = £2.22$. Under the NPV criterion, we get an unambiguous answer of 'accept this project'. Under the IRR criterion, we do not know which *IRR* value the target rate of return should be compared with, if any. For this and other reasons, financial analysts usually recommend the use of the NPV criterion in preference to the IRR criterion. We will follow this advice.

Activity:
- The *NPV* of the cash flow of –1400, +1000, +1000 at the beginning of years 1, 2, and 3, respectively at a discount rate of 25% is 40 (example of previous Activity). If the target rate of return is 20%, should this project be accepted? Why?
- Is its *IRR* less than 20%? larger than 20%? larger than 25%? Using the *IRR* criterion, should the project be accepted or rejected?
- If you know the value of the post-paid annuity, how do you get the corresponding prepaid annuity? What is the equivalent prepaid annuity for the CG project?

10.5 Choice of target rate of return

What is the appropriate discount rate to use in evaluating the worth of a project? This is a rather complex problem — it is a topic extensively discussed in the financial theory literature. We shall only give it a rather cursory treatment. Any text on Managerial Finance will fill in the details.

Opportunity cost basis

Since the basis for discounting is the opportunity cost associated with the use of funds, the most obvious choice for the correct discount rate is the rate of return foregone on the best alternative use of the funds. Unfortunately, the best alternative use of funds changes over time. It is affected by changes in the range of alternative uses of the funds available at any given point in time. This could result in rather inconsistent choices being made from one project to the next, as the best alternative may change within a short span of time. Furthermore, the decision maker may not really be aware of all possible uses of funds.

In real life, the concept of the best alternative use is not a practicable approach for setting a suitable discount rate. Furthermore, this approach may also ignore the difference in degree of risk between various uses of funds.

Desired rate of return — a policy choice

A logical alternative is to ask management or the decision makers to formulate a policy as to what the minimum acceptable rate of return is for investments of a given level of risk in the entity or organization under their control. This minimum acceptable rate is then used as the target discount rate. It will reflect the general economic climate and will therefore be less subject to short-term fluctuations. From an MS/OR point of view, this is the preferred approach. It puts the onus for setting the target rate where it belongs, namely with the decision makers.

A firm's average cost of capital

Any organization has recourse to a variety sources of funds to finance its assets — the things it owns. For example, a limited liability company in the manufacturing sector will have somewhere between 40 and 60% of its funds financed by the owners — its shareholders. These so-called equity funds are in the form of share capital and retained earnings (i.e. profits reinvested in the firm, rather than paid out as dividends to the shareholders). The balance will be financed by liabilities, such as mortgages, debentures, short-term bank loans, and trade credit from suppliers. The latter is regularly renewed through new purchases.

If a firm runs into financial trouble, i.e. the value of its assets is less than what investors put into the firm, and the firm goes into liquidation, then the holders of secured liabilities, such as mortgages, will be repaid first. Funds owed to unsecured creditors are paid next from what is left over, with the owners paid last. The unsecured creditors and the owners may lose part or all of their investment. Hence each source of funds is exposed to a different degree of risk of losing its investment. The higher the degree of risk, the more will be 'charged' for advancing funds. So the cost of each type of funds increases with the degree of risk involved, with secured creditors being the cheapest and equity funds being the costliest.

Furthermore, a firm wants to be viewed as a good investment prospect for existing and new owners and creditors. So it will try to maintain a composition of funds or a capital structure considered appropriate for the type of business it is in with its associated inherent business risk. Any significant departure from these norms will cause the firm to be perceived as a more risky investment, increasing the cost of all its potential sources of funds.

It follows that the compositions of funds used for financing a firm's operations and the cost of each source dictate what it needs to earn to be viewed as a good investment. If its earnings do not cover the total annual cost of all funds — interest due plus dividends and capital gains expected by the owners — the return the owners receive on their equity is below what the market expects. It may even result in their equity being gradually eroded and the firm ultimately defaulting on its creditors. Expressed differently, the firm's average return on its own investments must be at least equal to its **cost of capital**. The cost of capital is computed as the weighted average cost of all its funds — liabilities and equity — with the weights given by the proportion each source contributes towards the total capital of the firm.

Rather than base the cost of capital on the past, we take an opportunity cost approach. For each source of funds we determine the cost to the firm of raising additional capital. This cost is easy to define for liabilities, like a bank loan. It is equal to the interest rate charged. Finding the cost of equity funds is more difficult and controversial, and its study goes beyond the scope of this text. If the firm is financially sound and generates adequate profits, a simplified approach is based on the ratio of profits before taxes and the total equity.

The cost of capital is used as the minimum required rate of return and hence the target discount rate for any project proposal. Any project that has a positive *NPV* at that discount rate increases the net worth of the firm, since it recovers more than what is required on average for remunerating the firm's combined sources of additional funds. Projects that do not meet this criterion lower the net worth of the firm.

Note that it would be incorrect to simply use the cost of the funds actually raised for the project as the target discount rate. This would lead to inconsistent decisions, since this cost would change from project to project, as the firm endeavours to rebalance its capital structure to what investors expect.

If the risk associated with a project is different from the average business risk of the firm, the target discount rate may need to be adjusted — up if the risk is higher, down if it is lower. Again this is something that should clearly be left to the decision maker(s) to decide upon and not the analyst.

Effect of choice of target discount rate

The choice of target discount rate has a significant impact on the type of project an organization accepts. To be specific, the higher the target discount rate, the lower is the *NPV*. But more importantly, this will also give less weight to future cash flows, both positive and negative. It will thus favour projects that have a low initial cost and/or quick recovery of the funds invested. It will favour the purchase of cheap equipment and plant, rather than equipment and plant with low running costs but a higher initial investment, thus sacrificing quality for cost. You go for the low-cost second-hand car, rather than the Mercedes.

When dealing with environmental projects, a high r^* will favour quick resource exploitation and environmental degradation rather than conservation. Similarly, abandonment costs which are incurred way in the distant future tend to contribute very little to the *NPV*. This explains why construction of nuclear power stations may be seen as more attractive by generators than other power sources, like solar power, in spite of the fact that the cost of decommissioning a nuclear power plant 40 or 50 years in the future and the cost of the storage of nuclear waste material for hundreds of years afterwards may run into the billions. However, discounting reduces these costs to insignificance. Just consider that the present value of a £1 billion cost 40 years from now at a discount rate of 10% amounts to a mere £22 million — a small sum compared to the initial investment for a nuclear power plant. These are some of the reasons why environmentally concerned people argue that the discount rate appropriate for projects with high environmental impacts has to be very low or even zero.

Discounting of costs for public projects, in fact, raises serious ethical questions of equity between generations. Bluntly put, discounting implies that future generations do not count. The interested reader should consult a text like E.J. Mishan, *Introduction to Normative Economics*, Oxford University Press, NY, 1981.

Activity: Why is it advisable/essential that normal commercial ventures be evaluated on the basis of their discounted cash flows, while the discounting of costs and benefits of projects that involve safety, health, or environmental issues raises serious moral and ethical questions?

10.6 Spreadsheet financial functions

Spreadsheets have built-in financial functions that perform most discounting computations with a few easy keystrokes. They allow the user to specify the timing of each cash flow — end of period or beginning of period — with end-of-period timing usually being the default.

The four financial functions which you will need most often are the following (the form shown is for Microsoft Excel$^©$; they are similar for other spreadsheet packages; the major difference may be the sequence of the function arguments):

Net present value of a stream of cash flows: NPV(r, Xi:Yj), where [Xi:Yj] indicates the first and last in a row or column of cells containing the sequence of cash flows, occurring at the end of consecutive periods. Note that you may have to add the initial cash flow at the beginning of the first period as a separate undiscounted entry.

Present value of an annuity: PV(r, number of periods, annuity, fv, type), where the annuity is the constant payment per period, and 'fv' and 'type' are optional arguments with a default value of zero. If type = 0, then the annuity is assumed to occur at the end of each period, i.e. post-paid; if type = 1, then the annuity is assumed to occur at the beginning of each period, i.e. prepaid. (For Excel this function assumes that the annuity is a cash outflow, hence it returns a negative value if the annuity is listed as positive.)

Internal rate of return: IRR(Xi:Yj, initial guess for *r*), where [Xi:Yj] again denotes the first and last cells in a row or column of cells containing the sequence of cash flows, including the initial cash flow at the beginning of the first period. At least one value must be positive (a cash inflow) and one value negative (a cash outflow). This function finds the answer by an algorithm of successive approximations. If no convergence occurs by the end of 20 iterations, a corresponding message is shown. A better initial guess must then be supplied.

Equivalent annuity: PMT(r, number of periods, NPV, fv, type), where NPV is the net present value of the original sequence of irregular cash flows, including the cash flow at the beginning of the first period, with fv = 0 and type = 0 as defaults. For type = 0 the equivalent annuity is post-paid, while for type = 1 it is prepaid.

Figure 10-6 demonstrates the use of these functions for the CG project. The Excel formulas used are shown at the bottom and refer to the column and row identifiers listed at the margins. The equivalent annuity is computed as occurring at the end of each period.

Figure 10-6   The use of spreadsheet financial functions

	A	B	C	D	F	G
1	Champignons Galore Expansion Project Evaluation					
2						
3	Year	Cash flow				
4	0	−1,200,000				
5	1	320,000				
6	2	360,000				
7	3	450,000				
8	4	600,000				
9	5	800,000				
10						
11		Discount rate	0.12	0.18	0.24	0.3
12		NPV	528,258	262,777	54,885	−11,0464
13		Equiv.annuity	146,544	84,040	19,991	−45,354
14		IRR	0.258476			
15	Spreadsheet formulas in column C for discount rate of 0.12:					
16	C12	=NPV(C11,$B5:$B9)+$B4				
17	C13	=PMT(C11,$A9,-C12,0,0)				
18	C14	=IRR(B4:B9,0.5)				

(If you do not have access to a spreadsheet program, the equivalent post-paid annuity can be computed using financial tables for **annuity factors**. These are based on the following formula:

$$\text{Annuity factor} = \frac{r}{1-(1+r)^{-N}}$$

where r is the discount rate and N is the number of periods of one cycle. To find the equivalent post-paid annuity, the annuity factor is multiplied by the *NPV* of the project. Setting $NPV = 1$, the PMT function with type=0 gives the annuity factor for the desired discount rate and number of periods. Multiplying the post-paid annuity by the discount factor gives the prepaid annuity. For example, for a discount rate of 18%, the prepaid equivalent annuity is 84,040 times 0.847455, the discount factor for 18%.)

10.7   Dependent and mutually exclusive projects

In evaluating an investment proposal the analyst has to explore the possible inter-relationships of the project in question with other potential project proposals. So far we have assumed that the cash flow of a given project is not affected by whether any other project is also implemented. If this is the case, the project in question is economically independent. An accept-or-reject decision can be made on its own.

In many instances, the cash flow for a given project is affected by the con-current or subsequent acceptance of other projects, i.e. several projects together form an interdependent system. For example, the LOD (Chapter 5) was considering the replacement of its main can filling machine with a substantially faster machine. In order to take full advantage of the increased filling speed offered, the carton packing equipment also needed upgrading. The savings in operating costs for the new filling machine depended therefore on whether or not the carton packing equipment was also upgraded, and if yes, when. The two projects 'purchase of a new filling machine' and 'upgrading of carton packing equipment' are thus interdependent. It could well be that the purchase of the new filling machine is financially unattractive without upgrading the packing equipment, while undertaking both projects is highly attractive.

The interdependence may even be stronger. Project A may be a prerequisite for project B. For example, a power generating company may evaluate the construction of a hydroelectric power scheme that involves damming a river to create a water storage lake. It may also explore the possibility of extending the scheme by adding an agricultural irrigation system. The irrigation scheme assumes the existence of the dam which is part of the hydro project. It can therefore only be evaluated in conjunction with that project, while the hydro project itself can be evaluated independently.

At the other extreme, two or several projects are mutually exclusive — only one of them can be accepted. For instance, there may be several filling machines that would have the required hourly filling capacity and would be suitable for the LOD. Each machine may have slightly different characteristics and hence different operating costs. Only one of them will be purchased, if any at all.

It may be helpful to think of these cases as points along a continuum of relation-ships, as depicted in Figure 10-7. At one extreme there is the complete dependency — one project being the prerequisite of another. At the other extreme, the projects are mutually exclusive. To the right of 'prerequisite' we have decreasing degrees of complementarity. To the left of 'mutually exclusive' we have decreasing degrees of substitutability. At the centre, we have independence.

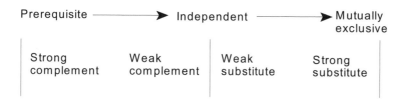

Figure 10-7 Range of interdependence of projects.

Mutually exclusive projects may differ not only in terms of the initial investment, but also in terms of their productive lives. To make the right decision, the evaluation has to take these differences correctly into account.

Differing initial investments

Which one of the following two projects should be accepted, if any?

Project	Cash flows in			NPV for
	year 0	year 1	year 2	$r = 0.2$
A	−2000	1440	1512	250
B	−3000	1500	2952	300

Both projects have a positive *NPV* and are therefore acceptable. Project B has the higher *NPV*. Hence it should be selected. By finding the present value of the difference between inflows and outflows, the *NPV* already takes into account that the two projects have a different initial investment. Both projects recover the initial investment plus more.

Figure 10-8 shows how the *NPV* of projects A and B vary as a function of the discount rate. Note that for discount rates of less than 23.1%, project B has a higher *NPV* than project A. For discount rates of more than 23.1%, this reverses. So for discount rates of less than 23.1% project B is preferred, while for discount rates of more than 23.1% project A is preferred.

However, if a fixed initial sum is available to undertake either project, the return that can be earned on the unused portion of funds must also be included in the analysis. Assume that £3000 are available for use. Project A leaves £1000 for investment elsewhere, such as another project or simply in bonds or a bank savings account. Say these £1000 are put into Project C that offers £1548 at the end of two years. The additional cash flow is then −£1000, 0, +1548. Discounted at the same *r* of 0.2, its *NPV* is £75. Hence the combination of projects A and C yields a combined *NPV* of £325, or £25 more than project B.

Differing productive lives

Often mutually exclusive projects have different productive lives. For example, a building contractor may have the choice between purchasing one type of utility vehicle or leasing it on a fixed-term contract. The purchased vehicle may have a

Figure 10-8   Comparison of *NPV*s as a function of the discount rate.

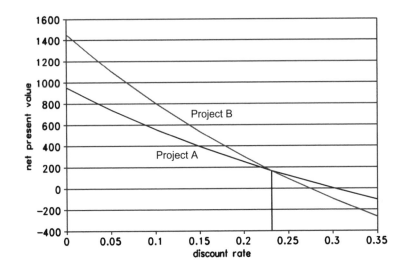

productive life of 5 years for the kind of usage considered, while the fixed-term lease may have to run for 4 years. The cash flow for each choice is shown in the top portion of the spreadsheet printout in Figure 10-9. The buy option has an initial purchase cost of £44,000 at the beginning of year 1 (= end of year 0), followed by operating costs each year. These increase as the vehicle gets older. At the end of year 5, the vehicle is sold for £14,000. Subtracting the operating cost for year 5 of £7,700, this results in a net cash inflow at the end of year 5 of £6,300. Both the 'buy' and the 'lease' options involve making some minor alterations to the vehicle at the beginning of year 1 at a cost of £1000. The rental cost for years 1 through 4 is £14,000 per year. The operating costs are identical under both options. For simplicity we assume that all cash flows occur at the end of each year, except for the initial outlays.

Management would like to know which option has the lower cost.

This is a cost minimization problem rather than one of maximizing profit or wealth. How should 'costs' be evaluated? Can we simply compute the *NPV* for each proposal as it stands and then select the one with the lowest *NPV* cost? The *NPV* for each option is listed in the 'Evaluations' portion under '*NPV* per cycle'.

The 'lease' option has a far lower *NPV* over its productive life. But note that the two options do not have the same productive life or life cycle length. The 'lease' option terminates after 4 years, while the 'buy' option goes to the end of year 5. What happens under the 'lease' option in year 5? We cannot ignore that.

Two mutually exclusive options that do not have the same productive life cannot be compared unless adjusted for that difference. There are several ways to make them comparable. We look at two. The first is to assume that each option is renewed

Figure 10-9 Mutually exclusive projects with different productive lives.

	A	B	C	D	E	F	G
1	NPV FOR "BUY" & "SELL" OPTIONS						
2	INPUT:						
3	Discount rate	0.2					
4							
5	Year	0	1	2	3	4	5
6	Purchase price	44,000					-14,000
7	Operating cost	1,000	5,600	5,800	6,400	6,900	$7,700
8	Leasing cost		14,000	14,000	14,000	14,000	
9							
10	Cash flow for options:						
11	Buy	45,000	5,600	5,800	6,400	6,900	-6,300
12	Lease	1,000	19,600	19,800	20,400	20,900	
13							
14	EVALUATIONS:						prepaid
15		NPV	Cycle	Repeats	NPV for	Annuity	Equivalent
16	Project	per cycle	length		N cycles	factor	annuity
17	Buy	58,194	5	4	94,756	0.278650	16,216
18	Lease	52,968	4	5	99,636	0.321908	17,051
19							
20	Excel Formulas for row						
21		B17 @NPV($B$3,C11:G11)+B11					
22		E17 @PV(((1+$B$3)^C17)-1,D17,-B17*(1+$B$3)^C17)					
23		F17 @PMT($B$3,C17,-1,,1)					
24		G17 @PMT($B$3,C17,-B17,,1)					

several times until both options reach the end of the productive life in the same period. There is no implication that this will actually be done in real life. It is only used as a trick to render the two options comparable.

In our example the 'buy' option would repeat itself four times and the 'lease' option five times. Both options reach the end of a life cycle at the end of year 20. This is depicted graphically in Figure 10-10.

The *NPV* cost for the 20-year interval is shown under the heading '*NPV* for *N* cycles' in Figure 10-9. The 'buy' option has now the lower *NPV* cost, which is the correct answer. (For E17 note that the Excel PV function assumes that each amount occurs at the end of a cycle; hence the *NPV* value of column B has to be recalculated as of that point in time, which explains the complexity of the last argument.)

Figure 10-10 NPV-calculations for projects with unequal productive lives.

Discounting of cycle present value to year 0

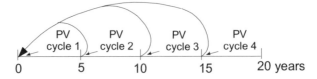

Lease Option
Discounting of cycle present value to year 0

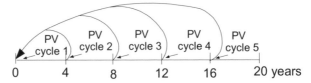

The last column of Figure 10-9 lists the equivalent annuities, computed from the *NPV* for one cycle using the PMT function. Again the 'buy' option is cheaper. In fact, the two approaches prefer the same option. The equivalent annuity approach is simpler and intuitively appealing. The interpretation of an equivalent annuity as a weighted average, with the discount factors as weights, is a more meaningful concept than the *NPV* covering several repetitions to a common date.

Activity:
- Comparing the 'Buy' and 'Lease' options, we used an equivalent prepaid annuity. Would the 'Buy' option also be the preferred one if we used an equivalent post-paid annuity for comparison? Why?
- 'Lease' payments have to be made monthly. Similarly, fuel costs have to be paid monthly. For the 'Buy' options, service and maintenance costs occur at least twice a year. Given the difference in the timing of costs for the two options, a comparison based on an equivalent monthly annuity is more accurate. How do the inputs into the analysis have to be adjusted to accommodate this?

10.8 Replacement decisions

This section considers an application of discounting concepts to an important optimization problem, namely the optimal time to replace a piece of equipment.

The performance of most machines or vehicles deteriorates with age. Aging equipment becomes increasingly prone to breakdowns, repairs become more frequent and more substantial, and the quality and volume of its output decreases. As a result operating and maintenance costs increase, while its potential for profit contributions decreases. Furthermore, its resale or salvage value also decreases, requiring a larger net outlay when it is replaced. Given these trends, it becomes more cost effective or more profitable to replace it with the latest model, even if the old equipment can still do its intended tasks and meet all capacity requirements adequately. This process is constantly going on — just look at the 'pre-loved' car market.

Situation summary of a replacement problem

Quiktrans is a small regional goods carrier. It currently operates three articulated AZ tractor–trailer units. Two are starting their third year of operation, while one is 3 years old. Carey Bumps, the owner–manager, has just studied advertising leaflets on the latest AZ model. He is impressed by the reduced operating costs. At first glance, these figures look very favourable compared to the operating costs of his oldest unit. Should he upgrade his fleet now or wait another two years?

Following the recommendations of the long-haul carrier association, Carey has kept careful records of operating and maintenance costs on his three units. The mileage run by each unit is very similar. Below is a summary of this information on an average per truck basis in euros:

Operating year	1	2	3	approximate timing
Insurance, licence	8,840	8,640	8,440	beginning of year
Maintenance	11,952	12,526	13,048	end of year
Mech. overhauls			3,041	beginning of year
Tyres		7,962	8,008	beginning of year
Paint & body work			11,951	beginning of year
Repairs		2,044	2,953	end of year
Variable running cost	1.62	1.64	1.67	per kilometre

The initial purchase cost of the existing units was €255,000. He has some information about the expected costs of operations for the three units. In particular, according to his mechanic, each unit will need a new motor every three years. So if the oldest unit is kept on, its motor will have to be replaced right away. This will push up the mechanical overhaul costs for year 4 to €22,000. Similarly, he expects that major body and paint work needs to be done every second year. Naturally, if a unit is sold at the end of a given year, it is put on the market as is, without these jobs being done. He has compiled the table below, outlining these costs, as well as the variable running costs/km. The latter decrease slightly in the year the motor is replaced, but in general accelerate steeply with age.

Predicted costs in	4th	5th	6th	7th	year of operation
variable running cost (€)	1.64	1.75	1.98	1.85	per kilometre
Repairs	4,000	4,000	8,000	15,000	[all at
Mech. overhauls	22,000	6,000	9,000	28,000	beginning
Paint & body work	-	15,000	-	15,000	of year]

The annual pattern for tyre replacement and regular maintenance is expected to continue as during the first three years.

Advertisements in the association's trade journal for second-hand units of a similar type, with initial purchase cost of €255,000, and typical annual mileage of between 90,000 and 110,000 km, give the following maximum and minimum asking prices in thousands of euros:

Age	1	2	3	4	5	6	7	years
Maximum	210	160	118	94	62	29	20	
Minimum	190	140	102	76	38	11	6	

The advertised characteristics for the new model AZ unit list the following variable running costs per kilometre:

Operating year	1	2	3	4	5	6	7
Running cost/km (€)	1.40	1.42	1.45	1.43	1.54	1.73	1.65

First year maintenance costs are predicted at about €10,000. Again replacement of the motor is expected after about 260,000 to 300,000 km. A replacement motor is tentatively priced at €24,000. This is €6,000 more than for the current models. The new unit is priced at €295,000 ready to roll. The insurance premium is expected to be €6,960, declining by €220 each year, while the licence cost remains constant at €2,200, rounded to the nearest €10. Carey's accountant suggests that an appropriate opportunity cost of capital is around 15%. What should Carey Bumps do?

Approach for analysing replacement problems

The old equipment should be replaced as soon as the total relevant cost for operating it for another period, say a year, is higher than the minimum average cost per period for the new equipment. This leads to a two-step procedure:

- Step 1: Find the optimal age at which the new equipment should be replaced, if it is acquired. Associated with this optimal replacement age is a corresponding average cost per period.

- Step 2: Compare this average cost with the total incremental cost incurred for keeping the current equipment for another period. If that cost is lower than the average cost for the new equipment, retain the old equipment for another period, otherwise replace it.

If the equipment is kept for another period, step 2 is repeated at that time by answering the question: is the incremental cost for operating the old equipment for a further period lower than the minimum average cost for the new equipment? This process continues until the incremental cost for operating the old equipment for another year becomes larger. At that point, the old equipment is replaced with the new.

The only complicating factor is that the cash flows occur at different points in time. They all have to be converted to a relevant common reference point in time.

Step 1: Finding the optimal replacement policy for the new unit

The manufacturer's advertisement contains estimates of the variable running costs per kilometre, but most other cost information has to be inferred from either the costs incurred or predicted for the current units. It is a fair assumption that many of these costs will be identical or follow a similar pattern. We shall assume that the costs for repairs, tyres, paint and body work, and mechanical overhauls for the new unit are the same as for the current units, except that the motor replacement costs at the beginning of years 4 and 7 are €6,000 higher. We shall assume that, starting from a base of €10,000, the annual maintenance costs also increase by about €500 per year. The resale value of the new unit is assumed to follow the pattern of the current model, but adjusted for the higher initial purchase price. For example, the resale value of a one-year old AZ model truck is set equal to 295/255 times the average of the corresponding maximum and minimum asking price for the old unit, i.e. 0.5(€210,000 + €190,000)(295/255), rounded to the nearest €100, or €231,400.

Finding the optimal replacement policy for the new unit boils down to a comparison of several mutually exclusive options, namely replacing the AZ unit after every N years, where $N = 1, 2, 3, \ldots$. In fact, we shall assume that Carey Bumps will never contemplate keeping a truck for more than 6 years, so $N = 6$ is the highest option. These options all cover different productive lives. Using the equivalent annuity approach, the optimal replacement policy is the one with the lowest equivalent annuity.

Figure 10-11 shows the spreadsheet computations for this analysis. As usual, the top portion of the spreadsheet lists all input data. Each cash flow item is assumed to occur at a given point in time, either at the end (**end/yr**) or at the beginning (**beg/yr**) of a given year. This is indicated under the column 'timing'. In reality, many cash flow items, in particular the variable running costs, are spread throughout each year. However, accounting for this more accurately would complicate matters somewhat. (We would have to go to continuous discounting — a topic not covered in this text.) So we will stick to this simplification, which will only result in small errors. The row for the variable running cost is simply equal to the running cost/km times the annual assumed mileage of 90,000 km.

The beginning-of-year and the end-of-year costs are summed separately. These two rows together with the row of resale values form the input into the NPV calculations. Each column in these computations refers to one of the six replacement options considered. The *NPV* for replacing the truck every N years is obtained as follows:

$NPV(N)$ = (Initial purchase price for new unit) +
(Cumulative present value of all costs over N years) −
(Present value of resale value for a unit N years old)

For example, for $N = 2$, the computations are:

Figure 10-11   Spreadsheet analysis for optimal replacement period.

QUICKTRANS TRUCK REPLACEMENT PROBLEM

DATA:	New truck cost	€285,000	Kilometres/year			90000
	Discount rate	0.15	Discount factor			0.869565

		Year of operation					
Cost item	timing	1	2	3	4	5	6
Running		€1.40	€1.42	€1.45	€1.43	€1.54	€1.73
Running cost/yr	end/yr	126000	127800	130500	128700	138600	155700
Maintenance	end/yr	10000	10500	11000	11500	12000	12500
Repairs	end/yr		2000	3000	4000	8000	15000
Tyres	beg/yr		8000	8000	8000	8000	8000
Mech. overhaul	beg/yr			3000	28000	6000	9000
Paint/body work	beg/yr			12000		15000	
Annual licence	beg/yr	2200	2200	2200	2200	2200	2200
Insurance	beg/yr	6960	6740	6520	6300	6080	5860
Cost summary by timing							
Total cost as of	beg/yr	9160	16940	31720	44500	37280	25060
Total cost as of	end/yr	136000	140300	144500	144200	158600	183200
Resale value	end/yr	231400	173500	127300	98300	57800	23100
EVALUATION							
Replace after year		1	2	3	4	5	6
PV cumulative costs		127421	248238	367234	478941	579108	670769
PV resale value		201217	131191	83702	56203	28737	9987
NPV of policy		221203	412047	578532	717737	845371	955783
Equiv. Annuity	pepaid	221203	220397	220334	218607	219293	219611

$$
\begin{aligned}
NPV(2) = \ & 295{,}000 + && \leftarrow \text{ initial purchase price} \\
& 127{,}421 + && \leftarrow \text{ } PV \text{ of year 1 costs} \\
& 16{,}940(0.869565 + && \leftarrow \text{ } PV \text{ of year 2 beg/y cost} \\
& 140{,}300(0.869565^2) - && \leftarrow \text{ } PV \text{ of year 2 end/y cost} \\
& 173{,}500(0.869565^2) && \leftarrow \text{ } PV \text{ of resale value end year 2}
\end{aligned}
$$

The cumulative present value of all costs over N years is recursively computed adding the year N present value costs to the $N - 1$ cumulative present value costs.

The equivalent annuity is expressed as prepaid. For this particular application, this approach seems to be more natural.

The lowest cost is obtained for $N = 4$. So the optimal policy is to keep the new AZ unit for four years and then replace it by a new one. Naturally, only one decision, namely the first purchase, would ever be implemented based on this analysis. Any subsequent replacement decisions would be based on a new analysis, using the latest up-to-date relevant information about new models and costs. (More on this in the next chapter.)

It is somewhat surprising that the equivalent annuity costs for the various options differ by less than €3,000 per year. The cost function is thus fairly flat. This is a valuable insight. The final decision made by Carey may well also reflect other factors not explicitly included in the financial analysis, such as the level of goodwill created by having relatively new trucks and replacing them more frequently than implied by the optimal policy.

The second surprising factor is that the high cost of replacing the motor just one year prior to disposing of the unit does not turn out to be a deterrent for keeping the unit for a fourth year — a counterintuitive result.

Step 2: When to replace the old units

We are now ready for the second step of the analysis, namely the decision about the timing of replacing the current units. These calculations are shown in the spreadsheet in Figure 10-12. It again lists all inputs in the top portion. The analysis is done for each current unit, one period at a time. For example, for the three-year-old unit, we want to establish if it is financially more attractive to operate it for a fourth year or replace it straight away. If it is replaced, then next year's annual

Figure 10-12   When to replace current trucks?

QUICKTRANS REPLACEMENT OF CURRENT TRUCKS						
DATA			Year of operation			
Item	timing	2	3	4	5	6
Running cost/km			€1.67	€1.64	€1.75	€1.98
Running cost/year	end/yr		150300	147600	157500	178200
Maintenance	end/yr		13000	13500	14000	14500
Repairs	end/yr		3000	4000	8000	15000
Tyres	beg/yr		8000	8000	8000	8000
Mech. overhaul	beg/yr		3000	22000	6000	9000
Paint/body work	beg/yr		12000		15000	
Annual licence	beg/yr		2200	2200	2200	2200
Insurance	beg/yr		6240	6040	5840	5640
Cash flow summary by timing						
Total cost as of	beg/yr		31440	38240	37040	24840
Total cost as of	end/yr		166300	165100	179500	207700
Total cost/year	beg/yr		176049	181805	193127	205449
Resale value	end/yr	150000	110000	85000	50000	20000
Incremental cost of running truck one more year (expressed as of beg/year)			230397	217892	234649	238057

cost is equal to €218,607 — the minimum equivalent annuity found in the previous analysis. If the incremental cost of keeping the 3-year-old unit for a fourth year is less than that, then it should be kept, otherwise it should be replaced.

Recall that the equivalent annuities shown in Figure 10-10 are expressed as prepaid annuities, rather than post-paid annuities. The incremental cost of keeping the old unit should therefore also refer to the beginning of the year. This cost consists of two elements:

Incremental cost = (Operating cost for another year) +
                            (Loss of resale value foregone by not selling now)

Since some of these costs are approximated as occurring at the beginning of the year, while others occur at the end of the year, all cash flows need to be expressed as of the same point in time, namely the beginning of the year. The operating costs are given by the column labelled year '4' in Figure 10-11. €38,240 of these occur at the beginning of the year, while the balance of €165,100 occur at the end of the year. Discounting the latter by one year and adding the two costs together equals €181,805 — the shaded entry in the intersection of row 'Total cost/year' and column year '4'.

If the unit were sold right away, it would net €110,000 (the resale value at the end of year 3). Sold one year later at the age of 4 years, it will only bring in €85,000. The difference in resale value foregone, expressed in pounds as of the beginning of the year, is equal to

Loss in resale value = (Resale value now) − (*PV* of resale value 1 period later)
              or €110,000 − €85,000(0.869565) = €36,087.

The total incremental cost of keeping the 3-year-old unit for a fourth year is €181,805 + €36,087 = €217,892. This is less than the minimum equivalent annuity of €218,607. Hence the three-year-old truck should be kept for a fourth year.

At the end of its fourth year of operation, this analysis is repeated. Verify that now the total incremental cost for keeping the (then four-year-old) unit for a fifth year is €234,649. This is more than the minimum equivalent annuity. Hence the unit should be sold at the end of its fourth year of operations.

Although these calculations should normally be done at the appropriate time with the latest up-to-date cost information, they are all shown in Figure 10-11. Note the counterintuitive conclusion that the two-year-old units should be sold right away, while the three-year-old unit should be kept running for a fourth year. This result seems to be due to the considerably larger loss in resale value suffered in the third year, given that these units are due for a new motor at the beginning of their next year of operations, as well as the higher running costs in year 3 as compared to year 4.

In conclusion, we stress again that this analysis only considers the financial side of things. The decision maker may need to take other factors into account, such as company image, safety, or quality, before reaching a final decision. This may lead to a choice different from the recommended one. However, the decision maker will know exactly the financial effect of this choice.

10.9 Chapter highlights

- For normal commercial ventures with cash flows spread over time, a valid comparison between alternative projects requires that all cash flows be expressed as net present values, i.e. discounted at the target discount rate. The latter reflects the organization's weighted average cost of funds or the desired rate of return on its investments, as well as the degree of risk involved in the project.
- If the *NPV* of a project is positive at that rate of discount, then it is an attractive project from a purely financial point of view. (Naturally, the financial return of a project is only one aspect in the decision of whether or not to undertake it. Other important considerations are the possible adverse effects on the organization's overall cash flow or the ability to raise the necessary funds.)
- Converting an uneven cash flow into an equivalent annuity provides additional insight into the project. The equivalent annuity can be viewed as an average cash flow in each period. It facilitates comparisons between projects, particularly those with different productive lives, such as finding the optimal replacement age.
- Financial evaluation of projects has been made simple by the various built-in financial functions of spreadsheets. (To avoid mistakes, it pays to carefully check the conventions used. They differ between software packages.)
- For public projects, the appropriate choice of discount rate is far from clear, particularly for projects that involve questions of public health or safety, or irreversible environmental consequences. We have to ask ourselves if there is any ethical or moral justification for discounting in such cases.

Exercises

All computational exercises should be done with the help of a computer spreadsheet.

1. The local town clerk of a seaside resort is considering two possible options for preventing or alleviating further encroachment of the sea on a newly developed housing estate for vacation houses. The first option is to build a rock wall, reinforced by concrete. It would have an initial cost of €700,000 and would require little maintenance for about 20 years. The property owners would be assessed an annual levy which would bring in €30,000 each year. The second option is to raise the protective sand dunes and plant them with grasses for stabilization, as well as building wooden crossings for beach access. This would have an initial cost of €100,000. It would require annual maintenance of €20,000. No levy could be raised in this case. The town can borrow funds from the local banks at 10% per year. Use a planning horizon of 20 years for each option.
    (a) Find the present value of each option. Which one is the preferred option from a purely financial point of view?
    (b) Since the annual levy would be paid by each property owner in two equal instalments and the maintenance costs would be occurred in early spring and early autumn in roughly equal amounts, the clerk thinks that annual discounting is not accurate enough.

He asks you to compute the present value based on half-yearly discounting.
(c) Find the equivalent annual annuity for each option evaluated under (a).
(d) Assume now that both options essentially have an infinite lifetime. Find their present value under annual discounting. Which one is the better option now?

2. Consider the following two projects:

Year	0	1	2	3	4	5
Cash flow project A	−1000	−200	400	500	600	300
Cash flow project B	−500	−700	0	800	200	600

(a) Find the net present value for each for a discount rate of 15%. Which one would you accept, if they are mutually exclusive?
(b) Find the discount rate for which both projects have the same net present value. Discuss the meaning of this rate.
(c) Find the internal rate of return for each project. Using the internal rate of return criterion, which one would you accept if the firm wishes to earn at least 15% on its investments?

3. You consider buying a car that has a cash price of £18,000. The dealer also offers you a monthly payment plan which requires an initial down-payment of £3000 followed by 36 monthly instalments of £525. As it happens, the dealer has offered you £3000 trade-in for your current car. This would just cover the down-payment. You could also take out a loan from your local savings bank. The bank's current interest rate is 15% per year on a declining balance basis. They would also insist that you repay the loan completely within 3 years. The minimum payment each month would be £400, covering both principal and interest. This would give you considerably more freedom in terms of choosing your payment schedule, as long as you repay the loan within three years. Which is the cheaper option?

4. A Canadian forest owner has just clear felled 200 hectares of hillside trees and is evaluating which one of two reforestation options is the more profitable one. Option A calls for planting at a rate of 1600 seedlings per hectare at a cost of $2000/ha. Thinning is scheduled at age 6 to a density of 800 trees per hectare at a cost of $400/ha. The remaining trees will be pruned at an additional cost of $600/ha. A second pruning is scheduled for age 10 at a cost of $800/ha. All trees will be clear felled at age 35 at a cost of $3000/ha. Their quality will make them suitable for saw milling. Hence the estimated revenue is $64,000/ ha. Option B calls for planting at a rate of about 1100 seedlings per hectare at a cost of $1500/ha. A thinning is scheduled for age 14 at a cost of $2000/ha. The thinned logs are then suitable for use as round wood and are estimated to fetch $3,600/ha. All remaining trees will be clear felled at age 27 for use as pulpwood. The clear felling cost is $2200/ha. The revenue from the logs is estimated to be $28,000/ha. Note that all prices are in terms of current dollars (i.e. either there is assumed to be no inflation, or future dollars have been adjusted to remove inflation effects). Which option is the better one if the forest owner wishes to earn a return of 5% on any investment?
(a) Build a spreadsheet for finding the NPV of all cash flows associated with each option over its productive life. Which spreadsheet functions do you need to use?
(b) Why can you not determine which option is better on the basis of these two present values? What is the recommended approach for comparing the two options? Do it. Which spreadsheet functions will you use?

5. A firm wants to determine which one of two different machine tools to purchase. The two machines differ in terms of purchase price and annual fixed and variable costs, as well as

maximum output capacity. However, the quality of their output is identical. The following data have been prepared:

Model	1	2
Initial purchase price	£30,000	£60,000
Variable operating cost/unit	£1.50	£1.45
Fixed annual operating cost	£18,000	£8,000
Maximum annual output capacity	100,000	120,000 units
Expected resale value end of year 3	£7,000	£19,000

Expected sales	year 1	year 2	year 3
amount	60,000	90,000	120,000

Each unit is sold at a price of 2.00. Note that if model 1 is purchased, not all of the demand of year 3 can be met. It is also expected that at the end of year 3 this particular product will become obsolete. It will then be replaced by another product, requiring different machinery. The firm's policy is to accept projects only if they reach a 20% rate of return. Which machine should the firm purchase, if it wants to maximize the net present value of all cash flows?

6. A firm considers buying a new piece of equipment. Its purchase price is £30,000. Its profile for the predicted annual output, predicted operating and maintenance costs, and resale value is as follows:

Year of operation	1	2	3	4	5	6
Annual output	12,000	12,000	11,500	10,800	10,000	9,000
Operating costs	£3,400	£3,600	£3,900	£4,500	£5,400	£6,800
Resale value	£27,000	£24,000	£20,000	£15,000	£9,000	£2,000

Each unit produced brings in a net contribution of £2.50 (= sales price less material and labour costs). The firm works with a rate of return of 20% on its investments.

(a) Assume that all cash flows occur at the end of the year. Develop a spreadsheet for finding the optimal replacement interval. Does it satisfy the firm's criterion of earning at least 20% per year?

(b) For greater accuracy, approximate all continuous cash flows, i.e. the net contribution and the operating costs, by four equal amounts spaced at 3-monthly intervals. Adapt your spreadsheet for this change. Does it affect the optimal replacement interval?

7. Management of ABC Printing is considering replacement of its current four-year-old guillotine. It has seen very heavy use. The production supervisor has looked into various possible options for upgrading the firm's cutting capacity. The two options which look the most promising are:

A Overhaul the current machine at a cost of €11,000. The machine would then gain at most another 4–5 years of productive use before it has to be sold for scrap. The manufacturer of the machine has provided some information on the expected operating cost and resale value of the overhauled machine:

Age of machine	5	6	7	8	9
Operating cost	€6,500	€7,200	€8,500	€10,100	€12,500
Resale value	€22,000	€18,000	€12,000	€6,000	€1,200

B Buy a new machine which has a current price of €35,000. The manufacturer is willing to take the old machine as a trade-in for €13,000 now. The operating cost and predicted resale value for the new machine are as follows:

Year of operation	1	2	3	4	5
Operating cost	€3,500	€3,600	€4,000	€6,000	€8,000
Resale value	€31,000	€26,000	€20,000	€12,000	€3,000

Naturally, if it is decided to overhaul the current machine, it still can be traded in at the resale values listed under option A for a new machine at a later date. The firm's policy is to require a rate of return of 18% on all new investments.
(a) Determine the optimal replacement interval for the new machine of option (B).
(b) Should the firm overhaul the current machine and only purchase the new machine at a later date, and if so how much longer should the current machine be kept?

8. It is early 2004. Silicone Plastics Ltd is considering the replacement of one of its current injection moulding machines, purchased at the beginning of 1999 for $164,000. The operating log of that machine shows the following picture:

Year	1999	2000	2001	2002	2003	2004
Down time hours	192	192	192	212	233	260
Reject rate	1%	1%	1%	1%	1.2%	1.6%
Repair costs	0	0	$146	$290	$590	$1180
Overhaul costs	0	0	0	$2867	0	0

Part of the down time includes the weekly cleaning of the machine, which takes about 4 hours. It is expected that a major overhaul will be required every 4 years from the fourth year on, at a cost of around $3000. The production supervisor also thinks that all other operating characteristics of the machine will continue at the same trend as up to now. Whenever possible, the machine is in use, producing at a rate of 78 kg per hour. The firm works one 40-hour shift per week, 48 weeks per year. The output of good parts (exclusive of rejects) required by the machine is 140,000 kg per year. This is expected to continue for the next few years. Overtime is scheduled as needed to meet this target. The amount of raw materials required is equal to the output produced. The current cost of the raw materials is $3640/1000 kg. Three people are needed during the operations: a machine operator and two labourers. The latter are in charge of loading the machine and packing the output produced. The operator is paid at $16/hour, while the labourers get $12/hour. All three are needed for the weekly cleaning of the machine. They also have to be paid during any down time of the machine due to breakdowns.

The accountant has provided the following breakdown of overheads, all assessed on the direct labour cost: employee fringe benefits 20%, other factory overheads 28% (building maintenance, building depreciation, general lighting and power, salaried production staff), general company overhead 52% (general administrative staff salaries, building maintenance and depreciation, salaries for research and development and marketing, insurance, interest on loan capital). The firm's current average return on capital is 18%. In the past, new investment projects have usually been accepted if their rate of return exceeded this target.

The latest version of this type of machine has an initial cost of $246,000. According to the manufacturer, its reliability should be substantially better than that of older models. In particular, the reject rate should only be about 80% of the current model. Similarly, down time other than regular weekly cleaning should also be about 50% less. The machine should be overhauled regularly every 3 years at a cost of about $4000. No information on other repair costs is available, except that most spare parts seem to be about 30% less expensive for the new machine. Information obtained from a second-hand machine dealer indicates the following pattern of prices, as a function of the age of the machine which has had regular overhauls (in $1000):

Age	1	2	3	4	5	6	7	8
Resale value	$144	$132	$122	$112	$88	$64	$40	$14

(a) Construct a spreadsheet to determine the optimal replacement period for the new machine and find the optimal replacement period. This spreadsheet should show sufficient details of how all costs are computed and manipulated.

(b) Add a section to the spreadsheet for determining when the current machine should be replaced. It is now the beginning of 2004. At the beginning of what year should the current machine be replaced?

9. KIWI WINES (KW) produces top class wines. In contrast to most other wines produced in New Zealand, some of KW's wines are best aged for several years to bring out their full flavour and rich bouquet. Sue Keller, KW's owner–manager, wonders whether the firm should do the aging of its wines itself or let its customers take responsibility for that aspect. In the past most wines were sold within one year of harvesting the grapes. This is about 3–4 months after bottling. Such wine is referred to as 'new wine'. However, Sue realizes that a substantial portion of those wines are drunk without being properly aged by the customers. The argument for having KW age its wines is really that the reputation of KW's wines will be considerably enhanced by making sure that the wines are properly aged. This can only be guaranteed if KW does the aging itself. However, this would mean that KW would have to build an addition to its bottle warehouse — a fairly expensive proposition, since the warehouse has to be air-conditioned to provide the right storing environment. The cost of building the warehouse extension is estimated at $300,000. It would be able to hold up to 360,000 bottles.

The cost of producing unaged wine is roughly proportional to the volume produced, since most of the costs incurred are the value of the grapes used and the labour of picking and processing the grapes. Although all grapes are produced on KW's own vineyards, Sue is of the opinion that any grapes used for wine making by KW itself should be valued at the going wine grape market price, although she is not sure whether this argument is in fact correct, since no money changes hands. Sue figures that once the wine has been bottled, the remaining cost of aging the wine consists mainly of the interest paid to the bank for the funds invested in the wine, the cost of maintaining the warehouse and running the air-conditioning installation. The current new wine bottle warehouse is owned by KW. There is no mortgage outstanding on it. The addition to the warehouse would need to be financed by a mortgage loan. Hence, Sue thinks that the warehousing cost would now also need to include the repayment of the loan and the interest incurred on it. Naturally, as the wine ages, its selling price goes up considerably. So at least some, possibly even all, additional costs might be recovered from the increased revenue generated through aging. However, the best age to offer wine for sale is not necessarily the age when its flavour and bouquet are judged to be at their peak — 4 to 5 years for the wine considered below. So before a decision can be made on whether the warehouse should be built, the question of the best age to sell the wines would also need to be settled.

The amount of grapes available each year allows producing more wine than can be stored in the warehouse addition, except possibly for a one-year aging interval. (Note that since wine making is an annual operation, if the wine is stored for 2 years, only 180,000 bottles of wine can be added to storage each year, given the warehouse capacity of 360,000 bottles. Similarly, storage for 3 years reduces the quantity that can be added to storage to 120,000, and so on.) Naturally the whole harvest would be processed. But the plan is to store as many bottles as either the harvest or the warehouse capacity permits.

Any excess bottles that cannot be stored are sold as new wine. Bottles stored for aging are kept on racks. Proper aging requires that they are turned several times per year. Just prior to selling, all wine, new or aged, is put into cartons of 12 bottles.

In the past, Sue has not accepted any new project that did not have a rate of return before taxes of 18% per year. The following additional data have been collected:

Warehouse addition:
    Total construction cost: $300,000; completion date: 3 months after start
    Expected useful life: 20 years
    Financed by a 10 year mortgage of $250,000 at an annual interest rate of 12%
    Annual repayment on principal: $25,000
    Additional storage capacity: 360,000 bottles
    Air-conditioning running cost: $32,000/year (independent of amount stored)
    Fixed maintenance cost: $10,000/year
    Building insurance: $1,600/year

Wine operation:
    Current market price for grapes: $1800/tonne
    Average size of harvest available: 240 tonnes
    Each tonne produces 920 litres of wine
    Picking cost for grapes: $250/tonne
    Cost of processing grapes, incl. fermentation and initial storage: $850/tonne
    Bottling cost, incl. bottle & label: $0.36/bottle
    Each bottle contains 0.7 litre
    Aging cost per year: $0.21/bottle
    Cost of packing, incl. case: $1.18/12 bottles

Wine wholesale selling price:

year sold	New	1	2	3	4	5	6
price/case ($)	72	86	110	136	148	156	160

(a) Determine how long the wine should be aged to maximize the annual contribution to profits. Note that part of the assignment is to identify which costs are relevant and which ones should be ignored as neither affecting the optimal time to age the wines nor whether the warehouse addition should be built. So you need to scrutinize carefully all costs listed to determine whether they are relevant or not. (Hints: You need to determine the total revenue and total relevant cost associated with the grapes harvested each year. Each total consists of cash flows occurring during the year of the harvest and cash flows occurring during the aging interval or at the end of the aging interval. Obviously, any costs that are unaffected by the length of time the wine is aged are irrelevant for finding the optimal aging time.)

(b) In view of the answer about the best age to sell wine, should the warehouse be built or not? Note that the optimal solution from (a) above would be implemented as follows: say the optimal age to sell the wines is 2 years (not necessarily the correct answer!). Then 180,000 bottles of the wine pressed from the zero-year harvest would be put into storage at the beginning of the first year, and 180,000 bottles from the first-year harvest would be added at the beginning of the second year to fill the warehouse. From then on, at the beginning of each year 180,000 of aged wine would be removed for sale and replaced with the same quantity of new wine for aging. At the end of the productive life of the warehouse addition, the aging process stops. You will have to make some reasonable assumption as to what will happen then. For instance, you could assume that at the end of year 20, the two- and one-year old wines in the warehouse are sold. Also, some costs that you could ignore for part (a) may become relevant for part (b).

10. Discounting is pretty much the norm for commercial decisions. It is also extensively used for many public projects that have mainly pecuniary effects or effects that lend themselves to be easily expressed in monetary terms, such as flood control projects and similar public works. However, for projects that involve environmental, health, or social aspects there is considerable debate as to whether discounting is appropriate for evaluating their merit. Examples of this sort are: pre-school education, vaccination and other health promoting programs, projects that involve prevention of loss of life, road safety campaigns, conservation and environmental projects, recreational facilities for which charging may be difficult or discriminatory, etc. What are the pros and cons of using discounting in such instances? What alternative criteria may be more suitable for evaluating their merit(s)? It may be interesting to do a limited literature search on this issue. The book by Mishan may be a good starting point.

11

Decision making over time

The types of decision process we have studied so far were concerned with making a single decision at a given point in time, usually the present. For instance, the Champignons Galore case in Chapter 9 explored whether the cycle length should be shortened. In Chapter 10 we considered which one of several mutually exclusive investments should be undertaken. The future, if it is explicitly considered, only enters in so far as it affects the costs and benefits flowing from the decision.

The inventory control problem of the Lubricating Oil Division in Chapter 6 considers a string of decisions, namely the periodic stock replenishment whenever the inventory for a given product has been depleted. At each decision point, the future in terms of the demand for the product and the incidence of costs, however, remains unchanged. In technical terms, the future is said to be **stationary**. As a consequence, each decision is identical to the first one.

In this chapter, the time element is explicitly incorporated into the decision process in several ways. All problems studied involve making decisions at several points in the future. Furthermore, the state of the system changes over time. Each future decision point may face a different state of the system — the latter being affected by changing inputs from the environment, as well as by prior future decisions. The future is not stationary, but **dynamic**. Hence consecutive decisions are not identical and independent of each other, but tailored to the state of the system at the decision point.

When the time element enters into the decision process, the first question that must be addressed is "how long into the future should we look?" The length of time that the model covers is called the **planning horizon**. We have already used the concept of a planning horizon in some of the examples and case studies of previous chapters. For example, for investment and replacement problems we included all costs and benefits over the productive life of the investment in the analysis. Hence the productive life of an investment became the planning horizon. For the stationary situation of the LOD stock control problem we looked at annual costs. Hence the planning horizon covered one year. However, the latter choice was arbitrary. The optimal replenishment policy would have been identical, even if the model had used a planning horizon of one month.

For dynamic situations, the choice of the planning horizon becomes more critical. The best sequence of decisions or the **decision policy** derived from the model may be affected by the length of the planning horizon. The analyst is now faced with a new consideration. What is its most appropriate length? Section 11.1 gives some tentative answers to this question. The same theme is taken up again in Sections 11.3 and 11.9. Sections 11.2, 11.4–11.7, and 11.8 study two production planning situations. Each one exhibits distinct features and calls for a different approach for choosing the planning horizon and finding the best sequence of decisions.

11.1 The planning horizon

The planning horizon is the length of time — number of weeks, months, or years — covered by the model. What is its most appropriate length for dynamic models? Before trying to answer this question, it is useful to carefully clarify our aim for modelling dynamic situations.

Aim of modelling dynamic situations

One of the rules of good MS/OR practice is to avoid taking any decision or action that will unnecessarily reduce the scope of future decision choices, as far as this is desirable and practical. In line with this, only those decisions are physically implemented which cannot be postponed any further without affecting costs and benefits unfavourably. No commitment is made on any decision that only has to be implemented at some later point in time. If the future is uncertain, the wisdom of this rule is obvious. The future may turn out to be different from what we expected and the decisions not yet implemented may now be far from optimal. By keeping our options open, we will be in a better position to respond effectively to unexpected situations. But even if we pretend that the future is known, following this rule is equally advisable. In most cases the assumption of a certain future is only a simplifying approximation.

But why may it be necessary to consider future actions if we do not intend to implement them? Because the best initial decision may depend not only on future events, but also on future decision choices available. Only by including these future choices in our analysis can we be sure that the initial decision is best.

We are now ready to give a general answer about the most appropriate length of the planning horizon. It goes without saying that the longer the planning horizon, the costlier is the data collection and the computation of the optimal policy. Furthermore, the further into the future we look, the higher the degree of uncertainty and the less reliable the information about distant events. Hence the analyst will want to keep the planning horizon as short as possible. Its minimum length should cover a time interval that includes all those aspects, activities, events, and decision choices in the future which would lead to one initial set of firm decisions being optimal when included and another when ignored.

Putting this into practice is far from simple. As the length of the planning horizon is extended, events and decisions towards the end of the planning horizon will in general influence initial decisions less and less. This is particularly true for costs and benefits. Even at a moderate discount rate of 10%, a pound received in 10 years is now worth only 38 pence, while after 20 years its value now is less than 15 pence.

In a few special instances, the mathematical structure of the model allows us to find a precise minimum interval or specify some conditions which, once satisfied, allow the future to be ignored. In most cases, however, the actual choice of the length of the planning horizon is a partially arbitrary compromise between all the factors mentioned and the cost of data collection and computations.

Systematic sensitivity analysis with respect to the time interval covered may help in assessing the effects of future events on the initial set of decisions. This may lead to a better choice for the most suitable length of planning horizon needed for a particular problem situation. But it will also increase the cost and the time incurred for completing the project. This is justified, if the project offers substantial benefits because of its size and importance. It is also justified if the model developed is intended for repeated and continued use on a regular basis. In either case the cost incurred in getting the length of the planning horizon right will be recouped through lower costs or higher benefits in using the model. In most other situations it pays to be conservative and select a planning horizon on the long rather than short side.

Planning horizons for seasonal processes

For some situations, the nature of the problem may strongly suggest a suitable length for the planning horizon. This is particularly the case for decision problems subject to a seasonal pattern for some of their crucial inputs. For example, a hydro reservoir used for electric power generation may go through a natural annual cycle. Spring snow melt and rainfall may tend to fill the reservoir to its full capacity. The water stored is then used for generating electricity either over the following summer period if the power is used mainly for air-conditioning or over the following winter period if power is mainly used for heating. In either case, at the end of the 'season' the reservoir is empty. There is no carry-over from one year to the next. A new cycle starts each year. A planning horizon of one year, starting with the beginning of the snow melt, is the natural and appropriate choice used by many hydroelectric power companies.

However, there are some very large hydro reservoirs, particularly in Ontario (Canada) and in Sweden, that take several years to fill or empty under normal inflow and usage conditions. Substantial volumes of stored water are carried from one year to the next. Although the water inflow into the reservoir and the water usage may be highly seasonal, the planning horizon needs to be substantially longer, covering several years of operation.

These two examples indicate that an annual planning horizon is a suitable choice for seasonal activities, provided that there is a natural break between consecutive seasonal cycles, with no or only insignificant carry-over from one cycle to the next. Such breaks clearly satisfy the conditions stated earlier that events occurring past the end of the planning horizon should not affect the optimality of the initial decisions. A substantial portion of agricultural production and processing falls into this category.

We may still choose to use an annual planning horizon, even if there is a significant carry-over from one cycle to the next. The trick used is to create an artificial break between consecutive cycles. For example, the consumption of soft drinks and beers also has a seasonal pattern, superimposed on a more or less steady base rate. The lowest point of the seasonal cycle is chosen as the starting point of the annual planning horizon. The break between consecutive cycles is created artificially by specifying ending conditions for the state of the system. These then become the beginning conditions for the next planning horizon. Specifying such ending/beginning conditions reduces or even eliminates the influence of later events on the current set of decisions. The size of finished product inventories, stocks of raw materials, or the workforce are excellent choices for the ending and starting conditions between consecutive cycles. Again, good levels for these conditions may be determined through sensitivity analysis.

Rolling planning horizon

For ongoing processes with no natural breaks or end points, **a rolling planning horizon** approach is used. This is depicted in Figure 11-1. A planning horizon of

Figure 11-1 Rolling planning horizon of constant length

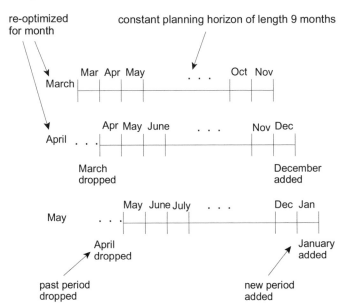

T periods, e.g. weeks, months, or years, is used for determining the initial set of optimal decisions. These decisions are then implemented and their effects on the state of the system recorded. One period later, the problem is again analysed based on the updated state of the system. The planning horizon used remains constant at *T* periods by dropping the period just passed and adding a new period at the end of the previous planning horizon. This scheme of dropping and adding periods at opposite ends of the planning horizon and re-optimizing the problem after each period based on the updated state of the system continues indefinitely. After each period, the planning horizon is, so to speak, rolled forward by one period, hence the label 'rolling planning horizon'.

Lead-up time, effective planning horizon, active planning horizon

The implementation of decisions may not be instantaneous, but may consist of a sequence of activities which take several days, weeks, months, or even years to plan in detail and to execute. Decisions of this sort, scheduled for implementation early on in the planning horizon, may need to be planned prior to the start of the actual planning horizon. Therefore, such a **lead-up time** becomes part of the **effective planning horizon**. Similarly, the time needed for developing the overall plan may take considerable time — weeks or even months. During this interval, no decisions that are part of the plan can normally be implemented. Hence this development time is also part of the lead-up time.

The effective planning horizon thus consists of two parts. The first part covers the lead-up time. During the lead-up time, firm commitments based on previous decisions will still get implemented as planned, since in most cases they can only be altered with heavy penalties. The second part is the **active planning horizon** for which decisions can still be made. It is the focus of the planning exercise. The role of the lead-up time is to update the state of the system to the position it will be in at the beginning of the active planning horizon.

Activity:
- If the set of future choices is different from the initial set, it seems reasonable that they need to be included in the analysis. But why is it necessary to consider them even if they are the same?
- Discuss the similarities and differences between the concept of a sunk cost and future decisions made, but not yet implemented.
- Can you think of other human-created activities which show regular cyclic behaviour (not necessarily annual) with clear breaks between each period?

11.2 Situation summary for seasonal production plan

The Crystal Springs Mineral Water Company of California produces carbonated mineral water with various flavours which it sells through supermarkets, corner groceries, hotels, and restaurants at $3.50 per case. It is a family-owned firm with

Sam Spring being the major shareholder. He is also Crystal's general manager, while his daughter and son do the selling. The company has a permanent staff of 18 people. Sales of its waters are highly seasonal, with demand during the summer months being three to four times larger than in the middle of winter. Since bottled water does not store well beyond two or three months, the rate of production has to follow the seasonal demand pattern to a large extent.

Crystal's output is pretty much limited by the capacity of its bottling machine. Normally, during the low season from November to April or May — the northern hemisphere winter — the bottling operation is run with one shift, staffed by a core of 12 employees who in the main have been with the company for many years. During the hot season, when sales soar, a second shift is operated by hiring temporary staff who work alongside the permanent staff. Since temporary staff have to undergo training, they have to be hired about two weeks prior to the time the second shift starts producing, with planning, hiring notices, and actual hiring adding another two weeks. Sam Spring estimates that the cost of hiring staff for a second shift, including advertising and interviewing, amounts to about $18,000. Similarly, once the second shift is abandoned, Crystal again incurs a cost of about $15,000 for laying off all temporary staff.

The bottles are sold in cases of 12. Hence all accounting and planning is in terms of cases, rather than bottles or volume. The production process is rather simple. Water is captured from a pristine natural spring on the firm's premises. Various minerals and flavourings are mixed into the water. The water is piped to the carbonating machine and immediately filled into bottles which are sealed and labelled, all in one sequence of operations. The bottles are then put into cases. The cost of all ingredients, packing materials and labels, including power to operate the machines, but excluding any labour costs, comes to $3.10 per case.

There is some temporary storage space for about one week's production right next to the bottling machine. The normal mode of operation is to ship cases to the various stores directly off the production floor without storing them first. This temporary storage is sufficient to absorb the normal daily fluctuations in selling and shipping. However, any excess has to be moved into the cool store warehouse, some 50 metres away. Moving and storing cases incurs a handling and holding cost of about $0.15 per case stored per month. Any cases stored are carefully rotated to avoid storage in excess of two months. Sam Spring reckons that if Crystal is unable to meet all potential sales, unsatisfied potential customers simply buy another brand. As a consequence, any unmet demand is lost. Sam attempts to meet demand whenever physically possible, since he is afraid that lost sales could mean more than simply $0.40 of profits foregone per case. It could imply losing some customers to the competition for good.

Although total annual sales have increased by about 5% in each of the past four years, the percentages of annual sales falling into each month have shown a remarkably stable seasonal pattern. Their averages are:

Month	1	2	3	4	5	6	7	8	9	10	11	12
Sales percentage	3.5	3.1	4.7	8.0	7.4	10.3	13.8	14.4	14.0	9.9	4.7	6.2

The regular time (RT) shift cost is the same regardless of whether the shift works at full capacity or below. A shift can work up to 25% overtime (OT). OT is paid at a 50% premium above the RT pay. The capacities for one- and two-shift operations, for RT and for OT, and the associated costs are as follows:

Operating mode	Capacity	Cost
1 shift on RT only	288,000 cartons	$24,000/month
OT capacity for one shift	72,000 cartons	$125/1000 cartons
2 shifts on RT only	540,000 cartons	$48,000/month
OT capacity for two shifts	125,000 cartons	$144/1000 cartons

OT capacity for a two-shift operation is less than twice the OT capacity for one shift due to reduced work efficiency. All other costs incurred are fixed overheads. They are not affected by the production schedule, and hence may be ignored.

It is now early December. Reviewing sales this year, Sam Spring expects that they will reach about 4,900,000 cartons. He wants to develop a tentative aggregate production schedule for the coming year. The intention is not to implement it blindly, but to use it as a guide for the planning of temporary staffing needs, purchasing of various ingredients, scheduling of bottle and carton deliveries to the plant, and developing the vacation roster for the permanent staff. Nevertheless, Sam would like an aggregate production schedule that maximizes profits for the year. In the past, he usually planned for an end-of-December inventory of 50,000 cartons of bottled water. He wishes to continue this practice.

As an exercise, we suggest you draw a rich picture for this problem situation. The issue to be analysed is the development of a production plan that maximizes profits. Next, you should define a relevant system, following the suggestions in Chapters 4 and 5. Armed with these preliminaries, you will be ready to formulate a mathematical model which we can explore using a spreadsheet approach.

11.3   Choice of planning horizon

This is a typical seasonal planning situation. Each calendar year forms a natural planning horizon. For Sam's intended use as an aggregate annual plan it will be sufficient to divide the planning horizon into monthly sub-intervals. This implies that any changes in shift levels or the production rate are assumed to occur at the beginning of each month. When it comes to actually implementing production decisions, Sam will break the planned monthly aggregates into detailed weekly production schedules which he will adjust in the light of the demand and shipment pattern actually observed at that time.

Do we need to include a lead-up time? Changing the number of shifts needs to be initiated at least one month ahead, while changes in the production rate can be imple-mented with only a day or two's notice. Similarly, it takes only a few hours to develop a new annual production schedule. So shift changes require the longest lead-up time, adding the month of December to the planning horizon. But Sam also knows that so far there has never been a need to introduce a second shift prior to April. As a consequence, no lead-up time has to be included for a possible shift change at the beginning of January. With monthly periods, the one or two days needed to institute a change in the production level can be ignored. Also, if Sam is able to predict how many cases will be shipped out prior to the end of December, he can adjust the December output such that he ends up with an inventory of bottled water of approximately 50,000 cases. Hence we can proceed without a lead-up time in the planning horizon, at least for the December planning exercise.

11.4 Influence diagram for production planning problem

Drawing an influence diagram for the relationships between inputs, system variables, and outputs will facilitate the formulation of a mathematical model from first principles. Figure 11-2 shows our version of such a diagram.

Figure 11-2 Influence diagram for multi-period production planning.

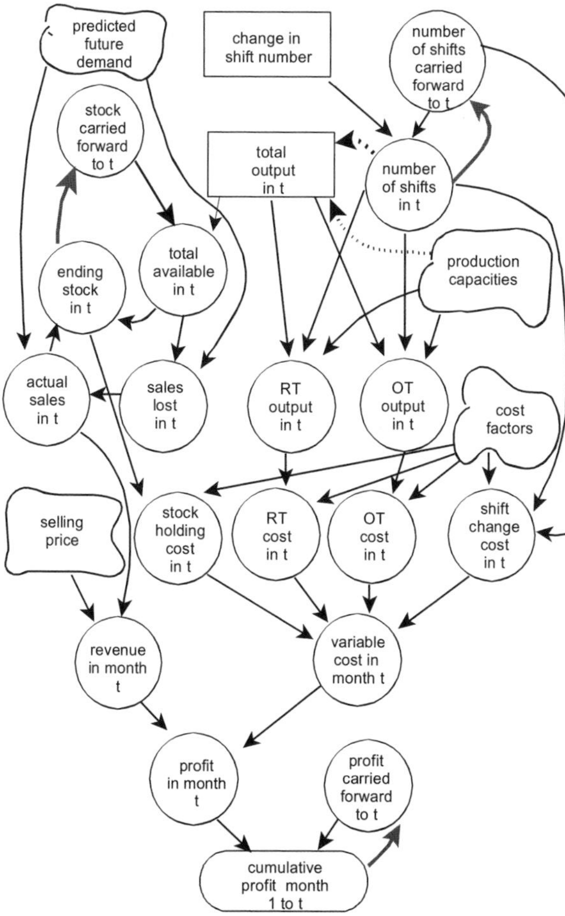

The inputs into the system are demand predictions, production capacities for the four shift configurations, and various revenue and cost factors. The major output of interest is the difference between total revenue and total relevant cost for the entire planning horizon. (Note that this difference is not the net profit, since all fixed costs have been excluded!)

For each month there are two decision variables: the number of shifts operated and the production level. The latter is only feasible if its value is within the production capacity for the shift level chosen, hence the broken lines from the shift level variable and the production capacities. Given the RT production capacity, the two decision variables also indirectly fix the OT output.

Each month is usefully viewed as a subsystem. The subsystems are linked by three system variables, namely the ending inventory of bottled water and the number of shifts operated in month $t - 1$, and the cumulative profit from month 1 to $t - 1$. In some sense they are pseudo-outputs of the subsystem for month $t - 1$ and become pseudo-inputs into the subsystem for month t. This feature calls for inventiveness in drawing the influence diagram. Rather than duplicating the subsystem relationships for each of the 12 months and connecting the subsystems through these pseudo-output/input linkages, we only show the relationships for one typical month t. The subsystem linkages are indicated symbolically by thick gray lines.

11.5 Spreadsheet model

Two different general purpose optimizing techniques could be applied to find the optimal production plan for this problem. One is dynamic programming, the other integer programming. Both are computationally expensive. Neither is discussed in this text, and using either would be like using a sledgehammer to crack a nut.

The mathematical relationships for this production planning model are relatively simple. Some have the form of accounting equations. Others require a table look-up. They are listed below. Their spreadsheet implementation is shown in Figure 11-3. (The compact layout used is not necessarily one that we would recommend for a business report. For space reasons and easy overview, all is displayed on a single page.)

In accordance with Sam Spring's policy, the beginning stock in January is entered as 50,000. All carton amounts are listed in thousands.

Functional relations of model

For the projected annual percentage growth of 5%, the sales forecast for the coming year is 105% of sales last year, or 5145 (1000 cases), as shown under 'Sales projections' in the top right-hand portion of the spreadsheet. Allocating these sales over the 12 months of the year according to the monthly sales percentage figures supplied at the bottom of page 287 gives the 'Potential sales'. (Due to rounding they add up to 5150 rather than 5145.)

The values of the decision variables are entered in the next two rows, shown

Figure 11-3 Spreadsheet implementation of CRYSTAL production plan — Schedule follows demand without shortages.

DATA:

	Capacity 1000 cases	Cost/month $1000
1 shift	288	24
1 shift o/time	72	9
2 shifts	540	48
2 shifts o/time	125	18

Other costs & revenue in $1000:

Raw materials/1000 cases	3.1
Holding cost/1000 cases	0.15
Shift change cost up	18
down	15
Revenue/1000 cases	3.5

Sales projections:

Sales last year in 1000 cases	4900
Annual percentage growth	5
Sales forecast coming year	5145
Desired ending stock in 1000 cases	50

Month:	JAN	FEB	MAR	APR	MAY	JUNE	JULY	AUG	SEP	OCT	NOV	DEC	TOTAL
Sales percent	3.5	3.1	4.7	8	7.4	10.3	13.8	14.4	14	9.9	4.7	6.2	100
Potential sales	181	160	242	412	381	530	711	741	721	510	242	319	5150
Total output	131	160	242	412	424	665	665	665	665	510	251	360	5150
Shift level	1	1	1	2	2	2	2	2	2	2	1	1	

Product transactions:

	JAN	FEB	MAR	APR	MAY	JUNE	JULY	AUG	SEP	OCT	NOV	DEC	TOTAL
Begin. stock	50	0	0	0	0	43	178	132	56	0	0	9	
R/T output	131	160	242	412	424	540	540	540	540	510	251	288	4578
O/T output	0	0	0	0	0	125	125	125	125	0	0	72	572
Am't available	181	160	242	412	424	708	843	797	721	510	251	369	
Actual sales	181	160	242	412	381	530	711	741	721	510	242	319	
Ending stock	0	0	0	0	43	178	132	56	0	0	9	50	
Lost sales	0	0	0	0	0	0	0	0	0	0	0	0	

Variable costs/month:

	JAN	FEB	MAR	APR	MAY	JUNE	JULY	AUG	SEP	OCT	NOV	DEC	TOTAL
Materials	406.1	496	750.2	1277.2	1314.4	2061.5	2061.5	2061.5	2061.5	1581	778.1	1116	15965
R/T shift cost	24	24	24	48	48	48	48	48	48	48	24	24	456
O/T shift cost	0	0	0	0	0	18	18	18	18	0	0	9	81
Shift change	0	0	0	18	0	0	0	0	0	0	15	0	33
Holding cost	0	0	0	0	6.45	26.7	19.8	8.4	0	0	1.35	7.5	70.2
Total cost	430.1	520	774.2	1343.2	1368.85	2154.2	2147.3	2135.9	2127.5	1629	818.45	1156.5	16605.2
Revenue	633.5	560	847	1442	1333.5	1855	2488.5	2593.5	2523.5	1785	847	1116.5	18025

Total revenue minus total variable cost   1419.8

shaded. The effects of the decision choices are traced out in the section entitled 'Product transactions'. The beginning stock in month t is equal to the ending stock in month $t-1$ (as depicted by the feedback loop in the influence diagram). Given the total output planned in month t, the RT and OT output is calculated from the table of production capacities on page 288 for the number of shifts scheduled. The RT output is equal to the total production or the relevant shift level capacity, whichever is smaller. Any excess is produced on OT. For example, the total output in June is 665,000 cases, with two shifts in operation. The two-shift capacities are 540,000 on RT and 125,000 on OT. Hence 540,000 are produced on RT and the balance of 665,000 − 540,000 or 125,000 on OT. In general

[RT output in t] = {[RT capacity for number of shifts in t], or
                          [Total output in t], whichever is smaller}

[OT output in t] = {[Total output in t] − [RT cap. for number of shifts in t]
                          if positive, and 0 otherwise}

Obviously, the two add up to the total output. The amount available for sale in month t is:

[Amount available in t] = [Beginning stock in t] + [Total output in t]

Comparing potential sales with the amount available indicates if there are any lost sales or any stock carried forward. Lost sales are subtracted from potential sales to give actual sales. This gives the following expressions:

[Lost sales in t] = {0 if [Potential sales in t] ≤ [Amount available in t], or
                          [Potential sales in t] − [Amount available in t] otherwise}

[Actual sales in t] = [Potential sales in t] − [Lost sales in t]

[Ending inventory in t] = [Amount available in t] − [Actual sales in t]

We now have all the entries needed for calculating costs, as shown in the bottom portion of the sheet. The material cost is the product of the unit material cost/1000 cases and the total output. The ending stock is penalized in month t by a stock handling and holding cost:

[Holding cost in t] = [Unit stock holding cost][Ending stock in t]

The RT shift cost for one or two shifts is obtained from the production cost table on page 288. The OT shift cost is proportional to the OT output. In our example for June, the RT output of 540,000 has a RT production cost of $48,000. The OT production cost for one shift is $144/1000 cases or $18,000 for 125,000 cases. In general:

[RT shift cost in t] = [RT shift cost for number of shifts in t]

[OT shift cost in t] = [OT output in t][OT cost/unit for shift level]

The shift change cost is only incurred if the number of shifts in month t is different from the number in month $t-1$. It is allocated to the month in which the capacity change takes effect. For example, an increase in the shift capacity effective for May means that the additional staff are hired and trained in the second half of April, but all costs are allocated to May. This approximation does not affect the total cost incurred over the entire planning horizon, while simplifying the spreadsheet computations. It is computed as follows:

[Shift change cost in t] = {[shift increase cost] if
　　　　　[number of shifts used in t] $\geq$ [number of shifts used in $t-1$],
　　　　　　or [shift decrease cost] if
　　　　　[number of shifts used in t] $\leq$ [number of shifts used in $t-1$],
　　　　　　and 0 otherwise}

The sum of all these costs is the total variable cost in month t:

[Total cost in t] = 　[Material cost in t]
　　　　　　　　+ [Holding cost in t] + [RT shift cost in t]
　　　　　　　　+ [OT shift cost in t] + [Shift change cost in t]

The revenue in month t is equal to actual sales in t times the unit selling price:

[Revenue in t] = [Actual sales in t][Unit selling price]

The profit in month t (without accounting for any fixed costs) is the difference between revenue and the total variable cost in month t:

[Profit in t] = [Revenue in t] − [Variable cost in t]

Finally, the cumulative profit from month 1 through month t is (another feedback loop in the influence diagram):

[Cumulative. profit to t] = [Profit in t] + [Cumulative. profit to $t-1$]

It took about an hour to develop this spreadsheet.

11.6　Finding the optimal production plan

Having set up a spreadsheet, an obvious approach is to try out various schedules and let the spreadsheet compute the corresponding annual profit. Sam Spring will be able to fully understand the logic used and can easily verify that it is correct. In contrast, he would have to accept the output of a sophisticated mathematical optimization technique on faith. He is more likely to trust the results of a spreadsheet that he can play around with himself.

　　The schedule tried first in Figure 11-3 uses a so-called 'chase strategy'. Production follows sales as closely as possible. No sales are lost, if possible. So we initially set the production level equal to the sales level, adjusting the number of shifts as needed. Since the two-shift capacity with overtime is insufficient to cover the high demands from July to September, we must backtrack and increase production to its maximum capacity level in the months just preceding July, until lost sales are eliminated. Production in June is thus increased to 665,000, needing another 43,000 cases to be produced in May in addition to the May demand. Note that the same sort of adjustment is made to cover the December requirements, including the provision of an ending stock of 50,000 cases. This policy has a total annual profit of $1,419,800.

This schedule does not use the RT production capacity efficiently. For instance, the March output is 242,000. This is 46,000 less than the one-shift RT capacity. Similarly, the two-shift RT capacity for May is underutilized by 116,000. By fully using the RT shift capacity in March and also producing 6,000 cases on overtime, it is possible to delay the start of the second shift by one month. This results in a small increase in profits of $6,450. The resulting schedule is shown in Figure 11-4.

Neither of these two schedules allows any lost sales. As a consequence, the amount of stock carried during the months of May to August is quite substantial. That stock is carried to cover demand in the three peak season months of July, August, and September, where the maximum production capacity is less than potential sales. However, the amount carried forward to month $t+1$ never exceeds the potential sales in that month. Hence the restriction on the limited shelf life of the product is not violated.

Reducing the amount of stock carried implies that some of the demand will not be met, resulting in some lost sales. For instance, if production in May is restricted to 381,000 cases — a reduction of 43,000 from the second schedule — then no stocks are carried forward from May to June, and the stocks at the end of June, July, and August are also reduced by the same amount. However, potential sales for September cannot be met completely, resulting in lost sales of 43,000. The saving in stock holding costs is $150 for each of these four months for every 1000 cases, or $150(43)(4) = $25,800. The loss in gross profit per 1000 cases is the difference between the sales price and the total material cost, i.e. $3500 – $3100 or $400 per 1000 cases. For 43,000 cases this amounts to $17,200, or $8600 less than the cost savings. Clearly, from a purely profit maximizing point of view this trade-off is advantageous. A similar (somewhat smaller) trade-off can be achieved by carrying no stocks from June to September.

The savings potential does not stop here. The new output for May still requires two shifts and is only 21,000 cases more than the maximum capacity of one shift with overtime. Delaying the introduction of the second shift until June, at the cost of additional lost sales in May, further increases total profits. These adjustments increase profits by $21,066 over schedule 2, as shown in Figure 11-5.

Given the ease with which such 'what-if' questions can be explored in a spreadsheet, we did not actually cost out such changes before trying them out. We simply reduced the production levels by successive small amounts first in May, then in June, and finally in July. If total profits increased we kept these changes. We reversed them

Figure 11-4 Crystal production plan — Schedule: delay 2nd shift by one month, no shortages.

DATA:

Capacity (1000 cases):

1 shift	288
1 shift o/time	72
2 shifts	540
2 shifts o/time	125

Cost/month ($1000):

1 shift	24
1 shift o/time	9
2 shifts	48
2 shifts o/time	18

Other costs & revenue in $1000:

Raw materials/1000 cases	3.1
Holding cost/1000 cases	0.15
Shift change cost — up	18
Shift change cost — down	15
Revenue/1000 cases	3.5

Sales projections:

Sales last year in 1000 cases	4900
Annual percentage growth	5
Sales forecast coming year	5145
Desired ending stock in 1000 cases	50

Month:	JAN	FEB	MAR	APR	MAY	JUNE	JULY	AUG	SEP	OCT	NOV	DEC	TOTAL
Sales percent	3.5	3.1	4.7	8	7.4	10.3	13.8	14.4	14	9.9	4.7	6.2	100
Potential sales	181	160	242	412	381	530	711	741	721	510	242	319	5150
Total output	131	160	294	360	424	665	665	665	665	510	251	360	5150
Shift level	1	1	1	1	2	2	2	2	2	2	1	1	
Product transactions:													
Begin. stock	50	0	0	52	0	43	178	132	56	0	0	9	
R/T output	131	160	288	288	424	540	540	540	540	510	251	288	4500
O/T output	0	0	6	72	0	125	125	125	125	0	0	72	650
Am't available	181	160	294	412	424	708	843	797	721	510	251	369	
Actual sales	181	160	242	412	381	530	711	741	721	510	242	319	
Ending stock	0	0	52	0	43	178	132	56	0	0	9	50	
Lost sales	0	0	0	0	0	0	0	0	0	0	0	0	
Variable costs/month:													
Materials	406.1	496	911.4	1116	1314.4	2061.5	2061.5	2061.5	2061.5	1581	778.1	1116	15965
R/T shift cost	24	24	24	24	48	48	48	48	48	48	24	24	432
O/T shift cost	0	0	0.75	9	0	18	18	18	18	0	0	9	90.75
Shift change	0	0	0	0	18	0	0	0	0	0	15	0	33
Holding cost	0	0	7.8	0	6.45	26.7	19.8	8.4	0	0	1.35	7.5	78
Total cost	430.1	520	943.95	1149	1386.85	2154.2	2147.3	2135.9	2127.5	1629	818.45	1156.5	16598.75
Revenue	633.5	560	847	1442	1333.5	1855	2488.5	2593.5	2523.5	1785	847	1116.5	18025

Total revenue minus total variable cost 1426.25

Figure 11-5   Crystal production plan — Best schedule, allowing some shortages.

DATA:

	Capacity 1000 cases	Cost/month $1000	Other costs & revenue in $1000:		Sales projections	
1 shift	288	24	Raw materials/1000 cases	3.1	Sales last year in 1000 cases	4900
1 shift o/time	72	9	Holding cost/1000 cases	0.15	Annual percentage growth	5
2 shifts	540	48	Shift change up	18	Sales forecast coming year	5145
2 shifts o/time	125	18	cost down	15		
			Revenue/1000 cases	3.5	Desired ending stock in 1000 cases	50

Month:	JAN	FEB	MAR	APR	MAY	JUNE	JULY	AUG	SEP	OCT	NOV	DEC	TOTAL
Sales percent	3.5	3.1	4.7	8	7.4	10.3	13.8	14.4	14	9.9	4.7	6.2	100
Potential sales	181	160	242	412	381	530	711	741	721	510	242	319	5150
Total output	131	160	294	360	360	576	665	665	665	510	251	360	4997
Shift level	1	1	1	1	1	2	2	2	2	2	1	1	
Product transactions:													
Begin. stock	50	0	0	52	0	0	46	0	0	0	0	9	
R/T output	131	160	288	288	288	540	540	540	540	510	251	288	4364
O/T output	0	0	6	72	72	36	125	125	125	0	0	72	633
Am't available	181	160	294	412	360	576	711	665	665	510	251	369	
Actual sales	181	160	242	412	360	530	711	665	665	510	242	319	
Ending stock	0	0	52	0	0	46	0	0	0	0	9	50	
Lost sales	0	0	0	0	21	0	0	76	56	0	0	0	153
Variable costs/month:													
Materials	406.1	496	911.4	1116	1116	1785.6	2061.5	2061.5	2061.5	1581	778.1	1116	15490.7
R/T shift cost	24	24	24	24	24	48	48	48	48	48	24	24	408
O/T shift cost	0	0	0.75	9	9	5.18	18	18	18	0	0	9	86.93
Shift change	0	0	0	0	0	18	0	0	0	0	15	0	33
Holding cost	0	0	7.8	0	0	6.9	0	0	0	0	1.35	7.5	23.55
Total cost	430.1	520	943.95	1149	1149	1863.6	2127.5	2127.5	2127.5	1629	818.45	1156.5	16042.18
Revenue	633.5	560	847	1442	1260	1855	2488.5	2327.5	2327.5	1785	847	1116.5	17489.5

Total revenue minus total variable cost   1447.32

if profits decreased. The same 'systematic' search by trial-and-error was used for exploring possible changes for April and May, etc.

It may be that Sam Spring is not willing to lose almost 3% of the potential sales forecasted (153,000/5,145,000) for an increase in profits of only $21,066. He may prefer the schedule in Figure 11-4 (note that it may be possible to improve upon that schedule without incurring shortages!), or one that lies between the second and the best schedule, allowing some lost sales in September, but none in August.

11.7 Considerations for practical implementation

Seasonal planning horizons have well-defined calendar start and end points. In the Crystal case, January 1 is the start and December 31 the end of the active annual planning horizon. The initial planning is done using these dates. As time progresses, more recent information about potential sales and stock levels becomes available and Sam will want to have a new look at the production schedule to see if any adjustments to the plan are advisable. For example, assume that it is now early April. Sales have been somewhat higher than expected, largely due to unseasonably warm weather. Long-term weather predictions indicate that this is likely to continue well into June. Should the second shift now be introduced in May rather than only in June? Should more stocks for future sales be built up?

To answer these questions, Sam will go back to the spreadsheet, update the sales forecasts from April on, and insert the current stock position at the beginning of April. The starting point of the planning horizon is now April 1, which now must also include a lead-up time of one month. Should the end point also be extended by another three months? Given the rather definite break in the annual cycle at the end of December, we keep this date as the end point. Hence, for subsequent updates of the production schedule, the planning horizon becomes shorter and shorter. So rather than talk about an annual planning horizon, it is more accurate to refer to it as a fixed date or fixed end point planning horizon.

Only towards the end of the current cycle, e.g. towards the end of the third quarter, may Sam wish to extend the planning horizon by a full annual season, in preparation for a preliminary mapping out next year's schedule.

Activity:
- Test your understanding of the computations by verifying each relationship numerically in the spreadsheet for several consecutive periods. March, April, May, and June cover most situations.
- If no shortages are allowed can material costs be ignored? Why or why not? Are there other aspects that could also be ignored?
- Since Sam uses the schedule to plan shift changes and build-up of stocks, would it be useful to go to shorter periods, say of one week or two week duration? What difficulties does this bring up in terms of forecasting and computations?

11.8 An example of a rolling planning horizon

A rolling planning horizon is suitable when activities are not subject to a pronounced seasonality, but just fluctuate in a predictable pattern. The following example of production planning in a manufacturing setting is a typical application where a rolling planning horizon approach is highly suitable.

For a particular household appliance, a manufacturer uses an electric motor type AC230/4. These motors are produced in batches of several hundred. Each new production run requires that the motor subassembly line is switched from one type of motor to another. That change-over has a cost of £960. No more than one run is made for any motor during any given week. However, a batch may well produce enough to cover the requirements for several consecutive weeks. Any motors not used in the week they are produced are stored. The storage cost for the AC230/4 motor is 26% per year on its unit production cost of £80. This amounts to £0.40 per unit per week. All other costs are not affected by the size and timing of production runs. They are either fixed costs or variable costs that only depend on the total amount produced per year, but not on individual run sizes.

Based on the assembly production plan, the manufacturer can predict the number of motors needed each week, although unforeseen events may result in changes. The production manager would like to determine a production schedule for the AC230/4 motor so as to minimize the total long-run relevant cost.

What would be a suitable length for the active planning horizon? A tentative answer can be obtained from a stationary type analysis. If the requirements for the motor were the same in each week, then we could use the EOQ model (see Section 6.13). The average weekly demand over the next four months is 460. Using the EOQ formula of expression 6-2 on page 142 for a weekly (rather than annual) model, we express all time-dependent inputs in terms of weekly figures. Hence $D = 460$, $s = 960$, $r = 0.26/52 = 0.005$, and $v = 80$. The resulting EOQ is 1486, covering 3.23 weeks of average requirements. (Verify that the answer would be identical if all time-dependent inputs had been expressed in annual figures!)

However, in view of the highly fluctuating weekly requirements — 750, 820, and 1200 in weeks 9, 1, and 4, respectively, while only 50 to 100 in weeks 6 to 8, as shown over the page — the planning horizon should be considerably longer than three to four weeks. We will arbitrarily settle for an active planning horizon of eight weeks.

It takes about one week to prepare a change-over on the motor assembly line. Hence, the lead-up time is one week. This gives a total planning horizon of 9 weeks. Since the first week is the lead-up time where no decision can be made, we will label it week –1. The first rolling planning horizon will cover weeks –1, 1, 2, ... through 8. Its active part covers weeks 1 to 8.

Remember again that the intention of this planning exercise is to implement only the first decision in the active part of the 9-week planning horizon. Subsequent decisions can wait. In fact, prior to implementing decisions for later periods, they will be re-evaluated in the light of the updated requirements and costs. The reason why they are included in the first place is simply to make sure that any possible effects they might have on the first decision are properly taken into account. Once the initial decision for week 1 has been implemented, the planning horizon is rolled forward by one week, the active portion covering weeks 2 to 9, and so on.

The following requirements are predicted over a 13-week period:

Week	−1	1	2	3	4	5	6	7	8	9	10	11	12	13
Number	460	820	220	450	1200	360	80	50	100	750	200	0	550	630

The Silver-Meal heuristic for dynamic replenishment problems

Rather than use an optimizing model, we will use a heuristic algorithm (see Section 6.19 for what both terms mean) — the Silver-Meal heuristic [E.A. Silver and R. Peterson (1985) *Decision Systems for Inventory Management and Production Planning*, Wiley, NY, pp. 232–9]. Extensive tests have shown that it tends to give close-to-optimal, if not optimal solutions.

Each replenishment covers the complete requirements for one or several consecutive periods. The Silver-Meal heuristic tries to minimize the average cost per period. The algorithm compares the average cost for successively longer and longer trial intervals. We continue adding additional periods as long as this average decreases. We stop when the average starts to increase. The only costs included are the change-over cost incurred for each replenishment and the holding cost on goods carried forward from the period in which they are produced to later periods.

First replenishment

Table 11-1 shows the calculations for weeks −1 through 8. No decision can be made for week −1. Hence no cost calculations need to be made. (Its entries are shown in *italics*.) The week −1 requirement of 460 units is met from the stock of 480 carried

Table 11-1 Replenishment schedule for weeks −1 through 8.

Week	Require-ment	Trial reple-nishment	Increm'l Cost	Total Cost	Average Cost	Best run size	Stock at end of week
−2					*stock carried forward*		*480*
−1	*460*		*no decision to be made*				*20*
1	820	800	£960	£960	£960	1470	670
2	220	1020	£88	£1048	£524		450
3	450	**1470**	£360	£1408	**£469**	**lowest**	0
4	1200	2670	£1440	£2848	£712		
4	1200	1200	£960	£960	£960	1790	590
5	360	1560	£144	£1104	£552		230
6	80	1640	£64	£1168	£389		150
7	50	1690	£60	£1228	£307		100
8	100	**1790**	£160	£1388	**£278**	**lowest**	0

into the planning horizon. The last column in Table 11-1 records the ending inventory in each week. Week 1 starts with a beginning stock of 20. These are allocated to the requirement in week 1. This leaves a net requirement of another 800 units to be catered for. Hence a replenishment has to be scheduled which covers at least this amount.

Let us now work through the algorithm. The first iteration covers a trial replenishment for week 1 only, i.e. the net requirements of 800. Since all units produced are used up in week 1, the only cost incurred is the change-over cost of £960. This is also the total cost as well as the average cost for this first trial replenishment. (Ignore the last two columns in Table 11-1 for the moment.)

For the second iteration, the trial interval covers two weeks, i.e. the trial replenishment in week 1 is extended to also include the week 2 requirements of 220. The size of the trial replenishment is now $800 + 220 = 1020$. The costs incurred consist of the change-over cost of £960 plus the incremental cost of carrying 220 units from week 1 to week 2. At £0.40 per unit per week, the holding cost is £220(0.40) or £88. The total cost for the two weeks is $£960 + 88 = £1048$, which averages to £524 per week. This is lower than the average cost for the first trial replenishment covering one week only. So the process continues.

The third iteration covers three weeks. Adding the week 3 requirement of 450, the trial replenishment goes to $1020 + 450 = 1470$. The total cost consists of the change-over cost, and the holding cost to cover the requirements for week 2 and week 3. But the first two items are simply the total cost for the two-week trial replenishment. So the 3-week total cost is found by adding the incremental cost to cover week 3 to the already computed 2-week total.

The week 3 incremental cost is the cost of holding the additional 450 units from week 1 to week 3 or two weeks. This amounts to 450(2)(0.40) or £360. The three-week total cost is $1048 + 360 = £1408$, or £469 per week. The average for a 3-week trial replenishment is lower than the one for 2 weeks.

Iteration 4 increases the trial replenishment by 1200 to also cover the week 4 requirement. The incremental cost for week 4 is the cost of holding these 1200 units for 3 weeks from week 1 to week 4, or £1440. The total for a 4-week trial replenishment is £2848, or an average weekly cost of £712. This turns out to be higher than the 3-week replenishment trial, so we have found the best batch size for the first replenishment in week 1. It is 1470, covering weeks 1, 2, and 3. The last column in Table 11-1 shows the inventory position at the end of each week.

Second replenishment

The process now restarts with finding the best run size for the replenishment to be scheduled in week 4. Verify that the average cost continues to decrease for the remainder of the planning horizon. We now have found the best replenishment schedule over the initial 9-week planning horizon. It consists of a replenishment of 1470 in week 1 to cover the requirements for weeks 1 to 3, and a replenishment of 1790 in week 4 to cover the requirements for weeks 4 to 8. Again, the last column records the resulting end-of-week inventory position.

Planning horizon roll-forward

Assume that it is a week later. Week −1 occurred as planned and a replenishment of 1470 units for week 1 was initiated. 800 motors of this first replenishment are still needed for the planned final assembly in week 1. This will leave a stock of 670 to be carried into week 2. The planning horizon is rolled forward by one week. We drop week −1 and add week 9. The active interval goes from week 2 to week 9.

Due to a rush order, the final product assembly schedule has been revised for weeks 2 and 3. It is now 320 and 350, respectively. No changes in requirements for weeks 4 through 9 are planned.

Table 11-2 finds the new production schedule covering weeks 2 through 9. As shown in the last column, the planned stock of units carried into week 2 still covers the revised requirements for weeks 2 and 3. It simply confirms the original plan that no replenishment is needed in these two weeks. Although the actual holding costs are different from the original plan, there is no point for computing them, since they are already committed by the original decision. The calculations for finding the best run size for week 4 are identical to the ones in Table 11-1. Adding week 9 confirms that the previously found best replenishment size for week 4 remains the same, with a new replenishment scheduled for week 9.

Table 11-2   Replenishment schedule for weeks 1 through 9.

Week	Require- ment	Trial reple- nishment	Increm. Cost	Total Cost	Average Cost	Best run size	Stock at end of week
−1					*stock carried forward*		*20*
1	*820*		*amount produced*			*1470*	*670*
2	320	previous decision confirmed					350
3	350	previous decision confirmed					0
4	1200	1200	£960	£960	£960	1790	590
5	360	1560	£144	£1104	£552		230
6	80	1640	£64	£1168	£389		150
7	50	1690	£60	£1228	£307		100
8	100	**1790**	£160	£1388	**£278**	**lowest**	0
9	750	2540	£1500	£2888	£481		
9	750	750	£960	£960	£960	750	0

The point of redoing these calculations was to find out whether the revised requirements caused a change in the planned decision of covering the week 2 requirements from the stock to be carried forward from week 1. Table 11-2 confirms that there is no change. In fact, regardless of any changes in requirements, as long as the planned stock carried forward into week 2 covers its requirement, the same conclusion will hold. Hence there was no need to perform the calculations in Table 11-2. However, if the stock carried forward had been less than the requirement for week 2, a completely new schedule would then have to be developed.

Time now advances to the beginning of week 2. The week 1 activities realize as per the revised plan. The planning horizon is again rolled forward by one week, covering weeks 2 to 10, with week 3 the first one where a new decision can be made. Again some changes in the final assembly schedule result in the following revised forecasts for the AC230/4 motor requirements:

Week	2	3	4	5	6	7	8	9	10	11	12	13	14
Number	320	210	1200	360	80	50	100	750	200	0	550	630	1050

The planned requirement for week 2 results in a planned stock of 350 to be carried forward to week 3. Does the smaller requirement in week 3 make it necessary do redo the calculations? The answer is 'No' for the following reasons. The smaller week 3 requirement results in a stock of 140 units carried into week 4. As a consequence the replenishment planned for week 4 will change. However, the decision to have no replenishment in week 3 still stands.

Time advances to the beginning of week 3. The planning horizon is again rolled forward by one week, with the first possible decision affecting week 4. Assume that the planned requirements for weeks 3 through 11 remain unchanged. Hence, the planned stock to be carried forward to week 4 is 140. The net requirement for week 4 is reduced from 1200 to 1060. The original schedule provided for a replenishment in week 4. This is still the case, but its size may be different due to the change in net requirements. A new production schedule has to be developed. This is done in Table 11-3. The new schedule has a run of size 1600 in week 4 and a run of 1100 in week 8. Note that the small change in the week 8 requirement results in the week 4 production no longer covering week 8.

This process of rolling the planning horizon forward one week at a time continues. No action is scheduled until the planned stock carried forward does not cover the requirements in the first period of the new active planning horizon. At that point a new schedule is developed.

Table 11-3   Replenishment schedule for weeks 3 through 11

Week	Require-ment	Trial reple-nishment	Increm. Cost	Total Cost	Average Cost	Best run size	Stock at end of week
2					stock carried forward		350
3	210		no decision to be made				140
4	1200	1060	£960	£960	£960	1600	540
5	360	1420	£144	£1104	£552		180
6	80	1500	£64	£1168	£389		100
7	100	**1600**	£120	£1288	**£322**	**lowest**	0
8	630	2330	£1008	£1388	£459		
8	630	630	£960	£960	£960	1100	470
9	220	850	£88	£1048	£524		250
10	200	1050	£160	£1208	£403		50
11	50	**1100**	£60	£1268	**£317**	**lowest**	0

11.9 Minimum length of planning horizon

As briefly mentioned in Section 11.1, in a few special instances, the mathematical structure of the model or the solution method used for solving it may allow identifying a minimum length for the planning horizon or specifying conditions which when satisfied allow the planning horizon to be truncated. The astute reader may have already guessed that this is the case for the solution approach to the replenishment scheduling problem of the previous section.

Recall that we are only interested in the 'best' initial decision, i.e. whether or not to schedule a replenishment in the first week of the active planning horizon and, if yes, what its best run size should be. For the situation of Table 11-1, the 'best' run size for week 1 is established once the trial replenishment covering the requirements for weeks 1 to 4 has been costed out and found to have a higher average than the trial replenishment covering only weeks 1 to 3. The rest of the analysis for finding the best run size for week 4 did not affect the best run size for week 1. There was, indeed, little point in continuing these computations. Similarly, the computations in Table 11-3 again did not need to go beyond week 8. At that point the best run size for week 4 had been identified as covering the requirements for weeks 4 to 7. Whatever happens after that will not affect this decision.

So we see that for this particular production scheduling problem, in those weeks where a replenishment is needed, the solution method used allows us to truncate the active planning horizon as soon as we have found that the average cost per week goes up, while in all other weeks, where the incoming stock is sufficient to cover the requirements of the first active week, the active planning horizon is only one week beyond the lead-up time.

Activity:
- Assume that there are no capacity constraints and that only one batch can be scheduled for a product in any given period. Why is a plan to carry any stock forward into a period in which you also plan to make a new batch always more expensive than increasing the new batch by the same amount, while at the same time decreasing the size of the previous batch?
- If setup costs are fixed, regardless of the batch size, why may it be necessary to adjust the length of the planning horizon used for the Silver-Meal algorithm in response to seasonal changes in requirement levels?

11.10 Chapter highlights

- The behaviour of many systems is dynamic in the sense that the uncontrollable inputs do not remain stationary but change over time. Decisions may have to be made at various future points. These decisions in turn affect the future state of the system. Their appropriateness or optimality may not only depend on external events, but also on alternative choices available for later decisions.

- Their influence tends to become weaker the farther in the future these events and decisions occur. One of the important problems faced by planners is how much of the future to take include — how long should the planning horizon be?
- The answer we gave was that the minimum length of the planning horizon should be such that any events happening later will have no significant effect on what is the best set of decisions for which the decision maker has to make a firm commitment. No action for implementation is taken on decisions planned for farther into the planning horizon. These will be reviewed later on.
- The effective planning horizon is made up of the lead-up time and the active planning horizon. New decisions can only be planned for the latter.
- For scheduling problems over time, we make use of a rolling planning horizon, i.e. after each decision point the planning horizon is shifted forward by one period — the first period (just past) is dropped and a new period is added at the end, thereby keeping the length fixed.

Exercises

1. Consider the Crystal Springs example. Develop a spreadsheet to reproduce the results in Figure 11-3. If you find more elegant ways to handle some aspects, do so. (Note that to get everything on one page, the format is rather crammed — not necessarily a model to follow.)

2. Still with Crystal Springs, assume now that, as indicated in Section 11.7, it is early April. Sales have been somewhat higher than expected. Actual sales and production for the first three months have been as follows:

Month	Jan	Feb	March
Actual sales	179	194	289
% increase over predicted	−1%	+21%	+19%
Actual production	129	206	320

Given the long-range weather forecast for another summer of heat and drought in California, Sam Spring expects that sales are likely to remain at a higher level well into September and only then revert back to the previous level. Then there is the problem with the union organizers who have been talking to his regular workforce. His workers seem to be unhappy about the way overtime was scheduled as needed. If any overtime is scheduled, they want it to be for a minimum of at least 1 hour per day (the current maximum is 2 hours per day). In other words, overtime for at least 36,000 cases for a one-shift operation and at least 62,000 cases for a two-shift operation should be scheduled, and any extra up to the maximum of 72,000 and 125,000, respectively. He also expects that, due to having to offer higher moving allowances, the cost of adding a second shift would increase to $24,000. Similarly, due to increases in interest rates, the implied cost of holding stock had increased to $180/1000 cases/month. Sam has also been experimenting with the processing speed of his filling machine. He is pretty certain that he can increase the filling speed by 5% without affecting the safety or accuracy of the machine operation. He plans to implement this starting April. Finally, Sam has been advised by his raw material suppliers that, due to inflation, prices will increase in July, adding another 14 cents to the cost of producing a case. Given all these changes, Sam wants to develop a new production/shift schedule for the rest of the year. Use the spreadsheet of exercise 1, making the necessary changes in input data to explore various possible schedules, trying to identify the highest profit solution.

3. A highway construction company rents specialized earth-moving equipment from a leasing company as needed during the various phases of a job. Such equipment has to be rented for one or more full weeks, even if it might only be required for part of the week. For a particular piece of equipment, the rental cost per week is £2000. Each time a unit is rented, there is a preparation and transport charge of £1200 by the leasing company. Each time a unit is returned, there is a service, cleaning, and transport cost of £1500. As an alternative to renting, the company can farm out some or all work during any given week to a local contractor at a cost of £1000 per unit short per working day. The weekly workload, shown in unit-days, i.e. the number of days work that needs to be done during each week with this equipment, is as follows:

Week	1	2	3	4	5	6	7	8	9	10
Unit-days	6	10	8	14	7	15	0	4	5	7

Assume that each week has 5 workdays. Hence a requirement of 8, for example, implies there is a need for one full unit and another unit for 3 days. But recall that rental charges cover full weeks only. At the beginning of the planning horizon, the company has one rental unit on hand. It can return it or keep it. There is no need for any units after week 10. Hence all units rented at that time are returned. Develop a spreadsheet and try to find the optimal renting schedule by trial and error.

4*. Study exercise 9 of Chapter 4 carefully. If you have not done that exercise yet, it may be advisable to do so now. The brief for the consultant is to propose several good shift patterns and suitable rosters for the staff which differ in terms of amount of overtime, total staff size, and total weekly cost. Consider the following additional data:

* Summer schedule of commercial flights: (PAX = estimate of passenger number)

Arrival	Day	Time	PAX	Departure	Day	Time	PAX
1	Mon	00:30	180	1	Mon	07:10	210
2	Mon	16:20	370	2	Mon	17:20	400
3	Mon	18:30	280	3	Mon	20:40	250
4	Mon	23:10	250	4	Tue	06:50	220
5	Tue	09:50	400	5	Tue	11:10	360
6	Tue	14:30	180	6	Tue	17:20	180
7	Tue	19:50	360	7	Tue	21:10	380
8	Tue	20:50	180	8	Tue	22:10	160
9	Wed	10:10	200	9	Wed	11:10	180
10	Wed	15:40	360	10	Wed	17:00	380
11	Wed	23:10	250	11	Thu	06:50	280
12	Thu	01:20	180	12	Thu	07:30	180
13	Thu	15:40	360	13	Thu	17:00	360
14	Fri	09:40	400	14	Thu	11:00	400
15	Fri	14:50	190	15	Fri	16:00	180
16	Fri	16:10	380	16	Fri	17:30	400
17	Fri	17:10	280	17	Fri	18:30	260
18	Fri	22:30	180	18	Sat	06:20	200
19	Fri	23:50	370	19	Sat	06:50	400
20	Sat	00:20	330	20	Sat	07:00	350
21	Sat	05:50	200	21	Sat	07:30	180
22	Sat	06:00	180	22	Sat	08:00	180
23	Sat	14:50	190	23	Sat	16:10	180

24	Sat	16:30	360	24	Sat	18:00	350
25	Sat	23:40	190	25	Sun	06:20	180
26	Sun	05:20	200	26	Sun	07:30	180
27	Sun	15:40	400	27	Sun	17:10	400
28	Sun	18:00	360	28	Sun	19:30	400

- Processing arriving passengers: It takes 1 minute to clear a passenger through immigration or passport control (primary processing). The maximum number of booths available is 10. For secondary processing, there is usually one officer for every 60 passengers arriving. In addition to this, one supervisor and two other customs officers are staffing the observation room which has a bank of TV monitors, one for each remote control camera in the arrival hall, or are roaming around in the arrival hall. Recall also that the officers form a team which assembles 30 minutes prior to the scheduled flight arrival for briefing and preparation of arrival hall.

- Processing of departing passengers: Regardless of the number of passengers on a departing plane, processing of departing customers starts 30 minutes prior to the scheduled departure and involves always just two custom officers. If several flights depart less than 30 minutes apart, no additional staff are scheduled. There is no extra time for briefing and preparation needed for departures.

- Deep Freeze mail schedule: usual arrival time of mail

Day	Mon	Tue	Wed	Thu	Fri	Fri	Sat	Sun
Time	09:00	09:00	09:00	15:00	09:00	15:00	15:00	9:00
Staffing	4	2	2	2	2	1	4	2

Assume that it always takes 60 minutes to process the mail.

- CIA freight office schedule: Daily 10:00 to 16:00, 2 staff required.

- Clerical tasks: 80 hours/day Monday to Friday, 48 hours/day Saturday and Sunday.

(a) Use the following approach for developing a schedule of shifts. Use regular graph paper to indicate the number of people required for processing flights and other regular scheduled duties. For each flight arrival, the number of people required has to be computed from the expected number of passengers on that flight, given the government processing standards, as well as the limitations of immigration booths. Let each square represent one person for 10 minutes. Elapsed time is measured along the x-axis, while the number of people required is shown along the y-axis. Use different colours for the various duties. If several duties occur at the same time, the duties are juxtaposed on top of each other. The resulting graph will look like the skyline of a city. You now super-impose on this pattern a set of shifts. The shifts do not have to start at the same time each day, but it would be highly desirable that each day has the same total number of shifts. Assigning people to shifts will also be considerably simplified if each shift always has the same number of members. For instance, you might have three shifts of 12 people, including one supervisor, and two shifts of 2 people each day. The latter are used for processing departures. Each shift should be 9 hours long. However, only 8.5 hours are working hours, since each officer will take off for a 30 minute break some time towards the middle of the shift. If a shift is relieved during a time when they are processing a flight, there must be a 30 minute overlap between the two shifts involved to allow for a smooth change-over. Draw the shifts in easy-erase pencil on top of the task schedule. Each shift is shown as a rectangle 9 hours long and up to 20 squares high (= 19 custom officers + one supervisor). If two shifts overlap, then for the duration of the overlap, one shift is shown above the other. Arrange the start times of the shifts in such a way that you can meet most of the flights, as well as the other scheduled tasks. Any flights not covered or only partially covered by a shift will require the scheduling of overtime. The aim is to minimize the amount of overtime scheduled, while at the same time keeping the total number of staff needed to a minimum. Obviously, there is a trade-off between the size of each shift and the amount of overtime. Note that overtime has a cost that is 50% higher than regular time. Develop two or three different shift schedules, differing in their timing and the size of the shifts.

(b) Develop a roster for the staff. A roster assigns staff to shifts. Contractual arrangements require that, on average, each staff member works 4 out of 6 days. The kinds of rostering patterns that seem to work well are cycles such as 4 days on/2 days off, or 5 days on/two days off/5 days on/3 days off. Such patterns have the effect that each staff member has the same number of weekends off. Indicate how many weeks it will take before a given person or whole shift team starts its cyclic pattern anew on the same day of the week.

5. An appliance manufacturer faces the following weekly requirements (in thousands of units) for a given subassembly, produced by the firm itself:

Week	1	2	3	4	5	6	7	8	9	10
Requirement	17	8	12	4	10	20	15	3	6	9

The cost of setting up a production run for this subassembly amounts to £500, while it costs £2 to store 1000 units from one week to the next, assessed on the ending stock on hand. Using the Silver-Meal heuristic, find the resulting schedule of production runs and stock holdings for the entire 10 weeks. (Note that once you find the size of the production run in period 1, you simply start the heuristic anew from the first period not covered by that run.) What is the minimum length of the planning horizon required?

6. Referring back to exercise 5 above, assume now that a production run of 25,000 subassemblies was scheduled for week 1. It is now the beginning of week 3. It turns out that due to a power failure only 22,000 subassemblies were actually produced. Furthermore, the actual usage in weeks 1 and 2 amounted to 20,000 subassemblies only. The revised predicted requirements are now as follows (in thousands of units):

Week	3	4	5	6	7	8	9	10	11	12
Requirement	15	10	20	4	15	3	6	9	2	20

Determine a revised production schedule for this subassembly to the end of week 12, using the Silver-Meal heuristic.

PART 4
Hard MS/OR methods

Chapter 6 explored in some detail an 11-step paradigm for hard OR. As depicted in Figure 6-9 on page 155, the hard OR approach deals with three systems:

- **System S:** the narrow system of interest which defines the interrelationships of the problem and how to judge system performance;
- **System M:** the modelling system that translates the interrelationships of system S and its performance measure(s) into a mathematical model; and
- **System O:** the improvement or optimization system that finds the preferred course of action or the most preferred values for the decision variables in the light of the performance measure(s) of system S.

While Parts 1 and 2 dealt mainly with system S, Part 4 deals exclusively with Systems M and O. This pursuit will lead us to study a number of MS/OR models and their associated solution and optimization techniques. However, the emphasis is not on the models, tools or techniques themselves. They are simply used as the vehicles to gain new insights into system behaviour and decision making when:

- the decision choices or decision variables are subject to constraints,
- there is uncertainty about the inputs into the system, causing the outcomes of decision choices to become uncertain themselves, and/or
- the performance is not measured by a single objective or goal, but by several, usually conflicting objectives.

So Part 4 is not a traditional introduction into MS/OR techniques and their solution methods. At an introductory level, although interesting and fun, they are often reduced to triviality, devoid of any practical application. Rather than study the intricacies of the techniques and solution methods with toy examples, we demonstrate the concepts and new insights using real-life practical case studies that we have been involved in or that have been reported in the literature. By necessity, some of them have been trimmed in order to reduce their complexity and render them amenable for inclusion in the limited space of a textbook, without robbing them of their original flavour.

In the course of this journey, you will be exposed in Chapter 12 to the ideas of marginal analysis from economics (ideas that in one form or another appear in a number of tools and techniques), how to deal with constraints in Chapters 13 and 14, including modelling using linear programming and the transportation problem, and the various meanings of uncertainty and the difficulties of capturing uncertainty in general in Chapter 15. Chapters 16 to 18 show a number of modelling approaches incorporating uncertainty, such as queueing and waiting lines, simulation, and decision analysis. Finally, Chapter 19 touches on the difficulties when faced with multiple objectives or goals and covers one of the simplest methods, i.e. the aggregate value function approach.

Whenever possible, the quantitative analysis uses the power and flexibility of spreadsheets. The text uses Microsoft Excel© and its solver capability, but this choice is one of convenience, rather than preference.

The use of spreadsheets implies that the level of mathematics involved remains at a fairly elementary level and does not go beyond high school mathematics and statistics. The emphasis of the exposure is not on the mathematics, but on the concepts and the process of quantitative decision making. The discussion lives on the principle of 'never let the mathematics get in the way of common sense!'

(As has already been the case in previous chapters, the format used for the spreadsheets is not necessarily one that we recommend you should use. While good practice usually has separate sheets for the inputs and the actual computations and outputs, for reasons of space and easy overview we show all three on the same compact sheet.)

12

Marginal and incremental analysis

Marginal analysis is one of the fundamental tools in economics. It forms the theoretical basis for deriving normative rules for a firm's optimal allocation of scarce resources to the production of goods and services, for the optimal output and activity levels, as well as for product and service pricing decisions.

MS/OR problems often deal with decisions about resource allocation. Furthermore, several MS/OR tools, both simple and sophisticated ones, have borrowed the mode of thinking underlying marginal analysis. In fact, you already have encountered this type of reasoning in the truck replacement problem in Chapter 10. A clear understanding of marginal analysis is essential for MS/OR analysts.

Sections 12.2 and 12.3 review the typical forms of total costs, total revenues, and total profits as functions of the level of activity or output of a firm. This will lead us in Section 12.4 to a short detour into breakeven analysis — a useful tool when these functions are all linear in the level of output. Section 12.5 studies the relationships between marginal costs and revenues and total profits, and derives the basic principle of marginal analysis, which are then demonstrated in Section 12.6. The discussion in Sections 12.2–12.6 will, with one exception, be in terms of variables that only assume integer values. Hence, the marginal output is always equal to the incremental output for a unit increase in the input. This will allow us to demonstrate the concepts with simple numerical examples.

The starred (optional) Sections 12.7 and 12.8 generalize these concepts to the case of continuous variables. Section 12.7 is somewhat more demanding and assumes a rudimentary understanding of differential calculus.

Sections 12.9–12.11 look at incremental analysis. Its usefulness is demonstrated with a transport problem for a leading US manufacturer of ketchup.

12.1 Marginal analysis versus incremental analysis

The term 'marginal' has a number of meanings. In everyday language, it usually implies 'just barely acceptable'. In economics, it relates to infinitesimally small changes occurring at the margin — a rather different meaning. For example, a wheat farmer applies 100 kg of fertilizer per hectare of land. This results in an output of 2000 kg of wheat per hectare. If the farmer increases the amount of fertilizer applied per hectare by a very small amount, say 0.5 kg, the wheat output goes up by 4 kg per hectare. This increase in output is called the marginal output. It relates to the change in output associated with a small change in the use of fertilizer from the current level or, in other words, at the margin. It is usually expressed in terms of a unit change in the factor that causes the output to change. For our example, the marginal output of wheat is 8 kg for 1 kg of fertilizer applied beyond the current level of 100 kg per hectare. Viewed in this way, the marginal output is the rate of change in the output of wheat at a level of 100 kg of fertilizer use per hectare. However, that rate may only be valid for a small increase in fertilizer use beyond 100 kg. Increasing the use of fertilizers by another 0.5 kg may only result in an additional 3.9 kg of wheat. The marginal output has already dropped to 7.8 kg at 100.5 kg of fertilizer use.

These are two important things to keep in mind when using the concept of 'marginal output'. Firstly, it is related to a **rate of change**, usually expressed in terms of a unit change in some input. Secondly, it is the rate of change at a given level of this input and may only be valid for a very small change in that input.

'Incremental' on the other hand relates to the actual numeric change in an output associated with a given increase of an input from its current level. In the above example, an increase in fertilizer use from 100 kg to 110 kg per hectare will increase the wheat output from 2000 kg to 2050 kg. The incremental output for increasing the use of fertilizers from 100 to 110 kg is therefore 50 kg.

In this example, the inputs and outputs are continuous variables that can assume any real value, integer or fractional. If the input can only assume integer values, such as the number of tellers used by a bank during a given time period, or the number of cars owned by a car rental company, the marginal output is equal to the incremental change in output for an additional unit of input. However, if the input is a continuous variable then marginal output and the incremental output for a unit increase in the input will in many cases be different.

Figure 12-1 depicts the relationship between marginal output and incremental output for the wheat production example. The incremental output is measured by the actually achieved increase in output in response to an increase in input from a specified level, e.g. 50 kg for a 10 kg fertilizer increase from 100 to 110 kg. The marginal output, on the other hand, is given by the slope of the total output curve at that level of input. This slope corresponds to the tangent to the curve. For instance, at an input of 100 kg of fertilizer, the slope of the output curve is 8 kg.

12.2 Total costs, marginal and average costs

Polycompound, or PC for short, produces silicone rubber for specific customer orders. Silicone rubber production is a two-step process. In step 1, the various ingredients, mostly PVC resin, plasticizer, fillers, stabilizers, pigment, and various other additives, are mixed in a specific sequence in individual batches of 80 kg in a

Figure 12-1   Marginal and incremental outputs.

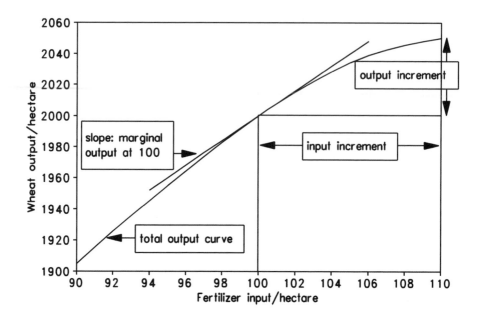

mixer. During mixing the blend is heated to temperatures of up to 140 °C. The mixed blend is cooled and dumped into the hopper of a compounding extruder that forms the PVC granules. These are aircooled and then packed into 40 kg bags, shrink-wrapped and labelled for delivery to customers. Customer orders are always in integer multiples of batches.

All operations need constant supervision and hence are labour intensive. Processing of the first two batches takes much longer than later batches, since numerous tests have to be performed to have the mixing and extruding operations properly adjusted. This reflects itself in higher labour costs for the first few batches. Up to 8 batches can be processed in a regular 8-hour shift. Once a run has been started, it has to be completed, even if this has to be done on overtime. If the extrusion section is stopped for more than 10 minutes, it requires a complete clean-down that results in a down time of 3 hours — the same as for a new setup.

The setup cost covers the cost of preparing a new run and the cleaning of both the mixer and the extrusion section after completion of a run. This avoids contamination between runs and prevents any residues left in the machines from hardening. The latter would require expensive scraping off and possible damage to the machines. Overtime requires the presence of two operators and a supervisor. This explains the rather large increase in labour cost from the ninth batch on. Table 12-1 lists the machine setup, material, and labour costs in pounds incurred for a production run requiring up to 12 mixing batches for silicone rubber PC312-X.

Table 12-1   Production costs per run.

Number of batches	Setup cost per run	Material cost	Labour cost	Total cost per run
1	80	10	72	162
2	80	20	108	208
3	80	30	132	242
4	80	40	144	264
5	80	50	156	286
6	80	60	168	308
7	80	70	180	330
8	80	80	192	352
9	80	90	228	398
10	80	100	264	444
11	80	110	300	490
12	80	120	336	536

As expected, the machine setup cost per run remains fixed, regardless of the number of batches needed. The material cost increases linearly at a rate of £10 per batch. Labour costs decrease from £72 for the first sub-batch to a low £12 for the fourth batch. Overtime increases the labour cost to £36 per batch.

Figure 12-2 shows the graph of the total costs as a function of the run size.

Figure 12-2   The graph of total costs versus run size.

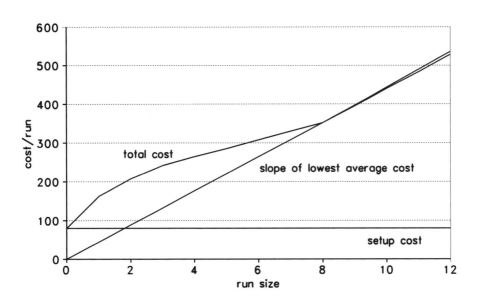

Although costs are only defined for multiples of full batches, for greater generality the total cost is depicted as a continuous curve. Starting from the fixed cost of £80, the total cost curve initially increases less than proportionately, then rises at a constant rate of £22 per batch. At a run size of 8 batches, the total cost curve has a kink, increasing at a rate of £46 from then on.

This general shape of the total cost function is fairly typical. Initially, total costs tend to increase less than proportionately due to such aspects as the learning effect — workers becoming more efficient in their tasks — and other economies of scale. Then for operating levels in the normal range of operations, costs rise proportionately with the increase in the level of activity or output. Finally, as the firm starts stretching its capacity to the limit, costs begin to increase more than proportionately. The result is a total cost curve in a shape of a stretched-out S.

Marginal costs

The marginal cost of an activity measures the rate of change in the total cost at a given activity level. As pointed out in Section 12.1, for an activity that assumes integer values only, the **marginal cost** $MC(Q)$ at the level of output Q is equal to the incremental cost, i.e. the difference in total cost for a unit increase in the level of activity, say from $Q-1$ to Q:

$$MC(Q) = T(Q) - T(Q - 1) \qquad (12\text{-}1)$$

For our example, a unit of output corresponds to a batch. The marginal cost of, say, the second unit (the second batch) is

$$MC(Q = 2) = T(Q = 2) - T(Q = 1) = £208 - £162 = £46.$$

Verify that for the fourth to the eighth unit, the marginal cost is £22, and then increases to £46 from there on. The marginal cost of the first unit includes the fixed setup cost. In terms of Figure 12-2, the marginal cost for Qth unit is equal to the slope of the total cost curve $TC(Q)$ between run size $Q - 1$ and Q.

The S-shape cost curve depicted in Figure 12-2 is rather typical of many operations. As the level of activity increases, the marginal cost first decreases (the slope of the total cost curve becomes less steep), then becomes constant (the slope remains the same), and finally starts to increase again (the slope becomes steeper). These three phases are also referred to as **increasing returns to scale**, **constant returns to scale**, and **decreasing returns to scale**. Obviously, most firms prefer to operate in the range of increasing or constant returns to scale.

In the short run, where only a limited number of input factors can be increased, while others have to remain constant, practically all production and service operations will ultimately exhibit increasing marginal costs for a variety of reasons — the additional output requires overtime, the factory floor becomes more congested, increasing delays and errors, etc. Increasing marginal cost is also seen in marketing. As the advertising budget increases, the gain in new sales generated will sooner or later fall off. These are all examples of the almost universal **law of decreasing mar-**

ginal returns, i.e. as the input of one variable production factor is increased, while all other production factors remain fixed in the short run, the resulting increase in the total output will, after some point, become progressively smaller.

The same result may not hold in the long run. In theory at least, it should be possible to simply duplicate existing operations and run all at their optimum levels of activity. Similarly, it is usually true that, by introducing more sophisticated capital equipment, it may even be possible to adopt production processes that have both lower fixed and variable costs than those obtainable through duplication. This may allow the firm to achieve the same or a higher level of activity at lower marginal costs. However, as the scale of operations increases, even more and more sophisticated equipment will ultimately follow the law of decreasing marginal returns.

In the long run, we should also expect that further technological developments will from time to time reduce marginal costs at most levels of output.

Average costs

The **average cost** $AC(Q)$ at the level of activity Q is defined as the ratio of total costs to output: $TC(Q)/Q$. This corresponds to the slope of the straight line from the origin to a given point on the $T(Q)$ curve. This is demonstrated in Figure 12-2 for $Q = 8$. The slope of the straight line from the origin to $T(Q = 8) = 352$ is equal to 44, i.e. 352/8.

Table 12-2 lists the marginal, total, and average costs for the PC case. (Ignore for the time being the last three table columns.) Observe what happens to the average cost as output or run size increases. Initially, the average cost decreases. This must be so

Table 12-2 Marginal, total, and average costs and revenues.

1 Run size Q	2 Marginal cost $MC(Q)$	3 Total cost $TC(Q)$	4 Average cost $AC(Q)$	5 Marginal revenue $MR(Q)$	6 Total revenue $TR(Q)$	7 Total profit $TP(Q)$
1	162	162	162	80	80	− 82
2	46	208	104	80	160	− 48
3	34	242	80.67	80	240	− 2
4	22	264	66	80	320	+ 56
5	22	286	57.20	80	400	+ 114
6	22	308	51.33	80	480	+ 172
7	22	330	47.14	40	520	+ 190
8	22	352	44	40	560	+ 208
9	46	398	44.22	40	600	+ 202
10	46	444	44.40	40	640	+ 196
11	46	490	44.56	40	680	+ 190
12	46	536	44.67	40	720	+ 184

as long as the marginal cost of the next unit added is less than the average cost up to then. For instance, the average cost for a run of two units equals £208/2 = £104. The marginal cost for the 3rd unit is £34. So the average cost decreases to £(208 + 34)/3 = £80.67. In this example, average cost continues to decrease up to the eighth unit, when it reaches £44. The marginal cost of the ninth unit is £46. This is more than the average cost for 8 units. As a result, the average cost for 9 units now increases to £44.22.

Relationships between marginal and average costs

From these observations we can deduce some general principles. First, as long as the marginal cost for another unit of output is less than the average cost up to the previous output level, the average cost continues to decrease as the output increases. This is in part due to the fact that the initial fixed setup cost can be spread over a larger volume. Second, as soon as the marginal cost becomes larger than the average cost, the latter starts to increase. Third, as a consequence, the lowest average cost is achieved just prior to the level of output where the marginal cost becomes larger than the average cost, or for a level of output Q^* where the following condition holds:

$$MC(Q^*) \leq AC(Q^*) < MC(Q^* + 1) \tag{12-2}$$

It is instructive to study the graph depicting these principles in Figure 12-2. Recall that the slope of $TC(Q)$ between two adjacent output levels $Q-1$ and Q is equal to the marginal cost of the Qth unit. For instance, the slope from $TC(Q = 7)$ to $TC(Q = 8)$ is $352 - 330 = 22$, the marginal cost of the eighth batch.

Similarly, the slope of the straight line from the origin to $TC(Q)$ represents the average cost for an output level Q. For output levels of 8 or less, the slope representing the marginal cost is everywhere less steep than the slope representing the average cost (except that both are the same for the first unit). From the ninth unit on, the relationship between these two slopes reverses. The slope representing marginal costs is now everywhere steeper than the slope representing average costs. The smallest (or the least steep) slope for the average cost is achieved when this reversal occurs.

The above explanations are all couched in terms of individual customer orders for a product made to order only. However, the concepts developed have a more general validity. They can be extended to the analysis of the level of a given activity of a firm during a specified time interval of, e.g. one year. Any positive level of output results in annual fixed costs in the amount of F dollars. (This covers all those fixed costs, such as administrative infrastructure and fixed production costs, directly incurred by that activity — costs which fall away if that activity ceases. It does not include other overheads shared with other activities!) As the annual level of activity increases, the marginal cost first tends to decrease, then becomes constant over the normal range of operations for that activity, and finally starts to increase beyond that range. The average cost will then be lowest at the level of activity where marginal cost is just less than or becomes equal to the average cost.

12.3 Total revenue and marginal revenue

PC is one of the smaller manufacturers for silicone rubber. It tends to follow the prices charged by the bigger manufacturers, competing on quality rather than price. Hence, the price charged for orders of up to 8 batches is £80 per batch of 80 kg. The price drops to £40 per batch for any amount in excess of 8 batches. This results in the total revenue pattern listed in the sixth column of Table 12-2. It is denoted as $TR(Q)$.

The rate of change of the total revenue at the level of activity Q is called the **marginal revenue**, denoted by $MR(Q)$. For a discrete variable, the marginal revenue for the Qth batch of an order is equal to the difference between the total revenue for an order of size Q and $Q-1$, i.e. $TR(Q) - TR(Q-1)$. Column 5 in Table 12-2 lists the marginal revenue for the PC example.

These concepts can again be extended to the behaviour of revenues for a product produced on a sustained basis over a specified time period, say one year. Furthermore, in many instances, the unit price a firm charges is constant, regardless of its output level. This is particularly so for standard type products, such as most food staples, but also many manufactured goods. Such products are typically sold by several firms in competition with each other. Each firm taken alone may be too small to affect the market in any significant way. The total revenue over one year is then simply equal to the quantity sold Q during the year times the unit price P, or $TR(Q) = PQ$. The marginal revenue is constant at P.

On the other hand, if one firm dominates the market for a particular product, it may have to reduce the unit price charged for its entire output, and not just for the additional output, if it wants to sell more in any given time period. In this case marginal revenue for selling an additional unit is given by the difference between the additional revenue obtained from that unit and the loss in revenue suffered on the previous output due to the reduction in price. Hence the marginal revenue tends to decrease by more than simply the reduction in price as the output level increases.

Activity:
- Average costs are affected by fixed costs. Why? For positive output or activity levels, marginal costs are not affected by fixed costs. Why?
- Are the concepts of increasing and decreasing returns to scale also applicable to non-commercial activities, e.g. learning, sports, safety? From your own experience, analyse what happens to your mastery of a subject as you devote more and more effort to it.
- Consider the following sequence of costs for an output of 1, 2, ..., 8 units: 130, 20, 30, 40, 80, 24, 40, 116. Show that the average cost is not lowest when condition (12-2) is satisfied for the first time. What conclusions can you draw from this with respect to the necessary shape of the cost function?

12.4 Breakeven analysis

Figure 12-3 superimposes the graphs for total revenue $TR(Q)$ and total cost $TC(Q)$ for the PC example, as listed in columns 3 and 6 of Table 12-2. The difference $TR(Q) - TC(Q)$ between the two curves corresponds to the total profit $TP(Q)$ for an order of size Q — the numbers listed in column 7 of Table 12-2.

Figure 12-3   Total cost and total revenue curves.

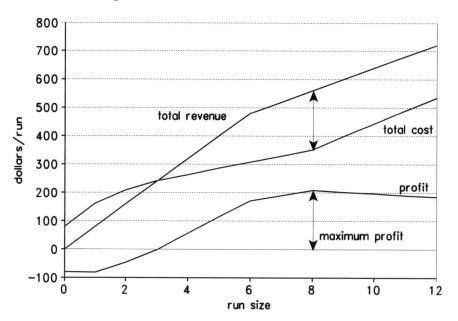

Observe what happens as the run size increases. For run sizes of three or fewer batches the total cost exceeds the total revenue. The firm is in a loss position. As the run size increases to 3, the size of the loss decreases. At a run size of 4 the firm starts making a profit on the order. Whenever possible, the firm would attempt to convince its customers to order the equivalent of at least four batches or 320 kg. If the firm could refuse to accept any orders of less than this amount without affecting its long-run sales prospects, it should do so. Alternatively, it could give customers a price incentive to order at least this amount by charging an even higher price for orders of three batches or less, if market conditions allowed such a pricing policy. For instance, a price structure of £104 for the first two batches, decreasing to £56 for the next two and £40 from batch 5 on would leave the total price for medium to large customer orders unchanged, only penalizing the very small orders. A loss would then only be incurred for orders of size 1.

The level of activity, Q_0, at which total revenue exactly recovers all fixed and variable costs incurred is called the **breakeven point**. At the breakeven point the total profit is zero. The firm would want to operate at a level of activity beyond the break-even point. If the level of activity is a continuous variable, then there exists an exact breakeven point. In the PC example where the output is discrete, there is no run size where the profit on the customer order is exactly equal to zero. So the run size of 4 batches at which the profit becomes positive is then the equivalent of the breakeven point. For the alternative price structure, the breakeven point would drop to 2 batches exactly.

If both the total cost and the total revenue are linear functions of the level of activity, the breakeven point can easily be determined mathematically. For linear functions, the total cost is given by

$$TC(Q) = F + VQ \qquad (12\text{-}3)$$

where F is the fixed cost, independent of the level of activity, and V is the variable unit production cost. The total revenue function is given by

$$TR(Q) = PQ \qquad (12\text{-}4)$$

At the breakeven point, the total cost is equal to the total revenue:

$$PQ = F + VQ \qquad (12\text{-}5)$$

Solving expression (12-5) for Q we get:

$$\text{Breakeven point} = Q_0 = \frac{F}{P - V} \qquad (12\text{-}6)$$

This derivation assumes that the level of activity Q can be varied continuously. If the output is in discrete units, then there may be no value of Q for which total revenue is exactly equal to total cost, as in the PC example. In such instances, the breakeven point Q_0 is the first value just larger than the ratio $F/(P - V)$.

Obviously, expression (12-6) only makes sense if the unit revenue exceeds the unit variable cost, i.e. $P > V$, otherwise that product should not be produced at all.

There is another way of looking at breakeven analysis. The denominator of expression (12-6), $(P - V)$, is the difference between the unit revenue and the unit variable cost. This difference is the **contribution** each unit (sold) makes towards covering of fixed costs and profits. The larger the contribution that each unit makes towards the recovery of fixed costs, the lower will be the breakeven point.

An example: Quiktrans

Remember Quiktrans in Section 10.8? Carey Bumps would like to know what the breakeven point is for the new AZ truck if he sells the 3-year old unit at the end of its fourth year of operation. In the first year, the fixed costs for the new AZ unit consist of the annual license and insurance cost of €9,160, interest cost of 12% on the net investment €210,000 (i.e. cost of AZ truck less resale value of a 4-year old truck of €85,000) equal to €25,200, and that portion of the depreciation of the truck that is attributable to age, rather than mileage, which he estimates as 60% of the loss of €63,600 in resale value (i.e. €295,000 – €231,400) in the first year, or €38,160. These costs sum up to €75,520.

The output of the truck consists of volume-kilometres carried. If we assume an average load for each trip, the output can be measured in terms of kilometres travelled only. So the variable cost refers to the cost of the truck travelling for one kilometre (with an average load). This consists of the 'running cost' of €1.40, as specified by the manufacturer, the maintenance and tire costs, and the mileage dependent depreciation. Using the estimates listed in Figure 10-11 on page 272, and based on an estimated annual mileage of 90,000 km, the latter two amount to €0.156/km for maintenance and mileage (i.e. €10,000 for maintenance plus half of €8000 for tyres divided by 90,000), and €0.283/km for depreciation (i.e. 40% of €63,600 divided by 90,000). All three costs add up to €1.839/km. It is reasonable to assume that this variable cost remains constant over a fairly large mileage range. Hence the total cost function is linear over this range.

Carey's accountant tells him that the revenue per kilometre for an average load amounts to €2.78. Again, this unit revenue can safely be assumed to remain constant over a wide mileage range, resulting in a linear revenue function.

From the assumptions about linearity of both costs and revenues, the contribution per 'unit output' towards fixed costs and profits is also constant and equal to €2.78 minus €1.839, or €1.171/km. Note also that the number of kilometres travelled is a continuous variable. Hence expression (12-6) can be used:

Breakeven point = €75,520/(€2.78 – 1.839) = 64,492 km

This breakeven point would change with the age of the truck as additional fixed costs are incurred and as the variable cost increases with the age and mileage.

Some words of caution

Expression (12-6) was derived on the assumption that both the total revenue and total cost functions are linear. This assumption made the mathematics simple, but is also the Achilles' heel of breakeven analysis. Although the total revenue is quite often proportional to sales, total costs are frequently nonlinear. Expression (12-6) can then no longer be used. This is the case for the PC example, where both the marginal cost and the marginal revenue vary with the run size and hence the total cost and total revenue are not linear.

Breakeven analysis also assumes that all costs involved and revenues are stationary, i.e. remain constant over time. If they change over the period covered by the breakeven analysis, then again expression (12-6) can no longer be used.

A graphical approach, i.e. plotting how total costs and total revenue behave over time, will usually find an approximate value for the breakeven point (which could be refined by search or enumeration). However, the breakeven analysis still remains a useful concept for the decision maker.

Activity:
- The average unit production cost for a run of 6000 units is £5. The variable production cost consists of the cost of raw materials (£2.50/unit) and wages (£1.50/unit). The item sells for £6.50. Was the run of 6000 units less than or larger than the breakeven point?
- Sales of an item are slower than expected. Lowering the selling price is likely to increase sales and hence output. The manager refuses to do this since output has not yet reached the breakeven point. Why is his reasoning faulty? (Hint: Section 9.3 on costs may help.)

12.5 Basic principle of marginal analysis

In a marginal analysis framework, a decision as to the best level of an activity is based on the comparison of the change in both revenues and costs resulting from a small change in the level of activity. Such a change in activity is desirable if the difference between total revenues and total costs, or in other words the total profit increases. The decision maker should continue making such small changes in the level of activity until no further increase in profit can be achieved. At that point, total profit is maximized.

An algorithm for marginal analysis

We now have to convert this principle into a practical approach — an algorithm for finding the optimal level of activity. It is an optimization system O terms of Figure 6-9. We start out with a relatively small level of activity Q. The breakeven point provides a good start. Next, we increase the level of activity by a small amount, say one unit. So the level of activity increases to $Q + 1$. This yields an increase in revenue, while simultaneously increasing costs. The increase in revenue is equal to the marginal revenue at the level $Q + 1$, i.e. $MR(Q + 1)$. The increase in cost is equal to the marginal cost at that level, i.e. $MC(Q + 1)$. If $MR(Q + 1)$ is larger than $MC(Q + 1)$, then the increase in the level of activity from Q to $Q + 1$ increases total profit. We continue this process of increasing the level of activity by 1 as long as the marginal revenue is larger than the marginal cost. We stop when the reverse becomes true, i.e. when for a further unit increase in the level of activity the marginal cost would be larger than marginal revenue, since this would cause the total profit to decrease. At that point we have found the optimal level of activity which maximizes the total profit.

In summary, the algorithm of marginal analysis uses the following principle: At the optimal level of activity Q^* the following condition holds:

$$MR(Q^*) \geq MC(Q^*) \text{ and } MR(Q^* + 1) < MC(Q^* + 1) \qquad (12\text{-}7)$$

You could visualize this process of successive small changes in the level of activity as resembling the strategy adopted by a myopic mountain climber (or climber trying to scale a mountain in foggy conditions) who does not know where or how far away the peak is. However, the climber is confident that, as long as each step goes uphill, he will reach the hidden top. By analogy with the firm, the height of the mountain is measured in pounds or dollars, etc., of profits, and the gain in height at each step is the additional profit achieved. As long as the latter is positive, continuing in the same direction is profitable. Once the top has been reached, steps in any direction go either on the flat or downhill again, i.e. no further gains in profit can be made.

> Activity: In the mountain climbing analogy above, what assumption is made about the shape or form of that mountain for this process to reach the true peak?

12.6 Applications of marginal analysis

Marginal analysis for the PC example

Table 12-3 lists again total revenue $TR(Q)$, total costs $TC(Q)$, and total profit $TP(Q)$ for the PC example as a function of the run size. The total profit is computed as $TR(Q) - TC(Q)$. The last three columns show the marginal revenue $MR(Q)$, the marginal cost $MC(Q)$, and the marginal profit $MP(Q) = MR(Q) - MC(Q)$. We wish to find the run size that maximizes the total profit for an individual customer order.

We start this process with the breakeven point of 4. For the fifth unit, the marginal revenue is £80, while the marginal cost is £22, giving a net increase in profit of £58. The same pattern holds for unit 6. For units 7 and 8, the marginal revenue drops to £40, while the marginal cost remains at £22 — still profitable. So we continue.

Table 12-3 Marginal analysis for the PC example

Run size Q	Total revenue $TR(Q)$	Total cost $TC(Q)$	Total profit $TP(Q)$	Marginal revenue $MR(Q)$	Marginal cost $MC(Q)$	Marginal profit $MP(Q)$
1	80	162	−82	80	162	−82
2	160	208	−48	80	46	+34
3	240	242	−2	80	34	+46
4	320	264	56	80	22	+58
5	400	286	114	80	22	+58
6	480	308	172	80	22	+58
7	520	330	190	40	22	+18
8	560	352	208	40	22	+18
9	600	398	202	40	46	−6
10	640	444	196	40	46	−6
11	680	490	190	40	46	−6
12	720	536	184	40	46	−6

For unit 9, the marginal cost increases to £46, or £6 more than the marginal revenue. We now encounter conditions (12-7) for the first time. For a run size of 8 the first part of condition (12-7) is satisfied, while a run size of 9 satisfies the second part. Hence, we stop at a run size of 8 with a maximum profit of £208. Verify that increasing the run size to 9 decreases the total profit.

In many cases, the optimal decision can more easily be found by evaluating the profit function. This is clearly the case here. However, there are many situations where a marginal analysis offers useful additional insights which remain hidden when looking at profits alone.

What can PC do with this information? The order sizes are controlled by the customers. PC can only exert an indirect influence by steering customers to an order size of 8. However, marginal analysis tells us two things. First, the drop in marginal revenue for an order of size 7 has a serious effect on marginal profits. So the firm may consider altering its pricing structure to give customers incentive for placing orders of size 8, such as a small discount for orders of that size alone. Secondly, the increase in the marginal production cost when an order has to be completed in overtime completely erodes any marginal profit. The firm could attempt to change the marginal cost pattern for larger orders, e.g. by eliminating the need for a supervisor to be on site for runs in excess of 8, thereby reducing labour costs.

Is marginal analysis of any help if the total cost and total revenue are linear? If unit revenue exceeds the unit variable cost, marginal revenues will always be larger than marginal costs. Hence the optimal level of activity is theoretically infinity. In practice, it will be equal to the maximum capacity of the operation.

In the discussion so far, we developed marginal analysis in a production frame-work. The aim was to find the optimal level of a given activity by comparing marginal revenues with marginal costs. However, the principles of marginal analysis have a much wider scope of application. In fact, the majority of MS/OR projects where this approach is useful are of a different type.

For many MS/OR projects the focus may be only on minimizing costs. No revenues are involved. Altering the level of some activity may increase certain costs, while offering savings in other costs. The savings achieved assume the role of 'revenues'. Marginal analysis then involves trading marginal costs for marginal savings. The next application is of that nature.

Finding the optimal economic order quantity

The EOQ model (see Section 6.13, in particular expression 6-1A) consists of two relevant costs: the annual setup cost sD/Q and the annual inventory holding cost $0.5Qvr$, where Q is the replenishment size, s the fixed setup cost per replenishment, D the annual demand, r the holding cost per dollar per year, and v the unit product value in stock. We derived the square root formula for the EOQ by calculus. We shall now find the EOQ using a marginal analysis approach. The product used as an example is packed into drums. The replenishment size is therefore a discrete variable, namely the number of drums produced per run.

As Q increases from its minimum of 1 unit, the average inventory increases, causing additional holding costs. But at the same time the number of replenishments decreases, hence saving some setup costs. So the change in holding costs becomes the 'marginal cost' and the savings in setup costs take the role of the 'marginal revenue'. The idea of marginal analysis is to continue increasing Q by small amounts as long as the marginal cost is less than the marginal savings gained. Once this condition reverses, we stop. The value of Q where this occurs is the EOQ.

Table 12-4 summarizes the iterations of the algorithm for an arbitrary starting level of $Q = 10$. Increasing Q from 10 to 11 gives a marginal saving of setup costs of $\$18(4140)/10 - \$18(4140)/11 = \$677.45$, while the marginal holding costs is $0.5(11)(\$320)(0.18) - 0.5(10)(\$320)(0.18) = \$28.80$. The 'marginal revenue' is substantially larger than the 'marginal cost'. So we continue increasing Q. Rather than increasing Q to 12, we make initially bigger jumps and backtrack if the last jump turned out to be too large. This will reduce the number of iterations needed and hence speed up convergence to the optimal solution. Condition (12-7) is next tested for $Q = 20$ and 21. Again, marginal savings exceed marginal cost. We continue in this vein. At $Q = 60$ and 61 marginal savings have become smaller than marginal cost. We now backtrack. The test for $Q = 51$ and 52 shows that even for that level marginal savings are smaller than marginal cost. We have now found the two values for Q which satisfy condition (12-7). The optimal Q is therefore 51.

Table 12-4   Marginal analysis for the EOQ model.

Data:	Product value $v = \$320$/unit		Holding cost penalty $r = 0.18/\$$/year		
	Annual demand $D = 4140$		Setup cost $s = \$18$/setup		

Q	Setup cost: sD/Q	Holding cost: $\frac{1}{2}Qrv$	$MR(Q)$	$MC(Q)$	Continue?
10	$7452	$288			
11	$6774.55	$316.80	$677.45	$28.80	yes
20	$3726	$576			
21	$3548.57	$604.80	$177.43	$28.80	yes
30	$2484	$864			
31	$2403.87	$892.80	$80.13	$28.80	yes
40	$1863	$1152			
41	$1817.56	$1180.80	$45.44	$28.80	yes
50	$1490.40	$1440			
51	$1461.18	$1468.80	$29.22	$28.80	yes
60	$1242	$1728			
61	$1221.64	$1756.80	$20.36	$28.80	no
51	$1461.18	$1468.80			
52	$1433.08	$1497.60	$28.10	$28.80	no

12.7* Marginal analysis for continuous variables

From the introductory discussion in Section 12.1 it follows that, if the activity is a continuous variable, such as the amount of flour produced by a flour mill, or the output of electricity of a power station, the marginal cost is the rate of change of the total cost function and the marginal revenue is the rate of change of the total revenue function at a given level of output. In graphical terms, they represent the slopes of the total cost or total revenue curves.

In some cases, the algebraic form of these total cost and revenue functions may be known or, at least, assumed to be known. As the next section will show, the marginal cost and marginal revenue may then be computed algebraically. In most instances, however, they must be approximated numerically.

Expression (12-1) is a reasonable approximation to the true rate of change in total cost when a unit change in the activity is relatively small in relation to the normal range of activity, e.g. the latter being in the hundreds or larger. However, when an increase by one unit is relatively large in relation to the normal range of activity, expression (12-1) may be a bad estimate of the true marginal cost. In such cases a better approximation to the true rate of change is obtained by taking the difference between $T(Q)$ and $T(Q - \delta)$, where δ is chosen arbitrarily, but sufficiently small, say 0.1 or 0.01, and then extrapolating this difference to a unit increase. Expression (12-1) then becomes:

$$MC(Q) = \frac{T(Q) - T(Q - \delta)}{\delta} \qquad (12\text{-}1A)$$

Condition (12-2), which defines at what level of activity the lowest average cost occurs, also changes. Since the change in the level of activity can be made infinitesimally small, the lowest average cost occurs at the level of output Q^* where marginal cost and average cost are equal, i.e. where

$$MC(Q^*) = AC(Q^*) \qquad (12\text{-}2A)$$

Condition (12-7) for the optimal level of Q^* also collapses to an equality:

At the optimal level of activity Q^*, $MR(Q^*) = MC(Q^*)$ \qquad (12-7A)

Consider again the example in Table 12-4, except that we now allow Q to be a continuous variable. From Table 12-4 we know that the optimal Q has to be around 51. Setting δ equal to 0.1 and $Q = 51$, expression (12-1A) gives a marginal holding cost of [\$1468.80 – 0.5(50.9)(\$320)(0.18)]/0.1 = \$2.88/0.1 = \$28.80. Since holding costs are proportional to Q this simply confirms our previous results. The marginal savings in setup cost are equal to the negative of the marginal setup cost. We can again use (12-1A): –[\$1461.18–4140(\$18)/50.9]/0.1 = \$2.87/0.1 = \$28.70. Marginal savings are just smaller than marginal cost. This shows that optimal Q must be just below 51.

We now repeat the same analysis for $Q = 50.9$. The marginal cost is constant at \$28.80. Marginal savings are now –[4140(\$18)/50.9–4140(\$18)/50.8]/0.1 = \$28.80, i.e. equal to the marginal cost after rounding to two decimal places. You should verify that for $Q = 50.8$ marginal savings are just larger than marginal cost. Hence the optimal Q is 50.9. Note that this result only differs 'marginally' from the more accurate value of 50.87 found using the EOQ formula. By decreasing the value of δ to 0.01, we could have derived the exact answer.

12.8* Marginal analysis and differential calculus

The graph in Figure 12-4 shows typical total revenue $TR(Q)$ and total cost curves $TC(Q)$ in the same quadrant. The vertical difference between the two curves for any level of output Q is the profit $TP(Q) = TR(Q) - TC(Q)$.

Figure 12-4   Marginal costs and marginal revenues.

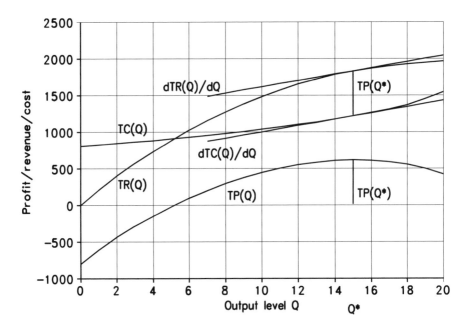

Remember that the marginal revenue and marginal cost are given by the slope of the total revenue and total cost curves. In the general case, the slope of a function for any given value of its argument, Q in our case, is given by the tangent of the corresponding curve at Q. But you will also remember that the tangent to a curve is equal to the first derivative of the corresponding function. Putting these two things together, we see that the marginal revenue at any given output level Q' is equal to the first derivative of the total revenue function, evaluated at Q':

$$MR(Q) = dTR(Q)/dQ \text{ evaluated at } Q = Q'$$

By the analogous reasoning, the marginal cost at the output level Q' is equal to the first derivative of the total cost curve evaluated at Q':

$$MC(Q) = dTC(Q)/dQ \text{ evaluated at } Q = Q'$$

For what level of output is the profit maximized? From the graph we see that the difference between the total revenue curve and the total cost curve is largest at the output level Q^*. At that point the tangents to the two curves have exactly the same slope, i.e. $dTR(Q)/dQ = dTC(Q)/dQ$, both evaluated at Q^*, or

$$MR(Q^*) = MC(Q^*).$$

This is again condition (12-7A) of 'marginal revenue equals marginal cost'.

The stock replenishment example in Table 12-4 will be used for demonstrating this result. Recall again that the 'total revenue' is represented by the savings in annual setup costs. Hence, $TR(Q)$ is the negative of annual setup costs, i.e. $-sD/Q$, while the 'total cost' $TC(Q)$ corresponds to the holding cost, i.e. $0.5Qvr$. Taking derivatives of both expressions with respect to Q and setting them equal, we get

$$sD/Q^2 = 0.5vr$$

Solving this expression for Q we obtain, to no surprise, the EOQ formula.

There is an alternative way to derive condition (12-7A), using the total profit function. As we have already seen in Section 6.10 of *ST&DM*, the value of x where the function $f(x)$ assumes its maximum can be found by setting the first derivative of $f(x)$ equal to zero and solving for x. Let us apply this to the profit function $TP(Q) = TR(Q) - TC(Q)$:

$$dTP(Q)/dQ = d(TR(Q) - TC(Q))/dQ$$
$$= dTR(Q)/dQ - dTC(Q)/dQ = 0$$

Rearranging this last expression we find again that, at the optimum, marginal revenue equals marginal cost:

$$dTR(Q)/dQ = dTC(Q)/dQ$$

Classical methods of differential calculus offer a simple and convenient optimization system O for determining the maximum or minimum value of a differentiable function.

12.9 Incremental analysis

Incremental analysis deals with the effect on revenue and the costs of discrete, and often large, changes in the level of an activity, such as adding a whole new machine or vehicle, in contrast to marginal analysis which allows arbitrarily small changes at the margin. The majority of decisions relating to changes in activity levels call for incremental, rather than marginal analysis.

Consider a transport firm operating long-haul trucks. Although the activity level of its fleet is measured in terms of tonne-kilometres that may assume any real value, any increase in the fleet size has to be in terms of whole trucks, even if the last truck added is not used to full capacity. Airlines face a similar situation which will affect their decision about of the number of each type of aircraft to have in their fleet.

The number of gasoline pumps installed at a service station, the number of telephone lines rented by a firm, the number of doctors on duty in an accident and emergency clinic, or the number of generators in operation at a power station at a given time, are all examples giving rise to incremental changes.

Our discussion in Sections 12.2, 12.3, and 12.5 was couched in discrete incremental changes. It was done so as to simplify the explanations, but applies without modifications to incremental analysis.

The next example is a somewhat simplified account of a logistic problem faced by Heinz USA, the leading US manufacturer of ketchup. It is adapted from the paper by Sunder Kerke *et al.*, 'A logistics analysis at Heinz', in the Sep.–Oct. 1990 issue of *Interfaces* (pp. 1–13). *Interfaces* is one of the more readable MS/OR journals.

12.10   A logistics analysis

Logistics deals with the transportation and distribution of goods. Many successful MS/OR applications worldwide involve such issues.

Situation summary

Over 80% of the US tomato crop is grown in California and harvested from early July to mid-October. Part of this crop is immediately processed into various finished tomato products. A large portion, however, is made into tomato paste in factories located close to the growing areas. This paste is later converted into various other finished products at a number of plants throughout the USA, with ketchup taking the biggest slice. Sales of finished products are also seasonal, but with a sizable steady demand throughout the year. The production pattern for finished products at the conversion plants tends to follow this seasonal demand.

Assume that this is January 1987. Heinz faces a vast logistics problem of how to transport large quantities of tomato paste from the factories in California to these conversion plants. This transport is done with a specialized fleet of railroad tankers. These are due to come off lease in early 1988. A team of analysts from finance and all major functional operating areas of Heinz, as well as three academics from Carnegie Mellon University, is set up to identify and analyse various transport strategy options.

Three options stand out:

1. Use a fleet of specialized railroad tankers only. This involves a substantial initial

investment, but low maintenance costs during the long life of the tankers. On the other hand, Heinz has to pay the return trip of the empty tankers. Hence round trip hauling costs for the tankers are considerably higher than the one-way transport cost for the same volume of goods in regular railroad box cars. If the tanker option is chosen, how many are needed?

2. Use giant pouches, similar in concept to the single-portion packets of ketchup you get in fast food restaurants, except that these pouches contain 300 gallons of paste (i.e. more than 1 cubic metre). They are called Scholle bags, after the company that commercialized them. They are not reusable — they last for one trip only. Only minor investments in filling and unloading equipment are required. Filled Scholle bags can be stored and transported in simple plywood cases which can be reused up to 40 times. Transportation is done in box cars, and hence is about 40% cheaper per gallon of ketchup than transport by tanker. This is, however, more than compensated by the cost of the bags. No decision on the number of bags needed has to be made. The number is proportional to the volume of tomato paste shipped.

3. A combination of options 1 and 2, with option 1 used for covering the steady transport needs all year round and option 2 used for meeting the excess demand for tomato paste at the conversion plants during the peak periods.

Note that options 1 and 2 are, in fact, simply limiting cases of option 3. In other words, option 3 includes the other two options. Hence the analysis only needs to consider option 3, since it allows the optimal solution to either be a true combination or options 1 or 2 as limiting cases.

Input data

Rather than look at this problem as a whole, we will demonstrate the approach used by considering the transportation of paste from factory X to conversion plant Y. (Since the report in *Interfaces* does not contain any real data, all cost and demand figures come from the inexhaustible store of numbers in our brains.)

The top portion of the spreadsheet output in Figure 12-5 lists cost components and other data, including the demand, ranked by size. (The rest of the table shows the computations, discussed later.)

Since the useful life of the tankers is 12 years, an obvious way of analysing this problem is to determine the net present value of all costs incurred over that 12-year planning horizon for all possible numbers of tankers. The best solution is then the one that minimizes the net present value (see Chapter 10). We shall take a more insightful approach, based on marginal analysis.

Usage of tankers by demand levels

The total annual volume to be transported is 24,000 tonnes. Note that a tanker carries 18 tonnes per trip. For an average of 30 round trips per year or 2.5/month, one tanker can carry an average of 45 tonnes per month. If the demand were constant throughout the year at 2000 tonnes per month, then a total of 2000/45 or

Figure 12-5   Spreadsheet evaluation of Heinz transportation problem.

DATA:	Rail:	Investment	$80,000	/tanker	Scholle bags:	Capacity of bag	1.1355	tonnes	COST EVALUATIONS:	
		Useful tanker life	12	years		Cost of bag	$59	/bag	Discount rate	0.15
		Tanker capacity	18	tonnes		Plywood case cost	$73	/case	Equivalent annuity/tanker	$14,758
		Tanker round trip	30	/year		Useful life of case	40	r'trips	Tanker hauling cost/tonne	$54.00
		Hauling cost	$972	/car		Rail hauling cost	$43	/case		
						Return cost	$2	/case	Bag cost/tonne	$93.20
		Total annual volume	24000	tonnes						

INCREMENTAL ANALYSIS BY DEMAND LEVELS (months ranked by increasing volume)

Months	Jan	Feb	June	July	Dec	May	Nov	March	Aug	April	Oct	Sep
Demand level	600	1100	1200	1300	1400	1800	2100	2300	2400	2900	3200	3700
Months at that level	12	11	10	9	8	7	6	5	4	3	2	1
Level increase	600	500	100	100	100	400	300	200	100	500	300	500
Additional volume	7200	5500	1000	900	800	2800	1800	1000	400	1500	600	500
Total volume	7200	12700	13700	14600	15400	18200	20000	21000	21400	22900	23500	24000
No. of tankers needed	13.33	24.44	26.67	28.89	31.11	40.00	46.67	51.11	53.33	64.44	71.11	82.22
No. of rankers used	13	24	26	28	31	40	46	51	53	64	71	82
Additional tankers	13	11	2	2	3	9	6	5	2	11	7	11
Volume by tankers	7020	12480	13400	14240	15360	18200	19820	20975	21340	22840	23490	23990
Volume by Scholle	16980	11520	10600	9760	8640	5800	4180	3025	2660	1160	510	10
Add. volume by tankers	7020	5460	920	840	1120	2840	1620	1155	365	1500	650	500
Marginal tanker cost/t	$81.33	$83.73	$86.08	$89.14	$93.53	$100.77	$108.66	$117.89	$134.87	$162.23	$212.93	$378.68
Marginal bag cost/t	$93.20	$93.20	$93.20	$93.20	$93.20	$93.20	$93.20	$93.20	$93.20	$93.20	$93.20	$93.20

TOTAL COST ANALYSIS (dollars)

by tankers	0	570,934	1,028,112	1,107,308	1,182,184	1,286,938	1,573,120	1,749,148	1,885,308	1,934,534	2,177,872	2,316,278	2,505,616
by bags	2,236,800	1,582,536	1,073,664	987,920	909,632	805,248	540,560	389,576	281,930	247,912	108,112	47,532	932
Total cost	2,236,800	2,153,470	2,101,776	2,095,228	2,091,816	2,092,186	2,113,680	2,138,724	2,167,238	2,182,446	2,285,984	2,363,810	2,506,548

about 45 tankers could do the job. However, the demand is unevenly spread over the year, with as little as 600 tonnes in January and a peak of 3700 tonnes in September. To meet the September demand 3700/45 = 82.22 or, rounded up, 83 tankers are needed — the 83rd car not fully used. The next highest demand month, October with 3200 tonnes, only requires 72 tankers. If Heinz acquired 83 tankers, 11 would be used only for one month per year, remaining idle for the rest of the year. The third highest demand month, April with 2900 tonnes, requires 65 tankers. So, another 7 cars would only be used during two months of each year. (Figure out how many will be idle 9 months of the year.) Only 14 tankers would be used every month of the year. This is depicted graphically in Figure 12-6.

Figure 12-6 Demand pattern for paste by levels.

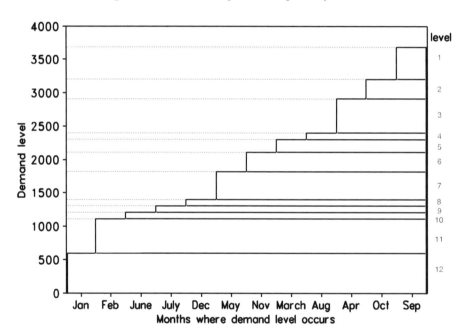

The monthly demands have been ordered by increasing size. The horizontal bands represent a monthly demand size that persists for $n = 12, 11, 10, ..., 1$ months during the year. We will refer to them as demand levels. Demand level 1 is the largest in size, level 12 the smallest. Each band requires an additional number of tankers which see use during n months and are idle during $12 - n$ months. For example, demand level 7 is a band 400 tonnes height persisting for May, November, March, August, April, October, and September. It would require an additional 9 tankers over the number needed to cover the tonnage of all bands up to level 6. These 9 tankers would be used in those seven months, and remain idle during the remaining five.

Incremental reasoning: a motivation

If a tanker is in use most of the time, its initial investment can be spread over many tonnes. The investment cost per tonne carried is low. On the other hand, if it is used only for a few months of the year, the tonnage carried is low. The initial investment is spread over fewer tonnes and the investment cost per tonne carried goes up. As more tankers are added, they are used for fewer and fewer months of the year. As a result, the incremental investment cost per tonne carried tends to increase as the demand level decreases from 12 to 1.

In contrast, the incremental cost of transporting paste in Scholle bags remains unchanged, regardless of the volume transported in any month, since there is little or no initial investment needed, and all the remaining costs — bags, case, and freight — are constant per tonne transported.

So we see that, as the amount transported by tanker increases, one incremental cost per tonne goes up, while the Scholle bag cost remains constant. The approach taken to find the optimal number of tankers uses this property.

We now cast this into the framework of incremental analysis, so that we can use the algorithm of Section 12.5 and apply condition (12-7) to find the optimal level of activity — the number of tankers to be bought. The trick is to interpret the incremental cost of transport by Scholle bag as savings — each tonne switched to a tanker saves that cost. It is the equivalent of the incremental revenue.

The starting point for the algorithm is to have all paste transported by Scholle bags. Next we consider adding one tanker at a time, replacing tonnage carried by Scholle bags in increasing order of incremental costs. We stop when condition (12-7) is satisfied, i.e. when the last tanker added implies an incremental cost per tonne carried that exceeds the 'incremental revenue', viz. the incremental savings by Scholle bags.

The incremental cost by tanker is lowest for demand level 12. So we start substituting tankers for Scholle bags at that level first and proceed down to lower levels, until condition (12-7) occurs.

Incremental analysis

Rather than add one tanker at a time — a considerable computational effort — we take advantage of the fact that the incremental cost within a given demand level remains constant until the last tanker added begins to eat into the tonnage of the next lower demand level. At that point the incremental cost increases by one or two discrete steps. So at each iteration of the algorithm, we add enough tankers to carry all or most of the tonnage up to this level. Once condition (12-7) gets invoked, all we need to do is to check whether one additional tanker that straddles the two corresponding demand levels is justified or not. This reduces the number of iterations to at most 12.

Activity:
• Why is the incremental tanker cost constant within each demand level (except maybe for the first few and the last few tonnes) and then increases by one or two steps

as we eat into the next lower level? (Try out some numbers.)
*   Why is the number of iterations needed at most 12?

Intermediate results of these iterations are shown in the central portion of Figure 12-5, under the heading 'Incremental analysis by demand levels'. We will demonstrate some of the calculations. First, we need to determine the annual cost implied by the initial investment of $80,000 for a tanker. This is the major cost incurred by Heinz for the use of the tankers over a 12-year productive life. We want to apportion this cost in equal amounts to each year, such that the NPVs of these costs add up to $80,000. This is the same concept we used in Chapter 10 of *ST&DM* for comparing different policies with different productive lives, namely the concept of an equivalent annuity. For a discount rate of 15%, the equivalent annuity amounts to $14,758. The other cost incurred for transport by tanker is the tanker hauling cost of $972 per round trip, carrying 18 tonnes. It is constant at $54 per tonne ($972/18). These are the numbers listed under 'cost evaluations' in the top right-hand corner of the spreadsheet in Figure 12-5.

The incremental cost per tonne for transport by Scholle bag is based on the sum of the bag cost ($59), the transport cost for full bags in cases ($43), the return freight for the boxes ($2), and a portion of the initial cost for the plywood case. Since that case can be used for about 40 round trips, this is equal to 1/40 of $73. Adding these costs and dividing them by the weight carried per bag (1.1355 tonnes) results in a constant incremental cost for transport by Scholle bag of $93.20 per tonne. (Note: Forty round trips at about 2.5 trips per month cover $1^1/_3$ years if the case is used all year round. But it could take several years if the case is only used for a few months. A more accurate treatment would express the case cost also in the form of an annuity, as a function of the number of years the case is in use. However, the added accuracy hardly justifies the complex calculations.)

The incremental tanker cost for demand level 12 is then computed as follows. Demand level 12 amounts to 600 tonnes for each of 12 months or a total of 7200 tonnes. This would require 600/45 = 13.33 or 14 tankers. Since the 14th tanker is only used to $1/_3$ of its capacity, we only add the 13 fully-used tankers. Hence only 7020 tonnes (13 tankers times 18 tonnes times 30 trips per year) are carried. The balance of 180 tonnes for level 12 still goes by Scholle bags, together with the remaining 16800 tonnes of the other 11 demand levels. These numbers are recorded in column 'Jan' in the spreadsheet.

The investment cost for 13 tankers is 13 times the equivalent annuity of $14,758, or $191,854. To express this on a per tonne basis, we divide by 7020 — the amount carried by these 13 cars. The resulting investment cost per tonne carried for demand level 12 is $27.33. Adding the constant hauling cost of $54 per tonne gives a incremental tanker cost of $81.33 per tonne. So, switching (most of) demand level 12 from Scholle bags to tanker increases tanker costs by $81.33 per tonne, but saves $93.20 per tonne in transport cost by Scholle bags. Hence this switch is advantageous.

We now consider switching demand level 11 to tankers (plus the balance of 180 tonnes from level 12). The calculations now become a bit more complicated. Recall that to cover level 12 completely, we need 13.33 tankers. To this we now add the number needed to carry the additional 500 tonnes for each month of level 11 (all except January, as shown in Figure 12-5 in the row 'Level increase'). Since each tanker can carry 45 tonnes per month, this requires 500/45 = 11.11 tankers. The total number of tankers needed to cover both demand level 12 and 11 is 24.44 (i.e. 13.33 + 11.11). Again, the 25th car is only used to 44%. So the second iteration only adds 11 new tankers serving both levels. The additional tonnage carried is then: the 180 tones remaining from level 12, which uses 180/(45)(12) = $^1/_3$ of the capacity of one tanker; leaving $10^2/_3$ of their capacity for level 11. This carries another $(10^2/_3)(45)(11)$ = 5280. The additional volume carried by these 11 tankers is therefore 5460 tonnes, and the total of the 24 tankers 7020 + 5460 = 12480, as shown in column 'Feb'.

Eleven tankers incur an additional investment cost of $162,338. Expressed on a per tonne basis, this is $29.73 (162,338/5,460). We add this to the tanker hauling cost of $54 and get a incremental cost of $83.73. This is still lower that the incremental savings from Scholle bags, so we continue.

The central portion of Figure 12-5 shows the results of these computations. We halt the process when the incremental tanker cost of the last iteration rises above the incremental savings from Scholle bags. This happens for demand level 8. Hence it pays to add at least 28 tankers to carry the tonnage of demand levels 12, 11, 10, and all but 360 tonnes of level 9. This amounts to a total tonnage carried by tanker of 14,240.

To carry the last 360 tonnes of level 9 would require 0.89 of an additional tanker. So we have to check if it is advantageous to add a 29th tanker. It would also carry a bit of tonnage for demand level 8, in fact 11% of 45 tonnes over 8 months, or 39.6 tonnes. The total tonnage carried by the 29th tanker is 399.6. Verify that the incremental cost per tonne for this additional tanker is (14,758/399.6) + 54 or $90.93. Since this is still below the incremental savings from Scholle bags, tanker 29 is added. There is no need to repeat this for a further tanker, since the incremental cost for demand level 8 is $93.53. We have found the optimal solution in five iterations of variable increments plus an additional iteration for one car.

Further discussion of solution

Although there is no need to continue these calculations beyond demand level 8, it is insightful to see how incremental tanker costs increase as more demand levels are switched to tanker. Since incremental tanker costs remain constant within each demand level, its graph is a step function, as shown in Figure 12-7. The steps become increasingly larg past demand level 4 (53 tankers).

The spreadsheet in Figure 12-5 also shows the total average annual cost as a function of the number of tankers used. It is an average because it includes not only the variable costs, but also the annual equivalent investment cost. Verify it! It also confirms that the minimum total cost is achieved around 28 tankers. The results are graphed in Figure 12-8.

Figure 12-7   Incremental costs for tanker and Scholle bags.

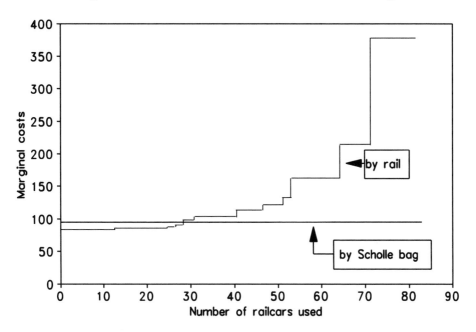

The total cost curve is quite flat over the range of 24 to 40 tankers. Given that the demand data used are future predictions whose reliability is not guaranteed, management has quite some leeway. A choice somewhere in that range will not affect total costs significantly. Any likelihood that demand may increase more than predicted will favour more rather than fewer tankers. Management may thus choose to be conservative and go for a higher number rather than a lower.

Before making a final decision, management would also want to know something about how robust the solution is with respect to certain important assumptions. One of those is the discount rate. However, the average of 30 round trips per year assumed in all calculations may be more critical. (Exercises 8 and 9 at the end of this chapter will ask you to investigate such aspects.)

Again the incremental analysis approach provides insights into the situation that cannot be readily inferred from a total cost approach. For example, the difference in incremental costs between the two modes is only $7.50 for demand level 7 (May) per tonne in favour of Scholle bags. A price increase for bags of less than 13% makes tanker the more attractive option also for May (and by implication for December). Unless Heinz can secure long-term price contracts with the bag manufacturer, the risk of a price increase may well sway the decision to purchase 40 tankers, rather than just 29.

The next example is of a completely different nature. Rather than analysing the optimal number of identical entities to get for a given activity, we have a set of

Figure 12-8   Total annual average costs for Heinz.

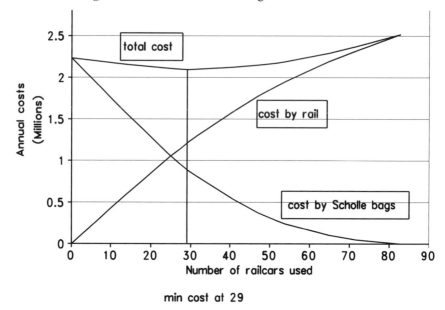

min cost at 29

distinct and different entities, each contributing towards the system's objectives and requiring the input of some shared resource.

12.11 An investment portfolio selection

The Sure-Bet Investment House has just completed the evaluation of nine potential investment projects. Each one has to be accepted or rejected in its entirety. Table 12-5 lists their ranking in terms of decreasing internal rates of return. Sure-Bet has currently also several firm offers for funds. In contrast to the projects, offers for funds can be taken up partially. Table 12-5 lists all relevant data.

Which projects should be accepted? Using the normal accept/reject principle for financial project evaluation (as described in Section 10.4), the temptation is great to say 'all of them', since even the last ranked project has an IRR higher than the cheapest source of funds. If this were done, the annual return would be £5.477 million. Subtracting the annual cost of £3.55 million — the interest on the £30 million of funds used — gives a net annual profit of £1.927 million. This naive approach, however, leads to the wrong decision. The correct method is to use incremental analysis.

An incremental analysis approach looks at the projects one at a time in order of decreasing IRRs — the equivalent to decreasing incremental revenues as the level of activity increases. The funds, on the other hand, are considered in order of increasing costs — the equivalent to increasing incremental cost as the level of activity increases. The level of activity is the amount of funds invested. This level

Table 12-5   Investment choices and sources of funds.

Project	Initial investment	Internal rate of return
A	1.8 million	32 %
B	6.9 million	26 %
C	2.5 million	23 %
D	1.1 million	18 %
E	7.3 million	15 %
F	3.2 million	14 %
G	0.9 million	13 %
H	2.2 million	12 %
I	4.1 million	10 %

Source	Funds offered	cost/year
1	up to 10 million	9.5 %
2	up to 4 million	12 %
3	up to 8 million	12.5%
4	up to 10 million	14 %

of activity can only be increased in unequal discrete amounts. We compare the incremental revenue per year for each additional project with the incremental cost per year of the funds used. Projects are accepted if the incremental revenue exceeds the incremental cost of the funds.

Table 12-6 summarizes the steps of the analysis. All dollar amounts are shown in millions. We start with project A. Its incremental annual revenue is 32% of £1.8 million or £576,000. Funded from the cheapest source of funds, the incremental annual cost is 9.5% of £1.8 million or £171,000. So project A is accepted. This reduces the amount of funds available at a cost of 9.5% to £8.2 million.

The second-ranked project B has an incremental annual revenue of 26% of £6.9 million or £1,794,000. It can be funded entirely from the cheapest source at an annual

Table 12-6   Incremental analysis for an investment portfolio.

Project	Funds needed	Incremental revenue	Incremental cost	Accept/ reject	Unused sources of funds			
					9.5%	12.0%	12.5%	14%
A	1.8	0.576	0.171	accept	8.2	4.0	8.0	10.0
B	6.9	1.794	0.6555	accept	1.3	4.0	8.0	10.0
C	2.5	0.575	0.2675	accept	0	2.8	8.0	10.0
D	1.1	0.198	0.132	accept	0	1.7	8.0	10.0
E	7.3	1.095	0.904	accept	0	0	2.4	10.0
F	3.2	0.448	0.412	accept	0	0	0	9.2
G	0.9	0.117	0.126	reject	0	0	0	8.3

cost of £655,500. This leaves £8.2 – £6.9 or £1.3 of the 9.5% funds. The third-ranked project C has an incremental annual return of £575,000. £1.3 million can be financed at 9.5%, and the balance of £1.2 million at 12%. This results in an incremental annual cost of £267,500. Hence C is accepted. The 9.5% funds have now been exhausted, and £2.8 million of the 12% funds remain. This process continues until we discover that the next ranked project fails to recover all annual interest costs. This occurs for project G.

The optimal solution is to accept projects A to F for a total annual revenue of £4.686 million. The amount of funds used is £22.8 million. This uses up the 9.5%, the 12%, and 12.5% funds, and £0.8 million of the 14% funds, with the balance of £9.2 million remaining unused. The total annual cost of the funds used is £2.542 million, leaving an annual total profit of £2.144 million, which is £217,000 more than the naive approach.

Note that in view of the order in which both the projects and the sources of funds were considered, there is no need to continue the analysis once a project has been rejected. Any project farther down in the rank order will stack up even more un-favourably.

12.12 Chapter highlights

• Marginal costs are the rate of increase in total costs as the level of activity increases. Typically, marginal costs initially exhibit increasing returns to scale, then constant returns to scale, and finally decreasing returns to scale, as the level of activity increases.

• The average cost is lowest for a level of activity where the (increasing) marginal cost becomes larger than average cost.

• Marginal revenues (or marginal benefits) are the rate of change in total revenues (or benefits).

• Marginal and incremental analysis are useful tools for solving many relatively simple MS/OR problems. 'Simple' means that they only have one decision variable or activity level and either a cost and a benefit or two cost aspects that vary in opposite direction as the level of activity increases. However, the ideas underlying marginal analysis also form the basis for a number of sophisticated mathematical OR tools.

• The principle of marginal or incremental analysis is to increase the activity level in small or incremental amounts until the gain in benefits (or savings of one cost) becomes less than the increase in costs.

• Breakeven analysis is a commonly used business tool. It determines the output or activity level for which total revenue (or benefits) become equal to or just larger than total costs (including the fixed costs directly associated with the activity). At the breakeven point profits are zero (or have just become positive).

Exercises

1. What is the practical difference between marginal and incremental analysis and why is the latter more useful for decision making?

2. An electrical goods manufacturer makes industrial transformers which it sells for £840 each. The material used in the manufacture consists of £120 for metal and plastic castings and wire costing £70 per km. The particular type of transformer produced on that machine requires 8 km of wire and 2 hours of labour per unit. The fixed annual cost of operating the machinery and overheads directly associated with the operation amount to £80,000. The machine operator is paid £800 per 40-hour week.
   (a) Assuming that the operator does other tasks when not working on this machine, determine the breakeven point in terms of the number of transformers to produce per year.
   (b) If the machine operator remains idle when not operating the machine, what is the breakeven point then?

3. A travel agent is contemplating opening another office in a different part of town. There is little or no overlap in potential clients expected. The cost of setting up a new agency is as follows: refurbishing of the office $24,000; computer equipment and software licences $17,500; initial training of staff $3,600; initial promotion $6,900. The annual operating cost of the office consists of: office rental $10,400; staff salaries, including fringe benefits $58,000; various fixed office costs, such as telephone rentals, power, heating, etc. $4,200; subscription to travel data sources, etc. $6000. Commission on travel ticket and accommodation sales, etc., averages 10% of gross sales. Other variable sales costs amount to about 3% of gross sales.
   (a) Determine the breakeven point for annual gross sales needed for the agency to remain viable.
   (b) The first office opened by the firm was able to operate at a sales level of 80% of the breakeven point for the first year, 30% above the breakeven point for the second year, and 50% above the breakeven point in the third year, and has maintained that level on average since then. If the same trend holds for the second office, how many years will it take to recover the initial investment?

4. An electric power company operates a number of hydro and thermal power generating stations. Although the actual variable cost of using hydro stations is essentially zero, power planners impute values for the water stored in hydro lakes based on the most expensive thermal power that they can replace at some later time of the year. The table below lists the power increments available at the various stations and the associated real or imputed generating cost per megawatt hour (MWh) of power produced, valid for a given week:

Station	A			B		C	D			
Power increments	1	2	3	1	2	1	1	2	3	4
Output in MWh	50	50	50	40	40	20	30	30	30	30
Cost 1000$/MWh	80	80	85	110	112	300	65	65	70	75

The company has firm contracts for supply of electricity of 170 MWh for that week. It can also offer additional power to other power companies at various prices: up to 40 MWh at $120,000/MWh, up to 50 MWh at $90,000/MWh, and up to 80 MWh at $82,000/MWh. What is the company's best power generating schedule for that week? Use marginal reasoning. It may help to set up a table similar to Table 12-3.

5. A firm produces ceramic tiles on a continuous basis. The daily output is 2 tonnes. They are stored temporarily at the plant and shipped periodically to its distribution warehouse in a box

car that can carry up to 28 tonnes. The hauling cost, regardless of the amount shipped is £1195. Each tonne has a value of £12,000. The storage cost at the plant is 30% on the average stock investment. Compute the optimal number of days each shipment should cover using marginal analysis, as demonstrated in Section 12.6.

6. Earth Care, Inc., sells beauty products through house calls by its 'certified personal advisors', more commonly known as door-to-door salespersons. A recent study revealed the following pattern between the number of 'advisors' assigned to urban areas, the total annual sales volume, and the total travel costs reimbursed to the 'advisors' for each 200,000 inhabitants (all in €1000):

'Advisors'	1	2	3	4	5	6	7	8	9	10
Sales	250	500	750	1000	1240	1470	1690	1890	2050	2170
Travel costs	2	4	6	8	10	12	14.5	17	20	23

The reason for the ultimate decrease in additional sales is partially due to the fact that less affluent urban areas have to be included. Travel costs increase more than proportionately for similar reasons. Each 'advisor' gets a basic annual salary of €15,000 and a commission of 5% on sales. Earth Care makes 9% gross profit on its sales, after subtracting any sales commissions, but before other selling costs. Use marginal or incremental analysis to determine the optimal number of 'advisors' to assign for each 200,000 inhabitants.

7. A soft drink bottling firm faces a seasonal demand (millions of bottles) as follows:

Period	Jan/Feb	Mar/Apr	May/June	July/Aug	Sep/Oct	Nov/Dec
Bottles sold	10	15	20	28	22	15

The firm can meet as much or as little of the demand as it wishes. The limited shelf life of bottled soft drinks means that no goods can be carried forward to a later period. The firm is currently modernizing its bottling plant by acquiring new bottling machines. Each bottling machine has a two-monthly capacity of 5 million bottles. The predicted total annual cost for each machine is $75,000. This includes all relevant fixed operating costs, as well as the recovery of the initial outlay less the salvage value at the end of its productive life, all expressed in terms of an equivalent annuity, as discussed in Section 10.3. The net contribution to profits is equal to $10,000 for each 1 million bottles sold. Use incremental analysis to determine the optimal number of machines to purchase.

8. Create a spreadsheet to reproduce the results in Figure 12-5.

9. Use the spreadsheet developed in exercise 8 above for the following sensitivity analysis, each done separately from the base case:
    (a) A change in the annual number of round trips from the current 30 to 25.
    (b) An increase in the cost of Scholle bags by 10%.
    (c) An increase in the carrying capacity of tankers from 18 to 20 tonnes.
    (d) An increase in the discount rate to 20%.

10*. For the Heinz logistics problem, assume now that there is a second conversion plant Z with the following monthly demands:

month	Jan	Feb	Mar	Apr	May	Jun	Jul	Aug	Sep	Oct	Nov	Dec
demand	400	700	1500	1600	2500	3000	2200	2500	3200	2800	600	300

The number of round trips from factory X to Z is 40 and the tanker hauling cost for a return trip is $794. The freight cost for Scholle bags is $38/tonne. The cost of returning the case remains at $2/case. Build a spreadsheet similar to the one in Figure 12-5 and find the optimal number of tankers to purchase. Hint: rather than expressing the demand levels in terms of incremental tonnes shipped, it is easier to express them in terms of incremental tankers needed. Determine for each destination the number of tankers needed in each month, add them for the two destinations, and then only rank the months in order of increasing number of tankers. Keep fractions here; only go to integer numbers for the subsequent analysis.

11. A firm has the following indivisible investment opportunities, with the investment in £1000 and the internal rate of return (IRR) in % per year:

Project	A	B	C	D	E	F	G	H	I	J
Investment	20	40	60	30	50	10	20	50	40	30
IRR	28	27	25	22	21	21	18	15	12	10

It has the following sources of funds available, each of which can be taken up in its entirety or only partially:

Funds source	1	2	3	4
Limit in $1000	150	120	90	80
Cost/year %	12	16	20	24

Determine which investment projects should be entered into.

13

Constrained decision making

The decision problems studied so far have not involved quantitative restrictions on the decision variables or on the combination of alternative courses of action. For example, in the LOD problem in Chapter 6 there was no restriction on the possible combinations of the stock replenishment quantity and the cutoff size for special production runs for the various products (except that negative values were implicitly ruled out). Their optimal values were determined without consideration of any resource constraints. Although the mixing and filling capacities and the warehouse space were limited, and had to be shared by all products, we assumed that the total capacities of these resources were ample and would not restrict the decision choices. This simplified the analysis considerably. It made it possible to look at each product individually, ignoring the fact that they shared the same resources. Similarly, when we evaluated investment projects we assumed that there was no restriction on the amount of funds available.

In this and the following chapter we study the effect of constraints on the decision choices or on system behaviour. These constraints can be in the form of limited resources, such as funds, machine capacities, and so on. They could also be in the form of other conditions, such as minimum output requirements, minimum quality standards, or fixed relationships between activities. Some of the constraints may be physical, such as maximum machine capacity — so-called **hard constraints**. Others may be the result of management or policy decisions — so-called **soft constraints**. An example of this is a budget allocation, e.g. the size of the advertising budget, which could be renegotiated or changed.

To keep things simple, this chapter only considers the case of a single resource constraint. In Chapter 14 we will study how to deal with several constraints when all mathematical relationships are linear.

Section 13.1 deals with a single activity using the limited resource. We then study the effect of relaxing the constraint by increasing the amount of the resource marginally, i.e. we perform sensitivity analysis on the resource (see Section 6.17). This will lead us to the concept of the **shadow price** of a resource — an important theoretical concept of constrained optimization. Section 13.5 shows how the ideas of marginal analysis can be extended to the allocation of a limited resource to several competing uses. The last section looks at the allocation of a scarce resource when its use occurs in discrete and possibly unequal increments.

13.1 Resource constraint on a single activity

In this section, some of the basic concepts of constrained optimization will be explored. Rather than do this in the abstract, I will refer to the simple EOQ inventory replenishment model developed for the LOD in Section 6.13.

The optimal unconstrained solution

One of the LOD products has to be stored under refrigeration. Any demand for this product is always met from stock. Whenever the stock is depleted, a replenishment of size Q is initiated. The situation thus corresponds to the basic EOQ model. The relevant annual cost is given by the sum of the annual stock holding cost and the annual replenishment setup cost, expression (6-1A), reproduced below:

$$T(Q) = 0.5Qvr + sD/Q \qquad (13\text{-}1)$$

where D is the predicted number of cans sold over the coming year, s is the production setup cost, v is the value of the product per can, and r is the annual investment holding cost per dollar invested. This total cost function is so-called well-behaved. In this context this means that it has a nice U-shape. (See Figure 6-8 on page 153.) Therefore, it follows that it has its minimum value at a single point corresponding to the economic order quantity, expression (13-2):

$$Q^* = \sqrt{(2Ds/vr)} \qquad (13\text{-}2)$$

Table 13-1 lists the input parameters for this product in the top portion. Verify that expression (13-2) gives an order quantity of 1857.7 cans. Since fractional cans cannot be stored, this is rounded to 1858 cans. Using expression (13-1), the relevant annual cost amounts to $3,274.

Cans are packed into boxes which are placed on pallets, with 12 cans per box and 8 boxes per pallet, or a total of 96 cans per pallet. A pallet area measures exactly 1 m². The pallets in turn are placed on shelves in the cool store. Therefore, 1858 cans require 19.35 pallets. Since any partially used pallet uses the same storage space as a full pallet, each replenishment occupies 20 pallet spaces. This is 20 m² of storage space. If there is no restriction on the amount of refrigerated space, then the optimal replenishment policy for this product is to make a run of 1858 cans whenever the inventory is depleted. This occurs, on the average, about 31 times per year, or about every 8 working days (assuming 250 working days/year). By definition, no other policy can have a lower annual cost.

Unfortunately, the current cool store only has a storage capacity of 8 m², or the equivalent of 768 cans. In other words, there is a constraint imposed on the values

Table 13-1   Stock replenishment with limited warehouse space.

DATA	
Annual demand in cans	57600 (*D*)
Value per can	$7.05 (*v*)
Production setup cost/setup	$52.80 (*s*)
Investment holding cost/$/year	$0.25 (*r*)
Warehouse space: cans/m^2	96
Warehouse space available: m^2	8
Unconstrained optimal solution:	
Economic order quantity Q in cans	1858
Total warehouse space needed in m^2	20
Annual cost	$3,274

Constrained optimal solution:

Available space	Order quantity		Annual cost	Cost increase	Shadow price
21	1858	(EOQ)	3,274		
20	1858	(EOQ)	3,274	0	0.00
19	1824		3,275	1	3.16
18	1728		3,283	8	13.18
17	1632		3,302	19	25.02
16	1536		3,334	32	39.15
15	1440		3,381	47	56.20
14	1344		3,447	66	77.03
13	1248		3,537	90	102.86
12	1152		3,655	118	135.40
11	1056		3,811	156	177.22
10	960		4,014	203	232.20
9	864		4,281	267	306.51
8	**768**		**4,637**	356	410.40
7	672		5,118	481	561.93
6	576		5,788	670	795.40
5	480		6,759	971	1,182.60
4	384		8,258	1,499	1,895.40

that the decision variable may assume. The unconstrained optimal policy of 1858 cans violates this constraint. Therefore, it is **infeasible**. To be a **feasible solution** the stock replenishment has to be decreased to at most 768 cans, with an annual cost of $4,637, an increase of $1,363 over the unconstrained solution.

Any deviation from the unconstrained optimal policy, by definition, results in a higher relevant annual cost. For what feasible value is this cost increase the smallest?

Incremental cost increases as available storage space is reduced

Fractional pallet areas cannot be used as storage space, since a pallet requires a shelf measuring one square metre. It only makes sense to consider reductions in the size of the replenishment equivalent to one pallet area, or 96 cans. We have, therefore, recourse to an incremental type analysis, except that this time we study the effect of decreases in an activity, rather than increases. This is demonstrated in the lower portion of Table 13-1 (ignore the last column, labelled 'shadow price' for the time being). Starting from the unconstrained optimal solution, we reduce the warehouse required by one square metre. Since the 20th pallet is only partially used, the increase in costs is small — in fact, only one dollar. Further reductions in area imply a reduction in Q by 96 cans and increase costs by larger and larger amounts. They are listed in the column labelled 'Cost increase'.

The constraint limits stock replenishments to values that require no more than 8 m² of storage space. The only values for the decision variable which satisfy this constraint are those involving a stock replenishment of 768 cans or less. From the 'Annual cost' listed in Table 13-1 we see that the cheapest feasible solution is the one that uses the entire space available. The optimal constrained replenishment quantity is therefore $Q = 768$ cans at an annual relevant cost of \$4,637. Any lower value for Q results in higher costs, while any larger Q is not a feasible solution.

Generalizing the results

We can now generalize this result for the case of a single resource constraint. If the unconstrained optimal solution violates the constraint, i.e. is not feasible, then the optimal constrained solution is to choose a value for the decision variable that just satisfies the constraint, i.e. uses up all of the resource available. We then say that **the constraint is binding**. On the other hand, if the unconstrained optimal solution does not violate the constraint, i.e. requires less of the resource than is available, we say that **the constraint has slack**. The amount of slack is the difference between the amount available and the amount used. Slack is the amount of unused resource.

This discussion was couched in terms of a resource constraint. However, the conclusions reached are no different for any other type of constraint. If there is only one constraint and it is violated by the optimal unconstrained solution, then the optimal constrained solution is to set the values of the decision variables so that they just satisfy the constraint, i.e. the constraint holds as an equality.

Procedure for finding the optimal solution subject to one constraint

This suggests the following optimization system O for finding the optimal solution if the values of the decision variables are subject to a single constraint:

Step 1: Ignore the constraint and find the optimal (unconstrained) solution.

Step 2: Verify if the constraint is satisfied by this solution. If 'yes', this solution is the optimal solution. If 'no', go to step 3.

Step 3: The optimal constrained solution is the one where the decision variables satisfy the constraint as a strict equality.

If there is only one decision variable, step 3 reduces to solving the constraint for the decision variable. For instance, in the LOD example we know that $Q/96 = 8$ m^2. Hence $Q = 8(96) = 768$. If there are two or more decision variables, step 3 is somewhat more challenging, as we shall see in Section 13.5.

Activity:
- For the data in Table 13-1, what is the optimal production run for a cool store capacity of 24 pallets? Why? Why is it not optimal to fill the cool store?
- Study the column labelled 'Cost increase' in Table 13-1. Note that successive reductions in the space available cause the cost to increase by larger and larger amounts. Try to explain why this is so. (Section 12.2 will help.)

13.2 Sensitivity analysis

How does the optimal value of the objective function respond to changes in a constraint? We shall use incremental analysis to study this.

With only 8 m^2 of cool store space available, the optimal constrained replenishment is 768 cans, using up all available space. How much is it worth to acquire additional storage space? This is the type of question regularly asked by a decision maker faced with limited resources. The worth of additional storage space is given by the decrease in the total annual cost. Increasing the available storage space from 8 to 9 m^2 results in a decrease in the annual cost of $356, as shown in Table 13-1 for the entry in column 'Cost increase' and row 'Available space 8'. If the annual cost of an additional square metre is less than $356, then it would be to the LOD's advantage to acquire at least one more square metre of space.

Often a resource can only be acquired or effectively used in a limited range of sizes or quantities. For instance, machine capacity may only be increased by adding further machines of the same type. In the LOD case it is possible to rent refrigerated containers that increase the storage capacity by 6 m^2 at an annual rental cost of $600 per container. Should the LOD rent one? With the container, the total storage space increases from 8 to 14 m^2. For 14 m^2 the optimal constrained order quantity is 1344 cans with a total annual cost of $3,447 — a decrease of $1,190 from the best solution with the space constraint at 8 m^2. After payment of the container rental, the LOD will still be better off by $590. Hence this option should be considered seriously if it is technically acceptable.

Should the firm consider renting two refrigerated containers, increasing the total storage space to 20 m^2? The storage space is not limiting any longer and the unconstrained solution becomes optimal, reducing the annual cost by another $173. This saving is less than the annual rental of the container. The total combined cost increases. The answer to the question is thus 'No'.

13.3 Shadow price of a constraint

Let us now study how the optimal value of the objective function responds to a gradual relaxation of a constraint.

The concept of shadow price

The rate of change of the optimal value of the objective function in response to a marginal change in a resource constraint is called the **shadow price** of the constraint. Two points are important in this definition. First, the shadow price is **a rate of change valid for a particular value of the constraint**. As the amount of the resource changes, so may the shadow price. Secondly, it refers to the rate of change in the objective function **at the optimal solution** for a given resource availability, not simply at any arbitrary solution.

Note the similarity of this definition with the concept of the marginal costs and revenues, discussed in Sections 12.2 and 12.3. Both refer to the rate of change of some 'output' for a marginal change in some input — a resource in this case. They differ, however, in one respect. The shadow price always refers to the rate of change at the optimal solution, while the marginal costs and revenues can be assessed for any arbitrary 'solution' that may or may not be optimal.

Given this similarity, determining the shadow price of a resource uses the same marginal reasoning as used in Section 12.7* for finding the marginal cost of an activity that is a continuous variable. What is the shadow price of the storage constraint at the present limit of 8 m²?

Procedure for finding the shadow price

Since a shadow price is a marginal concept, the first step is to abandon the assumption that storage space can only be increased in discrete increments of one pallet area, but by any arbitrarily small amount. Assume the storage space is increased by 1/96 of a square metre — just enough to store one additional can. By how much does the minimum cost decrease? Extrapolating this to a unit change in storage space gives an approximate value for the shadow price at the current constraint level of 8 m².

The minimum total annual cost for 8 m² of storage space (or the equivalent of 768 cans) is \$4,636.80, precise to two decimals. For $8^1/_{96}$ m² Q increases to 769 cans. Verify that the total annual cost decreases to \$4,632.53. So the cost decrease is \$4.27. Extrapolated to 1 m² (or 96 cans) this gives an approximate shadow price of \$4.27/(1/96) = \$409.92. At the current constraint of 8 m² the rate of change of the minimum cost is approximately \$409.92 per square metre of storage space. This though is only an approximation. As we shall see later on, there is a more accurate method for computing the shadow price. That method was used for finding the values listed in Table 13-1.

The shadow price is, however, quite sensitive to the amount of storage space. Consider another increase of $^1/_{96}$ m² to $8^2/_{96}$ m². This second increase lowers the minimum cost by \$4.25, resulting in an approximate shadow price of \$408. The graph in Figure 13-1 shows how the accurately computed shadow price behaves as the storage space available increases. Initially, the shadow price drops quite steeply. However, the curve starts to become flatter as we approach 20 m². At 20 m², the unconstrained optimal solution can be implemented. Additional increases in storage space available will not decrease the minimum cost any further. Hence they have a zero value, i.e. the shadow price drops to zero once the resource is not binding on the optimal solution.

Figure 13-1   The shadow price of storage space.

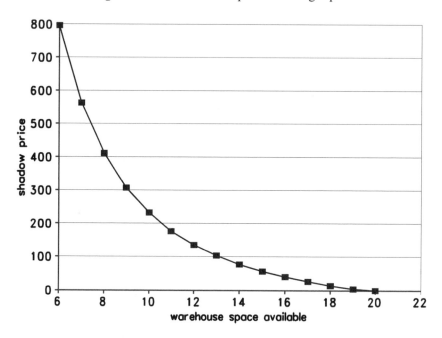

Analytic method for finding the shadow price of the storage constraint

In many problems, the numerical approach demonstrated above is the most efficient way to determine an approximate curve for the shadow price as a function of the resource availability. In some cases, there is a more elegant way. The idea is deceptively simple! The relevant cost in expression (13-1) only includes the annual replenishment setup cost and the annual inventory holding cost. The trick is to add a further penalty in the form of a yet unknown, annual charge π per square metre of storage space used. In our example, this additional charge for a replenishment of size Q amounts to $\pi Q/96$, since 96 cans can be stored on one square metre. Adding this term to the total cost expression (13-1), we get

$$T(Q) = 0.5Qvr + \pi Q/96 + sD/Q \qquad (13\text{-}3)$$

or

$$= 0.5Q(vr + \pi/48) + sD/Q$$

The optimal replenishment $Q*$ is now

$$Q* = \sqrt{\{2Ds/[vr + (1/48)\pi]\}} \qquad (13\text{-}4)$$

Note the similarity with EOQ formula (13-2). There is an additional term of $(1/48)\pi$ in the denominator. If π is set equal to zero, expression (13-4) gives the same answer as the EOQ formula. This must be so, since a zero charge implies that storage space is abundant and hence has no value. However, for any positive value of π, $Q*$ will be smaller than the EOQ.

Expression (13-4) can now be used for determining the value of this unknown charge π implied by a given amount of storage space available. As we saw in the previous section, if the storage space is restricted, the constrained optimal order quantity is set to a value q which exactly uses up all storage space. We now simply assign π a value such that expression (13-4) yields a $Q*$ equal to q. We can find the correct value for π by trial and error. However, in this instance, some simple algebra allows us to find a formula for the value of π we are looking for:

$$\pi = 48([2Ds/q^2] - vr) \qquad (13\text{-}5)$$

For example, for the current storage restriction of 8 m², we see from Table 13-1 that $q = 768$. Expression (13-5) then yields the following value for π:

$$\pi = 48([2(57600)(52.80)/(768^2)] - (7.05)(0.25)) = \$410.40.$$

Verify that if you insert this value into expression (13-4) you get $Q* = 768$. This shadow price is an exact value — not an approximation, unlike the one obtained by making small but discrete changes in the constraint and extrapolating the resulting cost decrease to a full unit of the resource. The difference is though small. The values listed under the heading 'Shadow price' in Table 13-1 are the exact shadow prices computed by the above formula.

Generalizing the meaning of shadow price

The concept of shadow price can be extended to any type of restriction on activities or decision variables. The shadow price always refers to the rate of change in the optimal value of the objective function for relaxing the constraint by one unit. Relaxing a constraint means making it less binding or less tight. For a resource constraint this means providing additional amounts of the resource. The optimal constrained solution will then get closer to the unconstrained optimal solution. Hence the value of the objective function should normally improve, i.e. decrease if we minimize costs or increase if we maximize profits.

Relaxing a constraint may take many different forms besides increasing the amount of a scarce resource. Here are a few examples to illustrate this.

Consider a water reservoir intended mainly for irrigation, with any excess water used to generate power. The irrigation contracts may require a minimum release of M m³ of water per day. Relaxing this constraint means lowering the minimum release and having more water available for power generation. The value of the additional power generated per m^3 gives the shadow price of the minimum release constraint.

The constraint may be in the form of a maximum amount of output of a by-product for a given activity, say the emission of air pollutants at a factory. Relaxing this constraint means allowing higher emissions, hence reducing the cost of emission control for the factory (but increasing the social cost of pollution, which is usually not included in the cost function of a private enterprise).

The constraint may refer to minimum quality standards, such as a minimum breaking strength for a cable. Relaxing this constraint means making it easier to satisfy this quality standard. This implies decreasing this minimum breaking strength required. It hopefully results in a decrease in manufacturing costs.

The shadow price also reflects the rate of change in the objective function for making a constraint marginally tighter, such as decreasing the amount of a resource available. Naturally, making a constraint tighter means that the optimal value of the objective function deteriorates, i.e. the effect is just the reverse of relaxing a constraint. Minimum costs go up, maximum benefits go down.

13.4   Interpretation and uses of shadow price

Value of additional resources

The discussion in the previous section immediately suggests that the shadow price of a resource constraint can be interpreted as the maximum price that the user entity, e.g. a firm, should be willing to pay for additional (but possibly very small) amounts of the resource. So, if the cost of the resource is less than the shadow price at the current constraint level, this is a signal for acquiring additional amounts of that resource. On the other hand, if the cost of the resource is more than the shadow price, this may be an indication that the firm either uses too much of the resource or uses it inefficiently.

Although the shadow price gives a signal whether to acquire more of the resource or dispose of some of it, there still remains the question of 'how much?' The answer to this question is made more difficult by the fact that the shadow price of a resource is a marginal concept and may be highly sensitive to changes in the constraint level.

As a first cut, we can study the curve of the shadow price as a function of the constraint level. For example, assume that the current cost of refrigerated storage space is about $100 per m^2. Figure 13-1 shows that for storage space of 13 m^2 or less the shadow price is more than $100. Hence if storage space can be purchased at that unit price in any arbitrary amount (within reason), the optimal decision for the LOD is to increase the refrigerated storage space to 13 m^2. So we see that knowing the shadow price at the current constraint level of 8 m^2 is not sufficient. In fact, we generally need to know part or most of the shadow price curve for answering the question of 'how much'.

If the resource can only be acquired in a limited number of sizes or amounts, 'how much' is not a question of marginal analysis, but one of incremental analysis. Section

13.2 demonstrated this approach for the storage problem. There, additional storage could be obtained in lots of 6 m^2 at a cost of $600. This is also $100 per m^2. We concluded that the optimal solution was to increase the storage space to 14 m^2. This is 1 m^2 more than the optimal solution derived from marginal analysis. The reason why the two answers differ is that marginal analysis assumes the resource is infinitesimally divisible, i.e. can be acquired in arbitrary amounts, while incremental analysis is based on the discrete realities of the real world.

Correct interpretation of shadow price

A clear grasp of the distinction between marginal and incremental analysis is the basis for a proper interpretation of the shadow price at a given constraint level. Only then will the use of shadow prices lead to the correct decisions.

There is a second source of potential confusion in the interpretation of shadow prices. If the objective function already includes a charge for the resource, say the going purchase price, the shadow price also reflects this cost. It then only represents the highest additional premium that should be paid for the resource at the current constraint level. For example, the scarce resource is hours of labour during regular work time. The regular-time labour cost is already included as a cost component in the objective function. Then the shadow price represents the maximum overtime premium the firm can afford to pay without being worse off. (Note that the question of 'how much' still needs to be answered!)

A shadow price may not necessarily be expressed in monetary terms. In fact, it is always expressed in terms of the units used in the objective function. If the latter deals for example with maximizing the amount of electric power produced, then the shadow price on the water in the hydro reservoir, which limits the amount of power that can be produced, will also be in terms of units of electric power.

In conclusion, shadow prices provide indicators on whether or not it may be advantageous to change the current constraint level and whether the change should be a relaxation or a tightening of the constraint. However, without further analysis, it does not tell us the best size of any change. To answer that question, we may need to have recourse to incremental analysis.

Shadow prices are one of the more difficult concepts. You may need to study this and the previous section again. They are a most important practical aspect of sensitivity analysis. They are also an important theoretical concept in OR/MS. We will demonstrate their usefulness in this as well as the following chapter.

Activity:
- Section 6-17 defines sensitivity analysis as the response of the optimal solution to changes in inputs (cost, demand, etc.). Compare sensitivity analysis with the concept of shadow price. What are the similarities?
- The shadow price of a resource used in a given activity falls to zero once it is abundantly available. But you will rightly respond that the value of that resource surely cannot be zero: that if the firm has no use for it, it could be sold. Discuss this apparent contradiction. (Hint: The shadow price only reflects what is in the model.)

13.5   Several activities sharing a limited resource

When several activities compete for the use of the same scarce resource, the optimal level of each activity cannot be determined individually for each activity. They are now linked together through the resource use. There will be trade-offs. Allocating more to one activity in order to capture high benefits will leave less for the other activities, reducing the benefits there. The optimal combination of activity levels needs to be determined jointly.

The Heinz logistics problem revisited

At this point, it is a good idea for you to reviewed the Heinz USA logistics case of Section 12.10, and in particular Table 12-5. Using the idea of marginal costs and marginal savings, we found the optimal number of rail tankers by stepwise increasing their number until their marginal cost became larger than the marginal savings from the reduction in Scholle bag usage. This approach was possible because we only looked at the transport of tomato paste from a single factory to a single processing plant.

Heinz operates several factories and many processing plants. If there is no constraint on the total number of tankers that can be purchased, then each combination of factory and plant can be solved individually. (We also make the assumption that the demand follows the same pattern of peaks and troughs. This implies that idle tankers cannot be switched to other routes in order to increase their usage and lower the marginal rail cost.) Let us now throw a spanner into the works by assuming that the manufacturer can only supply a total of 60 tankers. Again, to simplify things, we consider only four different combinations of factories and processing plants, each being a separate activity. How should we go about finding the optimal allocation of tankers to each activity?

As is often the case, the basic idea is very simple — it just needed somebody to think of it. We will demonstrate it with this little story. After having seen the film classic *Babette's Feast* with a group of friends, you invited them for a special treat. You planned to surprise them with 'caille au sarcophage' — the main course Babette offered to her guests. A crude translation is 'quail in a coffin'. But do not be deceived — it is delicious! Unfortunately you procrastinated over buying the quails. In panic you go to the local farmers' market. A quick check shows that several stalls still have a few suitable birds left and that the prices vary substantially. But no single stall can supply all the quails you need. Being a frugal gourmet — a rather interesting contradiction — you quickly note down prices and the number of quails at each stall. Your purchasing strategy is to start buying as many quails as are available at the stall with the lowest price, then proceed to the stall with the next lowest price, and so on, until you have bought the required number of quails. In other words, true to your character, you use a **greedy algorithm**. It will guarantee that you spend the least amount of money to buy the number of quails required.

A greedy algorithm for resource allocation

This same type of greedy algorithm can be applied to the allocation of rail tankers. All we need is a schedule of the difference between the marginal Scholle bag cost and the marginal tanker cost per tonne for each activity. We will call these differences 'the marginal advantage of rail over bags' or MARB for short. We allocate the rail tankers sequentially in order of decreasing value of MARBs until all 60 tankers have been allocated to the four activities.

Table 13-2 lists the MARBs for each factory-processing plant pair. Activity 1 is the one we analysed in Figure 12-5 on page 330. For example, the MARB for demand level 12 is the difference between $93.20 for Scholle bags and $82.70 for tanker per tonne transported. Only positive MARBs are shown, since we would never use tankers when the MARBs become negative (<0).

Table 13-2   MARBs in decreasing value for each activity.

Demand level	Activity 1 tankers	MARB	Activity 2 tankers	MARB	Activity 3 tankers	MARB	Activity 4 tankers	MARB
12	14	10.50 (6)	10	11.96 (2)	9	13.12 (1)	12	9.65
11	11	9.68 (8*)	8	10.98 (4)	7	11.63 (3)	9	9.03
10	2	9.68	4	10.02 (7)	1	10.63 (5)	3	9.03
9	2	6.40	1	7.03	2	7.45	2	6.74
8	3	<0	2	2.61	4	2.92	4	0.49
7			5	<0	6	<0	8	<0
allocation		21		22		17		0

Activity 3 has the highest MARB of $13.12 per tonne, valid for the first 9 tankers used. So, the first 9 tankers are allocated to activity 3. There are 51 tankers left to allocate. Activity 2 has the next highest MARB with $11.96 and gets allocated 10. This leaves 41. The third allocation is again to activity 3, and so on. (How about testing your understanding by doing the next few allocations?) The numbers in parentheses after the MARBs show the order in which the tankers are allocated. After the seventh allocation (to activity 2) there are only 7 tankers left. These are allocated to activity 1. The asterisk flags the fact that the eighth incremental allocation only covers a portion of the 11 tankers which have the MARB of $9.68. The bottom row summarizes the number of tankers allocated to each activity.

The shadow price of the current constraint level for tankers is given by the MARB for the 61st tanker available. That tanker would be used for increasing the eighth incremental allocation. It goes to activity 1, increasing that allocation for the 11th demand level from 7 to 8. Its MARB is $9.68 per tonne, valid for up to 11 tankers. Since the MARB is the difference between the rail cost and the Scholle bag cost per tonne transported, this shadow price must now be interpreted as a premium. It is the highest premium, in addition to the normal rail cost per tonne, that Heinz should be willing to pay to get an additional tanker. In contrast to the inventory control example, this premium remains the same for a total of 6 tankers, rather than changing continuously. Can you figure out why?

The answer to this question can be found in Figure 12-7 on page 335. It shows how the marginal rail cost increases step-wise with each progressive higher demand level, but remains constant for additional tankers within each demand level. As a consequence, the shadow price for additional tankers also remains constant within a demand level, and increases when stepping to a higher demand level.

There is a close similarity between the greedy algorithm and the algorithm for marginal analysis. As a result, both require that the objective function is well behaved. This means that the marginal costs have to be non-decreasing, i.e. they either stay the same or increase for additional allocations, and the marginal savings have to be non-increasing, i.e. they either stay the same or decrease for additional allocations. As a result, the marginal advantage will ultimately decrease as the amount allocated increases further and further. If costs or benefits do not satisfy this property, then the greedy algorithm fails to find the optimal solution. It may also fail if the allocation has to be done in irregularly discrete chunks. The next section will demonstrate this aspect.

> Activity: Think up a simple numeric example with two competing uses, where benefit
> functions are not well-behaved, and then show that the greedy algorithm fails.

13.6 Discrete and irregular sized requirements of a resource

A firm is considering its investments for the coming year. A list of possible candidates has been prepared from the proposals put forward by the various operating departments. Each proposal has been subjected to the usual financial accept/reject test in terms of the firm's desired rate of return on new investments. The first three rows in Table 13-3 list the candidate projects, their individual initial investment or cash outflow, and their NPV, i.e. the sum of the present values of all cash outflows (including the initial investment) and cash inflows associated with each project, all expressed in units of £1000.

The firm has an investment budget of £600,000. Which combination or portfolio of projects should be undertaken? The firm's objective is to maximize the NPV of the portfolio selected.

A naive application of the greedy algorithm would choose the projects in terms of decreasing NPVs. The second set of rows in Table 13-3 shows that the projects have already been ranked in this order. Hence A, B, and C are the first three projects chosen. They use up £490,000 of the £600,000 available. The fourth ranked project D has an initial investment of £133,000 and exceeds the balance

Table 13-3   Selection of investment portfolio.

Project	A	B	C	D	E	F	G	H	J	K
Initial investment	107	201	182	133	82	141	30	37	25	12
NPV	84	50	45	39	35	26	24	9	8	2
Ranking by decreasing NPV:										
NPV rank	1	2	3	4	5	6	7	8	9	10
Cumul. investm.	107	308	490	-	572	-	-	-	597	-
Cumul. NPV	84	134	179	-	214	-	-	-	222	-
Ranking by decreasing ratio of [PV of cash inflows / Initial investment]:										
PV cash inflow	191	251	227	172	117	167	54	46	33	14
Ratio	0.785	0.249	0.247	0.293	0.427	0.184	0.800	0.243	0.320	0.167
Ratio rank	2	6	7	5	3	9	1	8	4	10
Cumul. investm.	137	578	-	377	219	-	30	-	244	590
Cumul. NPV	108	240	-	190	143	-	24	-	151	242
Optimal solution:										
Cumul. investm.	107	-	289	422	82	-	534	571	596	-
Cumul. NPV	84	-	129	168	203	-	227	236	244	-

of funds left. Hence, it is skipped over. The initial investment of the fifth ranked project E can be accommodated, leaving a balance of unallocated funds of £28,000. Projects F, G, and H have to be again skipped. The final project selected is J, leaving an unused balance of £3000. The sum of the NPVs is £222,000.

This selection method has serious flaws. Just consider the extreme case where there is another candidate L with an initial investment of £600,000 and an associated NPV of £120,000. Since it has the largest NPV it is the first one chosen, exhausting the entire budget. This leads to a substantially inferior return than if project L had been ignored.

Some 50 years ago, two economists (J. Lorie and L. J. Savage) suggested that the projects be viewed in terms of the ratio [PV of all cash flows exclusive of the initial investment] to [the initial investment], also referred to as the benefit/cost ratio. A more sophisticated version of the greedy algorithm would then select projects in decreasing order of their benefit/cost ratios. This method is demonstrated in the third set of rows in Table 13-3. Verify that this method selects the first six projects G, A, E, J, D, B in that order. Project C is the seventh ranked one. Its initial investment exceeds the unallocated balance of £22,000. Hence it is skipped. So are projects F, G, and H. Only project K still fits into the budget. The NPVs of the projects chosen add up to £242,000, considerably better than the first method.

However, even the Lorie–Savage criterion cannot guarantee finding the optimal solution. The reason for this is that funds are allocated in discrete and uneven chunks. The Lorie–Savage criterion may leave a fairly large balance of funds unused, but smaller than the smallest remaining project. A different choice may use more of the funds budgeted and hence achieve a higher NPV total. For our example, the optimal solution is shown in the last set of rows. Note that it does not select the projects in terms of their decreasing benefit/cost ratio. More sophisticated solution algorithms are needed to find the optimal solution if the solution space is not well-behaved, as is the case here. However, for large problems with many relatively small projects, the Lorie–Savage criterion often finds the optimal solution or one very close to it.

13.7 Chapter highlights

- If the optimal unconstrained solution for a one-decision-variable problem violates the constraint, the optimal constrained solution is to set a value for the decision variable that satisfies the constraint exactly.
- The shadow price of a constraint represents the rate of change in the optimal value of the objective function (expressed in terms of a unit change in the constraint). If the objective function is a nonlinear function of the decision variable, then the shadow price may change continuously, becoming smaller and smaller as the constraint is relaxed. It is zero if the constraint has slack.
- When several activities compete for the same resource and the incremental improvement in the objective function is decreasing (or at least non-increasing) for any activity increase, then a greedy algorithm that allocates each additional unit of the resource in order of decreasing incremental improvements finds the optimal resource allocation.
- If the objective function is not well-behaved, then a greedy algorithm fails to find the optimal resource allocation.

Exercises

1. For the cost and demand data in Table 13-1, use a spreadsheet to analyse a restriction on the average investment in inventories. Reduce the investment limit initially to the nearest multiple of $100 and then by decrements of $100 to a minimum of $5000. Plot the incremental cost change as a function of the average investment, i.e. the x-axis increases from $5000 to the unconstrained optimal average investment.

2. For the data in Table 13-1, find the shadow price for a warehouse constraint of 12 m^2,
    (a) using first the approximation procedure in the second subsection of Section 13.3.
    (b) using expression (13-5).

3. Using the approximation procedure described the second subsection of Section 13.3,
    (a) Find a reasonably accurate shadow price for the situation in exercise 1 above for an average investment limit of $5,500.
    (b) What is the exact interpretation of this shadow price?
    (c) Show that the difference in cost between the unconstrained optimal solution and the constrained optimal solution for an investment limit of $5,500 is substantially less than the product of the shadow price and the difference between the unconstrained optimal Q and the constrained Q.

4*. For the problem in exercise 3 above, develop an analytic expression similar to expression (13-5) for determining the shadow price on the average inventory investment and use it to evaluate the shadow price for a $5,500 limit.

5. Determine the shadow price for the data given in exercise 6 of Chapter 2 if the number of 'advisors' is limited to 6.

6. Consider exercise 5 in Chapter 12. Assume that the box car can only carry 18 tons. Find the optimal constrained solution and its cost. Determine the shadow price of this constraint.

7*. The original data in the Heinz case of Chapter 12 had a limit of 30 round trips per year and a tanker capacity of 18 tonnes. Using a spreadsheet, apply the approximation procedure demonstrated in the second subsection of Section 13.3 to determine the shadow price
(a) for 30 round trips.
(b) for tankers of 18-tonne capacity.

8. A chain of supermarkets has just received the last shipment of strawberries of the season, packed in cases containing 24 punnets each. From past observations, the fresh fruit marketing manager is able to develop the following table of total sales revenues (in euros) for allocating n cases to each of the 6 stores of the chain:

Store		1	2	3	4	5	6
Allocation:	1 case	36	36	32	30	30	29
	2 cases	70	68	64	60	58	57
	3 cases	95	96	96	90	84	84
	4 cases	112	116	128	118	105	104
	5 cases	122	125	152	138	126	118
	6 cases	122	125	172	153	135	125
	7 cases	122	125	181	160	135	125
	8 cases	122	125	181	160	135	125

The difference in revenues is due to differences of location and customer propensity to buy strawberries. Each case has a cost of €20. Use a greedy algorithm for the following situation:
(a) If there is no restriction on the number of cases that can be obtained, how many cases should be purchased to at least break even? How many are allocated to each store? What is the total gross profit (difference between revenue and cost)?
(b) If the maximum number of cases that the manager can procure is 16, how should they be allocated to the various stores? What is the total revenue? What is the shadow price of case 17?

9. The table below shows the choices of an electric power generating company for generating incremental amounts of power for a given day, where the numbers in the table represent the actual cost of thermal generation or the imputed value of the water used for hydro generation for incremental units of one MWh in £1000.
(a) If the amount of power required is 9 MWh, what is the optimal output for each station, assuming that there are no fixed start-up costs for thermal power stations? What is the total cost? Use a greedy algorithm.
(b) Assume now that there is a start-up cost of £20,000 for each thermal station. This means that the first MWh of power produced costs £20,000 more than listed in the table above, but the cost of further increments is the same as above. Discuss why a greedy algorithm will fail to find the optimal solution.

		Incremental output		
Source of power	station 1	station 2	station 3	station 4
Type of station	hydro	hydro	thermal	thermal
1st MWh	56	75	80	110
2nd MWh	72	75	80	110
3rd MWh	84	82	80	110
4th MWh	95	90	96	120
5th MWh	110	110	96	120
6th MWh	110	110	96	120

10. Consider the investment opportunities in exercise 11 of Chapter 12. Assume now that only £270,000 of funds are available (i.e. only the first two sources of funds). Using the ratio method of Section 13.6, find the resulting choice of projects made.

14

Multiple constraints: linear programming

We saw in Chapter 13 that a constraint on the decision choices may force a solution that is less advantageous than the one achievable without a constraint. If the decision choices have to satisfy several constraints simultaneously, this is even more true. This chapter studies a special case of constrained optimization where the relationships between the decision variables are all linear. Although the assumption of linearity may look highly restrictive, there are, in fact, numerous applications in business, industry, agriculture, and the public sector, as well as in engineering, where linearity of all relationships between the variables holds or is at least a very good approximation over the normal range of operations.

As an example, consider the construction of a highway through hilly countryside. Soil and rocks has to be shifted from places where the road cuts through hills, or where it can easily be removed, to where fill is required to raise the road, or to be discarded at other suitable sites. The construction firm wants to do this as cheaply as possible. For any two sites, one where excess material is to be removed, called a source of material, and one where material is to be deposited or may be dumped, called a sink of material, the cost of shifting this material is approximately proportional to the amount that is transported. (However, this cost does not have to be proportional to the distance between the two sites.) The constraints imposed on the schedule for shifting material are, on the one hand, the amounts of excess material to be removed from each source and, on the other hand, the amounts of fill material required at each sink or the capacity of sinks serving as dumps for unwanted material. The schedule for shifting material consists of a detailed list of how much is transported from each source to each sink — the decision variables of the problem. Clearly, the constraints are linear. They simply consist of a sum of material shifted. For instance, if site A has a capacity for receiving 120,000 m^3 of dumped material, then the sum of the amounts transported from all sources to sink A cannot exceed this limit.

This chapter starts out with a short general discussion on optimization in the presence of multiple constraints. Section 14.2 gives a summary of a somewhat simplified, but typical, situation and shows the associated influence diagram. Its trans-

359

lation into mathematics is given in Section 14.3. The Appendix to this chapter shows the graphical representation of a simplified version of the problem and motivates the solution algorithm. Sections 14.4 and 14.5 show how spreadsheet **solvers** or **optimizers** find the optimal solution and discusses the output reports, particularly sensitivity analysis and its limitations. The ease with which sensitivity analysis can be performed in linear programming is one of the strengths of this tool. The chapter concludes with two, albeit somewhat simplified, practical applications of linear programming.

14.1 Constrained optimization

Section 13.1 suggests a three-step procedure for finding the best solution if there is a single constraint on the decision choices. We first determine the optimal solution ignoring the constraint. If this solution satisfies the constraint, we have found the optimal solution to the problem. If the constraint is violated, then we know that the best solution will satisfy the constraint as an equality, e.g. use up all of the available resource for continuous decision variables or use up as much as possible of the resource if the decision variables can only assume discrete values. Often a greedy algorithm will find the best constrained optimal solution.

New aspects with multiple constraints

Faced with many constraints, often in the hundreds or thousands, more powerful optimization systems are needed. Over the last 50 years a number of sophisticated mathematical algorithms have been developed. Some are of a fairly general nature, making few assumptions about the mathematical structure of the problem. The majority, however, deal with special classes of problems and take advantage of their special mathematical structure. For instance, as indicated above, if all relationships are linear and the variables are continuous, the solution technique of linear programming can be applied. If all decision variables can only assume values of 0 or 1, then network algorithms are often computationally highly efficient for finding the optimal solution. These algorithms are the topic of advanced university courses in operations research and are beyond the scope of this text. Our interest here is much more modest. We simply wish to get a better understanding of the nature of the difficulties and maybe gain some insights into the general form of the solutions.

In a multiple constraint decision problem, some of the constraints may be binding on the optimal solution, while others will not be. If the constraints are all in the form of scarce resources, a binding constraint implies that all of the resource is used up — in other words, the total amount of the resource consumed is equal to the amount available. A constraint that is not binding means that some of the resource remains unused — in other words, the constraint has slack.

From Section 13.1, we also know that the optimal constrained solution can never be better than the optimal unconstrained solution. In fact, unless all constraints have slack, the best constrained solution will be worse.

If we knew which constraints are binding on the decision variables at the optimal solution, we could simply discard all other non-binding constraints. These will, by definition, have no effect on the optimal constrained values of the decision variables. With fewer constraints to be considered, finding the optimal constrained solution would be computationally simpler. At the optimal constrained solution, all the binding constraints would be in the form of equations. The computational problem would then boil down to solving a system of equations, some or all of which could be nonlinear. Unfortunately, there is no simple way of identifying which constraints are binding and which constraints have slack.

An algorithmic analogy — South Sea island treasure hunt

So, how do the majority of these algorithmic methods go about finding the optimal constrained solution to a problem? The easiest way to explain the general principle is to take a geographical analogy. Consider this enchanting South Sea island. Your treasure map only tells you that the treasure is hidden under a round rock at the highest point on this island. You arrive on the island in the middle of a pitch black night. You cannot wait until daylight before starting the ascent to the highest point since one-eyed Jack is in hot pursuit of you. You also know that the island has a very rugged coastline, with high cliffs at various places. In fact, the highest point on the island could well be at some cliff top.

You need an approach — an algorithm — that will guide you ultimately to the highest point. Recall from Section 6.19 that an algorithm is an iterative method that starts with an initial or incoming solution. It applies a set of rules to find the new improved solution. This then becomes the next incoming solution to which the rules are again applied for a new iteration. The process stops when no further improvement can be found.

You reason as follows: You land at a suitable spot where the ground rises slowly from the shore. This is your initial solution. Since you could land there, it must be a feasible solution. You now want to move away from this spot to a higher point. Each step up means that you get closer to the summit of the island. The height you reach after each step is your measure of success — your objective function. But you also consider only steps that do not lead you over a cliff. The cliffs are constraints on your movements. They limit the direction you can travel or, if a constraint is still some distance away, how far you may travel in its direction. So your rules are: make steps in a direction that is feasible, i.e. do not go over a cliff, and at the same time go uphill, i.e. improve your objective function. Once you reach a point where you cannot take another step in a feasible uphill direction, you stop having reached a top.

Local and global optima

The question now is 'Is this the highest point on the island?' If the island has only a single peak and the ground rises from the shore steadily towards this single peak from every feasible direction, even along the cliff edges, then you can be sure that you have reached the highest point even in pitch darkness. Mathematically speaking, we say that the surface of the island is **well-behaved**. In this case your algorithm will find the optimal solution.

On the other hand, if the island has many high points with peaks of various heights and possibly also some plateaux and valleys part-way up, we say that the surface of the island is not well-behaved. Then there is no guarantee that this algorithm will lead you to the highest point on the island. You could easily end up at a plateau part way up or at one of the minor peaks, i.e. a local peak rather the highest or global peak. Had you started at some different initial point, you might have reached a different local peak or even the global peak. But in the dark you can never tell!

Back to the discussion of constrained optimization! If the mathematical form is well-behaved, an algorithm which at each iteration improves the value of the objective function, while remaining feasible, will ultimately find the optimal solution. If a problem does not have a well-behaved mathematical form, then no such guarantee can be given. You might have found a **local optimum** or the **global optimum**. The vexing question is that you will never know which one.

For some types of problem we can ascertain that the mathematical form is well-behaved and hence the solution algorithm is guaranteed to find the global optimal constrained solution. Linear programming — our focus — is one of those.

Activity:
- Compare the above process of ascent with the greedy algorithm in Section 13-5.
- What happens if you combine this process and the greedy algorithm?
- If a problem has several optima, how could you try to find the global one?

14.2 A product mix example

A situation summary

Consider the following highly simplified example: An office furniture company produces ergonomic computer workstations on rollers. Each consists of a tubular frame with adjustable shelves for the keyboard, monitor, computer, printer, and other accessories. Three models are made: basic, standard, and luxury. They are sold through the firm's own retail outlets. Manufacture of the workstations consists of five operations: cutting the tubular frame pieces, welding the frames, spray painting the frames, making the shelves, and final assembly of frames, shelves, and rollers. Table 14-1 lists the labour input required for the various operations, the production capacity for each operation, the costs of the parts and supplies used, and the wholesale price of the units.

The labour capacities imply that one worker cuts tubes, while two each weld and assemble, and three make shelves. Welding, shelf-making, and assembly all require a daily setup time, hence the lost hour of production. The spray painting and curing facility has a capacity for 32 frames per day, regardless of which type.

Table 14-1   Computer workstation production problem.

Product	Cutting tubes	Welding frames	Making shelves	Assembly of unit	Material cost	Wholesale price
Basic	16 min.	25 min.	36 min.	22.5 min.	$43	$143
Standard	12 min.	22.5 min.	50 min.	25 min.	$60	$180
Luxury	20 min.	36 min.	80 min.	40 min.	$86	$246
Capacity/day	8 hours	15 hours	23 hours	15 hours		

These five capacities are technical or physical output restrictions imposed by the current production process and the facilities used. They can only be increased by adding more workers, arranging for overtime, or a change in equipment. They are hard constraints of the production process.

Marketing considerations dictate that the number of standard units should be at least equal to one third of the number of basic units. In contrast to the five hard conditions above, this condition is the result of a deliberate management policy. It can be changed by a simple management decision. It is thus a soft constraint on the choice of product mix.

Management would like to know the product mix which uses its current production capacities most effectively, while also meeting the marketing restriction. We shall interpret 'most effectively' as that use of resources which maximizes profit. Profit is the difference between the revenue generated by the output and all costs incurred. We shall arbitrarily set the basic planning period at one day.

Certain costs are fixed, regardless of the product mix, such as the various types of overhead. In the short run, even labour costs are fixed, since each worker is paid for the entire 8 hours of each working day, even if he or she may be idle for a fraction of the time. In this example, the only cost items that vary as a function of the product mix are the material cost. Therefore, an appropriate measure of performance is given by the difference between revenues and material costs. We shall call this difference the gross profit (not the usual definition for this term).

An influence diagram

The influence diagram in Figure 14-1 depicts the chain of consequences associated with the control inputs — here the product mix choice (rectangle labelled 1). A product mix choice consists of specifying the exact number of each type of workstation to produce per day. The output of prime interest to us is the gross profit (shown as the oval labelled 24). However, there are several other outputs that we must observe, namely whether or not the various operations capacities and the marketing restriction are violated or not. These are the other six ovals (labelled 5, 9, 12, 16. 20, and 22).

Figure 14-1   Influence diagram for product mix problem.

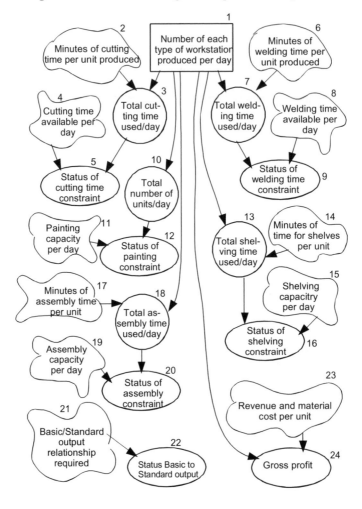

The uncontrollable inputs (shown as clouds) are given by the unit labour time for each operation and each model, the daily capacity in productive time or throughput for each operation, the Basic/Standard output mix restriction, and the unit material costs and unit revenues.

Just to remind you of the principles underlying influence diagrams (Section 5.6), we briefly review the relationships ending in output 5 ('Status of cutting time constraint'). Each model takes a given number of 'Minutes of cutting time per unit produced' (cloud 2). Given a choice of 'Number of each type of workstation produced per day' (rectangle 1), this results in the systems variable 'Total cutting time used/day' (circle 3). This total is compared to the 'Cutting capacity per day' (cloud 4). If it is less than or equal to the capacity, then the 'Status of cutting time constraint' (oval 5) is "OK", i.e. the decision choice is feasible with regard to this constraint, otherwise the status is "violated", i.e. the decision choice is infeasible with respect to this constraint.

A decision choice has to be "OK" for all six constraints to be a feasible solution. Obviously, we wish to find the feasible solution, or solutions, that maximize the 'Gross profit'. But remember, the influence diagram does not deal directly with optimization. It only traces the consequences of a given control input choice. In terms of Figure 6-9 on page 155, it only deals with system S — the narrow system of interest. Our next task is to translate system S into a mathematical model, using system M — in this case a linear programming model, to which we can then apply system O, the optimization system, to find the optimal solution.

14.3 A linear programming model

A linear programming model consists of an objective function and a set of constraints, all linear relationships. As we shall see, this means that the mathematical expressions used only involve sums of variables, where each may be multiplied by a coefficient. No expression contains products of two or more variables or powers of variables. The constraints may be in the form of inequalities, less than or equal to ($\leq$), greater than or equal to ($\geq$), or equalities ($=$).

Decision variables

A decision choice consists of the number of units produced per day for each product. Rather than denote the variables by letter symbols, such as x_1, x_2, and x_3, it is more helpful to use **mnemonic names** which suggest what the variables stand for. This is even more important if a problem involves hundreds or thousands of variables. You would need a huge list defining all subscripted letter symbol used — a nightmare! We will use the names BASIC, STANDRD, and LUXURY.

The modelling system M assumes that all decision variables may take on any value, integer or fractional that is **non-negative**. So we allow a daily production of 5.47 units of type Basic. This simply implies that a unit is started on a given day and then finished the next day. Such an assumption may reflect reality. The variable value represents the average output over many days. If this assumption is not correct, i.e. the variables can only assume integer values, then the problem has to be formulated as an **integer linear programming model**.

The non-negativity assumption reflects the nature of real-world activities, where negative activities rarely makes sense within an economic, industrial, or agricultural context. If an activity may be negative, a simple trick gets around this assumption. We replace the original variable with two variables, both non-negative, one measuring the 'positive' values, the other measuring the 'negative' values. If the 'positive' one is positive, then the 'negative' one is zero and vice versa. (Note most software now offers an option to allow negative values.)

The objective function

The 'Gross profit' (output oval 24 in Figure 14-1) is the objective function we wish to maximize. Table 14-2 how we construct the objective function from basic principles.

Table 14-2   Objective function for product mix problem.

Type	Revenue per unit	Material cost per unit	Difference per unit	Number of units/day	Gross profit per day
Basic	$143	$43	$100	BASIC	100 BASIC
Standard	$180	$60	$120	STANDRD	120 STANDRD
Luxury	$246	$86	$160	LUXURY	160 LUXURY
Total/day:		GROSSPROF = 100 BASIC + 120 STANDRD + 160 LUXURY			

The influence diagram shows that it is a function of the decision variables (rectangle 1) and the 'Revenue and material costs per unit' (cloud 23). The last line in Table 14-2 is the expression for the objective function, representing the 'Gross profit'. For any combination of values of the decision variables it has the value GROSSPROF. To indicate that it is to be maximized, we show it as

$$\text{Max GROSSPROF} = 100 \text{ BASIC} + 120 \text{ STANDRD} + 160 \text{ LUXURY} \quad (14\text{-}1)$$

The coefficients multiplying the decision variables are called the **objective function coefficients**. Note that the expression is the sum of products, each involving a decision variable and a coefficient. It is linear as required by the linear programming model.

(Figure 14-10 in the appendix to this chapter shows how an objective function in two variables can be represented graphically.)

Restrictions on decision variable choice

In addition to the non-negativity conditions, there are five hard and one soft constraints that restrict the combination of values the decision variables may assume. Each could be formulated by a pattern analogous to Table 14-2 above. Rather than write it out formally, we simply do it in our mind.

Cutting Time constraint: There are 8 hours or 480 minutes of 'Cutting time available' (cloud 4) to cut the tubular pieces that make up the frame. The 'Total time used per day' (circle 3) to produce any combination of workstations is the product of 'Minutes of cutting time per unit' (cloud 2) and 'Number of workstation produced per day' (rectangle 1), summed over all three types:

$$16 \text{ BASIC} + 12 \text{ STANDRD} + 20 \text{ LUXURY minutes}$$

This time cannot exceed 480 minutes. We show this by the symbol ≤. The cutting constraint thus becomes:

(CUTTING)   16 BASIC + 12 STANDRD + 20 LUXURY ≤ 480   (14-2)

This constraint says that the sum on the left-hand side (LHS) has to be less than or equal to the number on the right-hand side (RHS). The coefficients multiplying the decision variables are called the **left-hand side** or **LHS coefficients**, while the constant on the RHS is referred to as the **right-hand side** or **RHS parameter**. As required by the linear programming model, this constraint is again linear. (Figure 14-11 in the appendix to this chapter shows a graphical representation of an simpler version of this constraint.)

Welding time constraint: There are 15 hours or 900 minutes of welding time available per day. Hence:

(WELDING)   25 BASIC + 22.5 STANDRD + 36 LUXURY ≤ 900   (14-3)

Painting capacity constraint: Only 32 frames can be processed per day; so

(PAINTING)   BASIC + STANDRD + LUXURY ≤ 32   (14-4)

Note that an LHS coefficient of 1 is usually not shown explicitly.

Shelving time constraint:
(SHELVING)   36 BASIC + 50 STANDRD + 80 LUXURY ≤ 1380   (14-5)

Assembly time constraint:
(ASSEMBLY)   22.5 BASIC + 25 STANDRD + 40 LUXURY ≤ 900   (14-6)

Basic/Standard output mix: The daily output of Standard units has to be at least equal to one third of the number of Basic units produced. This gives the following greater-than-or-equal constraint:

$$STANDRD \geq ⅓ \ BASIC$$

The usual convention in writing down linear programming constraints is to have all parts that involve a decision variable on the LHS, while the RHS only shows a constant, which may be zero. So we subtract ⅓ BASIC from both sides. Adding or subtracting the same term on both sides or multiplying or dividing both sides by the same constant does not affect which values of the variables are admissible. This yields the following constraint:

(BAS/STD MIX)   − ⅓ BASIC + STANDRD ≥ 0   (14-7)

To be a **feasible solution** to the product mix problem, the three decision variables have to be non-negative and satisfy all six constraints (14-2) to (14-7). The **optimal solution** to the problem is the feasible solution that maximizes the objective function, as shown by expression (14-1).

This completes the formulation. The Appendix gives the graphical interpretation of a two-decision-variable version of this problem.

A linear programming model is often referred to as a **linear program** or as an **LP**. In comparison to real-life applications, the above LP is very small. Real-life product mix situations may easily have hundreds or more often even thousands of variables and constraints. Activity scheduling problems, such as the scheduling of aircraft and aircrews, or a representation of all operations of an oil company or forestry processing company — all classical applications for linear programming — may even have hundreds of thousands of variables and constraints.

Neither decision variables nor constraints need to be in the same measurement units. Some variables may be in number of units, others in kilograms, still others in tonnes, etc. Similarly, some constraints may be in minutes per day, e.g. constraint (14-2), while others may use a different measure, such as constraint (14-4) which is in units per day. All we have to make sure is that each constraint is dimensionally consistent, e.g. if the RHS is in a specified in minutes per day, each product of a LHS coefficient and decision variable must also be in minutes per day. Verify that this is the case for constraint (14-2).

14.4 Solution by computer

The optimization system O used for finding the optimal solution to an LP is known as the **simplex method**. It was developed in 1947 by the American mathematician George Dantzig. Its discussion goes beyond the scope of this text. Although it is possible to solve small LPs in a few decision variables and a few constraints by hand, the computations would take hundreds of years for even a moderate-size LP. Fortunately, there exists sophisticated LP computer software that finds the optimal solution to smallish problems of several hundred variables and constraints in seconds, and larger problems in minutes.

Some of the more sophisticated spreadsheet packages have built in **optimizer or solver functions** or **add-on mathematical programming routines**. Solvers can handle small problems quite effectively. Their accuracy deteriorates as the number of variables and constraints grows. In general, for LPs with more than 100 variables and/or constraints, you should use specialized commercial **LP software**, such as CPLEX, XPRESS, or OSL, or **mathematical optimization software**, such as AMPL, AIMMS, GAMS, or MPL, that also handle nonlinear relationships. LINDO is used as an educational LP package in some MS/OR textbooks, but is powerful enough to handle reasonable size problems.

Input to Excel Solver

Any LP computer software, whether in a spreadsheet or as a standalone package, needs to know the names of the variables and the constraints, the values of the objective function coefficients, the LHS coefficients, the RHS parameters, the form of each constraint ($\leq$, $=$, $\geq$), and whether the problem is to be maximized or minimized. This is most conveniently done as a table, like the Excel spreadsheet in Figure 14-2. The table has a column for each variable, a column for the sign of the constraint, and one for the RHS parameters. It has a row for the objective function and one for each constraint.

Figure 14-2   Microsoft Excel spreadsheet for product mix problem

	A	B	C	D	E	F	G	H
1	LP in detached coefficient form for product mix problem							
2			Decision variables					
3			BASIC	STANDRD	LUXURY		sign	RHS
4								
5	Objective: GROSSPROF		100	120	180		max	
6		CUTTING	16	12	20		$\leq$	480
7	Constraints	WELDING	25	22.5	36		$\leq$	900
8		PAINTING	1	1	1		$\leq$	32
9		SHELVING	36	50	80		$\leq$	1380
10		ASSEMBLY	22.5	25	40		$\leq$	900
11		BAS/STD MIX	-0.3333	1			$\geq$	0

The row for the objective function lists the objective function coefficient for each variable. Each LHS coefficient is inserted in the cell intersected by its corresponding constraint and variable. Fractions have to be rounded to the nearest decimal value. For greater accuracy, it pays to show sufficient decimal places, otherwise the accuracy of the results may suffer. Zero entries may be left blank.

Such a table is referred to as the **LP in detached coefficient form.** Multiplying the coefficients of each row with its corresponding variable, and summing across all variables generates the objective function and the LHS of each constraint, respectively. Hence, the table contains all information needed for expressing the mathematical relationships of the corresponding LP.

Note that row 4 and column F, both shown shaded, are unused. We will need those to prepare the input into Excel Solver. As shown in the screen image in Figure 14-3, the extra row 4 is named 'Changing cells'. These are the cells where Solver will display the values of the decision variables. Initially we leave them blank or set them to zero.

The unused column F, named 'sum' in Figure 14-3, contains the summation formulas for the objective function and for the LHS of the constraints. These formulas are simply the sum of the products of the entries in each row and the changing cells. In Excel these sums of products are obtained by the function

SUMPRODUCT(range 1, range 2),

Figure 14-3   EXCEL Solver dialog window for product mix problem.

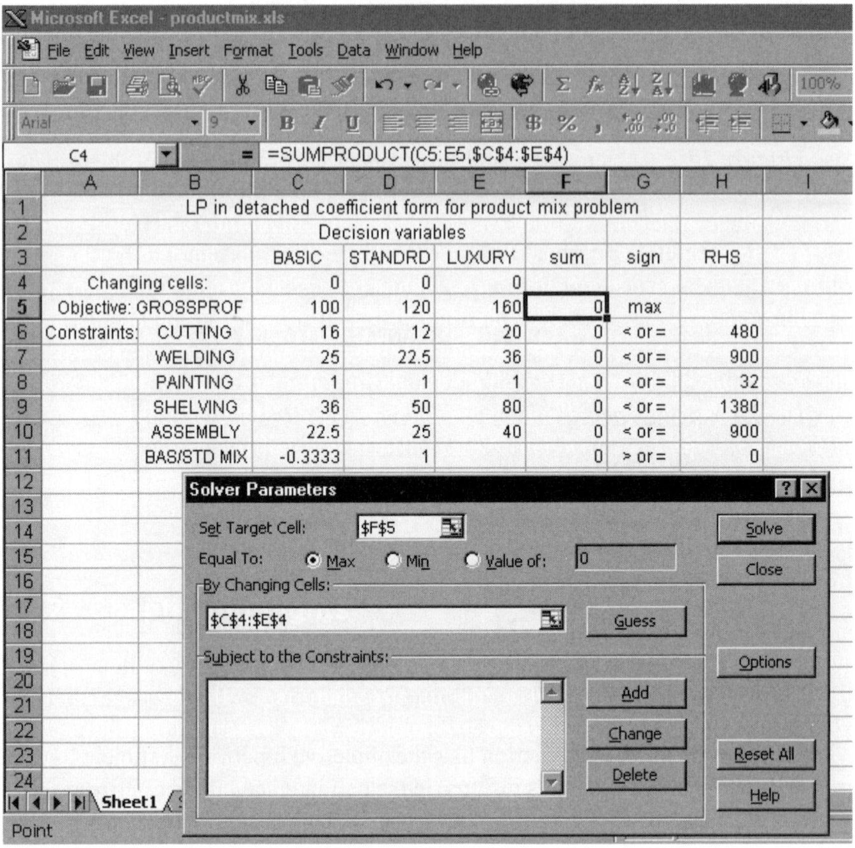

where 'range 1' refers to the objective function or LHS coefficients, and 'range 2' refers to the changing cells. The formula bar in Figure 14-3 shows an example for the value of the objective function corresponding to the values assumed by the decision variables. Since to start with the latter are all zero, the SUMPRODUCT is also zero. The formula is copied to cells F6 through F11 (with the changing cells shown as absolute cell references, using the $ sign). These values represent the level achieved by the LHS of the constraints for the values assumed by the decision variables, e.g. the resource use for constraints (14-2) to (14-6) or the excess of Standard output over its minimum of $1/3$ of Basic output.

We are now ready to invoke the Excel Solver from 'Tools' in the menu bar by clicking on 'Solver...'. The dialog box 'Solver Parameters' appears, as shown in the bottom portion of the screen reproduction in Figure 14-3, with the cursor in the top-most entry box, labelled 'Set Target Cell:'. This is the cell which computes the value of the objective function — in our example cell F5. If the problem has a feasible solution, Solver will store the optimal value of the objective function in it. To enter the cell reference, we move the cursor to the corresponding cell F5 in the spreadsheet and click on it. This is less prone to error than typing it in.

On the next line, labelled 'Equal to', we click the button for 'Max' or 'Min', depending on whether we want to maximize or minimize the objective function.

Next we click the entry box labelled 'By Changing cells' and select the cell range from C4 to E4.

Finally, we enter the constraints. These can be entered in groups, provided all constraints in a given group are of the same type, i.e. $\leq$, $\geq$, or $=$. For this reason, it is helpful to regroup the constraints into these three constraint sets first. Then only three sets of constraints have to be entered, rather than each constraint separately. The constraints in Figure 14-2 are already grouped that way.

To add a constraint or constraint set, we click 'Add...', which opens the new three-part dialog box, shown in Figure 14-4, with the cursor pulsing in the 'Cell Reference' box. Having done the preparatory summations in column F, every constraint set can simply be entered by highlighting first the corresponding range in column F, next selecting the appropriate sign in the middle box (Excel uses the forms '$<=$', '$=$', and '$>=$'), and then clicking the 'Constraint' box and highlighting the corresponding range of the RHS.

Our first set of $\leq$ constraints correspond to rows 6 to 10. So we highlight range F6:F10, select '$<=$', and then highlight range H6:H10. Clicking 'OK' enters that

Figure 14-4   Dialog box for entering constraints in Solver.

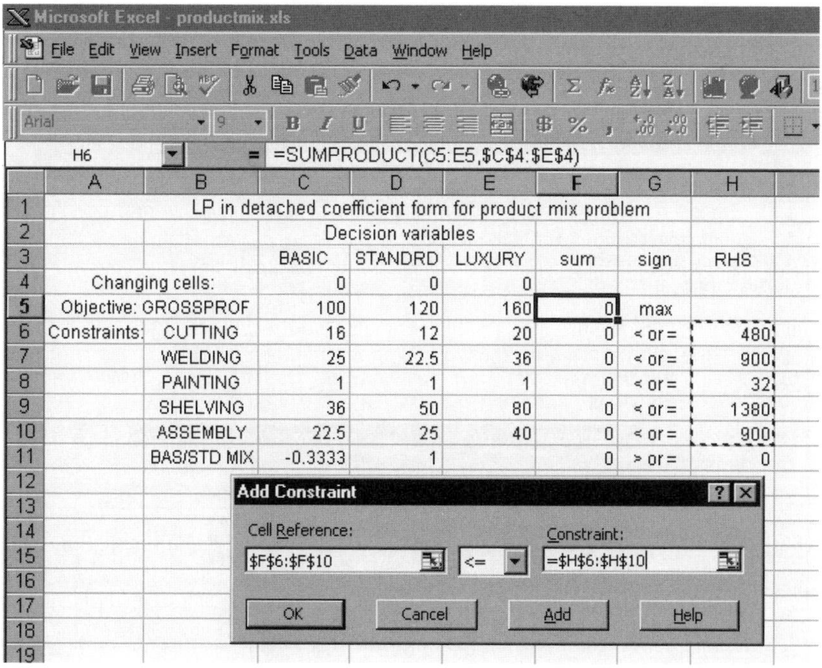

information into the dialog box in Figure 14-3. We repeat the same procedure for the group of ≥ constraints (only row 11 here).

Next we click on 'Options…', opening the 'Solver Options' dialog box, select 'Assume Linear Model' and 'Assume Non-Negative', and exit by clicking 'OK'. We now are ready to have the problem solved by clicking 'Solve'. For a problem of this size, Solver will complete all computations in less than a second. Larger problems of tens of variables and constraints may take several seconds.

Solution output of Excel Solver

At the end of the computations, Solver tells us if it found a feasible solution and if so offers us the results in three reports, as shown in the window of Figure 14-5. We must highlight those we want to see and have saved. Note that row 11 and column F in Figure 14-5 now show some non-zero values: row 11 contains the optimal values of the three decision variables, column F the optimal value of the objective function and the LHS constraint sums.

Clicking 'OK' produces the highlighted reports. You call each in by clicking on the corresponding label on the bottom line. They are reproduced in Figure 14-6 on pages 374–5. The 'Answer Report' has three parts. The top, labelled 'Target Cell' lists the optimal value of the objective function. Our product mix problem

Figure 14-5 Solver result window.

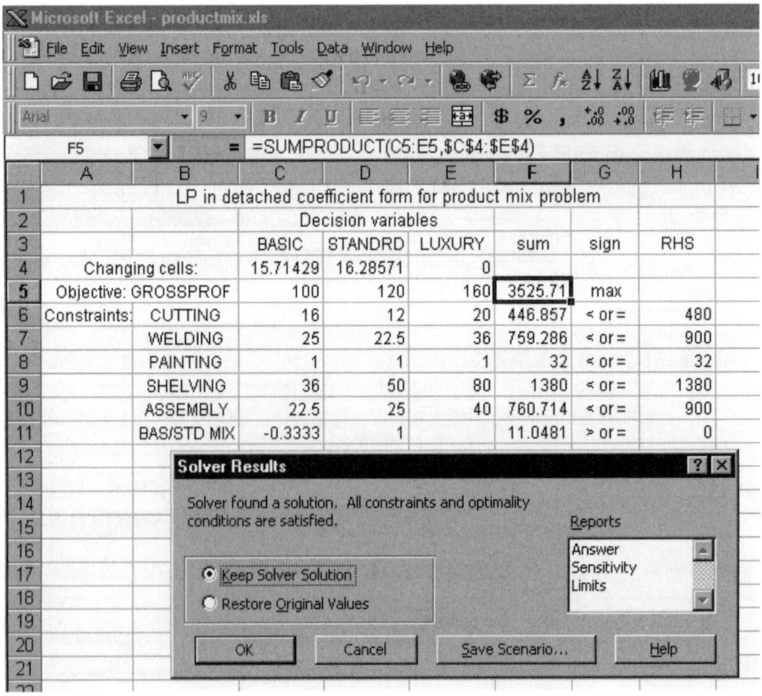

	A	B	C	D	E	F	G	H
1		LP in detached coefficient form for product mix problem						
2			Decision variables					
3			BASIC	STANDRD	LUXURY	sum	sign	RHS
4	Changing cells:		15.71429	16.28571	0			
5	Objective: GROSSPROF		100	120	160	3525.71	max	
6	Constraints:	CUTTING	16	12	20	446.857	< or =	480
7		WELDING	25	22.5	36	759.286	< or =	900
8		PAINTING	1	1	1	32	< or =	32
9		SHELVING	36	50	80	1380	< or =	1380
10		ASSEMBLY	22.5	25	40	760.714	< or =	900
11		BAS/STD MIX	-0.3333	1		11.0481	> or =	0

has a maximal value of the daily gross profit of \$3525.71. The cell is named 'Objective: GROSSPROF', reproducing the entry in the first cell to the left of the target cell that contains at least one alphabetic character. (If the width of the cell allows it will also show the content of the cell above the target cell, in our case "sum".)

The second part, labelled 'Adjustable Cells', shows the optimal values of the decision variables (the changing cells). Each is identified by its alphanumeric name entered above the corresponding variable column. The best product mix only produces 15.7143 Basic units ($15^5/_7$) and 16.2857 Standard units ($16^2/_7$) per day. Surprisingly, it is optimal not to produce any Luxury units at all in spite of their high gross profit contribution. This may not be desirable, and management may want to look into this aspect. We shall briefly do this in Section 14.5.

Recall that these numbers represent the average daily output over many days. In fact, on 5 out of 7 days 16 units are completed of each type, while on 2 out of 7, 15 units of Basic and 17 units of Standard are finished. It may also imply that work on some units is interrupted at the end of the day, to be completed the following day. If this is not possible or desirable, then some of the binding constraints may have to be marginally violated. In practice, this is usually of little concern for a problem of this sort. Not only are the LHS coefficients for the various operation times estimates of observed averages, but the actual times vary from unit to unit. The workers may on some days do a few minutes overtime, while quitting a few minutes early on others, or they simply vary their work speed a bit. Only if the constraints were of a hard physical nature would we have to adhere to them strictly. In modelling it is always important to use common sense, particularly if human aspects are involved.

The third part lists the constraints (named according to the column entries to the left of the first variable column), the constraint levels achieved (as also shown in Column F in Figure 14-5), the status of the constraints — 'Binding' or 'Not Binding'— and the differences between the RHS and the constraint level achieved, i.e. the amounts of **slack**. For the product mix problem, only two of the constraints turn out to be binding, namely the ones for the shelving time capacity and the Basic/Standard product mix. The other four operations all have various amounts of slack, e.g. there are about 33 minutes of cutting time unused.

The second report shows the result of sensitivity analysis on some of the inputs. The top part refers to the objective function. The '**Reduced Cost**' is always zero for those decision variables that assume a positive value — in our case for BASIC and STANDRD. For those whose optimal value is zero, the reduced cost represents the change in the value of the objective function resulting from forcing that decision variable to assume the value 1. (This would obviously mean that the values of some or all other decision variables would have to change for the solution to remain feasible and that the constraint set allows this.)

The reduced cost is negative or zero if the objective function is maximized, signalling a possible decrease in the objective function, and it is positive or zero if it is minimized, signalling a possible increase. So we see that setting LUXURY = 1, the

Figure 14-6 Excel LP reports.

Microsoft Excel 9.0 Answer Report

Worksheet: [productmix.xls] Sheet1

Target Cell (Max)

Cell	Name	Original Value	Final Value
$F$5	Objective: GROSSPROF sum	0	3525.714286

Adjustable Cells

Cell	Name	Original Value	Final Value
$C$4	Changing cells BASIC	0	15.71428571
$D$4	Changing cells STANDRD	0	16.28571429
$E$4	Changing cells LUXURY	0	0

Constraints

Cell	Name	Cell Value	Formula	Status	Slack
$F$11	BAS/STD MIX sum	11.04814286	$F$11>=$H$11	Not Binding	11.04814286
$F$6	CUTTING sum	446.8571429	$F$6<=$H$6	Not Binding	33.14285714
$F$7	WELDING sum	759.2857143	$F$7<=$H$7	Not Binding	140.7142857
$F$8	PAINTING sum	32	$F$8<=$H$8	Binding	0
$F$9	SHELVING sum	1380	$F$9<=$H$9	Binding	0
$F$10	ASSEMBLY sum	760.7142857	$F$10<=$H$10	Not Binding	139.2857143

Microsoft Excel 9.0 Sensitivity Report

Adjustable Cells

Cell	Name	Final Value	Reduced Cost	Objective Coefficient	Allowable Increase	Allowable Decrease
$C$4	Changing cells BASIC	15.71428571	0	100	1.333333333	13.6
$D$4	Changing cells STANDRD	16.28571429	0	120	18.88888889	0.909090909
$E$4	Changing cells LUXURY	0	-2.857142857	160	2.857142857	1E+30

Constraints

Cell	Name	Final Value	Shadow Price	Constraint R.H. Side	Allowable Increase	Allowable Decrease
$F$11	BAS/STD MIX sum	11.04814286	0	0	11.04814286	1E+30
$F$6	CUTTING sum	446.8571429	0	480	1E+30	33.14285714
$F$7	WELDING sum	759.2857143	0	900	1E+30	140.7142857
$F$8	PAINTING sum	32	48.57142857	32	1.260869565	4.4
$F$9	SHELVING sum	1380	1.428571429	1380	220	116
$F$10	ASSEMBLY sum	760.7142857	0	900	1E+30	139.2857143

Microsoft Excel 9.0 Limits Report

Cell	Target Name	Value
$F$5	GROSSPROF sum	3525.714286

Cell	Adjustable Name	Value	Lower Limit	Target Result	Upper Limit	Target Result
$C$4	Changing cells BASIC	15.71428571	0	1954.285714	15.71428571	3525.714286
$D$4	Changing cells STANDRD	16.28571429	5.237571429	2199.937143	16.28571429	3525.714286
$E$4	Changing cells LUXURY	0	0	3525.714286	0	3525.714286

objective function would change by $-2.85^5/_7$, i.e. a decrease of $\$2.85^5/_7$. This profit reduction can be explained as follows: At the optimal solution it is not advantageous to let LUXURY assume a positive value. If the solution is forced away from the optimum, its objective function value must decrease by definition.

What is the implication if the reduced cost is zero when the optimal value of the decision variable is zero? By the above definition, letting the variable become positive would cause no change in the objective function. It would remain at its current optimal value. In other words, the solution listed is not the only one that achieves that optimal value. There are **alternative optimal solution** with the same optimal objective function value.

> Activity: Explain why for variables with a zero optimal value the 'Reduced Cost' is positive (or zero) if the objective function is minimized.

The reduced cost can also be given an alternative, even more useful interpretation. If the original objective function coefficient is changed by adding to it the negative of the reduced cost, then there exist alternative optimal solutions where the corresponding variable assumes a positive value. For example, if the objective function value of LUXURY increases by $\$2.85^5/_7$ to $\$162.85^5/_7$ (i.e. we add the negative of $-2.85^5/_7$), then it would just become attractive to produce some Luxury units, reducing the number of Basic and/or Standard units accordingly. (The notation 'xE+p' means 'x times 10^p'; so '1E+30' is 1 multiplied by 10^{30}, a very large number standing for +infinity.)

For all decision variable, the Sensitivity Report also shows by how much the value of its objective function coefficient can be increased or decreased without affecting the optimal value of the decision variables. So the current optimal values of the three decision variables remain the same as long as the gross profit per unit of Basic is between $100 - 13.60$ and $100 + 2.85^5/_7$, although any change in an objective function coefficient will result in a change in the value of the objective function.

The second part of the Sensitivity Report lists, for each constraint, its **shadow price** (see Section 13.4 for the correct interpretation of this term). For example, adding one minute of overtime for the shelving operation will increase the optimal value of the objective function by $\$1.4286$ or about $\$85.70$ per hour.

In contrast to the analysis of Chapter 13, which involved a nonlinear objective function, the shadow price of an LP constraint does not change gradually as the RHS of the constraint is changed. Rather it remains constant over a given interval and then changes abruptly to a different value. This is the significance of the two columns 'Allowable Increase' and 'Allowable Decrease'. For the SHELVING constraint the optimal value of the objective function increases by $\$1.43$ for each additional minute up to a capacity of $1380 + 220 = 1600$ minutes/day, or decreases by that amount for a decrease of up to 116 minutes. So, we see that if each of the three workers in the shelving operation does 30 minutes of overtime per day (adding 90 minutes in total), profits would go up by 90 times $\$1.4286 = \$128.57$. Since this must surely be more than the cost of 1½ hours of overtime, the firm should be advised to investigate having some workers go on overtime. (Figure 14-13 in the appendix demonstrates how the shadow price for a two-decision variable problem can be derived graphically.)

Again recall that the shadow price for a constraint that has slack is zero.

The third report, entitled 'Limits Report', lists how the objective function value varies if each decision variable takes on its lowest and its highest feasible value, respectively. For instance, if STANDRD is reduced to 5.2376 (its minimum of ⅓ of BASIC), then GROSSPROF = $2199.94. Since none of the slack created is taken up by other variables, such as LUXURY, this report is of little usefulness.

> Activity: Using what you learned in Chapter 13 about shadow prices, explain why the shadow price for the SHELVING constraint will decrease (in discrete steps) as more shelving time becomes available, but will increase (in discrete steps) as the time available becomes smaller.

Number of binding constraints and number of positive optimal values of decision variables

Only two of the three decision variables in the product-mix problem assume a positive value in the optimal solution. Similarly, only two of the six constraints are binding. This is no coincidence. Regardless of the number of variables, the number that have positive optimal values is never larger than the number of constraints that are binding. Even if the choice of workstation types had been in the hundreds, at most six would ever have been chosen as optimal for production if only six constraints restricted their values. And if one or several constraints had been slack, the solution would have used even fewer types.

This relationship between the number of positive variables in the optimal solution and the number of binding constraints holds in general. It is a property associated with the mathematical structure of LP problems. For the non-mathematician — and most decision makers in business, industry, and government fall into this category — this property is a rather counterintuitive result. Most would expect that the larger number of choices that can all be pursued jointly, the larger the number that is actually used. Not so! The number of constraints dictates the variety of choice that is optimal.

Unsuccessful termination of solver

Solver may terminate without finding a solution. If no combination of decision variable values exists that satisfies all constraints simultaneously, the Solver Results window will have the message 'Solver could not find a feasible solution'.

The other unsuccessful termination is an **unbounded solution**. The Solver Result window will show the message 'The Set Cell values do not converge'. This means that the constraint set is such that some decision variables may be increased in value without upper bound and never be restricted by a constraint. Hence the objective function value can go to plus infinity.

Although theoretical problems can easily be devised that are infeasible or result in an unbounded solution, few economic or technical real-life problems are of this nature. Rather, getting this result is usually an indication of errors in the computer input or that something went wrong in the formulation of the problem. If you get either message you should painstakingly check the value of each LHS and objective function coefficient for each variable and each RHS parameter. A wrong sign — positive when it should be negative or vice versa — is an easy error to make. You may have left some LHS coefficients at zero by mistake. It is easy to enter a coefficient in the wrong column or row of the LP in detached coefficient form. Check in the 'Solver Parameter' window (Figure 14-3) whether the direction of each constraint ($\leq$ or $\geq$) has been correctly entered. A $\geq$ sign instead of a $\leq$ could let one or more variables go to infinity. If the input into your LP software is in equation form, carefully check the spelling of all variable names. One incorrect letter, and you have created a nonexistent variable which may allow another legitimate variable to become infinitely large.

If this does not remove the problem, carefully verify that all constraints have been correctly formulated. For instance, check that each constraint is dimensionally consistent. You may have to review your work more than once. Even better, have another person check it. If you are still unsuccessful you may have to go back even further and have another look at your system definition. You may have overlooked other crucial aspects — other decision choices or restrictions on them.

14.5   Effect of forcing production of luxury

The reduced cost for LUXURY is only $-2.85^5/_7$. Forcing the production of some Luxury units may thus cause only a small decrease in the daily gross profit, while giving the firm a more balanced product line. Management may consider that not offering any Luxury workstation may be detrimental to its market image. So they ask that the effect of forcing a minimum output of two Luxury units per day be studied. We add an additional constraint:

$$\text{LUXURY} \geq 2 \qquad\qquad (14\text{-}8)$$

The complete problem and its optimal solution are shown in Figure 14-7.

The CUTTING constraint now also becomes binding. The additional trade-off needed for BASIC and STANDRD to accommodate this means that the GROSSPROF (shaded F4 cell) decreases by \$5.71, i.e. by 2 times \$2.85$^5/_7$. Management should be pleased that adding a requirement of a minimum Luxury production has such a negligible effect on daily gross profits. However, the rather large shift from Standard to Basic production may be not be so desirable.

Figure 14-7   Expanded product mix problem with minimum Luxury output.

	A	B	C	D	E	F	G	H
1	LP in detached coefficient form for product mix problem							
2			Decision variables			status or slack		
3			BASIC	STANDRD	LUXURY		sign	RHS
4	Changing cells opt. values		20	10	2			
5	Objective: GROSSPROF		100	120	160	3520	max	
6		CUTTING	16	12	20	binding	≤	480
7		WELDING	25	22.5	36	103	≤	900
8		PAINTING	1	1	1	binding	≤	32
9	Constraints	SHELVING	36	50	80	binding	≤	1380
10		ASSEMBLY	22.5	25	40	120	≤	900
11		BAS/STD MIX	-0.3333	1		3.334	≥	0
12		MIN LUXURY			1	binding	≥	2

Limitations of sensitivity analysis

This little exercise also points to some of the limitations of the Sensitivity Report. It gives no information on the permissible increase in the decision variable for which it is valid. An even bigger shortcoming is the assumption of sensitivity analysis that only one input parameter or coefficient is changed at a time, with all other inputs remaining at their original values. In many situations, a change in costs or in production rates, etc., may affect more than one input. For instance in the product-mix problem, an increase in raw material costs will affect every single objective function coefficient. Similarly, management may feel obliged to offer overtime to all workers and not just those making the shelves. Again this means that several RHS parameters will change simultaneously. Furthermore, the change may affect one or several LHS coefficients. Sensitivity analysis with respect to them is very complex. In all three cases the analyst has no choice but to resolve the problem for each new configuration.

The Sensitivity Report's main value is to highlight further aspects for analysis.

14.6 Pineapple Delight case study

A situation summary

Pineapple Delight, Inc., of Queensland, Australia, owns its pineapple plantation. Most years it processes its entire harvest in its cannery. Exceptionally, some fruit is sold at the going market price to other processors. The current price for pineapple fruit sold on the market is $440 per tonne (= 1000 kg).

This coming season the crop is estimated at 24,000 tonnes. For processing, fresh fruit has to be skinned. This produces an average waste of 39.4%. Also the outer part of the skinned pineapple and its core, amounting to another 26.6%, can only be used for juice extraction. Juice is used in the finished pineapple product or sold at cost to beverage manufacturers. The balance of the flesh has traditionally been used for the premium pineapple rings. Offcuts in the form of crushed pineapple are used in fruit salad, and so on. With the market for canned pineapple rings becoming more competitive, Pineapple Delight has started to differentiate its products by marketing some output in novel shapes, such as spears and chunky pieces, or mixed with passion fruit.

Rings use 81% of the pineapple flesh, while 85% of the flesh can be cut into chunks. Flesh used for spears produces 60% spears and 28% chunks. In each case the balance of the flesh is offcuts, used for crush. Chunks are canned as chunky pieces or as passion fruit/pineapple chunks. Offcuts are used in fruit salad, fruit salad catering packs, and crush catering packs. The normal retail can has a net weight of 1 pound or 454 grams, while catering packs have a net weight of 4.54 kg. The actual fruit content of each can is about 70% of the net weight.

Table 14-3 lists the pineapple products sold by Pineapple Delight, the amount of skinned flesh, the price ex factory, and the sum of variable cutting, canning and ingredient costs (mainly sugar) for each product. It also lists the upper limit for potential sales of each finished product. Naturally, these are only forecasts. They could be affected by advertising. For simplicity, we will ignore this aspect.

Table 14-3   Pineapple Delight product information

Product	Flesh	Revenue	Cost*	Contribution	Upper limit
Rings delight	0.31 kg	$0.74	$0.12	$0.62	9 million cans
Spears delight	0.27 kg	$0.82	$0.13	$0.69	6
Passion fruit/pineapple	0.31 kg	$0.88	$0.19	$0.69	4
Chunky pieces delight	0.34 kg	$0.68	$0.10	$0.58	8
Fruit salad delight	0.16 kg	$0.92	$0.51	$0.41	7
Fruit salad catering packs	1.6 kg	$6.20	$4.05	$2.15	3
Crush catering packs	3.4 kg	$5.10	$0.88	$4.22	unlimited

*exclusive of pineapple fruit cost

The management of Pineapple Delight would like to develop an operating plan for the coming season's crop. Its objective is to maximize profits. This means determining how much of its crop should be processed in its own cannery, how much sold to other processors, and how to allocate the usable flesh from the pineapple processed in its own cannery to the various products it sells.

A material flow diagram

You will agree that the firm's operations are difficult to grasp from this account. The systemic relationships are more effectively captured by a material flow diagram.

Figure 14-8 shows the material flow associated with selling and processing pine-apples. Cloud 1 denotes the input of 24,000 tonnes of fresh pineapples. It is either processed in the firm's own cannery (circle 3) or is sold to other processors (circle 2). Some 34% of the pineapples processed in its own cannery become usable flesh (circle 5), while the rest is either waste or is used for juice (cloud 4). Most of it is used in the firm's finished products and the balance sold at cost to beverage manufacturers. Hence there is no need to keep track of the use of juice since it does not affect profits. Pineapple flesh is then allocated to the production of the three main pro-ducts: rings, spears, and chunks (circles 6, 7, 8). Each of these allocations is

Figure 14-8   Material flow for pineapple processing.

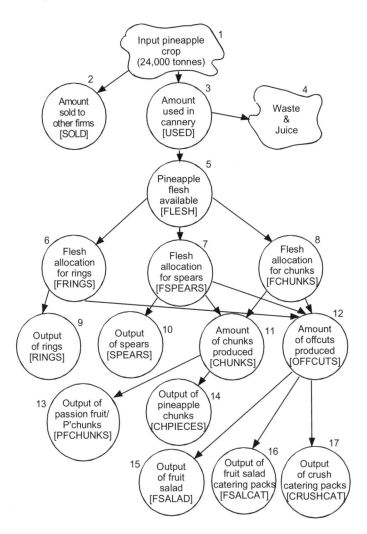

processed into its intended main product (circles 9, 10, 11), with part of it becoming offcuts (circle 12). Chunks are also a by-product of spears production. Finally, chunks and offcuts are allocated to the remaining five finished products (circles 13 to 17).

In this material flow diagram each circle represents a variable whose optimal value we wish to find. In the next section we shall see an example where it is more effective to let the arrows represent the variables.

Notice that some circles, i.e. 3, 5, 6, 7, 8, 11, and 12, refer to intermediate products, used as input into finished products, i.e. 9, 10, and 13 to 17. We will refer to all these variables as 'decision variables'. This may not be strictly true, since some of them are simply consequences of another variable, i.e. we do not have the freedom to choose their values independently of each other. For example, the amount of pineapple flesh we get for any quantity of pineapples used in the cannery is 34%. Choosing the quantity of pineapples used immediately fixes the amount of pineapple flesh available.

Variable names and units

The variable names used for formulating the mathematical relationships are the mnemonic labels shown in brackets in the material flow diagram of Figure 14-8. In the formulation all variables are measured in terms of units of 1000, either 1000 kg (= 1 tonne) or 1000 cans. This is referred to as **scaling**. It is done for two reasons. First it avoids writing all the extra zeros. More importantly, the accuracy of the computations performed by the LP computer packages increases if all LHS coefficients and RHS parameters are scaled such that they are close to 1, rather than some being extremely small, while others are very large. So, all intermediate products, including SOLD, are all measured in 1000 kg, while all finished products are all measured in 1000 cans of various weights. Also, all variables are non-negative.

Objective function

The objective is to maximize profits, i.e. the difference between revenues and costs. However, fixed costs can be ignored. They will not affect the optimal operating plans, unless it is better to close down the plant. Revenues consist of the net receipts from selling either fresh fruit or canned products, as listed under revenue in Table 14-3. The variable costs include the cost of preparing the fruit, cutting and canning it, as well as the cost of any ingredients used in the canning operation.

Should the cost of the pineapple fruit also be included? What is, in fact, the cost of the fruit? We could interpret it as the cost of harvesting it. If the entire harvest is used, either internally or sold, then this cost is a constant. Hence it can be ignored. However, if less than the entire potential harvest is used, either sold or processed, with some fruit left in the fields, then the harvesting cost becomes a function of the pineapple used and must be included. In our case, all fruit is either processed or sold, so we will exclude the harvesting cost.

Alternatively, we could say the fruit is valued at the opportunity cost of the best alternative use. This is selling it to other processors. But this is one of the options included in the linear programming model, with the receipts from selling fruit added to the total revenue. Hence, including the opportunity cost as part of the production cost would amount to double counting. This is another reason why the 'contribution' in Table 14-3 excludes the fruit cost in this example.

With the relevant variable costs directly allocated to the various finished products, the total contribution towards profit is simply given by the product of the amount of each finished product produced (and presumably sold) and its unit contribution, as listed in Table 14-3. To this we also add the receipts from fresh pineapples sold. The objective function therefore reads as follows:

$$
\begin{aligned}
\text{MAXIMIZE} \quad & 0.44 \text{ SOLD} + 0.62 \text{ RINGS} + 0.69 \text{ SPEARS} \\
& + 0.69 \text{ PFCHUNKS} + 0.58 \text{ CHPIECES} + 0.41 \text{ FSALAD} \qquad (14\text{-}9) \\
& + 2.15 \text{ FSALCAT} + 4.22 \text{ CRUSHCAT}
\end{aligned}
$$

Since all variables are in units of 1000, the objective function is also in $1000.

Processing constraints

The material flow diagram helps us in determining the constraints. We associate one constraint with the set of flows (or arrows) coming out of each cloud or circle and one constraint with each set of flows (or arrows) ending at a circle.

Starting at the top of the diagram we see two arrows coming from cloud 1 allocating the input of 24,000 tonnes of fresh fruit. One goes to SOLD, the other to USED in the firm's own cannery. Obviously, some of the crop could also be left over unused. Hence we get the following inequality constraint:

$$\text{SOLD} + \text{USED} \leq 24,000 \qquad (14\text{-}10)$$

Stepping down the diagram, the next element is the circle for the amount of pineapple flesh, denoted by FLESH, resulting from the decision USED. From the description of the operation, we know that only 34% of fresh pineapple fruit is suitable for further processing into canned products:

$$\text{FLESH} = 0.34 \text{ USED}$$

or expressed in the usual linear programming form:

$$\text{FLESH} - 0.34 \text{ USED} = 0 \qquad (14\text{-}11)$$

This is an accounting type **material balance** or **input–output constraint**.

The next constraint allocates the usable flesh for cutting into finished shapes, i.e. rings, spears, and chunks, represented by the three arrows leaving the circle for FLESH:

$$\text{FRINGS} + \text{FSPEARS} + \text{FCHUNKS} = \text{FLESH}$$

or   FRINGS + FSPEARS + FCHUNKS − FLESH = 0   (14-12)

The next layer in the diagram has four circles. So with the set of arrows leading into each one we have a separate constraint. The first one deals with the output of rings. Each unit of 1000 cans contains 0.31 tonnes of flesh. But only 81% of the flesh allocated for ring production is rings, the balance is offcuts. So we get the following relationship for rings:

$$0.31 \text{ RINGS} = 0.81 \text{ FRINGS}$$

or $0.31 \text{ RINGS} − 0.81 \text{ FRINGS} = 0$ (14-13)

and we get a similar constraint for the output of spears:

$$0.27 \text{ SPEARS} − 0.6 \text{ FSPEARS} = 0 \qquad (14\text{-}14)$$

Chunks are produced as a by-product from spears as well as from the flesh allocated specifically to chunk production, each flow associated with one of the two arrows leading into the circle for CHUNKS:

$$0.28 \text{ FSPEARS} + 0.85 \text{ FCHUNKS} = \text{CHUNKS}$$

or $0.28 \text{ FSPEARS} + 0.85 \text{ FCHUNKS} − \text{CHUNKS} = 0$ (14-15)

Verify that the amount of offcuts produced yields the following constraint:

$0.19 \text{ FRINGS} + 0.12 \text{ FSPEARS} + 0.15 \text{ FCHUNKS} − \text{OFFCUTS} = 0$ (14-16)

Finally, we have to allocate chunks and offcuts to their canned products:

$$0.31 \text{ PFCHUNKS} + 0.34 \text{ CHPIECES} − \text{CHUNKS} = 0 \qquad (14\text{-}17)$$
$$0.16 \text{ FSALAD} + 1.6 \text{ FSALCAT} + 3.4 \text{ CRUSHCAT} − \text{OFFCUTS} = 0 \qquad (14\text{-}18)$$

Note that with the exception of (14-10) all these constraints are equalities. They represent the flow of materials into or out of a node. For example, the total amount of material leaving circle 5 is equal to the sum sent along the arrows to circles 6, 7, and 8. Similarly, what is received by a given node, e.g. the circle 11, must be equal to the sum of the material coming along the arrows from circles 7 and 8.

Marketing constraints

The output of each finished product, with the exception of crush in catering packs, should not exceed its upper limit listed in Table 14-4. Hence we get the following so-called **upper bound constraint**:

RINGS ≤ 9000,	SPEARS ≤ 6000,	
PFCHUNKS ≤ 4000,	CHPIECES ≤ 8000,	(14-19)
FSALAD ≤ 7000,	FSALCAT ≤ 3000	

Optimal solution

This linear program was solved using the Microsoft Excel Solver. The maximal value of the objective function is 17,662.95. Since the objective function is in units of $1000, the total contribution is $17,662,950. Information on all variables and all inequality constraints at the optimum is listed in Table 14-4. The shadow prices for the equality constraints are not shown since their interpretation is rather complex and beyond the scope of this text. When interpreting these numbers, remember that they are in units of 1000 kg or cans, respectively. Similarly, the reduced costs and the shadow prices are in thousands of dollars.

Table 14-4 Optimal solution to Pineapple Delight.

Product	Variable	Optimal value	Reduced cost	
Pineapples sold	SOLD	0	−0.1215	
Pineapples processed	USED	24000	0	
Usable flesh	FLESH	8160	0	
Flesh allocated to rings	FRINGS	3444.4	0	
Flesh allocated to spears	FSPEARS	2700	0	
Flesh allocated to chunks	FCHUNKS	2015.6	0	
Chunks produced	CHUNKS	1280.8	0	
Rings	RINGS	*9000	0.0856	
Spears	SPEARS	*6000	0.2343	
Passion fruit chunks	PFCHUNKS	*4000	0.1612	
Chunky pieces	CHPIECES	3615.4	0	
Fruit salad	FSALAD	*7000	0.195	
Fruit salad catering packs	FSALCAT	100.5	0	
Crush catering packs	CRUSHCAT	0	−0.3487	

Constraint	Equation	Status	Slack	Shadow price
Total fresh fruit	14-9	binding	0	0.5615
Upper limit on rings	14-18	binding	0	0.0856
on spears	14-18	binding	0	0.2343
on passion fruit chunks	14-18	binding	0	0.1612
on chunky pieces	14-18	slack	4384.6	0
on fruit salad	14-18	binding	0	0.195
on fruit salad cat. packs	14-18	slack	2899.5	0

*variable at its upper limit

What-If analysis

No catering packs of crush are produced. The output of fruit salad catering packs is only 100,500 cans. It is conceivable that this is too small for effective marketing of this product. The firm may wish to increase its marketing effort for retail cans of fruit salad to absorb the crush allocated to catering packs. It would imply raising the upper limit on fruit salad by about 1000 units of 1000 cans or one million cans — one seventh of the current output. The shadow price for the upper limit on fruit salad is 0.195, or $195 per 1000 cans. It turns out that this shadow price is valid for any conceivable increase in the upper limit (not shown!). Hence if the upper limit on fruit salad can be lifted to at least 8 million cans through further advertising at a cost of less than $195,000 (= $195 times 1000), such a switch would be advantageous.

We could have obtained the same answer using the reduced costs. The reason is that the interpretation of the reduced cost is more complex for decision variables that are upper bounded, as is the case for most of the final pineapple products sold. These cannot exceed the limits imposed by marketing considerations. If such a variable has a zero value in the optimal solution, the meaning of the reduced cost is the same as defined for the product-mix problem. However, if the variable has an optimal value equal to its upper bound, such as is the case in this problem for RINGS, SPEARS, PFCHUNKS, and FSALAD, the reduced cost (for a maximizing problem) will be positive. It then indicates the improvement in the maximal value of the objective function resulting from increasing this upper bound by one unit. The reduced cost for FSALAD is 0.195 — the same as the shadow price for the upper bound constraint on fruit salad.

All fresh fruit is processed internally. None is sold. The reduced cost coefficient for SOLD indicates that the total profit contribution would decrease by 0.1215 (= $121.50/tonne) for every unit increase (= 1 tonne) of SOLD. It may be useful to ask 'What increase in price for fresh fruit would be required before selling some or all fresh fruit becomes attractive?' The reduced cost for SOLD again provides us with the answer. Its negative is the minimum price increase needed for the variable SOLD to assume a positive value without reducing the objective function. The market price for fresh fruit would need to increase by $121.50/tonne to at least $561.50 (= $440 + $121.50).

This is also the increase in contribution realized by increasing the amount of pineapple crop by 1 tonne, as indicated by the shadow price of the total fresh fruit constraint (14-9). Hence if the firm can acquire fresh fruit on the open market for less than $561.50 it could increase its profits by the difference for each additional tonne processed, up to a maximum of 5158.4 tonnes (not shown!).

14.7 A transportation problem

An application of high practical importance deals with transportation problems. Goods are available in limited quantities at several sources and required in given quantities at various destinations. There is a cost of transporting the goods between sources and destinations. The problem consists of satisfying the requirements at all destinations so as to minimize the sum of all transportation costs. The shifting of soil and rocks in the highway construction problem referred to in the introduction to this chapter is an example of a transportation problem.

A production/transportation problem situation

Remember the Heinz tomato paste logistics case in Section 12.10? The problem consisted in finding the optimal number of railcars for transporting tomato paste from factory X to conversion plant Y. Obviously, Heinz processes tomatoes at several factories and has quite a few conversion plants scattered all over the USA. Consider the following (hypothetical) example. There are tomato processing plants in Stockton and Riverside, California, and Tuscaloosa, Alabama. There are five conversion plants: Los Angeles, Dallas, Chicago, Atlanta, and Newark.

Table 14-5 summarizes the unit transportation cost from each tomato processing plant to each conversion station, the unit processing costs at each processing plant, the production capacity at each processing plant, and the tomato paste requirements at each conversion plant during a given 4-week period. For example, the transportation cost from Stockton to Chicago is $54 per tonne, Stockton's production cost is $524 per tonne, and it has a production capacity of 4600 tonnes for the given 4-week period, while Chicago has a requirement of 1600 tonnes for the corresponding 4-week period. (The 4-week requirement period for the conversion plants is offset by one week from the 4-week production period for the processing plants to take the transportation time delay into account.) The firm would like to determine the production schedule which has the lowest total production and transportation cost.

Table 14-5 Input data for a transportation problem.

Sources	Production cost	Capacity tonnes	Transportation cost to destinations				
			LA	Dallas	Chicago	Atlanta	Newark
Stockton	$524	4600	$25	$48	$54	$67	$75
Riverside	$541	2900	$11	$44	$57	$61	$81
Tuscaloosa	$612	1700	$57	$33	$32	$10	$36
Amount required in tonnes			2100	1700	1600	1300	2200

As in the previous example, a material flow diagram makes the transportation problem much more transparent. The network in Figure 14-9 depicts the flow of goods from the three source nodes to the five destination nodes. Each arrow from a source node to a destination node depicts a shipping option. For instance, the arrow from Stockton to Chicago represents the option of shipping goods from Stockton to Chicago. The amount shipped along that arrow is denoted by the mnemonic variable STCH, using the first two letters of each name, shown in bold next to the arrow.

Note that, in contrast to Figure 14-8, the flow of material from sources to destinations is represented by the arrows, rather than by the circles. If all options are available, the number of arrows leaving each source is equal to the number of

Figure 14-9   Goods flow diagram for transportation problem.

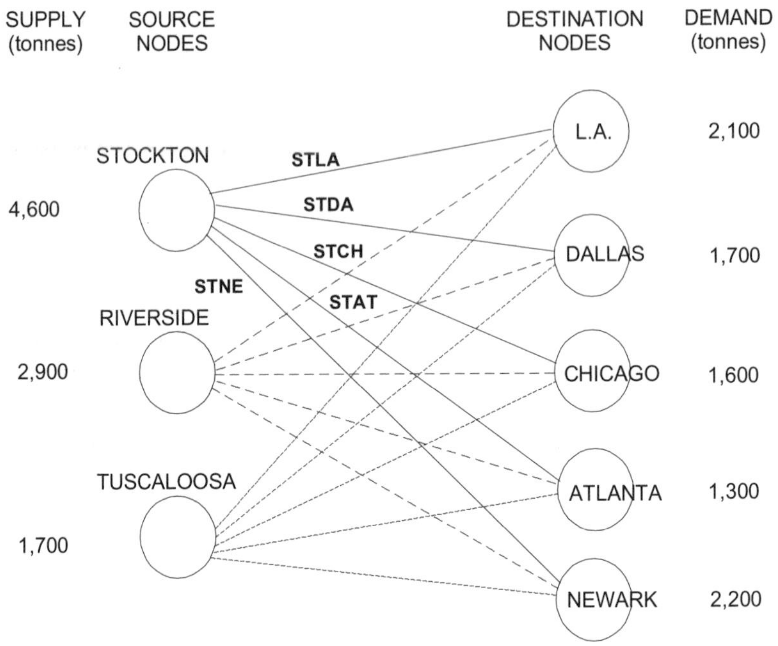

destinations, denoted by n, while the number of arrows entering each destination is equal to the number of sources, denoted by m. The total number of variables is therefore equal to m times n, i.e. 3 times 5, or 15.

The network flow diagram again helps us in determining all constraints. As in the previous example, we associate a constraint with each set of arrows leaving a source node (the nodes issuing material) and one with each set of arrows entering a destination node (the nodes receiving material).

Availability or supply constraints

Consider the five arrows leaving the Stockton node. Each represents the amount shipped from Stockton to one of the five destinations. It is obvious that the total amount shipped from Stockton cannot exceed Stockton's capacity of 4600 tonnes for the four-week period in question. So we get the following constraint, called **a supply constraint**:

$$\text{STLA} + \text{STDA} + \text{STCH} + \text{STAT} + \text{STNE} \leq 4600 \qquad (14\text{-}19)$$

Each of the other two sources has a similar supply constraint:

$$\text{RILA} + \text{RIDA} + \text{RICH} + \text{RIAT} + \text{RINE} \leq 2900 \qquad (14\text{-}20)$$

$$\text{TULA} + \text{TUDA} + \text{TUCH} + \text{TUAT} + \text{TUNE} \leq 1700 \qquad (14\text{-}21)$$

Requirement or demand constraints

The arrows entering the destination nodes represent the amount shipped from each of the three sources. We have to ensure that each destination gets exactly what it requires. So, we get the following **demand constraint** for Los Angeles:

$$STLA + RILA + TULA = 2100 \qquad (14\text{-}22)$$

The demand constraints for the other four destinations are:

$$STDA + RIDA + TUDA = 1700 \qquad (14\text{-}23)$$
$$STCH + RICH + TUCH = 1600 \qquad (14\text{-}24)$$
$$STAT + RIAT + TUAT = 1300 \qquad (14\text{-}25)$$
and $$STNE + RINE + TUNE = 2200 \qquad (14\text{-}26)$$

Obviously, this problem only has a feasible solution if the total amount available at all sources is at least as large as the total amount required at all destinations. Verify that our problem has an excess capacity of 300 tonnes.

Objective function

The objective is to minimize total costs. In a transportation problem the relevant cost includes only the transportation costs. However, in our example the variable production costs at the three tomato processing plants differ. Furthermore, there is 300 tonnes excess processing capacity. Hence, not all processing plants will operate at full capacity. The total production cost will depend on which plants are left with excess capacity. As a consequence the production costs become a relevant cost. For example, from Table 14-5 it follows that the relevant cost of allocating one tonne of goods from Stockton to Chicago is equal to the variable production costs at Stockton of $524 plus the transportation cost from Stockton to Chicago of $54, or a total of $578.

The total cost is equal to the product of the unit allocation cost, computed from Table 14-5, and the amount shipped, summed over all allocation options:

$$
\begin{aligned}
z = \ & 549\,STLA + 572\,STDA + 578\,STCH + 591\,STAT \\
& + 601\,STNE + 552\,RILA + 585\,RIDA + 598\,RICH \\
& + 602\,RIAT + 622\,RINE + 669\,TULA + 645\,TUDA \\
& + 644\,TUCH + 622\,TUAT + 648\,TUNE
\end{aligned}
\qquad (14\text{-}27)
$$

Activity: If the total supply is smaller than the total demand, the nature of the problem changes to one of allocating the goods so as to maximize net profits.
- How does this change the supply and demand constraints? (Hint: One of more of the destinations will not have their demand met completely.)
- What revenue and costs would enter into the objective function coefficients?
- Can variable production costs be ignored if total supply equals demand?

Optimal solution

The problem has $m + n$ or $3 + 5 = 8$ constraints, plus the 15 non-negativity constraints on the decision variables. It was solved using Microsoft Excel Solver. The optimal solution has a cost of $5,202,300. The production/transportation schedule is listed in Table 14-6. Note that Tuscaloosa ends up with an excess capacity of 300 tonnes.

Table 14-6   Optimal production/transportation schedule.

Destinations Sources	LA	Dallas	Chicago	Atlanta	Newark	Total shipped
Stockton	0	900	1600	0	2100	4600
Riverside	2100	800	0	0	0	2900
Tuscaloosa	0	0	0	1300	100	1400
Total received	2100	1700	1600	1300	2200	

The optimal solution has some interesting features. As expected, the expensive Tuscaloosa plant does not work at full capacity. Far more unexpected though is that the optimal transportation schedule does not necessarily select the cheapest options. For example, Stockton ships nothing to Los Angeles — its cheapest option — but supplies almost the entire Newark requirement — its most expensive option. How can this rather counterintuitive result be optimal?

The answer lies in the relative total unit cost differences between the various shipping options from a given source. If Stockton supplied Los Angeles while Riverside shipped to Newark, there would be a $3 unit cost saving for Stockton shipments, but a $21 additional cost for Riverside shipments, or a net increase of $18.

The third interesting feature is that all decision variables assume integer values, although we did not put any restriction into the formulation that all shipments had to be in integer tonnes. It turns out that this is a general characteristic of all transportation problem solutions, provided that the availabilities at all sources and the requirements at all destinations are also integers.

Other problem situations disguised as transportation problems

The tomato problem above involved transporting goods **over space**, i.e. from several locations to several other locations. However, goods can also be 'transported', figuratively speaking, **over time** from a given period to a later period. For example, a firm has a production capacity that fluctuates in a known pattern over time, while it also has to meet a demand that varies in a different pattern over time. So production in, say, March is stored in inventory until it is used in June. Obviously there is a cost associated with storing goods. Furthermore, the firm may in fact have the option of adding more production capacity by going to overtime, again at a cost. The firm would like to find a production and storage schedule, including the use of overtime, so as to minimize the total relevant cost. That cost includes the cost of storing goods for later use and the cost of regular and overtime production. (Any option that implies meeting demand in a given period by production in a later period is ruled out by simply penalizing it with a prohibitive cost.) This is often referred to as the **regular time/overtime production scheduling problem**.

A related situation is the **assignment problem**. Here we have a number of jobs that need to be done and a number of people to do them. Due to differences in training and experience, the people differ in their aptitude or suitability to do the various jobs. The problem is to find the best match of people and jobs. This can again be viewed as a sort of transportation problem. The people become the sources, the jobs the destinations. Each source has an availability of 1. Each destination has a requirement of 1. The objective function is to maximize the sum of the 'suitability indices' of the people-to-job assignments. With all RHS parameters equal to 1 and the optimal solution being integer, each job is assigned to one person only. There are no split or partial assignments.

(The assignment problem was actually used by George B. Dantzig, the inventor of the first efficient solution algorithm for LPs, to prove that monogamy is the optimal social structure. When asked at a press conference in the late 1940s to explain in lay terms what the linear programming 'model' was, he used the following allegory: Assume that 100 men and 100 women get shipwrecked on a deserted island with no hope of any rescue in their lifetime. They decide to pair off men and women. But they wish to find the optimal set of pairings that maximizes happiness for their isolated society. This is an assignment problem. Since its optimal solution will have no split assignments, say several men partially assigned to one women, but only all or nothing assignments, this proves that monogamy is the optimal solution, i.e. the optimal social structure. As in real life, not all matches will be ideal, but viewed overall no other assignment will have a greater total happiness. My difficulty with this little story is 'how did George Dantzig think he would be able to determine the happiness indices for all possible pairings?' By having all possible 100^2 pairing be tried out? This might well take for ever and the preferences might change over time!)

14.8 Chapter highlights

- If all relationships — constraints and the objective function — are linear and all variables continuous, then a constrained optimization problem can be formulated as an LP and solved by LP computer software using the Simplex algorithm. The optimal solution provides useful sensitivity analysis.
- At the optimal solution,
  - the number of decision variables that can assume positive values is at most equal to the number of binding constraints;
  - the shadow price of a binding constraint is (normally) positive; it is the change

in the optimal value of the objective function for a unit change in the RHS of the corresponding constraint;
- slack constraints have zero shadow prices;
- the reduced cost tells us by how much the original objective function coefficient has to increase or decrease before the corresponding variable becomes a candidate to assume a positive value in the optimal solution.
• The transportation problem deals with finding the optimal schedule of
  - transporting goods over space from sources with limited availabilities to destinations with minimum requirements, or
  - allocating production capacity in given periods to meet demand in the same or later periods, i.e. 'transporting goods over time'.
• The assignment problems assigns 'people' to 'jobs' to best use their skills.
• Both problems are special types of LP that result in integer solutions.

Exercises

1. A manufacturer of camping trailers is offered a contract with the leading local distributor for producing two types of trailers, A and B, to the specifications supplied by the distributor. Trailer A offers a net profit per unit of $600, while B's unit profit is $900. A and B would share the same assembly and painting facilities. Type A requires 2 person-weeks of assembly time per unit, B requires $3\frac{1}{3}$ person-weeks per unit. There are 20 person weeks of assembly time available per month (= 5 people for 4 weeks each). The painting facilities can handle a maximum of 8 trailers per month. The distributor would leave it to the manufacturer to determine the product mix, provided that at least two trailers of type A would be available, and the number of type A is at least $\frac{1}{3}$ of the number of type B produced. This is to guarantee an acceptable product mix.
   (a) Draw an influence diagram for this problem.
   (b) Use it to formulate the problem as an LP with the objective of maximizing total monthly profits.
   (c) Enter the problem in a spreadsheet as an LP in detached coefficient form and prepare it for input into Solver or similar software.
   (d) Use it to find the optimal solution and verify that all constraints are met. What is the optimal number of each trailer to produce? What is the monthly profit?
   (e) How much should the manufacturer be willing to pay for additional assembly time per person week? How much for increasing the throughput of the painting facility by one unit?

2. Management in the product-mix problem of Section 14.2 is dismayed that no unit of the Luxury workstation are recommended in the optimal solution. They therefore add a soft constraint, requiring a minimum output of at least 4 Luxury units per day.
   (a) Add an appropriate constraint for this requirement and resolve the problem by computer. How has the solution changed in terms of binding constraints?
   (b) What is the daily cost to the firm of this new requirement?
   (c) Interpret the shadow price of this constraint. Why is it correct that it is negative?

3. A cabinet maker would like to use the current excess capacity in the factory to produce a combination of three different types of bathroom cabinets. The table below lists labour requirements for the various operations per unit and other input data:

Product	Cutting time	Gluing time	Sanding time	Finishing time	Profit/ unit
Modern	24 min.	60 min.	20 min.	160 min.	$60.00
Provincial	36 min.	90 min.	60 min.	120 min.	$60.00
Colonial	48 min.	60 min.	60 min.	180 min.	$56.00
Capacity	8 hours	15 hours	8 hours	32 hours	per week

(a) Formulate this problem as an LP, maximizing weekly profits for the additional activity.
(b) Solve this problem. What is the optimal solution?
(c) The cabinet maker considers introducing overtime for some of the operations. Which ones are possible candidates and what is the maximum overtime premium the cabinet maker should consider paying?
(d) The optimal solution does not produce any colonial cabinets. The cabinet maker has been approached by a bathroom dealer to supply at least 1 colonial cabinet per week. Using the information on sensitivity analysis available from the computer printout, how much would the cabinet maker's weekly profit decrease if one colonial cabinet is produced per week? How much larger would the increase in the unit profit for colonial have to be before it would become attractive to produce colonial cabinets?

4. An insurance company has £100 million of funds available for investments. It has a choice of three types of investment of unequal risk: Blue-chip shares that offer an annual return of 6% with a risk rating of 1, government bonds at 4% with a risk rating of 0, and somewhat more risky industrial real estate that offers a return of 10% with a risk rating of 2.5. The choice is restricted by risk considerations, as well as legal constraints. Legal requirements are that at least 30% of the investment has to be in government bonds. The amount invested in real estate should not exceed 1.5 times the amount invested in blue-chip shares. The average risk rating should be no more than 1.2 (it is computed as the weighted average of the risk rating). The objective is to maximize the annual weighted return.
(a) Formulate this problem as an LP.
(b) Solve it by computer.
(c) How would you reformulate this problem so that you could give management an answer of how to plan their investments which meet these conditions regardless of the amount of funds that becomes available?

5. During the construction of a reservoir dam, large quantities of aggregate for concrete mixing have to be prepared at some or all the four possible sites with sufficient quantities of deposits and then transported to the concrete mixing plant near the dam:

Deposit site	Available m³	Cost/m³
River-dredge material site A	8,000	£3.20
River-dredge material site B	16,000	£4.50
Island aggregate site C	8,000	£2.80
River bar aggregate site D	6,000	£4.00

The costs cover preparation and transportation to concrete mixing plant. Three different aggregate blends are required at the quantities and additional costs shown:

Blend	Specifications	Cost/m³	Requirement
1	$(A + B) \leq 50\%$, $C \geq 10\%$, D no limit	£4.80	6,000 m³
2	$(A + B) \leq 60\%$, $C \geq 10\%$, $(C + D) \leq (A + B)$	£4.20	15,000 m³
3	$A \geq 20\%$, $(C + D) \geq 0.5(A + B)$	£5.40	8,000 m³

Formulate this problem as an LP minimizing total costs. Find the optimal solution.

6. The Western Paper Company (WPC) operates a cardboard plant in Seattle. The plant has been operating at only 75% capacity, producing 2700 tonnes per month at a total cost of $77.33 per tonne. Included in the total cost per tonne is the cost of wastepaper, one of the major raw materials used. For each 100 tonnes of product, 80 tonnes of wastepaper are required. Up to 1440 tonnes of wastepaper per month can be purchased locally at $18.75 per tonne. Additional wastepaper may be purchased through brokers at $27.50 per tonne delivered to the plant. Of the present total monthly costs at the plant, $59,400 is estimated to be fixed costs not dependent on the output level of the plant. The remainder of the cost varies in proportion to the output level. WPC has a second plant in Oregon. That plant is operated currently at 60% capacity, producing 3600 tonnes per month at a total cost per tonne of $85.00. Local wastepaper at the Oregon plant costs $20 per tonne and is limited to 4000 tonnes per month. Again, additional wastepaper can be purchased through brokers at the same conditions as for the Seattle plant. Of the present operating cost at the Oregon plant, $108,000 is fixed cost.
   (a) Determine the variable cost per tonne of producing cardboard at each factory.
   (b) The firm wants to determine the optimal output at each plant to produce the current combined output of 6300 tonnes per year. The objective is to minimize total combined production costs. Formulate this as an LP.
   (c) Find the optimal solution.
   (d) Using the information on sensitivity analysis provided by the LP computer printout, answer the following questions:
   • What is the additional cost of increasing the combined output to 6400 tonnes per year?
   • What are the shadow prices for locally available wastepaper at each plant?
   • Due to a slump in demand, the wastepaper broker approaches WPC offering the possibility of a substantial discount on wastepaper. What is the maximum price WPC would be willing to pay for wastepaper bought from the broker at each of the two plants?

7. BULL DIESEL produces two specialized lightweight diesel trucks. Production is done in four departments: the metal cutting and press department, engine assembly, Model A final assembly, and Model B final assembly. The monthly production capacities are as follows:
   • The metal cutting and press department can either produce 1200 Model A or 857.14 Model B, or any corresponding combination of the two.
   • The engine assembly department has an assembly capacity that can assemble either 800 Model A engines or 1200 Model B engines or any corresponding combination of the two.
   • The two final assembly departments have the following capacities: 800 Model A, 600 Model B. Note that each model can only be assembled on its own dedicated assembly line.
   BULL can currently sell as many trucks as they can produce. However, dealers insist on a balance between the two models. In particular, they want to receive no more than twice as many of Model A as of Model B. This has not been a problem in the last few years. BULL tended to produce considerably more Model B trucks than Model A, since according to the accountants standard cost imputations Model B is much more profitable than Model A, as can be seen from the table below (currency: euros):

Standard costs of production for:	Model A	Model B
Materials and purchased parts	7,400	5,900
Direct labour:		
Metal cutting and press	1,200	900
Engine assembly	900	1,300
Final assembly	2,400	1,800
total labour	4,500	4,000
Overhead allocation:		
Shared manufacturing overhead	1,512	1,584
Final assembly overhead	4,008	1,696
subtotal	5,520	3,280
General overhead 25% of above	1,380	820
total overhead	6,900	4,100
Total cost	18,800	14,000
Net selling price	20,000	18,450

Overheads for the two shared manufacturing departments (metal cutting and press, and the engine assembly), expected to total €1,404,000 per month, are allocated to the two models in terms of the direct labour costs for these two departments, based on the preliminary plan of producing 300 Model A and 600 Model B trucks each month. Monthly overheads for the two final assembly departments are forecast at €1,202,400 for the Model A assembly department and €1,017,600 for the Model B department. The predicted monthly general overhead of €906,000 is allocated to the two models as 25% of manufacturing overheads. Note that the manufacturing overhead included 20% fringe benefits (vacation pay, pension fund contributions, insurance, etc.) on direct labour costs. The figures shown for direct labour above are exclusive of fringe benefits.

At the regular monthly planning session, the chief executive voiced his concern about the company's profit performance. The marketing manager immediately pointed out that it was impossible to raise the price of Model A trucks to yield a profit comparable to the Model B truck. He suggested that serious consideration should be given to dropping this model from the product line. He asked the production manager by how much the output of Model B could be increased by such a move. The production manager took out his calculator and, after 20 seconds, responded: 'About 200 more, but only if the Model A assembly line is converted to the production of Model B trucks! That would cost roughly €500,000!' The marketing manager nodded and expressed the opinion that most dealers would welcome an increased output of Model B, particularly if they were made aware of the firm's current plans to develop two new models for introduction in about 18 months time. The company's vice-president of finance objected to this suggestion. She pointed out that the seemingly bad profit margin on Model A was caused by trying to absorb the entire fixed overhead of the Model A assembly department with only a small number of units produced. She suggested that the firm should explore the possibility of producing more Model A trucks. The production manager interjected that this would only be possible by reducing the output of Model B trucks, although he thought that it would be possible to buy in engines to the required specifications from another engine manufacturer. This would obviously be considerably more expensive. At this point in the discussions, the chief executive decided that additional information was needed before a decision could be reached. He asked the production manager to inquire about the cost of buying in engines and report to him as quickly as possible. He asked the marketing manager to investigate the response of some of the important dealerships about the possibility of dropping Model A, as well as whether the market could absorb up to 800 Model B trucks, as well as possibly more Model A trucks, without forcing a price reduction in either model. Five days later the production manager reported that engines to the required specifications could be purchased for €5,980 for Model A engines and for €6,910 for Model B engines. Purchasing engines from outside would also reduce material costs by €1600 for each truck. Obviously, no engine assembly costs would be incurred. Assume that you are the chief executive's analytic assistant. He asks you to analyse this situation. In particular, he wants recommendations about the following points:

(a) Should Model A be dropped from the production line and the output of Model B increased to 800 by converting the assembly line for Model A to Model B assembly?

(b) Should output of Model B trucks even be increased beyond 800 by purchasing engines from outside suppliers? If purchase of engines from outside suppliers is not on the cards at the current prices quoted, he would like to know the maximum price the firm would be willing to pay.

(c) Is the suggestion of the vice-president of finance to increase production of Model A units by reducing the output of Model B trucks or buying in engines a better solution than either of the two above? Again, he also wants to know the maximum price the firm should be willing to pay for engines purchased from outside.

Note that all questions can be answered by using a single model that allows all possible options and letting the model determine the optimal solution. Identification of relevant costs is an integral part of this exercise. (This exercise has been liberally adapted from an example in W.L. Berry *et al.*, *Management Decision Sciences*, Irwin, 1980, pp. 88–91.)

8. One of the earliest successful applications of linear programming deals with diet or feed-mix problems. A feedlot farmer has just bought a herd of 200 young steers for fattening up. He feeds his animals on a carefully chosen combination of various feeds, such that they get just the right combination of nutrients in the form of starch, protein, and fibre. The table below lists the currently available feeds, the percentage by weight of the three nutrients, and their cost per 100 kg:

Feed	starch	protein	fibre	cost (€)
Potatoes	18.8	0.82	0.89	8.00
Swedes	7.4	0.68	1.12	5.50
Lucerne	6.9	3.1	6.15	8.80
Meadow hay	33	3.8	25.5	10.40
Dried grass	52.4	9.5	19.6	15.60
Barley	71.1	6.4	5.3	17.80
Wheat	71.8	9.4	2.2	18.90
Soya beans	68.9	17.8	4.1	27.50

The Government farm consultant advises him that if he wants his steers to grow at a rate of 0.5 kg per day, each animal needs a daily nutrient intake of at least 4 kg of starch, 0.5 kg of protein, and 0.5 kg of fibre. The farmer would like to know which combination of feeds to choose so as to meet these requirements at least cost.

(a) Formulate this problem as an LP.

(b) Find the optimal solution by computer. What quantities of each feed does he have to prepare and mix each day to feed the herd? What is the total cost?

(c) How much cheaper would meadow hay have to become before it would become an alternative feed choice to use?

9. Continental Meats, a Dutch sausage factory in Tilburg, produces two types of sausages: beef frankfurters and luncheon meat. The firm uses by-products from other company divisions, in particular its chain of butcher stores, as major inputs into sausage production, namely pork trimmings, pork heads, beef trimmings, and mutton. The recipes for beef frankfurters and luncheon meats allow considerable flexibility in the inputs, as long as certain other specifications, such as fat and water content, are met. The production manager of Continental Meats is confident that these two products can be produced from a wide range of inputs, while still maintaining product quality in terms of flavour, colour, and texture. The specifications for beef frankfurters require that: (1) the total fat content cannot exceed 31% of the finished product; (2) the total moisture must not exceed four times the protein content; (3) the amount of pork must be between 20% and 40% of the finished product; (4) the content of mutton cannot exceed 30%; and (5) the content of beef trimmings has to exceed 45%. For luncheon meat the recipe states that it can contain any combination of mutton, beef trimmings, and pork, provided that: (1) the content of pork is at least 15%; (2) fat content cannot exceed 40%; (3) moisture content has to be at most 47%; and (4) the protein content has to be at least 12%; and (4) mutton cannot be more than 35% of the total input into luncheon meat.

   Although the different batches of the various inputs used vary slightly in terms of their fat, protein, and moisture composition, the production manager is confident that production plans can be based on past averages. These are as follows:

Input	Content of: Fat	Protein	Moisture
Pork trimmings	61.7%	6.5%	28.9%
Pork heads	70.2%	4.5%	23.8%
Beef trimmings	12.2%	19.1%	66.0%
Mutton	15.3%	18.7%	64.3%

   The current selling price per kilogram is 8.60 for beef frankfurters and 5.90 for luncheon meat. Although about 80% of the total inputs used come from other company divisions, with the balance purchased from external suppliers, the production manager considers that the value of the inputs received from other company divisions should be equal to the cost from external suppliers. The latest schedule specifies the following price schedule: pork trimmings 4.80; pork heads 2.85; beef trimmings 5.90; and mutton 2.80. However, the total amount of pork heads available from other company divisions, as well as other external sources is limited to about 2000 kg per week.

   Marketing has supplied the following information about average weekly sales requirements: beef frankfurters between 4000 and 8000 kg; luncheon meat between 4000 and 6000 kg. The firm's daily production capacity is 2000 kg. The factory works 5 days per week. The wage cost for the production workers amounts to 4236 per week. This includes variable overheads (fringe benefits) of 18%. Other production costs, such as other ingredients used (salt, pepper, spices, etc.), casings for the sausages, and electricity, amount to 0.27 per kg of output. The production manager's salary, including fringe benefits, is 2800 per month. The sausage production department also employs an office clerk who is paid 586 per week, including fringe benefits. The sausage department is assessed a charge for facility rental and general overhead contribution, totalling 8,800 per week.

   (a) The production manager would like to have a detailed weekly production schedule, specifying exact quantities of each sausage type produced, together with an exact schedule of input requirements. Obviously, that schedule should maximize profits.

Formulate this problem as an LP and find the optimal solution. Note that identification of the relevant cost factors is an integral part of this exercise.

(b) He would also like to know whether to schedule some overtime. Overtime amounting to up to 20% per week can be scheduled, at a wage premium of 50%. Overtime increases the maximum daily output proportionately. How much overtime should he schedule? Why?

(c) He has just learned from a colleague across the Belgian border that there are up to 500 kg of pork heads available there on a weekly basis. Pork heads sell for the same price as in Tilburg. However, there would be an additional cost of 0.70/kg incurred for the packing and transport under refrigeration from Belgium to Tilburg. Should he buy these pork heads? Why?

(d) The product quality supervisor approaches the production manager with the request that some pork trimmings should be used in place of pork heads in the production of beef frankfurters. This would improve the texture of the final product. Since the recent appearance of frankfurters imported from Germany, such an improvement might be important for Continental to maintain its share of the market. What effect would this have on the weekly profits?

10. A car rental firm projects the following distribution of its most popular rental model for the coming Monday, listed as 'available', in contrast to its ideal planned distribution, listed as 'planned':

Location	A	B	C	D	E	F
Available	18	6	22	11	7	4
Planned	12	9	15	18	6	6

Note that the planned distribution requires fewer cars than are available. Cars can be transferred between locations at the following cost/car in £:

To		A	B	C	D	E	F
From	A	0	48	92	65	74	126
	B		0	115	58	35	88
	C			0	50	78	105
	D				0	44	65
	E					0	38

(a) Draw a flow diagram similar to Figure 14-9.
(b) Use the diagram to formulate the corresponding LP.
(c) What is the least-cost redistribution schedule? Which location ends up with more cars than planned?

11. A firm faces a seasonal demand for its products. The firm has the policy to maintain a stable workforce, although the workforce can be scheduled to work overtime up to 25% of its regular time capacity. Goods produced in any given month are available for sale in the same months. Any goods produced in a given month can be stored in inventory for sale in a later month at a cost of £4 per unit per month stored, assessed on the ending stock of each month. The regular time capacity of the plant is 6000 units per month. Each unit produced during regular time has a cost of £250, while a unit produced on overtime has a cost of £260. The firm faces the following demands over the coming 6 months:

Month	1	2	3	4	5	6
Demand	3000	4500	6500	9000	7000	6500

Demand cannot be back ordered.
(a) Draw a flow diagram similar to Figure 14-9.
(b) Use it to formulate the corresponding LP.
(c) Find the optimal regular time/overtime production schedule.

12. Nordic Forest Corporation (NFC) of Norway is planning its production schedule for the coming month. NFC is currently logging two forests, F1 and F2. The logs harvested are used either in NFC's sawmill or in its pulp mill. Some of the logs can also be exported to England. The table below lists the average output of each forest per day, the maximum percentage of logs suitable for processing by the sawmill or for export (export logs need to be straight, otherwise they take too much space in the ship's hold), and the cost of harvesting and of transporting the logs from each forest to the plants or to the export port. Logs not suitable for the sawmill or for export can only be used for pulp. Export logs fetch €200/cubic metre.

Logs processed by the sawmill are converted into construction timber and dressed timber in the proportions shown below. Offcuts and scraps are transferred to the pulp mill for use there. The conversion proportions shown are fixed and cannot be altered, i.e. they are not decision variables.

Forest		F1	F2
Upper limit to log output in cubic metres		128	192
Maximum percentage of logs harvested			
suitable for sawmill and export		41%	55%
Cost of harvesting logs		€12.40	€13.20/cubic metre
Transport cost to	sawmill	€4.20	€6.60/cubic metre
	pulp mill	€3.20	€4.50/cubic metre
	port	€6.20	€5.60/cubic metre
Log conversion at sawmill: Construction timber		60%	40%
Dressed timber		30%	48%
Scrap and offcuts		10%	12%
Transport cost sawmill to pulp mill		€2.40/cubic metre	

The sawmill has an average capacity of 6 hours per day; the remaining 2 hours for the shift are used for maintenance. Processing one cubic metre of logs into construction timber takes 0.06 hours of sawmill capacity, while processing one cubic metre of logs into dressed timber takes 0.12 hours of sawmill capacity. Obviously scraps and offcuts are simply a by-product of the sawmill process. Construction timber sells for €150/cubic metre, while dressed timber sells for €300/cubic metre. NFC wants to meet the demand for construction timber of at least 32 cubic metres per day, while the output of dressed timber should not exceed 40 cubic metres per day. The processing cost for construction timber is €15/cubic metre and for dressed timber €25/cubic metre.

Logs, scraps, and offcuts are converted into chips at the pulp mill. The chips are then processed into pulp, used for newsprint production. Each cubic metre of wood yields 0.5 tonne of pulp which has a value of €340/tonne and incurs a processing cost of €40/tonne. The pulp mill can process up to 160 cubic metres per day. NFC has to meet firm contracts for pulp of 60 tonnes per day.

Management of NFC would like to know its best daily operating schedule, in terms of allocation of logs to the various uses, and output of final products, so as to maximize net profits. The fixed costs of operating the sawmill amount to €6,000 per day, while they amount to €12,000 for the pulp mill. Administrative overheads run at €5,000 per day.

(Note that most integrated forest products processing companies use OR/MS methods to help them determine suitable operating plans. Obviously, their problems are much more complex, involving logs of different qualities with different conversion rates into final products, as well as modelling their operations in greater detail.)

(a) Develop a diagram depicting the material flow for this situation, similar to the one shown in Figure 14-8. However, you may find it easier to have the flows associated with the arrows, and let the nodes represent either sources, processes, or uses. This will be helpful for part (b) below.

(b) Formulate this problem as a linear program. Use a formulation that corresponds to your material flow diagram, i.e. showing variables for intermediate and final products, as well as for the log supply. Use and define mnemonic names for the decision variables and label each constraint clearly (such as `sawmill capacity constraint'). Note that in this example, it may be easier to associate decision variables with the arrows, rather than the circles.

(c) Solve the problem using an LP computer package, e.g. Solver in Excel.

(d) Show the numerical values of your solution on the flow diagram developed under (a) above, by attaching to each arrow the value of the corresponding decision variable.

(e) Management is considering the possibility of shifting all or part of the maintenance work on the sawmill to overtime. What increase in profit can be achieved for an additional hour of capacity? It is also possible to add an additional logging gang to forest F1 at a daily cost of €480. The additional gang would be able to log up to 32 cubic metres of logs per day. Should NFC consider this option? Why or why not? The marketing manager would like to launch a campaign to increase sales of dressed timber, since it seems to provide such a high contribution towards profits. Should he be encouraged to do this? What would be the consequences of it and why?

You can find many LP formulation problems in any MS/OR introductory text.

Appendix: Graphical solution to an LP

Some insight into the form of the solution, the results of sensitivity analysis, and the general nature of the solution algorithm can be gained by studying the graphical representation of an LP and finding the optimal solution graphically. However, this restricts us to problems that have only two decision variables.

Recapitulation of revised product-mix problem

Since the product-mix problem does not recommend the production of Luxury work-stations, the problem reduces to a two decision variables, with BASIC and STANDRD as the only variables. Dropping the LUXURY variable from all expressions, we get the following LP:

Objective function:

$$\text{Maximize GROSSPROF} = 100 \text{ BASIC} + 120 \text{ STANDRD} \qquad (14\text{-}1\text{A})$$

subject to

Cutting constraint:	$16 \text{ BASIC} + 12 \text{ STANDRD} \leq 480$	(14-2A)
Welding constraint:	$25 \text{ BASIC} + 22.5 \text{ STANDRD} \leq 900$	(14-3A)
Painting constraint:	$\text{BASIC} + \text{STANDRD} \leq 32$	(14-4A)
Shelving constraint:	$36 \text{ BASIC} + 50 \text{ STANDRD} \leq 1380$	(14-5A)
Assembly constraint:	$22.5 \text{ BASIC} + 25 \text{ STANDRD} \leq 900$	(14-6A)
Basic/Standard mix:	$-\frac{1}{3} \text{ BASIC} + \text{STANDRD} \geq 0$	(14-7A)
Non-negativity:	$\text{BASIC} \geq 0, \text{ STANDRD} \geq 0$	

Graphical representation of LP

Each expression involves only two variables. Hence it can be graphed in two dimensions, with values of BASIC along the Y-axis and the values of STANDRD along the X-axis. Each point in the positive quadrant and along the two axes represents a combination of non-negative values for the two decision variables. For any given value of GROSSPROF, equation (14-1A) is a straight line. Any straight line is defined by two points. So, we simply find two points and then draw the straight line that goes through both. Say GROSSPROF = 3600. Two convenient points can easily be found by setting each variable in turn to zero and solving for the other one. For BASIC = 0, STANDRD must be 3600/120 = 30, and for STANDRD = 0, BASIC becomes 3600/100 = 36. So the two points are (30, 0), falling on the X-axis, and (0, 36), falling on Y-axis, as shown in Figure 14-10. Drawing a straight line through these points gives all combinations of BASIC and STANDRD that yield a GROSSPROF of 3600. It is called an **isoquant** or **equal profit line.** Two additional lines for a

GROSSPROF of $2400 and $1200 are shown. They are parallel to the first. As GROSSPROF increases the corresponding lines move parallel up and to the right.

Each of the constraints restricts the values of the decision variable to a given region. To identify that region, we draw the straight line corresponding to the constraint satisfied as an equality, using the same procedure as above. Figure 14-11

Figure 14-10   The graph of the objective function.

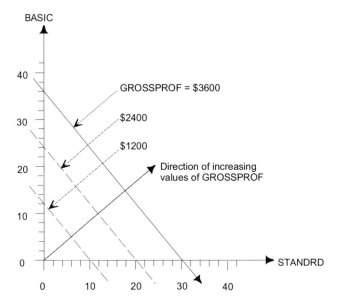

Figure 14-11   The graph of the cutting constraint.

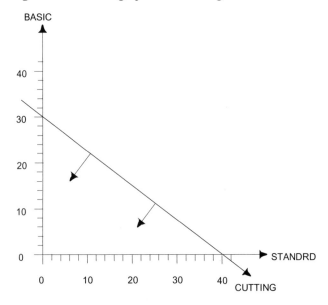

shows the region of permissible variable values for the cutting constraint as the area below and to the left of the constraint line.

Figure 14-12 shows the lines for all six constraints on the same graph. Only those combinations of values for BASIC and STANDRD that satisfy all constraints including the non-negativity conditions simultaneously are admissible. The set of all those admissible points is called the **feasible region**. It is the shaded area in the positive quadrant.

Figure 14-12 The feasible region and the optimal solution.

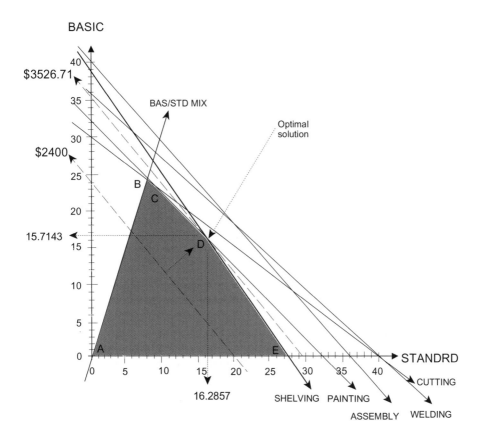

The feasible region is bounded by four of the six constraint lines — CUTTING, SHELVING, PAINTING, and BAS/STD MIX, as well as the non-negativity condition on BASIC, while the constraint lines for WELDING and ASSEMBLY lie outside the feasible region. Neither restricts the two decision variables. They are so-called **redundant**. We could delete them from the formulation. For problems in more than two variables, it is usually difficult to determine whether a constraint is redundant or not and no attempt is made to identify and drop them. With fast computers, it hardly matters that leaving them in marginally increases the computation time. Also, to get the correct ranges for the shadow prices it is essential that they remain.

For finding the feasible region we only needed the constraints. The objective function does not enter into consideration. It only becomes relevant when we want to find where in the feasible region the optimal solution is located. For this we see what happens when we push the equal-profit lines to higher and higher values.

For a value of $2400, the equal-profit line has a whole segment inside the feasible region with a multitude of other feasible solutions that lie on higher equal-profit lines. The highest permissible equal-profit line which still has at least one point in common with the feasible region is at the intersection of the PAINTING and SHELVING constraints. It has a value of $3525.71. All equal-profit lines for larger values are completely outside the feasible region. So $3525.71 is the maximal value of the objective function. It corresponds to values for BASIC of 15.7143 and STANDRD of 16.2857.

The optimal solution implies that painting and shelving time are completely used up — they are binding — while all other constraints have various amounts of slack.

Insights on the solution method

From the way the equal profit lines slide parallel to themselves through the feasible region it follows that the optimal solution must always lie somewhere along the boundary of the feasible region. It is either at a corner point, also referred to as an **extreme point**, such as in our example, or along any point on a segment of a constraint line that forms part of the boundary of the feasible region. The latter occurs if the isoquants for the objective function — the equal-profit lines in our example — are parallel to one of the constraint lines. If this is the case, there is an infinite number of alternative optimal solutions. Any point along the boundary segment that coincides with the optimal isoquant is a candidate, including its two adjacent corner points.

These insights motivate the solution algorithm used for finding the optimal solution. Remember the South Sea island treasure hunt! Hence we start at some corner, such as the origin — point A in Figure 14-12. At A, the objective function is zero, i.e. we are still at sea level. We want to move away from it in a direction that increases the value of the objective function. But we also know that we only need to search along the boundary of the feasible region — in fact only for corner points with a higher objective function value. So, rather than searching in an infinite number of direction through the interior of the feasible region, we stay on the boundary. At each iteration we try to find an adjacent corner point that is better. So, from A we could either move to point B (along the BAS/STD MIX constraint line) or to point E (along the X-axis). One possible selection criterion is to move in the direction that gives the steepest rate of increase in the objective function. It can be shown that this is in the direction of B. So we go along the edge of the BAS/STD MIX constraint. At point B we are stopped by the CUTTING constraint. We now have completed the first iteration of the search algorithm, ending at an improved solution. We start a new iteration, searching again for a direction of improvement. Of the two directions along an edge, one leads back to where we just came from — no good. The other follows along the edge of the CUTTING constraint to point C, where it intersects the PAINTING constraint — only a short hop. This further improves the objective function value. The third iteration leads us along the PAINTING constraint to point D, where it intersects the SHELVING constraint. The fourth iteration shows that no direction of improvement can be found anymore. We have reached the optimal solution.

This is, in very broad terms, what the simplex algorithm does.

Sensitivity analysis

In Figure 14-13, we briefly look at changes in the objective function coefficients and changes in the RHS parameters of resource-type constraints. The two slack constraints ASSEMBLY and WELDING are deleted to unclutter the diagram.

Figure 14-13 Increasing RHS parameter of SHELVING.

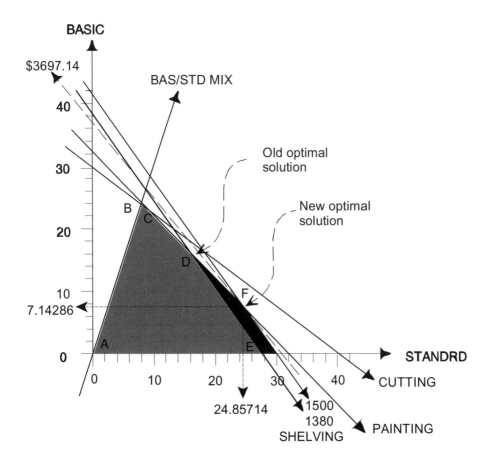

The slope of the isoquants for GROSSPROF determines at which corner point of the feasible region the optimal solution occurs. A change in one or the other objective function coefficient will change that slope. For example, if the gross profit contribution for BASIC increases (while the one for STANDRD remains the same), the slope will tilt counter-clockwise. When it is parallel to the PAINTING constraint line, point C becomes an alternative optimal solution, together with point D, as well as any point along the line from D to C. A little bit of thought will tell you that in this example the isoquant for the objective function is parallel to the PAINTING constraint line if both objective function coefficients are the same. So the change in the Basic gross profit needed is an increase of £20. Then both coefficients are £120. This is also what the Solver Sensitivity Report shows in the top line of the Adjustable Cells list.

Adding more shelving time shifts the SHELVING constraint line up and to the right, as shown in Figure 14-13. To achieve a clearer shift, I add two hours of shelving time. The RHS of the constraint goes to 1500. It intersects the PAINTING constraint line not at point D, but at point F. The feasible region is enlarged by the dotted area. The isoquant for the objective function can now be pushed up to point F also (broken line in graph). Its value increases by $170.43 to $3697.14, or by $170.43/120 = $1.42 $6/7$ per additional minute. This is again confirmed by the shadow price in the Solver Sensitivity Report in its 'Constraints' list.

15
Uncertainty

"Everybody complains about their memory, but no-one complains about their judgement."
La Rochefoucauld (1613–1680)

The approaches to decision making within systems discussed so far implicitly assumed that if we take a given action, we can predict the resulting effect on the system with (absolute) certainty. In many problems, our knowledge of the situation actually may be good enough to satisfy this assumption, at least in a practical sense, if not in theory. Situations of this sort are called **deterministic**.

For example, XL Bakers has a firm contract with the Big-G chain of supermarkets for delivery of 2000 loaves of white sandwich-sliced bread each day of the week. It enjoys a deterministic demand for that portion of its sales. Accordingly, it can make firm decisions regarding the number of loaves to be baked to meet that demand.

More often, however, the exact outcome that results in a given situation or from a given event may not be known in advance — in other words, may be **uncertain**. Take again XL Bakers. It has a firm contract to supply each of the 13 stores of the rival Bargain Barn chain daily with sufficient bread to satisfy customer demand, with the obligation to take back any bread that is not sold within 24 hours after delivery. On some days, all bread delivered to a given store is sold within the 24-hour period. In fact, had XL stocked more, all or a portion of the additional amount stocked might have been sold too. On other days it may have to take back from the same store dozens of unsold (stale) loaves. XL may be able to predict how many loaves are sold on average by each store, but not how many will be sold on any specific day. So, it faces an uncertain demand picture for that part of its daily operation.

And then there are situations which are unique, in the sense that they will not repeat themselves in similar way, or even if they do, we may have not experience about them or no way to make comparisons. We may be able to list some or most of the possible outcomes, but how could we assess the likelihood of each?

Situations where we cannot predict which particular outcome will occur are referred to as **uncertain, risky, stochastic, or probabilistic**. The approaches used for decision making under certainty may not be appropriate any longer. Even the form or structure of the decision itself may need to be different. Rather than using decisions in the form of open-loop controls, it may be more appropriate to resort to decision rules involving closed-loop or feedback controls. Such decision rules are referred to as **strategies**.

The first three sections of this chapter explore the meaning, causes, and types of uncertainty. Section 15.4 then looks at how uncertainty is expressed in everyday language, and how we try to deal with uncertainty through various approaches to forecasting future events. The concepts of objective and subjective probabilities and the biases, fallacies, and difficulties associated with assessing subjective probabilities are the topics of Sections 15.6 and 15.7. Sections 15.8 and 15.9 explore the meaning of random variables and their measures of central location and variation, while the last two sections address the problems of how to reduce uncertainty and the decision criteria relevant in the face of uncertainty.

The chapter does not deal with the computational rules of probability and statistical data analysis. It assumes that you are familiar with their most elementary operations. Its aim is to enhance your understanding of the meaning of uncertainty on a conceptual level. This will hopefully lead to a more informed grasp of decision making under uncertainty.

15.1   Linguistic ambiguity about uncertainty

Uncertainty is an everyday occurrence. Just consider the large number of words in the English language related to this concept: chance, probability, likelihood, possibility, risk, hazard, fortune, random, stochastic, odds, to expect, believe, feel, or guess that something will or might happen, to name just a few. In fact, this proliferation of words may be an indication of the ambiguity, even of a certain degree of confusion, associated with the notion of uncertainty.

What is the meaning of phrases like 'There is a possibility that...' or 'It is very unlikely that...'? Table 15-1 shows the responses to everyday language phrases indicating uncertainty to various degrees, with 0 denoting absolute impossibility and 100 absolute certainty. They were obtained from a group of over 500 students in a first-year university course. For comparison, a group of 40 older students (average age 33) in an executive-type MBA course was also asked the same questions. Their responses are shown in parentheses. The wide range of responses for both groups indicates highly divergent interpretations, even for statements suggesting a very high or a very low likelihood. No wonder that such statements lead to confusing and contradictory interpretations.

Such ambiguity is not only exhibited by the 'person in the street'. 'Experts' and professional people, such as economic advisers or national security advisers to governments, or judges in courts of law, are equally prone to it. C.W. Kelly and C.R. Peterson [*Probability estimates and probabilistic procedures in current-intelligence analysis*, Gaithersburg, MD: IBM, 1971, pp. 4-1, 4-2] report on a test involving a group of national security analysts. They were asked to give a numeric probability interpretation for the statement 'The cease-fire is holding, but it could be broken within the next week.' The author, a colleague of the group interviewed, intended the sentence to mean that there was a 30% chance of the

Table 15-1 Interpretation of statements about uncertainty.

Phrase	Assigned probability in percent		
	10th percentile	Median	90th percentile
It is highly likely that ...	75 (50)	90 (80)	95 (90)
There is a much better than even chance that ...	55 (50)	70 (65)	75 (75)
It is improbable that ...	5 (10)	20 (20)	40 (40)
There is a fair chance that ...	40 (35)	50 (50)	65 (70)
It is very unlikely that ...	5 (5)	10 (20)	25 (40)
It is quite possible that ...	30 (50)	60 (60)	80 (75)
It is almost impossible that ...	1 (3)	5 (5)	10 (30)
It was sunny today; it is likely to stay fine tomorrow.	40 (50)	50 (57)	75 (75)
The likelihood of a strong earthquake in the Los Angeles area next year is quite high.	10 (20)	60 (60)	80 (80)
The probability of a serious nuclear power plant accident anywhere is quite small.	2 (5)	10 (18)	40 (50)

cease-fire being broken. However, most of the other analysts thought that it meant a probability of 50% or higher.

Peter Wyden [*Bay of Pigs*, New York: Simon and Schuster, 1979, pp. 89–90] reports on an instance where such divergent interpretation may have led to a serious international incident. In early 1961, President Kennedy ordered the Joint Chiefs of Staff to study the CIA's plan for an invasion of Cuba by expatriate Cubans. The general in charge of the evaluation concluded that its chances of overall success were 'fair'. Interviewed on this affair several years later he revealed that he intended this to mean a 30% chance. He recalled "We thought other people would think that a 'fair chance' would mean 'not too good'." When the report was sent to the White House, it stated 'This plan has a fair chance of ultimate success.' It is quite possible that this misinterpretation of the word 'fair' led President Kennedy to authorize this mission, which ended in disaster for the invaders and humiliation for the USA.

Surveys of judges and jurors indicate that the commonly used court-room statement 'beyond a reasonable doubt' is variably interpreted as anywhere from 50 to 100% chance of guilt. This is rather alarming for both the innocent accused and the victim of a guilty accused.

The ambiguity of language and the widely differing interpretations given to statements about uncertainty suggest that numerical statements about the probability of an event would lead to clearer understanding and, consequently, to better decision making. Although this will be so in many cases, even probability statements may not be unambiguous, as we shall see in Section 15.7, nor will it necessarily lead to more rational decision making.

Activity: Cover the numerical answers shown in Table 15-1 and then fill in your own. Once finished, critically (in the sense of careful judgement and judicious evaluation) compare yours with those in the table. Explain the differences.

15.2   Causes of uncertainty

Uncertainty about the exact nature of some phenomenon, some process, or the precise state of a system at a given point is due to one or any combination of the following four reasons:

1. The most common reason is that the process or event in question is not known or understood in sufficient detail. Many physical phenomena, like the weather, or whether a coin flipped into the air will land head or tail, or the time, strength, and duration of the next earthquake at a given location, are all processes that we do not fully understand yet or for which it would be prohibitively expensive and time consuming to gather all relevant information. Clearly, if the processes that cause earthquakes could be understood to their last details, there would be nothing inherently random about the next earthquake in San Francisco, California, or in Wellington, New Zealand — two cities on highly active earthquake faults. So uncertainty is often a result of our ignorance or incomplete knowledge.

2. The second reason is that statements about a phenomenon or process are based on incomplete information. For instance, a statement about the percentage of all television viewers tuned in to a given station at a given time is, for cost reasons, usually based on a sample of some 500 to 1000 viewers, rather than the entire population of all viewers at that time. It is an estimate and hence it will only be exactly correct by coincidence. In other words its accuracy is uncertain. The uncertainty is again due to ignorance, except that this time it is ignorance by design. This type of uncertainty can be eliminated by surveying the entire population (provided no measurement errors occur).

3. A third important reason, particularly for economic phenomena, but also for competitive sports and games, is the inability to predict what moves other actors in the real world, like competitors, customers, employees, or the Government, will make, and which could affect the outcome. Such moves may be made completely independently of our own decisions or may be in response or in anticipation of our decisions. Take again the example of bread delivery. If — and this includes many sub-'ifs' — it were possible to ascertain by 6 p.m. each day exactly how many loaves of bread each of the supermarkets' potential regular and casual customers will buy over the 24-hour time span starting the next day at noon, then the bakery would know how many loaves of bread to bake and to supply. Clearly, such detailed information is not known, nor can it be reliably collected. Hence, the demand for bread remains uncertain.

In some team sports, such as football, it is often impossible to predict what kind of strategy the opposing team will attempt to use. In other sports, such as cricket or tennis, past observations of the players' favourite strokes or placement of the ball will give a good indication of the play.

4. The final and increasingly less important reason for uncertainty is measurement error about a phenomenon due to mistakes made by the observer or improper gauging or functioning of measuring instruments, both unknown to the observer. These measurement errors may lead to the conclusion that any variability observed is inherent in the phenomenon measured, rather than a result of the measuring process. But even if it is known that the measuring process may lack accuracy, the results obtained still involve uncertainty. They are estimates of the true values, not the true values themselves.

15.3 Types and degrees of uncertainty

Most of the uncertainties relevant to systems or faced by individuals or firms deal either with the numerical value (quantity, size, etc.), or the qualitative attribute (on, off; for against, etc.), associated with the phenomenon of interest, or with its timing. A firm being uncertain as to the size of the demand for one of its products during a given time period in the future, or at what price raw materials will have to be purchased next month on the commodity market, are examples of uncertainty about the numerical value of a phenomenon. The time between consecutive arrivals of patients at an accident and emergency facility is an example of uncertainty about timing, as well as the number of arrivals, since an ambulance attending an accident may bring in several people at the same time. Finally, the batsman in a cricket match does not know what kind of ball the bowler will deliver next—its qualitative attribute is unknown prior to being bowled.

The degree of uncertainty may vary from knowing almost nothing about the process or phenomenon to knowing almost everything. For instance, a firm preparing a cash flow budget (a plan of the timing and amounts of cash receipts and cash disbursements over a given time interval) may know exactly the timing and amounts of cash needed for disbursements over the first two weeks, have fairly accurate data on disbursements for the next four weeks, with less and less reliable information the further in the future these disbursements occur. For the far distant future, only rough average guesstimates may be available, since these events are influenced by many other unknown events, like the level of production, etc., which in turn depend on the level of sales in the far future.

When we are dealing with events involving competitors, any predictions about their responses may be even more precarious. We may not even have a complete list of all possible alternative courses of action available to them and their consequences for us. Similarly, for the introduction of a novelty product or service, a firm may have little to go on for predicting how successful it will be. Furthermore, knowledge about new technology, even just a few years from now, may be hazy or even completely absent — a case of complete uncertainty.

In the decision literature, we usually talk about **decision making under risk** if it is possible to list all outcomes and make numerical statements about the likelihood of each. If neither condition is met, then we talk about **decision making under complete uncertainty**. (However, 'decision making under uncertainty' is often loosely used for denoting both types!) As we shall see in later chapters, the approaches used for dealing with these two cases are radically different.

Activity:
- For each of the four causes/reasons listed in Section 15.2, find two new examples that differ in their nature and explain why they match the cause/reason.
- Find two new examples of uncertain size, uncertain timing, and both.
- Find two new examples that fit the case of risk and the case of complete uncertainty

15.4 Prediction and forecasting

Much of the uncertainty faced by decision makers deals with future events. How can we foresee the future? For thousands of years, the search for an answer has given rise to all sorts of professions: shamans, seers and soothsayers, travelling fortune-tellers, and high priests of all sorts, who often exploited their position of power and control over those that believed in their abilities. Economists and treasury officials are the modern version of these gurus (and they are usually highly paid too and too often no more successful in their predictions!).

Persistence prediction

At least a partial answer to 'How do we foresee the future?' is: 'By studying the past!' Even in the turbulent and often chaotic world we live in, there are some threads of continuity and stability. The phenomenon in question is said to be **stationary**. It does not change character, form or range of possible outcomes, or if its range changes, such a change itself is stable. So the first step toward prediction is the identification of characteristics that have persisted and have exhibited some degree of stability over time — hence the name persistence prediction. It is by far the simplest approach!

Persistence prediction is good for phenomena that remain at the current position or exhibit relatively small variations in a completely unpredictable pattern. It could be likened to the erratic movements of a drunk who, after struggling to his feet, is equally likely to simply fall right over again or teeter in any direction — a so-called **random walk**. Short-term daily fluctuations in share prices or foreign exchange rates, when these markets are in a stable phase, follow a random walk in response to the unpredictable entry of buyers and sellers .

In weather forecasting, persistence prediction is almost as good as the forecast developed with highly sophisticated monitoring equipment, complicated air-mass theories, and running computer programs on very fast computers for hours. In fact, in many areas with relatively stable weather patterns, comparisons show that the weather office is only about 10% more often correct than the simple prediction that tomorrow's weather will be the same as today's. This is not because the methods used by the weather office are so bad. Rather, it is because persistence prediction is so good.

So, predictions about the number of newspapers sold each day at a location subject to a highly regular and stable pedestrian traffic pattern, such as at a corner on Piccadilly Circus, or for that matter in most suburban shopping malls, can safely be based on the average number sold in the most recent past. The sales pattern is stationary. The prediction error — the difference between the forecast and the actual realization — will on most days be fairly small, particularly if such factors, as the day of the week, etc., are also taken into account in the prediction.

Trend prediction

A slightly more sophisticated scheme for forecasting the future is trajectory or trend prediction. This method assumes that, although there is change, the change itself is stable. If bread sales by XL Bakers in Glasgow have shown a fairly regular increase of 4% in each of the past few years, presumably due to the increase in the region's population, it will be reasonable to assume that this trend will continue, at least for another few years, unless a serious downturn in economic activity hits the area. In other words, the trend remains stationary.

Trend prediction is without doubt the most successful and most used forecasting approach. Tests have shown that it tends to give more reliable forecasts than much more sophisticated methods based on econometric models. It provides usually good short-run forecasts, but may lead to absurd long-range predictions, particularly if the trend is exponential.

Many phenomena initially exhibit an exponential-type growth, i.e. growth in successive time period is ever increasing. This could, for instance, be observed in the 1960s and 1970s for consumption of electricity and motor fuels, or more recently with the introduction and use of cell phones. But it is clear that such processes will ultimately change their pattern fundamentally. Electricity consumption is a case in point. Its growth pattern in the 1980s and early 1990s did not follow the exponential trends of the 1960s and 1970s. So the trend predictions for the 1980s based on the data of the 1960s and 1970s overestimated consumption systematically. Similarly, once the cell phone market has been saturated in a country, the sales growth will turn into sales decline, as several of the big cell phone manufacturers discovered.

Cyclic prediction

Cyclic predictions are based on the principle that history repeats itself. Cyclic predictions for seasonal phenomena are highly successful. They may be super-imposed on a trend prediction and hence give considerably better short-run forecasts. This is the case for demand forecasts for many products and services subject to seasonal consumption, like beverages, electricity use, or tourism. But cyclic predictions are equally fickle when they try forecast long-range phenomena, such as business cycles. Just look at the notoriously bad business forecasts made by economic research institutes or banks — fortunately as quickly forgotten by most people as they are issued by the forecasters — or the futile attempts to forecast stock exchange price cycles that in today's world of large-scale speculation may literally take a dive if the US president coughs.

Associative prediction

This method uses past data from one type of process (usually referred to as an independent factor) to predict another type of process (referred to as the dependent factor). It has given rise to powerful statistical techniques, such as regression analysis and its extension to econometrics.

Associative prediction is often expressed as the independent factor being the cause of the dependent factor, such as an increase in the amount of money in circulation 'causes' inflation, or a decrease in the number of building permits issued 'causes' a subsequent slump in the construction industry. In these cases, the cause precedes the consequence. However, there are many useful applications of associative predictions where there is no causal relationship between (what is used as) the independent factor and the dependent factor. Both could, in fact, be influenced by a third factor for which no data exists or which is difficult to observe directly. For example, the grade-point average of university students has a strong association with their IQ. But clearly, a high IQ is not the cause of a high grade-point average. Both are in fact a result of high intelligence, which cannot be measured directly. IQ tests are a crude attempt to measure intelligence. Similarly, the fact that an astute observer has discovered that there are remarkable parallels between the increase in university teachers' salaries and the consumption of wine hardly means that the former is the cause of the latter (or is it?).

Associative prediction greatly enlarges the area that is searched for clues. Much of regression analysis deals with discerning which independent clues are helpful — so-called statistically significant — for predicting a dependent process or event of interest. Trend prediction is a special form of associative prediction, time being the independent factor or variable.

But without doubt the method that uses all data available in the most effective way is hindsight prediction — the prediction of an event after it has already been observed and measured. Historians, TV commentators, economists, and politicians use this method to great effect. How often do you say "I told you so"?

Is the past valid for predicting the future?

With the exception of hindsight prediction, all approaches mentioned so far use past data to predict future events. The crucial systemic assumption underlying these approaches is that the past is a good basis for predicting the future. If this is not a well-founded premise, i.e. there are indications of structural or behavioural changes in the phenomenon observed, the validity of these methods becomes highly questionable. Structural changes could be due to changes in legislation, technology, or economic relationships governing the phenomenon in question. Behavioural changes could be the result of psychological, moral, or life-style changes in the population concerned.

There are, though, many instances in which there are no known past data that can be used for predicting future events. The occurrence and far-reaching consequences of technological innovations, like the invention of electronic computers, microchips, or laser technology clearly could not be predicted even by experts in the fields, except the very few actually involved in their development. Hence predictions based on past data without any knowledge of the imminence of such technological breakthroughs were badly off. But even for less spectacular events, such as next year's fashion trends or the Christmas sales volume for a given toy, predictions are difficult to make and are often unreliable. This is why fashion and toy stores only stock these goods just prior to the season and only in quantities that they are fairly confident to clear by the end of the season. However, the large number of end-of-season sales, with price reductions to a fraction of the original selling price for fashion items and toys, is a clear indication of the difficulty of demand predictions in these areas (although nowadays many sales items are in fact specially procured to attract customers during a sale).

Predictions should not be restricted to single estimates. The only way to assess the reliability of predictions is to obtain also some measure of the degree of variability inherent in the phenomenon predicted. If the predictions are part of an ongoing repetitive process, then it will be possible to compute some measure of the prediction error, such as an estimate of the standard deviation of the differences between corresponding pairs of predicted and actual values.

15.5 Predictions by expert judgement

In the second half of the 20th century, several other prediction methods have been developed that are regularly used by big business, market research consultants, and government. Firms test new products on consumer panels to get some indication as to their likely appeal. Larger firms and governments use various techniques involving experts in the field of interest — in an attempt to pool the combined and considered judgement of a group of experts.

Delphi method

The best known of these is the Delphi method. Consider the example of oil price predictions in the late 1970s, needed by the MS/OR group evaluating the economic desirability of the expansion of the only oil refinery then operating in New Zealand. A group of economic and energy experts from all over the world was asked to partake in a survey about the likely level of oil prices over a 30-year span. All participants were given a questionnaire. Their responses were collated and expressed in statistical form by a researcher. The results of the first questionnaire were then communicated in summarized form (averages, median responses, range of responses, etc.) to the experts, who were asked if, in the light of the first-round results, they wanted to change their original responses and how. Their new answers were again processed in the same manner. The Delphi method usually repeats this procedure through two or three iterations, with the responses of the last iteration being used as the final predictions. Note that complete anonymity of any responses received is preserved throughout the procedure.

The Delphi method has had many successful applications. It is not a cheap method and, unless the experts are all locally present, it takes considerable time to reach a conclusion. Each iteration can easily take weeks. It is therefore only suitable for relatively important projects. Before embarking on such an exercise, the analyst should perform considerable sensitivity analysis to determine how crucial it is to get a reliable estimate. In the oil price exercise reported above, the price for a barrel of the type of crude oil processed at the refinery in early 1978 was around US$35. The final predictions, made in early 1978, for the price by the end of the 1980s covered a range of US$60 to US$95. The analysis for the expansion option chosen established that it would remain economically viable as long as the price remained above about US$29. The actual price in 1989 was well below US$20, reaching lows of US$15 at times. So we see that even judgements by experts may be far off the mark.

Subjective or judgement predictions

What can be done for one-off cases, where no past history or comparable situations are available? In such instances, persons intimately familiar with the situation, usually the decision makers themselves, are asked to make a subjective prediction, based on general relevant experience, assessments obtained by other people, and pure 'gut feelings'. Such a prediction could, for instance, take the form of: "I estimate that the most likely outcome is X, with a 50–50 chance that the outcome will not deviate from X by more than 10%." The latter part of the statement provides an indication of the confidence that the respondent puts into the prediction. It can be used as a measure of the perceived degree of uncertainty in the prediction.

Unfortunately, many decision makers are very reluctant to make subjective predictions that involves a statement of odds. They are not used to think or reason in these terms and may be wary of being held accountable at some future time if their prediction turns out to be wrong. They may also be unfamiliar with or have forgotten the most basic statistical concepts. Either case will require skilful and sympathetic questioning on the part of the analyst. Furthermore, such judgemental assessments are prone to various biases, as discussed in Section 15.7.

So you may rightfully ask, why bother getting such predictions which smack of spurious accuracy, and then use them as input into some fancy decision model? Remember the principle of GIGO (garbage in, garbage out)! Why not ask the decision maker directly to choose the action he or she considers best? The answer is that the latter course solves nothing and may hide everything. The very process of obtaining subjective predictions will force the decision maker to a more thorough and logical analysis of the situation. Hidden elements become explicit. This in itself is of considerable value. The use of the model will allow the situation to be fully explored through sensitivity analysis on the very bones of contention — the subjective predictions — and hence to assess the robustness of the solution(s). It may also lead to re-evaluation of the boundary judgements made on the narrow and wider system of interest and even reveal hidden boundary judgements that may or may not need to be questioned. Finally, the reason for going through the modelling process is not to relieve the decision maker of the responsibility of making the final decision, but to provide a consistent and rational framework and insights for reaching the best decision.

Judgemental adjustments to forecasts derived by other methods

Quantitative forecasting methods, by necessity, are based on past data. As we have seen, there may sometimes be reasons for believing that such past data are not entirely representative of the future, due to events which are not reflected in the data yet or which are only appearing on the horizon. The seemingly obvious action is to use judgemental inputs to 'correct' the quantitative forecasts obtained on past data. In many instances this is a highly appropriate course of action to take. However, empirical research has shown that such adjustments are prone to bias and that certain rules should be followed (see, e.g. J. S. Armstrong, 'Research needs in forecasting', *Int. J. of Forecasting*, 1988, number 4, pp. 449–65, or S. Makridakis, 'Metaforecasting: Ways of improving forecast accuracy and usefulness', *Int. J. of Forecasting*, 1988, number 4, pp. 467–91). Some of the biases showing up in such adjustments are wishful thinking (more on this in Section 15.7) and the illusion of control, i.e. that making the forecast will, in fact, help reduce the variability of the phenomenon in question, such as sales.

There is general agreement among experts that judgemental adjustments should be restricted to take into account extra information or insider knowledge, but definitely not to reflect 'gut' feelings. Any adjustment made should be fully justified in writing (say, as a footnote). Experience shows that this often reduces the incidence of unjustified adjustments. Furthermore, the person(s) should be made aware of the common types of biases prevalent, as discussed in detail in Section 15.7. Finally, the persons making judgemental forecasts or judgemental adjustments to forecasts should receive timely and personalized feedback on their performance, with emphasis on 'timely'. Again, research has shown that such feedback helps improve forecasting and tends to reduce biases. However, it is important that such feedback is not used for fixing blame, but for learning. If it is used for blaming, the forecaster will try to protect him- or herself by making highly conservative predictions.

Activity: Find two new examples each for which the methods below are most suitable:
- persistence prediction
- cyclic prediction
- subjective or judgement prediction
- trend prediction
- associative prediction
- Delphi method

15.6   Probability measures and their interpretation

Uncertainty means that one of a number of possible outcomes will occur and that it is not possible to state, with certainty, which one of these outcomes will eventuate. The number of possible outcomes may be small (e.g. the number of cases of a rare notifiable disease in year XX or the price of Microsoft shares at the New York Stock Exchange will go up by 0, 1, 2, . . ., U cents or it will go down by 1, 2, 3, . . ., D cents by tomorrow, where both U and D are small numbers, like 5 to 15 cents); or it may be large (e.g. the number of CDs sold of the latest release by a famous band). In some instances, the potential or theoretical range of outcomes may be infinitely large (e.g. the time until the next earthquake in Paris, not located in an earthquake-prone region). The possible range of outcomes may not even be knowable — the case of complete uncertainty.

If we know the range of possible outcomes, the best thing we can do is to make a numeric statement about the likelihood of each if each outcome is discrete (e.g. the number of arrivals over a given period), or that the outcome falls into a given interval if the outcome is a real number (e.g. the time between consecutive arrivals).

How should we interpret statements of probability? Say I flip a fair coin. It repeatedly spins in midair and then lands on one of its sides. We all agree that the probability it will show heads is ½. How should we interpret this? Take a more complex problem, like the case of firm A having submitted a tender for a major construction job. A number of other firms have done the same. The manager of firm A estimates the probability that her firm will be awarded the contract to be 0.6. What is the meaning of such a statement?

There are at least four major schools of thought on this subject. Although the literature gives the impression that there are great differences between these schools, the differences are largely of a philosophical nature. (Facetious tongues warn us that in this quest we should be particularly aware of Academitis — a disease characterized by hairsplitting and, eventually, by *rigor mortis*.) All schools agree on the numerical values for all simple problems (particularly hypothetical ones), the rules of manipulating probabilities, and the broad principles of using them for decision making. So how do they differ? We shall now examine two of them.

Objective probabilities

For many simple situations, like games of chance, or any process that may repeat itself in more or less the same form time and again, the numerical value of the probability of a given outcome or event E, denoted by $P(E)$, can be interpreted as the long-run relative frequency with which this outcome occurs. However, for any given repetition of the process, the event E may or may not occur. We cannot state categorically for which repetition event E will or will not occur.

In terms of prediction, we would be fairly safe to predict that E will occur if the probability $P(E)$ is close to 1, say 0.9. In fact, in this situation we should always predict that event E will occur. In the long-run only in about 10% of all predictions would we be wrong. It would be completely illogical to use a pattern of predicting the occurrence of E in 90% of the cases and *Not E* in the other 10%. Our betting average would decrease from 90 to 82% correct.

Probability assessments that are either based on physical properties of the phenomenon, such as rolling dice, or based on a vast pool of past experience, such as the number of newspapers sold by a vendor at a given location on a given day of the week, or the probability that a male of age 25 of normal health will survive another t years, where t assumes values 0, 1, 2, 3, etc., as used by life insurance companies for setting their insurance premium, can all be given this long-run frequency interpretation. Such probabilities are referred to as **objective probabilities**. Powerful statistical data analysis can be applied to such phenomena.

Subjective probabilities

Difficulties of interpretation arise if we are dealing with one-shot deals — situations that are sufficiently unique and different from any previous experience. In fact, the majority of strategic decisions in business and government, such as the introduction of a new product, the effect of a given government intervention, or even a core meltdown at a nuclear power station, deal with unique situations. What is now the meaning of "the probability that outcome X occurs (e.g. sales of the new product exceed the break-even point) is 60%"? The repeatability argument cannot be applied — the product launch will not repeat itself ever under the same or similar circumstances. In fact, it may even be debatable whether assessing a probability measure makes logical sense.

It is in such cases that the subjective probability school comes to our rescue. It tells us that the numerical value, referred to as the **subjective probability** of an event, simply measures the confidence or degree of belief of a reasonable person, who is sufficiently informed about the situation, that the event in question will happen. Hence, two individuals, faced with the same situation, may assign different subjective probabilities to the same event. Their probability assessments are the personal, subjective perceptions of each individual, and hence both are valid — each for the individual who made it. Nor may that perception necessarily remain the same over even short time intervals of a day or a week.

It also seems obvious that if an event is repeatable and sufficient data on past outcomes have been collected, a reasonable individual's subjective probability assessment will coincide with the observed frequencies.

The use and validity of subjective probabilities sits rather uncomfortably with many people. Interestingly, we use them daily with such statements as 'it's highly probable' (about 0.9?), 'rather unlikely' (0.1?), 'impossible (0.01?), or '50–50'. Punters at the races use intuition or hunches to assess the odds of a horse winning — again subjective probabilities that are never explicitly stated, but still clearly enter into their choices. When you cross an intersection on your bike just in front of the oncoming car, you assess it as highly unlikely (about 0.02?) that you will not make it. So, rather than use such assessments implicitly, it makes good sense to render them explicit. Not only could this lead to a reassessment of what the best decision is, but it again allows us to do sensitivity analysis on these assessments. This helps in determining over what range of values for the subjective probability the decision remains unaffected. It will also lead to more consistent decision making.

Events whose occurrence is judged as highly unlikely are often ignored by decision makers. This is an implicit boundary judgement and its reasonableness should be justified. For example, the likelihood of a disaster may be so small that no protective measures are taken. The implicit boundary judgement is that the cost (monetary, social, or in human life) is zero.

Whether we are dealing with subjective probabilities, the event in question will either occur or will not occur. Since it is a one-shot deal, it would be nonsense to interpret its probability as 'it occurs x% of the time'. The probability measure only reflects our strength of belief in the event occurring.

A probability statement is an *a priori* concept. It is made before the uncertainty has been resolved — before we know which one of the various possible outcomes has occurred. Once 'the die has been cast', one and only one of these outcomes has occurred, and it could well be one which, *a priori*, had a low probability. If that outcome is known, no probability is associated with it any longer.

Activity:
- Find two new examples of a different nature where objective and where subjective probability measures are appropriate.
- Assume now that the probability of event E is $P(E)$ exactly 0.51 and you are repeatedly asked to predict the outcome. What sequence of predictions would you make and why?

15.7 Behavioural research on subjective probabilities

Research into how individuals assess uncertainty and make judgements under uncertainty shows up a number of rather disturbing behavioural patterns. G. Miller (*The Psychology of Communications: Seven Essays*. New York: Basic Books, 1967) states that people face severe limits in their capacity for processing information. This is particularly the case for understanding and processing complex multi-faceted relationships. Most people can only cope with about five to nine different unidimensional pieces of information at the same time, hence 'the magical number seven, plus or minus two'. Miller noted that once this threshold has been exceeded, people tend to reformulate information into bigger and less detailed chunks. This leads to stereotyping and other gross simplifications. These findings follow naturally from Herbert Simon's concept of **bounded rationality** (see page 7 in Chapter 1).

Simplifying heuristics for decision making under uncertainty

A. Tversky and D. Kahneman [1974, see also 1981, 1986] wrote a fascinating seminal paper on how human judgement tends to fail when faced with uncertainty — a must to read for any adult who strives for a position of responsibility. (See also the collection of papers in G. Wright and P. Ayton (eds) [1994].) They found that research into how the mind copes with uncertainty indicates that people tend to rely on a limited number of heuristic principles, rules, or patterns, known as **representativeness, availability,** and **adjustment and anchoring,** which they use for reducing the complex task of assessing probabilities and transforming predictions into simpler judgemental operations. This process happens most of the time outside their conscious awareness. Although these heuristics are often useful, they may also lead to serious errors in assessment and to systematic bias.

Research subsequent to the Tversky and Kahneman paper shows that the biases introduced by the use of these heuristic are reduced or attenuated when individuals have extensive experience and task familiarity and are motivated, e.g. by professional ethics, rewards or sanctions [Wright and Ayton, 1994, pp 116–25].

Representativeness

The likelihood or probability of an event is based on how closely it resembles a class of events for which it is seen as representative. For example, asked about the likely profession of a person described as 'very shy and withdrawn, invariably helpful, but with little interest in people or in the world of reality, a meek and tidy soul with a great need for order, structure, and a passion for detail', people tend to have recourse to **stereotyping.** Since that description is very representative of the mental image most people have about librarians, the likelihood that they will assign a person fitting this description to the class of librarians rather than the class of farmers is much larger. The fact that the proportion of farmers in the population is several times larger than the proportion of librarians does not enter into the assessment. The relative sizes of the corresponding statistical populations "librarians" and "farmers" are ignored. This is referred to as **base-rate neglect.**

Research also shows that the representativeness heuristic tends to **disregard the size of the sample** on which a probability judgement is based. A given outcome A in, say, $2/3$ of all observations is assumed (at least by people with little training in statistical analysis) as equally indicative of the true proportion of A regardless of whether it is based on 6 or 60 observation, when in fact the larger sample tends to provide more reliable estimates. The result is that too much confidence is placed in findings based on small samples. The extreme case is making a judgement based on a single observation, even if that observation consists of several aspects, such as happens in job applicant assessment tests. Unless the various aspects observed are largely independent of each other — in statistical terms have little or no correlation — the conclusion reached may be unreliable.

Another aspect of representativeness that is misunderstood or ignored is the tendency of **regression to the mean.** Stochastic phenomena where the outcomes vary randomly around stable values (so-called stationary processes) exhibit the general tendency that extreme outcomes are more likely to be followed by an outcome closer to the mean or mode than by other extreme values in the same direction. For example, even a bright student will observe that her or his performance in a test following an especially outstanding outcome tends to be less brilliant. Similarly, extremely low or extremely high sales in a given period tend to be followed by sales that are closer to the stable mean or the stable trend.

Availability

In many situations, people tend to assign a higher likelihood to the occurrence of an event where instances can be easily retrieved from past experience than to those that are difficult to recall. Events that have left a strong impression, such as accidents one was involved in or unpleasant episodes with the boss or a fellow employee, come more readily to one's mind and, hence, may be seen as more numerous that they really are. In contrast, more difficult to retrieve events, such as things that happened a long time ago or to other people, tend to be judged as occurring less frequently.

Similarly, having just experienced several such events in the recent past will again tend to overestimate their frequency. For example, having just gone through two floods in the space of three years, most people will scoff at the statement that both where one-in-a-hundred-years events.

However, the bias of availability even works for things that you may not have experienced personally, but for which possible contexts under which they might occur can easily be imagined. For example, the likelihood of being caught in a terror attack is overestimated by most people, since it is so easy to imagine potential scenarios.

Adjustment and anchoring

In most situations, people estimate something by starting from an initial value, usually based on past experience with comparable situations. Experiments have shown that, if people were fed with different starting points, any adjustment made to the starting point to account for the same additional information tended to be insufficient. The initial starting point acts like a ship's anchor that allows only a limited shift of position for the vessel in response to water currents or wind.

This has important consequences for how the quest for probability assessments or forecasts is framed, particularly for subjective probabilities. The frame may become such an anchor that leads to severe bias. It is therefore essential that considerable thought is given to framing the search for unbiased estimates of future events [Tversky and Kahneman, 1986]. Unfortunately, for people familiar with a given situation, the frame is already provided by what they know.

It is crucial that whoever is involved in developing estimates for future events is fully aware of the danger of anchoring. It may be useful to repeat such an exercise with a different frame and then reconcile any differences in results.

Overconfidence and wishful thinking

Other research indicates that people tend to be overconfident in their ability to assess probabilities — not justified by their actual performance. They tend to overestimate the probability of rare events and underestimate the probability of highly likely events.

People are prone to the **gambler's fallacy**, expecting that an outcome that has failed to occur for a while is likely to occur in the near future, disregarding the fact that each outcome may be independent of what happened before.

We may also overestimate probabilities of events that we would like to happen or desire, and underestimate those that we would rather did not happen. Experiments with MBA students and executives clearly reveal the existence of this type of wishful thinking. In one experiment, the subjects were presented with a sales history on a new product as shown in part (a) of Figure 15-1. Sales have increased dramatically after the product's launch, but then very recently have shown a small decline. The subjects were put into two groups. Group 1 were told to put themselves into the position of the marketing manager of the firm, while group 2 were told that they were the marketing manager of the firm's major competitor. Each group was then asked to predict the future sales pattern for that product. Most subjects in group 1 predicted that sales would recover promptly and continue their dramatic increase. In contrast, the subjects in group 2 predicted that the sales downturn would persist. This is depicted by the broken lines in part (b) of Figure 15-1. Clearly, each group seemed to reflect a high degree of wishful thinking.

This type of behaviour is true for the people in the street, as well as for experts and business executives, responsible for important decisions. Although some learning occurs in response to assessments that are discovered as being far off the mark, the degree of learning is hindered by the lack of accurate and immediate feedback about the correctness or otherwise of assessments made. The necessary feedback is often lacking because (a) outcomes happen later in time and may not be easily attributable to the causal action, (b) variability in the environment degrades the reliability of feedback, especially for outcomes of low probability, (c) there is often no information

Figure 15-1   Sales predictions by wishful thinking.

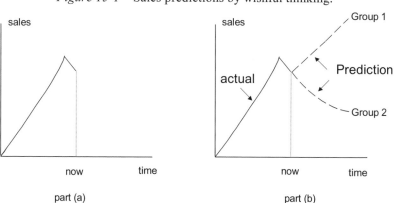

about what the outcome would have been if another action had been taken, (d) most decisions for which such assessments are made are unique and therefore provide little opportunity for learning [Tversky and Kahneman, 1986, p. 274], and (e) information for learning is often suppressed by subordinates or colleagues of decision makers out of fear that revealing it may backfire on them, i.e. is used for assigning blame rather than for learning.

Lessons to be learned

What lessons can we learn from this research? First, the individual making subjective probability assessments or predictions must be aware of the potential shortcomings of the heuristics of representativeness, availability, and the anchoring effect, as well as the tendency towards wishful thinking. It is best not to rush into an initial guess and then try to rationalize its validity. Instead, a good starting point is to decompose a complex problem situation and develop a complete list of all the factors that may affect it and how it is affected by each one, and then to weigh them carefully and deliberately against each other. It is also helpful to restate the same situation in a different framework, e.g. expressing a positive statement as the exact equivalent negative statement, and observe if this leads to a different assessment and why.

Rather than settle for a single number, it is more effective to select as the initial anchor or benchmark a fairly wide interval and then attempt to narrow it down in the light of the various influencing factors listed earlier. It is also useful to hold off on a definite assessment and first pool the judgement of other people who are sufficiently familiar with the situation. This is likely to lead to a more balanced and more representative answer and reduce the anchoring effect. A final assessment in the form of a narrow interval is usually a more honest and more useful piece of information than a single number.

Finally, once the final assessment has been made, it is important that the recommended decision is subjected to extensive sensitivity analysis with respect to all important subjective probability or prediction inputs. This will reveal how important it is to arrive at reliable assessments for each input of this nature.

When faced with unique situations, the tendency is to take an "inside" view by considering mainly the distinguishing features of the problem situation and ignore or even reject similarities or analogies to other situations of the same general type, when in fact it would be more insightful to take an "outside" view, i.e. see them as instances of the broader class of situations and learn from them.

Activity: From your own personal experience give examples of how you may have used each of the heuristics or biases: representativeness (stereotyping, disregard of sample size, estimates based on a single observation, misconception of regression), availability (ease of retrieving instances, lack or ease of imagining contexts), insufficient adjustment by anchoring, overconfidence, wishful thinking, and the gambler's fallacy. Clearly identify which aspect(s) of your judgement was affected. The same example often may have elements of several factors.

15.8 Random variables and probability distributions

Random variables

Assume now that a situation has several alternative outcomes and that with each outcome we can associate a real number. An example will help. Sales for XL Bakers' fruit loaves at supermarket K vary from day to day. On the odd day, none are sold. The largest number ever sold in recent history is 12. On most days, sales range somewhere between 4 and 8. Past history thus indicates that daily sales may assume any outcome between 0 and 12. Hence we can associate with each possible outcome (= daily sales) one of the integers from 0 to 12. These numbers represent the values that the **random variable** 'daily sales' may assume.

Frequency and probability distributions

The historical frequencies with which each sales amount has been observed could be used as an approximate model for the probabilities with which each of these sales amounts will occur in the future. These probabilities are now seen to be a function of the integers from 0 to 12. We call this function a **probability frequency function** of the random variable 'daily sales'. It is also sometimes loosely referred to as a probability distribution, although in probability theory this term has more precise meaning. The above case is an example of a discrete probability distribution. But remember again, on any given day only one of these outcomes will actually be realized. (By analogy, these concepts can also be applied to one-shot deals. The frequency interpretation is then replaced by 'the strength of belief' or 'the degree of confidence' in each possible value of the outcome.)

A probability distribution conveys considerably more information than does a single-valued prediction. Not only does it show the range of possible outcomes, but also their relative frequency in a reproducible situation, or the subjective strength of belief in each outcome for one-shot deals. It should thus lead to better and more informed decision making than that associated with single-valued predictions. However, it is also more costly to determine and usually leads to more complicated and hence costlier models.

Approximations by theoretical distributions

Since the determination of the exact probability distribution is difficult, we often have recourse to approximations. Events that occur singly and are relatively rare, like the breakdown of machines or the arrival of customers within a sufficiently small interval of time, are quite often approximated with a surprisingly good fit by a **Poisson** distribution. The Poisson distribution is completely specified by a single number: the average or expected value of the random variable, which is also its standard deviation.

If the outcome is affected by, or is the sum of, a large number of independent factors, with no factor having a predominant influence, the **normal distribution** provides an excellent approximation. Demand for bread — mentioned earlier — would be a good example. Daily sales are the result of many individuals independently making a decision to buy one or a few loaves, with no individual buying a very large number and thus having an undue influence over sales, whenever this occurs. It is completely defined by two parameters: the expected value and the standard deviation of the random variable.

The normal distribution is a continuous distribution, i.e. the random variable may assume any real value from minus infinity to plus infinity. In practice the outcomes tend to be clustered more or less tightly around the expected value. For example, there is a 95% probability that any particular realization of a normal random variable lies within two standard deviations of the expected value. The distribution's position and shape is completely defined by these two parameters.

Note that in the bread demand example, sales are in whole loaves. Hence daily sales is an integer variable. Still, if sales are sufficiently large, usually about 20 or more, then using a continuous random variable is a suitable and convenient approximation for many decision situations.

For a discrete distribution, each value that the random variable may assume has a positive probability. Not so for a continuous distribution. The probability that a continuous random variable assumes any given value is always zero, although the random variable will ultimately assume a value within its range. This may sound like a contradiction, but a little bit of reasoning shows that this is not so. There is a positive probability that a continuous random variable will assume a value in a specific interval within its range. But since there are an infinite number of possible values in each interval (part of the real line), the probability of any one of them occurring is zero. So for continuous distributions we only associate probabilities for intervals of the random variable, not for any specific value!

15.9 Expected value and standard deviation

For any group of observations about a phenomenon we can compute the average or mean value, which gives us an indication of their centre of gravity. We can also find the standard deviation, which provides us with a measure of how widely the observations are dispersed, although most of us have difficulties putting any intuitive meaning into a standard deviation. Sometimes comparing the average and the standard deviation helps in getting a better feel for the situation. For example, if the standard deviation is only a small fraction of the average, then the observations will tend to be bunched closely around the average.

The same types of measure can be computed for random variables. The average becomes the expected value of the random variable, while the standard deviation retains its name. The expected value shows where the centre of gravity of the possible outcomes is located. The standard deviation is a measure of the variability or dispersion of the possible outcomes.

Meaning or interpretation of the expected value

What is the meaning of the expected value of a random variable? As with an average of a set of numbers, only by coincidence will the actual value realized by a random variable ever fall exactly on its expected value. But for a repetitive phenomenon, the average of a large number of observations of the random variable will fluctuate around the expected value. Furthermore, by the **Central Limit Theorem**, as the number of observations gets larger, their average value tends to become closer and closer to the expected value of the random variable.

Often we may use the expected value as a convenient substitute for the long-run behaviour of a random variable and base our decisions on this number. However, it is only an approximation — a modelling simplification. It never implies that the random variable will, in fact, assume its expected value. For a discrete distribution, the expected value may not even be one of the possible outcomes, while for a continuous distribution it will be a pure coincidence if the realized value of a random variable falls exactly on its expected value.

For subjective probability distributions, particularly for one-shot deals, we do not even have the comfort of a long-run interpretation. No averaging can occur. The expected value has no meaning beyond its mathematical definition. Nevertheless, it can be shown that a decision based on the alternative which produces the highest expected value of the measure of performance is the best decision. But do not fall into the trap of assuming that the outcome when it occurs will be equal to the expected value. This point cannot be stressed enough!

15.10   Approaches to deal with/reduce uncertainty

Most decision makers would rather make decisions under certainty than under uncertainty. The higher the uncertainty, the higher their discomfort and anxiety. Hence it is not surprising that substantial efforts are made to create decision-making structures that reduce or avoid uncertainty. This is an important topic for theories in organizational behaviour and strategy. There are four basic approaches: we attempt to reduce uncertainty as such, we attempt to alleviate its effects, we postpone any firm commitments as long as possible (in the hope of dissolving some of the uncertainty as time passes), or we opt for greater flexibility for future responses by creating future options.

Collecting more information

The obvious approach to reduce uncertainty is to gather more information, and hence improve our predictions, be it in terms of a single-valued guesstimate or a probability distribution. For instance, a firm has experienced a steady growth for one of its main product lines over the last 18 months. If this trend continues, sales will increase by another 40% over the next year. The existing production facilities are now taxed to the limit. Substantial investments in new plant and equipment are needed to increase it. However, there is considerable uncertainty about the long-run potential for this product line. Will the growth trend be sustained, and if so, for how much longer? Faced with such a situation, most firms would undertake a comprehensive market research study to obtain a better picture of the market potential for the product line. In other words, they would gather more information to reduce the uncertainty faced.

Gathering more information is costly and time-consuming. This is only justified if the new information gained reduces uncertainty and leads to better decisions. There is a whole branch of statistical decision theory dealing with these aspects, namely **Bayesian decision analysis**. The underlying mathematics is, unfortunately, beyond an introductory survey. The basic idea though is simple and intuitively appealing. We start with some prior, albeit imperfect, information. This is used for making a preliminary decision which in turn will allow us to determine an approximation to the potential increase in benefits gained by gathering additional information. The additional information is obtained if its potential benefits justify its costs; otherwise the preliminary decision based on the current information is implemented.

Often the conditions for applying this analysis are not satisfied or the analysis is too complex. At that point, it is our natural creative instinct, more commonly referred to as a hunch, which will lead us either to get more information or to make do with what we have. If the information is easy and relatively cheap to get and we judge that it might bring a considerable improvement in the decision process — or at least alleviate our anxiety about it — we collect additional information, otherwise not. There still is a lot of 'art' in decision making, not just 'science'!

Sensitivity analysis

The second approach is to ascertain how crucial it is to get accurate information about uncertain events. Sensitivity analysis comes to the rescue. We systematically evaluate over what range of values for any uncertain parameters the best decision remains the same as for the guesstimates used for deriving it. If that range is small, then this may be an incentive to acquire more accurate information. If the range is wide and we feel fairly confident that the true value of the uncertain parameters lies well within that range, nothing will be gained by spending time and funds to get better information.

Keeping options open

The third approach is to select a decision strategy that closes the fewest doors for future action. In other words, any action which commits us firmly to a given direction and eliminates a large number of other possible future actions is either avoided or postponed until more and better information becomes available. Naturally, many decisions will narrow down future choices. It is a problem of finding a good balance between maximizing the benefit of the course of action to be chosen and keeping our options open — a version of the perennial problem in decision making, namely balancing benefits against costs, neither of which may be fully expressed in numerical terms only. Robustness analysis, a problem structuring method briefly discussed in Section 7.7, addresses such issues.

Creating future options

Rather than simply keeping options open, it may be strategically advisable to take actions that create new future options. For instance, a firm located in a growth area where suitable land is becoming scarce may decide to purchase a site now in anticipation of possible future expansion of its production facilities, although no decision or even exploratory planning has been made at the time of the purchase. It simply creates a new option for the future. If no expansion is made within 5 to 10 years, the land may be sold again — hopefully at a good profit.

Similarly, firms investing heavily into research clearly do this in anticipation of opening up new future options, i.e. new products.

Scenario analysis

Organizations invariably have to plan for events in the far future and often face a highly turbulent environment in terms of potential technological change, potential moves by competitors or adversaries, or high uncertainty as to the future economic climate. Rather than considering only one possible future that tries to accommodate the variability and uncertainty involved in all factors, it may be more effective and insightful to consider several possible futures or scenarios. Although an organization faces an infinite number of possible futures, the number of different scenarios explored is rarely more than three or four. Each scenario makes certain assumptions about crucial factors that drive what may happen in the future; in other words, each makes different boundary judgements, usually with regard to the system environment. It is important that these boundary judgements are clearly identified and justified as reasonable. Scenarios should not include decision choices and the possible response of the environment to such choices. That should be part of the subsequent analysis once the scenarios have been developed.

The practice is to start with two scenarios, one somewhat optimistic about various aspects of the future, the other somewhat on the pessimistic side. One or two other scenarios in between complete the set, one of which may be the continuation of the status quo. For commercial ventures, the choice of scenarios should be such that each has a reasonable chance of eventuating approximately. On the other hand, for disaster planning, it may be essential to also evaluate extreme scenarios that have a very small probability of occurring, but may have devastating consequences if they do.

For each of these scenarios, a preferred decision strategy that balances competing goals (see Chapter 19) is developed. Such a strategy should include contingency actions that allow recovery if another scenario occurs. Whenever possible, a strategy should consist of several stages, some to be implemented right away, others for future implementation and conditional or contingent on later events. Each decision strategy is assessed in terms of its robustness and risks with respect to the other scenarios, if this makes sense.

This process will enhance the understanding of the problem situation and thereby provide valuable insights for informed, rational decision making. It may even suggest actions that may increase the likelihood that the preferred scenario eventuates.

Any two or more of these five approaches may be used jointly for reducing the degree of uncertainty.

15.11 Decision criteria under uncertainty

When the outcome of each alternative course of action is known with certainty, the evaluation of which action is best boils down to identifying the one with the highest net benefit if the objective is maximizing benefits, or the lowest cost if the objective is minimizing costs. When the outcomes are uncertain, what criterion should be used for choosing the best decision? Chapters 16–18 will explore such questions with a number of examples. The discussion below is only intended as a cursory overview.

The most obvious approach is to adapt the criterion of maximizing benefits or minimizing costs for deterministic situations. Under uncertainty, each action leads to one of a number of possible outcomes. Which particular outcome will be realized is only known in terms of its probability. So, we substitute expected benefits or expected cost for benefits or costs in the above criterion. The best action is the one with the highest expected benefit or the lowest expected cost, whichever is relevant. Economic theory, in fact, shows that under fairly general conditions, this criterion achieves the best possible long-run results.

For repetitive risky situations, the meaning of this statement is the usual long-run frequency interpretation. Applied to one-shot deals, the meaning implied is that, using this criterion consistently will in the long-run produce superior results to any other criterion. However, for any particular one-shot deal, the outcome could still spell disaster!

In situations with extremely serious possible outcomes, such as large losses or bankruptcy, the decision maker may not be willing to make a decision based on the expected value criterion. Instead, he or she may select an outcome that has a lower expected benefit, but provides better protection against the risks involved. One such criterion chooses the best decision on the basis of reducing the probability of disastrous outcomes below a maximum acceptable level. In particular, the decision maker may eliminate any actions from further consideration if they imply that the probability of not achieving a certain minimum benefit or of exceeding a certain maximum cost is larger than a given threshold value. For instance, when comparing several mutually exclusive risky investment opportunities, the decision maker may eliminate any which have a probability of 5% of leading to a loss of more than a certain amount. The actions passing the threshold are then evaluated using a secondary criterion, such as maximizing expected benefits or minimizing expected costs.

Unfortunately, for many real-life complex and sequential decision situations, determining the probability distribution of the final outcomes may be difficult. Risk analysis — a topic briefly discussed in Chapter 18 — is one attempt to overcome some of these difficulties.

If there is a high degree of uncertainty about the outcomes and, furthermore, some may also involve serious adverse consequences, the decision maker may select the decision which offers the best protection against the worst outcomes. The probabilities are completely ignored. This criterion may be appropriate if some of the possible outcomes involve disasters, such as loss of life, serious injury, or irreversible damage to the environment, or if the outcomes are partially controlled by a vicious adversary who is out to get you. In a business context, a firm may resort to this criterion in order to avoid any possibilities of going bankrupt. Discussion of this and similar criteria is the subject of **decision analysis** (Chapter 18) and **game theory** (a topic not covered in this text).

15.12 Chapter highlights

- Few things in the real world are known with absolute certainty. Deterministic models are often convenient simplifying approximations. Uncertainty results in new types of system behaviour.
- Expressions in everyday language about uncertainty are prone to ambiguity. This may lead to misunderstandings about their intended meaning.
- Uncertainty has three major causes: insufficient understanding of the phenomenon, information based on samples from the unknown population, and measurement errors.
- The degree of uncertainty may range from almost complete ignorance about the phenomenon to well-understood principles about it or reliable and extensive observations of past occurrences.
- Much of decision making depends on having good information about future events. Methods for predicting the future fall into five groups: persistence prediction, trend prediction, cyclic prediction, associative prediction, and prediction based on expert judgement. The predictions are usually based on past behaviour. Hence, all methods assume to a lesser or larger extent that the past is a good predictor for the future.
- Objective probabilities can be interpreted as the frequency of various (usually repetitive) events occurring in the long-run. Subjective probabilities express a person's strength of belief in the occurrence of various (usually unique) events.
- Behavioural research shows that we tend to use simplifying heuristics when making judgements about uncertain events. These are prone to biases and systematic errors, such as stereotyping, disregard of sample size, disregard for regression to the mean, deriving estimates based on the ease of retrieving instances of the event, anchoring to the initial frame, the gambler's fallacy, and wishful thinking, which are all affected by our inability to consider more than a few aspects or dimensions of any phenomenon or situation at the same time.
- Certain theoretical probability distributions, such as the Poisson and the Normal, tend to approximate many phenomena in real life.

- Much of decision making is concerned with dealing with or reducing uncertainty or the effects of uncertainty, such as collecting more information, performing sensitivity analysis with respect to uncertain aspects, exploring more than one possible future via scenario analysis, and selecting decisions that keep open or create new future options.
- Decision criteria for selecting the best option need to reflect the degree of uncertainty. For repetitive-type decisions, maximizing or minimizing the expected value of the outcomes is most appropriate. Theoretical arguments show that even for unique or one-shot deals this remains the appropriate criterion, but the interpretation of the expected value changes. However, for decisions that can lead to extreme adverse outcomes, e.g. large monetary losses, environmental disasters, or serious injuries and loss of life, other types of decision criteria that offer additional protection may be more appropriate.

Exercises

1. One of the major causes of uncertainty listed in Section 15.2 is ignorance about or a lack of complete understanding of a given phenomenon. It is then conceivable that ultimately uncertainty will disappear since advances in science will allow us to understand all phenomena perfectly. Critically discuss this view.

2. A recent court case found a local council negligent for allowing the complainant to built a house on a 50-year flood plain. Although the council had actually informed the complainant of the danger, the court awarded him considerable damages, based on the fact that, within the first ten years after completion, the house was inundated in three of these years. The judge's verdict stated that the council's assessment of the flood risk clearly was in error, given that in three out of ten years flooding occurred. Assume that the council's assessment of the house being in a 50-year flood plain was correct. Discuss the validity or otherwise of the judge's reason for siding with the complainant.

3. An analyst asked an economist about whether or not he should collect additional data to have a more reliable basis for finding the best policy for a decision problem under uncertainty. The economist's answer was: 'You should collect additional information until the marginal cost of obtaining it is less than the marginal gain of improved decision making.' (This follows the principles developed in Chapter 12.) Why is this a rather naive recommendation? (Hint: consider the possible difficulties of doing this.)

4. "The probability that I will have a car accident on my way home from work is one in 700." Give an objective and a subjective interpretation of this statement.

5. Imagine you are in charge of an organization (business, school, sports club, government agency). Give an example for each of the following heuristics you may end up using for various uncertain events that you may face: stereotyping, disregarding sample size, making a judgement based on a single observation, disregard for the regression to the mean, the ease of recalling instances (based on past events), the difficulty of recalling instances, the ease of imagining a situation where the event occurs, the difficulty of imagining situations where the event might occur, insufficient adjustment due to anchoring, overconfidence, wishful thinking, and the gambler's fallacy.

6. Consider the heuristics discussed in Section 15.7. For each description listed below, identify which of these heuristics was or is likely to be used and the potential error or bias it could introduce. Some situations may fit more than one heuristic.

   (a) Discussing politics, Mike says to Sue: 'You can't trust a politician — they are all liars!'

   (b) When Mike went swimming in the ocean, his partner asked him to be careful of rips. "Oh, I'm more worried about sharks."

   (c) Five of John's friends recently won sizable sums in scratch lotto. John's aunt asks him whether the chances of winning in scratch lotto are good. He responds: 'Oh yes, just look how my friends are doing!'

   (d) Andrew goes to the supermarket. In the car park, raised on a slanted platform, is a beautiful cabriolet sports car — the latest model, offered as the first prize in a nationwide raffle organized on behalf of the Red Cross. He falls in love with the racy car. He has the firm feeling that if he buys a book of tickets for £10, he will win it.

   (e) Margaret got five A+ grades and three A grades in her first year at university. The head of department of her major subject is overheard making the following remark to one of his colleagues: 'I bet Margaret will top her class next year too!'

7. For each of the situations described below, indicate one or more possible approaches to deal with or reduce uncertainty and why each is a reasonable approach:

   (a) A firm has detailed data available of its sales, based on delivery documents for each sales transaction. However, for various reasons (suppliers' strikes and shipment delays, machine breakdowns, etc.) a substantial number of orders from customers could not be met. Due to these lost sales, the size of the true demand is therefore unknown.

   (b) A firm faces the dilemma of whether or not it should invest in an expensive expansion of its product research facility. There is hearsay evidence that the competition is considering similar action. Recent rapid advances in technology relevant for both research and production have created added uncertainty as to whether this trend will continue, in which case premature expansion may lock the firm in at a level of technology that may soon be partially obsolete. On the other hand, experience also indicates that advances in technology tend to go through cycles of high activity and stagnation.

   (c) A new prosthesis for artificial hips has come on the market. The manufacturer claims that it will increase the length of time before it fails, reducing the need for replacement. However, the manufacturer has only limited data which, although promising, is not sufficient to back up the claim fully. The health department (who pays for the cost of such operations, including the prostheses) wants to make a decision now whether it should switch to the new prosthesis, which is considerably more expensive than the one currently used, or whether is should stick with the current one for the foreseeable future.

16

Waiting lines: stochastic systems

As we saw in Chapter 15, uncertainty about the behaviour of a system can range from knowing almost nothing, to having fairly reliable information in the form of 'objective' probabilities about the various events that may occur in the system. This chapter studies system behaviour that is often the realization of a large sequence of random events. We assume that we know the probability distribution of each one. In practice this means that we have either compiled frequency distributions from past observations or fitted theoretical probability distributions as convenient approximations. We shall see that under these conditions a system may exhibit new and interesting types of behaviour — so-called emergent properties — behaviour that is not present in deterministic systems.

While in a deterministic system each alternative course of action leads to a corresponding known outcome, in a stochastic system each alternative course of action leads to one of a number of possible outcomes. *A priori*, we cannot specify which particular outcome will result from a given decision, but only with what probability each of the possible outcomes will occur. These probabilities are usually different for each different course of action. Seen from this perspective, each alternative course of action can be viewed as selecting a given probability distribution for the outcomes. The 'best' decision is the one that produces the most 'favourable' probability distribution for the outcomes. For most hard OR problem solving, the most favourable probability distribution is the one with the highest expected benefit or the lowest expected cost.

This chapter deals mainly with the long-run system behaviour of stochastic systems. This implies that the operation of the system continues (at least in theory) for a long time interval and that all inputs are stationary, i.e. the probability distributions governing all random events, as well as any other aspects, such as costs factors, remain unchanged.

We shall explore these ideas by studying a particular type of system, namely waiting lines. They are ideal for showing some of the emergent properties of stochastic systems, and how the long-run behaviour of such systems is affected by controllable and uncontrollable aspects. The first two sections of this chapter describe the structure of waiting line situations and demonstrate that stochastic systems may exhibit emergent properties that comparable deterministic systems do not have. The mathematics of waiting lines has been studied extensively since 1917. Section 16.3 summarizes some of the most basic results. The remaining sections of the chapter will study in detail a real-life application — the Forest Products weighbridge problem.

16.1 Waiting lines

We are all familiar with waiting lines or queues. We wait at a bus stop for the next bus, we wait for elevators, and we wait at checkout counters in supermarkets, the student cafeteria, or the library until it is our turn to be served. Queueing situations are also a common concern in commercial and industrial situations, leading to important decision problems. For example, ships in a harbor may have to wait for unloading cranes to become available. Every hour of waiting may cost several thousand dollars in operating costs for the ship. On the other hand, each additional crane installed represents a substantial investment. Port authorities do not want to have them sitting around idle. How many cranes should the port authorities operate so as to keep the waiting costs of arriving ships reasonably low, while at the same time keeping the cranes busy much of the time?

The first queueing models, developed by the Danish engineer A.K. Erlang in 1917, dealt with telephone exchanges. Communications remains one of the most common areas of application of queueing models. The very first example in Chapter 1 — the emergency services call centre — is an application of this kind. We want to know how many operators we need if we want, say, 99% of all incoming calls answered within ten seconds.

Basic structure

Figure 16-1 depicts the general structure of waiting line situations, while Table 16-1 lists a few typical examples.

Figure 16-1   General structure of waiting lines.

Customer Population   Arrival Process   Queue   Service

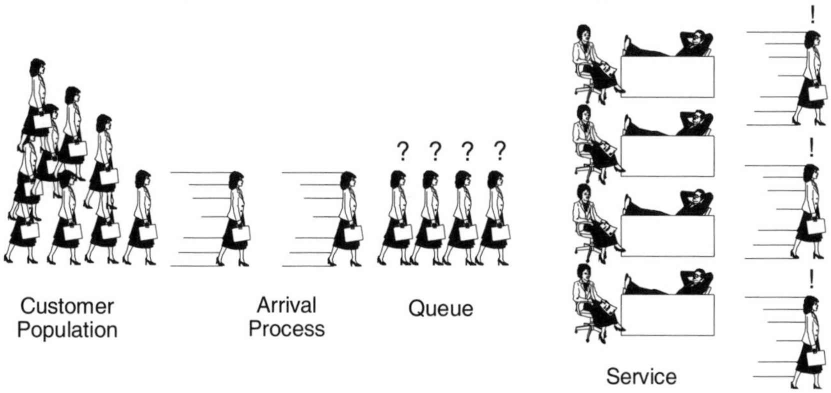

Table 16-1   Examples of waiting line situations.

Source of arrivals	Nature of service	Service facility
customers in stores	sales transactions	store attendant
telephone calls	enquiry	call centre
electronic messages	transmission	switch
aircraft	landing and take-off	runway
ships in harbor	berthing	dock
ships berthed at dock	loading and unloading	cranes or/and gangs
cars	sea crossing	ferry
machines	repairs, change-over, etc.	technician/operator
mechanics on shop floor	tools or parts	attendants at counter
computing jobs	processing on machine	computer
computing jobs	hard disk file handling	file server
emergency/accident victims	medical attention	nurses/surgeons
welfare applicants	processing of application	case worker
stock withdrawals	stock replenishment	supply facility

The three major components of a system involving queueing-type behaviour are:

• one or several sources of customers or **arrivals**,

• one or several **queues**, each with its corresponding **queue discipline**,

• one or several **service facilities**.

Arrivals from more than one source may all request service from the same service facility. For example, some arrivals at an accident and emergency clinic may suffer from a life-threatening condition that requires immediate attention, while others have had some minor accident, the treatment of which can be delayed within reason. Each group is viewed as a separate source of arrivals. Similarly, aircraft requesting permission to land may be large commercial airliners or small private planes. In each case, one source may get priority of service over the other source. Furthermore, each source of arrivals may have different characteristics in terms of the kind of service requested or the length of time needed to complete it.

The sequence or priority in which the server attends to the entities waiting in a given queue is called the queue discipline. In most queues, arrivals are attended to by the server on a first-come/first-served sequence. There are, however, instances where the service priority follows a different rule. For example, some blood banks issue blood for transfusions on a last-in/first-out basis. The reason for this is that the oxygen-carrying capacity of the blood deteriorates with age and hence using the freshest available blood is most effective from a medical point of view. In other instances, some arrivals meeting specified criteria are given priority over other arrivals. For example, customers may choose one or several charging rates for the service — the higher the charging rate, the higher the service priority. Or jobs arriving are classified by length of service required — the shorter the job, the higher the priority. However, within each priority class, jobs are processed on a first-come/first-served basis.

There may be one queue, several queues, or no queue at all. For example, most banks and post offices nowadays have all customers join a single queue. The person at the front of the queue is first in line for the first teller to become free. On the other hand, in supermarkets each check-out counter has its own queue, while the usual single-line telephone connection without a call-waiting option has no queueing facilities. If the line is already in use, any other caller gets a busy signal. He or she is not accepted as an arrival. Each caller has to redial to try for a successful connection.

The length of a queue may be limited. For example, a psychotherapist may limit the number of clients waiting for a weekly time slot to become available to at most three. Any potential clients arriving when the waiting list is full are referred to other therapists. Finally, potential arrivals may balk and depart immediately if they observe that the queue is too long. Some customers already in the queue may also become impatient and depart without service ('renege') if they expect that the additional waiting time will be too long. Arrivals finding the queue full, or balking and reneging customers are lost to the system. This may result in potential profits foregone.

As the examples in Table 16-1 indicate, the entities in the queues do not have to be at the same physical location, but may be awaiting service in separate locations, such as photocopiers owned or rented by different firms or organizations requiring repairs or service.

Service facilities may be arranged **in parallel** or **in sequence**. The check-out counters at a supermarket or tellers in a bank operate in parallel. Each service facility performs exactly the same type of service. Customers in the queue require service from only one such facility and may be serviced by any one of them. In contrast, an arrival may require service from several facilities in sequence. For example, a job in a machine shop may have to be cut first on a lathe, then drilled on a drill, and finally finished on a polishing machine. There may be a queue in front of each of these machines.

This brief survey shows that the variety of possible waiting line configurations seems almost unlimited. In this chapter we shall only study some rather simple situations. Chapter 17 on simulation looks at more complex configurations.

Activity: Show how each of the following situations can be viewed as a waiting line problem. Identify the source of arrivals and the nature of the service, and determine whether the server(s) act in parallel or in sequence.
- A fire station with a single crew to respond to fire calls.
- Lifeguards on a public beach.
- A hotel reception operation where guests check in at a desk, are shown to their rooms by a uniformed clerk, and brought their luggage by a porter.

16.2   What causes queues to form?

On the edge of the desert, east of Perth, Australia, is a small store with a single fuel pump. It displays a tall sign warning motorists that this is the last gas station for the next 300 km. As a result, no car ever drives past without filling up. On average, about four cars stop at the service station every hour. Jake, the owner of the store, having seen many cars stop at his station, is never rushed, regardless of how many cars are waiting for gas. If Jake takes a liking to a customer, he easily forgets himself and chats away for minutes. On average he takes about 10 minutes to serve each car. Let's study what happens to this simple system under various assumptions about the rate at which customers are served.

Constant arrival and service times

Assume first that cars arrive evenly spaced over time, i.e. the **interarrival time**, a, is constant. With four arrivals per hour, the interarrival time is exactly 15 minutes. We start observing the service station at 8 a.m. No cars are there, so the pump is idle. The first car arrives at 8:04. For some reason, Jake decides that today, he will spend exactly the same length of time, $s = 10$ minutes, serving each car. So he starts serving the first car immediately upon its arrival and finishes 10 minutes later at 8:14. The car departs. Jake goes back to his cup of coffee, kept warm on the stove. The next car arrives at 8:19, exactly 15 minutes after the first car. It gets immediate service, and leaves at 8:29. The third car arrives at 8:34, and Jake completes serving it at 8:44. This regular pattern continues all day long. No car ever has to wait. There is never a queue.

Because there is exactly one interarrival time and one service time for each customer, the service facility is busy a fraction of time equal to the ratio of the service time to the arrival time, or $s/a = 10/15 = \frac{2}{3}$ and it is idle a fraction of time equal to ($1 -$ [fraction busy]) or $1 - \frac{2}{3} = \frac{1}{3}$.

Next day, Jake decides to tell each customer in dramatic detail the story about how this snake had climbed up his pump and he mistook its tail for the nozzle of the hose. Hence each customer has to suffer through an agonizing 24 minutes before Jake finally sends them on their way. We again start observing the station at 8:00 with the first car arriving to an idle pump at 8:04. Jake completes the service at 8:28. In the meantime, the second car has arrived at the station at 8:19. It has to wait till 8:28 for the service on the first car to be completed before it gets its turn. The service is completed at 8:52. By then, third and fourth cars have arrived at 8:34 and 8:49. Service on the third car begins at 8:52 and ends at 9:16, well after the fifth car has joined the queue of cars waiting. In fact, the number of cars in the queue will slowly but surely increase throughout the day as long as Jake keeps up telling his snake story. No more coffee breaks for Jake!

We conclude that if the service time is longer than the interarrival time, or, equivalently, if the number of cars served per hour — the service rate — is lower than the number of cars arriving per hour — arrival rate, the queue length will get larger and larger.

Random arrival and service times

What happens when either or both the interarrival times and the service times are random variables, i.e. these times fluctuate randomly? We mimicked this for an eight-hour period, sticking to our previous assumption that the average rate of service is larger than the average rate of arrivals, or equivalently that the average service time is smaller than the average interarrival time. Figure 16-2 shows how the queue length

Figure 16-2   Queue behaviour for three different average service times and the same arrival pattern with a mean arrival rate of four cars per hour.

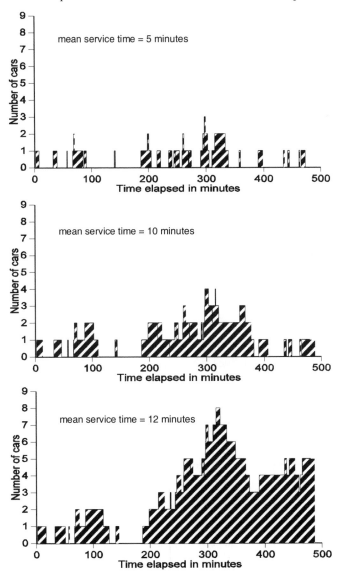

behaves for three values of the average service time, s, but the same average interarrival time of $a = 15$ minutes. We also assume that the standard deviations of both random variables are equal to the average times — a property of the negative exponential distribution assumed for both variables (see Figure 16-6, page 444, for a graph of this distribution).

Observe that for $s = 5$, queues occur only rarely and are usually of no more than 1 or 2 cars. However, as s increases, and gets closer to a, the frequency of queues increases and the length of the queues also tends to increase.

This happens even though, on average, the service capacity is sufficient to satisfy the service demand. Compare this with the deterministic case with constant interarrival and service times, where queues only occur if the service capacity is insufficient, but never if the service capacity exceeds the demand for service. Since the deterministic and the stochastic case only differ with respect to the variability in interarrival and service times, the forming of queues in the stochastic case can only be attributed to the variability in either or both the interarrival times and the service times. Therefore we can conclude that under uncertainty systems exhibit emergent properties or behaviours that are not present in a world of certainty. This is a very important finding.

Another interesting example which you might have experienced yourself is the following. You want to cross a busy highway. If there is a steady flow of cars driving by at equal distances between cars — akin to a constant interarrival time pattern — it may well be impossible to cross the highway safely because the time between cars is too short. However, if cars drive by in a random pattern of inter-distances — some tailgating, others with large distances — sufficiently long breaks between cars will occur from time to time for a safe crossing, even if the average number of cars using the highway over a given time interval is the same.

Cumulative arrival-departure diagrams

While Figure 16-2 shows us what the queue length is at any time, it is not easy to read off how long a particular customer has had to wait. A cumulative arrival and departure diagram overcomes this problem. We plot for each customer the arrival time and the service starting and departure times, using customer number as the vertical axis. Obviously, if a customer arrives when the server is idle, the arrival and service starting times are identical. Table 16-2 lists the times for the first six cars used in the third plot in Figure 16-2.

Table 16-2 Times for the first seven cars.

Car Number	Arrival Time	Service Starts	Time of Leaving
1	1.94	1.94	16.71
2	32.41	32.41	50.73
3	56.47	56.47	57.54
4	66.58	66.58	75.06
5	68.28	75.06	117.15
6	86.53	117.15	127.77
7	139.72	139.72	145.14

The cumulative arrival–departure diagram is plotted in Figure 16-3. From it we can see that cars 5 and 6 wait 6.78 and 30.62 minutes respectively (the horizontal lengths of the shaded areas.) If we considering these shaded areas vertically the diagram also tells us that there was one car waiting in the queue from 68.28 to 75.06 minutes, and one from 86.53 to 117.15 minutes.

Figure 16-3   A cumulative arrival–departure diagram.

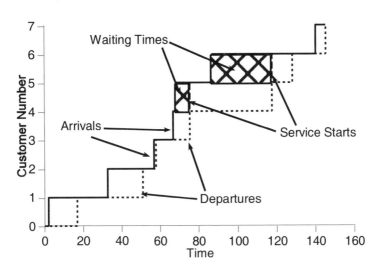

Two other useful facts that can be read from arrival–departure diagrams are that the slope of the arrival graph gives the arrival rate, and that during those times when the server is busy the service rate is given (approximately) by the slope of the departure times (or start of service times) graph.

A virtue of cumulative arrival–departure diagrams is that they can display situations in which the arrival rate of customers is temporarily greater than the service rate. Consider this situation. A self-service cafeteria has a rush of customers at lunchtime which is causing very long queues. The rush starts at about 11:30 a.m. and continues until 12:30 p.m. However, even with all the cashiers operating the queues do not empty out until about 1 p.m. Over a number of days we have recorded the arrival times, and then plotted the average cumulative arrival time curve in Figure 16-4. (Since it is an average we have joined the values up to give the relatively smooth curve in Figure 16-4, rather than a step graph like that in Figure 16-3.)

We have also found that when all cashiers are working they can serve 500 customers in 90 minutes. The middle portion of the dashed line gives the slope corresponding to this service rate. Given that the service times are very short, it is a good approximation to the service start times (as well as customer departure times), from the time when the system usually becomes very busy, until it meets the cumulative arrival curve again. When the system is not congested and waiting times are short, the dashed line follows the customer arrival curve closely.

Figure 16-4   The cafeteria average cumulative arrival–departure diagram.

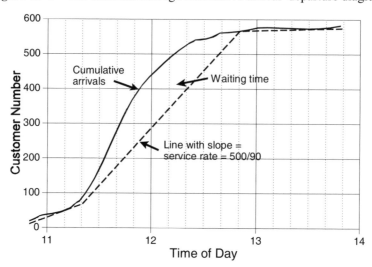

The area between the customer arrival curve — the continuous line — and the dashed line, representing the service rate, is the total waiting time of all customers who arrive during the rush. We can affect the size of that area by changing the slope of the dashed line and the point where the change occurs. This will allow us to estimate the effects of different service policies. For instance, the dotted line in Figure 16-5 corresponds to a service rate of 400/50 or 8 customers per minute. It reduces total waiting times by more than 80%. Such a result may be achieved by standardizing the service operations and adding more cashiers.

Figure 16-5   The effect of a faster service rate.

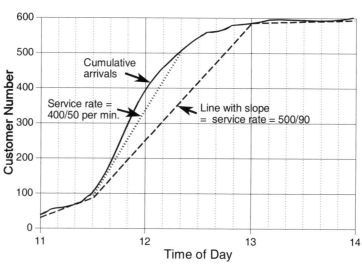

Furthermore, since the dotted line now meets the cumulative arrival curve at 12:20 p.m. it appears that this change removes most of the congestion by about that time too. Thus we see that faster service not only reduces the waiting times of individual customers, but also has a dramatic effect on the length of time during which the system is congested. Most of the customers who arrive during the rush will also now have much reduced waiting times. We can easily estimate the reduction in total customer waiting time by estimating the area between the two service-rate lines.

> Activity: For the following situations, would you expect the queues to be most of the time long or short, or to vary highly in length depending on the time of day. Why?
> - a life guard service at a beach (refer to previous activity).
> - a hotel reception operation (refer to previous activity).
> - a single-theatre cinema ticketing desk; a multi-theatre ticketing desk.

16.3 Formulas for some simple queueing models

Mathematical queueing models

Mathematical models of waiting line systems are the subject of **queueing theory**. *Queueing* is supposed to be the word in the English language with the most vowels in a row! Aside from this interesting fact, one of the nice aspects of queueing models is that some of them turn out to have surprisingly simple formulas for such system characteristics as the mean number of customers in the queue, denoted by L_q, and the mean time that a customer spends in the system, W. If we can determine that one of these theoretical models fits the situation studied reasonably well, then we can use these formulas for studying the performance of the system. This is usually much faster and less costly than determining approximate performance measures by directly observing the operation of the system.

In fact, queues can exhibit such highly variable behaviour patterns that in order to obtain reliable estimates of the mean waiting time and other system characteristics, we may find we have to observe the processing of several thousand arrivals. This may not be possible, both from a technical as well as a cost point of view. Furthermore, if the system studied is still being planned, actual observations are impossible. Simulation may be the only option for highly complex system structure and behaviour.

The simple models we will assume that the interarrival times come from a negative exponential distribution. The cumulative distribution function has the form $1 - e^{-\lambda t}$. It is completely specified by a single parameter, the arrival rate, λ, per unit time, e.g. per hour. As we have seen for Jake's service station, the reciprocal of the arrival rate is equal to the average interarrival time, i.e.

15 minutes = 0.25 hours = 1/(4 customers per hour), or $a = 1/\lambda$.

The standard deviation of a negative exponentially distributed random variable is also equal to a.

For this distribution, very short interarrival times occur more frequently than very long interarrival times. The longer the interarrival time, the less frequently it will occur. When we plot the fraction of interarrival times shorter than a certain time against time (the sample cumulative distribution), we get a graph consisting of a sequence of irregular steps with a slope that becomes less and less positive. This can be used as a rough check that a negative exponential assumption is reasonable.

Figure 16-6 plots these steps for a (small) sample of 40 interarrival times at Jake's service station. Note how there are many more short intervals in the sample than long ones, and hence the typical concave shape to the distribution function. The dashed line corresponds to the distribution function for a negative exponential random variable with a mean of 15 minutes. It appears from the obvious similarity between the two graphs that a negative exponential assumption for the interarrival times at Jake's service station is reasonable. (There are formal statistical **goodness-of-fit** tests available for a more scientific assessment, such as the Kolmogorov–Smirnov test. However, their discussion goes beyond the scope of this text.)

Checking that the assumptions of the mathematical model — in our case the form of the interarrival time distribution, the queue discipline, and the service-time distribution — are reasonable approximations to the characteristics of the actual queue are important steps in validating the mathematical model. In fact, because of the highly variable behaviour patterns noted above, this may be the only way in which we can validate the model against the actual system.

Figure 16-6   Shape of the negative exponential distribution.

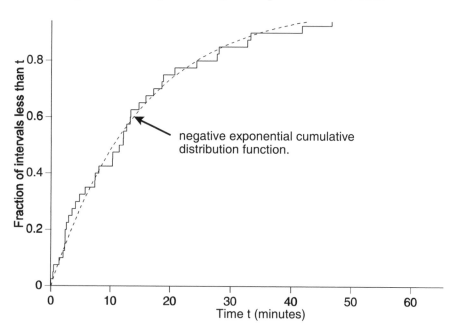

It turns out that for a surprisingly large number of waiting line situations, a negative exponential distribution is a very good approximation for the interarrival times. This is particularly the case if arrivals are generated independently of each other, such as individual customers or clients requesting a service, or individual machines breaking down.

The most basic queueing model assumes that the service times also follow a negative exponential distribution, with service rate μ, or a mean service time of $s = 1/\mu$. Although this may be an adequate first approximation for some cases, service times often follow a less variable distribution. Fortunately, the formulas for several important system characteristics of a basic class of models remain valid even if we allow the service time distribution to be of a more general form.

Formulas for the M/G/1 queue

A very useful class of queueing models is described by the shorthand notation of M/G/1, where 'M', short for '**Markovian**', refers to the fact that the time between arrivals comes from a negative exponential distribution with rate λ, the service times come from any positive probability distribution with mean s and variance σ_s^2 (i.e. a General service time distribution whose exact form does not need to be specified), and the "1" indicates that there is a single server.

The formulas listed below assume that the system has been running for a long time. This means that the system is in **steady state**, i.e. the state of the system no longer depends on the **initial state** of the system, such as how many customers were present at the start. (Check the precise meaning of steady state in the Glossary.) The system's characteristics calculated from these formulas are then valid representations of the long-run behaviour. Note that we are not saying that the waiting time and queue lengths are no longer changing over time, simply that the means of their distributions have stopped changing.

The mean number of customers in the queue will be given by:

$$L_q = \frac{\lambda^2 \sigma_s^2 + (\lambda s)^2}{2(1 - \lambda s)} \quad \text{provided } \lambda s < 1 \qquad (16\text{-}1)$$

λs is called the **traffic intensity**. Just as in the case of Jake's store, it can be interpreted as the fraction of time that the server is busy. For this class of models it is also the probability that an arriving customer will have to wait.

As was true for the deterministic case in Section 16.2, the traffic intensity has to be smaller than 1, or else the queue will continue to grow indefinitely. Hence we have the condition in Expression (16-1) that λs must be less than one. Rewriting this condition as $\lambda < 1/s = \mu$, we can see that it is just the condition of requiring that the arrival rate be less than the service rate, or equivalently that the average service time must be less than the average interarrival time.

Expression (16-1) rather nicely illustrates a couple of points that, in fact, hold for more models than just the M/G/1 class:

1. The mean queue length L_q (and the other operating characteristics) increase hyperbolically (i.e. in the shape of $1/(1-x)$) as the traffic intensity approaches 1. L_q is plotted in Figure 16-7 for an M/M/1 queue, where the service time distribution is also negative exponential.

From Figure 16-7 we note that reducing the traffic intensity (by providing faster service or by reducing the arrival rate) will gain us a great deal if the traffic intensity is high (say greater than 0.7), but that we make much smaller gains if the traffic intensity is already low. Changes in the traffic intensity that move us down from, say 0.8 above the 'knee' of the curve — roughly at 0.7 — to a point below the 'knee', say to 0.6, are more profitable than similar changes entirely below the 'knee', say from 0.6 to 0.4.

Figure 16-7 L_q for an M/M/1 queue.

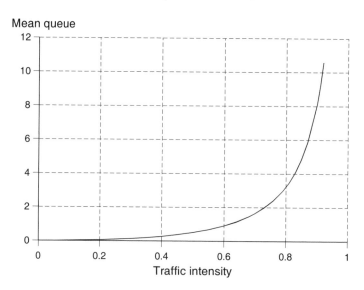

2. The average queue length (and hence the average delay, as we will show below) depends not only on how busy the server is, but also on how variable the service process is. Thus, for a given traffic intensity we can decrease the average delay also by reducing the variability of the service time. Fast food operations, for example, make explicit use of this by limiting the range (and hence variability in preparation time) of the items they sell. The same is also approximately true for arrival processes — the more variable the interarrival times, the longer the average waiting time.

L, the mean number of customers in the system, can be found from:

$$L = L_q + \lambda s \qquad (16\text{-}2)$$

This follows from noting that the mean number of customers in the system must be the sum of the mean number in the queue and the mean number in service, and that the latter is equal to the traffic intensity. The mean time that a customer spends in the queue, W_q, and the mean time that a customer spends in the system, W, are given by what are known as **Little's formulas**. They hold for a large number of queueing models.

Little's formulas: $\qquad L = \lambda W \qquad (16\text{-}3)$

$$L_q = \lambda W_q \qquad (16\text{-}4)$$

An elementary proof of (16-3) is given in the example below. Finally, the mean time a customer spends in the system is the sum of the mean time spent waiting in the queue and the mean service time:

$$W = W_q + s \qquad (16\text{-}5)$$

Activity: Referring to Figure 16-7, explain why successive 10% increases in the arrival rate tend to push the average queue length up by larger and larger amounts if the service rate remains the same.

An example

Consider the operation of a small container port. It has only one dock with a single container crane. Hence only one ship can be unloaded and loaded at any one time. Other container ships arriving while the dock is occupied will have to wait their turn until the dock becomes free. Suppose that a container ship arrives at the port, on average, every five days, i.e. $a = 5$. This implies that the arrival rate is $\lambda = 1/5$ ships per day. It takes $s = 4$ days to unload and load a ship. The standard deviation of the service time is $\sigma = 2$ days. To use the above formulas, we check first that the traffic intensity is indeed less than 1, i.e. $\lambda s = (1/5) \times 4 = 0.8 < 1$. Since it is, an estimate of the mean number of ships in the queue is given by expression (16-1):

$$L_q = [(0.2)^2 2^2 + (0.8)^2]/[2(1 - 0.8)] = 2.0,$$

and $L = L_q + \lambda s = 2 + 0.2(4) = 2.8$.

The average time in days that a ship spends waiting in the queue for the dock to become free is obtained by rearranging expression (16-4) as

$$W_q = L_q/\lambda = 2.0 / 0.2 = 10 \text{ days},$$

while expression (16-5) gives the average time a ship is in the system, i.e. waiting or being unloaded and loaded, as $W = W_q + s = 10 + 4 = 14$ days.

Suppose that it costs \$8,000 per day to operate a ship while in port. Hence each ship calling into port incurs a total cost of \$8,000 multiplied by the mean time a ship spends in the system, W, or $(\$8,000)(14) = \$112,000$. Another measure of interest is the average daily cost of the ships in port. This is given by \$8,000 times the mean number of ships in port, L, or $(\$8,000)(2.8) = \$22,400$. Both these costs seem to be rather high. Hence the port operator may wish to increase the unloading and loading capacity, either by installing a second crane on the dock or by replacing the current crane with another one of a higher capacity. You should verify that if the mean time to service a ship is reduced from 4 days to 2 days with a standard deviation of 1 day, the new system's characteristics are $L = 0.5667$ and $W = 2.8333$. Both measures are reduced substantially because we have reduced the traffic intensity from 0.8 to 0.4 (point 1 on page 446), and the standard deviation of the service time from 2 to 1 (point 2 on page 446). The average cost in port per ship falls to only $(\$8,000)(2.8333) = \$22,667$, while the average daily cost of ships in port falls to $(\$8,000)(0.5667) = \$4533$. A doubling of the service rate has resulted in an almost five-fold decrease in these costs.

We can use this example to demonstrate a proof of Little's formulas (expressions (16-3) and (16-4)). First consider (16-3). We have just established above that the average daily cost of ships waiting or being serviced in port is $(\$8,000)L$. On the other hand your friend works it out this way. Each ship spends an average of W days in port. On any given day, we expect on average λ ships to arrive, each of which is going to spend W days in port. Hence the additional cost, considering only that day's average number of arrivals, is $(\$8,000)W\lambda$. But this must also be the daily cost of all ships in port. Well, both arguments are right. Equating the answers, they produce expression (16-3).

Multiple server queues

What about a system where the customers form a single queue and go to the first available server out of a number, C, of servers? Such systems are often used at banks, post offices, and other service counters. We now only get simple formulas if we assume that the service time distribution is also negative exponential with rate parameter μ, i.e. an M/M/C queue. Then provided $\lambda/C\mu < 1$, the probability that there are no customers present in the system is:

$$P_0 = \cfrac{1}{\left[\displaystyle\sum_{n=0}^{C-1} \frac{(\lambda/\mu)^n}{n!} + \frac{(\lambda/\mu)^C}{C!(1-\lambda/C\mu)}\right]} \qquad (16\text{-}6)$$

and

$$L_q = \frac{(\lambda/\mu)^{C+1}}{C\,C!(1-(\lambda/C\mu))^2}P_0 \qquad (16\text{-}7)$$

The condition $\lambda/C\mu < 1$ ensures that the maximum service rate, when all the servers are busy, is greater than the arrival rate, as otherwise the queue will grow without limit. The characteristics for the number of customers in the system, L, the time in the system, W, and the waiting time, W_q, can again be found from (16-7) by using $L = L_q + \lambda/\mu$, $L_q = \lambda W_q$, and $W = W_q + 1/\mu$.

Repeated evaluation of (16-6) and (16-7), for instance, for sensitivity analysis, is best done by writing a short computer program or a spreadsheet macro. Many books (see for example Bunday [1986] or Gross and Harris [1998]) list examples of such programs and macros. Alternatively, there are books of tables, such as F.S.Hillier and O.S.Yu, (1979) *Queueing Tables and Graphs*, (Elsevier/North Holland, Amsterdam), which lists extensive tables for the M/M/C and other queueing models.

An example: queueing for toilets

In 1995 New Zealand Works Consultancy was contracted to revise the Building Standards for the number of toilets that needed to be provided in public buildings. Data was collected from thirteen types of building, including office buildings, schools, theatres, swimming pools and shopping plazas. Most of the data was collected electronically, with the times of arrival measured by the time a person cut a pair of infra-red beams. Occupancy times were measured either by magnetic switches on cubicle doors or infra-red beams. One can be seen to the right of the urinal in the picture below. The data was fed into a recorder which is in the box on the floor.

Let us suppose that the criterion to be used is that 'the average waiting time in the queue is to be no more that one minute.' In a building where the arrival rate is 60 customers per hour, and for a toilet type where the mean occupancy time is two minutes, how many toilets will we need? The assumption that the times between arrivals come from a negative exponential distribution is quite reasonable for the reasons discussed in Section 16.3. This was checked by drawing graphs of the interarrival times like Figure 16-6. We will also assume that the occupancy time distribution is negative exponential.

We start out by expressing all of our input information in the same time unit. Using hours, we have $\lambda = 60$, $\mu = 30$. Next we check for the minimum starting value for C to ensure that we have a feasible solution, i.e. that $\lambda/C\mu < 1$. Trying $C = 2$, we find that $\lambda/2\mu = 60/(2(30)) = 1$. Hence it is clear that at least three toilets will be needed. Is this sufficient or do we need more toilets to meet the criterion that $W_q \leq$ 1/60 hours?

For $C = 3$, we find

$$P_0 = \frac{1}{\left[\displaystyle\sum_{n=0}^{2} \frac{(60/30)^n}{n!} + \frac{(60/30)^3}{3!(1-60/(3(30)))}\right]} = 0.11111$$

$$L_q = \frac{(60/30)^4}{3(3!)(1-60/(3(30)))^2}(0.11111) = 0.88889$$

Now $W_q = L_q/\lambda = 0.014815$ hours or 53.3 seconds, so the criterion is just met. Three toilets will be enough to meet the Building Standard.

The benefits of pooling

We can also use the multiple server formulas to quantify the effects of alternative system configurations without actually observing the system. The alternative in which we are interested is **pooling**, i.e. combining separate servers into a central facility, as depicted in Figure 16-8.

Figure 16-8   Two alternative configurations.

Which is Better?

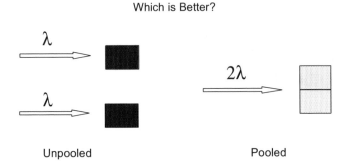

Unpooled   Pooled

Is it better to have arrivals join one of two separate queues, each feeding its own server, or have arrivals join a single queue that feeds both servers? In the 1980s, banks and post offices moved to the single-queue system. The reason for this is that it avoids the situation where one or more tellers are idle while other tellers have customers waiting. It appears likely that there would be some benefit in this change, but how large will it be? In Table 16-3, expressions (16-7) and (16-4) have been used for comparing the waiting times for the two systems.

Table 16-3 W_q for equivalent unpooled and pooled systems.

W_q (service rate = 1)		
λ	Unpooled	Pooled
0.3	.428	.099
0.5	1	.333
0.8	4	1.78
0.9	9	4.26

We see that, for these models, pooling similar service facilities can reduce waiting times by a factor of about four for low traffic intensities and by a factor of at least two when the servers are busier. In fact pooling together N service facilities can be shown to reduce average waiting times by at least a factor of N.

Provided other concerns, such as travel times or the quality of customer service, are taken into account, pooling similar service facilities will always reduce waiting times, often by a considerable amount. (The comparisons in Table 16-3 are valid for any equivalent ratio of λ/μ, even if $\mu \neq 1$.)

This effect can be partially described in terms of feedback loops, such as those described in Section 3.11 of Chapter 3. In the pooled system, as we move from only one customer in the system to two or more customers present, the service rate will definitely increase when the second server is called into action. Hence the waiting times are partially controlled by a self-regulating negative feedback loop. In the unpooled system the effect will only occur if the customers arrive at the appropriate server, hence there may be no feedback.

Activity:
- In queueing for toilets cubicle occupancy times were actually much less variable than a negative exponential distribution would imply (curiously, urinal occupancy times were remarkably close to negative exponential.) How would this show up in a graph like Figure 16-6? Would this necessarily invalidate results obtained using a negative exponential assumption? (Recall that we want to guarantee that 'the average waiting time in the queue is to be no more that one minute.')
- We just saw that pooling is better than servers with individual queues. Why is it not necessary to have all servers located at the same place in order to take advantage of the benefits of pooling? If the server has to travel to the physical location of the user, what other considerations may become important in allocating 'idle' servers to users? What may this imply in terms of the home base for servers? (Think of desirable properties for locating fire stations.)

16.4 The NZ Forest Products weighbridge case

The case history below comes from one of the author's involvement in a New Zealand company. However, any wood processing plant in any part of the world receiving truck loads of tree logs from forests may face a similar situation.

Description of the system

During the 1980s every year some 2,500,000 m^3 of cut logs were transported from the forest to a pulp mill operated by the New Zealand Forest Products Company. The cartage was done by trucks owned by private contractors. Every truck had to enter the NZFP complex over a single-lane weighbridge, as shown below. The weight of wood carried formed the basis of the payments to the contractors. The weighing records were also used for monitoring fellings in the forest.

When the complex was busy, more than 400 truck-loads passed over the bridge per day. A truck had to come to a complete halt on the weighbridge while it was weighed and documents were checked. If a truck arrived to find the weighbridge empty it drove straight onto it. If the weighbridge was already occupied, the next truck in line stopped some distance from it and, for safety reasons, was only allowed to proceed onto the weighbridge when the preceding truck was completely clear. Therefore a truck forced to wait lost additional time by having to drive onto the weighbridge as a separate movement. The resulting move-up time had the effect of slowing down the rate of progress of trucks. As a result, waiting times observed in 1989 sometimes exceeded 20 minutes per truck. This worried management: had the weighbridge reached its saturation point?

Various options to alleviate this problem were considered. One option was to build a second weighbridge in parallel with the existing bridge. Trucks would form a single queue and move to the first available weighbridge. It is important to note that the weighbridge forms a relatively small component in a very expensive complex, which had to be kept supplied with logs at all costs.

Data collection and system parameter estimation

To analyse this situation we needed data on the movement of trucks. For two days we observed the weighbridge, starting at 5.30 a.m. until the last load was allowed across at 5 p.m. The arrival time, the time of entering the weighbridge and the time of leaving it were recorded for each load. Table 16-4 reproduces a small sample of the data collected. The three numbers listed in each column are the hour, minute, and second at which the corresponding event occurred.

Table 16-4 A sample of weighbridge observations.

Load number	Arrival time	Time of entry	Time of leaving
...	...	...	...
100	8 22 53	8 22 53	8 24 52
101	8 23 42	8 25 18	8 27 22
102	8 24 45	8 27 56	8 28 36
103	8 26 13	8 28 53	8 29 45
104	8 29 11	8 29 59	8 31 44
105	8 31 09	8 32 08	8 34 34
106	8 36 16	8 36 16	8 37 23
107	8 36 43	8 37 43	8 38 38
...	...	...	...

Table 16-5 Weighbridge parameters.

Random variable	Mean (minutes)	Standard deviation
Interarrival time	1.6782	1.7459
Move-up time	0.3323	0.2735
Weighing time	1.207	0.7309

For load 100 the truck was able to drive straight onto the bridge. This follows from the 'arrival time' being equal to the 'time of entry'. Its weighing time was 1 minute 59 seconds — the difference between 'time of leaving' and 'time of entry'. Load 101 arrived 49 seconds after load 100, while that load was still being weighed. Hence it had to wait for 1 minute 10 seconds for the weighbridge to become available — the difference between 'time of leaving' for load 100 and the 'arrival time' for load 101. It then took the truck 26 seconds to move onto the weighbridge — 'time of entry' for load 101 less the 'time of leaving' for load 100. Its weighing time was 2 minutes 4 seconds.

Working in this way we can compile a list of interarrival times, move-up times, and weighing times. The averages and variances of these, as shown in Table 16-5, are estimates of the corresponding probability distributions

Generalizing the M/G/1 formulas to the weighbridge problem

Note that the mean and standard deviation of the truck interarrival times are in the same ball park. If truck arrivals are independent of each other, then a standard deviation equal to or very close to the mean is a good indication that the interarrival times are negative exponential — in this case with rate $\lambda = 1/1.6782 = 0.5959$. Statistical tests based on graphs like Figure 16-6 confirm that a negative exponential distribution gives an acceptable approximation. This discovery certainly increases our confidence in the use of an M/G/1 queueing model for the current operation of a single weighbridge. However, there are a couple of places where the system deviates seriously from the assumptions of the M/G/1 model.

1. The weighbridge starts from empty each morning. Hence the first few trucks tend to experience very small delays. On the other hand, the W_q obtained from the M/G/1 model assumes the system is in steady state. The true average waiting time per truck over the day will therefore be slightly lower than the theoretical W_q based on the steady state.

2. Trucks arriving when the weighbridge is occupied take some time to move on to it. In some sense the move-up time can be viewed as part of the service time. However, incurring this additional time depends on whether the bridge is 'free' or not. 'Not free' means that a truck occupies the weighbridge or that a truck is moving up. Hence we cannot assume that the service times are all drawn from the same probability distribution, independent of the state of the queue, which is an essential assumption of the M/G/1 model.

We can analyse the effect that this will cause by considering the weighbridge as a feedback loop (see Section 3.11). Figure 16-9 shows the feedback loop associated with the weighbridge.

Figure 16-9   The weighbridge described as a feedback loop.

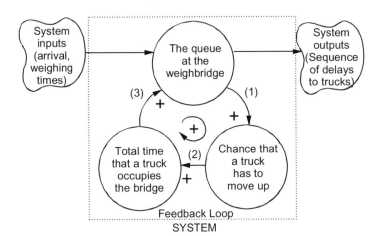

The bigger the queue at the weighbridge, the higher the probability that a truck will have to come to a complete halt and then move onto the weighbridge (arc 1 in Figure 16-9). The higher this probability the longer the total time that a truck occupies the weighbridge (arc 2), and the longer the total time that a truck occupies the weighbridge, the bigger the queue at the weighbridge will be (arc 3). Thus a positive change in any of these elements causes a positive effect on the next element in the loop, as indicated by the 'plus' signs on each arc of the loop. Since all of the effects are of the same sign the entire loop is clearly a positive feedback loop. As a queue starts to build up, the process generating the waiting times moves into a more unstable state, producing longer waiting times, which is only terminated when the weighbridge becomes idle.

Can we relate the actual characteristics of the weighbridge to those of the M/G/1 model? Recall that traffic intensity is the fraction of customers who wait:

$$\text{Fraction of customers waiting} = \text{Traffic intensity} = \lambda s$$

In the weighbridge case, the average service time s could be viewed as the average service delay a truck incurs for stopping at the weighbridge. This consists of the average weighing time plus the average move-up time for the fraction of trucks that have to wait. Now we use the interpretation of the traffic intensity as the probability that a customer will have to wait, giving:

$$s = \text{average weighing time} + [\text{traffic intensity}][\text{average move-up time}] \quad (16\text{-}8)$$

Putting these two expressions together and inserting the known values for $\lambda = 1/1.6782 = 0.5959$, the average weighing time $= 1.207$, and the average move-up time $= 0.3323$, we get:

$$\text{Traffic intensity} = (0.5959)(1.2070 + [\text{traffic intensity}]0.3323)$$

Rearranging this equation and solving it for the traffic intensity gives a value of 0.8968. As we have just seen, this is also the proportion of trucks that has to wait and incur a move-up time.

Now we consider the second way in which the actual weighbridge deviates from the M/G/1 model. Although an average of 89.68% of all trucks incur a move-up time, whether or not any particular truck is affected depends on the status of the weighbridge at the time of the arrival of that truck. As we have seen, this effect can be modelled as a positive feedback loop, which provides part of the explanation of the high waiting times. What if we simply ignored this and randomly assigned move-up times to trucks in this proportion? Now all the service delays of all trucks can be treated as if they were drawn from the same probability distribution and hence the M/G/1 model is more appropriate. This modification is equivalent to removing arc (1) of the positive feedback loop and hence breaks the entire loop. So this suggests that the theoretical M/G/1 formula should underestimate the delay. Note that a systems view has told us this quite valuable piece of information without any further mathematical analysis of the model. We hope that this underestimate and the overestimate produced by the start-up effect will partially cancel each other out.

Evaluation of system's performance using the modified M/G/1 model

We are now ready to determine the values of the parameters for the M/G/1 formulas. Inserting the estimates of Table 16-5 into expression (16-8) we compute the average service time, s, as

$$s = 1.2070 + 0.8968(0.3323) = 1.505.$$

For the variance of the service times we use the property that the variance of a weighted mixture of two random variables is given by

$$p\sigma_1^2 + (1-p)\sigma_2^2 + p(1-p)(m_1 - m_2)^2.$$

Here p and $1-p$ are the weights (in our case the traffic intensity and its complement), and m_1, m_2, σ_1^2, and σ_2^2 are the means and variances of the two random variables. So

$$\sigma_s^2 = 0.897[0.7309^2 + 0.2735^2] + (1-0.897)(0.7309^2) + 0.897(1-0.897)(0.3323^2) = 0.61.$$

We now have all input parameters needed for evaluating expressions (16-1) and (16-4). We get $L_q = 4.94$, and $W_q = 8.27$ minutes. The latter agrees quite well with the actually observed value of $W_q = 8.94$ minutes over the two days when data was collected.

Because we have a theoretical model which fits the observed system quite well, we can use it to show what the effect of varying some of the system parameters would be on the system performance. It is easy to write a short computer program for calculating values of W_q as a function of the arrival rate of loads. These are plotted in Figure 16-10. Note how the average waiting time increases hyperbolically as the traffic intensity tends to 1. The situation actually recorded in the two-day survey period corresponds to about 411 loads per day.

Figure 16-10   The effect of arrival rate on waiting times.

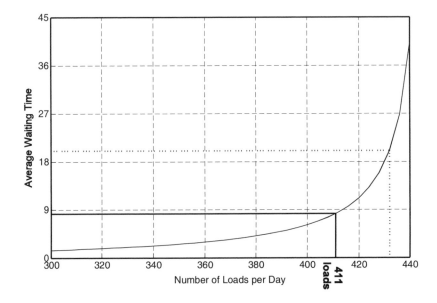

So it is clear that the weighbridge is dangerously close to its maximum practical capacity. An increase of only 5% in wood requirements and hence truck loads (the dotted lines in Figure 16-10) will lead to impossibly long waiting times.

16.5 The two-weighbridge option

To analyse the proposed extra weighbridge we will need a theoretical model of a two-server queue. Unfortunately the M/G/2 queue is one of the queueing models which does not have simple formulas for its operating characteristics.

Assuming that the service time distribution is also negative exponential implies that the standard deviation of service times is equal to the mean service time. In the weighbridge case, the standard deviation of service times is considerably smaller. From expression (16-1) we see that for the single-server case the larger the standard deviation of service times, the larger the mean queue length and mean waiting time. For multiple-server queues it is also a reasonably safe rule of thumb that the more variable the service process is (i.e. the larger the standard deviation of service times), the greater the average delay. So, using the M/M/2 model will result in overestimating the mean queue length and the mean waiting time. The M/M/2 model therefore provides a conservative upper bound on the average delay, and the savings estimated from the M/M/2 model will be smaller than those based on the true variability in service times. The M/M/2 model will thus give a lower bound on the potential savings of a second weighbridge. This is safer than overestimating savings.

What should we do about the move-up time problem? Intuitively we should expect that now very few trucks will have to wait. So our initial approach is to simply ignore the move-up time. If the results confirm that few trucks will wait, then this approximation is suitable. If the fraction of trucks waiting is still significant, then we would have to build a more accurate and hence more complex model.

Using the same arrival rate of $\lambda = 0.5989$ trucks per minute, a service rate of $\mu = 1/1.2070 = 0.8285$, and $C = 2$ servers, the formulas for the M/M/C model give an estimate for W_q of 0.18 minutes. So a good estimate of the minimum reduction in waiting time that will occur if a second weighbridge is built is $8.27 - 0.18 = 8.09$ minutes per load. Extrapolated to an average day's number of loads of around 400, this amounts to 400(8.09) minutes or almost 54 hours of truck time per day. This is the equivalent of the workload of about six trucks. Hence the current workload of hauling logs from the forests to the mill could be accomplished by six fewer trucks.

Remember that the trucks are paid by the amount of wood hauled. Eliminating most of the time wasted waiting at the weighbridge means that each truck can carry more loads per day. Therefore NZFP has a good case to negotiate a reduction in the haulage cost per load and still guarantee that each contractor's daily net earnings are at least as high as under the old system. At a running cost of $80 per truck-hour, the reduction in hauling costs for the mill is slightly over one million dollars (54 hours × 250 days × $80) annually. The additional wage bill for staffing the second weighbridge is less than $100,000 per year. The cost of building a second weighbridge is around $400,000. The cost of the second weighbridge can be recovered in the first six months of use. This sounds like a good proposition!

Activity:
- Why do we want to underestimate the savings due to the second weighbridge rather than overestimate them? Go through the sequence of models we have used and decide if we have achieved this objective.
- If we assume that the arrival process of trucks at the weighbridge is a Poisson process, estimate the maximum arrival rate of trucks that is possible (i.e. for which steady state exists). Verify your answer in Figure 16-10.

16.6 Some conclusions

It is interesting to see how the models we have used for this problem stack up against the properties of a good model listed in Section 5.3. Certainly they are simple, adaptive, and easy to manipulate. The formulas can easily be evaluated with a small computer program or even a calculator. Do they include all significant aspects of the problem? The assumption that the times between trucks arriving at the weighbridge can be drawn from a negative exponential distribution is critical for the use of simple mathematical models, yet the way the wood transport system operates raises serious questions about the validity of that assumption. In the actual system the trucks each make about 8 round trips per day. Hence it appears that a second weighbridge will change the arrival pattern since the round-trip time will be reduced. The key to resolving this worry is to note that the weighbridge is a very small part of a very expensive mill complex, which must be fed with the required amount of wood at all costs. Hence no matter how the weighbridge operation is altered, the flow of trucks across it will remain dictated by the needs of the mill. Knowing the part that the weighbridge plays in the entire system, we safely conclude that more extensive modelling of the arrival process would be very unlikely to change the recommendation for installing a second weighbridge.

With such great savings, was the second weighbridge built in 1989? The answer is 'no'. As often happens with projects of this sort, by the time the recommendations are submitted to the decision makers, or shortly thereafter, other events may change the economic picture. In this case it was a worldwide slump in the demand for newsprint. As a result, the level of operations of the mill was curtailed, reducing the number of daily loads required by the mill slightly. So the immediate pressure was off. There would be no further increase in wood demand until the market had recovered. The additional bridge was finally built in 1993.

However, the wood yard manager was able to put Figure 16-10 right away to good use in presenting a new proposal for a more effective operation of the wood yard. As Figure 16-10 shows, if the number of loads entering the yard during the time from 5:30 a.m. to 5 p.m. could be reduced to 350, the mean waiting time at the weighbridge would decrease to less than 3 minutes. This is one of those profitable changes that brings us down to below the 'knee' of the curve, as described in Section 16-3. One possible alternative would have been to extend the opening hours of the weighbridge by two hours or so to get the remaining 50 to 60 loads processed during this time. However, that would have required the entire workforce of the wood yard to be present, which would have been rather expensive.

A break-down of the type of wood coming in indicated that about 50 loads per day were thinnings. These were processed at a separate part of the yard employing only two people. The obvious solution was thus to restrict the loads coming in after hours to only thinnings. Hence, the congestion at the weighbridge could be reduced dramatically at a minimum of additional labour cost. Figure 16-10 was very valuable for judging the merit of this proposal.

16.7   Chapter highlights

- When we deal with stochastic phenomena, each alternative course of action leads to one of a number of possible outcomes. Prior to taking a particular action, all we may know is the probability distribution over the outcomes associated with that action. A decision is thus equivalent to choosing a particular probability distribution of outcomes.
- For stochastic systems, we are often primarily interested in their long-run behaviour. Hence the decision criterion used for evaluating a course of action is the expected value of the performance measure of interest.
- The simplest structure of waiting lines consists of customers arriving at a service facility, waiting in a queue until it is their turn for service and then being served on a first-come/first served basis. Queues form because both the time between consecutive customer arrivals and the service times are random variables.
- Simple queueing models assume that interarrival times have a negative exponential distribution and that service times are characterized by their expected value and their standard deviation. This leads to simple formulas for the average queue length, average waiting time, and average time in the system.
- Pooling of two or more service facilities results in lower waiting times than operating each facility with its own queue.
- By making judicious simplifications to the actual processes occurring in a waiting line system, it may often be possible to estimate conservative upper or lower bounds to crucial operating characteristics, such as the mean waiting time or the mean queue length which suffice to make safe recommendations for improving the system.

Exercises

1. A firm operates a 20-tonne crane truck on a job contracting basis. Going through the firm's records over the most recent 100 days shows that 140 requests for jobs were received. They took on average 4 hours or ½ day to execute, including the truck's travel time to the site and back to the yard.

   (a) Define the basic structure for this waiting line system, i.e. what constitutes an arrival, the service facility, and a service.

   (b) If you were to use an M/M/1 model, what assumptions must you make about the arrival and service processes? Indicate why or why not they are reasonable.

   (c) Assume now that the M/M/1 model fits. Find the average number of jobs waiting for the truck, and their average waiting time. What fraction of time is the truck idle? Busy?

   (d) If you were to use an M/G/1 model, what assumptions must you make about the arrival and service processes? Are they more likely to be satisfied than those for an M/M/1 model. Why?

   (e) Assume now that the M/G/1 model fits, with a service time standard deviation of 2 hours or ¼ day. Find the average number of jobs waiting for the truck and their average waiting time. What fraction of time is the truck idle? Busy?

2. A thermal power station operates its own coal mine. The mine is only a short distance from a barge loading port also owned and operated by the firm. The port consists of one berth with an automatic loading facility which takes 6 hours to load a barge, with a standard deviation of 1.5 hours. Given the distance between the port and the power station, as well as the variable ocean conditions, barges travelling back and forth between the power station and the port arrive at the port in an almost random pattern, with an average time between arrivals of 10 hours. (The port operates 24 hours/day.)

   (a) Find the fraction of time the port is idle. Compute the average time a barge is in the system, i.e. either waiting or being loaded in port, and the average total time in the system for all barges arriving at the port per day.

   (b) There is a fixed cost of $1200 to operate the port for one day. It costs $1500 to operate a barge for one day. Find the total cost for the port facility, consisting of the port's own operating cost and the cost of the time barges spend in the system.

   (c) The firm is considering upgrading the port's loading facility. The two options available are to decrease the average loading time to 4 hours at a daily operating cost of $1500 or to 3 hours at a daily operating cost of $1800, both with a one-hour standard deviation. Is any one of these options better than the current setup?

   (d) What additional assumption is implicit in your answer to (c)?

3. Consider again exercise 2 above. Assume now that the time to load a barge is deterministic, i.e. the standard deviation of loading times is zero. Reassess the daily average cost of each of the three choices of facilities.

4. Compute the average waiting time of an arrival for a single-server waiting line system with a service rate of 1 and the following set of arrival rates: 0.1, 0.2, 0.3, 0.4, 0.5, 0.6, 0.7, 0.8, 0.9, 0.95, 0.99. Show the average waiting times graphically as a function of the arrival rate. (This is a simple 10-minute exercise on a spreadsheet!)

5. Consider exercise 2 again. The power station plans to double its size, which will also result in a doubling of the number of barges that will transport coal from the mine to the power station. Management wishes to evaluate three possible options for upgrading the port facilities. Option 1 calls for the building of a second port at a new site that offers easier

access and better shelter. This would mean that the firm would operate two separate ports, each handling half of the volume. So barges would arrive at each port on average every 10 hours and each barge would take on average 6 hours to load. The new port would have a daily operating cost of $1000, while the cost of the existing port would remain unchanged. Option 2 calls for the building of a second identical loading facility at the existing port. Barges would arrive on average every 5 hours and then be loaded by the first berth becoming available. However, due to some economies of scale, the two facilities together would have a total daily cost of only $2000. Option 3 calls for the replacement of the current facility by a completely new facility which can load a barge in 3 hours. Its daily cost would be $2000. Barges would again arrive at that facility on average every 5 hours. So all three options have the same total capacity of being able to load 8 barges per day. Assume that the service times for all three options follow a negative exponential distribution.

(a) For each option, determine the average time the port facilities would be idle and the total average time in the system of all ships arriving for loading per day. Note that for Option 2 you will have to use expressions (16-7) and (16-8). What additional approximation will you have to make?

(b) Cost out each option. Which one is the cheapest one? Will the answer for Option 2 overestimate or underestimate the true cost?

6. (This problem is uses a similar model as the weighbridge project with move-up time.) Customers arrive according to a negative exponential distribution at a single-server queue with unlimited waiting space. The mean time between arrivals is two minutes. 30% of the customers require a service of exactly one minute and the remaining 70% require a service of exactly two minutes. The customers are randomly mixed in the arrival stream, i.e. the chance that the next customer will require a service of one minute is always 0.3.

(a) Calculate the steady state probability that an arriving customer does not have to wait.

(b) Calculate the mean number of customers in the queue and the mean time that a customer spends in the system.

7. In Section 16-3, Little's formulas were stated as relations between the system's characteristics for mathematical queueing models that applied only after the system had been running for a long time. Use two copies of an arrival–departure diagram to show that provided the server is idle at the end of the period Little's formulas are also exactly true over any finite period. In other words, provided L_q, W_q and λ are measured over the same period, then $L_q = \lambda W_q$.

8. (a) From Figure 16-4 estimate what the total waiting time of all the customers who arrive during the rush time at the cafeteria will be. Assume the service rate is 500/90 customers per minute. What is the average wait of any customer over the rush time?

(b) If the service rate is increased to 8 customers per minute, how much customer waiting time will this save? Although increasing the service rate obviously provides better service, it will also cost more staff time. From Figure 16-4 estimate approximately what is the maximum service rate that it would be sensible to consider?

(c) Management has agreed with your suggestion that they provide more service capacity, so that the maximum service rate is 8 customers per minute. However they are only prepared to provide this capacity from mid-day (12:00) until the congestion clears. Modify Figure 16-5 to demonstrate the effect of this change and estimate how this will affect the average waiting time.

9. Show that for an M/M/1 queue, where μ is the service rate, expression (16-1) can be rewritten as

$$L_q = \frac{(\lambda/\mu)^2}{(1 - \lambda/\mu)}$$

(a) Verify that expressions (16-6) and (16-7) give the same answer for L_q when $C = 1$.
(b) Use a spreadsheet to draw a graph of L_q versus the traffic intensity, which should be the same as Figure 16-6.

17

Simulation and system dynamics

In Chapter 16 we studied system behaviour under uncertainty with the aid of the theoretical mathematical models of queueing theory. If the problem situation can be captured adequately by fitting a theoretical model to it, this clearly is the preferred approach. However, there are many problem situations where either no suitable theoretical model exists or the problem is so complex that a theoretical model cannot represent the interrelationships properly. In such cases the management scientist often resorts to simulation.

What is simulation? *Webster's Collegiate Dictionary* defines simulation as 'the imitative representation of the functioning of one system or process by means of the functioning of another'. A film or a play is a simulation. In MS/OR, simulation is used to explore the dynamic behaviour or operation of complex commercial, industrial, or technical systems or subsystems. We do this by building a descriptive mathematical model of system behaviour over time. This model needs to include all aspects of the system that have been identified as essential to trace how the state of the system changes. It is then used to record in exact chronological order of **simulated time** (i.e. assumed or imitated time) each and every change in the state of the system that would have occurred had the actual system been operated in **real time** over the same time interval. At the end of the time interval various simulated measures for analysing the performance of the system are computed from the system state changes. (You may have to read this paragraph again to get its full meaning!)

Would it not be more accurate to observe the real operation directly? This may be true. It may though be neither economically affordable, nor technically feasible. It may take years of actual observations to accumulate reliable performance measures for a given mode of operation, let alone alternative modes. Any answers derived may be of little or no relevance by then. Even if observations can be done in a reasonable time interval, this may be too disruptive of the actual operation if alternative decision rules need evaluation. Finally, the system may still be on the drawing board. The simulation may be done precisely to finalize which of various options should be implemented.

On the other hand, a simulation can often be completed in a few days, weeks, or months, depending on the complexity of the system in question. Therefore, a simulation may turn out to be a far more effective approach.

Through simulation the management scientist has at her or his disposal a laboratory technique for experimentation on systems, similar to the experimental methods in the medical, biological, and earth sciences. It is also evident that it was the availability of faster and cheaper computers which allowed simulation to become a powerful MS/OR modelling tool. With the help of ever more friendly computer simulation software, the viability of proposed operating policies for existing and proposed systems can be explored and compared with ease.

The first part of this chapter is mainly devoted to **discrete event simulation**. Changes in the state of the system are triggered by events, such as the arrival of a customer, the start or end of an activity, and so on. Event simulation is particularly suitable for the study of the dynamic behaviour of complex waiting line situations which are beyond representation by theoretical queueing models.

Event simulation may also be used to verify if a queueing model used for modelling a waiting line situation that does not satisfy all assumptions of the theoretical model is a sufficiently good approximation. For example, in the weighbridge problem we incorporated the move-up time as a random component of the service time and argued that this will tend to slightly underestimate the true waiting times. Any reduction in waiting time for the two-weighbridge option would therefore be on the conservative side. A simulation that models the move-up time properly could be used to verify if our argument is correct.

Section 17.1 illustrates the simulation process, using the weighbridge example. Nowhere in MS/OR modelling is the systems view as evident as in simulation. Section 17.2 uses systems concepts to look at the basic structure of event simulation. Section 17.3 discusses strategic and tactical aspects, while in 17.4 we look at computer software.

Discrete event simulation is by far the most common type of simulation. However, there are other forms of simulation, such as fixed-time incrementation and Monte Carlo simulation, briefly described in Section 17.5.

The second part of the chapter deals with the simulation of continuous system, in particular a form which goes under the name of **system dynamics**. Section 17.6 introduces the topic. Section 17.7 gives a simple example, which is expanded into a case study of part of a health system in Section 17.8.

The last section discusses some of the pitfalls of simulation.

17.1   The weighbridge problem revisited

This section will demonstrate the process of simulation. We will use the original situation for one weighbridge. With simulation there is now no need to approximate the move-up process. We can easily model the real-life situation.

A detailed record of processing trucks at the weighbridge

The initial eight columns shown in Table 17-1 report in detail how the first 20 trucks

Table 17-1 Simulation of truck processing over weighbridge.

Column	1	2	3	4	5	6	7	8	9	10	11	12
Truck arriving	Arrival time	Move-up starts	Move-up time	Weighing starts	Weighing time	Weighing ends	Time in system	Waiting time	Interar-rival time	Random number	Random number	Random number
1	2			2	38	40	38	0	2	0.0166	0.0474	0.1064
2	23	40	61	101	59	160	137	78	21	0.1916	0.9531	0.3418
3	87	160	60	220	78	298	211	133	64	0.4706	0.951	0.5582
4	238	298	10	308	30	338	100	70	151	0.7756	0.4001	0.0113
5	506			506	54	560	54	0	268	0.9297	0.6985	0.2832
6	568			568	98	666	98	0	62	0.4603	0.8185	0.7864
7	584	666	28	694	48	742	158	110	16	0.1468	0.7524	0.2143
8	707	742	15	757	90	847	140	50	123	0.7059	0.5264	0.6932
9	717	847	22	869	82	951	234	152	10	0.0963	0.6721	0.6023
10	731	951	38	989	85	1074	343	258	14	0.1276	0.8513	0.6435
11	828	1074	16	1090	92	1182	354	262	97	0.6181	0.5496	0.7197
12	832	1182	13	1195	107	1302	470	363	4	0.0434	0.4808	0.8895
13	1308			1308	89	1397	89	0	476	0.9911	0.8391	0.6838
14	1387	1397	5	1402	53	1455	68	15	79	0.5412	0.2189	0.2785
15	1432	1455	42	1497	58	1555	123	65	45	0.3571	0.8806	0.3362
16	1435	1555	19	1574	77	1651	216	139	3	0.0259	0.62	0.5482
17	1442	1651	60	1711	115	1826	384	269	7	0.0627	0.9505	0.9785
18	1623	1826	9	1835	91	1926	303	212	181	0.8337	0.3561	0.7126
19	1867	1926	11	1937	74	2011	144	70	244	0.9114	0.4248	0.5106
20	1901	2011	9	2020	73	2093	192	119	34	0.2894	0.3669	0.5002
Average			26.13		74.55		192.80	118.25	95.05			

arriving at the weighbridge on a given day were processed. All times are expressed in seconds of time elapsed since the opening of the weighbridge. The first truck is just driving up to the weighbridge when it opens. Its 'arrival time' is recorded as '2' seconds (column 1). Since the weighbridge is unoccupied, there is no 'move-up' time (col. 2 and 3 are blank). 'Weighing starts' immediately at time '2' (col. 4). The 'weighing time' is 38 seconds (col. 5), hence 'weighing ends' at time '40' (col. 6), and truck 1 leaves the weighbridge, i.e. leaves the system. Truck 2 arrives at time '23'. It finds the weighbridge occupied; hence it has to wait until truck 1 leaves the weighbridge at time '40'. At time '40', truck 2 starts moving up to the weighbridge (col. 2). This takes 61 seconds (col. 3). As a result, weighing starts at time [40 + 61] or '101' (col. 4). Weighing takes 59 seconds and truck 2 vacates the weighbridge at time '160'. In the meantime, truck 3 arrives at time '87', finds the weighbridge occupied, and waits until time '160', when it starts moving onto the weighbridge, and so on.

Column 7 records the total time each truck spends in the system, i.e. the difference between its departure time from the weighbridge and its arrival time. Column 8 shows the unproductive time that each truck waits in the queue and moves up to the weighbridge. The time truck 1 spends in the system is simply equal to its weighing time, namely 38 seconds. Its unproductive time is zero. Truck 2 spends 78 seconds of unproductive time — the table entry in column 4 minus the table entry in column 1. Its total time in the system is 137 seconds.

These detailed records allow us to determine some overall measures of performance. For example, the average of column 7 tells us that each truck spends on average 192.8 seconds in the system. Of this, 118.25 seconds on average is lost either waiting in the queue or moving up to the weighbridge (average of column 8). The weighbridge was busy 71.2 % of the time. This percentage is calculated by dividing the sum of the weighing times of all 20 trucks by the 'weighing ends' time for truck 20.

Generating random events

So far we assumed that columns 1 through 8 of Table 17-1 are an actual reconstruction of how the first 20 trucks arriving after 5:30 a.m. on a given day were processed. For this we would have needed an exact record of arrival times, move-up times, and weighing times for each truck.

What if we have not collected such detailed records, but only have summary statistics on the arrival and processing pattern, as shown in Table 16-5 on page 453? Could we construct a table, similar to columns 1 through 8 of Table 17-1, that represents a good imitation of what might happen at the weighbridge at the start of a typical day? The answer is 'yes'. All we need is a method for generating for each truck an artificial but typical triplet of times consisting of an interarrival time, a move-up time, and a service time. These times should be consistent with what we know about their corresponding probability distributions. This is what simulation is all about! It is simply an imitation of the real process, based on artificially created times for the various activities and events that typically occur in the real thing.

How do we generate such artificial activity and event times? With the aid of **random numbers**. Random numbers are lists of the digits from 0 to 9, such as would be obtained by repeatedly drawing one ball at random from an urn that contains ten balls numbered 0 to 9. Each ball drawn is immediately returned to the urn after its number has been recorded, and the balls thoroughly mixed before the next draw.

We may need many thousands of random numbers for a single simulation. So sequences of numbers that have similar statistical properties to the digits obtained by drawing balls from an urn are usually produced by a computer program — a **random number generator**. Since the generation of such numbers is based on a formula, and hence the sequence of numbers that will be produced is in fact exactly known once you know the formula, they are also called **pseudo-random numbers.** All modern spreadsheet programs have a function that generates a random number, expressed as a decimal fraction between 0.000000 and .999999. Columns 10, 11, and 12 of Table 17-1 list 20 sets of three **random decimal fractions**, rounded to 4 significant digits. In Excel and many other packages the name of the function which generates random decimal fractions is RAND.

Random decimal fractions can be transformed into random numbers that have any desired distribution — so-called **random variates** or **deviates**. Consider the weighing times. According to Table 16-5, the weighing time has a mean of $\mu = 1.21$ minutes or 72.6 seconds and a standard deviation of $\sigma = 0.73$ or 43.8 seconds. Assume that the weighing time is normally distributed. Recall also that any value of a normal random variable can be expressed as its mean plus or minus a multiple of its standard deviation. We use the z-values from the normal distribution tables for this purpose. They measure how many standard deviations the value of the normal variable is away from its mean, either in a positive or a negative direction. The first random decimal fraction listed in column 12, $u = 0.1064$, can therefore be transformed into a normal random variate v as follows:

$$v = \mu + z_{u-0.5}\sigma \qquad\qquad (17\text{-}1)$$

$$= 72.6 + z_{(0.1064-0.5)}(43.8) = 72.6 + (-1.25)(43.8) = 17.85,$$

where $z_{u-0.5}$ corresponds to the normal distribution table entry $u - 0.5$. If $u - 0.5$ is negative, then you look up the z-value for the absolute value of $u - 0.5$ and make the z-value negative. This is the case in the above example. Since $0.1064-0.5 = -0.3936 < 0$, we look up the z-value closest to 0.3936, which is 1.25. Hence, $z_{(-0.3936)} = -1.25$. Excel has a function called NORMINV which performs this transformation for you.

For some distributions, the transformation can be done algebraically. For example, a random variate that is uniformly distributed over the range going from $a = 28.8$ to $b = 116.4$ seconds can be produced as follows, using again the first random decimal fraction listed in column 12, $u = 0.1064$:

$$v = a + u(b-a) \qquad\qquad (17\text{-}2)$$

$$= 28.8 + 0.1064(116.4\text{-}28.8) = 38.12 \text{ seconds.}$$

Sometimes we may have an empirical frequency distribution, compiled from observations of an actual process. In such instances, the preferred approach is to use this distribution directly for generating random variates, rather than some theoretical approximation to it. Assume that we have the following frequency distribution:

Observed value	0	1	2	3	4
Frequency	0.23	0.39	0.19	0.13	0.06
Cumulative frequency	0.23	0.62	0.81	0.94	1.00

Say the random decimal fraction to be transformed is $u = 0.7692$. We find the first cumulative frequency which is just larger than 0.7692. This is 0.81 in the above list. Its corresponding observed value is 2. This is the random variate associated with u. Had u been equal to 0.8100, then according to the above rule 0.94 would have been the cumulative frequency just larger than 0.8100, with an associated random variate of 3.

Figure 17-1 shows this transformation graphically. It plots the graph of the cumulative frequency distribution for the above example. Note that the vertical axis goes from 0 to 1, while the horizontal axis lists the values of the random variate. We first locate the point on the vertical axis corresponding to the random decimal fraction (0.7692), then go across until we meet the curve. Next we drop a vertical line down to the horizontal axis. This will identify the corresponding value

Figure 17-1   The Cumulative distribution function.

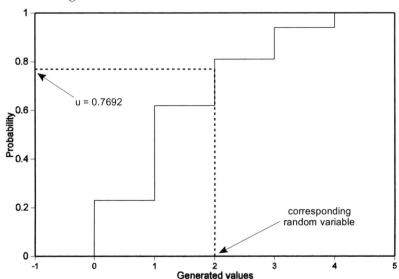

of the random variate. Because the vertical steps in the graph are in proportion to the frequencies of each value, the process will generate random variates with the correct frequencies. Since we use the graph in this inverted way, the method is known as the **inverse transform method**. It is the basis of most methods for generating random variates from empirical distributions, as well as from discrete probability distributions. Excel has macro functions for inverse transformations of this sort. In this example the random variate had only four possible values, but clearly the same look-across and then look-down process would apply to distributions with more values, and even, in the limit, to continuous distributions. Luckily, for a few random variables, notably negative exponential, the mathematical inverse of the distribution function is known.

Suppose that we want to a produce random variate from a negative exponential distribution with a mean of a. Let u be the random decimal fraction we have generated. Then the corresponding negative exponential variate is obtained from

$$u = 1 - e^{-v/a}$$

or $$v = a[-\ln(1 - u)] \tag{17-3}$$

ln denotes the natural logarithm to the base e. Thus a simple logarithmic operation transforms a random decimal fraction into a random variate with a negative exponential distribution. Figure 17-2 illustrates this process for generating the interarrival times of trucks at the weighbridge.

According to Table 16-5, the mean interarrival time of trucks at the weighbridge is $a = 1.68$ minutes or 100.8 seconds. Applying expression (17-3) to the same

Figure 17-2 The inverse transform for a negative exponential distribution.

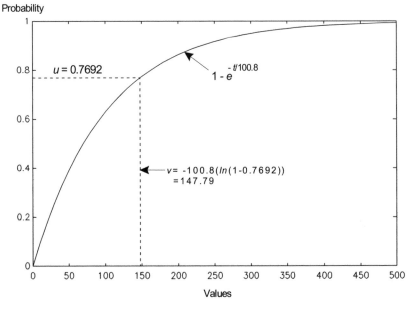

random decimal fraction (0.7692) produces an interarrival time of 147.79 seconds, as depicted in Figure 17-2. You should check your understanding by verifying that the first random decimal fraction in column 10 of Table 17-1 (0.0166) transforms into an interarrival time of 1.69 seconds.

Most random number generators available in computer software allow the user to specify a so-called **starting seed** — so-to-speak the first n-digit random decimal fraction used to start off the sequence of random numbers generated. It is, however, important to realize that for a given starting seed and random number generator exactly the same sequence of random numbers will be generated. Most spreadsheets, for example, have a built-in starting seed. So every new session when the spreadsheet is started up will always begin with the same seed. As a result it will produce exactly the same sequence of random numbers each time. This is a serious trap for the unwary, although as we shall see in Section 17.3, there are situations in which this property can have considerable modelling benefits.

Simulating the weighbridge operation

For each truck we have to generate an interarrival time, a move-up time if the truck has to wait, and a weighing time. Table 16-5 shows that the standard deviations of the truck interarrival times and move-up times are very close to their corresponding averages. If this is the case and each occurrence is independent of all other events, then the negative exponential distribution is often a good approximation. The inter-arrival time is thus assumed to have a negative exponential distribution with a mean of 1.68 minutes or 100.8 seconds, while the move-up time has a negative exponential distribution with a mean of 0.33 minutes or 19.8 seconds. (Note that for the negative exponential the standard deviation is equal to the observed mean — the only parameter of the distribution needed!)

The weighing time, on the other hand, seems to follow a different, but unknown, distribution. A tempting choice would be an approximation by a normal distribution with a mean of 1.21 minutes or 72.6 seconds and a standard deviation of 0.73 minutes or 43.8 seconds. However, given the relatively large standard deviation in comparison to the mean, very small random decimal fractions could easily result in negative weighing times, which is impossible. So we have to choose a different approximating distribution.

In a real application, the preferred approach would be the compilation of an empirical frequency distribution, based on a sample of some 100 observed weighing times. It would then be used in a table to generate directly corresponding random variates, using the method in Figure 17-1. Since we ultimately wish to use a spread-sheet for simulating the weighbridge problem, such an approach is computationally rather demanding. Hence we will use a somewhat rough approximation, based on a uniform distribution. Its range $[a, b]$ is chosen to correspond to $a = \mu - \sigma = 72.6 - 43.8 = 28.8$ and $b = \mu + \sigma = 72.6 + 43.8 = 116.4$ seconds, i.e. one standard deviation on either side of the mean. Although the true distribution is likely to be skewed, with a fairly long tail for high values, this approximation should underestimate the average waiting times. From a modelling point of view this is preferable. We do not want to represent the current situation as worse than it is in reality, and thereby produce a bias in favour of a change.

Consider again Table 17-1. The simulation starts at simulated time '0'. We now generate the first arrival. For this we need an interarrival time. For the first truck this is the time between the start of the simulation and the truck's arrival time. We use the random decimal fractions in column 10 to generate interarrival times. The first entry is 0.0166. We used it in expression (17-3) to generate a random variate from a negative exponential distribution. We obtained a value of 1.69 seconds, which we rounded to the nearest integer. So the first interarrival time is 2 seconds. This is the entry in column 9. Hence truck 1 arrives 2 seconds after the start of the simulation (entry in column 1). Since the weighbridge is empty, no move-up time has to be generated. The next random variate needed is the one for the weighing time of truck 1. We use the random decimal fractions in column 12 for that. The first entry is 0.1064, which we used above in expression (17-2) for demonstrating how to generate a uniformly distributed random variate in the range of 28.8 to 116.4. We got 38.12 seconds, which we round to 38 (entry in column 5).

We now create the arrival of truck 2. Using the second entry in column 10, 0.1916, expression (17-3) gives an interarrival time of $100.8(-\ln(1 - 0.1916)) = 21.44$ seconds, which we round to 21 (col. 9). Truck 2 arrives at simulated time $[2 + 21] = 23$ seconds (col. 1). It has to wait. So we now generate a move-up time from a negative exponential distribution with mean 19.8 seconds, using the random decimal fractions listed in column 11. The second entry in column 11, 0.9531, transforms into a move-up time of $19.8(-\ln(1 - 0.9531)) = 60.58$ seconds, rounded to 61 (col. 3). Note that if a truck does not have a move-up time, we simply skip the random decimal fraction reserved for this calculation in column 11. This was the case for truck 1. The second entry in column 12, 0.3398, gives a weighing time of $28.8 + 0.3398(116.4 - 28.8) = 58.57$ or 59 seconds (col. 5).

This process continues until the simulation is stopped. To test your understanding, verify the generation of random variates in the simulation for another few arrivals. In this example, the simulation was stopped after 20 arrivals. A more common **stopping rule** is to run the simulation until the simulated time reaches a specified time, such as a whole working day for the weighbridge problem. Table 17-1 covers only the first 40 minutes of simulating a full working day at the weighbridge. The lists of random decimal fractions in columns 10 to 12 were produced by the random number function of a spreadsheet program.

Activity:
- Why do trucks 5 and 6 each have no entry in the move-up time column?
- Verify the times in columns 2, 4, 6, 7, 8 of Table 17-1 for trucks 3 to 6.
- What if there were two weighbridges in parallel, where a truck goes to the first available one? Would this spreadsheet approach extend easily to this case? What implicit ordering of events are we relying on for the spreadsheet to work?
- How would you convert random decimal fractions into random variates from a uniform distribution with a range from −2 to +3?
- Take natural logs and verify the first term in (17-3) leads to the second equation.

17.2 The structure of simulation models

The simple spreadsheet approach to simulating the weighbridge problem worked because there was an inherent ordering of the events in the single queue model. A truck could not move onto the weighbridge until the previous arrival had left. For more complex situations we need a more general method of describing how the components of a system interact. In this section we will classify the components of a simulation system, and describe one method — entity life cycles — for capturing the complex interactions of these components.

In the terminology of event simulation, the components of the system are called **entities**. An event simulation traces the behaviour of entities through the system. There may be several types or **classes of entities**, such as people, machines, goods, or pieces of information, interacting with each other. For example, consider the simulation of a job shop, where various jobs arrive for processing on one or a sequence of machines. The sequence may be different from job to job. The jobs form one class of entities. Each group of interchangeable machines forms another class of entities.

Some types of entities may be **permanent**, such as the machines in the job shop. They remain part of the system throughout the entire simulation run. Others are **temporary** entities, such as the jobs. They are created at the time they arrive and are then cancelled or destroyed at the time they have finished all processing.

Entities engage in **activities**. For example, a job and a machine engage jointly in an activity, separate, and then may join another entity for a new activity, or become idle (for machines) or leave the system (for jobs).

The exact sequence of processing a given job in the job shop example is called an **attribute** of the job. This is an example of a permanent attribute. The machine on which a job is processed at any given point in simulated time is another attribute of the job — a temporary attribute in this case, since it changes once the processing at that machine ceases. Machines also have permanent attributes, such as the speed of processing, and temporary attributes, such as whether a machine is idle or busy.

At any given point in simulated time, the system has a given configuration, defined by the ongoing activities of the entities and the value(s) of the various temporary attributes of each entity. This is the **state** of the simulated system. A change in the state of the system is referred to as an **event**. For instance, in the job shop system the arrival of a new job, the start of processing a job on a machine, or the end of processing a job on a machine, are all events.

Some events may be imposed on the system from outside, i.e. they may be specified as an input to the system by the analyst. A typical example is the event that causes the simulation to stop, such as the value of the simulated time signalling the end of the simulation run. Other events are generated by the simulation itself, either by the completion of an activity or by another event. For example, in the job shop the event 'machine X starts processing job K' may be the consequence of the event 'machine X finishes job L', with job K waiting for processing at machine X (a temporary attribute of job K) or the event 'job K arrives at machine X', with machine X being idle at that time (a temporary attribute of machine X).

The weighbridge simulation structure

The weighbridge itself is a permanent entity. The weighing time distribution is its permanent attribute, while 'idle', 'waiting for a truck to move-up', and being 'busy' are its temporary attributes. The trucks are temporary entities. Their permanent attribute is their arrival pattern, as indicated by the interarrival time distribution. 'Waiting in the queue', 'moving-up', or 'being weighed' are their temporary attributes.

Trucks engage in three activities. They 'arrive', 'move-up', and are 'being weighed'. The weighbridge engages in one activity only, namely 'weighing'. However, it is standing by while a truck 'moves-up'. During that time the weighbridge is blocked — a sort of pseudo-activity it goes through if a truck has been 'waiting' while the bridge finished a 'weighing'. A truck engages in the activities 'arriving' singly, while for 'moving-up' and 'weighing' it also requires the presence of another entity, the weighbridge. So a truck and the weighbridge engage jointly in the activities 'moving-up' and 'weighing'. The events are 'the arrival of a truck', 'the start of moving-up', 'the end of moving-up', 'the start of weighing', and 'the end of weighing'. So, most events are associated with the start or end of an activity. There are two more events present in each simulation, namely 'the start' and 'the end of the simulation'.

Some activities and events can only occur if the state of the system satisfies a given condition. For example, the activity 'moving-up' can only start when two conditions are satisfied: a truck must be waiting and the event 'weighing' has been completed. On the other hand, once the truck has completed 'moving-up', it and the weighbridge unconditionally engage in the joint activity 'weighing'.

Entity life cycles

Each type of entity goes through a sequence of activities and changes of temporary state attributes. For example, a truck first 'arrives' and then 'waits in the queue' if the weighbridge is 'busy' or 'waiting for a truck to complete moving up'. Sooner or later the truck 'moves up', followed immediately by 'being weighed', and finally leaves the system. Alternatively, if a truck arrives while the weighbridge is in the 'idle' state, it goes through 'wait in the queue' without stopping and immediately engages in 'being weighed', and then leaves. So each truck goes through a **life cycle** of activities and inactivities or queues. This can be depicted graphically. Figure 17-3 shows the two paths for the truck life cycle. Activities are depicted as rectangles and queues as circles. The source and the sink of temporary entities are depicted as clouds.

This entity cycle diagram has a special feature, namely alternative paths that a truck could take, depending on whether or not the weighbridge is 'free' at the time of its arrival. A diamond is used to depict this switching mechanism. (Note that different authors may use different conventions.)

Figure 17-3   Life cycle diagram for truck entities

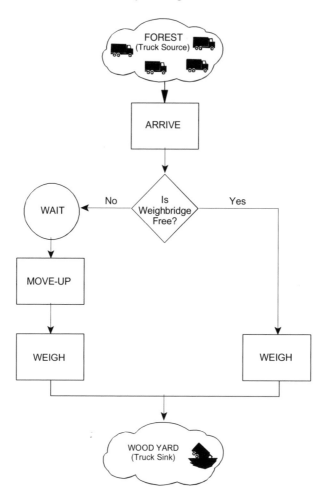

The entity weighbridge also has a life cycle, as shown in Figure 17-4. Since it is a permanent entity it repeats that life cycle for each truck it processes. As for trucks, the path involves a switch, depending on whether or not the queue of trucks is empty. If the weighbridge is 'idle', which can only happen if no trucks are 'waiting in the queue', then it remains 'idle' until a truck 'arrives'. At that point the weighbridge engages in 'weighing' (right-hand side of diagram) and then returns to the switch. If in the meantime a new truck has 'arrived' and is 'waiting in the queue', then the switch sends the weighbridge onto the left-hand path where it first 'waits for truck to complete move-up', after which it 'weighs' the truck, and returns again back to the switch for a new cycle.

Note that we show 'idle' as a queue. If there is only one weighbridge, it may not seem so obvious that being 'idle' has the nature of a queue. In state 'idle' the

Figure 17-4   Life cycle of weighbridge

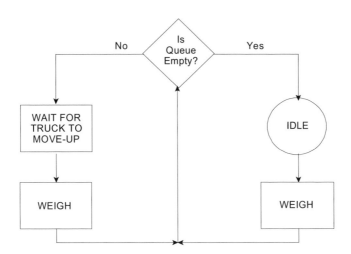

weighbridge is waiting for a truck to arrive. If there are several weighbridges that could be in the state 'idle', it becomes immediately clear that this is in fact a queue structurally no different from the queue 'wait' for trucks.

To show the interactions between the two types of entities we combine the two life cycles, such that they coincide for activities engaged in jointly by a truck and the weighbridge. This is shown in Figure 17-5. Since 'moving-up' and 'waiting for truck to complete move-up' always occur in parallel, in other words jointly, nothing is lost by referring to both as 'moving-up'. The two cycles merge for 'moving-up' and separate again after 'weighing'. For the alternative path, a truck and the weighbridge only join for 'weighing'.

Note that if trucks do not need to go through a 'move-up', but can directly enter the weighbridge once it becomes free, there is no need for a switch mechanism for either the truck or the weighbridge. In this case each has a single, unique path for its activity cycle. After 'arriving', a truck 'waits' until the weighbridge becomes 'idle' and then immediately joins with the latter for 'weighing' before departing. The weighbridge also remains in the queue 'idle' until a new truck arrives, at which point it joins the truck for 'weighing' and returns to 'idle'. If another truck is already waiting, it simply zooms through 'idle' and immediately starts another 'weighing'. As an exercise, draw the combined activity cycle diagram for this simpler situation.

The model used for the weighbridge creates the truck entities coming from the forest and then destroys them after weighing. In reality, the trucks are involved in round trips, picking up logs in various forests, bringing them to the mill over the weighbridge, unloading them in the wood yard, and returning to the forest, starting another round trip. Given that the weighbridge operation occupies only a small part

Figure 17-5   Truck and weighbridge life cycles combined

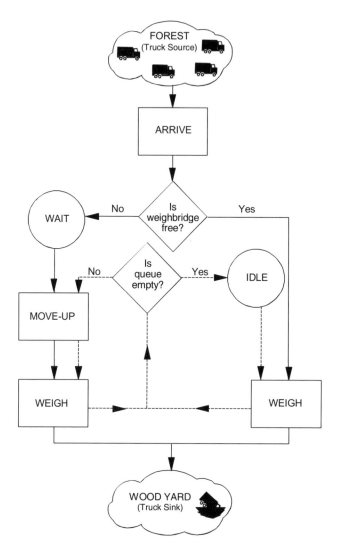

of each round trip, we use this as justification for separating it out from the round trip. However, any time lost waiting at the weighbridge will reduce the number of round trips a truck can undertake per day. As long as the congestion at the weighbridge remains minor, the reduction in round trips will be negligible. If the waiting times become excessive, say longer than 15 minutes, the effect may become significant.

A better approximation might be to model the round trips explicitly. The life cycle diagram for trucks is then also a closed loop, and the trucks become permanent entities, executing several new activities and queues, such as 'trip to forest and back', 'travel from weighbridge to wood yard', 'waiting for unloading', and 'unloading of logs'. Additional permanent entities, such as log unloaders, may have to be introduced. (Such a simulation would be very difficult or even impossible to set up for a spreadsheet. The use of specialized computer simulation software would be essential.)

As with influence diagrams, entity life cycle diagrams have several uses. They are a powerful display device for facilitating communication between problem owners and analysts or between analysts. They clearly show the interactions between entities and therefore facilitate better understanding of the complexities of the system. They can serve as a first step for writing a computer simulation program. In fact, a number of simulation packages explicitly or implicitly view event simulations in the form of entity life cycles. Some require the input to be organized and submitted in this form.

Activity: Get together a group of friends and play the following game (matchboxes can be substituted for friends):
- Divide into two groups of similar size and form two lines.
- Draw a circle on the ground between the two groups.
- The two persons at the head of each line must simultaneously and randomly decide to move into the circle. They hold hands for another randomly selected length of time and then each rejoin the back of their respective lines. Repeat this step a number of times.

You have been simulating a queue with a number of servers using the activity-cycle method. Does it matter which group represented the customers and which were the servers?

17.3 How is a simulation planned and run ?

Performing a simulation for a sufficiently large number of events or a sufficiently long period of time is called a **simulation run**. For all realistic practical applications this is done by computer. How should we plan such simulation runs in order to get useful and reliable results? This is a rather difficult question, so do not expect a comprehensive and definitive answer, if one even exists! We will simply be able to point out some of the more basic and obvious rules to follow and pitfalls to avoid.

Measures of performance

The analyst has to be very clear what kind of measures are needed to judge and compare the performance of alternative systems, such as one weighbridge versus two weighbridges. The simulation program has to be capable of collecting the information for compiling these measures. For instance, in the weighbridge problem we are interested in measures such as the average time a truck spends in the system, as well as how that time breaks down into waiting, moving-up, and being weighed. In a spreadsheet simulation these measures can be computed from the details recorded. Other simulation packages may require setting special accumulators to capture this information. Management may also wish to know what percentage of trucks has to wait longer than, say, 3 minutes. Hence the data collected may have to be organized in the form of a frequency distribution, rather than the simple cumulative totals needed for averages.

The performance of the real system usually varies over time. For example, in the weighbridge operation, there will be days when everything moves smoothly over the weighbridge, with few long delays. On other days, the congestion may be very bad, with many trucks delayed up to 20 minutes. So the average waiting time per truck varies from day to day. A good simulation of the weighbridge operation should, therefore, exhibit a comparable pattern of daily performance measures. Table 17-2 lists the results of 64 simulation runs, each for one day's operation covering about 400 truck arrivals. These results were obtained using the spreadsheet format of Table 17-1. With the help of a simple macro program, all 64 runs were made in succession, taking only a few seconds on a PC.

The average time trucks spent waiting in the queue and moving up varies widely from a minimum of 172 seconds for day 21 to a maximum of 1084 seconds for day 40. In fact, each run is one observation on a random experiment. Hence the times listed in Table 17-2 are 64 observations of the random variable 'average daily waiting time per truck'.

Variability of simulation results

In contrast to most MS/OR models, the inputs into a simulation model are often

Table 17-2   Sum of waiting and move-up times for 64 days.

Day	Time	Day	Time	Day	Time	Day	Time
1	426	17	173	33	405	49	560
2	915	18	278	34	582	50	835
3	327	19	641	35	302	51	317
4	954	20	199	36	400	52	329
5	782	21	172	37	426	53	350
6	330	22	394	38	325	54	241
7	289	23	331	39	607	55	308
8	475	24	386	40	1084	56	459
9	256	25	333	41	677	57	558
10	242	26	279	42	603	58	325
11	330	27	615	43	243	59	347
12	432	28	392	44	627	60	183
13	589	29	277	45	342	61	186
14	316	30	655	46	705	62	524
15	729	31	449	47	875	63	372
16	601	32	258	48	517	64	545
		Average	452.9		Standard deviation		207.8

sequences of random variates (such as the sequence of truck arrival times), rather than the single parameter estimates we might need for a theoretical queueing model. For example, although we based the generation of interarrival times on an average of 100.8 seconds, the observed average for the first 20 interarrival times shown in Table 17-1 is, in fact, 95.05 seconds. Hence the output measures of system performance collected from the simulation model will also reflect this variability. Figure 17-6 attempts to capture the problem we now face.

Figure 17-6   Variability of simulation results.

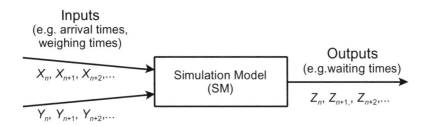

We want the variable inputs in order to have a valid model. However, as a result of this, we can expect to observe variable output measures, such as the waiting times in a queue. As we have seen in the example above, the variations observed may be surprisingly large. To get a sufficiently reliable picture of the long-run performance of the system simulated, it is therefore essential to make a sufficiently large number of simulation runs. This will not only give better estimates of the average values for all performance measures, but will also allow us to estimate their variation, such as their standard deviations. These can then be used to specify interval estimates for the performance measures of interest. Narrow interval estimates give more confidence in the reliability of the results. It is essential that the presentation of simulation results always includes some measures of the variability of the results as an indication of their reliability.

For our example, the overall average for the 64 days is 7 minutes and 32.9 seconds. This is fairly close to the values predicted by the theoretical model in Chapter 16. The standard deviation of average waiting times is 207.8 seconds. We can thus specify an approximate 95% confidence interval on the average total waiting time of 400.9 to 504.9 seconds (i.e. $452.9 \pm 1.96[207.8/\sqrt{64}]$; see a statistics text for details on how to find confidence intervals). Note that this is a rather wide interval. Unfortunately, the number of runs needed to get confidence intervals that bracket the overall average by just a few percent can easily be in the hundreds or thousands.

Much of the more sophisticated simulation methodology is, in fact, concerned with reducing some of the variability in the simulation output measures. Let us briefly touch on one of those, namely the use of common random numbers.

Simulations are usually done to explore how crucial performance measures are affected by different operating options or configurations, such as one or two weighbridges. If each option is simulated with a new set of random numbers, then the simulation results are affected by two sources of variability. The first is the variability inherent in the operation itself. That variability we want to measure. The second is the variability introduced by using different sequences of random numbers. That second variability we would rather do without. Fortunately, in many instances, this second variability can easily be reduced. The secret is to use the same sequence of random numbers in each configuration, for a given type of activity or event. This can be achieved by taking advantage of the property of random number generators mentioned in Section 17.1, that for any given starting seed the random number generator will always reproduce exactly the same sequence of random numbers.

We demonstrate this for the weighbridge example. There are three types of random activity: the arrival of trucks measured by the interarrival time between consecutive trucks, the move-up time, and the weighing time. All we need to do is to make sure that for the two-weighbridge simulation the times used for each truck arriving are identical to the ones used for the one-weighbridge simulation. This will eliminate the variability that would be introduced had we used different times generated by the use of different random number sequences. (In a spreadsheet simulation, the simplest way to guarantee this is to generate the required sequences of random numbers prior to the start of the simulation proper and store them somewhere in the spreadsheet for later use.)

Intuitively, what we are doing is just what you would do if you were running an agricultural experiment to determine the difference between the yields from two brands of carrot seed: you would ensure that as many as possible of the inputs (water, sunlight, fertilizer) to the two plots were the same, in order to reduce the variance of the difference of the outputs. In terms of Figure 17-6 we could say that we now have two models, SM_1 and SM_2, producing outputs $Z_n^1, Z_{n+1}^1, \dots$ and Z_n^2, $Z_{n+1}^2, \dots$ respectively. By ensuring that as many as possible of the inputs $X_n, X_{n+1}\dots$ and $Y_n, Y_{n+1},\dots$ are the same for the two models we hope that Z^1 and Z^2 will be positively correlated. If this is true then the variance of their differences will be less than the sum of their variances. Thus when the objectives of the model are taken into account, what initially appeared in Section 17.1 to be a serious defect of random number generators is indeed often exploited to produce more accurate model results.

Length of simulation runs

In the weighbridge system, the system starts at 5:30 a.m. every working day with an empty queue. No trucks arrive after 5:00 p.m., but any trucks waiting at that time will still be processed. There are many real-life applications with this daily or periodic pattern, with each period starting and ending with an empty system, i.e. with no temporary entities present. For periodic operations of this type, the system's performance is measured with respect to that period, e.g. a day.

In the job shop example, the operation is also interrupted at the end of each working day. However, the system starts each new day in exactly the state it was stopped the previous day. Any temporary entities in the system simply resume their life cycle at the point the system was interrupted at the end of the previous day. Hence the operation does not go through a regular daily cycle, but continues indefinitely.

Figure 17-7 shows how the performance measure for the cumulative average waiting time in a simple queueing model behaved in an simulation run of 1,000 arrivals. This is an M/M/1 queue with a mean time between arrivals of 15 minutes and a mean service time of 10 minutes. Because the first simulated customer arrives to an empty queue the average waiting time also starts from zero. Although initially it rapidly increases towards the steady state value of 20 minutes (calculated from formulas (16-1) and (16-4)), it is clearly affected by the initial empty state of the system. This effect is referred to as the **transient effect**. Note that even after the transient effect becomes small, the average waiting time continues to fluctuate up and down, although the magnitude of these fluctuations becomes smaller.

You should also note that in simulations we are often observing highly correlated random variables, such as the waiting times of successive customers in the queue or successive trucks at the weighbridge. If the 300th truck has to wait for an abnormally long time then there is a good chance that the 301st truck will also

Figure 17-7   Behaviour of waiting time with run length.

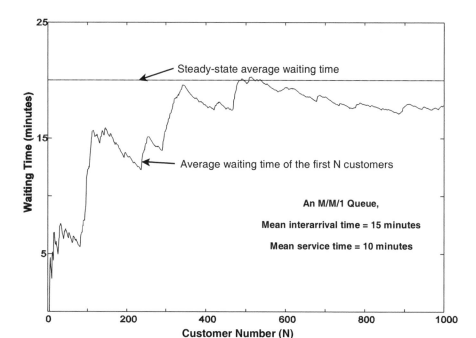

be abnormally delayed. (You may like to look at the graphs in Figure 16-2 to help confirm this point.) It is often this **positive serial correlation** that accounts for the very slow convergence of system characteristics towards their steady state values, both in simulations and in actual queue systems.

In view of this long-run behaviour, how should the length of a simulation run be chosen if we want to estimate the long-run characteristics of the system? The answer to this question is not simple. The stronger the initial transient effect is, the longer it takes for the system to settle down, and the longer the simulation must run. If we could start the system in an initial state which reflects the system's long-run behaviour, the transient effect would disappear or become negligible. As a consequence, the length of the simulation run could be shortened without affecting the accuracy of the performance estimates obtained.

Note that the fluctuations for the cumulative average waiting time in Figure 17-7 tend to decrease the longer the run. Hence the accuracy of the estimates obtained from each individual run increases with the run length. There is a second reason why the accuracy of the estimates increases with the run length. As we have seen in Table 17-1, the average interarrival time over the first 20 arrivals was 95.05. As the run length increases, the resulting average will get closer to its theoretical value of 100.8 seconds. Hence the simulation results become more representative. But long runs also take more computer time to execute.

Furthermore, measures of the variability of the results become more reliable if they are based on a sufficiently large number of runs. So, the accuracy of the final results can be increased by either increasing the run length of each simulation or the number of runs. Which strategy is more effective is hard to tell. There is a trade-off between the number of runs and the length of each run. As a rule of thumb, the number of runs should be at least 10 for small sample statistics to give acceptable results in terms of reliability. Similarly, most analysts would chose a run length for each simulation covering thousands of periods, say days, rather than just a few hundred.

Initial conditions

We saw above that, for some problems, a natural initial condition for starting the simulation is with no temporary entities present and all permanent entities in their natural 'parked' position. Such systems also end in the same 'empty state'. Hence, each simulation run starts with an empty state.

For other situations an empty state may occasionally occur too at random points in time. However, if used as a starting point, it may result in a long transient period before the performance measures settle down around their long-run averages. Getting rid of this transient period gives more accurate results even for shorter run lengths. In some situations, the analyst may be able to guess a suitable initial state for each run which shortens the transient period substantially. For example, setting the number of temporary entities in various queues equal to or close to their long-run average may have the desired effect.

A favourite trick used is to set the initial conditions for a simulation run equal to the ending state of the preceding run. This relieves the analyst from having to manually set initial conditions.

Another method that helps to eliminate the transient effect is to exclude all data for an appropriately chosen initial interval of the simulation, sometimes called a **warm-up period**. Data collection only starts after that interval. A good length for this initial interval can be found by some experimentation.

17.4 Computer simulation packages

Most simulations are performed by specialized computer software, such as GPSS, SIMSCRIPT, Simul8, or ARENA. For all but the simplest types of simulation, using one of these packages is recommended. Although spreadsheets can do rudimentary simulations, they lack not only many of the facilities needed, but also can only handle simple systems where each temporary entity can be processed through all operations with reference to event times of only the just preceding entity. This is the case for the single weighbridge problem. For the two-weighbridge problem, the two bridges may not necessarily process two trucks that arrived consecutively, but trucks that were separated by other truck arrivals. Writing spreadsheet macros to deal with this complexity would be tricky, increasing the computational time many-fold.

Computer simulation packages have facilities to generate random variates from many distributions, often with individually controlled random number generators. They automatically keep track of the state of the system and properly execute all events at their scheduled times. They automatically collect performance measures on all queues and allow the programmer to specify other statistics to be collected, including frequency distributions for various passage times, like waiting times. They contain automatic checking for errors in the simulation logic. They also allow the creation of output reports in the form needed for submission to the decision makers. The input to many of them consists simply of the various entity life cycles. Programming time is therefore reduced to a fraction of what it would take to use one of the general-purpose computer languages, like Visual Basic, Fortran, or C.

To give you an indication how simple such a program may be, Figure 17-8 lists the core of a GPSS/H program which was used for simulating the weighbridge problem. The entire program consists of only 37 lines. GPSS/H uses a slightly different problem representation method to that of entity cycles, called the **process-interaction** approach. The program consists of statements describing the process through which temporary entities pass. Specialized statements such as SEIZE and RELEASE then describe the way these entities interact with the model. For example, only one temporary entity is allowed to be present in the section of the program from SEIZE BRIDGE to RELEASE BRIDGE, thus modelling the way in which each truck has exclusive use of the weighbridge.

Recently, the availability of Windows and personal computers has contributed to the rise of visual interactive simulation packages such as ARENA and Simul8.

Figure 17-8   GPSS/H weighbridge program.

```
        GENERATE    RVEXPO(3,100.8),,,,,,1PH
        ASSIGN      EMPTY,F(BRIDGE),PH
        QUEUE       WAITQ
        SEIZE       BRIDGE
        DEPART      WAITQ
        TEST G PH(EMPTY),0,IDLE
        ADVANCE     FN(MOVUP)
  IDLE  ADVANCE  FN(WEIGH)
        RELEASE     BRIDGE
        TERMINATE
        GENERATE    41400
        TERMINATE  1
```

In these packages, the model is created by dragging and dropping pre-defined icons for various permanent entities onto the screen. For example, dragging and dropping the four icons in Figure 17-9 is enough to set up a Simul8 model of a simple queue like those discussed in Section 16.3. (The "8" in Simul8 was inspired by the minimum number of key strokes or mouse clicks needed to set up simple models!)

Figure 17-9   A simple queue modelled in Simul8.

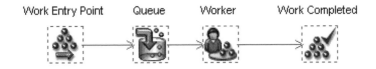

Temporary entities are created in the Work Entry Point. They wait for service in the Queue and then engage in the activity Being Served at the Worker. Finally they are destroyed and some statistics are gathered at Work Completed. A considerable advantage of these visual interaction packages is that an apparently realistic model can be created very quickly, even in front of the client. They are also much easier and more rewarding to learn initially. A disadvantage is that it may be difficult or even impossible to model particular kinds of complex entity behaviour if these are not provided by the predefined icons. Because the usual attributes of Simul8 temporary entities are less flexible than those of GPSS/H , for example, it is difficult to expand the model to capture the move-up behaviour of trucks at the weighbridge without external programming in Visual Basic.

An alternative strategy to programming would be to exploit the simplicity and speed of Simul8 to run a range of models which could be expected to over- and underestimate the results like the queueing models discussed in Section 16.4.

Figure 17-10 shows a screen of part of a model of a hospital accident and emergency department in Simul8. We changed the icons to more appropriate pictures and sketched an outline of the facility on the screen to enhance the appeal of the model to the client. Although the initial program was sketched out in less than a day, the model in Figure 17-10 again required substantial additional programming to model the complex behaviour of different classes of patient, and the different patterns of patient arrival over times of day and days of the week.

Activity:
- Describe in general terms how you might modify the spreadsheet simulations of the weighbridge in order to reduce the variability of the results due to using different sequences of random numbers.
- Does the transient effect present a problem for the weighbridge simulation?
- Does the problem of serial correlation apply to the results of separate days of the weighbridge simulation? Note that each day starts from empty.

17.5   Other simulation structures

Fixed-time incrementation

Event simulation is particularly suitable for queueing and sequencing situations of all sorts. Simulated time is always updated to the time when the next most imminent event is scheduled to occur.

For other situations it is more appropriate to update simulated time in equal discrete time intervals, such as a day or a month. Recall the production scheduling problem for the Crystal Springs Mineral Water Company in Chapter 11. There we traced out exactly what would happen month by month for a given shift level and production schedule. In fact, we simulated the response of the system to various policies, trying to identify the best policy. We did not refer to it as a simulation, but it was a deterministic simulation with monthly time intervals.

This type of time updating is called **fixed-time incrementation**. It is a suitable modelling approach if some events occur regularly in each period and it is not important to record exactly at which exact point in time within a period events occur, as this has little effect on the performance measures. It is usually convenient to assume that all events occur either at the beginning or the end of a period. For example, a simulation of a production/inventory control situation, like the one described in Chapter 6, would assume that any replenishments arrive in stock at the beginning of a day, while all stock withdrawals to meet customer orders occur at the end of each day. All costs would be assessed as of the end of each day.

Fixed-time incrementation is also used as an approximation for simulations of continuous systems, such as the operation of a series of hydro storage reservoirs.

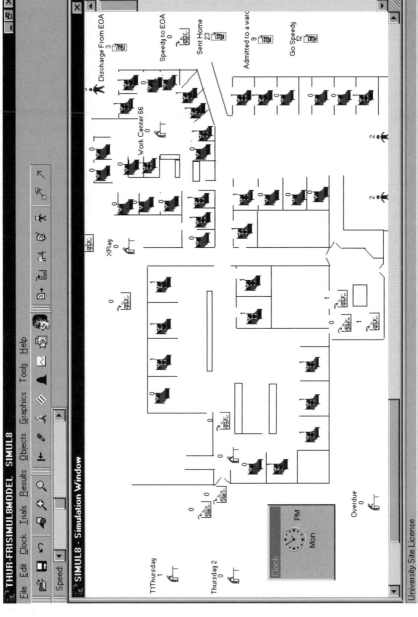

Figure 17-10
An accident and
emergency
department in
Simul8.

In such systems, some water flows into and out of each reservoir constantly. The control variables are the rate of water release for electric power generation. We do not have entities and events in the sense discussed in Section 17.2.

Although a number of computer simulation packages, like VENSIM, STELLA, and *ithink* (see Section 17-6), allow modelling of the continuous flow rate nature of such situations, we often approximate the behaviour of such systems by fixed-time incrementation. Water inflows and outflows are assumed to occur at constant rates over each planning subperiod: say, an hour. Any changes in rate also occur only at the beginning or end of a period. The inflow rate may be generated randomly from a theoretical probability distribution or an empirically obtained frequency distribution. With these assumptions the state of the system, such as reservoir levels or generators in use, at the end of each period can be assessed exactly. Each simulation run might cover a year and is repeated for different randomly generated inflows 30 to 50 times for each set of alternative policy rules.

Monte Carlo simulation and risk analysis

Sometimes the problem we are interested in refers directly to random sampling of probability distributions. For example how would you determine the probability distribution for the length of the **critical path** of a project, like that described in Figure 5-8 on page 101. Well, one way would be to simply draw a sample of the length of time that each task takes, use these times to determine the length of the critical path, and repeat this process for a thousand trials. The times generated are a sample probability distribution for the length of the critical path.

Such determinations of complex statistical distributions go under the name of **Monte Carlo** simulations. (In some books all stochastic simulations are referred to as "Monte Carlo," under the assumption that the name comes from an association with the famous gambling casino. It was, however, the code name given to models of neutron diffusion which were part of the effort to develop the first atomic bomb during the Second World War.) The use of Monte Carlo methods to provide estimates of the likely outcomes of multi-stage decision processes is known as **risk analysis** and will be studied further in Chapter 18.

17.6   System dynamics — continuous system simulation

Sometimes we do not need to know what happens to each individual entity in a simulation, but are happy enough to know simply the **level** and **rate-of-change** of a particular type of entity. Examples of such systems include large biological populations, money in an economy, chemical processes, staff recruitment systems for large organizations, such as the military or police, and ecological systems.

There are several simulation packages specifically for such problems, including STELLA, VENSIM, *ithink*, and DYNAMO. Usually, this kind of system modelling in terms of feedback loops (see Section 3-11 of Chapter 3) is associated with **system dynamics**. **Causal-loop diagrams**, as described in Section 5-5, are used for developing suitable models. In fact, the New Zealand Wine Industry planning model, depicted as a causal loop model in Figure 5-3 on page 94, served as the basis of a system dynamics model, evaluated using *ithink*.

When do we use these packages?

*   When there are lots, possibly an infinite number, of entities.
*   For simple entity behaviour — all entities of a given class must behave the same way. While the model may be complex, the interaction between entities can only be modelled simply, although it usually includes feedback loops.
*   When we are happy to know just the level of a type of entity over time.
*   When levels can be described by a system of equations that relate the levels to the rate of change or levels of other variables over time.

We will consider a model built using the *ithink* package, and use the notation of this package from now on. The two most important components in any continuous system simulation package are:

Levels: In *ithink* these are referred to as **stocks** and denoted by rectangles.

Flows: These represent activities which lead to changes in the magnitude of stocks, and in *ithink* have an icon which looks like a pipe with a valve on it. The valve ("flow regulator") contains an algebraic or graphical expression which determines the volume that flows through the pipe.

17.7   A simple health and social services model in *ithink*

We consider a simple model of part of a healthcare system. Elderly, infirm or mentally ill patients often receive much of their care either in their own homes or in facilities other than hospitals. This is known as "community care", and has become very popular as a means of both (ideally) providing appropriate care, and (often) reducing the total costs of care.

In our simple model patients are assigned from the community to a waiting list. They are then treated or assessed in hospital and then discharged into community care. Thus we have three stocks: *Waiting List*, *Hospital*, and *Community Care*. Four flows (*Assignment rate*, *Admission rate*, *Discharge rate* and *Leaving rate*) control the flow of patients through the model. The dynamic environment of the system, which provides inputs or receives outputs (infinite sources and sinks), is represented by clouds.

Since hospital capacity is limited we have used the two other remaining *ithink* building blocks to build a feedback loop to control the hospital admission rate. These building blocks are **converters** (circles), which typically take information in and transform or store it for use by another variable in the model, and **connecters** (arrows or wires). Connectors carry information, not flows, and in this case the information is: how full is the hospital? Thus *Fraction full* is calculated at each time step as the ratio of *Hospital* to *Hospital capacity*. The *Admission rate* is then modified, either by a formula, or here by a graph which shows how the *Admission rate* is to reduce as *Fraction full* increases towards one.

The system dynamics diagram for this model can be drawn interactively on the *ithink* screen window by the simple drag-and-drop facility provided. It is reproduced in Figure 17-11. Furthermore, *ithink* automatically creates most of the equations associated with the diagram, as listed in Figure 17-12.

Figure 17-11   A system dynamics diagram.

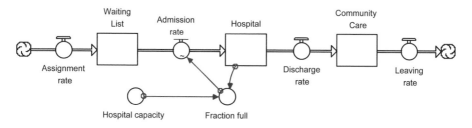

Figure 17-12   Automatically generated model equations in *ithink*.

```
Community_Care(t) =
Community_Care(t–dt) + (Discharge_rate – Leaving_rate) * dt
INIT Community_Care = 30
INFLOWS:
Discharge_rate = 19
OUTFLOWS:
Leaving_rate = 20

Hospital(t) =
Hospital(t–dt) + (Admission_rate – Discharge_rate) * dt
INIT Hospital = 40
INFLOWS:
Admission_rate = GRAPH(Fraction_full)
(0.00, 20.0), (0.333, 20.0), (0.667, 20.0), (1.00, 0.00)
OUTFLOWS:
Discharge_rate = 19

Waiting_List(t) =
Waiting_List(t–dt) + (Assignment_rate – Admission_rate) * dt
INIT Waiting_List = 10
INFLOWS:
Assignment_rate = 20
OUTFLOWS:
Admission_rate = GRAPH(Fraction_full)
(0.00, 20.0), (0.333, 20.0), (0.667, 20.0), (1.00, 0.00)
Fraction_full = Hospital/Hospital_capacity
Hospital_capacity = 100
```

The first lines in each section show the equations that the package has created. It solves these numerically to give the levels of the three stocks for each time step dt. The analyst specifies dt as an input, usually a small interval; in our case dt equals one month. For example, adding the net change in the level of patients in *Community Care* over the time step dt, (Discharge_rate – Leaving_rate)*dt, to the level at the previous time step, Community_Care(t–dt), gives the level at time t, Community_Care(t). The remainder of the program specifies initial values for the stocks (for example INIT Hospital = 40) and specifies the inflows and outflows for each stock. These are mostly set equal to constant values specified by the analyst except that Admission_rate is determined by a graphical relationship specified by four pairs of values showing how the admission rate is to reduce as Fraction_full approaches one.

Provided the *Assignment, Leaving*, and *Discharge rates* are all approximately equal, the process will be in balance. The three stocks in the system will buffer minor variations in inflow and outflow rates. We now describe an extended version of this model where this is not the case, and where a well-intended control system on part of the model created unintended and potentially disastrous consequences.

17.8   Process design in UK health care and social services

(This section is based on a case study first published in the "*ithink* Business Applications Guide" for versions 4-7. It is used with the permission of High Performance Systems, www.hps-inc.com and the authors, Professor Eric Wolstenholme, OLM Consulting, UK and Richard Stevenson, Cognitus Ltd., UK.)

In the United Kingdom, the National Health Service (NHS) provides all citizens with free medical care from cradle to grave, regardless of their financial or other circumstances. Recent reorganisations of the NHS have created an "internal market" for the purchase and provision of health services in the hope of providing better and more efficient services.

Another government department — Social Services — is responsible for those in society with special needs. In this context Social Services provides community care for elderly, disabled or mentally ill people, who often require medical treatment or assessment by the NHS in hospitals before and/or during their period under care by Social Services.

The interface between the NHS and Social Services subsystems is therefore crucial to considerations of patient welfare and efficient public spending. Patients flow back and forth across the boundary between these two organizations, and the processes which drive these flows are of particular interest, as the NHS reforms have placed new responsibilities on managers on both sides of the boundary. At this point you should look at the system dynamics diagram in Figure 17-13, which shows Wolstenholme and Stevens' generic model of such a community care system. The three subsystems — the community, the NHS and Social Services — are defined by rectangles. Representing them in this way allows each subsystem to be built up independently, and hidden when all the detail is not needed.

Before 1993 the discharge rate from hospitals was solely under control of the

Figure 17-13 Expanded *ithink* model of Health Care and Social Services interactions.

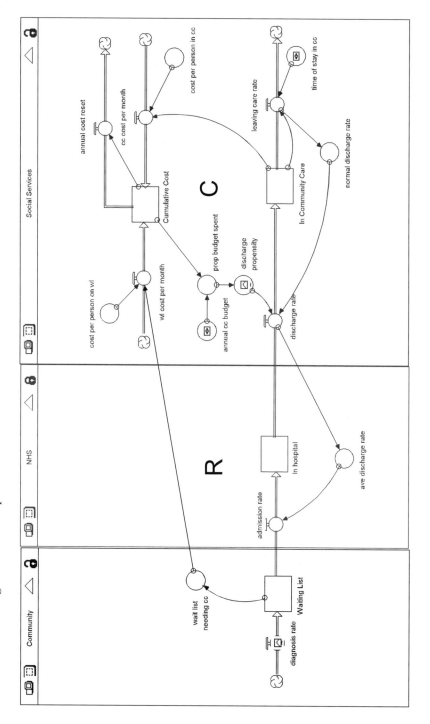

NHS. From 1993 on local social services managers became responsible for managing all community care under cash limited budgets. The discharge rate from hospitals thus moved at least partly under control of local social services managers. If cash resources were limited they could slow down the rate of acceptance of patients into community care, and hence reduce the discharge rate from hospitals. We model this change from the simple model in Figure 17-11 by shifting the *Discharge rate* regulator into the Social Service subsystem, where it is now controlled by the *leaving care rate*. This in turn is found by dividing the umber *in Community Care* by the *time of stay in community care*.

The intention is that this would assist local social services managers to adhere to their budgets, albeit possibly by adopting short-term and localized actions. In Figure 17-13 the feedback loop which models this intended behaviour is labelled "C". As the annual budget is used up, managers will be less willing to accept new patients from the NHS hospitals into Community Care (*discharge propensity*), which will reduce the *discharge rate*, and hence the number of patients *in Community Care*. The anticipated result is that the *Community Care cost per month* will reduce, and hence the *Cumulative Cost* will rise at a lower rate, allowing managers to meet annual budget targets. Thus we have a negative feedback loop. In *ithink* negative feedback loops are called Compensating loops, hence the letter C for compensating on it.

For clarity this feedback loop is reproduced in Figure 17-14. *ithink* drew this loop diagram directly from the systems map. This is a very useful attribute of the package. Separating out the causal loops from the clutter of the entire systems map makes it much easier to explain to stakeholders key aspects of the system which the model is attempting to capture.

However, if social services managers can now restrict the discharge rate from hospitals, one or more of three things must happen:

Figure 17-14 The intended consequences of controlling discharge rates.

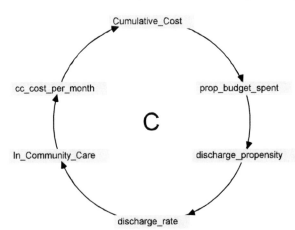

1. The number of patients in hospital will rise. But hospital capacity is limited.
2. Waiting lists will increase, as the admission rate must be reduced to ease congestion in the hospitals. This is the most likely outcome.
3. Primary healthcare providers recognise that hospital capacity is limited and assign fewer patients to the waiting list. Thus patients are deprived of appropriate care.

In practice we could expect all three of these things to occur simultaneously, but, in particular the waiting list, and the time which a patient spends on the waiting list, will rise. Many of these patients will need home care by nurses and social workers while they are on the waiting list. The increased cost of this will have to come from the very same Social Services budget which the original action was intended to control! In Figure 17-13 this is captured by connectors which go from the *Waiting List* through a convertor which calculates the number on the waiting list needing community care, and then feeds this (*wl cost per month*) into the *Cumulative Cost* in the Social Services sector of the model. The resulting loop is labelled "R", for **R**einforcing.

The causal loop associated with this aspect of the model is seen more clearly in Figure 17-15. As the *Waiting List* increases, so will the number of patients on the *wait list needing Community Care*. The cost of this is captured as the *wait list cost per month* and fed into the *Cumulative Cost*. As the budget is used up (*prop budget spent*), social services managers will be less inclined to accept patients from hospital into community care (*discharge propensity*). The *discharge rate* and hence the *admission rate* for hospitals reduce, causing still further growth in the *Waiting List*. It can thus be seen to be a positive feedback loop, or in *ithink* notation a **R**einforcing loop. This loop is particularly worrying as Social Services has no control mechanism for controlling community care expenditure in the community.

Figure 17-15   The unintended consequences.

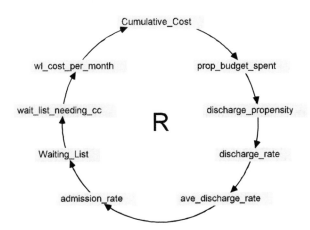

Positive feedback loops are discussed in Sections 3.11 and 5.5. In the absence of any control mechanism they lead to instability and the levels in them can explode. Thus the model suggests that there is a possibility that an action which was intended to impose control within part of the system, the Social Services, may have an opposite and unintended serious consequence on another part of the system, the community.

We ran the program over the time horizon of five years. *ithink* solves the system of differential equations over time using a numerical technique. The usual outputs from continuous system simulation packages are graphs showing the magnitudes of the stocks or levels over time. With the input variables originally specified by the authors for this problem, the system remains nicely in balance. Figure 17-16 shows that the annual expenditure on community care is comfortably less than the budget of £600,000 every year.

Figure 17-16   Annual costs and budget for community care.

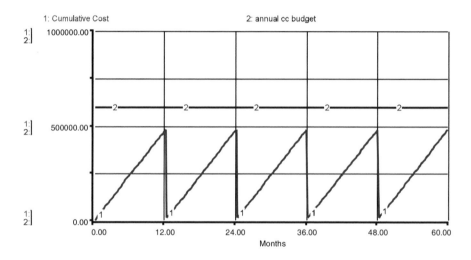

In fact, the annual expenditure on community care is always less than £500,000. So why not reduce the budget to this amount? The same amount of money that was previously adequate for community care would still be available, and the £100,000 released could be used for employing an additional social services manager. In Figure 17-13 there is a tiny "slider" on *annual cc budget* indicating that this change can easily be done from what *ithink* calls the **control panel** without altering the program. We make this change, and the surprising results can be seen in Figure 17-17.

For the first two years the expenditure remains exactly as expected, namely under £500,000. But from then on annual expenditure starts to rise, until by year 5 it is exceeding the budget by 60%. The reason for the budget blowout is easy to

Figure 17-17 Community care budget reduced to £500,000.

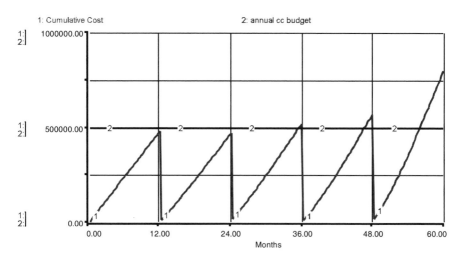

see if we look at the patient levels in the three subsystems, as shown Figure 17-18. In order to reduce the number of patients in community care and balance their budgets, social services managers reduce the discharge rate from hospital towards the end of every year. Thus the number of patients in hospital also rises sharply, until by the end of year 3 the NHS hospitals are almost continuously full. In the meantime, the number of patients on the waiting list rises at an increasing rate, from almost no-one to nearly 1,000. Since some of these will require home care while on the waiting list,

Figure 17-18 Patient levels in the three subsystems.

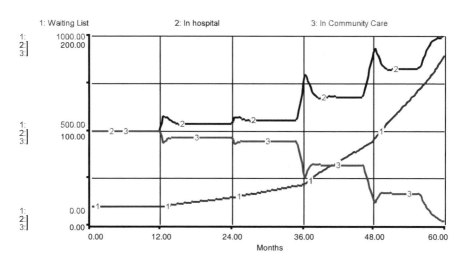

while on the waiting list, this further eats into the community care budget, which now can support fewer and fewer patients officially in community care.

Some comments on continuous system simulation

More than other kinds of simulations, system dynamics modelling requires careful thought about the formulation of the model and system boundaries. Many parameters must be estimated, often with little information. If the quantitative results of the model are to be taken seriously, extensive sensitivity analysis on input parameters is often needed, especially in the case of models with several feedback loops, to ensure that the results are not just artefacts of either the limitations of the model or specific parameter settings. In the case study above it would be equally unwise to assume that exactly the unstable behaviour depicted in Figure 17-18 would occur if the budget is cut, as it would also be to assume that a budget of £600,000 always leads to a system under smooth control.

Often a better way of using continuous simulation models is as a basis for discussion with all of the stakeholders, rather than to assume that the models can be fitted to the point where they exactly predict system behaviour.

As Wolstenholme and Stevenson say " The simple maps and models discussed here are only a starting point for investigation of overall system behaviour, which is certainly much more complex than this. Other strategies are available to Social Services (reducing the quality of care, or well care/preventative medicine.) These strategies can be implemented into the model and their effects assessed.... Management of these complex issues requires effective cross-boundary discussion between *all* of the players involved. The model provides a conceptual framework and a common language on which to base those discussions."

17.9   Conclusions on simulation as a tool

Simulation is one of the most spectacular MS/OR modelling techniques. Yet curiously, perhaps because of its obvious value and applicability, it also tends to be associated with more failed projects than any other technique. All too often, the results of effort spent on simulation are disappointing. All there is to show for six months of work is a 'nearly running' program, which may never produce useful results. The list of reasons for failure, discussed below, is adapted from the one published by the makers of SIMSCRIPT, a well-known simulation package. Most of the reasons relate to excessive concentration on the modelling phase of an MS/OR project — systems M and O in terms of Figure 6-9 on page 155 — with too little thought and effort spent on problem formulation — system S — and implementation(see Chapter 8).

So what aspects tend to go wrong in simulation modelling?

1. Selecting simulation because you don't know what else to do

Simulation, especially computer simulation, is sometimes described as a last-resort technique, to be used when attempts to fit some kind of analytical model have failed.

While this may sometimes be true, in practice it is not a particularly good way of thinking about the place of simulation in the range of MS/OR tools. As we have seen above, the use of simulation models in no way reduces the data requirements or the need for a thorough understanding of the system that is being modelled. This point is often vital, as starting to build a simulation model before the system has been fully understood may lead to excessively detailed modelling of unimportant parts of the system while crucial parts are overlooked. In addition, the analyst is faced with acquiring simulation software which is often very expensive, learning how to use it, and writing and debugging the simulation program.

A better way of thinking about simulation is that it is a technique that may require large inputs: data collection, study and understanding of the system being modelled, knowledge of the simulation software, and knowledge of the special statistical problems that occur in the analysis of simulation output. On the other hand, a simulation model:

- may produce detailed output on performance measures for various parts of the operations,
- may be a flexible model that can include aspects of the system for which no easy analytical model is available,
- has the ability to easily test the effect of varying system parameters, and
- in the case of a visual package, may be seen by management as more convincing than a model based on formulas.

2. Poor initial planning

Often a modeller simply drifts into simulation. The project is dumped on a junior team member who starts building the model so that at least something will appear to be getting done. No initial scoping assessments are made and a small model, using whatever language or package happens to be lying around, eventually grows into a monster. The time taken to complete the model is usually grossly underestimated. Practically all large computer program developments are late. Two major reasons for this are:

- **Premature coding:** The irresistible urge to begin coding before the system and the problem are properly defined.

- **Optimistic or lack of realistic scheduling:** Underestimating the time required for known tasks, such as problem scoping and data collection, and neglecting to allocate time for the inevitable, unanticipated problems.

3. Failure to define achievable goals or objectives

The goal of a simulation project should never be 'to model the ...'. As with all MS/OR projects, modelling itself is not a goal; it is a means of achieving a goal. An essential ingredient for successful simulation is a clearly articulated and agreed-upon set of realizable objectives. These depend on answers to questions like 'What is to be learned about the system under study?' or 'What decisions will be based on the simulation results?'.

The objectives cannot be correctly defined without the participation of the problem owner, and they must of course be realizable. Setting these objectives is an important early step in any MS/OR project.

4. Wrong simulation software

It is possible to write simple simulation programs in general-purpose languages such as Visual Basic. However, for a large model it is much easier to use a simulation package. These provide features like complex control of the flow of events, and reliable random variate generation. High-level simulation packages can substantially reduce both programming and project time. They offer language, program, and data structures that make models much easier to develop and modify.

If a special-purpose simulation package is available that fits the problem adequately, it is often better to purchase it rather than start developing your own. Usually such packages seem very expensive at first, but if they will do what you want they are usually much cheaper in the long run.

5. Incomplete mix of essential skills

A successful simulation project calls for a combination of at least four areas of knowledge and experience:

- **Project leadership:** The ability to motivate, lead and manage the simulation team.
- **Modelling:** The ability to design a conceptual model that imitates the system under study at the required level of detail.
- **Programming:** The ability to transform the model into a logical, modifiable, working computer program.
- **Knowledge of the modelled system:** Sufficient understanding of the system to guide the modelling and to judge the validity of the simulation results.

Teams have typically lacked specialists whose expertise and professional interests lie in modelling and simulation over and above programming. In addition, people knowledgeable about the system together with those who will use the results of the simulation study often do not track the development in sufficient detail to assure that the end product satisfies their needs.

6. Inadequate level of user participation

All too often, model developers simply go off by themselves for six months and then proudly drop the 'completed', never-to-be-used model on the project clients. Inevitably there will be some bug in the program or the results will exhibit odd and counterintuitive behaviour. Both immediately destroy confidence in the model.

The model-building team must work with the intended users of the results in order for both to have the confidence and understanding necessary to make and encourage effective use of the completed work. There should be regularly scheduled briefings, progress reports, and technical discussions with the users. The latter are also the only ones who can inform the team about realistic considerations, such as politics, bureaucracy, unions, budget limitations, and changes in the sponsoring organization. These can affect the success of the project as much as will the quality of the technical work.

7. Inappropriate level of detail

A model is a simplified representation of a system, and it should incorporate only those features of the system thought to be important for the users' purpose.

In modelling a complex system, difficult questions must be addressed — often for the first time. There is a tendency to spend a great deal of effort modelling in unnecessary detail those portions of the system that are well understood, while glossing over poorly defined portions that may be more important. This creates the illusion that great progress is being made, until it comes time to produce valid, usable results. The goals of the project determine the appropriate level of detail, which must be consistent with the availability of data and other resources.

8. Obsolete or nonexistent documentation

Many unsuccessful simulation projects end up with no documentation except the simulation model. Often even the programmer has difficulty understanding it a few weeks later. Most models evolve over a long period of time because of new and increased understanding of the system, changing goals, and availability of new data. Because of these evolutionary changes, flowcharts, prose documentation, detailed descriptions of routines and variables, and program comments are invariably incomplete, incorrect, and almost always out of date. The longer the model is around — many models in use today were developed five or more years ago — the more this type of documentation deteriorates.

9. Using an unverified or invalid model

Verification ('internal validation') involves comparing the programmed computer model with the system model. Does the program correctly implement the system model as designed? Validation ('external validation') involves comparing the system model with the real world (Section 6.4 discusses validation). Does the model adequately represent the real world? One effective verification–validation technique is a walk-through, with the programmer explaining what has been done to someone who is familiar with the system under study. This technique frequently turns up design and coding errors that can be corrected at an early stage.

10. Poor presentation of results

The results from simulation studies are often presented in a way that the user finds incomprehensible. A model that gives unexpected or illogical results may do so because certain parameters turn out to be far more or less significant than expected, or because unanticipated interactions between system elements, such as feedback loops, greatly affect system performance. Insight into hidden problems of this sort is often the major gain from a simulation. However, unexpected or unusual simulation results that cannot be explained are usually caused by errors, invalid assumptions, or lack of understanding of the real system. Someone familiar with the system under study must examine the simulation results to determine whether they are reasonable, and the simulation results must be presented in a way that the user can easily relate to the system under study.

17.10   A comparison of the weighbridge queueing and simulation models

In Chapter 16 we analysed the weighbridge problem by using queueing formulas. It is instructive to compare the advantages and disadvantages of the two approaches. Among the advantages of using simulation are:

* The move-up time can be easily and realistically modelled by a line in the GPSS/H simulation program (the second line in Figure 17-8), which assigns an arriving truck an attribute which takes the value '1' if the bridge is in use when it arrives. The value of this attribute is tested when the truck arrives at the head of the queue (line 6). If it is '1' the truck is delayed for a randomly generated move-up time, otherwise the truck jumps to the 8th line in the program, which delays it for a weighing time only.

* The simulation can be started with an empty queue and is stopped empty at the end of a (simulated) day. There is no need to use steady state formulas.

* It is easy to model the two-weighbridge situation because the computer package specifically provides for multiple servers in parallel.

* It is easier to convince management that we have a 'solution' to the problem because a visual version of the program made little trucks move across the computer screen. (Note, however, that this version of the program was far too slow to be of any practical use, and the extra programming effort required to produce the visual display increased the chance of introducing logical errors into the program.)

While the simulation model is easy to program and works well, its distinct disadvantage is the variability of the outputs that it produces, and hence the large number of simulation runs needed to produce sufficiently narrow confidence intervals for the results. Because the queue is so sensitive to slight variations in its parameters the simulated daily mean waiting time varied from 3 to 25 minutes. A total of 10,000 days was required to reduce the standard deviation of the mean daily waiting time down to 0.05 minutes.

For management, the most valuable part of the original study using the theoretical queueing model was the sensitivity analysis for the number of loads that could be carried per day, depicted in Figure 16-10 on page 456. Producing such a plot by simulation could easily take days of PC time.

We can also consider the two approaches in terms of the properties of good models listed in Section 5-3. Both approaches could be classed as **appropriate for the situation** and **relevant**. They produce the required economic information for management to make the decision about the second weighbridge at very small cost. We would probably conclude that while the simulation model is superior on the **completeness**, **simplicity**, and possibly the **credibility** criteria for a good model, it is distinctly inferior to the queueing formulas for **ease of manipulation**, being **easy to communicate with**, and **adaptivity**.

Some of the guidelines for modelling listed in Sections 5.3 and 5.4 can also be related to the weighbridge problem. In particular the ability to adequately model the arrival process of trucks at the weighbridge by assuming that the interarrival times were sampled from a negative exponential distribution is vital for the use of simple queueing models and also results in a much simpler simulation program. We are also applying **Ockham's Razor**, i.e. we exclude aspects that do not contribute to the predictive power of the model. For example, we exclude the fact that the trucks actually make round trips. We justified this simplification in Section 16.6.

Where the simulation model proved vital was in validating the queueing formulas that were used. These were slightly more complex than the ones shown in Chapter 16. (The analysis there was, in fact, our first attempt to produce a quick approximate answer to the problem. This was later refined into a more elegant method which gave very similar answers. Thus we were also following the advice given under 'An iterative process of enrichments' in Section 5.4.) By determining that the simulation and formula results are in close agreement for a few selected input values we can reasonably assume that the formulas will be correct for intermediate values, hence saving a substantial amount of computer time and data analysis. Management appeared to be happy with this validation and found the results of the analytical models acceptably accurate.

17.11 Chapter highlights

- Simulation is the management scientist's tool of experimentation for exploring the effect of different combinations of control inputs on aspects of dynamic system behaviour. It is also used for testing out solutions to stochastic problems derived by analytic means.
- Stochastic events or phenomena are imitated by generating random variates. Using the inverse transformation method, random variates for any theoretical probability or empirical frequency distribution can be obtained.
- Event simulations imply a system structure consisting of permanent and temporary entities, that have permanent or temporary attributes and engage individually or jointly in activities. The state of the system is given by the values of all attributes at a given point in simulated time. System behaviour is summarized by collecting statistics of these attributes.
- An entity cycle diagram captures the sequence of activities for a class of entities.

- When comparing different combinations of control inputs, the results of simulation runs are affected by two types of variability: the variability associated with the stochastic behaviour of the system proper, which is the one we wish to measure, and the variability introduced by the use of different sequences of random numbers. The latter we can often eliminate by using the same sequence of random variates for each configuration of control inputs.
- The reliability of performance estimates can be improved by having long simulation runs, by a large number of simulation runs, and where appropriate by reducing the transient effect through the judicious choice of initial conditions or a warm-up period.
- Computer simulation software contains features, such as random variate generators, updating of simulated time and entity attributes, and collection of statistics, that dramatically simplify simulation modelling.
- Event simulations update simulated time in variable increments by finding the next most imminent event. Fixed-time incrementation updates time in regular fixed periods. It is suitable for situations where events occur in most periods and it is not crucial when exactly in the period each event occurs.
- In continuous system simulation, such as system dynamics, system behaviour is modelled by the levels (stocks) and the rate of change of levels over time, rather than by the occurrence of individual events.
- Simulations hide many pitfalls for the beginner. Simulation should not be used in preference to suitable analytic or numeric methods which usually can produce valid and useful results more quickly and more cheaply. For no other MS/OR technique is the proper choice of the system boundaries, the system components and their interactions, and the appropriate level of modelling detail as important as for simulation. Great care must be taken in scoping and planning simulations, in seeking crucial user participation, in using the most suitable software, in adequate verification and validation of the model, and in producing up-to-date and complete documentation.

Exercises

1. Develop a spreadsheet similar to Table 17-1 to simulate the behaviour of the weighbridge and simulate the arrival and processing of 80 trucks. Determine statistics for the amount of idle time of the weighbridge and the total waiting time for the first 80 trucks.

2. The table below is a partial simulation of ships arriving at a port for unloading and loading. The average interarrival time between ships is 48 hours. Interarrival times follow a negative exponential distribution. It takes on average 12 hours to unload a ship. The unloading time also has a negative exponential distribution. The loading time is uniformly distributed between 8 and 32 hours. There is only one berth in the port. Thus only one ship can be unloaded and loaded at a time. Loading commences immediately after unloading has been completed. At the start of the simulation, no ship is in the port. This system is to be simulated for 12 ship arrivals, using the table format below. Note that the first 2 ships have already been processed to indicate the pattern.

(a) Define the structure of this system, i.e. the permanent and temporary entities, the activities, and associated events. What would you use to define the state of the system?

(b) Draw a combined life cycle diagram for the entities.

(c) Simulate the behaviour of this system by hand for 12 arrivals. Round all times to the nearest hour. The following set of uniformly distributed random decimal fractions should be used:

[.0196] [.0674] [.1064] [.1584] [.6801] [.9531] .4418 .1916 .7706 .6510 .5582 .0112
.9296 .6985 .2832 .4603 .8185 .7864 .1268 .7524 .2143 .7059 .5264 .6932 .0963
.6721 .8095 .4541 .6392 .1983 .8791 .5023 .1276 .8512 .6435 .6181 .5496 .7197

The random numbers already used for the first 2 ships are shown bracketed and resulted in the times listed below. Continue generating times starting with .4418.

ship #	interarrival time	arrival time	unload time	start unload	end unload	loading time	start of loading	end of loading
1	1	1	1	1	2	11	2	13
2	8	9	14	13	27	31	27	58
3								

(d) What is the waiting time for ship number 3? What is the total time the berth is idle, exclusive of the initial period at the start of the simulation?

3. A firm uses the following policy to control its inventory: Whenever the stock on hand has been reduced through sales to 8 units, a replenishment of size 24 is placed. This replenishment arrives at the firm's premises in the morning of the third day after it has been placed and becomes immediately available to meet customer demand. If the demand on a given day is larger than the stock on hand, then the amount short is lost, i.e. the customer goes elsewhere. The daily demand pattern is as follows:

Demand size	0	1	2	3	4	5	6	7
Frequency	0.25	0.20	0.15	0.12	0.10	0.08	0.06	0.04

Simulate the behaviour of this system by hand for an interval of 30 days. Use a table format that has one row for each day and appropriate columns for the amount of stock on hand at the beginning of each day, the demand generated using the set of random numbers listed in exercise 2 above, the stock level at the end of the day, the amount of goods on order (stock replenishment orders are placed at the end of the day after sales have been processed), and the amount of lost sales. To generate the random demands use the scheme described in Section 17.1, in particular the method demonstrated in Figure 17-1.

4. A product is assembled on a two-station assembly line. Station A assembles the first part (Part A) of the product, while Station B finishes the assembly of the product (Part B). Station A takes any time between 40 and 50 seconds to assemble one unit of Part A. The time is uniformly distributed. Station B takes on average 46 seconds to finish the assembly of one unit of Part B, with a standard deviation of 9 seconds. The distribution of the Part B assembly time is approximately normal. Station A starts assembling a new Part A immediately after having completed the previous unit. Any completed units are put on a counter within reach of the operator at Station B. Station B also starts a new assembly (Part B) after having completed the previous assembly, provided there are any Part A units

ready (waiting) on the counter for completion at Station B. If no Part A units are available, then the operator at Station B is temporarily idle until the next Part A has been completed at Station A. Assume that the work day begins at 8:00 a.m. and Station A starts the first Part A assembly. Station B starts work as soon as the first Part A has been placed on the counter.

(a) Define the structure of this system, i.e. temporary and permanent entities and their attributes, the activities, and the various events. How would you define the state of the system?

(b) Draw a combined life cycle diagram for the entities.

(c) Set up a computer spreadsheet and simulate this system for 60 assemblies. It should show when each event occurs. Use a new row for each new assembly started. Round all times to the nearest second. Use the following approach for generating approximate normal random variates with a mean of 0 and a standard deviation of 1: generate 12 uniformly distributed random decimal fractions and compute their average. (This needs to be repeated for each normal random variate.) You want to collect statistics for the length of time taken to complete the assembly of 60 complete items, as well as the fraction of time each of the two stations are idle during that time. Do not include the time at Station B at the beginning of the work day when Station B is waiting for the first partially completed assembly to be released by Station A as idle time.

(d*) Write a spreadsheet macro that allows you to repeat this simulation for 20 different runs, each one using a different set of random numbers. Compute the average of the statistics and a measure of the variation of the 20 runs.

5. An inner city service station has one pump and only space for two cars in total, i.e. the one being served and at most one waiting. Any potential customer intending to tank up at that station and seeing both spaces taken (i.e. two cars in the service station) will not enter and simply drives by to go to some other service station. These potential customers are thus lost to the system. Potential customers arrive at the service station at a rate of 10 per hour, or on average every 6 minutes. Given that each potential customer makes the decision to tank up or not independently, a negative exponential arrival distribution is a good assumption. The service takes on average 5 minutes. It is uniformly distributed over the range from 1 to 9 minutes. Service is on a first-come/first-served basis. The service station owner would like to determine the effect of the limited space available to serve customers, in particular the average number of customers lost due to lack of space. On average, each customer buys about 25 litres of petrol on which the service station earns $3.75. The owner would also like to know a number of other performance measures that could be of interest or useful. Think carefully about which performance measures you want to observe.

(a) Define the structure of the system, i.e. the temporary and permanent entities, the activities and the events. What would you use to describe the state of the system?

(b) Draw a combined life cycle diagram for the entities.

(c) Develop a computer spreadsheet and simulate this system for a total of 40 potential arrivals. Round all times to the nearest minute. It should enable you to collect/observe all performance measures of interest. List the formulas used for every cell in the row of your spreadsheet for the second arrival.

(d*) Write a spreadsheet macro that allows you to repeat this simulation for 10 different runs, each one using a different set of random numbers. Compute the average of the statistics and a measure of their variation for the 10 runs.

6*. Consider a somewhat simplified computerized system for telephone horse race betting. The system has two lines. When a punter calls, the call is answered by a free line and the punter connected to the computer touch-tone betting system to enter the bet(s). If both lines are occupied, the call is lost. When a punter has completed entering the bet(s), the line becomes free again. During the hour just prior to a given race, calls arrive at a rate of 1 per minute. It is reasonable to assume that interarrival times have a negative exponential distribution. Assume that a punter takes anywhere from 20 to 120 seconds to enter the bet(s), i.e. the time is uniformly distributed.

(a) Draw a combined life cycle diagram for all entities involved.
(b) Develop a computer spreadsheet and simulate the arrival of 60 calls. Round all times to the nearest second. Collect statistics on the total amount of idle time of the two lines together, and the number of calls lost.

18
Decision and risk analysis

The preceding two chapters explored dynamic systems behaviours where uncertainty can be captured by theoretical probability distributions or empirical frequency distributions. System behaviour is affected by a large number of random events occurring individually at random points in time. It is then appropriate to study the system's long-run behaviour. Its effectiveness can be judged on the basis of its average performance over a long period or a large number of trials or experiments.

In contrast, this chapter studies situations where uncertainty about future outcomes deals with a single event or a relatively small sequence of events. The problems analysed are often unique situations, where the decision maker has only one chance to get it right, such as the introduction of a new product or the acquisition of a new but risky venture. Uncertainty is often expressed in the form of subjective probabilities about future events. What the future holds in store is called the **state of the future** or the **state of nature**. The benefits and costs associated with the decision choices may be different for each possible state of the future. Furthermore, being one-shot deals, each situation is 'played' only once. There is no long-run behaviour to be observed.

What are effective and insightful ways for modelling such situations? What criteria are suitable for finding the 'best' alternative course of action? This chapter attempts to give partial answers to these questions. They are part of the vast topic of **decision analysis** and of **risk analysis**. Our purpose for studying aspects of decision analysis is not to give you a thorough working knowledge of these tools, but rather to let you gain further insights into systems modelling and decision making under uncertainty.

Although the focus of this chapter will be on unique and independent decision situations, there are some recurrent decision problems which have the same basic structure. A fast food stall or cafeteria daily faces the problem of how much of each of various dishes to prepare in anticipation of the coming day's sales. Similarly, 6 to 12 months prior to the start of the new clothing season a fashion goods manufacturer has to decide what assortment, in terms of sizes and materials, to produce. Usually only a single run is made, so it is important to get it right the first time.

Section 18.1 sets the stage with a simple, but by no means trivial decision situation that captures the basic aspects of decision and risk analysis. The problem is borrowed from the fascinating book *Quick Analysis for Busy Decision Makers* by Behn and Vaupel [1982, Chapter 2]. Sections 18.2–18.5 study decision analysis where random events can be captured by discrete probability distributions. Sections 18.2 and 18.3 discuss a business situation which involves risky monetary outcomes. They demonstrate the general approach of finding the 'best' solution and the kind of insights that can be gained from the analysis. Sections 18.4 and 18.5 explore approaches for dealing with situations where the monetary value of a risky outcome is not a true reflection of the intrinsic worth of the outcome.

The mathematics of decision analysis becomes intractable when the interdependencies between random outcomes over time become more intricate and some outcomes may be governed by continuous probability distributions. Furthermore, the decision maker may not be willing to make a decision on the basis of expected outcomes alone, as is the case with decision analysis, but may want to know something about the risk profile of a venture. The last two sections of the chapter look into risk analysis — a tool specifically designed to do just that.

18.1 Setting up a decision problem

Ollerton Watt, a busy executive, must make one of the most important decisions of his life. It has nothing to do with his job. Olly suffers from angina pectoris — chest pains often caused by hardening of the coronary arteries. This deprives the heart muscle of blood when the heart needs to pump harder in response to physical exertion, excitement, or stress. Medication prescribed to Olly relieved some of the symptoms, but was not successful in clearing the problem. So Olly has just had a complete cardiac examination. His doctor now sets out the options available to him. He can continue with his medication, taking it easy, and suffer the occasional angina attack. These are painful and frightening. He can elect to have bypass surgery. This will almost surely be successful in relieving the problem completely. There is only a small chance that the pain is not totally eliminated. However, the doctor also informs him that, in view of his age and previous medical history, there is one chance in ten that he could die on the operating table — more than twice the average death rate for this type of surgery! The doctor also explains to him that there is currently little medical evidence suggesting that surgery increases the patient's life expectancy. Olly could live as long with angina pectoris as with surgery, provided he took it easy. Should he decide to have surgery or not?

Olly's problem is far from unique. There are millions of people all over the world facing similar decision problems. Not all of them involve life-and-death decisions. Many may simply involve other risky outcomes, such as whether or not to accept the job offer in a new city, or getting into a stable relationship with a partner, or getting into a venture with possibly large monetary gains and losses.

Structuring the decision problem

A **decision tree** lays out sequential problems of this sort in a schematic form by decomposing it into simple single stage components. It clearly highlights the chronological structure of the problem and its sequential, conditional logic.

Figure 18-1 is a graphical representation of Olly's decision problem. This decision tree is read from left to right. It begins with a **decision node** — whether or not to undergo surgery — depicted as a square (labelled 1). The two branches leaving the square denote Olly's two decision choices 'Surgery' and 'No surgery'. The top branch 'No surgery' leads to the outcome 'Live with angina'. The bottom branch leads to a **chance node**, denoted by a circle (labelled 2). Each branch leaving the circle denotes one of the possible outcomes. In our example, there are two: 'Patient dies during surgery' and 'Patient survives'. The bottom branch 'Patient survives' leads to another chance node (labelled 3), also with two branches: 'No pain' and 'Some pain remains'. The 'Surgery' decision thus leads to one of three possible outcomes.

Figure 18-1   Decision tree for angina pectoris problem.

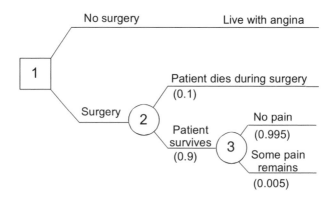

The branches leaving a chance node lead to uncertain outcomes. We associate a probability (subjective or objective) with each outcome. These are shown in parentheses below each branch. Since one of the outcomes must occur, the probabilities attached to the outcome branches originating at a given chance node add up to one. For example, according to the surgeon, there is a 10% chance that Olly dies during surgery. Hence, there must be a 90% chance that he survives. So we attach a probability of 0.1 to the top branch and a probability of 0.9 to the bottom branch. Similarly, Olly is told that if he survives the odds are 1 in 200 that 'Some pain remains'. Hence the odds for 'No pain' are 199 in 200. The probabilities attached to these two outcome branches are 0.995 and 0.005.

Evaluating the decision choices

We will initially ignore the small likelihood that, although Olly survives the surgery, some pain will remain. Surviving surgery is now assumed to mean 'surgery is successful'. With this small approximation, Olly faces a choice between a certain outcome 'Live with angina' if he decides on 'No surgery', and an uncertain outcome if he decides on 'Surgery'. That uncertain outcome — either 'Surgery is successful' or 'Patient dies during surgery' — is equivalent to participating in the following gamble with Nature. An urn contains 90 white and 10 black balls. If Olly decides on 'Surgery', Nature draws one ball at random from the urn. A white ball means 'Surgery is successful', a black ball means 'Patient dies during surgery'.

Whether or not Olly should choose 'No surgery' or 'Surgery' will depend on his assessment of the three possible outcomes. Clearly, he will view 'Surgery is successful' as the most preferred outcome, while 'Patient dies' is the worst outcome. 'Live with angina' will be somewhere in between these two outcomes in his preference ranking.

Olly could express these preferences on an arbitrary **point scale**. This point scale would be highly personal and subjective, reflecting his preference structure with respect to this particular situation at this point in time. It would be different for another person. For instance, Olly might assign the most preferred outcome 100 preference points and the least preferred outcome zero points. He would then assign 'Live with angina' more than zero but less than 100 points. If he judges it as only a little bit better than dying, he may assign it 5 points on his preference scale. On the other hand, if he views 'Live with angina' as a condition he is willing to live with, he may assign it 80 points.

A low preference point value for 'Live with angina' will push Olly towards 'Surgery' and willingness to accept the gamble this option entails. A high point value will tip the scale towards the 'No surgery' option. For example, he might prefer 'Live with angina' to the gamble if he positions 'Live with angina' at 25 points, but prefer the gamble if it is only 10. So as the point value decreases from 25 towards 10 his preferences switch from 'Live with angina' to the gamble. Somewhere along his preference scale there is a **switch point** where he will be indifferent between the two options.

In the above discussion we assumed that the probability of dying was given and known. An alternative way of looking at this problem is as follows. Assume that the proportions of white and black balls are not fixed yet. It is a fair guess that if the proportion of white balls is low, say only 50%, Olly like most people would opt for 'No surgery'. This choice may remain the same if the proportion of white balls increases to 70%. On the other hand, a very high proportion of say 95% would lead him to choose 'Surgery'. His choice would not change any more if the proportion were even increased to 99%. So, we see that as the proportion of white balls increases, there comes a critical level where Olly switches from the riskless 'No surgery' option to the risky 'Surgery' option. In our example, this critical level turns out to be higher than 70%, but less than 95%.

This critical level V is called the **switch probability** or **indifference probability**. If the proportion of white balls is just equal to V, then Olly would be indifferent between the two options. Neither is preferred over the other — he could let the decision be made by the toss of a coin. The two options are equivalent to each other.

One could be substituted for the other. However, if the proportion of white balls is less than *V* Olly prefers the riskless 'No surgery' option; if it is more than *V* he prefers the risky 'Surgery' option.

Viewed in this way, Olly's decision rule would be: choose 'No surgery' if the proportion of white balls is less than the indifference probability, choose 'Surgery' if it is more than the indifference probability, and flip a fair coin, with 'heads' meaning 'No surgery' and 'tails' meaning 'Surgery', if it is equal to the indifference probability. Finding this indifference probability is no simple matter. We will postpone this task to a later section.

The discussion in this section captures most of the conceptual features of decision analysis. It has given us some important insights. First, decision makers are able to rank final outcomes, even of a non-pecuniary nature, in order of their preference, from the least preferred outcome to the most preferred outcome. If the outcomes can be expressed in monetary terms, their values may well reflect the ranking order. In other instances, particularly highly risky situations, such as large financial gains or losses that could mean bankruptcy, or situations involving emotional, aesthetic, ethical, or environmental concerns, the decision maker may be willing to express the preferences along an arbitrary point scale. It is then possible to compare a riskless option with a risky option in terms of this scale.

Second, faced with three outcomes, A, B, and C, where A is preferred to B and B is preferred to C, we can compare an (assumed) riskless option B with a risky option involving outcomes A and C in either of two ways:

1. We find the switch point for which the decision maker is indifferent between the riskless and the risky option. If the valuation of B is higher than the switch point, the riskless option B is preferred to the risky option, and vice versa.

2. Alternatively, we find the indifference probability for A for which the decision maker is indifferent between the riskless option B and the risky option involving A or C. If the best assessment for the probability for A is higher than the indifference probability, then the risky option is preferred to the riskless option and vice versa. (Recall $P(C) = 1 - P(A)$.)

At the switch point or the indifference probability, the riskless option is equivalent to the risky option. The importance of this discovery is that it allows us to substitute a riskless option for a risky option in any further comparisons. We shall make use of this property in Section 18.5.

Activity: Explore the effect of having approximated the original risky option 'Patient survives surgery' with 'Surgery is successful':

- 'Patient survives surgery' leads to the uncertain outcome 'No pain or surgery is completely successful' and 'Some pain remains'. How would you rank those?
- Will the possibility of some pain remaining increase or decrease the points assigned to 'Patient survives' in relation to 'Patient dies'? How will this affect the switch point between the two outcomes from node 2?
- How will it affect the switch probability between the two outcomes?

18.2 A decision problem with monetary outcomes

Barry Low, the founder and major shareholder of FIRST US SOFTWARE (FUSS) has just been informed by his lawyer, Debbie Deft, that the Ying-Yang Computer Software House (YY) has informed her through their lawyer that YY plans to sue FUSS for copyright infringements by FUSS's EASY-OPT What-If Solver Release 2.1. YY claims damages of $500,000 for loss of sales plus triple punitive penalties of $1,500,000. Debbie Deft also tells Barry Low that YY's lawyer has hinted that YY would be willing to settle out of court by granting FUSS retroactively a flat-fee licence for using the software in contention for 2 million dollars. This would allow FUSS to continue selling Release 2.1. Barry Low estimates that the future revenue potential for Release 2.1 amounts to roughly 3 million dollars. If FUSS chose to defend the law suit and lost, these sales would also be lost. Debbie Deft estimates that the cost of defending the law suit will amount to $600,000. If FUSS wins, YY will have to refund FUSS about $500,000 of this. Similarly, if FUSS loses, it will have to refund YY an equal amount of costs.

Development of EASY-OPT Release 3.0 has just been started. With its completely new format, it will definitely not run any danger of infringing copyrights. Its development can be accelerated. This will allow Release 3.0 to be introduced four to eight months earlier than currently planned, provided it is initiated within a month. The difficulty is that without some preliminary analysis no prediction can be made by how much. Such a preliminary analysis has a cost tag of $100,000. Accelerating the development will also increase the cost by $200,000 for a 4-months early release and $400,000 for an 8-months early release. However, FUSS would recoup about $300,000 of the potential loss on abandoning Release 2.1 for every month of early introduction. Upon questioning Debbie Deft, Barry thinks that YY would be willing to accept an out-of-court settlement for $600,000 in compensation for past copyright infringements, if FUSS immediately stopped marketing the Release 2.1. He also thinks that YY would be willing to accept a licence fee of $1,250,000 if Release 3.0 is introduced 8 months earlier and $1,600,000 if it is introduced 4 months earlier.

Debbie stresses that Barry has at most 5 to 6 weeks available to make up his mind whether or not to accept an out of court settlement. Once YY has initiated the court case, there is little chance that they will still be interested in a deal.

There are two major uncertainties in this situation. What are FUSS's chances of successfully defending a court case? And, how much earlier can Release 3.0 be marketed if FUSS decides to accelerate its development? Debbie's subjective assessment is that FUSS has about a 70% chance of winning the case. Prior to a preliminary analysis, the EASY-OPT development project leader estimates that there is a 60% chance of accelerating completion of Release 3.0 by 8 months and a 40% chance of accelerating it only by 4 months.

Setting up a decision tree

What is the sequence of decisions and uncertain events? Within 5 weeks, Barry has to make up his mind whether to abandon marketing Release 2.1 immediately, or accept a licence agreement with YY, or defend the case in court. Which one of these decisions is 'best' may depend on whether or not Barry decides to accelerate development of Release 3.0. Indeed, acceleration or no acceleration must be Barry's first decision. This is the decision node labelled 1 in the decision tree in Figure 18-2. While 'Do not accelerate' has no immediate cost, 'Accelerate' incurs an immediate cost of $100,000. This is shown as –$0.1 (in millions).

Figure 18-2   Decision tree for Barry Low's copyright infringement problem.

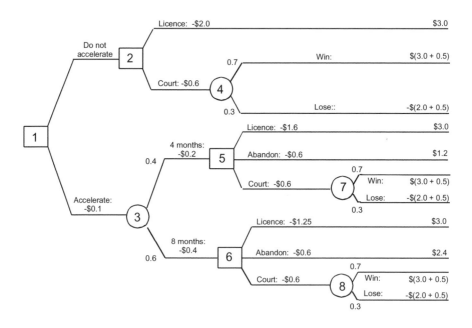

'Do not accelerate' leads to decision node 2. Since it is quite obvious that abandoning Release 2.1 without acceleration is a very unattractive option in comparison to taking out a 'Licence', there is little point in showing it as one of the decision alternatives. Hence, the two alternatives left are taking out a 'Licence' or going to 'Court'. The first one results in a licence fee of $2 million (shown as –$2.0), but will also generate revenues of $3 million. The second one incurs a cost of $0.6 million and leads to chance node 4 with branches 'Win' and 'Lose', with probabilities of 0.7 and 0.3, respectively. A 'Win' results in revenues of $3 million plus a refund of $0.5 in court costs, while 'Lose' means penalties and court costs paid to YY totalling $2.5 million. (Recall that costs are shown negative!)

'Accelerate' leads to chance node 3 with two branches: Release 3.0 is ready '4 months' earlier at an additional cost of $0.2 million with a probability of 0.4, and Release 3.0 is ready '8 months' earlier at an additional cost of $0.4 million with a probability of 0.6.

Each one of those branches leads to a new decision node, labelled 5 and 6, respectively. Both have the same choices, namely, take out a 'Licence', 'Abandon' Release 2.1 immediately, or go to 'Court'. Taking out a 'Licence' from node 5 has a cost of $1.6 million and will generate revenues from sales of $3.0 million. 'Abandon' causes costs of $0.6 million. With Release 3.0 ready '4 months' earlier, lost sales of $1.2 million can be recovered. Going to 'Court' has exactly the same structure as for the branch leaving decision node 2.

Activity: Figure out the net cash flows and probabilities from decision node 6 on.

Evaluating the decision tree by backward induction

What is Barry's 'best' choice of decisions? Before we can answer this question, we need a criterion for 'best'. One criterion listed in Section 15.11 (page 430) is to identify the decision or alternative course of action that **maximizes the expected monetary return**. For Barry this is the expected value of net cash flow. But 'wait' you may interject! 'Does it make sense to base the decision for a unique non-repetitive situation on an expected value concept?' It can indeed be shown that, under assumptions considered reasonable by most people, choosing the action that max-imizes the expected value of the outcomes is a rationally consistent criterion. What the expected value criterion implies is that the decision maker is willing to 'play the average' even for one-shot deals — the argument being that averaging over a string of unique decision situations is not necessarily different from averaging over recurring decisions. This does not mean that this approach sits well with everybody. Section 18.4 considers other criteria for selecting the 'best' action.

The first step in evaluating the decision tree is to find the cumulative net cash flow associated with each end point of the tree. We will refer to this as the **payoff** associated with the chain of actions and events leading to this end point. This is simply equal to the sum of the monetary outcomes attached to all branches on the path from the origin — node 1 — to each end point. For example, the path from node 1 to the top end point in Figure 18-2 goes through the branch from node 1 to node 2 ('Do not accelerate') and the branch labelled 'Licence'. The dollar amounts associated with these two branches are $0 and (–$2.0 + $3.0) million. Their sum is $1.0 million.

Figure 18-3 reproduces the tree of Figure 18-2. Instead of showing the detailed cash amounts associated with each branch, it only lists the cumulative payoff for each end point of the tree. So, the top end point shows $1.0 million. The second end point consists of the path from node 1 to node 2 to node 4 and branch 'win'. Figure 18-2 lists the sum of the cash flows associated with this path as (–$0.6 + $3.5) or $2.9. Check the payoff associated with the remaining ends in Figure 18-3! For evaluating the tree we only work with these payoffs. The cash flows associated with individual branches are now ignored.

Figure 18-3 Evaluating the decision tree by backward induction.

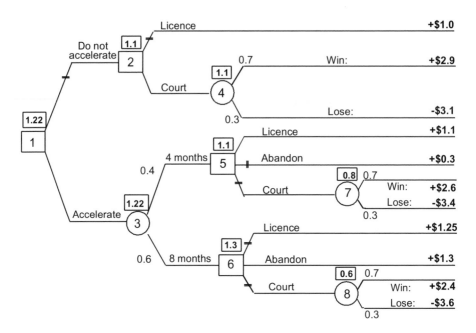

Using the expected value criterion, we find the best action by evaluating the nodes in the decision tree in reverse order. Evaluating a chance node means computing the expected value of the outcomes associated with all branches originating at that chance node. Take node 8. It has two branches. The top branch has a payoff of +$2.4 with probability 0.7 and the bottom branch has a payoff of –$3.6 with probability 0.3. The expected value is equal to the sum of the products of the payoffs and the corresponding probabilities. For node 8 this is (+$2.4)(0.7) + (–$3.6)(0.3) = $0.6 million. We insert this result above chance node 8 (shown in the small rectangular box).

Evaluating a decision node means finding which of the decision branches originating at that node has the highest monetary value. Consider decision node 6 in Figure 18-3. It has three decision branches. 'Licence' has a payoff of $1.25 million. 'Abandon' has a payoff of $1.3 million. We just computed the expected payoff for 'Court' at node 8 as $0.6. 'Abandon' has the highest value of $1.3 million. This is the amount inserted in the rectangle above node 6. Hence, at decision node 6, the best action to take is to 'Abandon' Release 2.1 immediately and wait for Release 3.0 to become available. To signal that this is the best decision, the other two actions are blocked off (shown by the two cross-bars).

Note that we used the expected payoff we computed for node 8 as an input into finding the expected payoff for the 'Court' branch at node 6. In fact, if we had not already evaluated node 8, we would not have been able to determine the expected payoff for 'Court' and hence evaluate node 6. Since we need the results of all successor nodes, if there are any, for evaluating a given node, the tree has to be evaluated by starting at the end and working backwards to the beginning — hence the term **backward induction** (also called rolling back the tree).

Verify that for chance node 7 the expected payoff is $0.8. Hence, for decision node 5, the three choices offer $1.1 for 'Licence', $0.3 for 'Abandon' and $0.8 for 'Court'. The best decision is 'Licence' with a value of $1.1 million — the amount listed above node 5 — while 'Abandon' and 'Court' are blocked off. With nodes 5 and 6 both evaluated, we can now evaluate chance node 3. This is again the expected value over the two branches originating at node 3, namely, ($1.1)(0.4) + ($1.3)(0.6) = $1.22, the amount listed above node 3.

Before decision node 1 can be evaluated, decision node 2, and hence chance node 4 need to be evaluated.

At decision node 1, decision 'Do not accelerate' has an expected payoff of $1.1, while 'Accelerate' has an expected payoff of $1.22. Hence the best decision is to 'Accelerate'. 'Do not accelerate' is blocked off.

We now have the best sequence of decisions. It is to 'Accelerate' development of Release 3.0. Then, if the results of the preliminary analysis indicate that only four months can be gained, Barry should take out a 'Licence'. On the other hand, if 8 months can be gained, then he should 'Abandon' Release 2.1 immediately. One of two possible final outcomes will occur: $1.1 million with probability 0.4 or $1.3 million with probability 0.6. The average of these two outcomes, weighted by their probabilities is $1.22 million.

Only the first decision is firm. The second decision, taken either at node 5 or 6, is conditional on what happens at the chance node 3. So under uncertainty, the best alternative course of action is not a single decision, but a sequence of conditional decisions. This is referred to as a **strategy**. Nor do we know what the final outcome will be. All we have is a list of possible final outcomes. Their corresponding probabilities can be inferred from the path of branches that leads to each final outcome, as the product of the probabilities of each chance branch. In contrast, in deterministic situations the best alternative course of action can be specified as a firm single decision or a firm sequence of decisions. There we know exactly what will happen and what the final outcome will be.

Sensitivity analysis

Remember that much of the input to Barry's problem was based on educated guesses. Would YY really settle out of court for the amounts used on the decision tree under the various options of abandoning Release 2.1 right away? And what about the probability of winning the case or of introducing Release 3.0 several months earlier than originally scheduled? Let us analyse what happens as the probability of winning, p, becomes larger than 0.7.

Verify that when the probability of winning increases to 0.72, 'Do not accelerate' also has an expected payoff (at chance node 4) of $(0.72)(2.9) + (0.28)(-3.1) = $1.22

million. (Note that an increase in p does not change the best choices at decision nodes 5 and 6.) So, as this probability increases beyond 0.72, the preferred sequence of decisions is 'Do not accelerate' at decision node 1, followed by go to 'Court' at decision node 2. These decisions are unconditional. However, the final outcome is still either \$2.9 million with probability $p > 0.72$, or –\$3.1 million with probability $1 - p < 1 - 0.72$. The best current strategy is, therefore, quite precariously poised on the probability of winning. A small increase in it will tilt the balance towards a different alternative course of action. If Barry is even a bit of a gambler he may well decide to go to court regardless.

Activity: Assuming all data remain the same, except for the probabilities of accelerating development by 4 or by 8 months, will a change in these probabilities affect the optimal strategy? Why or why not? (Hint: compare expected outcomes of 'Do not accelerate' with those of '4 months' and '8 months'.)

18.3   The expected value of perfect information

Debbie Deft suggests that Barry Low consult with this famous soothsayer, who, it is said, has a perfect record in predicting the future. Unfortunately, this person does not come cheap. How much should Barry be willing to spend, at most, for acquiring a 'perfect' prediction on which state of the future will become true? If Barry had such perfect knowledge, he could plan exactly what he has to do to get the best result for that future state. However, prior to receiving such **perfect information** Barry can only make contingency plans about which strategy is best for each possible future state. Then, knowing the probability for each future state, he can compute an expected payoff associated with his contingency plans. Comparing the expected value of his contingency plans, based on receiving perfect information, with the expected value of the best strategy without it, he can then see how much better off he will be with perfect information.

The states of the future are given by the various combinations of the two types of events, i.e. the outcomes of the court case and the acceleration of Release 3.0. The four possible combinations of events are listed under the heading 'Joint state of nature' in Table 18-1. The probability of each of the combinations occurring is given by the product of the corresponding probabilities of each type of event. For example, based on the currently available (subjective) information about the future, the probability of the joint outcome 'Court case win' and '4 months gained by acceleration' is the equal to the probability of winning (0.7) times the probability of accelerating Release 3.0 by 4 months (0.4) which equals 0.28. Verify the remaining three joint probabilities, listed in the bottom row of Table 18-1. Note that the joint probabilities for the four combinations of outcomes must add up to 1, since one of them will occur.

The combinations of 'Do not accelerate' or 'Accelerate', and 'Get licence', or 'Abandon', or 'Go to court' yield six possible strategies. ('Do not accelerate' and 'Abandon' is listed here for completeness, but was left out in Figure 18-2.) The

Table 18-1   Payoff table for combined actions and joint states of nature.

STRATEGY	EVENT	JOINT STATE OF NATURE			
Months gained by acceleration		4	4	8	8
Court case outcome		win	lose	win	lose
A: Not accelerate & get licence		$1.0	$1.0	$1.0	$1.0
B: Not accelerate & abandon		–$0.6	–$0.6	–$0.6	–$0.6
C: Not accelerate & go to court		$2.9	–$3.1	$2.9	–$3.1
D: Accelerate & get licence		$1.1	$1.1	$1.25	$1.25
E: Accelerate & abandon		$0.3	$0.3	$1.3	$1.3
F: Accelerate & go to court		$2.6	–$3.4	$2.4	–$3.6
Best strategy for state of nature		C	D	C	E
payoff		$2.9	$1.1	$2.9	$1.3
Probability of state of nature		0.28	0.12	0.42	0.18

entries at the intersections of strategy rows and state of nature columns are the payoffs (in $1 millions) — hence the name **payoff table**. For some strategies, such as 'A: Do not accelerate & get licence' the monetary outcome does not depend on the state of nature. Hence, it is the same for all states. This also occurs for strategy B. For C, the outcome only depends on 'win' or 'lose', but not whether the firm accelerates or not. The probabilities for the combinations win/4 months and win/8 months acceleration add up to 0.7, as they should, and so on.

For each state of nature, the best strategy can now easily be identified. It is given by the strategy with the most favourable monetary outcome of its column of payoffs, shown shaded. For example, for '4 months gained and court case win', the strategy with the highest payoff is 'C: Do not accelerate & go to court'. Its payoff is $2.9. Check out the other three states.

So, prior to receiving this perfect information, the expected value of the payoffs for the best strategies is given by the sum of the products of these payoffs with their corresponding probabilities, or

$$\$2.9(0.28) + \$1.1(0.12) + \$2.9(0.42) + \$1.3(0.18) = \$2.396 \text{ million}$$

But remember that the actual payoff will be one of the four payoffs, not their weighted average.

Without getting any information about the true state of the future, all Barry can 'expect' for using his optimal strategy is a weighted average payoff of $1.22 million. Getting perfect information, the expected payoff goes up to $2.396 — a gain of $1.176 million. This increase in the expected payoff is called the **expected value of perfect information**. It represents the upper limit that Barry should be willing to pay to get perfect information. Naturally, the perfect predictor does not exist, and imperfect information is worth considerably less.

So we get a new, albeit not unexpected, insight into decision making under uncertainty. It may pay to acquire better information about the true state of the future. Furthermore, we can put an upper limit on how much the decision maker should be willing to spend for better information.

The decision maker may be able to obtain better information through various means, such as market research and test markets (i.e., trying out the product on a small, reasonably self-contained market), additional scientific research to gain a better understanding of the underlying principles and causes, or by having recourse to expert advice, e.g. through a Delphi study (see Section 15.5).

18.4   Capturing the intrinsic worth of outcomes

In many situations, the intrinsic worth of an outcome can be adequately measured by its monetary outcome. This is particularly so for routine type decisions, where the monetary outcome falls well within the decision maker's normal range of experience. However, for strategic or unique decisions the monetary outcomes are usually outside this range. Furthermore, the outcomes may involve a high degree of uncertainty. In such instances, few decision makers are willing to 'play the averages'. Other factors, such as the decision maker's financial ability to absorb large losses or the personal likes and dislikes of engaging in risky situations, may well influence how such uncertain outcomes are viewed.

You can easily check this out by imagining the following situation. It is the 20th of the month and you have £80 left for food and other necessities to carry you through to the end of the month, when you get your next sustenance payment. You have no other means to get money. A 'friend' takes you to a party where you are invited to participate in a game. Upon payment of £60 you can flip a coin. If it falls heads you win £360, tails you get nothing. If you take the offer, you end up with either £380 or £20 in your pocket. The expected value of your financial situation is (0.5)(£380) + (0.5)(£20) or £200. Given that right now you have just barely enough to get through the remainder of the month, would you be willing to participate in this game? You might have to live on watery porridge for 10 days! If you are like most people, you would decline. The great majority of people in such a dire financial position would rather have £80 in their pocket for certain, than a 50–50 chance of £20 or £380. But then 'hope springs eternal!'

Similarly, most of us carry insurance on our cars and other property. Some of us buy lottery tickets or gamble at the races. Clearly, these decisions are not based on a simple criterion of maximizing the expected monetary outcome. How else could insurance companies or lottery and gambling operators cover their operating costs, their payouts on claims or wins, and at the same time also make handsome profits? Should we infer from this that decisions to buy insurance or to gamble are not made on a rational basis? Far from it! It simply means that factors other than simply monetary outcomes affect how decision makers view outcomes that involve a great degree of uncertainty and other possible thrills or anxieties.

Furthermore, for many decision situations the outcomes often cannot be measured in monetary terms alone without introducing rather questionable value judgments. This is clearly so for Olly's problem. What is the monetary equivalent for 'Living with angina' or 'Dying in surgery'? Similarly, for many decisions in the public sector the outcomes of various courses of action could be the preservation or the destruction of scenic beauty, wilderness areas, or other important sites of public interest, changes to public safety, public health, or equity, and so on. Assigning monetary values to such things is fraught with controversy.

Take the notorious proposals to build a third international airport for London in the late 1970s. The preferred option offered by the planners would have destroyed a Norman church built in the 11th century. The analysts valued the church at its fire insurance value (to be ridiculed in the public hearings held)! In such cases, a simple criterion of maximizing expected monetary values will not do. Some of the approaches discussed in this and the next section may help. In other instances, decision criteria that explicitly consider multiple conflicting objectives may have to be invoked. Dealing with multiple conflicting objectives is the topic of the next chapter.

To measure the intrinsic worth or desirability of highly risky outcomes outside our normal range of experience we have to go beyond monetary values. This section discusses two approaches which are not based on 'playing the averages'. The next section gives a short introduction to **utility theory** — an approach to express the intrinsic worth of outcomes along a numeric scale that expresses the decision maker's world view, her or his personal value judgment and attitude towards risk.

The minimax criterion

Consider again Barry Low's problem, but with an additional twist. Losing the court case would mean that Barry's firm goes bankrupt. Barry is not so much of a gambler to run that risk. So any action which runs this risk is excluded. In fact, Barry is even more of a risk averter. He really wants to play it safe. So he wants to choose a decision strategy that guarantees him at least the best of the worst outcomes possible over all alternatives, no matter what happens. In this example, this means finding the strategy with the maximum lowest payoff. This decision rule is known as the **minimax criterion** (derived from **mini**mizing the **max**imum loss; when dealing with benefits, it is also referred to as the **maxmin criterion**, derived from **max**imizing the **min**imum benefit).

Finding the minimax strategy could be done on the decision tree. However, since we have already summarized the information of the decision tree in the form of a payoff table, it is simpler to work directly with this table. Table 18-2 reproduces those parts of Table 18-1 that we need for this evaluation. We find for each strategy its worst outcome or payoff (shown shaded) and enter it in the last column of the table. For example, for strategy 'C: Do not accelerate & go to court', the worst payoff is −$3.1, obtained for two of the states of nature.

Table 18-2   Payoff table for combined actions and joint states of nature.

STRATEGY EVENT	JOINT STATE OF NATURE				Worst payoff for action
Months gained by acceleration	4	4	8	8	
Court case outcome	win	lose	win	lose	
A: Do not accelerate & get licence	$1.0	$1.0	$1.0	$1.0	$1.0
B: Do not accelerate & abandon	–$0.6	–$0.6	–$0.6	–$0.6	–$0.6
C: Do not accelerate & go to court	$2.9	–$3.1	$2.9	–$3.1	–$3.1
D: Accelerate & get licence	$1.1	$1.1	$1.25	$1.25	$1.1
E: Accelerate & abandon	$0.3	$0.3	$1.3	$1.3	$0.3
F: Accelerate & go to court	$2.6	–$3.4	$2.4	–$3.6	–$3.6

The best of the worst outcomes or, in our case, the maximum of the minimum payoffs is $1.1 million, obtained for strategy 'D: Accelerate & get licence' — the cell with the heavy lines. It is the **minimax strategy**. Interestingly, it is the same as the one which maximizes the expected payoff. But this is by coincidence rather than by rule.

Note that at no point did the probabilities of the various outcomes at chance nodes enter into the decision process. So even if the chance of losing the court case is, say, only one in a 1000, or 1 in a million for that matter, the minimax criterion will choose the same strategy. This seems to be rather unreasonable. In business, conservative decision makers of that sort end up accepting only riskless ventures. But most riskless ventures are also low-return. They miss most good opportunities. Their businesses stagnate and ultimately will be squeezed out by competitors who are willing to assume some reasonable risks.

On the other hand, if the decisions involve ethical, safety, or environmental aspects, such as life-and-death outcomes, or the possible destruction of unique eco-logical or scenic areas, a minimax approach may be more appropriate as a decision criterion than maximizing the expected payoff.

A risk threshold approach

In this approach, any decision choices that carry a probability of certain specified adverse outcomes larger than some critical level are eliminated. The 'best' alternative course of action is then chosen from the remaining ones, based on some other cri-terion, such as maximizing the expected net cash flow.

Referring back to Figure 18-3 on page 514, assume that Barry is not willing to run a risk of more than 1 in 5 of going bankrupt. Any strategy which has a probability of more than 0.2 of resulting in bankruptcy is eliminated. 'Do not accelerate' followed by 'Court' has a probability of 0.3 of bankruptcy. Hence it is ruled out. This leaves only 'Licence' to follow 'Do not accelerate', at a net cash flow of $1.0 million. 'Accelerate' can lead to bankruptcy for both chance outcomes at node 3 if 'Court' is the follow-on choice. However, using an expected value criterion, 'Court' is not a contender. The 'best' follow-on choices for 'Accelerate' have a zero chance of bankruptcy. Based on that reasoning, the expected net cash flow for 'Accelerate' is $1.22 million (as for the original problem situation). This turns out also to be the best strategy under the constraint of a probability of bankruptcy of at most 0.2. It turns out to be a robust strategy.

Sensitivity analysis on this subjectively fixed limit for going bankrupt gives additional insight into how critical it is in terms of its effect on the expected outcome of the best decision strategy. If the expected value is highly sensitive to the constraint, this may lead the decision maker to review and possibly change it.

Rather than impose a constraint on the probability of a certain type of outcome, the constraint could be imposed on the maximum possible loss.

The risk threshold approach has considerable appeal. It formalizes the intuitive decision behaviour used by many decision makers and produces more consistent and insightful decision making, particularly when coupled with systematic sensitivity analysis. Its major difficulty is that it may become quite intractable for complex decision situations with a large number of possible combinations of decision choices and random events.

The literature on decision analysis discusses several other criteria. Most are mainly of academic interest, with little or no practical use for real-life situations.

> Activity: Consider a controversial issue, such as the development of medical treatment based on gene technology, where typically the proponents claim that the chances of inadvertently creating dangerous genes are minimal and opponents argue that if anything goes wrong it could threaten life on earth as we know it. Discuss these stands in terms of various decision criteria.

18.5 Utility analysis

In 1944, Von Neumann and Morgenstern, a mathematician and an economist, proposed an index designed to quantify the personal subjective worth of a risky outcome to a given decision maker, valid for a particular decision situation at a particular time. They called it **utility** — a rather unfortunate choice, given the traditional and discredited usage made of this term in economic theory. For this reason, some authors prefer the term **preference theory**.

A **utility function** expresses a decision maker's valuation of risky outcomes on a numerical scale. We have already used this concept for capturing Olly's preference structure. The scale used is arbitrary; it could cover a range from 0 to 1, 0 to 100, or −1000 to +1000. The lower limit reflects the worth of the least desirable outcome, the higher limit the most desirable outcome, with all other outcomes in between.

Basic forms of utility functions

Figure 18-4 shows three different shapes of utility functions. The horizontal axis measures the monetary outcomes. The vertical scale shows the intrinsic worth of that outcome on the arbitrary scale chosen — here the range 0 to 1. The straight line in the middle represents the utility function for a person who is **risk neutral**. Such a person does not need to have recourse to a utility function — the 'best' decision will be the same as for maximizing expected monetary outcomes. Most of us are risk neutral when we deal with outcomes which are clearly within our everyday range of experience. This may be a few dollars for an individual, but could be in the hundred thousands for large business corporations.

Figure 18-4   The three basic shapes of utility functions.

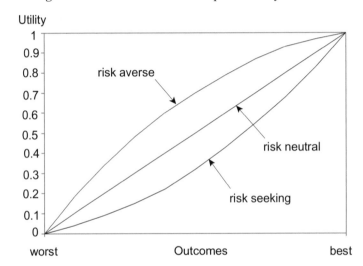

The concave curve above the straight line is the general shape of the utility function for a decision maker who is **risk averse**. Consecutive equal increments in the monetary outcome result in smaller and smaller increments in utility. Most people exhibit some degree of risk aversion, particularly for large monetary gains or losses in their private and professional lives.

The convex curve below the straight line depicts the utility function for a person who is a **risk taker**. Doubling the monetary outcome increases the utility more than proportionately. Few people exhibit such a pattern for outcomes of important business and private decision choices. The exception is the pathological gambler. However, all of us are occasionally risk takers when we are looking for thrills or fun, such as gambling at the races, playing cards, or taking part in a dangerous sport.

So, we see that the same person may make some decisions from a risk-neutral position, others from a risk-averse position, and a few from a risk-seeking position. Each position is perfectly rational within its proper context and consistent with the person's world view.

A five-point assessment procedure

Recall the insights we gained from Olly's problem situation. We concluded that, given a risky option with outcomes A or C, we can construct an equivalent riskless option with outcome B, where A is preferred to B which is preferred to C, such that the decision maker is indifferent between choosing the risky or the riskless option. The equivalent riskless option can be constructed either by adjusting the value of B or by adjusting the probabilities of the risky option. Indifference between the two options implies that their intrinsic worth is the same. These surprisingly simple ideas form the basis for finding the utility function for a given decision situation.

We will now demonstrate the procedure with Barry's problem. We start out by assigning the worst outcome an intrinsic value or a utility of zero, and the best outcome a utility of 1. The choice of these values is arbitrary. It will not affect the relative ranking of the various decision strategies open to Barry. In Barry's case, the worst outcome is –$3.6 million (i.e. a loss of $3.6 million), the best outcome a gain of $2.9 million.

We now offer Barry a choice of two options: (1) a 50–50 gamble involving the best and the worst outcomes, and (2) a riskless option involving a net cash flow somewhere in between the worst and the best outcomes. The technical term for the gamble is **reference lottery**. We could start out with a cash flow exactly halfway, i.e. –$0.35 million. (Keep in mind that negative outcomes represent losses!) Knowing that Barry is risk averse, we expect that he will prefer the sure payoff of –$0.35 million to the gamble. This is indeed the case. So we know that his utility for –$0.35 million is higher than the utility of the gamble. We now lower the monetary value of the riskless option. Say we reduce it to –$2.0 million. We again ask him to rank the original gamble and the sure outcome of –$2.0 million. He now says that he prefers the gamble. This implies that his utility for –$2.0 is lower than the utility of the gamble. Our next try is a value between –$0.35 and –$2.0 million. We continue presenting Barry with a choice of the original gamble and a sure outcome of X dollars, increasing the value of X if he prefers the gamble and decreasing it if he prefers X. After a few more trials, he finally settles on a value of –$1.5 million, for which he is indifferent between the gamble and the riskless outcome. Indifference between the original gamble and the sure thing of –$1.5 implies that these two options have the same intrinsic worth or the same utility. But we know the utility of the gamble. It is equal to the expected utility of the outcome of the gamble. For a 50–50 gamble this is $(0.5)(1) + (0.5)(0)$, where 1 and 0 are the arbitrary utility values assigned to the best and worst outcomes. So, the utilities of the gamble and of the riskless outcome of –$1.5 million are both 0.5.

We now repeat this procedure a second and third time. But instead of choosing a 50–50 reference lottery involving the worst and best outcomes, we replace either the worst outcome or the best outcome with the value –$1.5 million just found. So the second reference lottery is given by a 50–50 chance of –$1.5 and $2.9 million. Again we can easily compute the expected utility of this reference lottery as $(0.5)(1) + (0.5)(0.5)$ or 0.75. After a number of trials Barry agrees on an equivalent riskless option of $0.4 million. Hence an outcome of $0.4 million must have a utility of 0.75, the same as the second reference lottery. For the third round we set the reference lottery to a 50–50 chance of –$3.6 and –$1.5. Verify that the expected utility of this reference lottery is 0.25. After a few more trials Barry settles on an equivalent riskless option of –$2.8 million. Hence –$2.8 must have a utility of 0.25.

We have now determined the utility of five outcomes in the range from the worst to the best outcome for this particular decision situation under uncertainty. They are depicted in Figure 18-5 by the solid squares. Fitting a smooth curve through these five points yields a good approximation to Barry's utility function for this problem. As expected, Barry is clearly risk averse. His utility function is everywhere above the straight line representing a risk neutral utility function.

Figure 18-5   Barry Low's utility function.

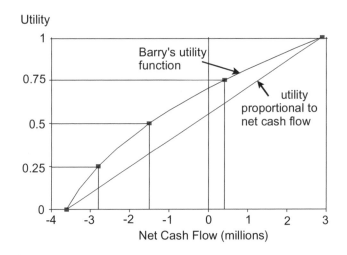

Activity
- You worked hard to accumulate savings of £3000 that will allow you to complete the last year of your degree only needing to work weekends and assured of getting good average grades. You get an invitation to from a reputable stockbroker to participate in a risky venture that if it pays off would yield £10,000 — no need to work and hence offering a good chance of getting those important top grades. But if it goes wrong, you lose all your savings, opening up the possibility of failing some courses and needing a further miserable year to complete the degree.
- Having some £20 spare cash, you go to the races for an afternoon of fun. Your fancy is caught by a particular horse which offers rather long odds of £26 per pound placed on it. So if you put your entire £20 on a win, you will make £500 net for a win, but lose £20 for a loss.

Finding the best decision using utility functions

If the full worth of an outcome can be measured on a monetary scale, the best decision strategy is based on an expected monetary value criterion. If the intrinsic worth of outcomes is measured by utilities, it can again be shown that the best strategy is the one that **maximizes expected utility**. We simply replace the net cash flows at all end points in the decision tree by the corresponding utility values, and then proceed to evaluate the tree by backward induction as before. I suggest that you read off Figure 18-5 the utility values corresponding to all end point net cash flows, insert them into Figure 18-3, and evaluate all the nodes again. For Barry's utility function, the overall best strategy remains the same. (However, the best action at the blocked-off node 2 switches from 'Court' to 'Licence'.)

Some reflections on utility measures

It is important to stress that the utility measures obtained in this manner reflect not only the decision maker's valuation of outcomes, but also the attitude towards risk. So these utility functions are not valid for decisions that do not involve uncertainty. Furthermore, they are valid for the particular situation for which they were assessed at a particular point in time. Each new situation needs to be assessed anew. Similarly, a decision maker's attitude towards risk may change over time. Therefore, even when facing the same type of situation at some later time, he or she may need to reassess her or his utility function.

The procedure can also be easily adapted to situations that do not involve monetary outcomes, such as is the case in Olly's problem. In fact, there have been serious efforts made since the early 1980s to introduce utility-type concepts into decision situations in the health and medical fields.

As we have seen, the method for assessing approximate utility functions is surprisingly simple. Increased accuracy for drawing the curve can easily be obtained by finding equivalent riskless options for additional utility values between the ones assessed in the five-point procedure. It may also be possible to fit algebraic functions to the points found.

So, given the simplicity of the procedure, why have utility functions largely remained an academic curiosity, and this in spite of the fact that this topic has been part of the curriculum of most college and university business courses since the early 1960s? There are a number of reasons. Although the procedure is simple, most decision makers find it difficult to think in terms of reference lotteries and equivalent riskless options. Hence they are reluctant to be pinned down to definite answers. Their answers may not be consistent, requiring a delicate process of re-assessment. In fact, it needs a fairly skilful analyst to get results which the decision maker feels truly reflect her or his preference structure for the problem situation in question. Up to now few real-life applications outside academic institutions have been reported.

Research by M. McCord and R. de Neufville ['Lottery equivalents': Reduction of the certainty effect in utility assessment, *Management Science,* Jan. 1986, pp. 56–60] and by P. Delquié [Inconsistent trade-offs between attributes: New evidence in preference assessment biases, *Management Science*, Nov. 1993, pp. 1382–95] indicates that the utility functions derived may differ depending on the exact sequence and form of assessments made and the framing of the assessment, as well as other unexplained factors. Hence this casts serious doubts on their validity.

However, even if the utility functions derived are never explicitly used in finding the 'best' decision strategy, the process of assessing such utility functions will enhance the decision maker's awareness of her or his preference structure and thereby lead to better and more informed decision making.

18.6   Risk analysis: basic concepts

(Sections 18.6 and 18.7 require basic knowledge of simulation concepts, in particular the generation and use of random variates (Section 17.1) and the concept of Monte Carlo simulation (Section 17.4). Similarly, they assume familiarity with discounting of cash flows over time (Sections 10.1 and 10.2) and the associated spreadsheet function in Section 10.6.)

For investment decisions, the exact amounts of future cash flows are usually not known with certainty, particularly on the revenue side. They are random variables. Conventional methods of investment evaluation approximate these random cash flows by their expected values or other conservative estimates. Similarly, the cost and revenue figures attached to the end points of decision trees are also expected values for that particular sequence of events. Furthermore, decision trees suffer from the need to restrict any chance events to only a few discrete outcomes, or else the tree explodes in size and becomes unwieldy and difficult to use.

Backward induction or rolling back the tree eliminates all but a few endpoints that are possible payoffs of the best strategy. For instance, in Barry Low's problem, the best strategy results either in an outcome of $1.1 million (accelerate/4 months/ licence) with probability 0.4, or $1.3 million (accelerate/8 months/abandon) with probability 0.6. In reality, acceleration may result in a reduction of development time ranging anywhere from 3 to 10 months, each with different development costs. Similarly, the cost of the preliminary analysis is hardly $100,000 exactly, but could be between a low of $50,000 and a high of $200,000; the guess as to the size of the licence fee that YY is willing to accept may be off. It is a random variable, and so are the costs of defending the law suit, or the revenues generated from sales under the various conditions. Most are continuous variables. They are not restricted to a few values. The decision tree reduced all this myriad of possible outcomes to just two numbers: 1.1 and 1.3 million.

Faced with risky situations, few decision makers will be satisfied with such scant information. They would want to see a better profile of the true variability of outcomes associated with a given strategy. They would want to be able to get answers to such questions as: What is the probability that the strategy threatens the survival of the firm? What is the probability that the monetary outcome is less than the break-even point? And so on.

To answer such questions about the risk of a venture, what is needed is a probability distribution over the possible range of outcomes. Except for the simplest and hence trivial situations, there is no analytical way to determine the probability distribution of the final outcome if some of the intermediate chance events are in turn conditional continuous random variables. Risk analysis is an attempt to find an empirical approximation based on the idea of Monte Carlo simulation.

Risk analysis repeatedly simulates the sequence of unconditional and conditional random events that result from a given decision strategy and records their effect on various performance measures, such as the project's cumulative cash flow and its profitability. For investment ventures that span several years, the measures may well be expressed as net present values (NPVs). The results over all these simulations are then captured by frequency tables and histograms.

Repeating this process for various possible good strategies, and performing sensitivity analysis on some of the more 'uncertain' aspects will provide the decision maker with the insight as to the risk profile of such ventures.

Commercial software, such as @RISK, 1-2-Tree, or SIM.xla (see Bibliography), considerably simplifies performing risk analysis. SIM.xla is used in the next section for assessing the risk profile of an investment in a new ski-field.

18.7 Risk analysis for a ski-field development

Situation summary and definition of narrow system of interest

ITALIA NEVE is considering launching a new ski-field in a north-facing valley on Mount Aetna, adjacent to a rival facility. Based on a comprehensive investigation of the development design, it has accumulated information about

- construction costs for each of 3 years;
- operating costs for various patronage levels;
- effect of pricing structure on market share;
- number of skiable days in the region based on records over the past 20 years for the neighbouring ski-field;
- future levels for the region's skiing market over time.

All of these aspects involve considerable uncertainty. The values they will assume in any given year are random variables. Furthermore, they are affected to various degrees by three other factors. The first is the general economic conditions affecting the main customer catchment area, in this particular instance a major metropolitan region within driving range. An economic slump may reduce the patronage by up to ½. The second is the fact that the area is on the slopes of a mountain which over the last 100 years has shown regular volcanic activity. Just a few years previously, a major eruption necessitated the temporary closure of the neighbouring ski-field, thereby ruining the better part of the ski season for that year. A conservative estimate is that patronage will be reduced by 40% in any year an eruption occurs. Finally, the amount of natural snowfall, the average temperature, and the frequency of warm sirocco winds during the skiing season — all three captured by the catch-all term 'weather conditions' — can only partially be 'corrected' by artificial snow-making facilities, and hence they affect the number of skiable days and patronage for that year.

The firm would like to get a better feel for the economic viability of this project, in particular the financial risks, in terms of both profitability and the cash flow profiles over time. The latter could lead to liquidity problems even if the project has a satisfactory rate of return on investment. Risk analysis is the ideal tool for this. I will arbitrarily select a planning horizon of 10 years (as otherwise the spreadsheet will not fit on one page).

The first step is to get a clearer picture of the narrow system of interest S. Based on S we can then build a quantitative model, using the spreadsheet technology and SIM.xla as the mathematical modelling system M, which will allow us to explore the solution space. An influence diagram seems the ideal vehicle for defining S. This is done in Figure 18-6.

First, some conventions used. A number of inputs are in the form of random variables, depicted as input clouds with a tilde (~) above the name. The actual variate values generated are system variables, depicted by circles.   Construction occurs in the first three years. Its 'Actual cost' — generated from the assumed probability distribution for 'Construction cost' — is affected by the overall 'Weather' conditions — another random input. In year three the field begins partial operations. The 'Actual operating cost' is also affected by the general 'Economic conditions'. The latter may change from year to year. An economic slump means less patronage, and hence fewer staff hired. 'Actual patronage' is affected by the 'Weather', by 'Volcanic activity', and by the general 'Economic conditions'. It affects 'Actual revenue'. The various cash flows of year 3 produce the 'Total cash flow' in year 3, which added to the 'Cumulative cash flow' to the end of year 2 results in the 'Cumulative cash flow' to the end of year 3. The year 3 pattern for the operating costs and patronage, as well as the revenue flows is then repeated for year 4 and on through year 10, as indicated by the broken arrows.

Spreadsheet implementation

To formulate a spreadsheet model, we need to specify probability distributions for each of the random aspects. The construction costs are assumed to follow a normal distribution with means and standard deviations entered as input into the top portion of the spreadsheet in Figure 18-7 (page 530), cells C5 to E6. For example, costs in year 1 have a mean of €4.1 and a standard deviation of €0.2 million.

Based on the advice received from meteorologists, the effects of the weather conditions in each year can be approximated adequately by a triangular distribution, as shown in Figure 18-8 on page 531. It generates a weather factor between 0.9 and 1.1, with the majority falling around 1, as indicated by the peak of Figure 18-8, shown on page 531. Multiplying these factors by the patronage produces the desired effect. The distribution parameters are listed in cells J4 to L4.

Similarly, engineering estimates indicate that bad weather will increase the construction cost by up to 11%, while good weather will decrease it by at most 9%. Again we can get the desired effect, but this time by dividing the construction cost

Figure 18-6 Influence diagram for ski-field project.

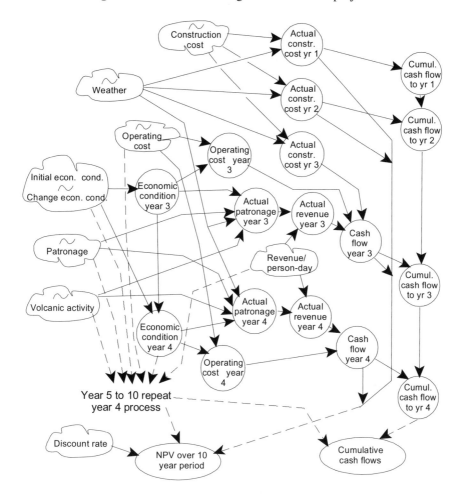

by the weather factor.

Our vulcanologist adviser estimates that the chance of an eruption serious enough to disrupt operations in any year is about 5% (input cell L5). During a year of volcanic eruptions patronage is assumed to be reduced to 60% of a normal year (input cell L6).

Economics consultants guess that a change in the general economic conditions occurs on average in three out of ten years. So in each year there is a 30% probability that the economic conditions change, either from 'Good' to 'Bad' or vice versa (input cell L2), while there is a 70% chance of no change.

'Bad' economic conditions mean that operating costs are only 80% (input cell L3) of those under 'Good' conditions (input rows 12 and 13). To reflect the impact of the economic conditions on patronage, we use a different normal distribution for each

Figure 18-7
Risk analysis for ski-field investment (one run).

#	A	B	C	D	E	F	G	H	I	J	K	L
1	SKI-FIELD DATA: (all monetary outcomes in millions of Euros)						Discount rate					0.12
2	Current economic conditions		GOOD				P(economic conditions change)					0.3
3	Revenue per skier-day			78			Cost reduction					0.8
4	Predicted construction cost		year 1	year 2	year 3		Weather triangular dist.			0.9	1	1.1
5	Average cost		4.1	5.2	1.6		P(volcanic eruption)					0.05
6	Standard deviation		0.2	0.4	0.3		Reduced patronage due to volcanic eruption					0.6
7	Year		1	2	3	4	5	6	7	8	9	10
8	Good patronage: average				0.1	0.2	0.3	0.33	0.35	0.36	0.37	0.38
9	(million skier-days) standard deviation				0.02	0.05	0.08	0.06	0.06	0.06	0.06	0.06
10	Bad patronage: average				0.05	0.1	0.2	0.22	0.23	0.24	0.25	0.25
11	(million skier-days) standard deviation				0.01	0.02	0.05	0.05	0.05	0.05	0.05	0.05
12	Nominal operating cost: average				8	12	16	17	17	17	17	17
13	standard deviation				0.2	0.3	0.4	0.4	0.4	0.4	0.4	0.4
14	SIMULATION OF STOCHASTIC EVENTS:				(patronage in million skier-days)							
15	Weather factor		1.0391	0.9794	1.0019	0.9909	0.9845	0.9799	0.9664	1.044	1.005	0.9643
16	Volcanic eruption		NO	NO	NO	NO	NO	NO	NO	NO	NO	NO
17	Patronage multiplier for volcanic eruptions				1	1	1	1	1	1	1	1
18	Unadjusted good patronage				0.0859	0.1938	0.3447	0.2498	0.3575	0.4292	0.5022	0.2735
19	Unadjusted bad patronage				0.0371	0.1116	0.2911	0.1962	0.3157	0.2649	0.3145	0.2875
20	Change in econ. cond.				NO	NO	YES	YES	NO	YES	YES	YES
21	Economic conditions				GOOD	GOOD	BAD	GOOD	GOOD	BAD	GOOD	BAD
22	Actual patronage				0.0861	0.192	0.2865	0.2448	0.3455	0.2765	0.5047	0.2772
23	CASH FLOWS: (in millions of Euros)											
24	Actual construction cost		3.85	5.097	2.194							
25	Actual operating cost				7.793	12.09	12.756	17.2	17.484	13.393	17.102	13.013
26	Actual revenue				6.712	14.975	22.35	19.092	26.95	21.568	39.365	21.62
27	Net cash flow		-3.85	-5.097	-3.275	2.885	9.594	1.892	9.466	8.175	22.263	8.607
28	Cumulative cash flow		-3.85	-8.947	-12.222	-9.337	0.257	2.15	11.615	19.79	42.053	50.66
29											NPV over planning horizon	16.787

Figure 18-8 Triangular distribution.

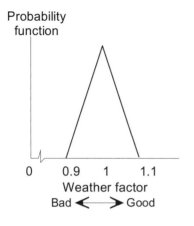

Probability
function

0   0.9   1   1.1
Weather factor
Bad ←——→ Good

case: input rows 8 and 9 for 'Good', 10 and 11 for 'Bad'. These are guesstimates, made by a committee of top staff and advisers.

Even for this cut-down problem, we needed to specify 30 probability distributions, as well as guesstimates for several other uncertain factors. There is no doubt that for any real-life risk analysis, assembling the needed information about all uncertain aspects (for many of which little hard data may be available) easily escalates into a massive data collection and data fitting exercise.

The last two parts of Figure 18-7 show one simulated realization of the project over all ten years. It largely follows the sequence of events depicted in the influence diagram. Row 15 generates the weather factor and row 16 volcanic eruptions (yes or no), while row 17 shows the corresponding multiplier on patronage (1 for no, 0.6 for yes). Rows 18 and 19 are the normal random variates for unadjusted patronage for both good and bad economic conditions, based on the input rows 8 to 11. Although only one of the two entries will ever be used in any given year, calculating both at this point simplifies the formulas for actual patronage in row 22. Row 20 then finds whether a change in economic conditions occurred or not. Its effect is reflected in row 21. The first change occurs in year 5. Hence the economic conditions in years 1 to 4 carry forward the initial conditions 'Good' (input cell D2), and only changes to 'Bad' in year 5. The actual patronage (row 22) is calculated by multiplying the product of the weather factor (row 15) and the volcanic eruption multiplier (row 17) by the entry in row 18 if the corresponding cell in row 21 shows 'Good' or the entry in row 19 if it shows 'Bad'.

The bottom section calculates the resulting cash flows. The construction costs in cells C24 to E24 are the ratios of the normal random variates generated from the input data cells C5 to E6 and the weather factors in row 15. Operating costs are equal to the random variates generated from rows 12 and 13, reduced to 80% (input cell L3) if the economic conditions are 'Bad'. Finally, the actual revenues (row 26) are computed as the product of the unit revenue per skier-day (input cell D4) and the actual patronage in row 22. The net cash flow in each year (row 27) is equal to actual revenue less actual construction cost and actual operating cost. The row 28 entries are the cumulative sums of row 27, while the NPV (cell L29) is the sum of the discounted net cash flows, using the discount rate in cell L2.

This particular simulation results in a healthy €16.8 million NPV and recovers the initial investment by the end of year 5. However, it would be foolhardy to make a decision as to the desirability of a risky project on only one simulation. Usually, several hundred simulations are needed and the results combined.

Results of risk analysis

To get risk profiles for the project, we made a run of 1000 simulations. Risk analysis software automatically produces frequency tables and histograms. The top portion of Table 18-3 shows that the average NPV is close to €8 million. What is rather alarming, however, is that the standard deviation is almost equally large. The bottom portion reveals that there is almost a 15% probability that the NPV is negative — a sizable risk. There is little chance of recovering the construction costs within the first five years, and even by the end of seven years it is still more than 35% likely that not all funds have been recovered. What is also alarming is that the worst case scenario may end up with a net loss of more than €10 million.

Table 18-3   Result of 1000 simulations for ski-field project.

Output Name	NPV (million €)	Cum. Cash 5 years	Cum. Cash 7 years	Cum. Cash 10 years
Average	7.8904	−7.0757	5.2837	30.067
Std Dev	7.6259	7.9739	11.609	16.274
Std Err	0.2412	0.2522	0.3671	0.5146
Max	31.12	23.733	40.116	77.258
Min	−14.44	−25.907	−28.145	−15.778
Percentiles				
5%	−4.4361	−18.949	−12.454	3.8675
10%	−1.6469	−16.841	−9.687	9.2121
15%	0.2949	−14.87	−6.5996	13.383
20%	1.2716	−13.961	−4.4087	15.981
25%	2.4641	−12.786	−2.2758	19.004
30%	3.4939	−11.864	−0.9672	21.125
35%	4.6243	−10.836	0.4911	23.3
40%	5.9074	−9.8556	1.7113	25.557
45%	6.7367	−8.6597	2.9305	27.914
50%	7.6708	−7.8001	4.5685	29.836
55%	8.5	−6.7862	6.0283	31.221
60%	9.6692	−5.5628	7.5339	33.675
65%	10.778	−4.7338	9.6204	36.279
70%	11.648	−3.3039	10.873	38.386
75%	12.872	−1.7827	12.655	41.085
80%	14.154	−0.1583	14.74	43.709
85%	15.758	1.4817	17.169	46.947
90%	17.884	3.913	21.07	51.952
95%	21.182	7.6418	25.071	57.948
100%	31.12	23.733	40.116	77.258

A second run of 1000 simulations, using a different stream of random variates, yielded very similar overall results.

Since the average NPV of €7.8904 million is larger than the mode of 7.6708 (the 50% percentile), this means that distribution is slightly skewed to the left. Its right tail, extending to 31.12, is longer than its left tail, going to –4.4361.

Figure 18-9 shows the graph for the risk profile of the NPV, while Figure 18-10 maps the profiles for the cumulative cash flows after 5, 7, and 10 years.

Properly used, risk analysis is a powerful tool for quantifying the risk involved in a venture. It has the potential for providing valuable insights that cannot be gleaned from decision trees. However, it is important to realize that, if the project is implemented,

Figure 18-9   Risk profile of NPV over a ten year planning horizon.

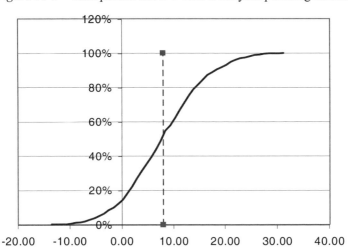

Figure 18-10   Risk profile of cumulative cash flows after 5, 7, and 10 years.

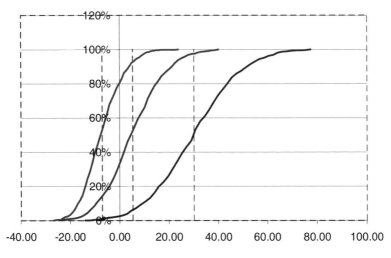

the outcome will not be a distribution, but a single point in the range of possible outcomes, e.g. €16.8 million for the run in Figure 18-7. Potentially, it could even fall outside the range produced by the risk analysis. Furthermore, the reliability of the results is only as good as the reliability of the inputs and, in particular, how well the various uncertainties have been captured by the probability distributions used. For this reason it is important to do extensive sensitivity analysis. For our example it is crucial to explore what happens to the risk profiles for

(a) different levels of reduction in patronage due to volcanic eruptions,

(b) different unit revenues per skier-day, and

(c) wider ranges of the distribution for weather conditions (e.g. 0.8 to 1.2).

Sensitivity analysis is greatly facilitated by commercial software. Systematic exploration of the response to changes in the various inputs will reveal which ones are critical and need to be assessed with extra care. This will allow the analyst to direct data collection into these areas. The size and the difficulties of the data collection effort needed to get reliable results are, without doubt, the Achilles' heel of risk analysis.

18.8 Chapter highlights

- Decision trees graphically depict the sequence and conditional dependence of multi-stage decision processes involving uncertain events. They are a useful aid for forcing the decision maker to clearly and comprehensively map out all possible sequences of decisions and contingent events that lead to all possible final outcomes.

- The best sequence of decision choices is usually in the form of a strategy of conditional actions that achieves the highest expected value of benefits or the lowest expected cost. It is determined by backward induction, blocking off decision branches that lead to inferior outcomes.

- Given that some of the input used may be of a subjective nature, it is important to perform extensive sensitivity analysis. This will identify which inputs are critical. These should be assessed with extra care.

- For single- or two-stage processes, it is possible to determine the value of perfect information. This provides an upper limit to the amount that may be spent on collecting better and more reliable input data.

- For decision problems that are subject to high degrees of uncertainty or that involve outcomes with serious environmental, health, or security implications, or for which the monetary outcome may not reflect the true intrinsic value, decision criteria based on other than maximizing or minimizing expected values may be more appropriate. The minimax criterion minimizes the maximum possible loss, regardless of the probability associated with the various outcomes. Threshold criteria eliminate actions that lead to extreme outcomes or have unacceptably high probabilities for unfavourable outcomes.

- Utility functions are another approach to measure the intrinsic value of numeric outcomes, both monetary and other, particularly those that fall outside the every-day range of experience. Such utility functions are, however, specific for a given risky situation experienced by a given decision maker at a specific point in time. They are not valid for other decision problems of a different nature or for other decision makers. They may change over time. Based on the concepts of in-difference or switch points, it is possible to derive empirical approximations to the utility function for a given risky outcome using a five-point assessment procedure.

- Risk analysis is an approach for assessing the risk profile associated with a particular strategy used for multi-stage and/or multi-period ventures that involve uncertain events, some of which may be conditional upon other events. It allows random events to be represented in the form of discrete or continuous probability distributions or empirical frequency functions. Each simulation represents one particular realization of the venture. By performing a large number of such simulations, it is possible to derive frequency distributions of the outcomes associated with that strategy.

Exercises

1. Sally Smart is planning how to survive, in financial terms, the 2004/5 academic year. The way matters stand right now, she will lose her government assistance since her parents have just joined the class of 'nouveau riche' created by the government to raise the morale of the country's population. With another brother struggling to finish his engineering degree, the chances are nil that her parents will be able to support her with more than an occasional carrot cake. Her choices are:
    - She could drop out and join the ranks of the unemployed. Using her skills in present value calculations recently acquired in MSCI 101 she calculated that the NPV of her lifetime loss in earning power would amount to £25,000 if the finance minister's ECON 101 policies continue to depress the economy, while the loss would only be £5,000 if the prime minister finds the courage to sack her with most of her Treasury advisers. Sally figures that the chance that the prime minister can find the necessary courage is only 25%.
    - She could take out a loan, finish her degree and then pay it back over the next 10 to 20 years. The NPV cost of that action is £15,800 with the present finance minister remaining in office and £12,400 if she is replaced.
    - She could enter into a marriage of convenience with another student and then automatically retain her government assistance. With the cost of the parties her friends would insist she throw for both 'tying the knot' and 'cutting it again after graduation', as well as the potential 'intangible' costs associated with this action, she figures that the net cost to her would be £4000 with the present finance minister remaining in office, but £16,000 without her (due to having gotten married without really any need for it).
    (a) Develop a decision tree, attaching costs and probabilities to the various branches. Using this tree, find the best action for Sally based on monetary considerations only.
    (b) Using the method of Section 18.3 determine the value of perfect information.

2. After making her choice, Sally decides to sleep on it for a few days before taking any irrevocable action. On the second morning, it dawns on her that the minister of education might stumble on the marriage of convenience scheme. She figures that there is in fact a 40% chance that the Government would introduce a questionnaire asking embarrassing personal questions about the civil state of the applicants for government assistance. She might then have incurred the expense of getting married (£4,000) only to find out that she does not qualify for assistance anyway, given that her marriage is one of convenience only. She would then be back to the drawing board, but obviously still could settle on one of the first two choices above. (The 4,000 would then have been incurred in addition to the cost of these choices.)

(a) Draw up a new decision tree for this problem and find the strategy that minimizes expected costs now.

(b) Using the method of Section 18.3, determine the value of perfect information.

3. In the mid-1970s a small car was blown off the access road to a ski-field in the Southern Alps of New Zealand, resulting in a fatality. The car's owner had in fact ignored warnings not to use the road during gale force winds that had sprung up in the early afternoon. Several other cars had close shaves during other storms. The management of the ski-field was faced with the dilemma as to what action to take, if any, to prevent further accidents of that sort. Three alternatives were investigated: (1) Relocation of the road away from exposed areas at a cost of $2.5 million, completely eliminating any further danger. (2) Erection of protective wind barriers at a cost of $1.5 million, which would prevent any vehicle from being blown off the road, except under the most severe storm conditions. The chance of such a storm occurring over the next 10 years was estimated at 20%, but, since the road would be closed to traffic if such a storm was predicted, the chance that a car would actually be caught in such a storm was only 10%. If, however, an accident were to happen, the ski-field company would be liable to punitive damages and possible loss of income due to adverse publicity to an amount of $4.2 million. Furthermore, the company would have little choice but to relocate the road then. (3) Do nothing, but close the ski-field whenever there was the slightest danger of any winds in excess of 20 knots. This would not involve any immediate costs, but would lose considerable revenues. These are estimated at $1 million. Furthermore, there still remained a residual 10% chance of a major accident due to the inability to predict the often sudden weather changes in the region. An accident would have the same financial consequences as for option (2), i.e. punitive damages and the cost of relocating the road. Assume all amounts are already expressed in present values.

(a) Develop a decision tree for this problem, attaching costs and probabilities to the various branches.

(b) Determine the action with the lowest expected cost.

(c) Using the method of Section 18.3, determine the value of perfect information.

4. In 2004, The British Columbia tourist industry experienced a drop in tourist tour bookings of over 25%. According to the latest forecast, the tourist trade is unlikely to pick up significantly before the middle of 2005. In fact, one of the tour operators, Green Tours, using The Airport Château has just notified Michel d'Hôtelier, the Quebec-born manager, that they might cancel their bookings for 2005. Green Tours booked on average 20 rooms for 250 days of the year (i.e. 5000 room nights). Michel thinks that this may be a ploy to get reduced room rates. He expects that there is a 50–50 chance they will renew the contract if he reduces the room fee from $150 per night to $130 for 2005. If Green Tours abandons its bookings, it will be too late to fill the empty rooms by arranging a contract

with another tour operator. However, he thinks that there is a 75% chance he will be able to negotiate a contract with another tour operator for 5000 room nights for 2005 at a price of $140. This alternative will however incur a $20,000 cost, regardless of whether the negotiations are successful or not. If Green Tours continues its bookings for 2005, Michel is 80% certain that Green Tours will renew their contract for 2006 at the old price of $150. If not they would certainly do it again at the $130 price. If no firm contracts can be arranged with a tour operator, then all Michel can expect is to sell about 1000 room-nights per year on a casual basis to individual tourists at a room rate of $180 per night, leaving some 4000 room-nights empty.

Michel can also look for alternative business for 2005/6. By far the most reliable business is in so-called 'air-crew contracts', where an airline books a fixed number of rooms every night at a fixed contractual sum for the entire year, regardless of whether the rooms are used or not. Michel has already been approached by Bamboo Airlines, which serves the lucrative tourist trade to South East Asia, with a contract proposal for 20 rooms for a two-year period at a fixed contract sum of $1,200,000. This averages to about $82 per room per night, considerably less than the price paid by tour operators, although it is guaranteed for the entire two years. Unfortunately, he will have to make a decision on the Bamboo Airlines contract before being able to conclude the negotiations with Green Tours for 2005.

In any case, he expects that by 2006 his Airport Château will again be fully booked with tour operators. The hotel's operating costs are obviously dependent on its occupancy rate. If Michel clinches any deals with tour operators or the airline, he will need a full staff complement. The hotel's annual operating costs will be $300,000 higher than if it only relies on casual tourist traffic.

(a) Develop a decision tree for this situation. Show the revenues and costs associated with each branch, as well as any probabilities. Also show the cumulative cash flow associated with each end point of the tree. You do not have to use discounting on the cash flows.

(b) Use the tree developed under (a) to find the best strategy. What is the best strategy and its expected profit?

(c) Using the method demonstrated in Section 18.3, determine the value of perfect information.

5. The BlueSky Recording company is faced with the decision as to whether or not to record and market an album for a promising, but so far unknown and untested, Continental rock band. The usual method to reach a decision is as follows: Two songs of the group's repertoire are recorded in the firm's Belgium studio. These are then submitted for appraisal to a consumer panel. These two steps have a cost of €3000. The panel is asked to rate the songs as 'potential hits' or 'questionable'. The talent scout and the music director of the firm agree that from what music they have heard of the group and the perceived current preference patterns of the potential buyers, the probability that the panel will rate the songs as 'potential hits' is 0.7. If the panel rates the songs as 'questionable', the firm normally decides not to go ahead with any further recordings of the band. If the panel rates the songs as 'potential hits', the firm will record a full album and prepare its release to the market. This has a fixed cost of €50,000. The decision to be made then is whether to make an initial production run of a combined total of 10,000 or 40,000 disks, records, and cassettes. Two months after the release, the market response will be evaluated. It is either 'success' or 'failure'. 'Success' means all disks, etc., will be sold at a gross unit profit of €7. 'Fail-ure' means that the majority will have to be dumped at a heavy discount, at an average gross profit of €1.50 if 10,000 are made and €0.50 if 40,000 are made. Past experience

shows that out of 10 cases where the panel rated the songs as 'potential hits', 8 turned out to be a 'success'.

(a) Draw a decision tree for this situation, attaching costs, gross revenues, and probabilities to the various branches.

(b) Find the best action for the firm for this particular band.

(c) Find the payoff table corresponding to this problem and determine the value of perfect information.

6. A firm has just placed an order for a special-purpose machine. Since this is one of a kind, it is cheaper to also order some essential spare parts for the machine at the time when the original order for it is placed, rather than wait until later when they might be needed. Consider a particular part. If ordered with the machine, each part has a cost of £2,100. If ordered later on at the time of an actual breakdown, the cost of the part is £6,000. In addition, the loss in profits caused by the machine being down for several weeks amounts to another $4,000. Past experience with similar machines indicates that the probability of needing n spare parts over the machine's productive life is as follows:

number of parts needed	0	1	2	3	4
probability	0.1	0.3	0.3	0.2	0.1

Any parts remaining unused at the end of the machine's productive life have only a scrap value of £100. (Ignore the fact that various cash flows may occur over a span of several years.) The decision is the number of spare parts to be included in the original machine order. Develop a decision tree for this situation and find the best action.

7. A bookshop is considering how many copies of an exclusive connoisseur art calendar to buy. The purchase price is £240 per copy. They would be sold for £440 each. From past experience the owner predicts the following probability distribution for the demand for this calendar:

Demand	4	5	6	7	8
Probability	0.4	0.3	0.15	0.1	0.5

Any calendars not sold are disposed of below cost for £50.

(a) Draw a decision tree depicting the decision choices and associated outcomes for this problem. Show the revenues and costs associated with each branch and the probabilities associated with all branches issuing from chance nodes.

(b) Use the decision tree to determine the optimal number to procure and find the associated expected profit.

(c) Interpret the meaning of the expected profit in terms of the possible outcomes.

8. Consider again the decision tree developed for the ski-field case in exercise 3 above. Find its corresponding payoff table and determine the minimax strategy. Note that in this case it is the strategy that minimizes the maximum cost.

9. Consider again the decision tree developed for the recording company in exercise 5 above. Find its corresponding payoff table and determine the minimax strategy.

10. Assume that your mechanic just told you that there is a 50–50 chance that your beloved BMW's motor will seize within the next 6 months. If this happens, other major damage will occur to your motor. The total repair bill will amount to about €2000. He advises you to have the motor overhauled now at a fraction of that cost. What is the maximum amount that you personally would be willing to spend on an overhaul, such that you would just be indifferent between the 50–50 chance of the motor seizing and the overhaul? Using the other steps of the five-point assessment procedure, determine the approximate shape of your personal utility function for expenditures on your BMW.

11. Gérard Mousse, manager of Champignons Galore (see Chap. 9) want to determine the risk involved in exporting mushrooms to London from his French factory. He contemplates daily shipments. The truck freight forwarding company is willing to reserve a daily fixed volume 10 tonnes of cargo space (= one truck) at a daily cost of €2,400. The current excess production capacity for mushrooms at his factory is 9.6 tonnes ± 25%. If actual excess production is less then 10 tonnes, only that excess will be shipped. If it is more than 10 tonnes, the amount shipped is 10 tonnes. Mushroom shipments are auctioned in London and fetch on average £1800 ± 400 per tonne. The fluctuations in the currency exchange rate of £ into € is a random variable with an expected change of zero from week to week and a range of €0.03. The current rate is £1 = €1.515. Bob Moss would like to get an indication of the weekly revenue in €. Note that the exchange rate is always rounded to three decimal places. Assume a uniform distribution for changes in the exchange rate, while the actual production and the London price both follow a normal distribution. (Take the ranges given as covering 90% probability.)

(a) Map out the sequence of events.
(b) Use a spreadsheet to simulate 50 days of outcomes and use them to construct a histogram of net € revenues. Plot it. What percentage of days is the net € revenue below €24,000? (If you have access to risk analysis software, use it.)

19
Decisions with multiple objectives

In most of the examples and case studies discussed in Chapters 9–14 and 16–18 we assumed that for any given decision problem the decision maker pursues a single objective. Often that objective was minimizing costs or maximizing net benefits. You will rightly point out that, in real-life, most decision makers attempt to satisfy a variety of objectives and goals simultaneously. Some of these objectives or goals are fully or partially conflicting. Multiple conflicting objectives and goals are an integral part of each person's *Weltanschauung* — a word you have not heard for a while! It is not just politicians who promise to deliver the 'maximum benefits' to the 'largest number of people' at the 'least cost' (sic!). Few business people are so single-minded as to only look for maximum returns on their investment. Most also wish to provide high-quality products or services, maintain the best customer services possible, keep a happy and cooperative workforce, and achieve the largest market share possible. Similarly, most decisions dealing with environmental and social issues strive to meet multiple and usually conflicting goals. On a personal level, have you not allowed yourself to dream of that ideal job that offers daily challenges, involves a variety of interesting duties, has responsibility and prestige, has excellent promotional opportunities, has a pleasing work environment, is high paying with lots of fringe benefits, and involves extended stays on the French Riviera? In each instance, the actual decision taken is usually a compromise. It does well on some objectives or goals, worse on others.

But even our daily life is a sequence of compromises between conflicting goals and objectives. This means that we must in fact be experts in decision making with multiple objectives! And we do this without any support of a formal approach. So why should we need such support in a managerial or planning context? In part, it is for the same reasons that led us to have recourse to formal decision models when we ignored all but one objective, namely as a means for overcoming at least in part the complexity of the situation. Remember our discussion in Section 15.7 on people's limited cognitive abilities for processing complex, multi-faceted relationships? This is not only a reality when faced with decision making under uncertainty, but becomes even more pronounced when faced with weighing several partially conflicting objectives.

There are other reasons. A formal approach allows a fuller exploration of the solution space, thereby providing deeper insight into the problem — one of the prime aims of MS/OR. The joint performance of the objectives in response to the various potential decision alternatives can be observed, compared, and weighed. This may reveal that certain objectives are much more sensitive, while the performance of others is hardly affected, no matter what action is taken. The decision maker is thus provided with a more effective basis for finding the most preferred compromise. It may lead to a partial or complete re-evaluation of the importance of the various objectives and ultimately to better, more defensible, and wiser decision making.

This chapter will only lightly scratch the surface of this vast topic. To set the stage, we will summarize three real applications reported in the literature. Section 19.2 reviews how 'traditional' MS/OR methods deal with multiple objectives. Sections 19.3 and 19.4 give a brief overview of the difficulties and aims of multi-criteria decision making, commonly abbreviated as MCDM — not a roman numeral — and the approaches to MCDM suggested in the literature. The discussion is largely restricted to the case where the choice has to be made from a set of discrete alternatives. This sidesteps the rather more complex situation of continuous decision variables, for which multiple objective mathematical programming techniques, similar to linear programming, have been invented. Sections 19.5 and 19.6 then apply one of the simplest MCDM approaches to the selection of the 'best' venue for a conference of a software users' group.

19.1 Three real MCDM problem situations

Multiple land use planning

The Federal Land Policy and Management Act, passed by the 94th US Congress in 1976, gave the following mandate to the Bureau of Land Management (BLM) for the management of the over 400 million acres of federally owned land under its control: Land management is

- to be on the basis of multiple use and sustained yield;
- to protect the quality of scientific, scenic, historical, ecological, environmental, air and atmospheric, water resource, and archaeological values;
- where appropriate, to preserve and protect certain public lands in their natural condition;
- to provide food and habitat for fish, wildlife, and domestic animals;
- to provide for outdoor recreation and human occupancy and use.

Many of these objectives are in direct conflict with one another. For some areas, the BLM would be under fire from different pressure groups to have their vested interest prevail. These groups include farm lobbies who want more grazing land, mining companies who want prospecting rights, and conservation groups who want to keep some areas in their natural state. How should the BLM resolve these conflicts?

Assume that a BLM district officer has to develop a multiple-use land program for an area in his district which is mainly used for grazing, but for which a geological survey indicates the likely presence of oil or gas deposits of potentially economic significance. The area's recreational value is mainly for big game hunting and winter use by snow-mobiles. BLM's assessment procedure consists of compiling detailed inventories of the area's topography, soil, vegetation, other physical features, and of its existing uses. This is followed by a detailed assessment of the area's unlimited potential for each possible use — grazing, recreation, mineral exploitation, habitat conservation for native flora and fauna — without regard to any other uses. Independently of this, a socioeconomic profile is compiled that provides relevant information on attitudes of current and prospective users of the area, on special interest groups, and on the economic importance of exploitable natural resources. Armed with these documents, the area manager attempts to develop a compromise solution that reflects both the best intrinsic uses of the area and relevant socio-economic factors. This is a very difficult task of weighing conflicting objectives against each other.

A pilot study by K.F. Martinson at the University of Colorado 1977, implemented on a trial basis by some BLM districts, demonstrated how a multiple-objective linear programming approach can be used for gaining deep insights into how the various objectives respond to each other, leading to more effective and more defensible management plans. (Section 22-5 in Daellenbach *et al.* [1983] has a simple, but detailed example of this approach.)

The Mexico City Airport development

One of the classical examples deals with the Mexico City airport development, done in 1971 for the Ministry of Public Works (MPW) of Mexico by two MIT professors, H.R. de Neufville and H. Raiffa, both pioneers in the field of decision analysis. As in many other large urban centres, the growth in the volume of air traffic, the difficulties of further expansion of the existing major airport, with its take-off and landing flight patterns largely over built-up areas, lent considerable urgency for providing an acceptable airport service development strategy over the next 30 years. The then existing Texcoco airport was sandwiched between the remains of Lake Texcoco to the east and the sprawling city expanse to the west. Upgrading Texcoco on the highly unstable former lake bed or by displacement of large populations would make construction and maintenance very expensive. The continued increase in air traffic that this would allow would further aggravate the current noise problem and increase the danger of serious air accidents with potentially numerous casualties among the residents in the densely populated surrounding areas. The advantage of upgrading Texcoco was its close proximity to the city centre. The most attractive alternative sight was at Zumpango, an un-developed rural area some 25 miles north of the city. It would not suffer any of Texcoco's problems, but would increase travel times to and from the city substantially.

Based on a consensus of the directors of the MPW, a partial list of objectives included:

- minimizing total construction, maintenance, and operating costs;
- minimizing travel times to and from the airport;
- maximizing airport operating safety;
- minimizing the effect of air traffic noise pollution;
- minimizing social disruption and displacement of the population; and
- raising the air traffic service capacity for Mexico City.

There were many uncertainties associated with any decisions. For instance, what was the future growth in air traffic likely to be? Would the noise levels of future aircraft engines be considerably lower? What safety standards were the IATA and international pilot associations going to impose for future airport operations?

Faced with the multiple objectives and these uncertainties, how should the MPW go about developing a strategy that is 'best' in terms of social, economic, safety, and political considerations? After attempts by the MPW to 'solve' this problem using traditional cost/benefit analysis (a version of the project evaluation method of Chapter 10, adapted for public projects), the two professors, together with the senior staff of the MPW, applied a form of decision analysis based on multi-attribute utility functions to come up with a set of recommendations.

This method develops individual utility functions for the performance on each objective. These are then combined into a single complex aggregate utility function which is used for comparing various development strategies. (See R.L. Keeney and H. Raiffa, *Decisions with Multiple Objectives*, Wiley, 1976, for a detailed account of that and other case studies. Chapter 22 of Daellenbach *et al.* [1983] applies this approach to a search and rescue service.)

As happens with the recommendations of many major projects, their findings — to have a staged move to Zumpango — were never implemented. Thirty years later, Texcoco is still Mexico City's major international airport and is still facing the same problems. (As a footnote, at about the same time, a similar planning exercise, based on an expensive cost/benefit analysis and public hearings, was done to select the location of the third London airport. Its recommendations to convert the small Stansted airport into a full-fledged international airport were not implemented either at that time.)

Blood bank stock management

Blood banks maintain stocks of various blood products, including fresh blood, for use in emergencies and scheduled operations. Unfortunately, fresh blood has a limited shelf life of anywhere from 35 to 49 days, depending on the type of preservatives added. Any unused blood past its limited shelf life is outdated and has to be destroyed. Blood bank managers try to avoid two types of undesirable event: (1) running short of blood needed for emergencies and scheduled operations, and (2) outdating of unused blood. The first may have serious consequences, such as endangering life, or require expensive remedial action, such as calling up suitable emergency donors and/or postponing elective surgery. The second is a waste of a valuable product. If donors give blood without compensation, outdating of blood is morally undesirable. Avoiding both shortages and outdating of blood are the major objectives of fresh blood management. Cost considerations may not enter into the picture.

Relatively large stocks of each type of blood will help to keep shortages to low levels. On the other hand, outdating can be kept to a minimum by keeping low levels of blood stocks. The achievement levels of the two objectives thus vary inversely with each other. The solution must be a compromise. Naturally, most managers will view blood shortages as more serious than outdating of blood. They will thus risk more outdating of blood in order to keep shortages to acceptably safe low levels.

In the 1970s and 1980s a lot of research was devoted to this problem. The policies derived from the models developed have led to a reduction in outdating of blood from well over 25% of all blood collected in the early 1970s to well below 5% by the late 1980s, without an increase in the rate of shortages.

19.2 Traditional MS/OR approach

The traditional approach for modelling multiple objectives is to optimize what is considered the most important objective, while meeting minimal performance targets on all other objectives. In other words, arbitrary boundary choices are used as a substitute for all but one objective. Often no or little justification is given for these choices. For instance, for most issues involving safety, such as the operation of means of transport or plants, like a nuclear power station, an acceptable 'solution' is obtained by minimizing operating costs, subject to meeting arbitrarily specified safety standards. Usually, cost minimization is considered to be the most important objective, while safety and other objectives are subordinated to it.

In this approach the lesser objectives are replaced by minimal performance targets that have to be met, i.e. by firm surrogate constraints. Therefore, they restrict (in fact, dictate), the best level of achievement that is possible for the most important objective. In other words, this approach first guarantees that the targets on the lesser objectives are satisfied, before it allows any look at the most important objective. So, by a rather ironic twist, the most important objective becomes subordinated to what are seen as the less important objectives.

Mind you, when dealing with safety issues, this may be preferable. However, there are many situations where this inadvertent reversal of priorities is more questionable. In particular, these minimal performance targets may involve a considerable degree of arbitrariness, nor do the performance targets chosen have the inviolate nature of hard constraints. They are often the result of a policy decision, hence soft constraints. They reflect what is seen as a reasonable or a desirable level of achievement — both rather fuzzy and highly subjective notions. Furthermore, they may even result in a suboptimal solution when other feasible solutions exist that perform better on several objectives without being worse on any of the others — a highly undesirable outcome.

It is, therefore, important that the MS/OR analyst does extensive sensitivity analysis with respect to all these surrogate constraints. The decision maker should be presented not simply with the 'optimal' solution for the target levels chosen, but also with the insights gained from an extensive sensitivity exercise.

The traditional approach is a fairly arbitrary *ad hoc* procedure. It really shirks the fundamental issues in MCDM. The next two sections look at some of these.

> Activity:
> - In the LOD problem in Chapter (Sections 6, 6.7 to 6.1 and 6.13 to 6.17) the objective used was cost minimization. There were other objectives, such as achieving a high inventory turnover rate, as specified by the vice-president of finance, providing top service to customers in terms of fast execution of their orders, smoothing the level of mixing and filling capacity usage over time. How were these handled?
> - Consider the NuWave Shoes case. List Elly's possible objectives. How did she deal with them?

19.3 Some basic issues in MCDM

A new meaning for 'optimal solution'

Finding the optimal solution with respect to a single objective has a precise meaning. It identifies that solution which either achieves the maximum 'benefit' or the minimum 'cost' — taking these two terms in their broadest sense — whichever is the aim of the optimization. What is the meaning of an optimal solution in the presence of several objectives?

Clearly, it cannot be a maximum or a minimum of something. Only by coincidence will all objectives take on, for instance, their maximum outcome simultaneously for the same decision choice. If this should happen, the objectives are not conflicting and the problem is trivial in this respect. In general, one decision choice does better with respect to some objectives, while another fares better for others. By necessity, the decision chosen as the 'best' one is a compromise between them. It may achieve the optimum outcome for some objectives, but falls short to various degrees on others. So, rather than refer to the solution finally chosen as 'the optimal solution', it makes more sense to call it the **most preferred** solution.

Dominance

Some decision choices can be ruled out as potential candidates for the most preferred solution. If a decision choice A performs no better than another decision choice C with respect to all objectives and worse for at least one, then A is **dominated** by C. A can be eliminated from further consideration. A rational decision maker will never consider A as a potential candidate for the most preferred solution (provided the objectives used capture everything that counts about the decision choices).

Figure 19-1 depicts dominance graphically for the case of two conflicting objectives. Each axis measures the achievement level on one objective. The higher the level, the more desirable it becomes. The joint achievement levels on both objectives for each decision choice represent a point in the positive quadrant.

Figure 19-1   Dominance and efficient solutions.

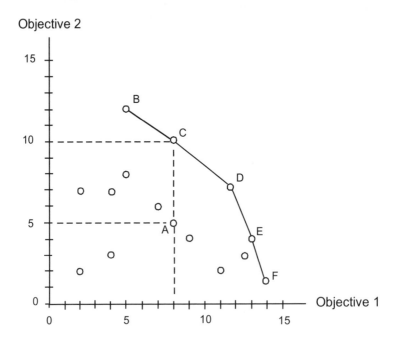

For example, alternative A achieves an outcome of 8 on objective 1 and 5 on objective 2, while alternative C achieves 8 on 1 and 10 on 2. A is no better than C for objective 1, but worse for objective 2. Hence A is dominated by C. On the other hand, alternative B, with outcomes of 4 on objective 1 and 12 on objective 2 does not dominate either A or C and is dominated by neither

The solid line in Figure 19-1 from B to F connects all those alternatives that are not dominated by any other alternative. They are referred to as **efficient solutions**. They should be the only candidates for the most preferred solution. (In economics, the concept of dominance is also referred to as **Pareto optimality**.)

Activity: In the light of the discussion on dominance what do you see as another potential serious shortcoming of the traditional MS/OR approach of substituting targets or constraints for all but the most important objective?

Measuring outcomes for objectives

The performance of a decision choice is given by a set of outcomes, one for each objective. Some objectives may readily be measured in terms of a natural physical unit — pounds, dollars or euros, or pollutant emission levels in parts per million. For others, such as beauty or convenience, no natural measuring scales exist. Ultimately, the various decision choices must be compared with one another in some way. This comparison is either made indirectly in terms of some combined performance derived from the individual outcomes over all objectives, or on a holistic basis which ranks alternatives from best to worst. In the latter case, the outcomes achieved for the objective need not be measured along a cardinal scale.

Sometimes the measurement units used for different objectives are commensurable. For example, the overall performance of a blood bank can be expressed in terms of the average number of pints of blood outdated that have to be destroyed over a given time interval because the blood has outlived its useful life, and in terms of the average number of units of blood requested for transfusions which cannot be delivered, i.e. pints of blood short. Although the consequences of outdating and shortages of blood are vastly different, the two measures can readily be compared. Shortages may be seen as ten times worse than outdating.

Contrast this to a safety problem, where the outcomes of any decision choice are expected total cost and the expected number of injuries of various severities and deaths. How can monetary values be compared with numbers of people injured or numbers of deaths? Economists would suggest that we express injuries or deaths in terms of the loss of future earnings. However, that ignores all intangible aspects, such as the pain and trauma suffered, the potential loss of life enjoyment, or the emotional personal loss of relatives of a dead person. Furthermore, how can we even measure such intangible aspects in a meaningful way?

The commonly accepted way out of many of these difficulties is to express outcomes in terms of a **score** along an arbitrary scale from say 0 to 1 or 0 to 100, similar to what we did to assess utilities in the previous chapter. The worst possible outcome is given a score of 0, while the best possible outcome is given a score of 1 or 100. All other outcomes are scored inside the interval selected.

This approach is used for all objectives. For outcomes with a natural unit of measurement the scores are simple linear transformations. For example, if the range of monetary benefits runs from $10,000 to $260,000 over the various alternatives, the maximum outcome is assigned a score of 100, with all other scores proportionately less. $20,000 then gets a score of 4. For intangible objectives, the scores assigned are, by necessity, highly subjective to the person doing the scoring. The scores assigned are not valid for another person, nor may they remain the same over time even for the same person.

The difference in the scores achieved by pairs of alternatives for a given objective reflects the differences in desirability. For example, if alternatives A, B, and C have scores of 10, 50, and 70, then a switch from A to B is interpreted as being twice as desirable as a switch from B to C, since the gain in the score is 40 for the first and only 20 for the second. The same conclusion is reached if the three scores are 20, 60, and 80. It is not affected by the initial choice of a score of 10 or 20 for A. It only depends on the difference between scores. However, the ratio of two scores is not assumed to have any meaning. So, the ratio of scores for B and A of $50/10 = 5$ does not mean that B is five times more desirable than A. That ratio is affected by the initial choice of the score for A. It reduces to 3 if A is scored at 20 and B at 60, while the difference between them remains at 40.

If the scores range from 0 to 100, then each score may also be interpreted as the percentage achieved on a given objective by the alternative in comparison with the highest scoring alternative.

The decision maker's preference structure

How decision makers value various outcomes forms part of their **preference structure**. The latter reflects their world view. It is therefore highly personal to each decision maker. Naturally, it also enters into the valuation of outcomes for single-objective decision making, as we have seen in the discussion on utility functions in Chapter 18. However, in MCDM a new dimension is added. It is now not simply a question of valuing the outcomes of individual objectives, but also a question of the relative importance of each objective. In order to assess the relative worth of an alternative we need a measure of both. Only then can the alternatives be ranked from best to worst.

Multiple decision makers

Situations with more than one decision maker raise a new difficulty. All decision makers bring their own personal preference structure into the evaluation. They may not only assign different scores to the same outcome, but also give each objectives a different importance weight. As a result, each decision maker may end up with a different ranking of the alternatives. Furthermore, the various people may have a different personal stake in the problem, so that it is a legitimate question whether each should have the same degree of say in the matter. For example, one may be the major investor in the firm, while others may be employees at different levels in the hierarchy. Should their inputs all be given equal weight?

The group as a whole will ultimately have to agree on a common single ranking. This calls for at least a partial reconciliation of the individual preference structures and 'rights' of the participants. A discussion of suitable processes for resolving such conflicts goes beyond the scope of this text. Problem structuring methods, covered in Chapter 7, may help to resolve them.

19.4   The process of evaluating choices

The two predominant approaches for finding the most preferred of a set of discrete alternatives are **aggregate value function methods**, mainly used and developed in the USA, and **outranking methods**, originating in France and Belgium.

Aggregate value functions

These methods in their most basic form assume that

- a favourable outcome for one objective can be traded off against a less favourable outcome on another objective; and
- the overall or aggregate score of an alternative is a function of the outcome scores and the weights for the relative importance of the individual objectives.

Usually, the weights are normalized such that their sum adds up to 1. So each weight is a number in the range from 0 to 1.

An example may help. To keep things simple, I use a linear aggregate value function. This means that the overall score is equal to the weighted sum of the individual scores, with the relative importance of each objective serving as the weights. Say there are only two objectives X and Y. Objective X is considered the less important and objective Y is viewed as 3 times more important than X. X is therefore assigned a raw weight of 1 and Y a raw weight of 3. The sum of the raw weights is 4. We normalize the raw weights by dividing each by the sum of the raw weights. Hence, objective X gets a normalized weight of $1/(1 + 3) = 0.25$ and Y one of $3/(1 + 3) = 0.75$. Their sum adds up to 1 as desired. Assume further that alternative A achieves outcome scores of 90 and 60 for objectives X and Y, while B has outcome scores of 75 and 65. The overall scores are then

$$\text{Alternative A: } 0.25(90) + 0.75(60) = 67.5$$
$$\text{Alternative B: } 0.25(75) + 0.75(65) = 67.5$$

They are the same. If a choice is made exclusively on the basis of the overall scores, the decision maker would be indifferent between the two alternatives. So we can conclude that a loss of 15 score points on objective X from 90 to 75 is compensated by a gain of 5 points on objective Y from 60 to 65. In other words, score points of one objective can be traded off for score points on another objective, such that the aggregate score remains unchanged.

Outranking methods

In contrast, outranking methods assume that the decision maker is unwilling or unable to define trade-offs between objectives. This implies that no aggregate value function can be derived. Any ranking of the alternatives has to be done on the basis of pairwise comparisons of alternatives. These comparisons indicate that one alternative is preferred to the other, that the two alternatives are indifferent to one another, or that the comparison is inconclusive. These relationships are derived from indices based on the outcome scores and the relative importance of the objectives for each pair of alternatives. The end result of this process is a partial or complete ranking of the alternatives.

The various methods offer little theoretical justification for how these indices are computed. In contrast, the theoretical justification for the aggregate score of aggregate value function methods is based on utility theory.

19.5 Conference venue selection

We shall now study an application of the aggregate value function method to the selection of a conference venue where the final choice should be the best compromise over several desirable features.

The alternatives

Nancy Clare, the promotions manager of XL SOFTWARE has to decide on the venue for next year's European XL Users' Group conference. Such meetings are always preceded by one or more workshops for new users of XL's products. Geneva has been chosen as the location for that conference. Nancy visited the four potential venues on the short list and made the following brief comments:

Venue A: A first class airport hotel; well-known for hosting international meetings, with experienced, helpful and flexible staff, good conference facilities, all-round good accommodations, and reasonable catering; social meeting places limited to its several busy in-house restaurants and bars; direct access to airport and railway station; fairly expensive.

Venue B: A luxury city centre hotel; extensively used for international conferences of all sorts, with experienced, helpful, but overworked staff, well-equipped modern conference facilities, including computer networking, and luxury accommodations; good but rather expensive catering; a wide choice of in-house and close-by social meeting places; fast and easy access from the airport and the railway station; very expensive.

Venue C: The university conference venue; used mainly for scientific and cultural conferences; its staff somewhat bureaucratic and not known to be helpful; with a wide choice of good, but somewhat stark conference facilities, including computer labs; modest, barely adequate accommodation and catering; few attractive close-by social meeting places; a nice park-like environment; reasonable access to transport means; cost-wise by far the cheapest.

Venue D: A newly renovated chateau in a near-by village, overlooking Lake Geneva with the Alps as a backdrop; a recent newcomer on the scene of conference venues, with limited staff experience, reasonable facilities for small conferences, and excellent modern accommodations; famous for its catering; good social meeting places on its facilities and in the several small restaurants in the village; access from the airport and the railway station would have to be organized by bus; still reasonably priced.

Nancy recently studied Professor Belton's tutorial on MCDM (in L.C. Hendry and R.W. Eglese, [1990]) which demonstrates various aspects of the use of MCDM on exactly the type of problem she is facing now. She wants to give the simple multi-attribute value function approach a trial.

Selecting objectives

The first step is to come up with a list of objectives considered important for evaluating each alternative venue. In fact, this step has to be done before making up a list of possible venues. It tells the analyst(s) what aspects to look out for and what information to collect about each venue.

In consultation with the conference director and the preconference workshop leaders, Nancy develops the following list:

1. low overall cost of the facilities,
2. easy transport access,
3. a wide range of top-quality conference rooms and other conference facilities,
4. high quality of accommodations,
5. outstanding catering for conference meals,
6. a high level of staff experience and helpfulness available to organizers and participants,
7. a wide range and high quality of informal social meeting places and restaurants easily accessible to the participants, and finally
8. a congenial, pleasant overall environment of the venue.

These objectives fall into three groups: (a) those associated with the 'Location' of the venue, (b) those associated with the 'Facilities' offered by the venue, and (c) its 'Cost'. They become the **first level objectives**, while the original list with the exception of 'Cost' is referred to as the **second level objectives**. It is conceivable that even some of the latter might already be groupings of third level objectives. This **hierarchy of objectives** is depicted in Figure 19-2. Objectives that are not broken down further are called **end objectives**.

Figure 19-2   Hierarchy of objectives for evaluating conference venue.

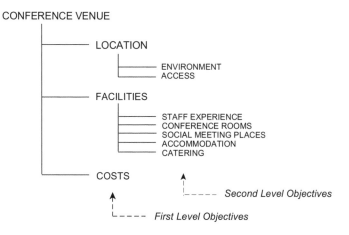

Setting importance weights

The next step is to assess weights of the relative importance of each objective. These are numbers between 0 and 1. They are usually chosen so that the weights of the first-level objectives add up to one, and similarly the weights of the second level objectives associated with each first level objective also add up to one (and so on for further level objectives). This is demonstrated in the two columns headed 'level 1' and 'level 2' of Table 19-1. Note that column 2 sums to one, and similarly the weights for each grouping of second level objectives also sum to one. Again, Nancy settles on these weights after two animated sessions with the conference director and workshop leaders. These may not be the final weights, but serve as a good starting point.

Table 19-1   Spreadsheet evaluation of conference venues.

DATA	WEIGHTS		SCORES FOR VENUE			
OBJECTIVES	level 1	level 2	A	B	C	D
Location:	0.35					
Environment		0.50	0	25	40	100
Access		0.50	100	80	35	0
Facilities:	0.45					
Staff experience		0.10	100	80	40	0
Conference rooms		0.30	75	100	50	0
Social meeting places		0.15	25	100	0	75
Accommodation		0.20	80	100	0	90
Catering		0.25	60	70	0	100
Cost	0.20		5	0	100	60
EVALUATION	Location score		50	52.5	37.5	50
	Facilities score		67.25	90.5	19	54.25
	Cost score		5	0	100	60
	Overall score		48.76	59.1	41.68	53.92
	Rank		3	1	4	2

Setting weights that truly reflect the importance that a decision maker attaches to the objectives is no easy task. The decision maker may well be prone to similar biases as in the assessment of subjective probabilities (see Section 15.7 for a discussion on potential biases). Naturally, being aware of these biases is the first step towards overcoming them. However, it is essential that the analyst provides the decision maker with meaningful information about the sensitivity of the overall scores and their ranking in response to changes in the weights.

Assessing achievement scores

Assessing the scores achieved by each alternative for each end objective is step 3. Since Nancy is the only person who has inspected the facilities, this task falls exclusively upon her shoulders. After much agonizing and a few phone calls to Geneva, she comes up with the scores in the last four columns of Table 19-1.

For all end objectives with the exception of 'Cost', the higher the level of achievement of a given venue the more attractive it becomes. Hence the highest achievement level is assigned a score of 100, while the lowest achievement level gets a score of 0, with all other scores in between. On the other hand, the higher the cost of a venue the less attractive it becomes. The highest cost is therefore given a score of 0 and the lowest cost a score of 100.

These scores are relative only with respect to the four alternatives. Adding other alternatives may require some scores to be reassessed. Say we add a new venue E that does better for 'Accommodation' than venue B which previously had the highest score of 100. Then venue E would get a score of 100, while all other venues, except the one with the score of 0, would have their relative scores adjusted down. A similar readjustment could occur if an alternative is dropped. Although these readjustments may be a nuisance, relative scores based only on the alternatives included are generally easier to assess.

Another approach is to use scores for each end objective that are relative to arbitrary worst and best reference achievement levels. For example, the scores for 'Catering' could be with reference to the Paris Ritz and a typical university student cafeteria. Adding or deleting alternatives would then not require readjustments of any scores. Such **absolute scores** require considerably more effort to derive, since a suitable set of reference pairs has to be selected for each objective. This effort is, however, well justified if we are dealing with a repetitive decision problem. For example, if XL has several such conferences in different parts of the world every year, then developing such an absolute scale could well be worthwhile. It would also lead to a more consistent assessment over time between successive uses.

Evaluating the alternatives

Armed with this information, we can now compute a weighted overall score for each alternative. The steps are similar to the roll-back procedure in a decision tree. We first determine a weighted score for each grouping of end objectives. These weighted scores become an input into the next higher level in the hierarchy of objectives, until we can determine the weighted score for the first level objectives. In our example, using the second level objectives that make up 'Location' and 'Facilities', we find the weighted scores for these two first level objectives. For example, for venue A the weighted score for 'Location' is equal to $0.5(0) + 0.5(100) = 50$ and for 'Facilities' $0.1(100) + 0.3(75) + 0.15(25) + 0.20(80) + 0.25(60) = 67.25$. The first level score for 'Cost' is simply its score of 5. The first level scores are shown under 'Evaluation' at the bottom of Table 19-1.

With all first level scores computed, the 'Overall score' can now be obtained. Again, for venue A it is found by summing the products of the first level weights and the first level scores, i.e. $0.35(50) + 0.45(67.25) + 0.2(5) = 48.76$ (rounded).

As a first cut, the four alternatives are ranked from best to worst in the order of B – D – A – C. The city centre hotel scores highest, with the chateau coming in as a respectable second. However, this ranking should not be taken as the final answer. It should be used as a catalyst for discussion and for learning more about the problem. But more on this in the last section of this chapter!

Activity: Is it possible that an alternative, A, that is dominated by another alternative, B, can end up with an overall score that is better than B? Why or why not?

Graphical representation

As usual, displaying the results in graphical form allows the decision maker to gain a better 'feel'. Figures 19-3 and 19-4 show two different charts for the first level objectives. Similar charts can be constructed for the second level objectives.

Figure 19-3 shows a profile of the performance of each alternative on the first level objectives. The three objectives are spaced along the *x*-axis. Their scores are measured along the *y*-axis. Each line connects the scores on the three objectives for a given alternative. Such a chart shows whether a given alternative dominates another alternative. But even if no strict dominance occurs, it reveals whether such dominance is close. In our example, no venue dominates, although Venue B comes close to topping A. It is just a bit better for 'Location', far outstrips it for 'Facilities', and is just marginally worse for 'Cost'. On this basis, Nancy Clare may well eliminate Venue A as a serious contender.

Figure 19-3   Performance profile of alternatives.

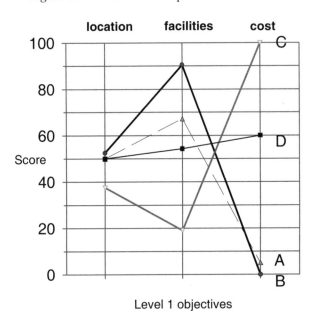

Level 1 objectives

However, that dominance of first level objectives does not imply dominance over all end objectives, as defined in Section 19.2. First level scores may be weighted averages over end objectives farther down the hierarchy. (Just compare the scores for 'Environment' and 'Access' of A and B. There is no dominance there, although the weighted score for 'Location' of B is better than for A.)

The graph also helps clarify the overall performance pattern of an alternative. Is it a good all-rounder or does it have significant weaknesses? A good all-rounder may be an attractive choice, even if it does not achieve the highest overall score. In our example, Venue D comes close to being a good all-rounder — its 'Facilities' score being a minor weakness. The chart also clearly highlights that 'Cost' is the major weakness of venue B — our highest scoring venue.

Figure 19-4 contrasts the overall score of the alternatives and how each breaks down into first level objectives. Each first level objective score has been scaled by its corresponding weight. This reveals the relative weighted contribution of each objective towards the overall scores. An alternative's weakness with respect to a particular objective, as revealed in the performance profile chart (like Figure 19-3), may be viewed as less damaging if the importance weight of the objective is relatively small in comparison to all other objectives.

Figure 19-4   Composition of overall performance scores.

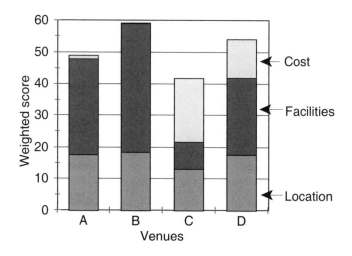

In our example, the striking features are the high contributions made by 'Facilities' for venue B and 'Cost' for venue C, amounting to more than 50% of their overall scores. Contrast this with the much more even distribution of venue D. It now has an even more pronounced image of a good all-rounder.

19.6 Sensitivity analysis

Subjectivity of MCDM methods

As for decision analysis, personal subjective judgments play an important role. In fact, every step requires some subjective inputs. The choice of objectives, their grouping into a hierarchy, the choice of importance weights for the objectives, the assessment of the end objective scores for each alternative, all involve subjective judgments. Even the choice of the evaluation criterion is in part subjective. In the conference venue example we used a criterion for maximizing the weighted overall score. An alternative criterion could have been to maximize the lowest weighted score on any first-level objective (similar to the minimax criterion in decision analysis). Given this high degree of subjectivity, it is essential to perform extensive and thorough sensitivity analysis, at least for those aspects that involve numerical inputs, such as the importance weights and the end objective scores.

Sensitivity analysis with respect to importance weights

Table 19-2 shows the results of sensitivity analysis on the importance weights. The first set of three rows shows the response of the overall score distribution as the importance weight for 'Location' decreases from 0.45 to 0.25 in steps of 0.1, with the weights of the other two objectives increasing by 0.05 at each step. The second set of three rows decreases the weight for 'Facilities' from 0.55 to 0.35, the third set the weight for 'Cost' from 0.3 to 0.1, while adjusting the other two weights accordingly. The striking feature of this analysis is the fact that the overall score for Venue D only changes marginally, in contrast to the scores for the other three venues. The performance for D is thus very robust, reinforcing its quality as a good all-rounder. However, note that B remains the highest scoring venue as long as 'Facilities' has a relatively high importance weight.

Table 19-2   Sensitivity analysis for conference venue selection.

Weights			Venues			
Location	Facilities	Cost	A	B	C	D
0.45	0.40	0.15	50.2	59.8	39.5	53.2
0.35	0.45	0.20	48.8	59.1	41.7	53.9
0.25	0.50	0.25	47.4	58.4	43.9	54.6
0.30	0.55	0.15	52.7	65.5	36.7	53.8
0.35	0.45	0.20	48.8	59.1	41.7	53.9
0.40	0.35	0.25	44.8	52.7	46.7	54.0
0.30	0.40	0.30	43.4	52.0	48.9	54.7
0.35	0.45	0.20	48.8	59.1	41.7	53.9
0.40	0.50	0.10	54.1	66.3	34.5	53.1

Firming up the preference structure

When embarking on such an analysis, the decision maker(s) may often have somewhat vague ideas about the relative importance of the various objectives. In other words, the preference structure is not yet clearly defined. Helping the decision maker(s) to firm up the preference structure is frequently an essential and integral part of an MCDM analysis. Access to an appropriate spreadsheet template or a dedicated MCDM computer package will facilitate this task.

In our example, notice the relatively subdued response of the scores to major changes in the relative importance of 'Location', as revealed by the first three rows in Table 19-2, in contrast to the much stronger response to major changes in each of the other two weights. 'Location' is a less discriminating objective than either 'Facilities' or 'Cost'. This could well lead Nancy to reappraise the importance she initially attached to 'Location'. She might settle for the weight distribution in row 3 of Table 19-2. Although this does not change the relative ranking, it reduces the difference between Venues B and D further, with the all-rounder D becoming even more attractive.

19.7 Chapter highlights

- For many real-life situations, the decision maker has multiple objectives or goals. The traditional MS/OR approach substitutes target constraints for all but the most important objective and then finds the best solution for this objective, subject to the targets.
- MCDM approaches try to find the best compromise solution that balances the achievement levels for all objectives to meet the decision maker's preference structure.
- The decision maker should never settle for a dominated solution, but should select an efficient solution.
- The two major approaches in MCDM are aggregate value function methods and outranking methods. The first allow trade-offs between objectives; the second do not and derive a ranking of the alternatives by different means.
- The simplest aggregate value function approach assigns for each decision choice an achievement score for each objective. Each objective is given an importance weight. An overall score for an alternative is given by the weighted average over all objectives. The alternative with the highest overall score is the most preferred one according to the decision maker's preferences.

Exercises

1. Assume that you are two months away from graduating and you are already actively looking for a job. You have arranged three interviews with prospective employers. Think about possible things and aspects that you are looking for in a job and arrange them into a hierarchy of first and second level objectives. These have to be chosen such that appropriate measures for their

performance levels can be determined, either using a natural or a point scale. Indicate how each would be measured. What are their importance weights? Such information will be essential in order to know what questions you will want to have answered from the firms about the job(s) for which they are recruiting.

2. Consider the Blood Bank problem in Section 19.1. Assume that there are three areas of concern: shortages, outdating, and costs. What numerical attributes would you use to measure each? Think about how you could get the necessary data to determine their values for a given policy.

3. The waters discharged in Deep Cove from the Manapouri Power Station in Fiordland National Park at the bottom of New Zealand's South Island are so pure that they do not need any chemicals to neutralize harmful bacteria or other contaminants. A firm applied for the rights to capture this water and transport it in large ocean-going tankers to the US West Coast and Middle Eastern countries. It would have entailed building a floating dock close to the tail race of the power station in order to allow water to be pumped into the tankers. The project would provide employment for about 30 people in an economically depressed area, and the NZ Government would collect a substantial water royalty. The firm showed considerable environmental concern: no permanent staff residence inside the park, all staff flown in by helicopter; all rubbish removed; extensive safety measures to avoid oil spills, etc. Not surprisingly, environmental groups opposed the project: non-tourist commercial activities are against the charter of National Parks; removal of up to 60% of the tail race water would affect the sound's unique flora and fauna that has evolved over millions of years; large tanker traffic would speed up the mixing of the surface fresh water layer with the salt water underneath, affecting flora and fauna even more; due to the severe weather conditions accidents resulting in oil spills would be difficult to prevent with potentially disastrous consequences; it would make poaching of rare birds easier and could introduce rats into the park; it would reduce wilderness enjoyment by tourists. Assume you have been asked by the NZ Government to assess this project. Define a first and second level hierarchy of suitable objectives. How would you measure each?

4. Consider Sally Smart's problem described in exercises 1 and 2 of Chapter 18. Indicate why a single objective approach dealing with monetary outcomes alone may not really capture all the essential aspects of the problem situation. Define a set of three to four suitable objectives, goals, or targets which any option chosen should either meet or achieve as well as possible. These have to be chosen such that appropriate measures for their performance levels can be determined, using either a natural or a point scale. Indicate how each would be measured.

5. Consider the following hierarchy of objectives, associated importance weights, and achievement scores for selecting a location for a factory:

	Weights		Locations			
Objective	level 1	level 2	A	B	C	D
Locality	0.5					
transport access		0.6	0	60	100	50
water availability		0.4	80	100	0	50
Cost	0.5					
construction		0.3	100	30	0	50
operating		0.7	70	0	100	50

Using a weighted average scoring approach, which location is the highest scoring one? Is there a close second? Show your results in performance profile graphs.

6. The manager of a BLM district office has been asked to come up with a management plan for a 16 square mile area in southern Colorado. The area consists of two mesas with adjoining gullies and deep canyons. The vegetation consists of low brush, junipers, and other bushes that thrive in the semi-arid low rainfall area, with a few stands of pines and other trees in sheltered parts. The few open places on the mesas are currently used for sheep grazing at a very low stocking rate. The current run holder would like to get permission for clearing brush and increasing the stocking rate. The mesas and canyons get the occasional visit from backpackers. One of the gullies between the two mesas contains an abandoned silver mine which was worked in the late 19th century. It has the potential for being developed into a tourist attraction, as have the interesting rock formations in the canyons. The area has considerable wildlife, particularly deer and various large birds. The deer stalkers' association would like the area preserved for hunting, excluding all grazing by domestic animals, which severely compete for the limited fodder available. No human habitation is currently in the area. Seven management options have been put forward by various interest groups. The district manager would like to select the option which best achieves the intrinsic values and characteristics of the area. He has captured these by four objectives: (A) preservation of scenic beauty, (B) recreational potential, (C) economic potential, (D) watershed protection, each being a first level objective. (There are no second level objectives.) All objectives are to be maximized. The table below lists the seven management options and their achievement scores for each objective:

Option	A	B	C	D
Exclusive intensive grazing of mesas*	50	0	$50,000	30
Exclusive 4-wheel vehicle recreation*	30	80	–$40,000	0
Exclusive hunting*	90	60	$40,000	90
Canyons tourism, grazing of mesas	60	80	$100,000	50
Canyons tourism, 4-wheel use of mesas	40	100	$30,000	20
Continuation of current usage	70	40	$20,000	70
Exclusive wilderness area use	100	30	$0	100

The options marked by an asterisk assume that most of the current other low-intensity recreational use would continue.

(a) The district manager, after extensive consultation with various experts, comes up with the following set of importance weights: A 0.2, B 0.4, C 0.15, D 0.25. Which option would you recommend on the basis of an aggregate value function approach? Note that to apply this method you will need to convert the economic achievement levels into a suitable point scale. Show your results in a performance profile graph.

(b) Perform some sensitivity analysis, increasing and decreasing the weight of each objective individually by 0.15 at the expense or benefit of the other three objectives. How does this affect your conclusion derived under (a)?

20
Reflections on MS/OR

It is now time to take stock of the vast and rugged landscape of MS/OR. In fact, since the 1960s it has grown to the point where most practitioners and academics of MS/OR can claim to have expertise in only a small niche of it, and no more than a superficial knowledge of the scenery beyond. As a result, there is often the danger that they try to fit any problem into one of their three or four favourite methods or techniques by making questionable boundary judgements. The risks are obvious. They end up with an elegant solution to the wrong problem.

Unfortunately, the vast majority of practitioners fall either into the camp of 'hard OR' or 'soft systems and soft OR', when it would enhance their professional effectiveness if they had a more balanced background and view.

Although this text has a partial bias towards hard OR, it is firmly based on the principles of systems thinking and thus shares this focus with soft OR. It also exposes hard OR practitioners to a brief overview of the underlying philosophy of soft OR and a few of the more widely applied problem structuring methods — not to allow them to apply any of these without further in-depth study, but as an incentive to step back when they approach a problem situation and evaluate whether a hard OR approach is really the most appropriate one.

The methodology for hard OR presented here unashamedly borrows aspects of soft approaches, particularly for the problem formulation phase, if they contribute to a more comprehensive picture of the problem and its wider context. This is in stark contrast to the narrowly focussed treatment given in most MS/OR textbooks, which blind the reader with the beauty, the power, and intricate computational details of various quantitative techniques, as if their mastery guarantees good MS/OR, at the neglect of the most important aspect of successful problem solving: identifying the real problem within its full context.

Problem situations, not problems

Although the occasional MS/OR project starts out with a relatively well-structured, well-defined problem, most projects begin life as vague feelings of dissatisfaction or concern about the current or future state of affairs. So much of the time, what analysts face is not a problem but a problem situation of interconnected issues. Getting a proper grasp of the context in which they occur is a crucial and critical phase for any project. The seeds of success or failure are quite often sown there. Homing in on a 'problem' without exploring its full context can be costly. The issue that has given rise to dissatisfaction may not be the 'real' problem or can only be tackled once one or several other issues have been resolved. It may be solved at the wrong level of resolution or the form of the solution may not be appropriate for decision making. Even its true nature may be misunderstood, as the following telling story demonstrates.

For several years, the management of a high-rise office building was inundated by complaints about the excessive time people had to wait for elevators in the main lobby. Successive MS/OR teams were asked to investigate the 'problem of excessive waiting times'. A number of 'solutions' were tried out, such as having some lifts operate exclusively for the lower floors, while others were express lifts to the higher levels. But each project team reached the conclusion that waiting times could only be reduced effectively by installing additional lifts — precluded by its horrendous cost. Each team basically took the problem as it was defined by management, namely one of excessive waiting times, except for the last team, where one team member suggested studying why people objected to waiting for lifts in the main lobby. They discovered that it was mainly boredom. So if boredom could be overcome, then complaints about excessive waiting times would to a large extent disappear. The same team member suggested that they install mirrors along all the walls in the main lobby. This would surely alleviate boredom. Some people would take advantage of the mirrors to make last minute checks on how they looked and put on some finishing touches. Others could observe people standing around without being too obvious about it. This was the essence of his argument, although he put it rather more bluntly by stereotyping people by gender. This surprisingly cheap solution was implemented and complaints almost completely disappeared. Nowadays, instead of or in addition to mirrors, TV screens showing the latest stock exchange prices would do the same trick. The lesson of this story clearly is that it pays to look at the problem situation in very broad terms, rather than launching immediately into the 'problem' that may have triggered off the study.

The aim of MS/OR

The aim of MS/OR is not to come up with 'optimal' solutions, as more traditional textbooks profess, but to provide a basis for more insightful decision making. As we have seen, optimality is a rather misleading concept. Any solution recommended is only optimal with respect to the model chosen to capture the system. Both the system definition and the model imply boundary choices, some of which are arbitrary, affected by the resources available for the analysis (time, funds, computing power, etc.), the experience and background of the analyst, and last but not least the particular world view on which it is based. Widen any of these, and the 'optimal' solution may not be optimal any longer. What is optimal for a particular narrow system, may only be suboptimal for the wider system, and each system is always embedded in a wider system. So, the concept of optimality loses much of its gloss. All MS/OR can really strive for is to achieve some degree of improvement over the previous situation or an *ad hoc* decision process. This is why one of the founders of OR defined it as "the art of giving bad answers to problems to which otherwise worse answers are given."

If the focus shifts from optimality to improvements, the insights gained from sensitivity analysis about to boundary choices becomes even more important.

Hard OR methodologies ≠ scientific method of natural sciences

Hard OR methodologies are not a version of the 'objective' scientific method of the natural sciences, consisting of formation of hypotheses, experimental design, data collection, and refutation or conditional confirmation of the hypotheses, performed under conditions that allow replication. While the scientific method aims at advancing scientific knowledge, MS/OR is aimed at problem solving within a real context with much of its complexity preserved. Most problem situations are unique, subject to change due to external factors. The analysis can rarely be replication under exactly the same conditions. MS/OR practice does not claim to be 'objective', but recognizes that many of its aspects are tainted with a fair degree of subjectivity. There is no distinct data collection phase. Different data are collected throughout most phases. All that hard OR shares with the scientific method is that the methodology should be transparent, all assumptions and boundary choices should be spelled out and justified, data used should be conserved, and full documentation should be written up.

Potential improvements from widening boundary of system

Focussing on the narrow problem as presented by the decision maker, without exploring its context fully, may also make you miss the potential for really big savings that can be made at little or no cost. Here are three examples. A firm experienced high container shipping costs for its products, a variety of electrical cables wound on wooden drums of various sizes. The problem was presented to the MS/OR team — OR students — as a container packing problem, i.e. which items of a shipment to load into each container and in what sequence, so as to minimize the number of containers needed and the extra cost of less-than-full container loads for any goods left over. A plethora of heuristic algorithms exist to deal with such problems. Rather than launch into the search of which algorithms suited this particular problem best and then write appropriate software, the students watched an experienced dispatcher direct the loading of several shipments. In one shipment for large-size drums, only two layers of drums could be inserted into the container. A third layer would have exceeded the container dimension by 4 cm. Hence almost a third of the container capacity remained unused. Tough luck! Similar observations were made for other shipments. While the firm has no control over the dimensions of the shipping containers, it has control over the dimensions of its drums. One of the students asked if the diameter of the wooden drums could not be reduced by 2 cm, which would allow 100% usage of the container capacity. *A priori*, there seemed to be no obstacle to this, even without reducing the length of cable, since most drums had enough unfilled space. So by enlarging the boundaries of the system, i.e. allowing drum sizes to become part of the problem, huge savings in shipping costs could be achieved, even without the use of a container packing algorithm. Further savings from applying such algorithms were small in comparison.

Another team of students was presented with a trim problem for an appliance manufacturer. For certain sizes of steel sheets available from the supplier, the unusable off-cuts amounted to 15 and 20% — an expensive waste of raw material. Optimization algorithms shave trim losses by only a few per cent over those of an experienced scheduler. Again, one of the students asked if it would be possible to procure different sheet sizes from the supplier. The procurement clerk's answer was "no"; these were the standard sizes available. He also speculated that special sizes, more suitable for their needs, would be more expensive, since the supplier would have to make special setups for them. The student did not give up that easily. He requested permission to approach the supplier. To his surprise, the latter said that since the appliance manufacturer was one of their important customers they would be willing to cut the steel sheets to any feasible length. A bit of further analysis showed that with different sheet lengths the trim losses could be reduced by 10 to 15% using the method currently used by the staff, without the use of any optimization techniques.

Finally, in the LOD problem, the grease manufacturing supervisor claimed that greases produced in huge pressure mixers required the mixer to be full. He had thirty years of experience. So the problem was reduced to allocating grease manufacture to the three sizes of mixers available, leaving little or no room for lowering overall costs. Again, the analyst did not give up. He checked with the engineering section of the firm and after some study was told that grease quality would not be affected if the mixers were filled to at least 40% capacity, opening up room for considerable savings in total inventory and production costs.

Each of these examples shows that often small changes in the boundaries of the system, in particular in what are taken as uncontrollable inputs, can give rise to improvements that may in fact exceed the ones that 'optimization' of the originally defined problem could have produced. Without exploring the wider context in which the problem occurs, such improvements may be missed. Another lesson from these examples is the importance of asking "why?" and then following up the answer with another "why?", until a sufficiently comprehensive picture has been obtained.

A systems thinking approach is no guarantee of effective problem solving. However, by its very nature of rendering explicit all boundary choices made in the analysis and their implications, it leads to more comprehensive, more balanced, less biassed, and hence more insightful and more effective decision making.

Bibliography

Encyclopaedic texts

Daellenbach, H.G. and Flood R.L. (2002) *The Informed Student Guide to Management Science*, Thomson, London. Short, introductory descriptions of all major OR/MS concepts and tools.

Gass, S.I. and Harris, C.M. (2000) *Encyclopedia of OR and MS*, Kluwer Academic, Hingham MA. Authoritative, succinct treatment of concepts and techniques. Requires good mathematics background.

Systems thinking and MS/OR methodologies

Implementation and Validation

Churchman, C.W. and Schainblatt, A.H. (1965) 'The researcher and the manager: A dialectic of implementation', *Management Science*, Feb.. Philosophical analysis of the activities and attitudes of analysts and problem owners which are most appropriate for a climate conducive to proper implementation. See also the October 1965 issue of *Management Science* for a follow-up on this very provocative paper, particularly the comments by W. Alderson.

Interfaces (1987) Special Issue: Implementation, May–June. The entire issue is devoted to implementation with particular emphasis on management information systems.

Landry M., Malouin, J.-L. and Oral, M. (1983) 'Model validation in operations research', *European Journal of Operational Research*, 14/3, Nov., 207–20.

Landry, M. and Oral, M. (1993) Special Issue: Model Validation, *European Journal of Operational Research*, 66/2, April. A series of articles on model validation. The first by Landry and Oral gives a comprehensive and comparative survey of the other six. Their conclusions show that the validation issue cannot be divorced from the questions of 'What is science?' and 'Is OR/MS science?' Extensive bibliographies on validation and the process of science.

Schultz, R.L. and Slevin, D.P., (eds) (1975) *Implementing of Operation Research/ Management Science*, Elsevier. A collection of papers on implementation. Read the one by A. Reisman and C.A. de Kluyver 'Strategies for implementing systems studies' for a pragmatic view of how to improve the chances for successful implementation.

Urban, G.L. (1974) 'Building models for decision makers', *Interfaces*, May. Looks at the process of building implementable models.

MS/OR methodologies, problem structuring, critical systems thinking

Beer, S. (1985) *Diagnosing the System for Organizations*, Wiley, Chichester. Stafford Beer is the creator around 1959 of the 'viable system model', a cybernetic model of organizations, which Beer started to implement for the restructuring of the Chilean economy under Allende.

Checkland, P. (1983/1999) *Systems Thinking, Systems Practice, includes a 30-year retrospective*, Wiley, Chichester. Chapters 6 and 7 give a detailed account of his soft systems methodology. The whole book covers interesting and thought provoking material.

Checkland, P. and Scholes, J. (1999) *Soft Systems Methodology in Action, includes a 30-year retrospective*, Wiley, Chichester. Shows how SSM has evolved since its inception in the 1970s, with authoritative accounts of several real-life applications.

Eden, C.L., Jones, S. and Simms, D. (1983) *Messing About in Problems*, Pergamon Press, Oxford. First extensive coverage of SODA by its developers.

Eden, C.L., Ackermann, F. and Cropper, S. (1995) *Getting Started with Cognitive Mapping*, documentation for COPE v2, Banxia Software, Glasgow (http://www.banxia.com/).

Daellenbach, H.G. (2001) Systems Thinking and Decision Making, REA Publications, Christchurch. A detailed coverage of the hard OR methodology in Chapters 5–8.

Flood, R.L. and Jackson M.C. (1991) *Creative Problem Solving, Total Systems Intervention*, Wiley, Chichester. Chapters 1 and 2 cover systems concepts, the remainder deals with TSI.

Friend, J.K. and Hickling, A. (1987) *Planning under Pressure: the Strategic Choice Approach*, Pergamon, Oxford. Coverage by its developers.

Jackson, M.C. (2000) *Systems Approaches to Management*, Kluwer/Plenum, New York. A comprehensive and critical review of all systems methodologies based on systems thinking. A must for any serious student in systems thinking. Hull School of CST. Bibliography.

Mason, R.O. and Mitroff, I.I. (1981) *Challenging Strategic Planning Assumptions*, Wiley, New York. Original coverage of SAST by its developers.

Mingers, J.C. and Gill, A. (1997) *Multimethodology — The Theory and Practice of Combining Management Science Methodologies*, Wiley, Chichester. Combining different methods or parts of methods for analysis of different aspects of the same problem.

Naughton, J. (1984) *Soft Systems Analysis: An Introductory Guide*, Technology Course T301: Block 4, The Open University Press, Milton Keynes. Down-to-earth text. Together with its *Workbook* this is one of the best accounts of the use of rich pictures and other systems diagrams.

Pidd, M. (1996) *Tools for Thinking*, Wiley, Chichester. Incisive introductory treatment of SSM, cognitive mapping and SODA in Part II.

Rosenhead, J. and Mingers, J.C. (eds) (2000) *Rational Analysis for a Problematic World Revisited*, Wiley, Chichester. An overview of the important properties of soft systems approaches, followed by a detailed account with case studies of several methodologies, written by various contributors. Good starting point for the 'basics' of and a 'feel' for the subject (1989 edition by Rosenhead.)

Ulrich, W. (1983) *Critical Heuristics of Social Planning: A new Approach to Practical Philosophy*, Haupt, Berne. Reprinted in 1994 by Wiley, Chichester. Philosophical foundation of critical systems thinking and CSH. Highly demanding.

Ulrich, W. (1996) *A Primer to Critical Systems Heuristics for Action Researchers*, Centre for Systems Studies, University of Hull. Useful, practical guide for applying CSH.

Ulrich, W. (2003) 'Beyond methodology choice: critical systems thinking as critically systemic discourse,' *Journal of the OR Society*, April, 54:325–42.

Systems and Systems Thinking

Russel L. Ackoff has written widely on the need for systems thinking to 'resolve' today's decision problems. He is also of the opinion that OR/MS is not living up to the ideals of its originators. Controversial but thought-provoking. See for instance:

Ackoff, R.L. (1974) 'The Systems Revolution', *Long-Range Planning*, 2–20.

Ackoff, RL (1973) 'Science in the Systems Age. Beyond IE, OR, and MS', *Operations*

Research, May–June, 661–71.

Ackoff, R.L. (1979) 'The Future of OR is Past', *J. of the OR Society*, Feb., 93–104.

Ackoff, R.L. (1979) 'Resurrecting the Future of OR', *J. of the OR Society*, March, 189-99.

Ackoff, R.L. (1978) *The Art of Problem Solving*, Wiley, New York. Part 1 deals with problem solving, Part 2 shows six cases. Includes Ackoff's fables. Enjoyable. Many valuable lessons. A clear must and reminder for analysts with some practical experience. The emphasis is on 'Art' — something largely learned from experience, and consequently somewhat lost on the beginner.

Beishon, John, and Peters, Geoff (eds) (1981) *Systems Behaviour*, 3rd ed., Harper & Row, London. A collection of articles and applications on systems and systems thinking.

Peter Checkland, one of the most articulate proponents of soft systems methodologies, has written numerous articles and several books dealing with systems thinking:

Checkland, P. (1983/1999) *Systems Thinking, Systems Practice, includes a 30-year retrospective*, Wiley, Chichester. Chapters 1–5 have a most authoritative discussion of the systems movement. The whole book covers thought-provoking material.

Checkland, P. (1985) 'From Optimization to Learning: A Development of Systems Thinking for the 1990s', *J. of the Operational Research Society*, Sept., 757–67.

C. West Churchman, a mentor and then colleague of R.L. Ackoff. His philosophy of MS and the role of the problem analyst is reflected in this text. He says that the moment the analyst starts tinkering with a system, he or she becomes part of it. His writings have shaped many of the systems approaches to problem solving, particularly Soft OR. His approach is in the form of a 'critical debate among the opposing views of systems protagonists' is well captured in:

Churchman, C.W. (1968) *The Systems Approach*, Dell Publishing Co., New York, Provocative.

Churchman, C.W. (1971) *The Design of Inquiring Systems*, Basic Books New York. A scholarly text.

Cooke, Steve and Slack, Nigel (1991) *Making Management Decisions*, 2nd ed., Prentice Hall, Englewood Cliffs NJ. Broad coverage, including behavioural aspects of management, at the expense of systems modelling. Relevant chapters: 1–5, 8–10.

Habermas, J. (1971) *Knowledge and Human Interests*, Beacon Press, Boston. Advanced.

Hill, P.H. *et al.* (1986) *Making Decisions – A Multidisciplinary Introduction*, University Press of America, Lanham. Delightful book. Chapters 1 and 2 are relevant for systems thinking.

Jackson, M.C. (2000) *Systems Approaches to Management*, Kluwer/Plenum, New York. A comprehensive and critical review of various systems methodologies. A must for any serious student in systems thinking. Bias towards Hull School of CST. Bibliography up to 2000.

Klirr, G.J. (1991) *Facets of Systems Science,* Plenum Press, New York. Part 1 gives a guided tour of systems science at a mathematical level. Part 2 is a collection of papers on general systems theory. Neither are for the faint-hearted. (There is an extensive literature on **general systems theory**, dealing with concepts, principles, properties of systems, and systems behaviour, not specific to a given field of application. At its inception in the 1940s and 1950s, great hopes were put on this theory to enhance and unify our understanding of systems and their use for the betterment of the human race. Unfortunately, it has not lived up to these expectations. Much of the theory is of such a general nature that it is of little practical use.)

Mayon-White, Bill and Morris, Dick (1982) *Systems Behaviour - Module 1: Systems and how to describe them*, Technology Course T241, The Open University Press, Milton Keynes. The major part of the text is devoted to a detailed analysis of two systems.

Pidd, M. (1996) *Tools for Thinking*, Wiley, Chichester. Excellent text. Systems concepts covered in Chapters 1, 3, and Introduction to Part 2.

Watson, Lewis (1984) *Systems Paradigms – Studying Systems Failures*, Technology Course T301: Block 2, The Open University Press, Milton Keynes. As its companion text by Bignell, V, and Fortune, J, *Understanding Systems Failures*, Manchester University Press, 1984, this text applies systems thinking to explore why and how major disasters, such as the Three Mile Island nuclear power station accident, could occur, and what we can learn from such failures.

Uncertainty

Armstrong, J.S. (1985) *Long-Range Forecasting: From Crystal Ball to Computer*, Wiley, New York. Extensive coverage. Armstrong is a provocative writer.

Bross, Irwin D.J. (1953) *Design for Decision*, Macmillan. The date of publication makes this a classic. It is a classic! Humorous, insightful discussion of many issues associated with uncertainty. Our discussion in Chapter 15 has been strongly influenced by this book. The relevant chapters are 1 to 5.

Delquié, P. (1993) 'Inconsistent trade-offs between attributes: New evidence in preference assessment biases,' *Management Science*, Nov., pp. 1382–95.

Hogarth, R.M. and Makridakis, S. (1981) 'Forecasting and planning: an evaluation,' *Management Sciences*, Feb., 115–38. This seminal paper first reviews some of the psychology of human judgment, followed by a review of reported applications of formal forecasting methods. It finds that the latter are prone to similar problems to the former. It then concludes with some suggestions for overcoming some of these problems.

Tversky, A. and Kahneman, D. (1974) 'Judgment under uncertainty: heuristics and biases', *Science*, Vol. 185, Sept., pp. 1124–31. The classic article discussed in Section 15.7.

Tversky, A. and Kahneman, D. (1981) 'The framing of decisions and the psychology of choice,' *Science*, Jan., 453–8. A popular follow-on article to 'Judgment under uncertainty' that shows that preferences and, hence, decision choices are highly dependent on how the problem in question is presented or framed.

Tversky, A. and Kahneman, D. (1986) 'Rational choice and the framing of decisions,' *Journal of Business*, No. 4, part 2, S251–8. The more academic version of the same theme as their 1981 paper above.

Wright, G. and Ayton, P. (eds) (1994) *Subjective Probability*, Wiley, Chichester. A collection of academic papers extending the Tversky and Kahneman research.

Wright, G. and Goodwin, P. (eds) (1998) *Forecasting with Judgment*, Wiley, Chichester. An authoritative series of articles on how judgement affects and biasses predictions and ways to overcome some of the difficulties.

Wright, G. (2001) *Strategic Decision Making: A Best Practice Blueprint*, Wiley, New York. Popular, easy reading on fallacies and pitfalls when dealing with uncertainties.

Hard OR techniques

General OR texts

Daellenbach, H.G., George, J. and McNickle D.C. (1983) *Introduction to O.R. Techniques*, 2nd ed., Allyn and Bacon, Boston. Partially outdated, but contains aspects not covered in other general OR texts.

Hillier, F.S. and Lieberman, J. (2001) *Introduction to Operations Research*, 7th edn., McGraw-Hill, New York.

Winston, W.L. (1999) *Operations Research — Applications and Algorithms*, 3rd edn., Duxbury, Belmont CA.

Decision making over time

Silver, E.A., Pyke, D.F. and Peterson, R. (1998) *Inventory Management and Production Planning and Schedulingt*, 3rd ed., Wiley, New York.

Constrained optimization and linear programming

There are a number of sophisticated mathematical algorithms or methods to find the optimal solution to single-constraint problems. If both the objective function and the constraint are differentiable in the decision variable, the **Lagrange multiplier approach** can be used. See Section 19-7 in Daellenbach *et al.* [1983] above, or any other intermediate level OR text for an introductory discussion. If the functions are not differentiable or not well behaved, **dynamic programming** is the most commonly recommended approach. See Chapter 9 of Daellenbach *et al.* [1983] above.

Most OR/MS introductory texts contain several formulation examples, as well as full coverage of the Simplex method for finding the optimal solution. The latter will require a fair background in linear algebra. We think that the emphasis given to the Simplex method in introductory texts is misplaced. The ordinary user of linear programming will never need to know its details. Instead he or she should have some familiarity with a commercial LP computer software or spreadsheet optimizer, like Excel's Solver.

There are a few specialized linear programming texts around. Most of them will be beyond your reach, unless you have a good working knowledge of linear algebra, including matrix and vector notation. One of the few exceptions is:

Daellenbach, H.G. and Bell, E.J. (1970) *User's Guide to Linear Programming*, Prentice Hall, Englewood Cliffs NJ. Its treatment is at a similar level to this chapter. It contains a number of real-life examples, including a scaled-down version of a planning model for an integrated oil company with several sources of crude oils, two refineries, and several marketing areas. Except for its use of a simple LP computer code, it still is up-to-date in terms of formulation examples and its treatment of sensitivity analysis.

Decision analysis and utility analysis

Behn, R.D. and Vaupel, J.W. (1982) *Quick Analysis for Busy Decision Makers*, Basic Books, New York. A fascinating book on a wide range of close-to-real-life decision situations under risk and uncertainty. Aims to convince current and future decision makers of the usefulness of decision analysis and make it easily accessible to the lay person. No mathematics background required.

Goodwin, P. and Wright, G. (1999) *Decision Analysis for Management Judgement*, Wiley, New York.

Jennings, D. and Wattam, S. (1998) *Decision Making*, Financial Times, Prentice Hall, Englewood Cliffs NJ.

Keeney, R.L. and Raiffa, H. (1976) *Decisions with Multiple Objectives*, Wiley, New York. Authoritative treatment of utility functions and their use, particularly for multi-attribute outcomes. Chapter 4 deals with single-attribute utility functions.

Samson, Danny (1988) *Managerial Decision Analysis*, Irwin, Homewood IL. Comprehensive introductory treatment of decision analysis, including the use of the Arborist decision analysis package for PCs. Contains numerous fully worked out examples, case studies, and real-life applications.

Multiple Criteria Decision Making

Belton, Valerie (1990) 'Multiple criteria decision analysis – Practically the only way to choose', in L.C. Hendry and R.W. Eglese, *Operational Research Tutorial Papers 1990*, Operational Research Society, Neville House, Waterloo St., Birmingham B2 5TX, England, 53–102. This is an elementary, but highly instructive introduction to the basics of MCDM, similar in level to the coverage here, but rather more extensive. It also has an extensive bibliography and shows an application of the VISA software for the aggregate function value approach.

Gal, T., Stewart, T.J. and Hanne, T. (eds) (1999) *Multicriteria Decision Making: Advances in MCDM Models, Algorithms, Theory and Applications*, Kluwer, Boston.

Keeney, R.L. and Raiffa, H. (1976) *Decisions with Multiple Objectives: Preferences and Value Tradeoffs*, Wiley, New York. Classic text for multi-attribute utility analysis, with several case studies done by the authors. Demanding in parts, both mathematically and conceptually.

Risk analysis

Evans J.R. and Olson, D.L. (1998) *Introduction to Simulation and Risk Analysis*, Prentice Hall, Englewood Cliffs NJ. Basic introduction. Includes a student version of Crystal Ball, a risk analysis software.

Hertz, D.B. (1979) 'Risk Analysis in Capital Investment', *Harvard Business Review*, v57#5. A popularized first introduction to risk analysis by its inventor.

Hertz, D.B. and Thomas, H. (1983) *Risk Analysis and its Applications*, Wiley, New York. Chapters 1 and 2 give an introduction to the basics of risk analysis.

Savage Sam L. (1998) *Insight.xla – Business Analysis Tools for Microsoft Excel*, Duxbury Press, Belmont CA. A low-cost primer and software add-ons for Excel for risk analysis (and simulation, forecasting, Markov chains, decision trees). SIM.xla has most of the capabilities of @RISK and can be downloaded from the Web. XLSIM is its full-fledged commercial extension.

Vose, D. (1996) *Quantitative Risk Analysis*, Wiley, Chichester. A more advanced treatment of risk analysis. Particularly useful in terms of the discussion on various probability distributions.

Winston, Wayne (1998) *Financial Models Using Simulation and Optimization*, Palisade Corp., Newfield NY. A detailed, step-by-step guide for Excel and Palisade's Decision Tools software covering risk analysis using @RISK for financial modelling.

Simulation and system dynamics

Banks, J., Carson, J.S. and Sy, J.N. (1995) *Getting Started with GPSS/H 2nd Edition*, Wolverine Software Corporation, 4115 Annandale Road, Annandale, VA 22003-3910. The introductory manual for the GPSS/H package mentioned in Section 7.3. It includes a functioning version of the software. http://wolverinesoftware.com/

Law, A.M. and Kelton, W.D. (2000) *Simulation Modeling and Analysis*, 3rd ed., McGraw-Hill, Boston. A very good reference for details of data analysis, modelling strategy, and output analysis in simulation, co-authored by a leading practitioner.

Maani, K.E. and Cavana R.Y. (2000) *Systems Thinking and Modelling – Understanding Change and Complexity*, Prentice Hall, Auckland, An introduction to system dynamics with computer models, including the New Zealand Wine Industry planning model.

Pidd, M. (1998) *Computer Simulation in Management Science, Fourth Edition*, Wiley, Chichester. A readable, general introduction to simulation either using packages or general-purpose (Pascal, Basic) programs. Also includes a section on system dynamics modelling.

Simul8 is published by Simul8 Corporation. Check their informative website: http://www. Simul8.com/

The INFORMS College on Simulation maintains lists of other simulation software and useful simulation resources on its website: http://www.informs-cs.org/index.html.

Waiting lines and queueing

Bunday, B.D. (1986) *Basic Queueing Theory*, Edward Arnold, London. Easier coverage of the simpler theoretical models than Gross and Harris, cited below.

Gross, D. and Harris, C.M. (1998) *Fundamentals of Queueing Theory*, 3rd edn, Wiley, New York. There has been a vast amount of work on theoretical models for queueing systems. This is the best general reference on them. Spreadsheets for calculating queueing formulas are available from the Wiley ftp site.

Hall, R.W. (1991) *Queueing Methods for Services and Manufacturing*, Prentice Hall, Englewood Cliffs NJ. Unique graphical methods for control and modelling of queues like the arrival–departure diagram.

Kleinrock, L. (1975) *Queueing Systems, Volumes I and II*, Wiley-Interscience, New York. Another very comprehensive general reference on the theory of queueing models. Many interesting applications of waiting lines are concerned with computer/ communications systems. Volume II concentrates on them.

McNickle, D.C. and Woollons, R.C. (1990) 'Analysis and simulation of a logging weighbridge installation', *N.Z. J. Forestry Science*, 20, 111–19. Analysis of the weighbridge problem.

McNickle, D.C. (1991) 'Estimating the average delay of the first N customers in an M/Erlang/1 queue', *Asia–Pacific J. of Operational Research*, 8, 44–54. The final theory that was actually used for the weighbridge problem.

McNickle, D.C. (1998) 'Queueing for toilets', *O. R. Insight*, 11, 2–5. The analysis of toilet standards was done using the method described in Section 16-3, except that the criterion used was that 90% of customers should wait less than one minute.

Glossary of technical terms

Refer also to the index (pages 592–598). Bold-faced terms indicate glossary entry.

abstract system

A **system** that has no physical components, consisting only of abstract concepts, rules, interactions, and relationships. Ex.: a classification system; the legal system.

activity life cycle, see **life cycle**

aggregate value function methods

A **multi-objective** solution method that allows **tradeoffs** between **objectives** (Ex.: $x\%$ of objective 1 is worth $y\%$ of objective 2) and forms an overall aggregate score that is the weighted average of the individual objective scores, with the relative importance of each objective serving as the weights.

algorithm

A set of logical and computational operations performed to prescribed rules, often **iteratively**. Most **optimization** methods are algorithmic. Ex.: **greedy algorithm**.

analogous model

A representation of an entity or operation by mimicking its properties and behaviour by alternative means. Ex.: position and movement of aircraft on radar screen; representing size of numbers by length of lines in a graph.

attributes

Properties of **system** components, measured by **state variables**. Used for describing the **state of a system**. Ex.: status of machine (component: machine, attribute: 'idle' or 'busy', state variable: 0 for 'idle', 1 for 'busy'); number of people waiting in a queue (component: queue; attribute: size; state variable: number waiting).

backward induction, see **decision analysis**

Bayesian decision analysis (see also **expected value of information**)

A **decision analysis** method that uses information obtained through sampling to update the initially assumed or derived **probabilities** of **random events**.

'black box', systems as black box

A mathematical representation that produces the results of the system **transformation** process in aggregate form without attempting to reproduce the details of the relationships and activities inside the system. Ex.: transforming crude inputs in a refinery into refined products using an aggregate yield structure.

breakeven analysis, breakeven point

A **mathematical model** for finding the level of output or activity, called the breakeven point, where total revenues just recover total costs, including all **fixed costs**. An output below the breakeven point implies a loss, while an output above the breakeven point yields a profit.

boundary, see **system boundary**

boundary judgements

Critical assessment and evaluation of the consequences on all **stakeholders** of (1) where to place the **boundary** between the **system** and the relevant **environment**, and (2) which aspects are part of the relevant environment and which ones are ignored.

bounded rationality
The inability of the human mind to deal simultaneously with several conflicting or incommensurate aspects or factors (usually more than 5 to 9), and the brain's limited computational power, preventing us from being fully rational when faced with complex situation. It leads to **satisficing** behaviour.

CATWOE
An acronym standing for the six elements that make up a problem situation: Customers/victims/beneficiaries, Actors/users, (system) **Transformation** (process), **World view**, (problem) Owners, **Environment**.

causal-loop diagram, cause-and-effect diagram
A system representation in the form of a network that depicts the **cause-and-effect relationships** between various aspects, concepts, entities, **systems components** and their **attributes**, where the arrows indicate the causal direction. A sequence of arrows that lead back to the originating aspect is called a **feedback loop**.

cause-and-effect relationships and thinking
A causal relationship between concepts or events, usually occurring in chains of multiple links, Ex.: aspect A produces, affects, or influences aspects B and C, B and C affect D. Cause-and-effect thinking explains phenomena or **system behaviour** through chains of cause-and-effects links. Ex.: room temperature exceeding 20 °C trips an electric switch, cutting the flow of electricity.

CSH, see **critical systems heuristics**

closed-loop control or feedback control
A control signal that responds to the **state of the system** or to specific system **outputs**. Ex.: heating system where thermostat controls heat output in response to room temperature changes; driver response to road traffic and conditions.

closed system
A self-contained **system** that has no **environment,** receives no **inputs** and has no **outputs**. Its behaviour is **deterministic**. No natural or **human activity systems** are closed. For experimental purposes, such system are sometimes approximated as closed if inputs occur only as part of the starting conditions, but not later on. Ex.: deterministic **simulation** for specified starting conditions.

cognitive map, cognitive mapping (see also **SODA**)
A cognitive map is a network representation that captures the **subjective**, personal perceptions of an individual about a **problem situation** — ideas, goals, concerns, preferences, actions and their contrasts or opposites — called constructs. The arrows indicate which construct leads to which other constructs, implying a logical or evocative relationship, not necessarily causal. Since language contains connotations personal to the individual, the constructs are expressed in the individual's own words.

Sets of highly interlinked constructs, but few links to the rest of the map, form emerging themes. Constructs with many arrows out or in are core constructs.

complexity
Intricate **system behaviour** that is difficult to trace and comprehend because of a multiplicity of highly interrelated elements, influence and response patterns, **feedback loops**, mutual causality, and **uncertainties**, even if the behaviour of each part by itself may be fully or partially understood. Ex.: the greenhouse effect; share price fluctuations; group behaviour.

components, parts
Individual aspects, entities that belong to the **system** or make up the system. Components may have **attributes** and exhibit behaviours. Ex.: the customers in a bank (**waiting in line**, being served by teller); bank tellers (idle or serving customers).

conceptualization
Something conceived in the mind, a **mental** interpretation or representation of a phenomenon, entity or group of entities, that is not necessarily a true picture of **reality**. Its aim is to gain understanding or insight. Ex.: heaven or hell; customer traffic in a bank seen as a **waiting line** system; the mathematical queueing model.

constraints (also see **shadow prices**)
Restrictions imposed on the **feasible** decision choices and/or **system variables** or function of system variables, often in the form of limited **resources** (funds, time, capacity, materials); Policy decisions or a legal edicts. Some constraints are **hard** (Ex.: physical capacity of equipment, availability of natural resources), others are **soft**, imposed by management decisions (Ex.: quality standards, budget allocations).

constructs, see **cognitive map**

continuous system (contrast with **discrete system**)
A **system** where the **system variables** are real valued. Ex.: heating system measuring temperature as a continuous variable; chemical plant measuring flows in litres.

control input
An **input** into a **system** over which the decision maker has control in the form of: a discrete action (alternative course of action A or B); setting the values of decision variables (size of production run); a decision strategy or rules or a **control mechanism** (if condition X occurs, take action Y); a **policy** (quality standards); amount of **resources** made available ($X to spend per year; Y days to complete project).

control mechanism
Device or procedure that monitors **system behaviour** and issues **feed-back control** signals to adjust system behaviour. The settings or rules used are a **control input**. Ex.: the thermostat of a heater; set of rules used for replenishing goods when stock level falls below a trigger point.

control signal, see **control mechanism**, **closed-loop control**.

counterintuitive outcome
A **system behaviour** that contradicts common sense or that cannot be readily explained by **reductionist** and/or **cause-and-effect thinking**. Ex.: chemical binding of hydrogen and oxygen, two gases, producing water, a liquid.

credibility (see also **robust**)
Degree of confidence **problem owners** and/or **problem users** have in the model of how well it 'solves' the **real-world** problem.

critical systems heuristics (CSH) (see also **boundary judgements**)
A **critical systems thinking** approach developed by Ulrich [1983] to externalize **boundary** choices on the **system** and **environment** implied by a given system definition and subject them to critical assessment.

critical systems thinking (CST)
A set of systems perspectives aimed to develop a valid philosophical foundation for **systems thinking**, based on the work of philosophers, such as Kant, Churchman, Habermas and others, and to develop a framework for professional practice through critical awareness and understanding of the strengths an weaknesses of various approaches, appropriate for

the nature of the problem situation. **Critical systems heuristics** and **total systems intervention** are CTS approaches.

CST, see **critical systems thinking**

cumulative distribution function

A function ranging from 0 to 1 which gives the **probability** that a given **random variable** will assume a value of less than or equal to some specified number.

data

Facts or patterns, real or inferred, quantitative or qualitative, incorporated in or used as inputs into a **mathematical model**. Ex.: numerical (unit costs; machine capacity); **attributes** (age, income, profession of a person); **probability distributions** (demand for a product; age distribution of target population).

decision analysis, decision node, decision tree

An approach to determine the **optimal** strategy in a **multi-stage decision process** where the outcomes are **random** and often conditional on the results of previous stages. It can be laid out in schematic form of a decision tree. Each branching point is either (1) a decision node (a square), each branch representing a decision choice, or (2) a chance node (a circle), each branch leading to a possible random outcome with a given **probability**. Each path from the initial trunk node to a final branch end is an outcome with a net benefit or total cost. A **solution** consists of a **strategy** of conditional actions which specifies which decision choice is made at each decision node. The best strategy is evaluated by working backwards from all final branch ends, node by node, to the initial trunk node (backward induction).

decision criterion

The value process or standard used for judging or evaluating which decision or **solution** should be selected. Not to be confused with the **objective** or the **objective function**. Ex.: (1) The objective function is profit; the criterion is to maximize the expected value of profit. (2) When allocating parking spaces to apartments, the objective may be to keep the distance between pairs of apartments and spaces allocated as low as possible. The criterion used interprets the meaning of 'low overall distance'. It could mean (a) minimize the sum of the distances, (b) minimize the sum of the squared distances, or (c) minimize the maximum distance between any apartment and its allocated parking space. Criteria (b) and (c) lead to a more equitable allocation.

decision flow chart

A chart of the logical sequence of steps (tests, actions) that lead to a final decision.

decision maker

A person, often the **problem owner**, holding the authority over the **decision choices**.

decisions, decision variables, alternative courses of action, see control input

Delphi method

An **iterative** method for pooling expert judgments. A group of experts are asked to supply qualitative or quantitative assessments about a phenomenon. The combined results are fed back to the experts, allowing them to revise their original assessments in the light of the combined results. This process may be repeated several times.

deterministic system (contrast with **stochastic system**)

A system whose behaviour can be predicted exactly for any given initial **state of the system** and **control inputs**. No **random** inputs or random behaviour occur. Few natural and **human activity systems** are truly deterministic. Used as an approximation to **stochastic systems** if randomness is small. Ex.: traffic lights set on a fixed pattern.

discrete system (contrast with **continuous system**)

A system where **system variables** are integer valued. Ex.: **waiting line** (system variables: number of entities in queue; status of tellers: 0 for idle, 1 for busy).

dominance, dominated decision choices, Pareto optimality

A decision alternative A is said to be dominated by another choice B if A performs no better than B for all **objectives** and worse for at least one. A choice that is not dominated by any other choice is called an efficient choice, an efficient solution, or Pareto-optimal. The set of all efficient solutions is called the efficient frontier.

economic order quantity (EOQ)

The most basic inventory control model, minimizing the sum of holding and setup costs. Its optimal solution is the famous square root formula.

effectiveness (contrast with **efficiency**)

Effectiveness measures the degree of achieving the **objective(s)** of a **system**, operation, or activity. Ex.: an immunization drive resulted in 89% of the target population being immunized — it was 89% effective.

efficacy

The ability of an activity to produce the desired effect. Ex.: increasing the capacity of a bottleneck operation will increase output; adding another machine when the first one always has excess capacity will not produce more output (its efficacy is nil).

efficiency (contrast with **effectiveness**)

Increasing output for the same **resource** use, maintaining effectiveness at same level with fewer resources. Efficiency is concerned with the best use of resources. Ex.: travel farther with the same amount of fuel.

efficient solution, efficient frontier, see **dominance**

emancipatory systems approaches (see also **critical systems thinking**)

A **subjectivist** approach to **systems thinking** that attempts to deal with conflicting and irreconcilable views between **stakeholders** on the **system**, its **boundaries**, and its purposes and goals, and where there exist differences in the power (as given by authority, knowledge and information, intellectual abilities, resources) between stakeholders which may lead to coercion.

emergent property

System behaviour or a system **output** that none of the system **components** has individually. Achieving desirable emergent properties is the reason for building systems. Ex.: telephone communication is not attributable to a single telephone component, but requires their interaction.

enrichment (of model) (contrast with **reformulation**)

Adding more features to a model to capture more of **reality** without changing its basic structure. Ex.: increase number of periods covered; introduce more constraints.

entity life cycle, see **life cycles**

environment (of system) (also see **wider system of interest**, **hierarchy of systems**)

All aspects of universe that affect the **system** (provide **inputs**), or are affected by it (receive **outputs**). Ex.: local economy is environment of a firm (input: local demand, etc.; output: percentage of demand satisfied); local population, education policy, etc., form environment for a local school.

EOQ, see **economic order quantity**

equilibrium, state of equilibrium, see **steady state**

error analysis (contrast with **sensitivity analysis**)

Analysis of the potential reduction in benefits or increase in costs for using erroneous or incorrect input **data**. Usually done prior to implementation. Ex.: projected actual inventory costs increase by 2.1% by overestimating demand by 50%.

event simulation, see **simulation**

expected value of perfect information (see also **decision analysis**)

The difference between (1) the expected **payoff** for the optimal decision or **strategy** and (2) the expected payoff that would be achievable if, just prior to having to select a decision or strategy, it is revealed which **random events** will eventuate at each chance node and adjusting the best decision or strategy accordingly. It is the maximum amount the decision maker should be willing to pay to obtain perfect information.

expected value of a random variable

The weighted average of all possible outcomes of a discrete **random variable**, where the **probabilities** serve as weights. Expected value, mean, and average are synonymous and all measure the central tendency for a **random** numeric outcome.

fault tree

A **cause-and-effect** arrow diagram that shows in detail how various aspects and conditions combine to produce or cause a failure, breakdown, or disaster.

feasible solution

A **solution** that satisfies all **constraints** imposed on the decision variables and on **system behaviour**.

feedback control, see **closed-loop control**

feedback loop (see also **causal loop diagrams**)

The results of the effects of component A on component B are fed back directly or in-directly to A. The feedback may be via a sequence of **cause-and-effects** links. Example: a rise in room temperature causes the thermometer level to rise which turns off the heating system which causes the temperature to drop gradually, etc.

feed-forward control

A control that takes into account projected future **system behaviour** (as a result of the cur-rent **state of the system** or in anticipation of future inputs) to steer it in a desired direction. Ex.: heating system that measures changes in outside temperature to predict effect on inside temperature and then adjusts heating inputs accordingly.

fishbone diagram, see **spray or fishbone diagram**

fixed cost (see also **overhead, variable cost**)

A cost that remains constant, regardless of activity level. Ex.: machine start-up cost.

flow chart, see **decision flow chart, material flow chart, precedence chart, spray or fish-bone diagram, fault tree**

frequency distributions

A frequency distribution summarizes how the observed outcomes of a **random** experiment are distributed over all its possible values. It associates with each discrete (attribute or numeric) outcome, or each interval of numeric outcomes, the corresponding absolute or relative frequency of the outcomes. If expressed in relative terms, the frequencies over all values sum to one. A frequency distribution is often used as an empirical approximation for an unknown theoretical **probability distribution**.

functionalist systems approaches

The **system** definition is viewed as independent of the observer, capturing **reality**.

Stakeholders see the same system and share the same goals. All **hard OR** is functionalist.

games, game theory

The process of selecting a decision (or **strategy**) option by each of two or more players in a potentially adversarial setting, where each combination of options chosen results in a **payoff** for each participant. Examples: chess players in a chess game; several commercial competitors in a price war; a military encounter of opposing forces.

global optimum

The best of several **local optima** of the objective function. Also used for denoting the unique maximum or minimum to the objective function.

goodness of fit

Fitting a line, or curve, or a set of numbers to **data** and performing a statistical test to assess how good the fit is. Routinely used for assessing how well a theoretical **probability distribution** fits a set of observations on a **random** phenomenon.

greedy algorithm

An **algorithm** that allocates a scarce **resource** to competing uses in the order decreasing **marginal or incremental returns**. Only finds the **global optimal** solution if each individual return function has decreasing marginal or incremental returns.

hard facts, soft facts

Hard facts are aspects and data relevant to describe the **problem situation** that all **stakeholders** tend to interpret in the same way without disagreement. Soft facts are aspects that may be interpreted in different ways or that are controversial, often leading to disagreement. They usually deal with human aspects and interactions. Ex.: physical layout of a facility (hard fact); records of past sales (hard fact); gossip (soft fact); prediction of future sales during times of economic instability (soft fact).

hard OR

A **functionalist approach** to **systems** intervention, usually involving **mathematical modelling**, most often aimed at **optimizing** a system **performance measure**.

heuristics, heuristic problem solving (see also **satisficing**)

Problem solving rules based on discovery, experience, learning, human ingenuity, using **algorithms** of heuristics to improve system performance or to reach an **objective**. Ex.: to reach the mountain top, hidden in fog, at each step go in the direction of the steepest slope; pack goods into a container in decreasing order of size.

hierarchy

A ranking of things into two or more levels, where lower levels are subclasses of higher levels, Ex.: major objectives, each consisting of subgoals, measured by attributes.

hierarchy of systems

Several levels of systems, where each system is a **subsystem** or is contained completely by the next higher level, except for the highest level. Ex.: A 'school class' (lowest level system), contained by the 'school' (next higher level system), which in turn is contained by the 'education system' (highest level system).

human activity system (contrast to **natural systems**)

A system created by and for the use of humans.

iconic model

A reproduction of something in a different (e.g. reduced) scale. Ex.: a matchbox car.

implementation

Planning, preparation, and execution of all activities for getting the proposed **solution** adopted for use, including writing of users manuals and training of personnel.

incremental analysis, cost, see **marginal ...**

influence diagram

A formal version of a **causal loop diagram** that shows the system **transformation process** from uncontrollable and **control inputs** to system **outputs**, via **system variables**. It delineates the system **boundary**.

inputs

Aspects (**resources**, information, **data**) from the **environment** which are fed across the system **boundary** into the system. Ex.: cost data, machine processing rates (uncontrollable inputs); operating rules (**control inputs**).

inside-us view of systems (contrast with **out-there view, reality**)

A **conceptualization** of a **system**, created by an individual for a given purpose. There is no claim that it resembles or mimics the real thing faithfully, although there will often be corresponding counterparts and it performs the same system **transformation**. Ex.: a traffic network, measuring vehicle flows along all arterial routes (no track kept of individual cars, etc.); all **human activity systems**.

intangible cost

Loss of returns, loss of savings, or a cost that are difficult to assess since it involve unobservable, imponderable, and uncertain aspects, or consequences that cannot be measured in monetary terms. Ex.: loss of goodwill by losing sale; value of a life lost.

integer linear programming or IP

A **mathematical model**, similar to **linear programming**, where all relationships are also linear, but where some or all decision variables may only assume integer values.

interarrival times (see also **waiting lines**)

The time between two consecutive arrivals at a service facility.

interpretive systems approaches

A **subjectivist** approach to **systems thinking**, allowing multiple goals and a certain divergence of views of what the **system** is and its **boundaries**, but where there is sufficient sharing of interests and goals that cooperation and compromise is possible. The majority of **problem structuring methods** are interpretive.

intrinsic worth

The worth that a person assigns to a thing or an outcome in a given context, reflecting her/his personal **preference structure** and perception of the context, as opposed to the value assessed by the market or society in general, devoid of its context.

investment portfolio

The composition (types and amounts) of securities (stocks and bonds, etc.) and other investments held by an investor (an individual or a firm).

iteration, iterative (see also **algorithm, recursive**)

Executing a sequence of steps or operations repeatedly. Each complete repetition is an iteration. Iterative may also refer to returning to earlier steps rather than the start.

lead time

Elapsed time before action becomes effective. Time between initiating an activity and its effects being felt or the activity being completed. Ex.: the time interval between initiating a production run and the items becoming available for use or sale.

lead-up time (see **planning horizon**)

Inactive part of the planning horizon, where no changes to decisions can be made.

life cycles (also called activity or entity cycles)

The sequence of events and **attribute** transformations that an entity (in a **simulation**) undergoes over time. It can be expressed as a flow diagram. For permanent entities, this cycle repeats itself iteratively over time. For temporary entities, the entity is created, goes through the cycle, and then is cancelled.

linear programming or LP

A **mathematical model** where all relationships (the objective function and the **constraints**) are linear functions of continuous, non-negative decision variables.

management science/operations research, MS/OR

An eclectic group of methodologies for problem solving based on **systems thinking** using systems **models**. Its aim is to provide insights to the **decision maker** for **effective** and informed decision making.

marginal ...

Infinitesimally small changes; the rate of change at a given value of a function.

marginal and incremental analysis, law of marginal returns and marginal costs

Based on the assumption that as the activity level increases, the **marginal cost** increases more than proportionately (= increasing marginal cost) and the **marginal revenue** increases less than proportionately (= decreasing marginal revenue) — properties often observed in business, industry, or agriculture. Additional increases in activity level are desirable as long as the increase in revenue exceeds the increase in costs. The optimal output is achieved where marginal cost equals marginal revenue.

If changes can only occur in discrete steps, then the optimal output level occurs just prior to when incremental cost exceeds incremental revenue.

marginal, incremental cost, revenue

The rate of change in total cost (or revenue) at a given activity level per unit increase in the activity. If cost (revenue) is nonlinear, the rate of change varies continuously. For activities that only occur in discrete units or amounts, it is the increase in total cost (revenue) associated with the discrete increase in activity at a given level.

Markovian ...

Andrei Markov, a Russian mathematician at the turn of the 20th century, is known for the concept of Markov chains — a **mathematical model** describing the probabilistic process of how certain **systems** change their **state**. Some **queueing system** can be modelled as Markov chains if their interarrival times and service times both follow **negative exponential distributions**, hence the terminology 'Markovian'.

material flow chart

An arrow diagram that depicts how materials, goods, documents, or/and information travel (or flow) through a **system**.

mathematical model, mathematical modelling

A set of numeric relationships between system **inputs**, **system variables**, and system **outputs** that describes the numeric behaviour of the system. Examples: the expression for the distance travelled by a free-falling body; the expression for the net present value of a sequence of cash transactions over time as a function of the discount rate.

General purpose **models** satisfy clearly defined structures (Ex.: in linear programming, all expressions are linear). MS/OR uses a number of powerful general purpose models (Ex.: **linear programming, waiting line models**). For dynamic systems, the model describes the detailed changes in the **state of the system** over time. Mathematical modelling is the process of formulating a mathematical model.

MCDM, see **multiple objectives**

measure of performance, see **performance measure, objective function**

mental construct, see **conceptualization**

mind map

A **situation summary** showing each aspects of a **problem situation** in titles, slogans or in few words, arranged on a sheet of paper (or computer screen) with arrows and links showing causal effects and other relationships. A word form of a **rich picture**.

minimax, maximin strategy

A conservative **decision criterion** that identifies the decision or **strategy** which *mini*mizes the *max*imum loss (or *max*imizes the *min*imum return) associated with any decision choice.

model (see also **abstract, symbolic, mathematical, iconic, and analogous models**)

Any formal **mental construct** or representation of an operation, a system's **transformation** process, or an entity's behaviour. It may reproduce the perceived structure, relationships, and interactions of all components involved in detail or in aggregate form. Its form may be symbolic, iconic, or analogous.

Monte Carlo simulation (see also **simulation, risk analysis**)

Repeated simulated execution of **random** phenomena using a different **random number** sequence, where each execution generates one sample point. The results of many runs are summarized by a **frequency distribution**.

multimethodology

Several different **hard** and/or soft OR methods or parts of different methods are used either in sequence or in combination for a systems intervention.

multiple objectives, multicriteria decision problem, MCDM

A decision problem where each outcome is evaluated in terms of several, partially or wholly conflicting **objectives** or goals. Example: job selection (objectives: income, working conditions, promotional opportunities, challenge, location).

multi-stage decision process

A decision situation that requires the choice of a **strategy**, often over time, where subsequent decisions may be dependent on the outcome of earlier decisions and/or the outcomes of **random events**. Examples: development and launch of a new product; most competitive games.

narrow system of interest (see also **wider system of interest, hierarchy of systems**)

The smallest system that can achieve the **objectives** set by **decision maker** and whose performance will be measured. It receives **control inputs** from the wider system which controls its **resources**. Ex.: the firm as a whole (wider system) controls the resources (funds) of the production department (narrow system).

natural systems (see also **self regulation**)

Phenomena occurring in nature or the universe without human intervention, represented in systems terms. Ex.: the solar system; an estuary (a type of eco-system).

negative exponential distribution

A **probability distribution** where the frequency of outcomes of larger and larger values becomes smaller and smaller. The **interarrival times** of individual independently acting customers at a **waiting line** often follow a negative exponential distribution. It is characterized by a single parameter λ which corresponds to the rate of arrival. $1/\lambda$ is the expected value and standard deviation of the **random variable**.

Normal distribution (see also **Central limit theorem**)

A **probability distribution** which has the outcomes of the random variable symmetrically distributed around the **expected value**, with lower and lower interval frequencies the farther away from the expected value. It is defined by two parameters: its expected value and its standard deviation. It fits **random** phenomena that are made up as the sum of a large number of independent, small **random events**, such as the daily demand for bread at a supermarket, which is the sum of purchases of individual small customers that each make their decision independently.

objective function (see also **performance measure**)

A mathematical expression measuring the system performance level. Ex.: total cost.

objective probabilities, see **probability**

objectives, goals, and targets

Things that the **decision maker** wants to achieve. Objectives and goals are used interchangeably as desirable directions to move towards. Ex.: maximize profits, minimize **resource** use. Targets are levels of achievements to be approached as closely as possible. Ex.: attain a 50–50 female/male representation in parliament.

objectivity, objective (contrast with **subjective**)

Expressing aspects, phenomena, facts, or conditions without distortion by personal feelings, prejudices, or interpretations, i.e. independent of the observer's mind. In practice, objectivity thus defined is an impossibility, because **reality** can never be known. Our mind can only capture our subjective perceptions. An operational meaning of objectivity is a (temporary) consensus of many individual subjective views.

Ockham's razor

Principle of keeping a **model** as simple as possible by including only aspects that significantly contribute to the explanation of the phenomenon modelled.

open-loop control (contrast with **closed-loop controls**)

Control inputs to the **system** based only on the assumed **system behaviour**, with no **feedback** from the system. Usually in the form of a sequence of unconditional steps or actions. Ex.: some cooking recipes; operating instructions for a video recorder.

open system (contrast with **closed system**)

A system that receives **inputs** from the **environment** and provides **outputs** to it. **Natural** and **human-activity systems** are always open.

operations research, OR, see **management science, hard OR**

opportunity cost

Potential return or cost saving that could be obtained by using a **resource** for its best use that is foregone by an alternative use. Usually assessed as a penalty on resource use. Ex.: penalty reflecting to cost of funds used; revenue forgone for losing a sale.

optimal, optimality, optimization (see also **decision criterion**)

A **feasible** solution that achieves the **objectives** to the highest possible level, i.e. maximizes benefits or minimizes penalties while satisfying all **constraints**. Optimization is the process of finding the optimal solution. Ex.: maximize profit; minimize elapsed time; find the highest output for a given fixed amount of resources available.

outputs (see also **environment**)

System outputs are the outcomes or consequences (often **emergent properties**) of **system behaviour**. Some are planned and desired; some may be undesired and/or unplanned. Those of prime interest to the **decision maker** measure the **system performance**. Ex.:

profit of firm (planned), number of redundancies (unplanned).

outranking methods
A group of methods and **decision criteria** used for ranking the decision choices from best to worst for problems with **multiple objectives** where the **decision maker** is unwilling to make **tradeoffs** between **objectives**. Decision choices are ranked by pairwise comparisons of alternatives, holistically or separately for each objective.

out-there view of systems (see also **inside-us view**)
Viewing a set of **components**, their relationships, and their activities as existing or planned to exist in that form in the **real world**, rather than as a convenient **conceptualization**. There is a one-to-one correspondence between the system components, relationships, and activities, and their real-world counterparts. Ex.: wiring diagram of a sound system, the hardware of the telephone system.

overhead
Costs that cannot be directly attributed to an activity, but are shared among several activities and do not depend on the level of activity within the normal range of operations. Ex: salary of executives; mortgage interest cost; building insurance.

Pareto optimality, see **dominance**

payoff table
A two-way table where each row corresponds to a decision alternative and each column to a **state of nature**, and the entries at their intersections are the numeric outcomes associated with each pair. The term is also used for two-person **games**, where rows and columns refer to the **strategy** choices for each of two players.

performance measure (see also **objective function**)
System output used for measuring the system performance as a function of the **control inputs**. Examples: course grade as a function of study effort; distance travelled by a vehicle as a function of road itinerary chosen; profit as a function of output level.

planning horizon
The time interval, usually divided into periods (weeks, years) covered by the analysis. It consists of an active part during which decisions can be made and an inactive part or **lead-up time** when no new decisions can be implemented. Ex. the expected productive life of a machine; an annual planning cycle for a farmer.

point scale
A numeric score over an arbitrarily interval (Ex.: 0 to 1, 0 to 100) that reflects the **intrinsic worth** of a given outcome. Ex.: Likert scale for worst to best (1 to 5).

Poisson distribution (see also **waiting lines**)
A slightly asymmetric, discrete **probability distribution**, defined by the **expected value** of the random variable (= variance). It is particularly suitable for (relatively) rare events that occur singly and independently, such as the number of individual customers arriving at a service facility over a given length of time. (The latter implies that the interarrival time follows a **negative exponential distribution**.) If the expected value exceeds 20, the normal distribution is an excellent approximation.

policy, see **strategy**

precedence chart
An arrow diagram that shows the logical sequence of how a complex, interconnected set of tasks that make up a project, process, or job have to be performed, i.e. which tasks have to be completed before other tasks can be started. Used as a basis for project planning (and

critical path scheduling).

preference structure
The set of values and preferences which reflect a person's **world view** and which dictate how that person assesses the **intrinsic worth** of various decision choices.

probability
For **random events** that can be repeated under exactly the same conditions, the probability associated with each possible outcome measures the relative frequency with which that outcome occurs (objective probability). For random events that are rare or even unique (i.e. cannot be repeated under exactly the same conditions), the probability associated with each possible outcome is an expression of the strength of belief of a person that this outcome will eventuate (subjective probability). It is a number in the range of 0 to 1, inclusive, where 0 means impossibility and 1 means certainty that the event occurs. The sum of probabilities over all events equals 1.

probability distributions
A probability distribution for a discrete **random variable** is a function that associates with each discrete outcome a probability of its occurrence (Ex.: the **Poisson distribution**). A probability distribution for a continuous random variable is a function that associates a probability that the outcome of the random variable falls into a given interval on the real line (Ex.: the **normal distribution**).

problem customer (see also **stakeholders**)
Beneficiaries or victims of the consequences of the problem solution (if implemented) and who may or may not have any input in determining its form. Ex. the decision maker who reaps the benefits; patients affected by staff scheduling in an emergency clinic; future generations; non-human species (the last three have no voice).

problem owner (see also **stakeholders**)
A person who owns the problem, usually the **decision maker**, who has control over the project, in particular whether the project proceeds or is terminated, and its resources.

problem situation (see also **situation summary**)
A contextual and situational framework within which a given problem is embedded. All aspects that help in understanding the **systemic** relationships and content of the problem or issue selected. However, it is not intended to be a **system** description.

problem solver or analyst (see also **stakeholders**)
A person formulates the problem, does the **mathematical modelling**, finds an appropriate solution, and helps in the planning and execution of its implementation.

problem structuring methods (PSMs) or soft OR or soft systems methodologies
A branch of management science, based on systems thinking, that uses a non-mathematical or **interpretive systems approach**. PSMs attempt to deal with the human aspects and **soft facts** of problem solving, usually calling for the active involvement of all **stakeholders** and aiming to bring about a shared understanding and a consensus agreement of what steps to follow for solving or resolving the issue(s).

problem user (see **stakeholders** for an example)
A person who uses the **solution** derived or execute the actions recommended.

process interaction approach
A modelling approach used by some computer **simulation** software where the simulation **model** is described by the process through which temporary entities pass.

pseudo- (see also **random numbers**)

Not the real thing, but an imitation that tries to mimic the real thing.

qualitative

Expressing aspects in descriptive, non-quantitative terms, showing distinguishing, characteristic, general or individual traits or features. Ex.: written description of a process or the nature of aspects, often by qualifiers (good, best, serious; well, highly, seriously); preference ranking in terms of strength of feeling or perceived worth.

queue discipline (see also **waiting lines**)

The order in which arrivals at a service facility are processed. Ex.: first-come/first-served; last-come/first-served; by importance measure, e.g. highest severity of the accident processed first; smallest service time required processed first.

queueing, queueing theory, see **waiting lines**

random, randomness (see also **random event**, **random variable**, **uncertainty**)

Something that is subject to uncontrollable variations or fluctuations which cannot be predicted individually, usually as a result of unknown or unknowable aspects, always represented as an uncontrollable system input. The pattern of random outcomes may often be captured by a **probability distribution**. Example: the possible outcome of rolling a die; the occurrence of an earthquake next week at a given location; the arrival pattern of customers requesting service in a bank.

random event

An event whose exact outcome is unknown prior to its occurrence; something that is **uncertain** before it happens or before it can be observed. Usually, the range of possible outcomes or a list of possible outcomes is assumed known.

random numbers, random variates

Random numbers are lists of artificially generated digits from 0 to 9 such as the list of digits obtained by repeatedly drawing with replacement one ball at random from an urn containing ten balls numbered from 0 to 9. In the long run, each number would appear about equally often and there would be no **serial correlation** between any possible sequences of balls drawn. Generated by using a numeric computer **algorithm**.

Random variates are independent and uncorrelated random numbers that follow a specified **probability distribution**. Both are used in **simulation**.

random variable (see also **probability distribution**, **expected value**)

A variable that represents the yet unknown numeric outcome of a **random event**. Once the result is known, its value is a constant, i.e. it is one of the possible numeric outcomes, not a random variable anymore.

reality, real world

What exists out there (**objectively**). It can never be known without doubt, but only inferred from observations or logical reasoning, which is subject to our perceptions and interpretations. Its everyday substitute is the critical consensus view of a group of open-minded, like-minded, informed people.

recursive

A relationship that refers back to itself. Ex.: mutual causality; an **iterative** sequence of computational evaluations, where each new **iteration** uses the results of the previous iterations as the starting point.

reductionist thinking, reductionism (see also **cause-and-effect thinking**)

Assumes that all phenomena or events can be reduced, decomposed, or disassembled sequentially into more and more basic elements. In terms of decision making, this implies that a problem can be broken into simpler and simpler subproblems, and the **solution** to the original problem built up from the solutions to the subproblems.

reformulation (of model) (contrast with **enrichment**)
A complete or partial abandonment of the original model, changing the type and form of the **systems variables** and the structure and form of their relationships. Ex.: changing discrete decision variables to continuous; substituting a **stochastic** model for a **deterministic** model; replacing linear relationships with non-linear ones.

resolution level
Degree or level of detail depicted in a representation, **system** definition, or **model**. The higher the resolution level, the more detail is included.

resources
System inputs that are used by system activity; availability often restricted.

response lag
Elapsed time between the moment an action or event occurs and its effects are felt or can be observed. Ex.: the time taken for a Web site to respond.

rich picture (see **problem situation**)
A cartoon-like pictorial representation of a **situation summary**. Not a **system** view.

risk, see **uncertainty**, **random**

risk analysis
A **Monte Carlo simulation** for **multi-stage decision processes**, particularly risky investment projects or other operations that involve high **uncertainty**. A particular policy or **strategy** is simulated many times and the results for aspects of interest are summarized in the form of **frequency distributions** and histograms.

robust, robustness
How well a **model** can accommodate changes in **inputs**, and its ability to give valid answers under varied and changing conditions. The better a model copes, the more robust it is. Robustness is a desirable property of models.

robustness analysis
A **problem structuring approach** for analysing strategic planning problems, subject to high degrees of **uncertainties**, by identifying actions or **strategies** that avoid foreclosing potential future actions, i.e. keep future actions open until uncertainties become resolved. Such actions are referred to as **robust**.

roles of participants, see **stakeholders**

root definition, see **soft systems methodology**

SAST, see **strategic assumption surfacing and testing**

satisficing (see also **bounded rationality**, **heuristics**)
Searching for a good or satisfactory **solution** that meets the important **objectives** to a high degree, without aiming for the best or **optimal solution**. A satisficing approach strikes a balance between costs of search and benefits obtainable.

SCA, see **strategic choice approach**

scenario analysis
Analysing strategy options for a problem situation with high future uncontrollable environmental, technical, and/or competitive **uncertainties** for several different plausible

versions of the future, e.g. optimistic, pessimistic, and average view of future.

scientific, scientific method
Guided by principles of science, usually in the pursuit of knowledge; a **systematic**, unbiased, **objective** investigative procedure for confirming or falsifying hypotheses or properties of things or phenomena by collection of **data** through observation or experiments (often by proper statistical methods) used for testing the hypotheses.

self-regulation
The response of a **natural system** to environmental disturbances to maintain or restore its natural **equilibrium** or find a new ecological equilibrium. Ex.: the human body's mechanism to keep the body temperature stable around 37 °C.

sensitivity analysis (see also **error analysis**)
Systematic exploration of how the **optimal solution** responds to changes in model **inputs**, usually done separately for each input, keeping all other inputs unchanged. Ex.: the reduction in profit as raw material costs increase by 10, 20, … x per cent.

serial correlation
Lagged correlation between values in a sequence of numbers, Example: correlation between consecutive entries, or correlation between every third value.

shadow price
The rate of change (= a **marginal** value) of the **objective function** for a unit increase in a **constraint** at a given level (ex.: **resource**). For problems with nonlinear relationships, this rate may change continuously. For linear problems, such as a **linear program**, the shadow price may remain constant over a given interval. For resource constraints, it is the marginal value of additional resources at a given resource level.

simulation (see also **Monte Carlo simulation, risk analysis, system dynamics**)
Mimicking the behaviour of an existing or proposed **system** or process by means of a **model**, rather than using the real thing. Reproducing, tracing, and recording in detail over simulated time the change in the **state of the system**, and collecting information on **state variables** useful for evaluating the system **performance**. If changes in the system state at any given point in simulated time are discrete quantities (ex.: number of arrivals; items removed from stock), we talk about **discrete event simulation**. **Stochastic** simulations use **random numbers** and **random variates** to generate **random events**. One execution of a simulation for a given length of simulated time is a simulation run. To obtain reliable results for **stochastic systems**, many simulation runs, each using different random numbers, need to be made to determine reliable estimates of average behaviour and its variation. See **system dynamics** for continuous changes in system state.

situation summary (see also **mind map, rich picture**)
A description of all aspects, hard and soft facts, and related issues, contributing to an adequate understanding of the **problem situation**. It is not a representation of a suitable **system** for a problem under study.

SODA, see **strategic option development and analysis**

soft facts, see **hard facts**

soft OR, see **problem structuring methods**

soft systems approaches, see **problem structuring methods**

soft systems methodology
A **problem structuring method** developed by Checkland [1993/99], based on iterative

learning about the **problem situation**. Its aim is to enhance mutual appreciation of the views of different **stakeholders** and develop alternative views of the problem (root definitions) and corresponding systems definitions (conceptual models) that are compared with what exists, in view of bringing about changes which are **systemically** desirable and culturally **feasible**.

solution

A given alternative course of action or a given combination of values for decision variables and the associated level of the **performance measure** or **objective function** to a problem or a **model**. It is not necessarily **optimal** or even **feasible**. Contrast with day-to-day meaning of solution as 'the answer.'

solution/implementation audit

A review or analysis of how well the implemented **model** achieves its original aims and the degree of effective use of the model.

solution method

A procedure or mathematical or computational approach for finding a **feasible solution** to the **model**. Partial list of methods: ranking outcomes by preference, enumeration, search, an **algorithm**, classical calculus, **heuristics**, **simulation**.

solution space

Set of all possible **feasible solutions** for a given problem or a **model**.

spray or fish-bone diagram

A tree-like **cause-and-effect** diagram that shows all potential final (or elementary) aspects or causes that may produce a given outcome (individually or in combination). The main outcome is split into two or more main potential causes, each of which is in turn decomposed into more elementary potential causes, and so on.

SSM, see **soft systems methodology**

stakeholders (see also **problem owner, -user, -customer, -solver or analyst**)

Various roles assumed by the active and passive participants of a **problem situation**. A person may assume several of these roles. Ex.: problem: developing a staffing roster for a fast-food outlet; stakeholders: the manager (problem owner, problem user), the staff (problem users and customers), the patrons (problem customers), the manager or a consultant, whoever does the analysis (problem solver).

state of nature or state of future

One of the combinations of potential or possible outcomes of future (or yet unobserved) **random events**. If **probability distributions** are known for all random events, then we can associate a **probability** with each possible state of nature. Example: the states of nature faced by a student in her final year looking for a job could be given by the 3×3 combinations of 'graduating with high grades', 'graduating with low grades', 'failing', and 'job market buoyant', 'job market average', 'job market bad'.

state of a system, state variable

A state variable is the numeric value of a component **attribute**. The state of the system is the configuration, at any given point in time, of the values of all system variables. It represents a snapshot of the system status at that time. Ex.: In a bank teller system, the number of customers waiting to be served, the number being served, the length of time each is waiting or being served, the status (busy, idle) of each teller and time that status has been held since the last change, total waiting time for all customers, total idle time for all servers, etc., up to each point in time.

stationarity

The property of a **system** input or the pattern or **probability distribution** of a **stochastic** event to remain unchanged over time. Examples: stable cost structure; the rate of arrivals at a **waiting line** remaining unchanged over time. Stationarity is often a simplification to reality and may hold only for a limited time. A trend can also be stationary.

steady state or equilibrium

Long-run behaviour of a **stochastic system** under the assumption of **stationarity** of **inputs**. It is independent of the initial starting state.

Steady state is an unfortunate misnomer, since the concept refers to the average stable long-run behaviour of the **state of the system** — an equilibrium, not a specific state, defined by particular values of all **state variables**. A system is in 'steady state' if the long-run average behaviour, such as the average waiting time of customer, remains more or less constant. Some systems are unstable — they tend to veer off with averages increasing or decreasing constantly. Other systems undergo cyclic fluctuations (e.g. weather pattern). No stochastic system ever reaches steady state, but only approaches it, random disturbances throwing it off course from time to time.

stochastic (see **random, random variables**)

Refers to events or phenomena that are random, and whose behaviour or pattern can be expressed by an empirical **frequency distribution** or the **probability distribution** (Ex.: a **normal distribution**), showing the relative frequency with which each outcome tends to occur in the long run. Stochastic is derived from a Greek word that means 'proceeding by guesswork.' Examples: customer arrivals at a bank; temperatures on a given day of the year, foreign exchange fluctuations.

stochastic system (contrast with **deterministic system**)

A system that is subject to **random**, uncontrollable **inputs**. Example: traffic flow in a network; price fluctuations on stock exchange.

strategic assumption surfaces and testing (SAST)

A **problem structuring method** to externalize assumptions (or **boundary judgements**) implied in the position taken by conflicting groups of **stakeholders** and rate them in terms of importance and degree of **uncertainty**. The findings are debated in an adversarial setting with a facilitator in view of producing a shared view.

strategic choice approach, SCA

A **problem structuring method** developed at the Tavistock Institute that iterates between four modes of working (identifying and selecting decision areas, identifying actions for each, comparing their performance, committing to actions) which help a group of **stakeholders** structure interrelated decision problems and cope with environmental, technical, structural, and political uncertainties associated with various aspects of the problem situation. The aim is to bring about a strategy commitment package for immediate and contingent future actions.

strategic map, see entry below

strategic option development and analysis (SODA)

A **problem structuring method** developed by Eden [1983], for the resolution of conflicting views between stakeholders. It aggregates individual **cognitive maps** for all stakeholders into a strategic map that may reveal emerging themes and core constructs which are analysed and discussed in a workshop under the guidance of a facilitator. The aim is to get a commitment for mutually agreed upon action.

strategy (see also **multi-stage decision process, decision analysis**)

A sequence of conditional actions or decisions for a **multi-stage decision process**, spelling out in detail what action to take for each possible **state of nature**.

subjective, subjectivist, subjectivity (contrast with **objectivity**)

A view, observation, interpretation, or judgment of events, phenomena, things or 'facts', as perceived and processed by an individual's mind rather than as independent of the mind. Full reality can never be known. A person's perception of reality is always interpreted through her or his world view and therefore subjective to some degree.

subjective probabilities, see **probability**

subsystem (see also **hierarchy of systems**)

A **component** of a **system** which itself can be viewed as a system. Examples: the electronic library catalogue inquiry service is a subsystem of the university-wide computer network; a given school is a subsystem of the national education system.

sunk cost

A cost incurred in the past that cannot be recovered or undone any more; it is not relevant for decision making. Ex.: the loss in car value after purchasing and driving the car from the dealer yard; the repair cost already spent.

symbolic model

A **model** that represents the relationships between **system components** by means of symbols, abstract logic functions or expressions, mathematical expressions, graphs or diagrams, or qualitative verbal expressions, or a combination of them.

system (see also **inside-us** and **out-there view**)

An organized collection of things or **components** (which may be **subsystems**) that does something and exhibits behaviours that none of its components exhibits individually, i.e. **emergent** behaviours. It has a **boundary** that separates it from its **environment**. It receives **inputs** from the environment, which it **transforms** into **outputs** to the environment. The dynamic system behaviour is captured by the change in the **state of the system**. In MS/OR, seeing something as a system is a **mental construct** or human **conceptualization**; hence its definition is to some extent **subjective**. The **narrow system of interest** is the focus of a study whose behaviour we want to observe. The **wider system of interest** is the one that controls the **resources** and provides the **control inputs** for the narrow system of interest.

systematic (contrast with **systemic**)

Use of a methodical procedure or operation, marked by thoroughness and regularity.

system behaviour

A change in the **state of the system**.

system boundary (see also **boundary judgements**)

An imaginary line that separates the system **components** from the system **environment**. Choosing the boundary is a fundamental part of defining a system.

system dynamics

A **simulation** model of a dynamic **system** (usually **deterministic**) where the **state variables** can assume continuous values and the behaviour of the system changes in a continuous manner over time. It usually involves (lagged) **feedback loops**, expressed in the form of differential equations. The **state of the system** is captured by the values of all state variables (stocks or levels) and by their rate of change (rates or flows). System dynamic software simulates differential equations by difference equations, simulating the system changes over small intervals of time.

systemic (contrast with **systematic**)

Referring to the relationships between system **components**, using systems ideas, viewing things in terms of their role in a **system** or pertaining to a system.

systems thinking

Study of phenomena or processes in terms of their **systemic** properties and role; something is viewed as an interdependent part of a larger whole — a **system** — and its behaviour is explained by its role in that system. Contrast to **reductionist** or **cause- and-effect thinking** which explains **system behaviour** by the behaviour of individual components. In systems thinking, the whole is greater than the sum of its parts.

system variable

Attribute value assumed by a system **component**. A circle in an **influence diagram**.

total systems intervention (TSI)

A **meta-methodology**, based on **critical systems thinking**, i.e. critical awareness of the strengths and weaknesses of various methods, for guidance of practical **system** interventions, where the methodology applied is appropriate for the analogy used for viewing an organization (i.e. viewed as a machine, a brain, a culture, a political system, or a coercive system). For example, a **functionalist approach** is suitable for a machine or a brain view, while an **interpretive approach** is better for a culture view.

tradeoff (see **aggregate value function methods**)

A **marginal** exchange of one thing for another thing (Ex.: x per cent of achievement level of objective 1 for y per cent of achievement level of objective 2).

traffic intensity (see also **waiting lines**)

The ratio of the rate of arrivals at a service facility and the rate of service. It is equal to the fraction of time the server is busy or the **probability** of finding the server busy at a **random** point in time (in **steady state**).

transformation process

A process of a **system** that changes system **inputs** into system **outputs**. Ex.: Raw materials + labour + machine capacities transformed into finished products or profits; a computer + a computer game + a player + time transformed into enjoyment.

transportation problem

A type of **linear programming model** that involves transportation of goods in space or over time from sources (locations or time slots) to destinations (locations or time slots), subject to supply and demand **constraints**.

uncertainty (see also **stochastic, probability distributions**)

The lack of complete knowledge or the inability to explain fully an event or phenomenon. In **decision analysis**, uncertainty is means complete lack of predictive ability. Partial uncertainty (where **probabilities** of **random events** are known) is referred to as **risk**. Examples: complete uncertainty as to the next move of competitors; some information about the risk involved in a given company share.

utility

A numeric score, using a **point scale** (usually between 0 and 1 or 0 and 100), that expresses the subjective, relative **intrinsic value** of an outcome, usually under conditions of **uncertainty**, for a given person at a given time in a given context.

validation (see also **verification**)

Establishing whether a **model** is a sufficiently close approximation to the existing or planned **reality** such that it is able to provide appropriate and useful answers.

variable cost (contrast with **fixed cost**)

A cost that varies with the level of activity, often proportionately. Ex.: cost of raw material used; fuel cost for distance travelled.

verification (see also **validation**)

Establishing whether a **model** is logically and mathematically correct and consistent and that its **data** inputs are correct.

waiting line

A process where customers arrive at a service facility, join a queue if all servers are occupied, take their position and advance in the queue according to a given queue discipline (Ex.: first-come/first-served), are being served, and then depart. There may be more than one server at the service facility, working in parallel or in sequence. There may be several customer populations with different arrival patterns and service needs, both of which are usually **random**.

Weltanschauung, **or world view** (see also **subjective**)

An individual's personal values, beliefs and biases, as affected by upbringing, cultural and social background, education, and experience, used as a filter to interpret and give meaning to the observed, perceived, or experienced reality. Few people are fully aware of their own world view. Disagreements often arise because of differing world views. Problems are seen differently by different people because of differing world views.

wider system of interest (see **narrow system of interest**, **hierarchy or systems**)

The system that controls the **resources** and provides the **control inputs** to the narrow system of interest. Ex.: (funds) of the production department (narrow system).

Index

Bold entries in Glossary (pages 571–591)